SYSTEMS ANALYSIS AND DESIGN

Sixth Edition

D0080391

Gary B. Shelly

Thomas J. Cashman

Harry J. Rosenblatt

THOMSON COURSE TECHNOLOGY

25 THOMSON PLACE

BOSTON MA 02210

SHELLY CASHMAN SERIES®

Australia • Canada • Denmark • Japan • Mexico • New Zealand • Philippines • Puerto Rico • Singapore

South Africa • Spain • United Kingdom • United States

Systems Analysis and Design
Sixth Edition

Gary B. Shelly

Thomas J. Cashman

Harry J. Rosenblatt

Managing Editor:
Alexandra Arnold

Senior Acquisitions Editor:
Dana Merk

Product Manager:
Reed Cotter

Editorial Assistant:
Selena Coppock

Print Buyer:
Laura Burns

Director of Production:
Patty Stephan

Production Editor:
Aimee Poirier

Production Assistant:
Jill Klaffky

Development Editor:
Mali Jones

Copy Editor:
Nancy Lamm

Proofreader:
Lori Silfen

Interior Designer:
Joel Sadagursky

Cover Image:
John Still

Compositor:
GEX Publishing Services

Indexer:
Jay Kreider

Printer:
Banta Menasha

ISBN 0-619-25510-2

BRIEF CONTENTS

TABLE OF CONTENTS

PHASE 1: SYSTEMS PLANNING

Chapter 2

Analyzing the Business Case

PHASE 2: SYSTEMS ANALYSIS

Chapter 3

Requirements Modeling

Chapter 4

Data and Process Modeling

Chapter 5

Development Strategies

Chapter 8

System Architecture

PHASE 4: SYSTEMS IMPLEMENTATION

Chapter 9

Systems Implementation

PHASE 5: SYSTEMS OPERATION, SUPPORT, AND SECURITY

Chapter 10

Systems Operation, Support, and Security

THE SYSTEMS ANALYST'S TOOLKIT

Toolkit 1

Communication Tools

Toolkit 2

CASE Tools

Toolkit 3

Financial Analysis Tools

Toolkit 4

Project Management Tools

Toolkit 5

Object-Oriented Tools

Toolkit 6

Internet Resource Tools

PREFACE

The Shelly Cashman Series® offers the finest textbooks in computer education. We are proud that previous editions of Systems Analysis and Design have been so well received by instructors and students. *Systems Analysis and Design, Sixth Edition* continues with the innovation, quality, and reliability you have come to expect from the Shelly Cashman Series.

Overview

Systems Analysis and Design, Sixth Edition presents a practical approach to information technology and systems development. Many two- and four-year colleges and schools use this book in information systems, computer science, and e-commerce curriculums. The textbook emphasizes the role of the systems analyst in a dynamic, business-related environment.

Using this book, students learn how to translate business requirements into information systems that support a company's short- and long-term objectives. Case studies and assignments teach analytical, problem-solving, and decision-making techniques. A new Case in Point feature offers numerous in-chapter analytical opportunities, and extensive end-of-chapter exercises emphasize the development of critical-thinking skills.

Objectives of this Textbook

Systems Analysis and Design, Sixth Edition is intended for a three credit-hour introductory systems analysis and design course. This textbook is designed to:

- Present the material in an appealing full-color format, with an easy-to-read style that invites students to learn
- Describe important IT developments and trends, using numerous screen shots of selected Web sites and links
- Describe the five phases of the systems development life cycle (SDLC): systems planning, systems analysis, systems design, systems implementation, and systems operation, support, and security
- Give students an in-depth understanding of how information technology (IT) supports operational and business requirements in today's intensely competitive environment
- Explain how systems analysts interact with users, management, and other IT professionals in a typical business organization
- Provide case studies and exercises that promote critical-thinking skills and encourage students to apply their skills and knowledge
- Provide students with a comprehensive Systems Analyst's Toolkit that highlights six major cross-functional tools that all systems analysts need, including: communications tools, CASE tools, financial analysis tools, project management tools, object-oriented tools, and Internet resource tools

New to this Edition

Systems Analysis and Design, Sixth Edition offers many exciting new features:

- **New** IT Security section in Chapter 10 provides comprehensive explanations of physical, network, application, file, and user security
- **New** coverage of RFID technology, wireless networks, and mobile computing trends in Chapters 1 and 8, and new emphasis on offshore outsourcing, e-business,

ERP, application service providers, client/server architecture, network concepts, and Web-based applications in Chapters 1, 5, and 8

➡ **New** Case in Point feature in each chapter provides four embedded mini-case opportunities for analysis and application of chapter skills and concepts

➡ **New** Chapter Capstone Case provides in-depth coverage of chapter material and a set of individual and team-based tasks, while the companion Chapter Introduction Case continues to highlight key objectives in each chapter

➡ **New** Case-Sim® SCR Associates case study enhancements now include 20 realistic voice mail messages and more than 30 e-mail messages that students receive in this interactive, Web-based simulation

➡ **New** *Systems Analyst's Toolkit* enhancement adds strategically placed *Toolkit Time* tips throughout the textbook to remind students to visit the six-part Toolkit to learn text-related IT support skills in six cross-functional areas, including Communication Tools, CASE Tools, Financial Analysis Tools, Project Management Tools, Object-Oriented Tools, and Internet Resource Tools

➡ **New** chapter alignment provides comprehensive coverage and continuity, with Output and User Interface Design material moved to Chapter 6, followed by Data Design concepts in Chapter 7

➡ **New** Glossary – Index feature offers students additional learning support

➡ **New** Brief Table of Contents provides overview of content

➡ **New** faculty support feature includes the full text of all Web simulation case e-mail and voice mail messages, which are located in the Additional Faculty Files folder on the Instructor Resources CD

Organization of this Textbook

Systems Analysis and Design, Sixth Edition contains 16 learning units in ten chapters and a six-part integrated Systems Analyst's Toolkit.

Chapter 1 – Introduction to Systems Analysis and Design Chapter 1 provides an up-to-date overview of IT issues, major trends, the systems development life cycle, and the important role of systems analysis and design in supporting business objectives.

Chapter 2 – Analyzing the Business Case Chapter 2 offers a business-related starting point for successful systems analysis. Topics include strategic planning, review of systems requests, how to conduct a feasibility study, and the steps in a preliminary investigation.

Chapter 3 – Requirements Modeling Chapter 3 describes fact-finding techniques and team-based modeling methods, including JAD and RAD, that systems analysts use to model and document a new system.

Chapter 4 – Data and Process Modeling Chapter 4 explains how systems analysts create a logical model for the new system by using data flow diagrams and process description tools, including structured English, decision tables, and decision trees.

Chapter 5 – Development Strategies Chapter 5 focuses on software acquisition options, including outsourcing and offshore outsourcing options, application service providers, and other trends that view software as a service rather than a product.

Chapter 6 – Output and User Interface Design Chapter 6 highlights output and report design, the interaction between humans and computers, including usability issues, graphical screen design, input issues, and data entry guidelines.

Chapter 7 – Data Design Chapter 7 describes data design terms, concepts, and skills including entity-relationship diagrams, cardinality, data normalization rules, data warehousing, data mining, a comparison of logical and physical records, and data control measures.

Chapter 8 – System Architecture Chapter 8 explains the elements of system architecture, with emphasis on RFID, ERP, supply chain management, client/server architecture, and network topology including wireless trends.

Chapter 9 – Systems Implementation Chapter 9 includes coverage of application development and implementation topics, including structure charts, documentation techniques, system testing, user training, data conversion, changeover methods, and post-implementation evaluation.

Chapter 10 – Systems Operation, Support, and Security Chapter 10 describes user support, maintenance techniques, and factors that indicate the end of a system's useful life. This chapter includes a comprehensive description of IT security concepts, techniques, and tools, and specifically addresses five security levels: physical, network, application, file, and user security. Chapter 10 also explains future challenges and opportunities that IT professionals will face in a dynamic workplace.

Toolkit Part 1 – Communications Tools Part 1 of the Toolkit describes oral and written communication tools that can make a systems analyst more effective. Topics include guidelines for successful communications, tips for better readability, how to organize and plan an oral presentation, and effective speaking techniques.

Toolkit Part 2 – CASE Tools Part 2 of the Toolkit focuses on computer-aided software engineering (CASE) tools that systems analysts use to document, model; and develop information systems. Examples of several popular CASE tools are provided, along with sample screens that show CASE tool features.

Toolkit Part 3 – Financial Analysis Tools Part 3 of the Toolkit explains various tools that systems analysts use to determine feasibility and evaluate the costs and benefits of an information system. Specific tools include payback analysis, return on investment (ROI), and net present value (NPV).

Toolkit Part 4 – Project Management Tools Part 4 of the Toolkit explains project management, cost estimating, and change control for information systems. This section also includes hands-on skills that systems analysts can use to create Gantt charts and PERT charts.

Toolkit Part 5 – Object-Oriented Tools Part 5 of the Toolkit explains how systems analysts use object-oriented analysis methods. This section describes object-oriented terms and concepts and shows how the Unified Modeling Language can be used to document, analyze, and model an information system.

Toolkit Part 6 – Internet Resource Tools Part 6 of the Toolkit explains Internet-based information gathering strategies. Topics include search engines, subject directories, the invisible Web, advanced search techniques, Boolean logic and Venn diagrams. This section also discusses newsgroups, newsletters, mailing lists, Web-based discussion groups, chat rooms, instant messaging, and online learning opportunities.

FOR THE STUDENT

The Shelly Cashman Series wants you to have a valuable learning experience that will provide the knowledge and skills you need to be successful. With that goal in mind, we have included many activities, games, and learning tools, that we hope you will find interesting, challenging, and enjoyable. The following sections describe features at the beginning, learning tools within, and exercises at the end of each chapter. Other support tools accompanying this textbook are also described.

Chapter Opening Features

Each chapter contains the following features to help you get started:

- ➡ **Chapter Introduction** Read the Chapter Introduction for a brief overview of the chapter
- ➡ **Chapter Objectives** The Chapter Objectives lists the main skills and knowledge you will have when you finish the chapter
- ➡ **Chapter Introduction Case: Mountain View College Bookstore** The Mountain View College Bookstore case is a continuing case study that introduces each chapter and provides a real-world overview of the topics that will be covered in the chapter. As you work through the textbook, you will see how the Mountain View IT team discusses the issues, identifies the key points, and creates specific task lists

Learning Tools within the Chapter

As you work through each chapter, you will find these helpful tools and features:

- ➡ **Case in Point** This exciting new feature provides four embedded mini-case opportunities for you to analyze and apply the skills and concepts you are learning in the chapter
- ➡ **Toolkit Time** The Systems Analyst's Toolkit explains skills that you can apply at any point in the textbook. Toolkit Time marginal notes remind you about the Toolkit, where to find it, and how it might help you address the issues or material in the chapter
- ➡ **More on the Web** Learn more about a topic by visiting the suggested Web sites and exploring the links we have provided

End-of-Chapter Exercises

The following exercises are in every text chapter:

- ➡ **Learn It Online** Each chapter features a Learn It Online page comprised of six exercises. These exercises utilize the Web to offer chapter-related reinforcement activities that will help you gain confidence in systems analysis and design. These exercises include True/False, Multiple Choice, Short Answer, Flash Cards, Practice Test, and several learning games
- ➡ **CASE SIM: SCR Associates** complete this interactive case study using the Web. Log on to the company intranet, read e-mail messages addressed to you, listen to voice mail messages, and perform assigned tasks in a realistic corporate setting. In this simulation you report to Jesse Baker, but you e-mail your completed assignments to your instructor. Detailed instructions on how to use this case are available at www.scsite.com/sad6e/scr. To log on to the SCR intranet, you will be required to provide a password. Your password is **sad6**. When you log on to the SCR intranet, you also will be asked to enter your first and last name so your e-mail can be addressed to you correctly

➡ **Chapter Exercises** In this section, you will find 10 Review Questions, four Discussion Topics, and four Projects. These exercises allow you to apply your understanding of the material and will help to prepare you for tests and assessments

➡ **Apply Your Knowledge** This section includes four mini-cases per chapter. Each mini-case requires you to use the knowledge and skills you learned in the chapter

➡ **Case Studies** Case studies provide practical experience and allow you to practice specific skills learned in the chapter. Each chapter contains several case studies, two of which (New Century Health Clinic and Personal Trainer, Inc.) continue throughout the textbook. You can complete your assignments using Microsoft Word and Excel forms, available at www.scsite.com/sad6e/forms

➡ **Chapter Capstone Case: SoftWear, Limited** SoftWear, Limited (SWL) is a continuing case study providing students the opportunity to act as members of the SWL systems development team and perform various tasks pertinent to material in each chapter

Additional Support Tools

These additional tools are provided to enhance your learning experience:

GLOSSARY This edition of the textbook includes a new glossary feature. Check your understanding of key terms and phrases, or use the glossary as a quick reference tool.

STUDENT STUDY TOOL This CD-ROM, provided in the back of your book, contains:

➡ Detailed outlines of every chapter that highlight key topics covered and can be used as a guide when reviewing for an exam

➡ Chapter glossaries that allow you to look up all key terms in one place. They also provide page references where key terms can be found if you need more information

➡ Web Links, Figures, and Test Yourself questions that provide additional reinforcement of chapter concepts

COMPANION WEB SITE Broaden your learning experience and enhance your understanding of the material in each chapter with the Companion Web site. Visit scsite.com/sad6e for access to:

➡ On the Web links

➡ Learn It Online exercises, including True/False, Multiple Choice, Short Answer, Flash Cards, Practice Test, and several learning games

➡ SCR Associates Internet and intranet sites

➡ Forms Library

FOR THE INSTRUCTOR

The Shelly Cashman Series is dedicated to providing you all of the tools you need to make your class a success. Information on all supplementary materials is available through your Thomson Course Technology representative or by calling one of the following telephone numbers: Colleges and Universities, 1-800-648-7450; High Schools, 1-800-824-5179; Private Career Colleges, 1-800-477-3692; Canada, 1-800-268-2222; and Corporations and Government Agencies, 1-800-340-7450.

Instructor Resources CD

The Instructor Resources CD (0-619-25512-9) for this textbook includes both teaching and testing aids. The contents of the CD are listed below:

- **Instructor's Manual** The Instructor's Manual is made up of Microsoft Word files. The Instructor's Manual includes detailed lecture notes with page number references, teacher's notes, classroom activities, discussion topics, and projects to assign.

- **Course Syllabus** A sample syllabus is included, and can be customized easily customized for your course.

- **PowerPoint Presentations** PowerPoint Presentations is a multimedia lecture presentation system that provides PowerPoint slides for each chapter. Presentations are based on the chapters' objectives. Use this presentation system to present well organized lectures that are both interesting and knowledge based. PowerPoint Presentations provides consistent coverage at schools that use multiple lecturers in their programming courses.

- **Figure Files** Illustrations for every figure in the textbook are available in electronic form. Use this ancillary to present a slide show in lecture or to print transparencies for use in lecture with an overhead projector. If you have a personal computer and LCD device, this ancillary can be an effective tool for presenting lectures.

- **Solutions to Exercises** Solutions are included for all end-of-chapter exercises, as well as the Chapter Reinforcement activities.

- **Test Bank & Test Engine** The test bank includes 110 questions for every chapter (25 multiple-choice, 50 true/false, and 35 fill-in-the-blank) with page number references and, when appropriate, figure references. A printable version of the test bank also is included. The test bank comes with a copy of the test engine, ExamView. ExamView is a state-of-the-art test builder that is easy to use. ExamView enables you quickly to create printed tests, Internet tests, and computer (LAN-based) tests. You can enter your own test questions or use the test bank that accompanies ExamView.

- **Data Files for Students** The forms that students can use to complete the Case studies are included. You can distribute the files on the Instructor Resources CD-ROM to your students over a network, or you can have them follow the instructions on the inside back cover of this book.

- **Additional Activities for Students** Two additional case studies and solution files are provided for every chapter. You can assign them as homework, extra credit, or to assess student understanding of the chapter. Also included are SCR Associates Data Library, e-mail and voice mail text, and Interview Summaries for the New Century Case Study.

- **Additional Faculty Files** Word document versions of the e-mail and voice mail messages posted for students on the SCR Web site are available for instructor reference. Students should be able to access these on their own as part of the simulation, but if necessary, instructors can supply text versions.

- **Software** A copy of the powerful CASE tool, Visible Analyst – Student Edition, is provided for your evaluation. Several sample solutions to case study tasks also are included.

Online Content

Thomson Course Technology knows what it takes to develop and deliver an online course that will keep you and your students engaged from start to finish. That's why we provide you with all the tools you need to teach an interactive, informative class. From ready-to-use online content to our own content delivery platform, tools from Thomson Course Technology make teaching online easier than ever.

➤ **MyCourse 1.0** A flexible, easy-to-use course management tool, MyCourse 1.0 allows you to personalize your course home page, schedule your course activities and assignments, post messages, administer tests, and file the results in a grade book. You also can use text-specific preloaded content for this book, add your own content, select from a pool of test bank questions, or create questions yourself. MyCourse 1.0 is hosted by Thomson Learning, allowing you hassle-free maintenance and student access at all times. For more information, visit www.course.com/onlinecontent.

➤ **Blackboard and WebCT Online Content** Thomson Course Technology offers you options for online content. For those who want online testing, we provide a Blackboard test bank and a WebCT test bank, available for download in the Instructor Resources section on course.com. For those who desire more content, we offer course management and access to a Web site that is fully populated with content for this book. For more information, visit www.course.com/onlinecontent.

SOFTWARE BUNDLING OPPORTUNITIES *Systems Analysis and Design, Sixth Edition* can be bundled with several popular software programs:

➤ **Visible Analyst, Student Edition** Whether you are designing e-business applications, developing a data warehouse, or integrating your legacy systems with new enterprise applications, Visible Analyst has all the power you need. Educating tomorrow's developers today, Visible Analyst helps students become more marketable with advanced, affordable, application development and training tools. This "special" version of Visible Analyst is a separate product with a unique goal of educating the future application development workforce. A network version, called the Visible Analyst University Edition, is available to colleges and universities for installation in computer labs.

➤ **Microsoft Visio® 2003** Create business and technical diagrams that document and organize complex ideas, processes, and systems. Diagrams created in Visio 2003 enable you to visualize and communicate information clearly, concisely, and effectively in ways that text and numbers cannot. Visio 2003 also automates data visualization by synchronizing directly with data sources to provide up-to-date diagrams, and it can be customized to meet the needs of your organization.

➤ **Microsoft Office Project 2003** Project managers everywhere rely on Microsoft Office Project Standard to plan and manage their projects. With Microsoft Office Project Standard 2003, efficiently organize and track tasks and resources to keep your projects on time and within budget. Extensive help resources and printing assistance make Project Standard 2003 easy to learn, so that you can be productive quickly. Project Standard 2003 is an integral part of the Microsoft Office System, so you can smoothly use products like Microsoft Office PowerPoint® 2003 and Microsoft Office Visio® 2003 to present project status effectively. And, as a user of the leading desktop project management program, support is readily available through a broad community of solution providers and user groups.

ACKNOWLEDGMENTS

Special thanks go to Mali Jones, development editor; Raymond Enger, author of the current Student Study Tool; and reviewers Alfred Benoit, Johnson & Wales University; Dr. Carol E.B. Choksy, Indiana University; Bernice Howard, Florida Community College; Michael Michaelson, Palomar College; and Martin Sheridan, TekResults Ltd. We would also like to thank the students at College of the Albemarle who provided valuable input, and security consultant Owen Stevens for his comments and suggestions about the system security topics discussed in Chapter 10.

CHAPTER

Introduction to Systems Analysis and Design

Chapter I introduces you to the role of information technology in today's dynamic business environment. You will learn about the development of information systems, systems analysis and design concepts, the systems development life cycle, and various systems development methods, tools, and techniques. This chapter also describes the role of the information technology department and the people who work there.

INTRODUCTION

OBJECTIVES

When you finish this chapter, you will be able to:

- Discuss the impact of information technology on business strategy and success
- Define an information system and describe its components
- Use profiles and models to understand business functions and operations
- Explain how the Internet has affected business strategies and relationships
- Identify various types of information systems and explain who uses them
- Explain systems development tools, including modeling, prototyping, and CASE tools
- Distinguish between structured analysis and object-oriented methodology
- Describe the systems development life cycle
- Discuss the role of the information technology department and the systems analysts who work there

The headlines in Figure 1-1 offer dramatic examples of how information technology affects businesses, large and small. Companies use information as a weapon in the battle to increase productivity, deliver quality products and services, maintain customer loyalty, and make sound decisions. In a global economy with intense competition, information technology can mean the difference between success and failure.

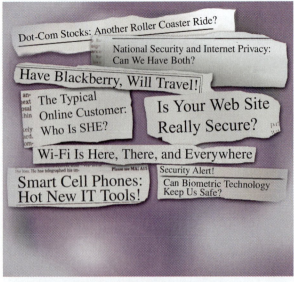

FIGURE I-I   These headlines show the enormous impact of information technology.

CHAPTER INTRODUCTION CASE: Mountain View College Bookstore

Background: Mountain View College is located in a large southwestern city. The school has grown rapidly and now has 8,000 students at three campuses, each with a branch bookstore. Wendy Lee, manager of college services, is responsible for all bookstore operations. Wendy wants a new information system that will increase efficiency and improve customer service.

As the case begins, Florence Fullerton, a systems analyst in the college's information technology department, is talking with Harry Boston. Harry is majoring in information systems at Mountain View College and is earning credit toward his degree by working part-time as a student intern.

Participants:	Florence and Harry
Location:	Florence's office, 10 a.m. Monday morning, September 12, 2005
Project status:	Initial discussion
Discussion topics:	Basic systems analysis and design concepts

Florence:	Welcome aboard, Harry.
Harry:	*I'm glad to be here. What's on the agenda?*
Florence:	Well, there's been some talk about a new bookstore information system. Wendy says nothing is definite yet, but she suggested that we should get ready.
Harry:	*So we start by learning about the bookstore business?*
Florence:	Yes, the best system in the world isn't worth much unless it supports business and information needs. But let's not get ahead of ourselves. First, we need to talk about business information systems in general. Then we'll build a business model so we can understand the specific operations and processes at the bookstore. We'll also discuss systems analysis and design tools and techniques. Let's start with an overview of information systems and their characteristics. Companies need different types of information systems, and individual employees have specific information needs.
Harry:	*That makes sense. What about the basic systems analysis techniques you mentioned? Can you tell me a bit more?*
Florence:	Several approaches exist, but I generally use what's called a structured method, which is based on the concept of a systems development life cycle, or SDLC for short.
Harry:	*How does that work?*
Florence:	The SDLC involves a series of phases. Think of it like constructing a building. First, you would list specific objectives for the project. Then you might hire an architect to present an overall concept and create a set of drawings to show how the building will fulfill your objectives. Later, you'd need detailed blueprints for the workers who would do the actual construction. When the building is done, you would check it out, test everything, turn it over to the new occupants, and make sure they're happy with the results.
Harry:	*And that's how we'll develop new information systems?*
Florence:	It sure is. I used Microsoft Project to create a list of tasks we can work on.

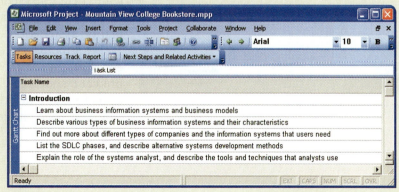

FIGURE 1-2

THE IMPACT OF INFORMATION TECHNOLOGY

Information technology (**IT**) refers to the combination of hardware and software products and services that people use to manage, access, communicate, and share information. Successful firms treat information as a vital asset that must be used effectively, updated constantly, and safeguarded carefully. Although fictitious, the headlines in Figure 1-1 on page 2 show the impact of IT on businesses, large and small.

The Future of IT

ON THE WEB

For more information about The Future of IT, visit **scsite.com/ sad6e/more**, locate Chapter 1 and then click The Future of IT link.

More than ever, business success depends on information technology. In a report titled *Digital Economy 2003*, the U.S. Department of Commerce stated that, "After two years of retrenchment, IT producing industries now show signs of resuming the dynamic role they played during 1996–2000." The report estimated that the IT sector accounted for almost 30 percent of economic growth during 2003, and pointed out that IT has created a new economy, where advances in hardware, software, and connectivity provide unprecedented benefits to businesses and individuals around the world. According to the report, an explosion in Internet use is driving this growth.

As the table shown in Figure 1-3 indicates, the world online population increased by 106 percent between 2000 and 2004. The statistics show rapid global growth.

Although economic trends affect IT spending levels, most businesses give IT budgets a relatively high priority, in good times or bad. The reason is simple — during periods of growth, companies cannot afford to lag behind the IT curve. Conversely, when the economy slows down, firms often use IT to reduce operating costs and improve efficiency.

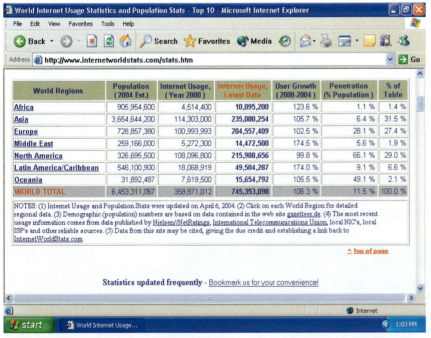

FIGURE 1-3 Internet World Stats is a firm that provides Internet usage figures and online population data.

The Role of Systems Analysis and Design

Systems analysis and design is a step-by-step process for developing high-quality information systems. An **information system** combines information technology, people, and data to support business requirements. For example, information systems handle daily business transactions, improve company productivity, and help managers make sound decisions. The IT department team includes **systems analysts** who plan, develop, and maintain information systems.

With increasing demand for talented people, employment experts predict a shortage of qualified applicants to fill IT positions. Many companies list employment opportunities on their Web sites, as shown in Figure 1-4.

Who Develops Information Systems?

Traditionally, a company either developed its own information systems, called **in-house applications**, or purchased systems called **software packages** from outside vendors. Today, the choice is much more complex. Options include Internet-based application services, outsourcing, custom solutions from IT consultants, and enterprise-wide software strategies.

Regardless of the development method, launching a new information system involves risks as well as benefits. The greatest risk occurs when a company tries to decide *how* the system will be implemented before determining *what* the system is supposed to do. Instead of putting the cart before the horse, a company must begin by outlining its business needs and identifying possible IT solutions. Typically, this important work is performed by systems analysts and other IT professionals. A firm should not consider implementation options until it has a clear set of objectives. Later on, as the system is developed, a systems analyst's role will vary depending on the implementation option selected.

INFORMATION SYSTEM COMPONENTS

A **system** is a set of related components that produces specific results. For example, specialized systems route Internet traffic, manufacture microchips, and control complex events like the Mars mission shown in Figure 1-5. A **mission-critical system** is one that is vital to a company's operations. An order processing system, for example, is mission-critical because the company cannot do business without it.

Every system requires input data. For example, your computer receives data when you press a key or click a menu command. In an information system, **data** consists of basic facts that are the system's raw material. **Information** is data that has been transformed into output that is valuable to users. For example, Figure 1-6 on the next page shows an order processing system that displays an order form. When a sales representative enters data (customer number, product code, and quantity ordered), the system creates a customer order with all the necessary information. Large businesses with thousands or millions of sales transactions require company-wide information systems and powerful servers such as those shown in Figure 1-7 on the next page.

FIGURE 1-4 Hewlett-Packard, a leader in information technology, advertises jobs and opportunities for students and graduates on its Web site.

FIGURE 1-5 Systems can be simple or complex. Imagine the systems used to send a space vehicle to explore the planet Mars and send back images to Earth.

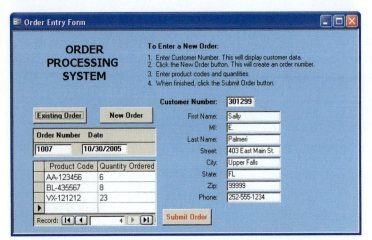

FIGURE 1-6 After a sales representative enters data, the order processing system creates a sales order.

FIGURE 1-7 Multiple servers provide the power and speed that modern IT systems require.

ON THE WEB

For more information about Moore's Law, visit **scsite.com/ sad6e/more**, locate Chapter 1 and then click the Moore's Law link.

An information system has five key components, as shown in Figure 1-8: hardware, software, data, processes, and people.

Hardware

Hardware consists of everything in the physical layer of the information system. For example, hardware can include servers, workstations, networks, telecommunications equipment, fiber-optic cables, handheld computers, scanners, digital capture devices, and other technology-based infrastructure. As new technologies emerge, manufacturers race to market the innovations and reap the rewards.

Hardware purchasers today face a wide array of technology choices and decisions. Almost 40 years ago, a concept called **Moore's Law** accurately predicted that computer processing power would double every 18 to 24 months, as shown in Figure 1-9. Fortunately, as hardware became more powerful, it also became less expensive.

Software

Software refers to the programs that control the hardware and produce the desired information or results. Software consists of system software and application software.

System software manages the hardware components, which can include a single workstation or a global network with many thousands of clients. Either the hardware manufacturer supplies the system software or a company purchases it from a vendor. Examples of system software include the operating system, security software that protects the computer from intrusion, device drivers that communicate with hardware such as printers, and utility programs that handle specific tasks such as data backup and disk management. System software also includes a **network operating system (NOS)**, which controls the flow of data, provides data security, and manages network accounts. In today's interconnected business world, network software is vitally important.

Application software consists of programs that support day-to-day business functions and provide users with the information they require. Application software can serve one user or thousands of users throughout the organization. Examples of company-wide applications, called **enterprise applications**, include order processing systems, payroll systems, and company communications networks. On a smaller scale, individual users increase their productivity with tools such as spreadsheets, word processors, and database management systems.

FIGURE 1-8 Components of an information system.

Application software includes horizontal and vertical systems. A **horizontal system** is a system, such as an inventory or payroll application, that can be adapted for use in many different types of companies. A **vertical system** is designed to meet the unique requirements of a specific business or industry, such as a Web-based retailer, a medical practice, or a video chain.

Most companies use a combination of software that is acquired at various times. When planning an information system, a company must consider how a new system will interface with older systems, which are called **legacy systems**. For example, a new human resources system might need to exchange data with an older payroll application.

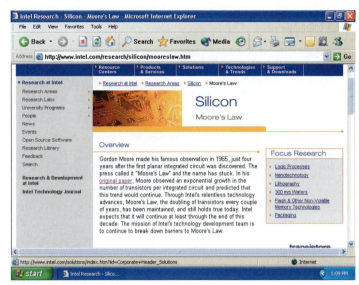

FIGURE 1-9 According to Moore's Law, processing power (measured by the number of transistors per integrated circuit) doubles every 18 months. This concept has held true for almost 40 years.

Data

Data is the raw material that an information system transforms into useful information. An information system can store data in various locations, called tables. By linking the tables, the system can extract specific information. Figure 1-10 shows a payroll system that stores data in four separate tables. At the end of a pay period, the payroll system produces a paycheck that accurately reflects the employee's hours worked, gross pay, current deductions, and net pay.

Processes

Processes describe the tasks and business functions that users, managers, and IT staff members perform to achieve specific results. Processes are the building blocks of an information system, because they represent actual day-to-day business operations. To build a successful information system, analysts must understand business processes and document them carefully.

People

The primary purpose of an information system is to provide valuable information to users. **Users**, sometimes called **end users**, are the people who interact with an information system, both inside and outside the company. Internal users include administrators, managers, technicians, sales staff, and corporate officers. External users include customers who track their orders on the company's Web site and suppliers who use a customer's system to plan their manufacturing schedules. The success or failure of a system usually depends on whether users are satisfied with the system's output and operations.

To serve users, successful information systems depend on skilled professionals, such as systems analysts, programmers, network administrators, and other IT staff members.

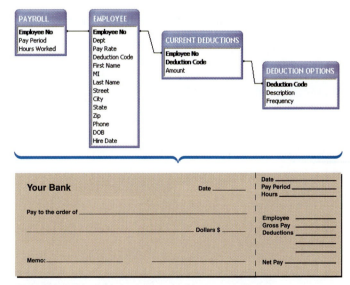

FIGURE 1-10 By linking several tables, a payroll system can extract specific information to produce a paycheck that accurately reflects the employee's hours worked, gross pay, current deductions, and net pay.

BUSINESS MODEL: HANDLE SALES ORDER

FIGURE 1-11 A simple business model might consist of an event, three processes, and a result.

UNDERSTANDING THE BUSINESS

IT professionals must understand a company's business operations in order to design successful systems. Each business situation is different. For example, a retail store, an Internet auction site, and a hotel chain all have unique information systems requirements. Systems analysts use a process called **business process modeling** to represent a company's operations and information needs. Business process modeling requires a business profile and a series of models that document various business processes.

As the business world changes, systems analysts can expect to work in new kinds of companies that require innovative IT solutions, including Web-based systems that serve customers and carry out online transactions with other businesses.

Business Profile

A **business profile** is an overview that describes a company's overall functions, processes, organization, products, services, customers, suppliers, competitors, constraints, and future direction. To develop a business profile, a systems analyst investigates a company's products, services, and Internet opportunities. The analyst also studies interactivity among the firm's information systems, specialized information needs, and future growth projections. Armed with a business profile, the analyst then creates a series of business models.

Business Models

Business models make it easier for managers and systems analysts to understand day-to-day business operations. A **business model** is a graphical representation of one or more business processes that a company performs, such as accepting an airline reservation, selling a ticket, or crediting a customer account. A **business process** describes a specific set of transactions, events, tasks, and results. For example, Figure 1-11 shows a business model called HANDLE SALES ORDER. Notice that the model represents an event, three separate business processes, and a result. Complex business operations require a series of linked models in order to show the overall picture.

When companies attempt to simplify operations or reduce costs, a popular strategy is to have managers and systems analysts perform **business process reengineering (BPR)**. The BPR OnLine Learning Center shown in Figure 1-12 offers comprehensive resources for business process reengineering, including articles, tutorials, and information on reengineering toolkits and templates.

FIGURE 1-12 The BPR OnLine Learning Center offers comprehensive resources for business process reengineering.

New Kinds of Companies

Traditionally, companies were identified as product-oriented or service-oriented. **Product-oriented** companies manufacture and sell products, such as computers, routers, or the microchip shown in Figure 1-13. Motorola, Intel, Compaq, Cisco, and Sun Microsystems are examples of product-oriented companies. **Service-oriented** companies primarily offer information or services or sell goods produced by others. Oracle, Amazon.com, and Office Depot are examples of service companies.

FIGURE 1-13 Motorola is an example of a product-oriented company that manufactures technology products, such as the microchip shown here.

In a growing trend in the IT industry, many companies offer a mix of products, services, information, and technical resources to customers. In many firms, the IT services sector is the fastest growing business segment. In its 2003 annual report, for example, IBM reported that 50 percent of its total revenue came from the sale of IT services. IBM's services include an international consulting division, a global leasing unit, and a financial services branch. According to the report, hardware accounted for only about one-third of total sales in 2003.

The newest company category is the **Internet-dependent** firm, often described as a **dot-com (.com)** company because its primary business depends on the Internet rather than a traditional business channel. Yahoo.com and eBay.com are examples of pure dot-com companies. At the other end of the spectrum are traditional companies, sometimes called **brick-and-mortar** companies because they conduct business from physical locations. Many brick-and-mortar firms have added Web-based marketing channels to increase sales and serve customers more effectively.

In recent years, many Internet-based companies enjoyed spectacular growth, and the value of their stock soared — only to plummet when the economy softened. Many IT observers wonder whether dot-com companies will be able to survive and prosper in uncertain economic times.

CASE IN POINT 1.1: CLOUD NINE FINANCIAL ADVISORS

Cloud Nine provides its clients with a monthly newsletter that offers recommendations about stocks to buy or sell. Doug Layton, Cloud Nine's president, has asked your opinion on whether dot-com stocks might be good investments for the future. He specifically mentioned Google, eBay, Amazon.com, and Yahoo!, but he said you could suggest other companies. Doug wants you to do some Internet research to learn more about these Web-based companies and their future prospects. You can use a search engine, or start by visiting the Web sites of publications such as *Forbes, Fortune Magazine, Business Week,* or *The Wall Street Journal,* among others.

IMPACT OF THE INTERNET

Internet-based commerce is called **e-commerce (electronic commerce)** or **I-commerce (Internet commerce)**. E-commerce includes two main sectors: **B2C (business-to-consumer)** and **B2B (business-to-business)**.

B2C (Business-to-Consumer)

Using the Internet, consumers can go online to purchase an enormous variety of products and services. This new shopping environment allows customers to do research, compare prices and features, check availability, arrange delivery, and choose payment methods in a single convenient session. Many companies, such as airlines, offer incentives for online transactions because Web-based processing costs are lower than traditional methods. By making flight information available online to last-minute travelers, some airlines also offer special discounts on seats that might otherwise go unfilled.

B2C commerce is changing traditional business models and creating new ones. For example, a common business model is a retail store that sells a product to a customer. To carry out that same transaction on the Internet, the company must develop an online store and deal with a totally different set of marketing, advertising, and profitability issues. Some companies have found new ways to use established business models. For example, eBay.com has transformed a traditional auction concept into a new, popular, and successful method of buying goods and services.

In recent years, B2C transactions accounted for a small portion of total retail sales, but B2C activity is expected to grow significantly. The surge in B2C marketing has created strong competition among Web designers to create attractive sites that increase online sales. The B2C trend also means more demand for systems analysts and programmers who can develop Web-based information systems and applications.

B2B (Business-to-Business)

Although the business-to-consumer (B2C) sector is more familiar to retail customers, the volume of business-to-business (B2B) transactions is many times greater. Industry observers predict that B2B sales will increase to over $10 trillion by 2006.

Because it allows companies to access the global marketplace, B2B is especially important to firms under pressure to reduce costs. B2B enables smaller suppliers to contact large customers, and allows purchasers to obtain instant information about market prices and availability. For example, Wal-Mart operates an online marketplace where suppliers can offer their products, submit specifications, and quote prices.

On an industry-wide scale, B2B sites exist where buyers, sellers, distributors, and manufacturers transact business, exchange information, and collaborate. For example, the ENI-Net site shown in Figure 1-14 brings together buyers and sellers of environmental equipment, supplies, and services. ENI-Net offers clients a Web-based process to increase procurement efficiencies, reduce costs, and mitigate risks. Many IT observers believe this type of digital marketplace will reduce purchasing costs dramatically and result in enormous B2B growth.

Online trading marketplaces initially were developed as company-to-company data-sharing arrangements called **electronic data interchange (EDI)**. EDI enabled computer-to-computer transfer of data between companies, usually over private telecommunications networks. Firms used EDI to plan production, adjust inventory levels, or stock up on raw materials using data from another company's information system. As B2B volume soared, the development of **extensible markup language (XML)** enabled company-to-company traffic to migrate to the Internet, which offered standard protocols, universal availability, and low communication costs. XML is a data description language that allows Web-based communication between different hardware and software environments. XML is extremely flexible because it is concerned with the data itself rather than the output format. For example, a user could view XML customer data as a Web page on a notebook computer or as a contact list on a PDA. The unique advantage of XML is that data description is not linked to output formatting. This is just the opposite of **HTML (hypertext markup language)**, where the language controls the way the information is displayed on a Web browser.

FIGURE 1-14 Many IT observers believe that digital marketplaces such as ENI-Net will reduce purchasing costs dramatically and result in enormous B2B growth.

Web-Based System Development

Internet-based systems development is changing rapidly, as software industry giants compete in market for overall software services, rather than individual products. These services include powerful Web-development environments and software solutions. For example, IBM claims that its **WebSphere** strategy is best, while Microsoft counters with a broad vision called **.NET** that redefines that company's approach to Web-based application development. These alternatives are discussed in more detail in Chapter 5, Development Strategies. Web-based databases are discussed in Chapter 7, Data Design, and Chapter 8, System Architecture. In addition, many firms offer **Web services**, which are Internet-based support programs that can be executed as an integral part of an information system. For example, a real estate brokerage Web site might offer instant mortgage calculations, which are performed by a Web service provided (for a fee) by a third-party company.

Internet-based systems involve various hardware and software designs, but a simple model is a series of Web pages that provides a user interface, which communicates with one or more levels of data management software and a Web-based database server. As companies build more Internet-based systems, career opportunities will expand for IT professionals, including Web designers, database developers, and systems analysts. The demand will come from brick-and-mortar firms, as well as dot-com companies.

Although they got off to a slow start in the e-commerce wars, many brick-and-mortar companies have substantial assets and worldwide brand recognition. Armed with these resources, many traditional firms developed e-commerce channels to enhance their core business and successfully fend off dot-com competitors. For example, Figure 1-15 shows how Wal-Mart, a brick-and-mortar firm, competes with online vendors of Mother's Day flowers and gifts.

FIGURE 1-15 Wal-Mart, a brick-and-mortar company, uses its Web site to compete aggressively with online vendors of Mother's Day flowers and gifts.

HOW BUSINESS USES INFORMATION SYSTEMS

In the past, IT managers divided systems into categories based on the user group the system served. Categories and users included office systems (administrative staff), operational systems (operational personnel), decision support systems (middle-managers and knowledge workers), and executive information systems (top managers).

Today, traditional labels no longer apply. For example, all employees, including top managers, use office productivity systems. Similarly, operational users often require decision support systems. As business changes, information use also changes in most companies. Today, it makes more sense to identify a system by its functions and features, rather than by its users. A new set of system definitions includes enterprise computing systems, transaction processing systems, business support systems, knowledge management systems, and user productivity systems.

Enterprise Computing Systems

Enterprise computing refers to information systems that support company-wide operations and data management requirements. Wal-Mart's inventory control system, Boeing's production control system, and American Airlines' reservation system are examples of enterprise computing systems. The main objective of enterprise computing is to integrate a company's primary functions (such as production, sales, services, inventory control, and accounting) to improve efficiency, reduce costs, and help managers make key decisions. Enterprise computing also improves data security and reliability by imposing a company-wide framework for data access and storage.

In many large companies, applications called **enterprise resource planning (ERP)** systems provide cost-effective support for users and managers throughout the company. For example, a car rental company can use ERP to forecast customer demand for rental cars at hundreds of locations.

By providing a company-wide computing environment, many firms have been able to achieve dramatic cost reductions. Other companies have been disappointed in the time, money, and commitment necessary to implement ERP successfully. A potential disadvantage of ERP is that ERP systems generally impose an overall structure that might or might not match the way a company operates. ERP is described in more detail in Chapter 5, which discusses system development strategies.

ON THE WEB

For more information about Enterprise Resource Planning, visit **scsite.com/ sad6e/more**, locate Chapter I and then click the Enterprise Resource Planning link.

Because of its growth and potential, many hardware and software vendors target the enterprise computing market and offer a wide array of products and services. Figure 1-16 shows an IBM Web site that is dedicated to marketing enterprise computing software and solutions.

Transaction Processing Systems

Transaction processing (TP) systems process data generated by day-to-day business operations. Examples of TP systems include customer order processing, accounts receivable, and warranty claim processing.

TP systems perform a series of tasks whenever a specific transaction occurs. In the example shown in Figure 1-17, a TP system verifies customer data, checks the customer's credit

FIGURE 1-16 IBM maintains a site dedicated to enterprise computing.

status, posts the invoice to the accounts receivable system, checks to ensure that the item is in stock, adjusts inventory data to reflect a sale, and updates the sales activity file. TP systems typically involve large amounts of data and are mission-critical systems, because the enterprise cannot function without them.

TP systems are efficient because they process a set of transaction-related commands as a group rather than individually. To protect data integrity, however, TP systems ensure that if any single element of a transaction fails, the system does not process the rest of the transaction.

Business Support Systems

Business support systems provide job-related information support to users at all levels of a company. These systems can analyze transactional data, generate information needed to manage and control business processes, and provide information that leads to better decision-making.

FIGURE 1-17 A single sales transaction consists of six separate tasks, which the TP system processes as a group.

The earliest business computer systems replaced manual tasks, such as payroll processing. Companies soon realized that computers also could produce valuable information. The new systems were called **management information systems (MIS)** because managers were the primary users. Today, employees at *all* levels need information to perform their jobs, and they rely on information systems for that support.

A business support system can work hand-in-hand with a TP system. For example, when a company sells merchandise to a customer, a TP system records the sale, updates the customer's balance, and makes a deduction from inventory. A related business support system highlights slow- or fast-moving items, customers with past due balances, and inventory levels that need adjustment.

To compete effectively, firms must collect production, sales, and shipping data and update the company-wide business support system immediately. The newest development in data acquisition is called **radio frequency identification (RFID)** technology, which uses high-frequency radio waves to track physical objects, such as the items shown in Figure 1-18. RFID is expected to grow dramatically as the Defense Department and companies such as Wal-Mart begin to require suppliers to add RFID tags to their goods.

An important feature of a business support system is decision support capability. Decision support helps users make decisions by creating a computer model and applying a set of variables. For example, a truck fleet dispatcher might run a series of **what-if** scenarios to determine the impact of increased shipments or bad weather. Alternatively, a retailer might use what-if analysis to determine the price it must charge to increase profits by a specific amount while volume and costs remain unchanged.

FIGURE 1-18 RFID technology allows companies to track physical objects, such as inventory items, by using small RFID tags that respond to radio frequency signals.

Knowledge Management Systems

ON THE WEB

For more information about Knowledge Management Systems, visit **scsite.com/ sad6e/more**, locate Chapter 1 and then click the Knowledge Management Systems link.

Knowledge management systems are called **expert systems** because they simulate human reasoning by combining a knowledge base and inference rules that determine how the knowledge is applied. A **knowledge base** consists of a large database that allows users to find information by entering keywords or questions in normal English phrases. A knowledge management system uses **inference rules**, which are logical rules that identify data patterns and relationships.

Figure 1-19 shows a knowledge management system that Novell maintains for its customers and users. After a user enters a symptom, problem, or question, Novell's Knowledgebase searches for a solution and displays the results.

Knowledge management systems do not use strict logical rules. Instead, many knowledge management systems use a technique called **fuzzy logic** that allows inferences to be drawn from imprecise relationships. Using fuzzy logic, values need not be black and white, like binary logic, but can be many shades of gray. The results of a fuzzy logic search will display in priority order, with the most relevant results at the top of the list.

User Productivity Systems

Companies provide employees at all levels with technology that improves productivity. Examples of **user productivity systems** include e-mail, voice mail, fax, video conferencing, word processing, automated calendars, database management, spreadsheets, desktop publishing, presentation graphics, company intranets, and high-speed Internet access. User productivity systems also include groupware. **Groupware** programs run on a company intranet and enable users to share data, collaborate on projects, and work in teams. GroupWise, offered by Novell, is a popular example of groupware.

When companies first installed word processing systems, managers expected to reduce the number of employees as office efficiency increased. That did not happen, primarily because the basic nature of clerical work changed. With computers performing most of the repetitive work, managers realized that office personnel could handle tasks that required more judgment, decision-making, and access to information.

Computer-based office work expanded rapidly as companies assigned more responsibility to employees at lower organizational levels. Relatively inexpensive hardware, powerful networks, corporate downsizing, and a move toward employee empowerment also contributed to this trend. Today, administrative assistants and company presidents alike are networked, use computer workstations, and need to share corporate data to perform their jobs.

Information Systems Integration

Most large companies require systems that combine transaction processing, business support, knowledge management, and user productivity features. For example, suppose an international customer has a problem with a product and makes a warranty claim. A customer service representative enters the claim into a TP system. The transaction updates two other systems: a knowledge management system that tracks product problems and warranty activity, and a quality control system with decision support capabilities. A quality control engineer uses

FIGURE 1-19   Novell's Web site includes a searchable knowledge management system.

what-if analysis to determine if it would be advantageous to make product design changes in order to reduce warranty claims. In this example, a TP system is integrated with a knowledge management system and a business support system with decision support features.

INFORMATION SYSTEM USERS AND THEIR NEEDS

Corporate organizational structure has changed considerably in recent years. As part of downsizing and business process reengineering, many companies reduced the number of management levels and delegated responsibility to operational personnel. Although modern organization charts tend to be flatter, an organizational hierarchy still exists in most companies.

A typical organizational model identifies business functions and organizational levels, as shown in Figure 1-20. Within the functional areas, operational personnel report to supervisors and team leaders. The next level includes middle managers and knowledge workers, who in turn report to top managers. In a corporate structure, the top managers report to a board of directors elected by the company's shareholders.

A systems analyst must understand the company's organizational model in order to recognize who is responsible for specific processes and decisions and to be aware of what information is required by whom.

Top Managers

Top managers develop long-range plans, called **strategic plans**, which define the company's overall mission and goals. To plot a future course, top managers ask questions such as "How much should the company invest in information technology?" or "How much will Internet sales grow in the next five years?" or "Should the company build new factories or contract out the production functions?"

Strategic planning affects the company's future survival and growth, including long-term IT plans. Top managers focus on the overall business enterprise and use IT to set the company's course and direction. To develop a strategic plan, top managers also need information from outside the company, such as economic forecasts, technology trends, competitive threats, and governmental issues.

Middle Managers and Knowledge Workers

Just below the top management level, most companies have a layer of middle managers and knowledge workers. **Middle managers** provide direction, necessary resources, and performance feedback to supervisors and team leaders. Because they focus on a somewhat

FIGURE 1-20 A typical organizational model identifies business functions and organizational levels.

shorter time frame, middle managers need more detailed information than top managers, but somewhat less than supervisors who oversee day-to-day operations. For example, a middle manager might review a weekly sales summary for a three-state area, while a local sales team leader would need a daily report on customer sales at a single location.

In addition to middle managers, every company has people called knowledge workers. **Knowledge workers** include professional staff members such as systems analysts, programmers, accountants, researchers, trainers, and human resource specialists. Knowledge workers also use business support systems, knowledge management systems, and user productivity systems. Knowledge workers provide support for the organization's basic functions. Just as a military unit requires logistical support, a successful company needs knowledge workers to carry out its mission.

Supervisors and Team Leaders

Supervisors, often called **team leaders**, oversee operational employees and carry out day-to-day functions. They coordinate operational tasks and people, make necessary decisions, and ensure that the right tools, materials, and training are available. Like other managers, supervisors and team leaders need decision support information, knowledge management systems, and user productivity systems to carry out their responsibilities.

Operational Employees

Operational employees include users who rely on TP systems to enter and receive data they need to perform their jobs. In many companies, operational users also need information to handle tasks and make decisions that were assigned previously to supervisors. This trend, called **empowerment**, gives employees more responsibility and accountability. Many companies find that empowerment improves employee motivation and increases customer satisfaction.

SYSTEMS DEVELOPMENT TOOLS AND TECHNIQUES

In addition to understanding business operations, systems analysts must know how to use a variety of techniques, such as modeling, prototyping, and computer-aided systems engineering tools to plan, design, and implement information systems. Systems analysts work with these tools in a team environment, where input from users, managers, and IT staff contributes to the system design.

Modeling

Modeling produces a graphical representation of a concept or process that systems developers can analyze, test, and modify. A systems analyst can describe and simplify an information system by using a set of business, data, object, network, and process models.

A **business model**, or **requirements model**, describes the information that a system must provide. A **data model** describes data structures and design. An **object model** describes objects, which combine data and processes. A **network model** describes the design and protocols of telecommunications links. A **process model** describes the logic that programmers use to write code modules. Although the models might appear to overlap, they actually work together to describe the same environment from different points of view.

🔧 TOOLKIT TIME

The CASE tools in Part 2 of the Systems Analyst's Toolkit can help you develop and maintain complex information systems. To learn more about these tools, turn to Part 2 of the six-part Toolkit that follows Chapter 10.

Modeling involves various techniques, including data flow diagrams and entity-relationship diagrams (described in Chapters 4 and 7), and unified modeling language diagrams (described in Part 5 of the Systems Analyst's Toolkit).

Prototyping

Prototyping tests system concepts and provides an opportunity to examine input, output, and user interfaces before final decisions are made. A **prototype** is an early working version of an information system. Just as an aircraft manufacturer tests a new design in a wind tunnel, systems analysts construct and study information system prototypes. A prototype can serve as an initial model that is used as a benchmark to evaluate the finished system, or the prototype itself can develop into the final version of the system. Either way, prototyping speeds up the development process significantly.

A possible disadvantage of prototyping is that important decisions might be made too early, before business or IT issues are understood thoroughly. A prototype based on careful fact-finding and modeling techniques, however, can be an extremely valuable tool.

Computer-Aided Systems Engineering (CASE) Tools

Computer-aided systems engineering (CASE), also called **computer-aided software engineering**, is a technique that uses powerful software, called **CASE tools**, to help systems analysts develop and maintain information systems. CASE tools provide an overall framework for systems development and support a wide variety of design methodologies, including structured analysis and object-oriented analysis.

Because CASE tools make it easier to build an information system, they boost IT productivity and improve the quality of the finished product. Part 2 of the Systems Analyst's Toolkit explains how analysts use CASE tools to create business profiles, build business models, and document complex processes. After developing a model, many CASE tools can generate program code, which speeds the implementation process. Figure 1-21 shows the Visible Systems Corporation Web site, and Figure 1-22 shows the Web site for Popkin Software. Both firms are leading vendors of CASE tools.

FIGURE 1-21 Visible Systems Corporation offers a wide array of software engineering tools, including Visible Analyst, a popular CASE tool.

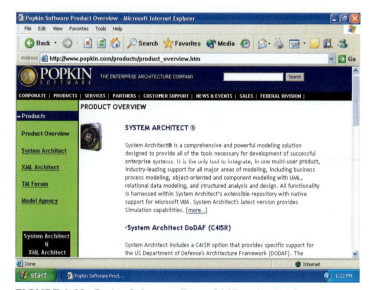

FIGURE 1-22 Popkin Software offers a CASE tool called System Architect, which supports a wide variety of methodologies and strategies.

In addition to traditional CASE tools, system developers often use project management tools, such as Microsoft Project, and special-purpose charting tools, such as Microsoft Visio, which is shown in Figure 1-23. A systems analyst can use Visio to create many different types of diagrams, including block diagrams, building plans, forms and charts, maps, network diagrams, and organization charts. Visio is described in more detail in Part 2 of the Systems Analyst's Toolkit.

SYSTEMS DEVELOPMENT METHODS

This section discusses various methods for developing computer-based information systems. Structured analysis is the most popular method, but a newer strategy called object-oriented analysis and design also is used widely. Each method offers many variations. Some organizations develop their own approaches or adopt methods offered by software suppliers, CASE tool vendors, or consultants. Most IT experts agree that no single, best system development strategy exists. Instead, a systems analyst should understand the alternative methodologies and their strengths and weaknesses.

Structured Analysis

Structured analysis is a traditional systems development technique that is time-tested and easy to understand. Structured analysis uses a series of phases, called the **systems development life cycle (SDLC)**, to plan, analyze, design, implement, and support an information system. Although structured analysis evolved when most systems were based on mainframe processing, it remains a dominant systems development method.

Structured analysis uses a set of process models to describe a system graphically. Because it focuses on processes that transform data into useful information, structured analysis is called a **process-centered** technique. In addition to modeling the processes, structured analysis includes data organization and structure, relational database design, and user interface issues.

Process modeling identifies the data flowing into a process, the business rules that transform the data, and the resulting output data flow. Figure 1-24 shows a simple process model that represents a school registration process with related input and output.

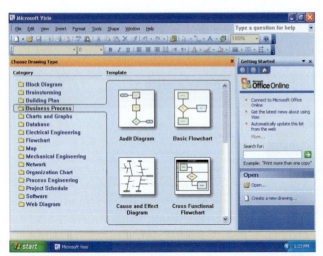

FIGURE 1-23 Microsoft Visio is a popular charting tool that systems analysts use to create many different types of diagrams.

FIGURE 1-24 This Visible Analyst screen shows a process model for a school registration system. The REGISTER STUDENTS process accepts input data from two sources and transforms it into output data.

Object-Oriented Analysis

TOOLKIT TIME

The Object-Oriented tools in Part 5 of the Systems Analyst's Toolkit can help you visualize and work with object-oriented information systems. To learn more about these tools, turn to Part 5 of the six-part Toolkit that follows Chapter 10.

Whereas structured analysis treats processes and data as separate components, **object-oriented analysis (O-O)** combines data and the processes that act on the data into things called **objects**. Systems analysts use O-O to model real-world business processes and operations. The result is a set of software objects that represent actual people, things, transactions, and events. Using an O-O programming language, a programmer then writes the code that creates the objects.

An object is a member of a **class**, which is a collection of similar objects. Objects possess characteristics called **properties**, which the object inherits from its class or possesses on its own. As shown in Figure 1-25, the class called PERSON includes INSTRUCTOR and STUDENT. Because the PERSON class has a property called Address, a STUDENT inherits an Address property. A STUDENT also has a property called Major that is not shared by other members of the PERSON class.

In O-O design, built-in processes called **methods** can change an object's properties. For example, in a Web-based catalog store, an ORDER object might have a property called STATUS that changes when a CUSTOMER object clicks to place, confirm, or cancel the order.

One object can send information to another object by using a message. A **message** requests specific behavior or information from another object. For example, an ORDER object might send a message to a CUSTOMER object that requests a shipping address. When it receives the message, the CUSTOMER object supplies the information. The ORDER object has the capability to send the message, and the CUSTOMER object knows what actions to perform when it receives the message.

O-O analysis uses object models to represent data and behavior, and to show how objects affect other objects. By describing the objects (data) and methods (processes) needed to support a business operation, a system developer can design reusable components that allow faster system implementation and decreased development cost.

O-O methodology is popular because it is flexible, is efficient, and provides an easy transition to O-O programming languages such as Visual Basic, Java, and C++. Part 5 of the Systems Analyst's Toolkit covers O-O analysis and design and describes O-O terms, concepts, tools, and techniques in detail.

Joint Application Development and Rapid Application Development

In the past, IT departments sometimes developed systems without sufficient input from users. Not surprisingly, users often were unhappy with the finished product. Over time, many companies discovered that systems development teams composed of IT staff, users, and managers could complete their work more rapidly and produce better results. Two methodologies became popular: **joint application development (JAD)** and **rapid application development (RAD)**. Both JAD and RAD use teams composed of users, managers, and IT staff. The difference is that JAD focuses on team-based fact-finding, which is only one phase of the development process, while RAD is more like a compressed version of the entire process. JAD and RAD are described in more detail in Chapter 3.

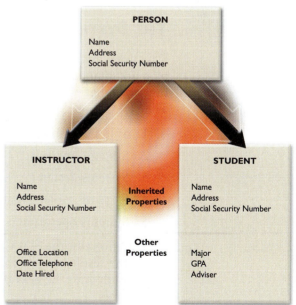

FIGURE 1-25 The PERSON class includes INSTRUCTOR and STUDENT objects, which have their own properties and inherited properties.

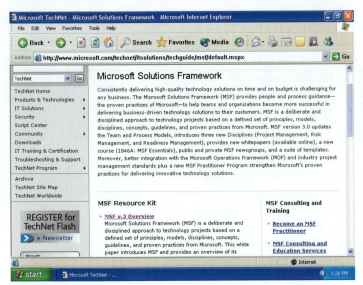

FIGURE 1-26 Microsoft offers a systems development strategy called Microsoft Solutions Framework (MSF), which relies on a set of concepts and models.

Other Development Strategies

In addition to structured analysis and O-O methodologies, you might encounter other systems development techniques. For example, Microsoft offers an approach called **Microsoft Solutions Framework (MSF)**, which documents the experience of its own IT teams, as shown in Figure 1-26.

Using MSF, systems analysts design a series of models, including a risk management model, a team model, and a process model, among others. Each model has a specific purpose and output that contributes to the overall design of the system. Although the Microsoft process differs from the SDLC phase-oriented approach, MSF developers perform the same kind of planning, ask the same kinds of fact-finding questions, deal with the same kinds of design and implementation issues, and resolve the same kinds of problems. MSF uses O-O analysis and design concepts, but also examines a broader business and organizational context that surrounds the development of an information system.

Companies often choose to follow their own methodology. Using CASE tools, an IT team can apply a variety of techniques rather than being bound to a single, rigid methodology. Many CASE tools offer a complete set of analysis and modeling tools that support various methods and strategies. If a systems analyst wants additional choices, he or she can choose from an entire industry of IT software companies and consulting firms.

THE SYSTEMS DEVELOPMENT LIFE CYCLE

Structured analysis uses a concept called the systems development life cycle (SDLC) to plan and manage the systems development process. The SDLC describes activities and functions that all systems developers perform, regardless of which approach they use. The SDLC model includes the following steps:

1. Systems planning
2. Systems analysis
3. Systems design
4. Systems implementation
5. Systems operation, support, and security

Traditionally, the SDLC is pictured as a **waterfall model** shown in Figure 1-27, where the result of each phase, which is called a **deliverable** or **end product**, flows sequentially into the next phase. Typically, the adjacent phases interact, as shown by the dotted lines.

Figure 1-28 represents an alternative model of the SDLC, where planning, analysis, and design interact continuously, followed by implementation and operation and support. An interactive model depicts real-world practice and the constant dialog among users, managers, and systems developers.

Systems Planning

The **systems planning phase** usually begins with a formal request to the IT department, called a **systems request**, that describes problems or desired changes in an information system or a business process. In many companies, IT systems planning is an integral part of overall business planning. When managers and users develop their business plans, they usually include IT requirements that generate systems requests.

A systems request can come from a top manager, a planning team, a department head, or the IT department itself. The request can be very significant or relatively minor. A major request might involve a new information system or the replacement of an existing system that cannot handle current requirements. In contrast, a minor request might ask for a new feature or a change to the user interface.

The purpose of this phase is to perform a **preliminary investigation** to identify the nature and scope of the business opportunity or problem. The preliminary investigation is a critical step because the outcome will affect the entire development process. A key part of the preliminary investigation is a **feasibility study** that reviews anticipated costs and benefits and recommends a course of action based on operational, technical, economic, and time factors.

Suppose you are a systems analyst and you receive a request for system changes or improvements. Your first step is to determine whether it makes sense to launch a preliminary investigation at all. Often you will need to learn more about business operations before you can reach a conclusion. After an investigation, you might find that the information system functions properly, but users need more training. In some situations, you might recommend a business process review, rather than an IT solution. In other cases, you might conclude that a full-scale systems review is necessary. If the development process continues, the next step is the systems analysis phase.

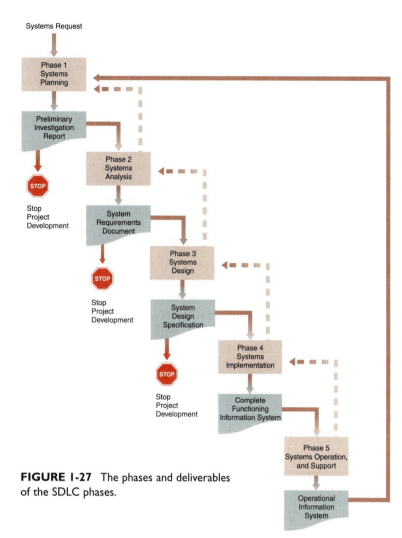

FIGURE 1-27 The phases and deliverables of the SDLC phases.

FIGURE 1-28 An alternative model of the SDLC focuses on the interaction of planning, analysis, and design tasks, which leads to implementation, followed by operation and support.

Systems Analysis

The purpose of the **systems analysis phase** is to build a logical model of the new system. The first step is **requirements modeling**, where you investigate business processes and document what the new system must do. Requirements modeling continues the investigation that began during the systems planning phase. To understand the system, you perform fact-finding using techniques such as interviews, surveys, document review, observation, and sampling. You use the fact-finding results to build business models, data and process models, and object models.

The end product for the systems analysis phase is the **system requirements document**. The system requirements document describes management and user requirements, costs and benefits, and outlines alternative development strategies.

Systems Design

The purpose of the **systems design phase** is to create a blueprint that will satisfy all documented requirements for the system. At this stage, you design the user interface and identify all necessary outputs, inputs, and processes. In addition, you design internal and external controls, including computer-based and manual features to guarantee that the system will be reliable, accurate, maintainable, and secure. During the systems design phase, you also determine the application architecture, which shows programmers how to transform the logical design into program modules and code.

The result of this phase is documented in the **system design specification** and presented to management and users for review and approval. Management and user involvement is critical to avoid any misunderstanding about what the new system will do, how it will do it, and what it will cost.

Systems Implementation

During the **systems implementation phase**, the new system is constructed. Whether the developers used structured analysis or O-O methods, the procedure is the same — programs are written, tested, and documented, and the system is installed. If the system was purchased as a package, systems analysts configure the software and perform any necessary modifications. The objective of the systems implementation phase is to deliver a completely functioning and documented information system.

At the conclusion of this phase, the system is ready for use. Final preparations include converting data to the new system's files, training users, and performing the actual transition to the new system. The systems implementation phase also includes an assessment, called a **systems evaluation**, to determine whether the system operates properly and if costs and benefits are within expectations.

Systems Operation, Support, and Security

During the **systems operation, support, and security phase**, the IT staff maintains, enhances, and protects the system. Maintenance changes correct errors and adapt to changes in the environment, such as new tax rates. Enhancements provide new features and benefits. The objective during this phase is to maximize return on the IT investment. Security controls safeguard the system from both external and internal threats.

A well-designed system will be secure, reliable, maintainable, and scalable. A **scalable** design can expand to meet new business requirements and volumes. Information systems development is always a work in progress. Business processes change rapidly, and most information systems need to be updated significantly or replaced after several years of operation.

SYSTEMS DEVELOPMENT GUIDELINES

With experience as a systems analyst, you will develop your own style and techniques. Although each project is different, you should consider some basic guidelines as you build an information system.

Planning

Stick to an overall development plan. If you use the SDLC as a framework for systems development, complete the phases in sequence. If you use an O-O methodology, follow a logical series of steps as you define the components.

Involve the Users Throughout the Development Process

Ensure that users are involved in the development process, especially when identifying and modeling system requirements. Modeling and prototyping can help you understand user needs and develop a better system.

Listening Is Very Important

Listen carefully! The best system is the one that meets user needs most effectively. When you interact with users, you must put aside any preconceived notions and listen closely to what they are saying to you. Chapter 3 describes the interview process and contains many tips about getting the most out of face-to-face communication.

Create a Timetable with Major Milestones

Identify major milestones for project review and assessment. At those milestones, managers and systems developers must decide whether to proceed with the project, redo certain tasks, return to an earlier phase, or terminate the project entirely. The SDLC model requires formal assessment of end products and deliverables. O-O analysis involves a continuous modeling process that also requires checkpoints and project review.

Identify Interim Checkpoints

Establish interim checkpoints between major milestones to ensure that the project remains on schedule. Regardless of the development methodology, the systems analyst must keep the project on track and avoid surprises. Create a reasonable number of checkpoints — too many can be burdensome, but too few will not provide adequate control. An example of a checkpoint might be the completion of interviews conducted during a preliminary investigation.

Remain Flexible

Be flexible within the framework of your plan. Systems development is a dynamic process, and overlap often exists between the phases of systems planning, analysis, design, and implementation. For example, when you investigate a systems request, you begin a fact-finding process that often carries over into the next phase. Similarly, you often start building process models before fact-finding is complete. The ability to overlap phases is especially important when you are working on a system that must be developed rapidly.

Develop Accurate Cost and Benefit Information

Provide accurate and reliable cost and benefit information. Managers need to know the cost of developing and operating a system. At the start of each phase, you must provide specific estimates.

INFORMATION TECHNOLOGY DEPARTMENT

The information technology (IT) department develops and maintains a company's information systems. The structure of the IT department varies among companies, as does its name and placement within the organization. In a small firm, one person might handle all computer support activities and services, whereas a large corporation might require many people with specialized skills to provide information systems support. Figure 1-29 shows a typical IT organization in a company that has networked PCs, enterprise-wide databases, centralized processing, and Web-based operations.

FIGURE 1-29 A typical IT department organization chart shows the major functions.

The IT group provides **technical support,** which includes six main functions: application development, systems support and security, user support, database administration, network administration, and Web support. These functions overlap considerably and often have different names in different companies.

Application Development

Traditionally, IT departments had an **application development** group composed of systems analysts and programmers who handled information system design, development, and implementation. Today, many companies use development teams consisting of users, managers, and IT staff members for those same tasks. A popular model for information systems development is a project-oriented team using RAD or JAD, with IT professionals providing overall coordination, guidance, and technical support.

Systems Support and Security

Systems support and security provides vital protection and maintenance services for system hardware and software, including enterprise computing systems, networks, transaction processing systems, and corporate IT infrastructure. The systems support and security group implements and monitors physical and electronic security hardware, software, and procedures. This group also installs and supports operating systems, telecommunications software, and centralized database management systems. In addition, systems support and security technicians provide technical assistance to other groups in the IT department.

CASE IN POINT 1.2: GLOBAL HOTELS AND MOMMA'S MOTELS

Suppose you work in the IT department of Global Hotels, a multinational hotel chain. Global Hotels runs several specialized business support systems, including a guest reservations system that was developed in-house to meet the requirements of a large company with worldwide operations. Guests can make one-stop online reservations by visiting Global's Web site, which has links to all major travel industry sites.

Global Hotels just acquired Momma's, a regional chain of 20 motels in western Canada. Momma's uses a vertical reservations package suitable for small- to medium-sized businesses, and a generic accounting and finance package. Should Momma's use Global Hotels' information systems or continue with its own? In your answer, consider issues such as business profiles, business processes, system interactivity, EDI, XML, e-commerce, and the characteristics of both information systems. What additional information would be helpful to you in making a recommendation?

User Support

User support provides users with technical information, training, and productivity support. The user support function usually is called a **help desk** or **information center** (**IC**). A help desk's staff trains users and managers on application software such as e-mail, word processors, spreadsheets, and graphics packages. User support specialists answer questions, troubleshoot problems, and serve as a clearinghouse for user problems and solutions.

In many companies, the user support team also installs and configures software applications that are used within the organization. Although user support specialists coordinate with other technical support areas, their primary focus is user productivity and support for user business processes.

Database Administration

Database administration involves database design, management, security, backup, and user access. In small- and medium-sized companies, an IT support person performs those roles in addition to other duties. Regardless of company size, mission-critical database applications require continuous attention and technical support.

Network Administration

Business operations depend on telecommunication networks that enable company-wide information systems. **Network administration** includes hardware and software maintenance, support, and security. In addition to controlling user access, network administrators install, configure, manage, monitor, and maintain network applications. Network administration is discussed in more detail in Chapter 8.

Web Support

Web support is the newest technical support function. Web support specialists, often called **webmasters**, support a company's Internet and intranet operations. Web support involves design and construction of Web pages, monitoring traffic, managing hardware and software, and linking Web-based applications to the company's existing information systems. Reliable, high-quality Web support is especially critical for companies engaged in e-commerce.

CASE IN POINT 1.3: WHAT SHOULD LISA DO?

Lisa Jameson has two job offers. One is from Pembroke Boats, a boat manufacturer that employs 200 people in a small Ohio town. Pembroke does not have an IT department and wants her to create one. The job position is called information coordinator, but she would be the only IT person.

The other offer, which pays about $7,500 more annually, is from Albemarle Express, a nationwide trucking firm located in Detroit. At Albemarle Express, Lisa would be a programmer-analyst, with the promise that if she does well in her position, she eventually will move into a systems analyst position and work on new systems development. Lisa has heard a rumor that another company might acquire Albemarle Express, but that rumor has occurred before and nothing has ever happened. What should Lisa do, and why?

THE SYSTEMS ANALYST POSITION

A systems analyst investigates, analyzes, designs, develops, installs, evaluates, and maintains a company's information systems. To perform those tasks, a systems analyst constantly interacts with users and managers within and outside the company. On large projects, the analyst works as a member of an IT department team; on smaller assignments, he or she might work alone.

Most companies assign systems analysts to the IT department, but analysts also can report to a specific user area such as marketing, sales, or accounting. As a member of a functional team, an analyst is better able to understand the needs of that group and how information systems support the department's mission. Smaller companies often use consultants to perform systems analysis work on an as-needed basis.

Responsibilities

The systems analyst's job overlaps business and technical issues. Analysts help translate business requirements into IT projects. When assigned to a systems development team, an analyst might help document business profiles, review business processes, select hardware and software packages, design information systems, train users, and plan e-commerce Web sites.

A systems analyst plans projects, develops schedules, and estimates costs. To keep managers and users informed, an analyst conducts meetings, delivers presentations, and writes memos, reports, and documentation. The Systems Analyst's Toolkit at the end of this book includes various tools to help you with each of those important skills.

Required Skills and Background

A systems analyst needs solid technical knowledge, strong oral and written communication skills, good analytical ability, and an understanding of business operations and processes. Companies typically require that systems analysts have a college degree in information systems, computer science, business, or a closely related field, and some IT experience usually is required. For higher-level positions, many companies require a master of science degree and additional experience.

A systems analyst needs good interpersonal skills to interact with people at all levels, from operational staff to senior executives, including people outside the company, such as software and hardware vendors, customers, and government officials.

Often an analyst must lead an IT development team. As a team leader, an analyst plans, estimates, and manages the project, and uses leadership and team-building skills to coach and motivate team members.

State-of-the-art knowledge is extremely important in a rapidly changing business and technical environment. The Internet offers numerous opportunities to update technical knowledge and skills. Many Web sites, such as the TechRepublic site shown in Figure 1-30, offer free subscriptions and enable IT professionals to learn about the latest technical developments, exchange experiences, and ask questions.

Analysts also maintain their skills by attending training courses, both on-site and online. Networking with colleagues is another way to keep up with new developments, and membership in professional associations also is important. A systems analyst, like any other professional, needs to manage his or her own career by developing knowledge and skills that are valuable and expected in the marketplace.

Certification

Many hardware and software companies offer certification for IT professionals. **Certification** verifies that an individual demonstrated a certain level of knowledge and skill on a standardized test. Certification is an excellent way for IT professionals to learn new skills and gain recognition for their efforts. Although certification alone does not guarantee competence or ability, many companies regard certification as an important credential for hiring or promotion. You can learn more about certification by visiting the Web sites of individual companies such as Microsoft, Cisco Systems, Sun Microsystems, and Novell.

Career Opportunities

The demand for systems analysts is expected to remain strong well into the twenty-first century. Companies will need systems analysts to apply new information technology, and the explosion in e-commerce will fuel IT job growth. The systems analyst position is a challenging and rewarding one that can lead to a top management position. With an understanding of technical and business issues, a systems analyst has an unlimited horizon. Many companies have presidents and senior managers who started in IT departments as systems analysts.

The responsibilities of a systems analyst at a small firm are different from those at a large corporation. Would you be better off at a small or large company? Where will you find the best opportunity for experience and professional growth? Each person looks for different rewards in a job. What will be important to you?

JOB TITLES First, do not rely on job titles alone. Some positions are called systems analysts, but involve only programming or technical support. In other cases, systems analyst responsibilities are found in positions titled computer specialist, programmer, programmer/analyst, systems designer, software engineer, and various others. Be sure the responsibilities of the job are stated clearly when you consider a position.

FIGURE 1-30 The TechRepublic Web site offers support for IT professionals. Features include newsletters, forums, product information, and a searchable knowledge base.

COMPANY ORGANIZATION Find out all you can about the company and where the IT department fits in the organization chart. Where are IT functions performed, and by whom? A firm might have a central IT group, but decentralize the systems development function. This situation sometimes occurs in large conglomerates, where the parent company consolidates information that actually is developed and managed at the subsidiary level. Where would you rather work?

COMPANY SIZE If you like more variety, a smaller firm might suit you best. If you want to specialize, however, then consider a larger company with state-of-the-art systems. Although you might have more responsibility in a smaller company, the promotional opportunities and financial rewards often are greater in larger companies. You also might want to consider working as an independent consultant, either on your own or with others. Many consulting firms have been successful in offering their services to smaller business enterprises that do not have the expertise to handle systems development on their own.

CORPORATE CULTURE In addition to having goals, methods, and information systems requirements, every firm has an underlying **corporate culture**. A corporate culture is the set of beliefs, rules, traditions, values, and attitudes that define a company and influence its way of doing business. To be successful, a systems analyst must understand the corporate culture and how it affects the way information is managed. Companies sometimes include statements about corporate culture in their mission statements, which are explained in Chapter 2.

SALARY, LOCATION, AND FUTURE GROWTH Finally, consider salary, location, and the company's prospects for future growth and success. Think about your impressions of the company and the people you met during your interviews. Most important, review your short- and long-term goals very carefully before deciding which position is best for you.

CASE IN POINT 1.4: JUST-IN-TIME AIRFREIGHT, INC.

Suppose you are the IT director at Just-in-Time Airfreight, and you have received authorization to hire another systems analyst. This will be an entry-level position, and the person will assist senior systems analysts on various projects involving the reservations and the human resources systems. Using the information in this chapter, draft an ad that would appear in *The Wall Street Journal*, local newspapers, and online. You can get some ideas by visiting monster.com, or a similar site. In your ad, be sure to list desired skills, experience, and educational requirements.

CHAPTER SUMMARY

In this chapter, you learned that information technology (IT) refers to the combination of hardware and software resources that companies use to manage, access, communicate, and share information. IT supports business operations, improves productivity, and helps managers make decisions. Systems analysis and design is the process of developing information systems that transform data into useful information.

Traditionally, companies either developed in-house applications or purchased software packages from vendors. Today, the choice is much more complex, but it is always important for companies to plan the system carefully before considering implementation options.

The essential components of an information system are hardware, software, data, processes, and people. Hardware consists of everything in the physical layer of the information system. Software consists of system software, which manages the hardware

components, and application software, which supports day-to-day business operations. Data is the raw material that an information system transforms into useful information. Processes describe the tasks and functions that users, managers, and IT staff members perform. People who interact with a system include users, from both within and outside the company.

A systems analyst starts with a business profile, which is an overview of company functions, and then he or she creates a series of business models that represent business processes, which describe specific transactions, events, tasks, and results. Companies engage in business process reengineering to simplify operations or reduce costs.

Companies are product-oriented, service-oriented, or a combination of the two. The newest business category is the Internet-dependent (dot-com) firm, which relies solely on Internet-based operations. E-commerce includes business-to-consumer (B2C) sales, and business-to-business (B2B) transactions that use Internet-based digital marketplaces or private electronic data interchange (EDI) systems.

Based on their functions and features, business information systems are identified as enterprise computing systems, transaction processing systems, business support systems, knowledge management systems, or user productivity systems. In most companies, significant overlap and integration exists among the various types of information systems.

A typical organization structure includes top managers, middle managers and knowledge workers, supervisors and team leaders, and operational employees. Top managers develop strategic plans, which define an overall mission and goals. Middle managers provide direction, resources, and feedback to supervisors and team leaders. Knowledge workers include various professionals who function as support staff. Supervisors and team leaders oversee operational employees. Each organizational level has a different set of responsibilities and information needs.

Systems analysts use modeling, prototyping, and computer-aided systems engineering (CASE) tools. Modeling produces a graphical representation of a concept or process, whereas prototyping involves the creation of an early working model of the information or its components. A systems analyst uses CASE tools to perform various systems development tasks.

Various development methods exist, including structured analysis, which treats data and processes as separate components, and object-oriented (O-O) analysis, which combines data and processes into objects. Companies also use teams of IT staff, users, and managers to speed up system development and produce better results. Two popular methodologies are joint application development (JAD) and rapid application development (RAD). JAD focuses on team-based fact-finding, which is only one phase of the development process, while RAD is more like a condensed version of the entire process. Another popular development strategy is Microsoft Solutions Framework (MSF).

The systems development life cycle (SDLC) is a structured approach that consists of five phases: systems planning, systems analysis, systems design, systems implementation, and systems operation, support, and security. The SDLC is pictured as a waterfall model, where the deliverable result or end product of each phase flows into the next phase.

The IT department develops, maintains, and operates a company's information systems. IT staff members provide technical support, including application development, systems support, user support, database administration, network administration, and Web support. These functions overlap considerably and often have different names in different companies.

A systems analyst investigates, analyzes, designs, develops, installs, evaluates, and maintains information systems. Systems analysts need a combination of technical and business knowledge, analytical ability, and communication skills. In addition to education and experience, various certifications are available to systems analysts. A systems analyst's responsibilities depend on a company's organization, size, and culture. Systems analysts need to consider salary, location, and future growth potential when making a career decision.

Key Terms and Phrases

application development 24
application software 6
B2B (business-to-business) 9
B2C (business-to-consumer) 9
brick-and-mortar 9
business model 8, 16
business process 8
business process modeling 8
business process reengineering (BPR) 8
business profile 8
business support systems 13
CASE tools 17
certification 27
class 19
computer-aided software engineering 17
computer-aided systems engineering (CASE) 17
corporate culture 28
data 5
data model 16
database administration 25
deliverable 20
dot-com (.com) 9
e-commerce (electronic commerce) 9
electronic data interchange (EDI) 10
empowerment 16
end product 20
end users 7
enterprise applications 6
enterprise computing 12
enterprise resource planning (ERP) 12
expert systems 14
extensible markup language (XML) 10
feasibility study 21
fuzzy logic 14
groupware 14
hardware 6
help desk 25
horizontal system 7
HTML (hypertext markup language) 10

I-commerce (Internet commerce) 9
inference rules 14
information 5
information center (IC) 25
information system 4
information technology (IT) 4
in-house applications 5
Internet-dependent 9
joint application development (JAD) 19
knowledge base 14
knowledge management systems 14
knowledge workers 16
legacy systems 7
management information systems (MIS) 13
message 19
methods 19
Microsoft Solutions Framework (MSF) 20
middle managers 15
mission-critical system 5
modeling 16
Moore's Law 6
.NET 11
network administration 25
network model 16
network operating system (NOS) 6
object-oriented analysis (O-O) 19
object model 16
objects 19
operational employees 16
preliminary investigation 21
process model 16
process-centered 18
processes 7
product-oriented 9
properties 19
prototype 17
prototyping 17
radio frequency identification (RFID) 13

rapid application development (RAD) 19
requirements model 16
requirements modeling 22
scalable 22
service-oriented 9
software 6
software packages 5
strategic plans 15
structured analysis 18
supervisors 16
system 5
system requirements document 22
system software 6
systems analysis and design 4
systems analysis phase 22
systems analysts 4
systems design phase 22
system design specification 22
systems development life cycle (SDLC) 18
systems evaluation 22
systems implementation phase 22
systems planning phase 21
systems request 21
systems operation, support, and security phase 22
systems support and security 24
team leaders 16
technical support 24
top managers 15
transaction processing (TP) systems 12
user productivity systems 14
user support 25
users 7
vertical system 7
waterfall model 20
Web services 11
Web support 25
webmasters 25
WebSphere 11
what-if 13

Learn It Online

Instructions: To complete the Learn It Online exercises, start your browser, click the Address bar, and then enter the Web address **scsite.com/sad6e/learn**. When the Systems Analysis and Design Learn It Online page is displayed, follow the instructions in the exercises below. Each exercise has instructions for saving your results, either for your own records or for submission to your instructor.

1 Chapter Reinforcement

TF, MC, and SA

Below SAD Chapter 1, click the Chapter Reinforcement link. Print the quiz by clicking Print on the File menu for each page. Answer each question.

2 Flash Cards

Below SAD Chapter 1, click the Flash Cards link and read the instructions. Type 20 (or a number specified by your instructor) in the Number of playing cards text box, type your name in the Enter your Name text box, and then click the Flip Card button. When the flash card is displayed, read the question and then click the ANSWER box arrow to select an answer. Flip through the Flash Cards. If your score is 15 (75%) correct or greater, click Print on the File menu to print your results. If your score is less than 15 (75%) correct, then redo this exercise by clicking the Replay button.

3 Practice Test

Below SAD Chapter 1, click the Practice Test link. Answer each question, enter your first and last name at the bottom of the page, and then click the Grade Test button. When the graded practice test is displayed on your screen, click Print on the File menu to print a hard copy. Continue to take practice tests until you score 80% or better.

4 Who Wants To Be a Computer Genius?

Below SAD Chapter 1, click the Computer Genius link. Read the instructions, enter your first and last name at the bottom of the page, and then click the Play button. When your score is displayed, click the PRINT RESULTS link to print a hard copy.

5 Wheel of Terms

Below SAD Chapter 1, click the Wheel of Terms link. Read the instructions, and then enter your first and last name and your school name. Click the PLAY button. When your score is displayed on the screen, right-click the score and then click Print on the shortcut menu to print a hard copy.

6 Crossword Puzzle Challenge

Below SAD Chapter 1, click the Crossword Puzzle Challenge link. Read the instructions, and then enter your first and last name. Click the SUBMIT button. Work the crossword puzzle. When you are finished, click the Submit button. When the crossword puzzle is redisplayed, click the Print Puzzle button to print a hard copy.

Case-Sim: SCR Associates

Background

SCR Associates is a consulting firm that offers IT solutions and training. SCR needs an information system to manage operations at its new training center. The new system will be called TIMS (Training Information Management System). As a newly hired systems analyst, you will report to Jesse Baker, systems group manager. You will work on various tasks and practice the skills you learned in this chapter.

Using the Case

The SCR Associates case study is a Web-based simulation that allows you to practice your skills in a real-world environment. The case study transports you to SCR's company intranet, where you can complete 10 work sessions, each aligning with a chapter. As you work on the case, you will receive e-mail and voice mail messages, obtain information from SCR's online libraries, and perform various tasks. The first time you enter the SCR Case, you should go to the starting page at **scsite.com/sad6e/scr** for detailed instructions.

Preview: Session 1

This is your second day on the job as a systems analyst at SCR Associates. You spent most of yesterday filling out personnel forms and learning your way around the office. This morning, you sit at your desk and examine SCR's Internet site. You explore the entire site, which reflects SCR's history, purpose, and values. You especially are impressed with the emphasis SCR puts on its relationships with clients. When you finish examining the site, you are more convinced than ever that SCR will be a great career opportunity for you. You are excited about your new job, and eager to get started.

To start a work session, you log on to the SCR intranet. When you enter your name and password, an opening screen displays links to the work sessions, and you select Session 1. At this point, you check your e-mail and voice mail messages carefully. You then begin working on your task list, which includes the following items:

Tasks: Introduction

Jesse wants me to learn as much as possible about SCR, and she gave me a checklist to get me started:

1. Investigate SCR's Internet site and learn about the company's history, purpose, and values. Send Jesse a brief memo with suggestions to expand or improve these sections.

2. On the SCR intranet, visit the data, forms, and resource libraries and review a sample of the information in each library.

3. Using the SCR functions and organization listed in the data library, create an organization chart using Microsoft Word, Visio, or a drawing program.

4. Jesse says that SCR has plenty of competition in the IT consulting field. Get on the Internet and find three other IT consulting firms. She wants a brief description of each firm and the services it offers.

FIGURE 1-31 Task list: Session 1.

Chapter Exercises

Review Questions

1. What is information technology, and why is it important to a business?
2. Define business profiles, business models, and business processes.
3. Identify the main components of an information system.
4. Explain the difference between vertical and horizontal systems packages.
5. How do companies use EDI? What are some advantages of using XML?
6. Describe five types of information systems, and give an example of each.
7. Describe four organizational levels of a typical business and their information requirements.
8. Describe the phases of the systems development life cycle.
9. Explain the use of models, prototypes, and CASE tools in the systems development process.
10. What is object-oriented analysis, and how does it differ from structured analysis?

Discussion Topics

1. Some experts believe that the growth in e-commerce will cause states and local governments to lose a significant amount of sales tax revenue, unless Internet transactions are subject to sales tax. Do you agree? Why or why not?
2. Present an argument for and against the following proposition: Because IT managers must understand all phases of the business, a company should fill top management vacancies by promoting IT managers.
3. The head of the IT group in a company often is called the chief information officer (CIO) or chief technology officer (CTO). Should the CIO or CTO report to the company president, to the finance department, where many of the information systems are used, or to someone or somewhere else? Why would it matter?
4. Computers perform many jobs that previously were performed by people. Will computer-based transactions and expanded e-commerce eventually replace person-to-person contact? From a customer's point of view, is this better? Why or why not?

Projects

1. Contact at least three people at your school or a nearby company who use information systems. List the systems, the position titles of the users, and the business functions that the systems support.
2. Research newspaper, business magazine articles, or the Web to find computer companies whose stock is traded publicly. Choose a company and pretend to buy $1,000 of its stock. What is the current price per share? Why did you choose that company? Report each week to your class on how your stock is doing.
3. Create an organization chart of your school or a local company by using Microsoft Word or a similar program, or you can draw it by hand. If you have Microsoft Word 2003 or Microsoft Word 2002, you can click the Insert Diagram or Organization Chart button on the Drawing toolbar, then click the Organization Chart button. If you have an older version of Word, you can click Insert – Object – MS Organization Chart.
4. In recent years, technology stocks have climbed to staggering heights, only to fall sharply. Imagine that you are a financial advisor, and an investor has to come to you for advice. Perform Internet research to learn more about investing in technology stocks. Would it be important to know something about the investor, including his or her goals and risk tolerance? How would you decide what companies to invest in?

Apply Your Knowledge

The Apply Your Knowledge section contains four mini-cases. Each case describes a situation, explains your role in the case, and asks you to respond to questions. You can answer the questions by applying knowledge you learned in the chapter.

1 Low-Voltage Components

Situation:

You are the IT manager at Low-Voltage Components, a medium-sized firm that makes specialized circuit boards. Low-Voltage's largest customer, TX Industries, recently installed a computerized purchasing system. If Low-Voltage connects to the TX system, TX will be able to submit purchase orders electronically. Although Low-Voltage has a computerized accounting system, that system is not capable of handling EDI.

1. Should Low-Voltage develop a system to connect with TX Industries' purchasing system? Why or why not?
2. What terms or concepts describe the proposed computer-to-computer relationship between Low-Voltage and TX Industries?
3. Is Low-Voltage's proposed new system a transaction processing system? Why or why not?
4. Before Low-Voltage makes a final decision, should the company consider an ERP system? Why or why not?

2 Systems Analyst Salaries

Situation:

As part of your job search, you decide to find out more about salaries and qualifications for systems analysts in the area where you would like to work. To increase your knowledge, search the Internet to perform the following research:

1. Find information about a career as a systems analyst.
2. Using the Internet, determine whether the Federal Bureau of Labor Statistics lists salary information for systems analysts. If so, summarize the information you find.
3. Find at least two online ads for systems analysts and list the employers, the qualifications, and the salaries, if mentioned.
4. Find at least one ad for an IT position that specifically mentions e-commerce.

3 MultiTech Interview

Situation:

You have an interview for an IT position with MultiTech, a large telecommunications company, and you want to learn more about the firm and its organizational structure. To prepare for the interview, you decide to review your knowledge about corporations, including the following questions:

1. What are the four organizational levels in a typical company?
2. How can you classify companies based on their mix of products and services?
3. What is empowerment?
4. What types of information systems might a large company use?

4 Rainbow's End Interview

Situation:

Your MultiTech interview seemed to go well, but you did not get the job. During the meeting, the interviewer mentioned that MultiTech uses structured analysis and relies heavily on modeling, prototyping, and CASE tools. Thinking back, you realize that you did not fully understand those terms. As you prepare for an interview with Rainbow's End, a large retail chain, you decide to review some IT terms and concepts. You want to be ready for the following questions:

1. What is the main difference between structured analysis and O-O analysis?
2. What is a CASE tool and what does it do?
3. What is modeling and how is it done?
4. What is prototyping and why is it important?

Case Studies

Case studies allow you to practice specific skills learned in the chapter. Each chapter contains several case studies that continue throughout the textbook, and a chapter capstone case.

New Century Health Clinic

New Century Health Clinic offers preventive medicine and traditional medical care. In your role as an IT consultant, you will help New Century develop a new information system.

Background

Five years ago, cardiologists Timothy Jones and Dolores Garcia decided to combine their individual practices in Brea, California, to form New Century Health Clinic. They wanted to concentrate on preventive medicine by helping patients maintain health and fitness and by providing traditional medical care. Dr. Jones recently asked you to work with him as an IT consultant. He wants you to help New Century develop an information system that will support the clinic's operations and future growth. During an initial meeting, he provided you with some background information and asked for your suggestions about how to get started.

At your desk, you begin to review New Century's situation. The clinic is located near a new shopping mall in a busy section of the city. New Century's staff includes four doctors, three registered nurses, four physical therapists, and six office staff workers. The clinic currently has a patient base of 3,500 patients from 275 different employers, many of which provide insurance coverage for employee wellness and health maintenance. Currently, New Century accepts 34 different insurance policies.

Anita Davenport, who has been with New Century since its inception, is the office manager. She supervises the staff, including Fred Brown, Susan Gifford, Tom Capaletti, Lisa Sung, and Carla Herrera. Fred Brown handles office payroll, tax reporting, and profit distribution among the associates. Susan Gifford is responsible for the maintenance of patient records. Tom Capaletti handles most of the paperwork concerning insurance reporting and accounting. Lisa Sung has the primary responsibility for the appointment book, and her duties include making reminder calls to patients and preparing daily appointment lists. Carla Herrera is concerned primarily with ordering and organizing office and clinic supplies.

Each of the six office staff people has one or more primary responsibilities; however, all members of the staff help out whenever necessary with patient records, insurance processing, and appointment processing. In addition to their regular responsibilities, all six office workers are involved in the preparation of patient statements at the end of each month.

Using this information, you begin to prepare for your next meeting with Dr. Jones.

Assignments

1. Create an organization chart of New Century's office staff by using Microsoft Word or a similar program, or you can draw it by hand. If you have Microsoft Word 2003 or Microsoft Word 2002, you can click the Insert Diagram or Organization Chart button on the Drawing toolbar, then click the Organization Chart button. If you have an older version of Word, you can click Insert – Object – MS Organization Chart.

2. Identify at least three business processes that New Century performs, and explain who is responsible for the specific tasks.

3. Explain how New Century might use a transaction processing system, a business support system, and a user productivity system. For each type of system, provide a specific example, and explain how the system would benefit the clinic.

4. During the systems development process, should New Century consider any of the following: B2B, vertical and horizontal system packages, or Internet-based solutions? Explain your answers.

PERSONAL TRAINER, INC.

Personal Trainer, Inc. owns and operates fitness centers in a dozen Midwestern cities. The centers have done well, and the company is planning an international expansion by opening a new "supercenter" in the Toronto area.

Background

Cassia Umi, president, heads Personal Trainer's management team. Three managers report to her at the firm's Chicago headquarters: Janet McDonald, manager, finance; Tai Tranh, manager, sales and marketing; and Reed Cotter, manager, operations. The managers who run the 12 existing centers all report to Reed.

Cassia wants the new supercenter to emphasize a wide variety of personal services and special programs for members. If the supercenter approach is successful, it will become the model for Personal Trainer's future growth. Cassia personally selected Gray Lewis, a manager with three years of fitness center experience, to run the new facility.

The new supercenter will feature a large exercise area with state-of-the-art equipment, a swimming pool, a sporting goods shop, a health food store, and a snack bar. In addition, the center will offer child care with special programs for various ages, a teen center, and a computer café. Cassia also wants members to have online access to customized training programs and progress reports.

Personal Trainer currently uses BumbleBee, a popular accounting package, to manage its receivables, payables, and general ledger. Membership lists and word processing are handled with Microsoft Office products.

Cassia believes the new supercenter will require additional data management capability, and she decided to hire Patterson and Wilder, an IT consulting firm, to help Personal Trainer develop an information system for the new operation. The firm assigned Susan Park, an experienced consultant, to work with the Personal Trainer team.

Susan's first task was to learn more about business operations at the new center, so she requested a meeting with Gray. After some small talk, the discussion went like this:

Susan: Tell me about your plans for the new operation. I'm especially interested in what kind of information management you'll need.

Gray: *Cassia thinks that we'll need more information support because of the size and complexity of the new operation. To tell the truth, I'm not so sure. We've had no problem with BumbleBee at the other centers, and I don't really want to reinvent the wheel.*

Susan: Maybe we should start by looking at the similarities — and the differences — between the new center and the existing ones.

Gray: *Okay, let's do that. First of all, we offer the same basic services everywhere. That includes the exercise equipment, a pool, and, in most centers, a snack bar. Some centers also sell sporting goods, and one offers child care — but not child-fitness programs. It is true that we've never put all this together under one roof. And, I admit, we've never offered online access. To be honest, I'm not absolutely sure what Cassia and Kerry have in mind when they talk about 24/7 Web-based access.*

Susan: So, with all this going on, wouldn't an overall system make your job easier?

Gray: *Yes, but I don't know where to start.*

Susan: Gray, that's why I'm here. I'll work with you and the rest of the team to come up with a solution that supports your business.

(continued)

Gray: *Sounds good to me. When can we start?*

Susan: *Let's get together first thing tomorrow. Bring along an organization chart and think about how you plan to run the new facility. We'll try to build a model of the new operation so we can identify the business functions. When we know what the functions are, we can figure out what kind of information is needed or generated by each function. That will be our starting point.*

Assignments

1. Develop a business profile for Personal Trainer, based on the facts provided. List at least three of Personal Trainer's business processes.

2. Create an organization chart for Personal Trainer, Inc., using Microsoft Word or a similar program, or you can draw it by hand. If you have Microsoft Word 2003 or Microsoft Word 2002, you can click the Insert Diagram or Organization Chart button on the Drawing toolbar, then click the Organization Chart button. If you have an older version of Word, you can click Insert – Object – MS Organization Chart.

3. Review the conversation between Susan and Gray. In your opinion, is Gray totally supportive of the new system? Why or why not? Do you agree with the way that Susan responds to Gray's comments? Why or why not?

4. Should Personal Trainer consider any of the following systems: enterprise computing, transaction processing, business support, knowledge management, or user productivity? Why or why not? What opportunities might Personal Trainer have for Web-based B2C transactions in the future? What about B2B?

Original Kayak Adventures

Original Kayak Adventures (OKA) offers guided eco-tours and kayak rentals along the Hudson River.

Background

John and Edie Caputo, who are avid kayakers and amateur naturalists, founded OKA two years ago. The Caputos spent many weekends and vacations exploring the Hudson's numerous creeks and tributaries. John was a sales representative and Edie worked for a Web design firm. Two years ago, John's division was purchased by a rival company, which announced plans to move operations to another state. Rather than relocate, the Caputos decided to launch OKA. They reasoned that Edie could leave her job and work as a free-lance Web designer, which would provide some income while John tried to build OKA into a profitable business. John and Edie are convinced that the eco-tourism market will expand greatly, and they look forward to sharing their experience and knowledge with others who enjoy nature and kayaking.

Original Kayak Adventures advertises in regional magazines and maintains a Web site, which Edie designed. Customers say that the site is attractive and informative, but the Caputos are not sure of its effectiveness in attracting new business. At this time, no other kayak rental firms operate within 20 miles of OKA's location.

So far, the Caputos' plan is working out well. OKA rents space at a nearby marina, where Edie runs the office and operates her Web design business. She also handles rentals when John is giving lessons or busy with a tour group. On summer weekends and holidays, Janet Jacobs, a local college student, handles telephone inquiries and reservations.

OKA's inventory includes 16 rental kayaks of various types, eight car-top carriers, and a large assortment of accessories and safety equipment. Based on customer requests, Edie is considering adding a selection of books and videos about kayaking and eco-tourism.

OKA has three main business segments: rentals, instruction, and guided tours. Most customers make advance reservations for scheduled tours and instruction sessions, but sometimes space is available for last-minute customers. Rentals are split evenly between reservations and walk-in customers.

Reservations are entered in a loose-leaf binder, with separate tabs for each business activity. Edie also created a Microsoft Access database to record reservations. When she has time, she enters the reservation date, the reservation details and kayak type, and the customer information into a table, which is sorted by reservation date. Each day, she prints a reservation list. For quick reference, Edie also displays kayak availability on a wall-mounted board with color-coded magnets that show the available or reserved status of each rental kayak. In addition to the database, Edie uses an inexpensive accounting package to keep OKA's books.

Although the OKA database handles the basic information, the Caputos have noticed some drawbacks. For example, reservations for guided tours or instruction sessions sometimes conflict with John's or Edie's availability. The Caputos also would like to get more information about rental patterns, customer profiles, advertising effectiveness, and future business opportunities. John and Edie have talked about updating the system, but they have been too busy to do so.

Assignments

1. Develop a business profile for Original Kayak Adventures. The profile should include information about OKA's business activities, organization, resources, customers, and potential opportunity to engage in e-commerce.

2. List OKA's main functions and business processes. Draw a model of an OKA business process, including possible events, processes, and results.

3. What types of information systems does OKA use? Do these systems support its current and future business objectives? Why or why not?

4. From an object-oriented viewpoint, OKA treats reservations as a class. Based on the background information provided, what are some properties of reservation objects?

CHAPTER CAPSTONE CASE: SoftWear, Limited

SoftWear, Limited (SWL) is a continuing case study that illustrates the knowledge and skills described in each chapter. In this case study, the student acts as a member of the SWL systems development team and performs various tasks.

Background

SoftWear, Limited, manufactures and sells casual and recreational clothing for men and women. SWL was formed about 10 years ago when a national firm sold the division during a corporate downsizing. A group of managers obtained financing and became owners of the company. With clever marketing, competitive pricing, and efficient production, SWL has grown to more than 450 employees, including the corporate headquarters and manufacturing plants. Last year, SWL had sales of $700 million.

The company employs 90 people at its Raleigh, North Carolina, headquarters, including officers, managers, and support staff. Another 30 salaried and 340 hourly people are employed at production facilities in Haskell, California, and Florence, Texas. The company also is considering new factories in Canada and Australia.

SWL maintains a Web site with information about the company and its products. SWL's Web site features text, graphics, and audio and allows customers to send e-mail, order products from the SoftWear catalog, and request special promotional items, including beach umbrellas, hats, and T-shirts customized with the purchaser's logo. SWL also is studying other ways to use the Internet to boost product sales and expand its marketing efforts, including a special European promotion designed to increase awareness of SWL's Web site.

Organization

SWL's headquarters includes the executive, operations, marketing, finance, and human resources departments. Figure 1-32 shows the organization chart of the management positions within SWL. Notice that the director of information technology, Ann Hon, reports to Michael Jeremy, vice president of finance. The director of the payroll department, Amy Calico, also reports to Mr. Jeremy.

FIGURE 1-32 Organization chart of SoftWear, Limited.

CHAPTER CAPSTONE CASE: SoftWear, Limited (continued)

SWL

The IT department includes Ann Hon, the director; Jane Rossman, the systems support manager; Kerry Krauss, the user support manager; and Altovise Martin, the Web support manager. Figure 1-33 shows the organization of the IT department. At SWL, the systems support group also handles new systems development, network administration, and database administration.

FIGURE 1-33 Organization chart of the IT department of SoftWear, Limited.

Systems analysts and programmers report to Jane Rossman, systems support manager. Systems analysts primarily analyze and design information systems. Programmers primarily develop, test, and implement code necessary for systems development, enhancements, and maintenance. In addition to the current staff, SWL is planning to hire a programmer-analyst who will divide his or her time between systems analysis and programming duties.

The technical support staff members are responsible for the system software on all SWL computers. They also provide technical advice and guidance to the other groups within the IT department.

The operations staff is responsible for centralized IT functions, including SWL's mainframe computer, and provides network and database administration.

Current Systems

SWL uses a manufacturing and inventory control system at its factories, but the system does not exchange data with SWL's suppliers at this time. The company's sales processing system handles online and catalog transactions, and produces sales reports. The marketing staff, however, wants even more information about sales trends and marketing analysis data. A company intranet connects employees at all locations, and provides e-mail, shared calendars, and a document library. Most administrative employees have workstations with Microsoft Office applications, but SWL has not provided company-wide training or help desk support.

CHAPTER CAPSTONE CASE: SoftWear, Limited (continued)

SWL Team Tasks

1. Write an employment advertisement for a new systems analyst position at SWL. Perform Internet research to locate examples of advertisements for systems analysts, and consider SWL's business profile when you write the advertisement.

2. Should SWL consider any of the following systems: ERP, business support, or knowledge management? Why or why not?

3. What opportunities might SWL have for Web-based B2B transactions in the future?

4. Should SWL consider ways to increase a sense of empowerment among its employees? Why or why not? Could user productivity software play a role in that effort? How?

PHASE | **SYSTEMS PLANNING**

Systems planning is the first of five phases in the systems development life cycle (SDLC). In this phase, you will learn how IT projects get started and how a systems analyst evaluates a proposed project and determines its feasibility. A systems analyst's first task is to review an IT request to determine whether it presents a strong business case, or justification. To do this, the analyst considers the company's strategic plan and studies its mission, objectives, and IT needs. Next, the analyst conducts a preliminary investigation, which requires fact-finding to see whether the request is feasible from an operational, technical, economic, and schedule standpoint. At the conclusion of the investigation, the analyst prepares a report and makes a recommendation to management.

PHASE TOPIC
Chapter 2
Analyzing the Business Case

DELIVERABLE
Preliminary investigation report

TOOLKIT SUPPORT
Primary tools: Communications, financial analysis, and project management tools.
Other tools as required.

CHAPTER

2 Analyzing the Business Case

CHAPTER 2 explains systems planning, which is the first phase in the systems development life cycle (SDLC). This chapter explains why it is important to understand business operations and requirements, how IT projects support a company's overall strategic plan, how systems projects get started, and how systems analysts conduct a preliminary investigation and feasibility study.

INTRODUCTION

OBJECTIVES

When you finish this chapter, you will be able to:

- Explain the concept of a business case and how a business case affects an IT project
- Describe the strategic planning process and why it is important to the IT team
- Explain the purpose of a mission statement
- Describe the SDLC, and explain how it serves as a framework for systems development and business modeling
- Describe risks and risk management features
- List the reasons for information systems projects and the factors that affect such projects
- Explain the initial review of systems requests and the role of the systems review committee
- Define operational feasibility, technical feasibility, economic feasibility, and schedule feasibility
- Describe the steps in a preliminary investigation and the end product of an investigation

During the systems planning phase, the IT team reviews a proposal to determine if it presents a strong business case. The term **business case** refers to the reasons, or justification, for a proposal. A strong business case suggests that the company should pursue the alternative, above other options, because it would be in the firm's best interest to do so. To analyze the business case for a specific proposal, the analyst must consider the company's overall mission, objectives, and IT needs.

This chapter begins with a discussion of strategic planning, because the IT team must understand, support, and help plan long-term strategic goals. Along with financial, marketing, and human resources, companies need information technology to achieve growth and success.

Systems development typically starts with a systems request, followed by a preliminary investigation, which includes a feasibility study. You will learn how systems requests originate, how they are evaluated, and how to conduct a preliminary investigation. You also will learn about fact-finding techniques that begin at this point and carry over into later development phases. Finally, you will examine the report to management, which concludes the systems planning phase.

CHAPTER INTRODUCTION CASE: Mountain View College Bookstore

Background: Wendy Lee, manager of college services at Mountain View College, wants a new information system that will improve efficiency and customer service at the three college bookstores.

In this part of the case, Florence Fullerton (systems analyst) and Harry Boston (student intern) are talking about justification for the new system and the project's feasibility.

Participants:	Florence and Harry
Location:	Mountain View College cafeteria, Monday afternoon, October 3, 2005
Project status:	Florence has received a systems request from Wendy Lee for a new bookstore information system.
Discussion topics:	Analysis of business justification and project feasibility

Florence:	Hi, Harry. Are you ready to get started?
Harry:	*Sure. What's our next step?*
Florence:	Well, when we analyze a specific systems request, we need to see how the proposal fits into the overall picture at the college. In other words, we have to analyze the business case for the request.
Harry:	*What's a business case?*
Florence:	A business case is the justification for a project. A strong business case means that a proposal will add substantial value to the organization and support our strategic plan.
Harry:	*What's a strategic plan?*
Florence:	A strategic plan is like a road map for the future. Without a long-range plan, it's hard to know if you're heading in the right direction. Our plan starts with a mission statement, which reflects our purpose, our vision, and our values.
Harry:	*I see what you mean. I read the mission statement this morning. It says that we will strive to be an efficient, customer-friendly bookstore that uses a mix of interpersonal skills and technology to serve our students and support the overall objectives of the college. That says a lot in just one sentence.*
Florence:	It sure does. Now, let's get to the specifics. I just received a systems request from the college business manager. She wants us to develop a new information system for the bookstore.
Harry:	*Do we have a green light to get started?*
Florence:	Yes and no. Mountain View College doesn't have a formal procedure for evaluating IT requests, and we don't have a systems review committee. Maybe that's something we should consider for the future. Meanwhile, we need to conduct a preliminary investigation to see whether this request is feasible.
Harry:	*What do you mean by "feasible"?*
Florence:	To see if a systems request is feasible, we have to look at four separate yardsticks: operational feasibility, technical feasibility, economic feasibility, and schedule feasibility. If the request passes all the tests, we continue working on the system. If not, we stop.
Harry:	*How will we know if the request passes the tests?*
Florence:	That's our next step. Here's a task list to get us started:

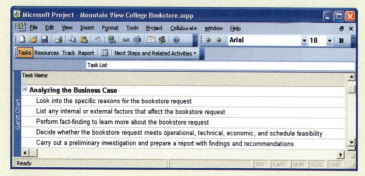

FIGURE 2-1

STRATEGIC PLANNING — A FRAMEWORK FOR IT SYSTEMS DEVELOPMENT

ON THE WEB

For more information about Strategic Planning, visit **scsite.com/sad6e/ more**, locate Chapter 2 and then click the Strategic Planning link.

Companies develop and maintain IT systems to support their current and future business operations. Some IT needs are immediate, such as fixing a logic problem in a payroll system. Other needs might be further on the horizon, such as planning IT support for a new factory, a future merger, or a corporate restructuring. In most companies, the IT team reviews each IT-related proposal, project, and systems request to determine if it presents a strong business case, or justification.

Most successful IT managers engage in long-range planning, even as they handle day-to-day maintenance and support. To carry out this task effectively, they must understand and participate in the firm's strategic planning process. **Strategic planning** is the process of identifying long-term organizational goals, strategies, and resources. Strategic planning looks beyond day-to-day activities and focuses on a horizon that is 3, 5, or even 10 years in the future.

Strategic Planning Overview

Why does a systems analyst need to know about strategic planning? The answer might be found in an old story about two stonecutters who were hard at work when a passerby asked them what they were doing. "I am cutting stones," said the first worker. The second worker replied, "I am building a cathedral." So it is with information technology: one analyst might say, "I am using a CASE tool," whereas another might say, "I am helping the company succeed in a major new business venture." Systems analysts should focus on the larger, strategic role of IT as they carry out their day-to-day responsibilities.

During strategic planning, top managers ask a series of questions that is called a **SWOT analysis** because it examines a company's strengths (S), weaknesses (W), opportunities (O), and threats (T). Each question may lead to an IT-related issue, which in turn requires more review, analysis, and planning. For example:

➡ What are our major strengths, and how can we maximize them in the future? What must we do to strengthen our IT function, including our people and technology infrastructure?

➡ What are our major weaknesses, and how can we overcome them? How should we address weaknesses in IT resources and capability?

➡ What are our major opportunities, and how can we take full advantage of them? What IT plans do we have to support business opportunities?

➡ What major threats do we face, and what can we do about them? What can we do to deal with potential threats to IT success?

POSSIBLE STRENGTHS

Excellent Web design staff
Low systems analyst turnover
Recently upgraded network

POSSIBLE WEAKNESSES

Still using several legacy systems
Budget increase was turned down
Documentation needs updating

POSSIBLE OPPORTUNITIES

Well-positioned for expansion
Can be first with new software
High potential for B2B growth

POSSIBLE THREATS

Aggressive new Web competition
Impact of new FCC rules
Other firms offer better benefits

FIGURE 2-2 A SWOT analysis might produce results similar to those shown here.

A SWOT analysis contributes to the strategic planning process by identifying technical, human, and financial resources. For example, suppose that a typical company assessed its IT resources by performing a SWOT analysis. Figure 2-2 shows some possible examples of strengths, weaknesses, opportunities, and threats.

From Strategic Plans to Business Results

Figure 2-3 shows the strategic planning process. A company develops a mission statement based on the firm's purpose, vision, and values. The mission statement is the foundation for the company's major goals, shorter-term objectives, and day-to-day business operations.

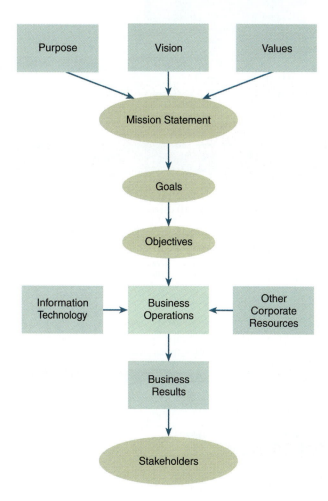

FIGURE 2-3   In the strategic planning process, a company's purpose, vision, and values shape its mission statement, which in turn leads to goals, objectives, business operations, and business results that affect company stakeholders.

A **mission statement** describes a company for its stakeholders and briefly states the company's overall purpose, products, services, and values. **Stakeholders** include anyone affected by the company's operations, such as customers, employees, suppliers, stockholders, and members of the community. Figure 2-4 on the next page shows examples of mission statements from three organizations.

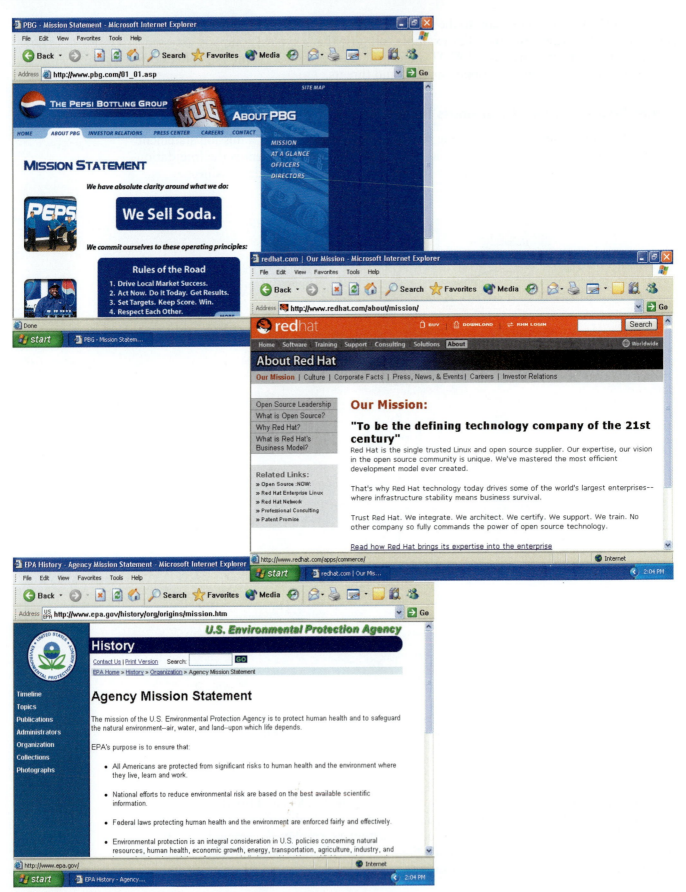

FIGURE 2-4   Three examples of mission statements.

A mission statement is just the starting point. Next, the company identifies a set of **goals** that will accomplish the mission. For example, the company might establish one-year, three-year, and five-year goals for expanding market share. To achieve those goals, the company develops a list of shorter-term **objectives**. For example, if a goal is to increase Web-based orders by 30 percent next year, a company might set quarterly objectives with monthly milestones. Objectives also might include tactical plans, such as creating a new Web site and training a special customer support group to answer e-mail inquiries. Finally, the objectives translate into day-to-day business operations, supported by IT and other corporate resources. The outcome is a set of business results that affect company stakeholders.

ON THE WEB

For more information about Mission Statements, visit **scsite.com/sad6e/ more**, locate Chapter 2 and then click the Mission Statements link.

CASE IN POINT 2.1: LO CARB MEALS

Lo Carb is a successful new company that has published several cookbooks, and marketed its own line of low-carbohydrate meals. Joe Turner, Lo Carb's president, has asked your opinion. He wants to know whether a mission statement really is necessary. After you review the chapter material, write a brief memo with your views. It might be a good idea to include online references that illustrate good (or not-so-good) examples of mission statements.

A Business Example

Suppose you are a systems analyst working in the IT department of an international hotel chain. The IT director favors the SDLC as an overall framework for system development and uses Popkin Software's System Architect CASE tool to organize and guide the tasks. Because you have no experience with that tool, you decide to complete a tutorial, which leads you through a series of screens similar to the one in Figure 2-5 on the next page.

As you work through the tutorial, you learn that you can organize and enter information and build a business enterprise model, a business model, an organizational model, a location model, an application model, a data model, and a technology model.

You also find that you will study the company's mission statement, business objectives and strategies, critical success factors, and critical business issues. **Critical success factors** are vital objectives that must be achieved for the enterprise to fulfill its mission, and **critical business issues** are the key problems, opportunities, and constraints that affect and shape the firm's decisions, just like a SWOT analysis. You learn that at some point in the systems development process, you will present a **case for action**, which is a summary of the project request and a specific recommendation.

The Role of the IT Department in Project Evaluation

Management leadership and information technology are linked closely, and remarkable changes have occurred in both areas. Ten years ago, a typical IT department handled all aspects of systems development and consulted users only when, and if, the department wanted user input. Today, systems development is much more team-oriented. New approaches to systems development, such as joint application development (JAD) and rapid application development (RAD), typically involve groups of users, managers, and IT staff working together right from the start.

Although team-oriented development is the norm, some companies see the role of the IT department as a gatekeeper, responsible for screening and evaluating systems requests. Should the IT department perform the initial evaluation, or should a cross-functional team do it? The answer depends on the company's size and organization, and whether IT is tightly integrated into business operations. In smaller companies or firms where only one person has IT skills, that person acts as a coordinator and consults closely with users and managers to evaluate systems requests. Larger firms are more likely to use an evaluation team or systems review committee.

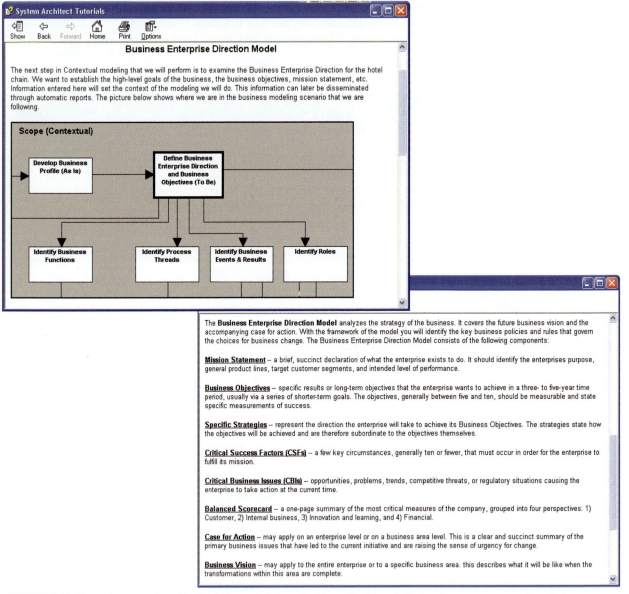

FIGURE 2-5 Tutorial screens from Popkin Software's System Architect CASE tool. Notice the references to the mission statement, critical success factors, critical business issues, and a case for action.

The Future

If you could look into the future, here is what you might see: New industries, products, and services emerging from amazing advances in information technology, customers who expect world-class IT support, a surge in Internet-based commerce, and a global business environment that is dynamic and incredibly challenging. To some firms, these changes will be threatening; other companies will see opportunities and take advantage of them by creating and following a strategic plan.

CASE IN POINT 2.2: ATTAWAY AIRLINES, PART ONE

You are the IT director at Attaway Airlines, a small regional air carrier. You chair the company's systems review committee, and you currently are dealing with strong disagreements about two key projects. Dan Esposito, the marketing manager, says it is vital to have a new computerized reservation system that can provide better customer service and reduce operational costs. Molly Kinnon, vice president of finance, is equally adamant that a new accounting system is needed immediately, because it will be very expensive to adjust the current system to new federal reporting requirements. Molly outranks Dan, and she is your boss. The next meeting, which promises to be a real showdown, is set for 9:00 a.m. tomorrow. How will you prepare for the meeting? What questions and issues should be discussed?

INFORMATION SYSTEMS PROJECTS

This section discusses reasons for systems projects, internal and external factors that affect systems projects, systems request forms, and project management tools.

Main Reasons for Systems Projects

The starting point for most projects is called a **systems request**, which is a formal way of asking for IT support. A systems request might propose enhancements for an existing system, the correction of problems, or the development of an entirely new information system.

As Figure 2-6 shows, the main reasons for systems requests are improved service to customers, better performance, support for new products and services, more information, stronger controls, and reduced cost.

IMPROVED SERVICE Systems requests often are aimed at improving service to customers or users within the company. Allowing mutual fund investors to check their account balances on a Web site, storing data on rental car customer preferences, or creating an online college registration system are examples that provide valuable services and increased customer satisfaction.

FIGURE 2-6 Six main reasons for systems requests.

SUPPORT FOR NEW PRODUCTS AND SERVICES New products and services often require new types or levels of IT support. For example, a software vendor might offer an automatic upgrade service for subscribers; or a package delivery company might add a special service for RFID-tagged shipments. In situations like these, it is most likely that additional IT support will be required.

BETTER PERFORMANCE The current system might not meet performance requirements. For example, it might respond slowly to data inquiries at certain times, or be unable to support company growth. Performance limitations also result when a system that was designed for a specific hardware configuration becomes obsolete when new hardware is introduced.

 ON THE WEB

For more information about Biometric Devices, visit **scsite.com/sad6e/ more**, locate Chapter 2 and then click the Biometric Devices link.

MORE INFORMATION The system might produce information that is insufficient, incomplete, or unable to support the company's changing information needs. For example, a system that tracks customer orders might not be capable of analyzing and predicting marketing trends. In the face of intense competition and rapid product development cycles, managers need the best possible information to make major decisions on planning, designing, and marketing new products and services.

STRONGER CONTROLS A system must have effective controls to ensure that data is secure and accurate. Some common security controls include passwords, various levels of user access, and **encryption**, or coding of data to keep it safe from unauthorized users. Hardware-based security controls include **biometric devices** that can identify a person by a retina scan or by mapping a facial pattern. A new biometric tool scans hands, rather than faces. The technology uses infrared scanners that create images with thousands of measurements of hand and finger characteristics, as shown in Figure 2-7.

In addition to being secure, data also must be accurate. Controls should minimize data entry errors whenever possible. For example, if a user enters an invalid customer number, the order processing system should reject the entry immediately and prompt the user to enter a valid number. Data entry controls must be effective without being excessive. If a system requires users to confirm every item with an "Are you sure? Y/N" message, internal users and customers might complain that the system is not user-friendly.

REDUCED COST The current system could be expensive to operate or maintain as a result of technical problems, design weaknesses, or the changing demands of the business. It might be possible to adapt the system to newer technology or upgrade it. On the other hand, cost-benefit analysis might show that a new system would be more cost effective and provide better support for long-term objectives.

FIGURE 2-7 This hand scanning device is used by Johnson & Wales University to identify students. The scanners provide quick and easy identification for dormitory residents.

CASE IN POINT 2.3: TRENT COLLEGE

Trent College is a private school in a small Maryland town. The college has outgrown its computerized registration system and is considering a new system. Althea Riddick, the college president, has asked you to list the reasons for systems projects, which are described on pages 51 – 52, and assign a relative weight to each reason, using a scale of 1 – 10, low to high. She said to use your best judgment, and support your conclusions in a brief memo to her. She also wants you to create an Excel spreadsheet that will calculate the weighted values automatically for each reason.

Factors that Affect Systems Projects

Internal and external factors affect every business decision that a company makes, and IT systems projects are no exception. Figure 2-8 shows the main internal and external factors.

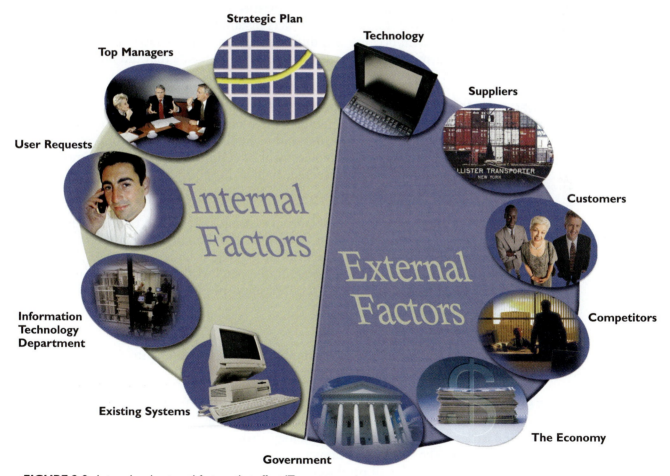

FIGURE 2-8   Internal and external factors that affect IT systems projects.

Internal Factors

Internal factors include the strategic plan, top managers, user requests, information technology department, and existing systems.

STRATEGIC PLAN A company's strategic plan sets the overall direction for the firm and has an important impact on IT projects. Company goals and objectives that need IT support will generate systems requests and influence IT priorities. A strategic plan that stresses technology tends to create a favorable climate for IT projects that extends throughout the organization.

TOP MANAGERS Directives from top managers are a prime source of large-scale systems projects. Those directives often result from strategic business decisions that require new IT systems, more information for decision making, or better support for mission-critical information systems.

USER REQUESTS As users rely more heavily on information systems to perform their jobs, they are likely to request even more IT services and support. For example, sales reps might request improvements to the company's Web site, a more powerful sales analysis report, a network to link all sales locations, or an online system that allows customers to obtain the status of their orders instantly. Or, users might not be satisfied with the current system because it is difficult to learn or lacks flexibility. They might want information systems support for business requirements that did not even exist when the system was developed.

INFORMATION TECHNOLOGY DEPARTMENT Many systems project requests come from the IT department. IT staff members often make recommendations based on their knowledge of business operations and technology trends. IT proposals might be strictly technical matters, such as replacement of certain network components, or suggestions might be more business oriented, such as proposing a new reporting or data collection system.

EXISTING SYSTEMS Errors or problems in existing systems can trigger requests for systems projects. Systems errors must be corrected, but analysts often spend too much time reacting to day-to-day problems without looking at underlying causes. This approach can turn an information system into a patchwork of corrections and changes that cannot support the company's overall business needs.

External Factors

External factors include technology, suppliers, customers, competitors, the economy, and government.

TECHNOLOGY Changing technology is a major force affecting business and society in general. For example, the rapid growth of telecommunications has created entire new industries and technologies. Technology also dramatically reshapes existing business operations. The success of scanner technology resulted in universal bar coding that now affects virtually all products. Most companies have a mix of software and hardware that must work together effectively. As technology changes, companies make decisions that trigger systems requests.

SUPPLIERS With the growth of electronic data interchange (EDI), relationships with suppliers are critically important. For example, an automobile company might require that suppliers code their parts in a certain manner to match the auto company's inventory control system. EDI also enables **just-in-time** (**JIT**) inventory systems, as shown in

ON THE WEB

For more information about JIT Systems, visit **scsite.com/ sad6e/ more**, locate Chapter 2 and then click the JIT Systems link.

Figure 2-9, which rely on computer-to-computer data exchange to minimize unnecessary inventory. The purpose of a JIT system is to provide the right product at the right place at the right time.

CUSTOMERS Customers are vitally important to any business. Information systems that interact with customers usually receive top priority. Many companies implement **customer relationship management (CRM)** systems that integrate all customer-related events and transactions, including marketing, sales, and customer service activities. CRM components can provide automated responses to sales inquiries, Web-based order processing, and online inventory tracking. Because an efficient warehouse is just as important as a successful Web site, suppliers use *smart* forklifts that can read RFID tags or UPC numbers and transmit data to a CRM system, as shown in Figure 2-10.

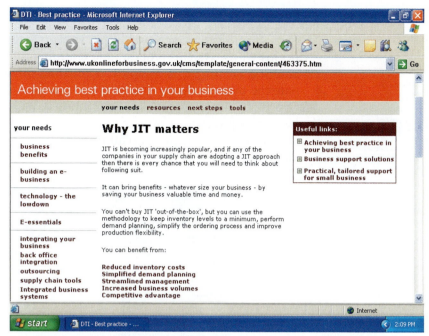

FIGURE 2-9 Just-in-time (JIT) inventory systems rely on computer-to-computer data exchange to minimize unnecessary inventory.

ON THE WEB

For more information about CRM Systems, visit **scsite.com/ sad6e/more**, locate Chapter 2 and then click the CRM Systems link.

COMPETITORS Competition drives many information systems decisions. For example, if one cellular telephone provider offers a new type of digital service, other firms must match the plan in order to remain competitive. New product research and development, marketing, sales, and service all require IT support.

THE ECONOMY Economic activity has a powerful influence on corporate information management. In a period of economic expansion, firms need to be ready with scalable systems that can handle additional volume and growth. Predicting the business cycle is not an exact science, and careful research and planning is critically important.

GOVERNMENT Federal, state, and local government regulations affect the design of corporate information systems. For example, income tax reporting requirements must be designed into a payroll package. The debate about Internet sales tax issues could profoundly affect e-commerce, as well as traditional retail businesses.

FIGURE 2-10 In an efficient warehouse, *smart* forklifts can read RFID tags or UPC numbers and transmit data to a CRM system.

Project Management Tools

TOOLKIT TIME

The Project Management Tools in Part 4 of the Systems Analyst's Toolkit can help you plan, manage, and control complex information systems projects. To learn more about these tools, turn to Part 4 of the six-part Toolkit that follows Chapter 10.

All IT projects, large and small, must be managed and controlled. Project management begins with a systems request, and continues until the project is completed or terminated. If the project is complex, companies often designate a project manager to coordinate the overall effort.

A popular project management tool is Microsoft Project, as shown in Figure 2-11. Using this program, a project manager can use a project map to define project tasks, list activities and participants, plan the sequence of work, estimate project milestone dates, and track all costs.

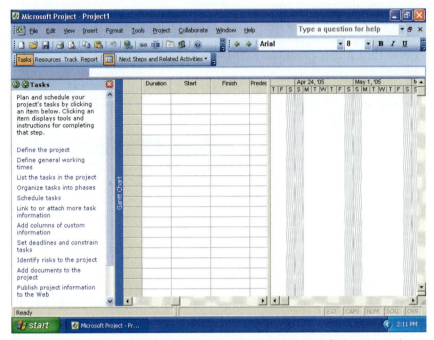

FIGURE 2-11   Microsoft Project enables a project manager to define project tasks, list activities and participants, plan the sequence of work, estimate project milestone dates, and track all costs.

Risk Management

Every IT project involves risks that systems analysts and IT project managers must address. A **risk** is an event that could affect the project negatively. **Risk management** is the process of identifying, evaluating, tracking, and controlling risks to minimize their impact. Risk management can be done manually, or by using software such as Microsoft Project, which includes a risk management feature. For example, with Microsoft Project software, a user can enter the following information for each risk:

- Probability, which represents the probability that the risk will happen, expressed as a percentage.

- Impact, which indicates the degree of adverse effect should the risk occur, on a scale of 1 to 10.

- Cost, which indicates the potential financial impact of the risk.

- Category, which specifies the risk type.

- Description, which specifies the nature of the risk.

- Mitigation plan, which identifies plans to control or limit the risk.

➡ Contingency plan, which specifies actions to be taken if the risk occurs.

➡ Trigger, which identifies a condition that would initiate the contingency plan.

Armed with this information, the IT team can make a recommendation regarding the risks associated with the project. Depending on the nature and magnitude of the risks, the final decision might have to be made by management.

EVALUATION OF SYSTEMS REQUESTS

In most organizations, the IT department receives more systems requests than it can handle. Many organizations assign responsibility for evaluating systems requests to a group of key managers and users. Many companies call this group a **systems review committee** or a **computer resources committee**. Regardless of the name, the objective is to use the combined judgment and experience of several managers to evaluate systems projects.

Systems Request Forms

Many organizations use a special form for systems requests, similar to the online sample shown in Figure 2-12. A properly designed form streamlines the request process and ensures consistency. The form must be easy to understand and include clear instructions. It should include enough space for all required information and should indicate what supporting documents are needed. Many companies use online systems request forms that can be filled in and submitted electronically.

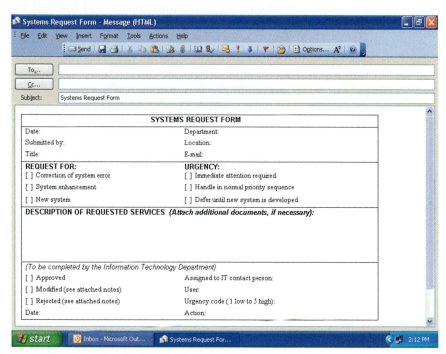

FIGURE 2-12 Example of an online systems request form.

When a systems request form is received, a systems analyst or IT manager examines it to determine what IT resources (staff and time) are required for the preliminary investigation. A designated person or a committee then decides whether to proceed with a preliminary investigation. Occasionally a situation will arise that requires an immediate response. For example, if the problem involves a mission-critical system, an IT maintenance team would attempt to restore normal operations. When the system is functioning properly, the team conducts a review and prepares a systems request to cover the work that was performed.

Systems Review Committee

Most large companies use a systems review committee to evaluate systems requests. Instead of relying on a single individual, a committee approach provides a variety of experience and knowledge. With a broader viewpoint, a committee can establish priorities more effectively than an individual, and one person's bias is less likely to affect the decisions. A typical committee consists of the IT director and several managers from other departments. The IT director usually serves as a technical consultant to ensure that committee members are aware of crucial issues, problems, and opportunities.

Although a committee offers many advantages, some disadvantages exist. For example, action on requests must wait until the committee meets. To avoid delay, committee members typically use e-mail and teleconferencing to communicate. Another potential disadvantage of a committee is that members might favor projects requested by their own departments, and internal political differences could delay important decisions.

Many smaller companies rely on one person to evaluate system requests instead of a committee. If only one person has the necessary IT skills and experience, that person must consult closely with users and managers throughout the company to ensure that business and operational needs are considered carefully.

Whether one person or a committee is responsible, the goal is to evaluate the requests and set priorities. Suppose four requests must be reviewed: a request from the marketing group to analyze current customer spending habits and forecast future trends; a request from the technical support group for a cellular link so service representatives can download technical data instantly; a request from the accounting department to redesign customer statements and allow Internet access; and a request from the production staff for an inventory control system that can exchange data with major suppliers. Which of those projects should the firm pursue? What criteria should be applied? How should priorities be determined? To answer those questions, the individual or the committee must assess the feasibility of each systems request.

OVERVIEW OF FEASIBILITY

A systems request must pass several tests, called a **feasibility study**, to see whether it is worthwhile to proceed further. As shown in Figure 2-13, a feasibility study uses four main yardsticks to measure a proposal: operational feasibility, technical feasibility, economic feasibility, and schedule feasibility.

Sometimes a feasibility study is quite simple and can be done in a few hours. If the request involves a new system or a major change, however, extensive fact-finding and investigation is required.

How much effort needs to go into a feasibility study? That depends on the request. For example, if a department wants an existing report sorted in a different order, the analyst can decide quickly whether the request is feasible. On the other hand, a proposal by the marketing department for a new market research system to predict sales trends requires more effort. In both cases, the systems analyst asks these important questions:

- Is the proposal desirable in an operational sense? Is it a practical approach that will solve a problem or take advantage of an opportunity to achieve company goals?

- Is the proposal technically feasible? Are the necessary technical resources and people available for the project?

→ Is the proposal economically desirable? What are the projected savings and costs? Are other intangible factors involved, such as customer satisfaction or company image? Is the problem worth solving, and will the request result in a sound business investment?

→ Can the proposal be accomplished within an acceptable time frame?

To obtain more information about a systems request, you might perform initial fact-finding by studying organization charts, performing interviews, reviewing current documentation, observing operations, and surveying users. If the systems request is approved, more intensive fact-finding will continue during the systems analysis phase.

FIGURE 2-13 A feasibility study includes tests for operational, technical, economic, and schedule feasibility.

Operational Feasibility

Operational feasibility means that a proposed system will be used effectively after it has been developed. If users have difficulty with a new system, it will not produce the expected benefits. Operational feasibility depends on several vital issues. For example, consider the following questions:

→ Does management support the project? Do users support the project? Is the current system well liked and effectively used? Do users see the need for change?

→ Will the new system result in a workforce reduction? If so, what will happen to affected employees?

→ Will the new system require training for users? If so, is the company prepared to provide the necessary resources for training current employees?

→ Will users be involved in planning the new system right from the start?

→ Will the new system place any new demands on users or require any operating changes? For example, will any information be less accessible or produced less frequently? Will performance decline in any way? If so, will an overall gain to the organization outweigh individual losses?

→ Will customers experience adverse effects in any way, either temporarily or permanently?

→ Will any risk to the company's image or goodwill result?

→ Does the development schedule conflict with other company priorities?

→ Do legal or ethical issues need to be considered?

Technical Feasibility

Technical feasibility refers to the technical resources needed to develop, purchase, install, or operate the system. When assessing technical feasibility, an analyst must consider the following points:

→ Does the company have the necessary hardware, software, and network resources? If not, can those resources be acquired without difficulty?

→ Does the company have the needed technical expertise? If not, can it be acquired?

➥ Does the proposed platform have sufficient capacity for future needs? If not, can it be expanded?

➥ Will a prototype be required?

➥ Will the hardware and software environment be reliable? Will it integrate with other company information systems, both now and in the future? Will it interface properly with external systems operated by customers and suppliers?

➥ Will the combination of hardware and software supply adequate performance? Do clear expectations and performance specifications exist?

➥ Will the system be able to handle future transaction volume and company growth?

Economic Feasibility

Economic feasibility means that the projected benefits of the proposed system outweigh the estimated costs usually considered the **total cost of ownership** (**TCO**), which includes ongoing support and maintenance costs, as well as acquisition costs. To determine TCO, the analyst must estimate costs in each of the following areas:

➥ People, including IT staff and users

➥ Hardware and equipment

➥ Software, including in-house development as well as purchases from vendors

➥ Formal and informal training

➥ Licenses and fees

➥ Consulting expenses

➥ Facility costs

➥ The estimated cost of not developing the system or postponing the project

In addition to costs, you need to assess tangible and intangible benefits to the company. The systems review committee will use those figures, along with your cost estimates, to decide whether to pursue the project beyond the preliminary investigation phase.

Tangible benefits are benefits that can be measured in dollars. Tangible benefits result from a decrease in expenses, an increase in revenues, or both. Examples of tangible benefits include the following:

➥ A new scheduling system that reduces overtime

➥ An online package tracking system that improves service and decreases the need for clerical staff

➥ A sophisticated inventory control system that cuts excess inventory and eliminates production delays

Intangible benefits are advantages that are difficult to measure in dollars but are important to the company. Examples of intangible benefits include the following:

➥ A user-friendly system that improves employee job satisfaction

➥ A sales tracking system that supplies better information for marketing decisions

➥ A new Web site that enhances the company's image

You also must consider the development timetable, because some benefits might occur as soon as the system is operational, but others might not take place until later.

ON THE WEB

For more information about TCO, visit **scsite.com/sad6e/ more**, locate Chapter 2 and then click the TCO link.

TOOLKIT TIME

The Financial Analysis tools in Part 2 of the Systems Analyst's Toolkit can help you analyze project costs, benefits, and economic feasibility. To learn more about these tools, turn to Part 2 of the six-part Toolkit that follows Chapter 10.

Schedule Feasibility

Schedule feasibility means that a project can be implemented in an acceptable time frame. When assessing schedule feasibility, a systems analyst must consider the interaction between time and costs. For example, speeding up a project schedule might make a project feasible, but much more expensive.

Other issues that relate to schedule feasibility include the following:

- ➡ Can the company or the IT team control the factors that affect schedule feasibility?
- ➡ Has management established a firm timetable for the project?
- ➡ What conditions must be satisfied during the development of the system?
- ➡ Will an accelerated schedule pose any risks? If so, are the risks acceptable?
- ➡ Will project management techniques be available to coordinate and control the project?
- ➡ Will a project manager be appointed?

Part 4 of the Systems Analyst's Toolkit describes various project management tools and techniques.

ON THE WEB

For more information about Project Management Tools, visit **scsite.com/ sad6e/more**, locate Chapter 2 and then click the Project Management Tools link.

EVALUATING FEASIBILITY

The first step in evaluating feasibility is to identify and weed out systems requests that are not feasible. For example, a request would not be feasible if it required hardware or software that the company already had rejected.

Even if the request is feasible, it might not be necessary. For example, a request for multiple versions of a report could require considerable design and programming effort. A better alternative might be to download the server data to a personal computer-based software package and show users how to produce their own reports. In this case, training users would be a better investment than producing reports for them.

Also keep in mind that systems requests that are not currently feasible can be resubmitted as new hardware, software, or expertise becomes available. Development costs might decrease, or the value of benefits might increase enough that a systems request eventually becomes feasible. Conversely, an initially feasible project can be rejected later. As the project progresses, conditions often change. Acquisition costs might increase, and the project might become more expensive than anticipated. In addition, managers and users sometimes lose confidence in a project. For all those reasons, feasibility analysis is an ongoing task that must be performed throughout the systems development process.

SETTING PRIORITIES

After rejecting systems requests that are not feasible, the systems review committee must establish priorities for the remaining items. The highest priority goes to projects that provide the greatest benefit, at the lowest cost, in the shortest period of time. Many factors, however, influence project evaluation.

Factors that Affect Priority

When assessing a project's priority, a systems analyst should consider the following:

- Will the proposed system reduce costs? Where? When? How? How much?
- Will the system increase revenue for the company? Where? When? How? How much?
- Will the systems project result in more information or produce better results? How? Are the results measurable?
- Will the system serve customers better?
- Will the system serve the organization better?
- Can the project be implemented in a reasonable time period? How long will the results last?
- Are the necessary financial, human, and technical resources available?

Very few projects will score high in all areas. Some proposed systems might not reduce costs but will provide important new features. Other systems might reduce operating costs substantially but require the purchase or lease of additional hardware. Some systems might be very desirable but require several years of development before producing significant benefits.

Whenever possible, the analyst should evaluate a proposed project based on tangible costs and benefits that represent actual (or approximate) dollar values. For example, a reduction of $8,000 in network maintenance is an example of a tangible benefit.

Often, the evaluation involves intangible costs or benefits, as described in the section on economic feasibility. In contrast to tangible benefits, such as the network cost reduction example, it is more difficult to assign dollar values to intangible benefits such as enhancing the organization's image, raising employee morale, or improving customer service. Intangible costs and benefits often influence systems decisions and priorities and must be considered carefully.

Discretionary and Nondiscretionary Projects

Is the project absolutely necessary? Projects where management has a choice in implementing them are called **discretionary projects**. Projects where no choice exists are called **nondiscretionary projects**. Creating a new report for a user is an example of a discretionary project; adding a report required by a new federal law is an example of a nondiscretionary project.

If a particular project is not discretionary, is it really necessary for the systems review committee to evaluate it? Some people believe that waiting for committee approval delays critical nondiscretionary projects unnecessarily. Others believe that by submitting all systems requests to the systems review committee, the committee is kept aware of all projects that compete for the resources of the IT department. As a result, the committee assesses the priority of discretionary projects and can schedule them more realistically. Additionally, the committee might need to prioritize nondiscretionary projects when funds or staff are limited.

Many nondiscretionary projects are predictable. Examples include annual updates to payroll, tax percentages, or quarterly changes in reporting requirements for an insurance processing system. By planning ahead for predictable projects, the IT department manages its resources better and keeps the systems review committee fully informed without needing prior approval in every case.

PRELIMINARY INVESTIGATION OVERVIEW

A systems analyst conducts a **preliminary investigation** to study the systems request and recommend specific action. After obtaining an authorization to proceed, the analyst interacts with managers and users, as shown in the model in Figure 2-14. The analyst gathers facts about the problem or opportunity, project scope and constraints, project benefits, and estimated development time and costs. The end product of the preliminary investigation is a report to management.

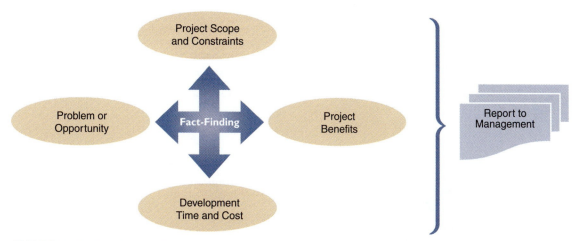

FIGURE 2-14 Model of a preliminary investigation.

Interaction with Managers and Users

Before beginning a preliminary investigation, a memo or an e-mail message should let people know about the investigation and explain your role. You should meet with key managers, users, and IT staff to describe the project, explain your responsibilities, answer questions, and invite comments. This starts an important dialog with users that will continue throughout the entire development process.

A systems project often produces significant changes in company operations. Employees may be curious, concerned, or even opposed to those changes. It is not surprising to encounter some user resistance during a preliminary investigation. Employee attitudes and reactions are important and must be considered.

When interacting with users, you should be careful in your use of the word *problem*, because generally it has a negative meaning. When you ask users about *problems*, some will stress current system limitations rather than desirable new features or enhancements. Instead of focusing on difficulties, you should question users about additional capability they would like to have. Using this approach, you highlight ways to improve the user's job, you get a better understanding of operations, and you build better, more positive relationships with users.

Planning the Preliminary Investigation

During a preliminary investigation, a systems analyst typically follows a series of steps, as shown in Figure 2-15. The exact procedure depends on the nature of the request, the size of the project, and the degree of urgency.

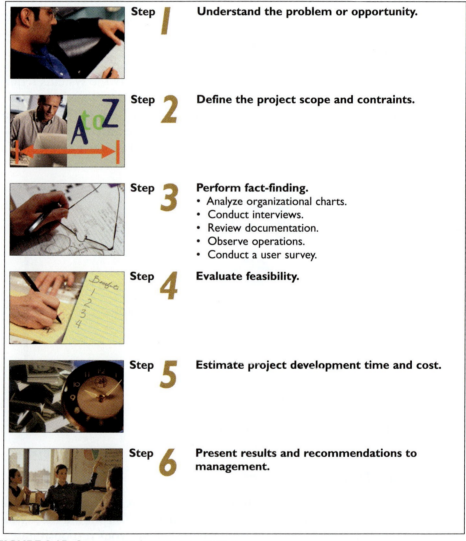

Step 1 Understand the problem or opportunity.

Step 2 Define the project scope and contraints.

Step 3 Perform fact-finding.
- Analyze organizational charts.
- Conduct interviews.
- Review documentation.
- Observe operations.
- Conduct a user survey.

Step 4 Evaluate feasibility.

Step 5 Estimate project development time and cost.

Step 6 Present results and recommendations to management.

FIGURE 2-15 Steps in a preliminary investigation.

Figure 2-16 shows how a systems analyst might use Microsoft Project to plan and manage the preliminary investigation. Notice that the analyst has listed the tasks, estimated the duration of each task, and designated a specific order in which the tasks must be performed.

Step 1: Understand the Problem or Opportunity

If the systems request involves a new information system or a substantial change in an existing system, systems analysts might need to develop a business profile that describes business processes and functions, as explained in Chapter 1. Even where the request involves relatively minor changes or enhancements, you need to understand how those modifications will affect business operations and other information systems. Often a change in one system has an unexpected effect on another system. When you analyze a systems request, you need to determine which departments, users, and business processes are involved.

In many cases, the systems request does not reveal the underlying problem, but only a symptom. For example, a request to investigate mainframe processing delays might reveal improper scheduling practices rather than hardware problems. Similarly, a request for analysis of customer complaints might disclose a lack of sales representative training, rather than problems with the product.

A popular technique for investigating causes and effects is called a **fishbone diagram**, or **Ishikawa diagram**, as shown in Figure 2-17. A fishbone diagram is an analysis tool that represents the possible causes of a problem as a graphical outline. When using a fishbone diagram, an analyst first states the problem and draws a main bone with sub-bones that represent possible causes of the problem. In the example shown in Figure 2-17, the problem is *unhappy workers*, and the analyst has identified four areas to investigate: *environment*, *workers*, *management*, and *machines*. In each area, the analyst identifies possible

FIGURE 2-16 A systems analyst might use Microsoft Project to plan and manage a preliminary investigation.

FIGURE 2-17 A fishbone diagram is an analysis tool that represents the possible causes of a problem as a graphical outline.

causes and draws them as horizontal sub-bones. For example, *too hot* is a possible cause in the *environment* bone. For each cause, the analyst must dig deeper and ask the question: what could be causing *this* symptom to occur? For example, *why* is it too hot? If the answer is insufficient air conditioning capacity, the analyst indicates this as a sub-bone to the *too hot* cause. In this manner, the analyst adds additional sub-bones to the diagram, until he or she uncovers root causes of a problem, rather than just the symptoms.

Step 2: Define the Project Scope and Constraints

Determining the **project scope** means defining the specific boundaries, or extent, of the project. For example, a statement that *payroll is not being produced accurately* is very general, compared with the statement *overtime pay is not being calculated correctly for production workers on the second shift at the Yorktown plant.* Similarly, the statement, the project scope is to *modify the accounts receivable system,* is not as specific as the statement, the project scope is to *allow customers to inquire online about account balances and recent transactions.*

Some analysts find it helpful to define project scope by creating a list with sections called *Must Do, Should Do, Could Do,* and *Won't Do.* This list can be reviewed later, during the systems analysis phase, when the systems requirements document is developed.

Projects with very general scope definitions are at risk of expanding gradually, without specific authorization, in a process called **project creep**. To avoid this problem, you should define project scope as clearly as possible. You might want to use a graphical model that shows the systems, people, and business processes that will be affected. The scope of the project also establishes the boundaries of the preliminary investigation itself. A systems analyst should limit the focus to the problem at hand and avoid unnecessary expenditure of time and money.

Along with defining the scope of the project, you need to identify any constraints on the system. A **constraint** is a requirement or condition that the system must satisfy or an outcome that the system must achieve. A constraint can involve hardware, software, time, policy, law, or cost. System constraints also define project scope. For example, if the system must operate with existing hardware, that is a constraint that affects potential solutions. Other examples of constraints are: the order entry system must accept input from 15 remote sites; the human resources information system must produce statistics on hiring practices; and the new Web site must be operational by March 1. When examining constraints, you should identify their characteristics.

PRESENT VERSUS FUTURE Is the constraint something that must be met as soon as the system is developed or modified, or is the constraint necessary at some future time?

INTERNAL VERSUS EXTERNAL Is the constraint due to a requirement within the organization or does some external force, such as government regulation, impose it?

MANDATORY VERSUS DESIRABLE Is the constraint mandatory? Is it absolutely essential to meet the constraint, or is it merely desirable?

Figure 2-18 shows five examples of constraints. Notice that each constraint has three characteristics, which are indicated by its position in the figure and by the symbol that represents the constraint. The constraint in Example A is present, external, and mandatory. The constraint in Example B is future, external, and mandatory. The constraint in Example C is present, internal, and desirable. The constraint in Example D is present, internal, and mandatory. The constraint in Example E is future, internal, and desirable.

Regardless of the type, all constraints should be identified as early as possible to avoid future problems and surprises. A clear definition of project scope and constraints avoids misunderstandings that arise when managers assume that the system will have a certain feature or support for a project, but later find that the feature is not included.

Examples of Constraints

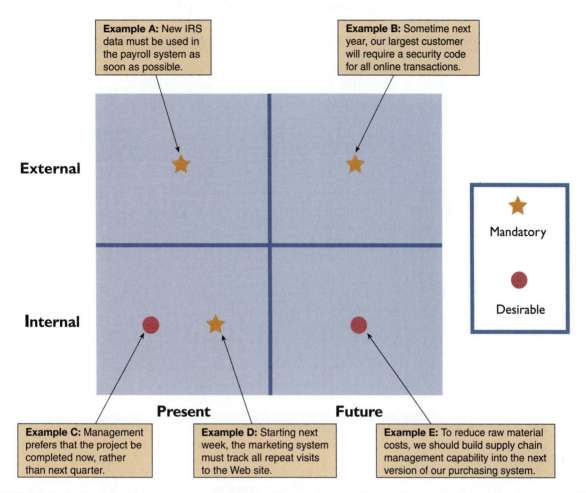

Example A: New IRS data must be used in the payroll system as soon as possible.

Example B: Sometime next year, our largest customer will require a security code for all online transactions.

External

Internal

Mandatory

Desirable

Present   Future

Example C: Management prefers that the project be completed now, rather than next quarter.

Example D: Starting next week, the marketing system must track all repeat visits to the Web site.

Example E: To reduce raw material costs, we should build supply chain management capability into the next version of our purchasing system.

FIGURE 2-18 Examples of various types of constraints. The constraint in Example A is present, external, and mandatory. The constraint in Example B is future, external, and mandatory. The constraint in Example C is present, internal, and desirable. The constraint in Example D is present, internal, and mandatory. The constraint in Example E is future, internal, and desirable.

Step 3: Perform Fact-Finding

Fact-finding involves various techniques, which are described below. Depending on what information is needed to investigate the systems request, fact-finding might consume several hours, days, or weeks. For example, a change in a report format or data entry screen might require a single telephone call or e-mail message to a user, whereas a new inventory system would involve a series of interviews. During fact-finding, you might analyze organization charts, conduct interviews, review current documentation, observe operations, and carry out a user survey.

ANALYZE ORGANIZATION CHARTS In many instances you will not know the organizational structure of departments involved in the study. You should obtain organization charts to understand how the department functions and identify individuals you might want to interview. Organization charts often can be obtained from the company's human resources department. If such charts are unavailable, you should obtain the necessary information directly from department personnel and then construct your own charts, as shown in Figure 2-19.

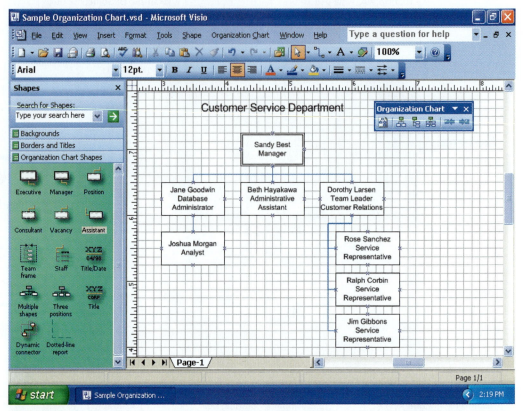

FIGURE 2-19 Microsoft Visio includes an organization chart drawing tool that is powerful and easy to use.

When organization charts are available, you should verify their accuracy. Keep in mind that organization charts show formal reporting relationships but not the informal alignment of a group, which also is important.

CONDUCT INTERVIEWS The primary method of obtaining information during the preliminary investigation is the interview, as shown in Figure 2-20. The interviewing process involves a series of steps:

1. Determine the people to interview.

2. Establish objectives for the interview.

3. Develop interview questions.

4. Prepare for the interview.

5. Conduct the interview.

6. Document the interview.

7. Evaluate the interview.

These seven steps are discussed in detail in Chapter 3, which describes fact-finding techniques that occur during the systems analysis phase of the SDLC.

Remember that the purpose of the interview, and of the preliminary investigation itself, is to uncover facts, not to convince others that the project is justified. Your primary role in an interview is to ask effective questions and listen carefully. If you plan to talk to several people about the same topic, you should prepare a standard set of questions for all the interviews. Also be sure to include open-ended questions, such as "What else do you think I should know about the system?" or "Is there any other relevant information that we have not discussed?"

When conducting interviews during the preliminary investigation, you should interview managers and supervisors who have a broad knowledge of the system and can give you an overview of the business processes involved. Depending on the situation, you might talk to operational personnel to learn how the system functions on a day-to-day basis.

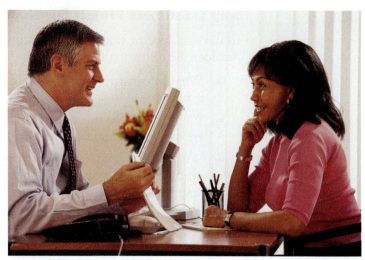

FIGURE 2-20   The interview is the primary method of obtaining information.

REVIEW DOCUMENTATION   Although interviews are an extremely important method of obtaining information, you also may want to investigate the current system documentation. The documentation might not be up-to-date, so you should check with users to confirm that you are receiving accurate and complete information.

OBSERVE OPERATIONS   Another fact-finding method is to observe the current system in operation. You might see how workers carry out typical tasks. You might choose to trace or follow the actual paths taken by input source documents or output reports. In addition to observing operations, you might want to sample the inputs or outputs of the system. Using sampling techniques described in Chapter 3, you can obtain valuable information about the nature and frequency of the problem.

CONDUCT A USER SURVEY   Interviews can be time-consuming. Sometimes you can obtain information from a larger group by conducting a user survey. In this case, you design a form that users complete and return to you for tabulation. A survey is not as flexible as a series of interviews, but it is less expensive, generally takes less time, and can involve a broad cross-section of people.

Step 4: Evaluate Feasibility

You have analyzed the problem or opportunity, defined the project scope and constraints, and performed fact-finding. Now you must evaluate the project's operational, technical, economic, and schedule feasibility.

You can use the financial analysis tools in Part 3 of the Systems Analyst's Toolkit to evaluate economic feasibility. In addition, fact-finding results (including answers to the feasibility questions listed on pages 58–59) will help you evaluate operational, technical, and schedule feasibility.

Step 5: Estimate Project Development Time and Cost

To develop specific time and cost estimates for the next development phase, you should consider the following issues:

→ What information must you obtain, and how will you gather and analyze the information?

→ What sources of information will you use, and what difficulties will you encounter in obtaining the information?

→ Will you conduct interviews? How many people will you interview, and how much time will you need to meet with the people and summarize their responses?

→ Will you conduct a survey? Who will be involved? How much time will it take people to complete it? How much time will it take to prepare it and tabulate the results?

→ How much will it cost to analyze the information gathered and to prepare a report with findings and recommendations?

In addition to time and cost figures for the next development phase, you should provide an estimate for the overall project, so managers can understand the full cost impact and timetable. Exact figures might not be available, but an estimated range of time and costs can be useful, particularly when forecasting a best versus worst scenario.

Step 6: Present Results and Recommendations to Management

At this stage, you have several alternatives. You might find that no action is necessary or that some other strategy, such as additional training, is needed. To solve a minor problem, you might implement a simple solution without performing further analysis. In other situations, you will recommend that the project proceed to the next development phase, which is systems analysis.

The final task in the preliminary investigation is to prepare a report to management, and possibly deliver a presentation, as shown in Figure 2-21. The report includes an evaluation of the systems request, an estimate of costs and benefits, and your recommendation. Part 1 of the Systems Analyst's Toolkit helps you achieve effective written and oral communications.

The format of a preliminary investigation report varies from one company to another. A typical report might consist of the following sections:

1. *Introduction* — the first section is an overview of the report. The introduction contains a brief description of the system, the name of the person or group who performed the investigation, and the name of the person or group who initiated the investigation.

2. *Systems Request Summary* — the summary describes the basis of the systems request.

3. *Findings* — the findings section contains the results of your preliminary investigation, including a description of the project's scope, constraints, and feasibility.

FIGURE 2-21 Oral presentations often are required during systems development, and systems analysts need to develop strong presentation skills.

4. *Recommendations* — recommendations for further action, with specific reasons and justification, are explained in this section. Management will make the final decision, but the IT department's input is an important factor.

5. *Project Roles* — this section lists the people who will participate in the project, and describes each person's role.

6. *Time and Cost Estimates* — this section describes the cost of acquiring and installing the system, and the total cost of ownership during the system's useful life.

7. *Expected Benefits* — anticipated tangible and intangible benefits and a timetable that shows when they are to occur are included in this section.

8. *Appendix* — an appendix is included in the report if you need to attach supporting information. For example, you might list the interviews you conducted, the documentation you reviewed, and other sources for the information you obtained. You do not need detailed reports of the interviews or other lengthy documentation. It is critical that you retain those documents to support your findings and for future reference.

TOOLKIT TIME

The Communication Tools in Part 1 of the Systems Analyst's Toolkit can help you develop better reports and presentations. To learn more about these tools, turn to Part 1 of the six-part Toolkit that follows Chapter 10.

CHAPTER SUMMARY

Systems planning is the first phase of the systems development life cycle. Effective information systems help an organization support its business processes, carry out its mission, and serve its stakeholders. Strategic planning allows a company to examine its purpose, vision, and values and develops a mission statement, which leads to goals, objectives, day-to-day operations, and business results that affect company stakeholders.

Systems projects are initiated to improve performance, provide more information, reduce costs, strengthen controls, or provide better service. Various internal and external factors affect systems projects, such as user requests, top management directives, existing systems, the IT department, software and hardware vendors, technology, customers, competitors, the economy, and government.

During the preliminary investigation, the analyst evaluates the systems request and determines whether the project is feasible from an operation, technical, economic, and schedule standpoint. Analysts evaluate systems requests on the basis of their expected costs and benefits, both tangible and intangible.

The steps in the preliminary investigation are to understand the problem or opportunity; define the project scope and constraints; perform fact-finding; estimate the project's benefits; estimate project development time and cost; and present results and recommendations to management. The report must include an estimate of time, staffing requirements, costs, benefits, and expected results for the next phase of the SDLC.

Key Terms and Phrases

biometric devices 52

business case 44

case for action 49

computer resources committee 57

constraint 66

critical business issues 49

critical success factors 49

customer relationship management (CRM) 55

discretionary projects 62

economic feasibility 60

encryption 52

feasibility study 58

fishbone diagram 65

goals 49

intangible benefits 60

Ishikawa diagram 65

just-in-time (JIT) 54

mission statement 47

nondiscretionary projects 62

objectives 49

operational feasibility 59

preliminary investigation 63

project creep 66

project scope 66

risk 56

risk management 56

schedule feasibility 61

stakeholders 47

strategic planning 46

SWOT analysis 46

systems request 51

systems review committee 57

tangible benefits 60

technical feasibility 59

total cost of ownership (TCO) 60

Learn It Online

Instructions: To complete the Learn It Online exercises, start your browser, click the Address bar, and then enter the Web address **scsite.com/sad6e/learn**. When the Systems Analysis and Design Learn It Online page is displayed, follow the instructions in the exercises below. Each exercise has instructions for saving your results, either for your own records or for submission to your instructor.

1 Chapter Reinforcement

TF, MC, and SA

Below SAD Chapter 2, click the Chapter Reinforcement link. Print the quiz by clicking Print on the File menu for each page. Answer each question.

2 Flash Cards

Below SAD Chapter 2, click the Flash Cards link and read the instructions. Type 20 (or a number specified by your instructor) in the Number of playing cards text box, type your name in the Enter your Name text box, and then click the Flip Card button. When the flash card is displayed, read the question and then click the ANSWER box arrow to select an answer. Flip through the Flash Cards. If your score is 15 (75%) correct or greater, click Print on the File menu to print your results. If your score is less than 15 (75%) correct, then redo this exercise by clicking the Replay button.

3 Practice Test

Below SAD Chapter 2, click the Practice Test link. Answer each question, enter your first and last name at the bottom of the page, and then click the Grade Test button. When the graded practice test is displayed on your screen, click Print on the File menu to print a hard copy. Continue to take practice tests until you score 80% or better.

4 Who Wants To Be a Computer Genius?

Below SAD Chapter 2, click the Computer Genius link. Read the instructions, enter your first and last name at the bottom of the page, and then click the Play button. When your score is displayed, click the PRINT RESULTS link to print a hard copy.

5 Wheel of Terms

Below SAD Chapter 2, click the Wheel of Terms link. Read the instructions, and then enter your first and last name and your school name. Click the PLAY button. When your score is displayed on the screen, right-click the score and then click Print on the shortcut menu to print a hard copy.

6 Crossword Puzzle Challenge

Below SAD Chapter 2, click the Crossword Puzzle Challenge link. Read the instructions, and then enter your first and last name. Click the SUBMIT button. Work the crossword puzzle. When you are finished, click the Submit button. When the crossword puzzle is displayed, click the Print Puzzle button to print a hard copy.

Case-Sim: SCR Associates

Background

SCR Associates is a consulting firm that offers IT solutions and training. SCR needs an information system to manage operations at its new training center. The new system will be called TIMS (Training Information Management System). As a newly hired systems analyst, you will report to Jesse Baker, systems group manager. You will work on various tasks and practice the skills you learned in this chapter.

Using the Case

The SCR Associates case study is a Web-based simulation that allows you to practice your skills in a real-world environment. The case study transports you to SCR's company intranet, where you can complete 10 work sessions, each aligning with a chapter. As you work on the case, you will receive e-mail and voice mail messages, obtain information from SCR's online libraries, and perform various tasks. The first time you enter the SCR Case, you should go to the Starting page at **scsite.com/sad6e/scr** for detailed instructions.

Preview: Session 2

During your orientation, you found your way around the office and had a chance to explore the SCR Internet site. Now, after a week on the job, your supervisor, Jesse Baker, has explained the new TIMS system and asked you to lead the systems development effort. She suggested that you review SCR's mission statement, think about a systems review committee, draft a project scope statement, and prepare to interview people to learn more about the new system.

To start a work session, you log on to the SCR intranet. When you enter your name and password, an opening screen displays links to the work sessions, and you select Session 2. At this point, you check your e-mail and voice mail messages carefully. You then begin working on your task list, which includes the following items:

Tasks: Analyzing the Business Case

1. *We need a corporate goal for SCR that refers to our new training activity. Prepare a draft to show Jesse.*

2. *Jesse wants my opinion on whether or not SCR needs a system review committee. Need to prepare a recommendation and reasons.*

3. *Draft a project scope statement for the TIMS system and describe the constraints. She said be specific.*

4. *Need to identify the people I want to interview to learn more about the new training activity, and prepare a list of the questions I will ask.*

FIGURE 2-22 Task list: Session 2.

Chapter Exercises

Review Questions

1. What is a business case? How does a business case affect an IT project?
2. What is a SWOT analysis and why is it important?
3. What are five common reasons for systems projects?
4. What are some internal and external factors that affect systems projects?
5. What are some advantages and disadvantages of a systems review committee?
6. What is feasibility? List and briefly discuss four feasibility tests.
7. How do tangible benefits differ from intangible benefits?
8. What are the steps in a preliminary investigation?
9. What is project scope? What is a constraint? In what three ways are constraints classified?
10. What are three fact-finding techniques that systems analysts use during the preliminary investigation?

Discussion Topics

1. Directives from top management often trigger IT projects. Suppose that the vice president of marketing tells you to write a program to create mailing labels for a one-time advertising promotion. As the IT manager, you know that the labels can be prepared more efficiently by simply exporting the data to a word processing program with a mail merge feature. How would you handle this situation?
2. The vice president of accounting says to you, the IT director, "This systems development life cycle stuff takes too long." She tells you that her people know what they are doing and that all systems requests coming from her department are necessary and important to the organization. She suggests that the IT department bypass the initial steps for any accounting department request and immediately get to work at the solution. What would you say to her?
3. One of your coworkers says, "Mission statements are nice, but they really don't change things down here in our department where the work gets done." How would you reply?
4. Would you continue to work for a company if you disagreed with the firm's mission statement? Why or why not?

Projects

1. Use the Internet to find an example of a corporate mission statement.
2. Risk management is an important part of information systems planning and project management. Perform Internet research to learn more about risk management, and write a summary of the results. Be sure to search for a book titled *Waltzing with Bears*, by Tom Demarco and Timothy Lister.
3. Suppose you own a travel agency in a large city. You have many corporate clients, but growth has slowed somewhat. Some long-term employees are getting discouraged, but you feel that there might be a way to make technology work in your favor. Use your imagination and suggest at least one strength, weakness, opportunity, and threat that your business faces.
4. Write a mission statement and at least three goals for the travel agency described in Project 3.

Apply Your Knowledge

The section contains four mini-cases. Each case describes a situation, explains your role in the case, and asks you to respond to questions. You can answer the questions by applying knowledge you learned in the chapter.

1 Last Chance Securities

Situation:

The IT director opened the department staff meeting today by saying "I've got some good news and some bad news. The good news is that management approved the payroll system project this morning. The new system will reduce clerical time and errors, improve morale in the payroll department, and avoid possible fines and penalties for noncompliance. The bad news is that the system must be installed by the end of December in order to meet new federal reporting rules, costs must be within the budgeted amount, the new system must interact with existing systems, and the vice president of finance insists on approving the final design."

1. Name the constraints and indicate whether each is present, future, internal, external, mandatory, or desirable.
2. Explain why it is important to define the payroll project's scope. Explain how to define project scope.
3. Identify tangible and intangible benefits of the new payroll system.
4. What topics should be included in a report to management at the end of the preliminary investigation?

2 Way Out Bikes

Situation:

The owner of Way Out Bikes asked you for advice about acquiring an information system for her business. The company specializes in helping customers select exactly the right bicycle for their needs and lifestyles. Way Out cannot compete on price with mass merchandisers, but it seeks to offer value and expertise for which customers are willing to pay. You ask the owner whether she has long-range plans for the company, and she replies that she has not really thought beyond a one-year time frame.

1. Explain the concept of strategic planning to Way Out's owner.
2. Decide what else you might want to know about Way Out. Consider the internal and external factors described on page 53, and make a list of questions to ask the owner.
3. Draft a mission statement for Way Out.
4. Make a list of Way Out's stakeholders.

The Monday IT Department Staff Meeting

Situation:

Your boss, the IT manager, was ready to explode. "Why can't we get our priorities straight?" he fumed. "Here we go again, working on a low-value project, just because it's a favorite of the marketing group. I wish we could get away from departmental politics! I want you to draft a memo that proposes a systems review committee for this company. Explain the advantages, but don't step on anyone's toes!"

1. Write a draft of the proposal, as your boss requested.
2. Write a memo to your boss explaining potential disadvantages of the committee approach.
3. Draft a set of ground rules for committee meetings. Try to suggest rules that will minimize political differences and focus on the overall benefit to the company.
4. Most people serve on a committee at some point in their lives. Write a brief memo describing your committee experiences, good or bad.

The Friday IT Department Staff Meeting

Situation:

By the end of the week, things quieted down. The IT staff discussed how to prioritize IT project requests, taking into account technical, operational, economic, and schedule feasibility. The IT manager asked for suggestions from the group.

1. Provide three examples of why a project might lack technical feasibility.
2. Provide three examples of why a project might lack operational feasibility.
3. Provide three examples of why a project might lack economic feasibility.
4. Provide three examples of why a project might lack schedule feasibility.

Case Studies

Case studies allow you to practice specific skills learned in the chapter. Each chapter contains several case studies that continue throughout the textbook, and a chapter capstone case.

NEW CENTURY HEALTH CLINIC

New Century Health Clinic offers preventive medicine and traditional medical care. In your role as an IT consultant, you will help New Century develop a new information system.

Background

New Century Health Clinic's office manager, Anita Davenport, recently asked permission to hire an additional office clerk because she feels the current staff can no longer handle the growing workload. The associates discussed Anita's request during a recent meeting. They were not surprised that the office staff was feeling overwhelmed by the constantly growing workload.

Because the clinic was busier and more profitable than ever, they all agreed that New Century could afford to hire another office worker. Dr. Jones then came up with another idea. He suggested that they investigate the possibility of computerizing New Century's office systems. Dr. Jones said that a computerized system could keep track of patients, appointments, charges, and insurance claim processing and reduce paperwork. All the associates were enthusiastic about the possibilities and voted to follow up on the suggestion. Dr. Jones agreed to direct the project.

Because no member of the staff had computer experience, Dr. Jones decided to hire a consultant to study the current office systems and recommend a course of action. Several friends recommended you as a person who has considerable experience with computerized business applications.

Assignments

1. Dr. Jones has arranged an introductory meeting between the associates of New Century Health Clinic and you to determine if mutual interest exists in pursuing the project. What should the associates try to learn about you? What should you try to learn in this meeting?
2. Does the proposed system present a strong business case? Why or why not?
3. For each type of feasibility, prepare at least two questions that will help you reach a feasibility determination.
4. You begin the preliminary investigation. What information is needed? From whom will you obtain it? What techniques will you use in your fact-finding?

PERSONAL TRAINER, INC.

Personal Trainer, Inc., owns and operates fitness centers in a dozen Midwestern cities. The centers have done well, and the company is planning an international expansion by opening a new "supercenter" in the Toronto area. Personal Trainer's president, Cassia Umi, hired an IT consultant, Susan Park, to help develop an information system for the new facility. During the project, Susan will work closely with Gray Lewis, who will manage the new operation.

Background

At their initial meeting, Susan and Gray discussed some initial steps in planning a new information system for the new facility. The next morning, they worked together on a business profile, drew an organization chart, discussed feasibility issues, and talked about

various types of information systems that would provide the best support for the supercenter's operations. Their main objective was to carry out a preliminary investigation of the new system and report their recommendations to Personal Trainer's top managers.

After the working session with Gray, Susan returned to her office and reviewed her notes. She knew that Personal Trainer's president, Cassia Umi, wanted the supercenter to become a model for the company's future growth, but she did not remember any mention of an overall strategic plan for the company. Susan also wondered whether the firm had done a SWOT analysis or analyzed the internal and external factors that might affect an information system for the supercenter.

Because the new operation would be so important to the company, Susan believed that Personal Trainer should consider an enterprise resource planning strategy that could provide a company-wide framework for information management. After she finished compiling her notes, Susan listed several topics that might need more study and called Gray to arrange another meeting the following day.

Assignments

1. Based on the background facts described in Chapter 1, draft a mission statement for Personal Trainer. Consider the firm's overall direction, and the services, products, and experiences the company might want to offer its customers in the future. In your statement, consider all the stakeholders affected by Personal Trainer's operations.

2. Susan and Gray probably will need more information about the proposed system. Make a list of people whom they might want to interview. Also, suggest other fact-finding techniques they should consider.

3. Consider the internal and external factors that affect information systems. Which factors, in your opinion, will have the greatest impact on the system proposed for the new supercenter? Explain your answer.

4. At the conclusion of the preliminary investigation, Susan and Gray will deliver a written summary of the results and deliver a brief presentation to Personal Trainer's management team. Prepare a list of recommendations that will help make their written and oral communications more effective. Put your list in priority order, starting with what you consider to be the most important suggestions. Before you complete this task, you should review Part 1 of the Systems Analyst's Toolkit, which provides suggestions for oral and written presentations.

ACTION OFFICE PRODUCTS

Background

Four months ago, Action Office Products hired David Jackson away from an advertising agency and made him the director of marketing. David recently submitted a systems request to redesign the company's customer statements.

Hannah Holt, the systems analyst assigned to do the preliminary investigation, interviewed David to learn the reasons for the request. David explained that the current statements are unattractive and dull. "We need to update our image," he said. "We have to show our customers that Action Office Products has contemporary ideas and tastes. The best place to start is with our monthly statements. We need something more colorful, more eye-catching, more artistic, more upbeat!"

Hannah next interviewed the director of accounting, Karen Alexander, who oversees the accounts receivable system, which produces the monthly customer statements. Karen told Hannah that she has never received any complaints from customers about the statements. She assured Hannah that the current forms were clear and easy to understand.

Confused, Hannah decided she should talk with Cecil Collier, the manager of customer relations. Cecil assured Hannah that Action Office Products was having no problems with its customers. She even showed Hannah the latest annual report, which showed that company's annual sales were increasing at a healthy pace.

Assignments

1. The chapter identifies five major reasons for systems projects. Has David made his systems request for one or more of those five reasons? If so, which one(s) and why? If not, why not?
2. Do you think this is a feasible project? Why or why not?
3. Of the four tests of feasibility — operational, technical, economic, and schedule — which would you perform first to measure the system project's feasibility? Why?
4. What should Hannah do next?

ORIGINAL KAYAK ADVENTURES

Original Kayak Adventures (OKA) offers guided eco-tours and kayak rentals along the Hudson River.

Background

In Chapter 1, you learned that John and Edie Caputo founded OKA two years ago. Now John and Edie are thinking about replacing their current system, which is a mix of manual and computer-based techniques, with a new information system that would meet their current and future needs. Before you answer the following questions, you should review the fact statement in Chapter 1.

Assignments

1. Does a strong business case exist for developing an information system to support the Caputos' business? Explain your answer.
2. In a small- to medium-sized business, such as OKA, is it really important to use a structured approach for information systems development? Why or why not?
3. Based on the facts provided, draft a mission statement for OKA. In your statement, consider all the stakeholders who might be affected by OKA operations.
4. What internal and external factors might affect OKA's business success?

TOWN OF EDEN BAY

The town of Eden Bay owns and maintains a fleet of vehicles. You are a systems analyst reporting to Dawn, the town's IT manager.

Background

Eden Bay is a medium-sized municipality. The town has grown rapidly, and so has the demand for town services. Eden Bay currently owns 90 vehicles, which the town's equipment department maintains. The fleet includes police cars, sanitation trucks, fire trucks, and other vehicles assigned to town employees. The maintenance budget has risen sharply in recent years, and people are asking whether the town should continue to perform its own maintenance or outsource it to private firms.

This morning, Dawn called you into her office to discuss the situation. A summary of her comments follows.

Dawn (IT manager): When I came here two years ago, I was told that Eden Bay had a computerized information system for vehicle maintenance. What I found was a spreadsheet application designed by a part-time employee as a quick answer to a much more complex problem. It's probably better than no system at all, but I can't justify spending any time on it. The system should never have been designed as a spreadsheet in the first place.

I've discussed the situation with the equipment department people. Rather than tinker with the current system, I think we should press for a new information system project, and I've developed an initial proposal. I've code-named the new system RAVE, which stands for Repair Analysis for Vehicular Equipment. I know that commercial fleet maintenance packages exist, but they are very expensive.

I did some fact-finding, and I want you to start by reading the interview summaries I prepared.

Before You Begin ...

Review the following interview summaries from Marie (town manager), Martin (equipment department manager), Phil (maintenance supervisor), Alice (maintenance clerk), and Joe (mechanic).

Marie (town manager): Maintenance costs have risen 14 to 16% annually. I'm not sure that we have any real control over these costs. Some members of the town council think we should get out of the maintenance business and contract it out to a private firm. That might mean laying off current employees, and I'm not sure whether outsourcing is the right way to go.

Both the equipment department manager and the IT manager tell me that our current record-keeping system is outdated, and I wonder if a new information system would give us a better handle on the problem. My own view is that if there's a way we can become more efficient, we should continue to perform our own maintenance.

Dawn, our IT manager, tells me that she has developed a proposal for a maintenance information system. I plan to bring it up at the next council meeting.

Martin (equipment department manager): I hear a lot of criticism about the maintenance budget, but I'm doing the best I can. We operate from one budget year to the next, without a long-term plan. I belong to a professional association of fleet maintenance managers, and I know that we should be developing a strategic plan instead of juggling annual budget figures.

I'd like to build this department into a first-class organization. Our people are great, but they could use more technical training. Our shop and equipment are generally adequate for what we do, but we haven't kept up with some of the newer diagnostic equipment. We have a real problem in record keeping. Instead of a short-term solution, Eden Bay should have developed a maintenance information system years ago. Prior to taking this position, I was assistant maintenance manager in a medium-sized city, and they had developed a system that handled scheduling and cost analysis, in addition to day-to-day maintenance operations.

Phil (maintenance supervisor): I'm in the middle — I get pressure from above to cut costs, and I get complaints from below that management doesn't know what it's doing. One thing for sure — short-term solutions are not the answer. I hope they don't ask me to cut back on preventive maintenance. The last time we did that, we extended routine oil changes and servicing, and we ended up with even more repairs than we had previously.

My mechanics are capable people, and they're doing the best they can. One problem I see is that it's hard to pull up a history for a particular vehicle. We keep the data on a computer, but different people used different codes and procedures over the years, and the system probably needs a good overhaul.

Alice (maintenance clerk): I'm in charge of maintenance record keeping. We use a spreadsheet system that was designed by a part-time employee who is no longer around. Because we work on a monthly budget, the spreadsheet has a separate page for each month. When the year is over, we start a new set of monthly pages. The spreadsheet is supposed to record labor and parts used, and assign the cost to a specific vehicle, but it doesn't always work out that way.

I also use a notebook to keep track of vehicle mileage and scheduled service intervals, so I can let the department heads know when a vehicle needs to come in for service. I write up work orders for scheduled service or necessary repairs, but often a mechanic finds other problems and has to write up an additional charges form.

Each time a vehicle comes into the shop, I start a new row on the spreadsheet. I enter the vehicle number, mileage, and date. Then I enter the rest of the data into the columns for parts, labor hours, job code, shop supplies, and miscellaneous charges. At the end of the month, I calculate total costs from the spreadsheet, and we compare these to actual payroll and parts vouchers for the month. If the totals are close, everyone is happy. If not, we try to figure out what work didn't get reported and entered into the spreadsheet.

The labor codes also are a problem. Specific codes are assigned for certain types of shop labor, but these were changed three years ago when the new Director arrived. Also, about half the labor can be coded, but the rest has to be entered manually — and there are no standards. Two mechanics might do the same job, and one records four specific tasks, while the other calls it a tune-up.

I know the mechanics don't like paperwork, but what can I do? I asked the IT manager if she could do anything to help, but she says that it isn't worthwhile to update the current system. She says she has heard some talk about developing a new information system specifically designed for vehicle fleet maintenance. It can't be soon enough for me.

Joe (mechanic): I love my job, but I hate the paperwork. We get a work order from the clerk for all scheduled maintenance, but if we find other problems, we have to handwrite an additional work ticket. Personally, I think some of these vehicles should be retired before they get too expensive to maintain.

I would hate to see the town contract out the maintenance. I've put in 17 years here, and I don't want to lose my job, but I know that some specialized repairs would be less expensive on the outside. Most of the mechanics realize this, but let management figure it out — they're the ones with the fancy computer system.

Assignments

1. Upon investigation, you learn that the town does not have a strategic plan or a mission statement. In your view, does this affect the current situation? Why or why not?

2. Based on the fact statements provided, summarize the maintenance department's most important strengths, weaknesses, problems, and opportunities.

3. Describe the specific steps you will follow during a preliminary investigation, including any fact-finding techniques you will use.

4. Of the four tests of feasibility — operational, technical, economic, and schedule — which would you perform first to measure the system project's feasibility? Why?

CHAPTER CAPSTONE CASE: SoftWear, Limited

SoftWear, Limited (SWL), is a continuing case study that illustrates the knowledge and skills described in each chapter. In this case study, the student acts as a member of the SWL systems development team and performs various tasks.

Background

SWL outsources the company's payroll processing to an outside firm called Business Information Systems (BIS). SWL's payroll department submits data to BIS, which uses its own hardware and software to produce employee paychecks and generate payroll reports. BIS performs payroll processing for dozens of companies. Contractual agreements between BIS and its customers identify specific information processing services and prices.

SWL's information technology department is located at the company headquarters in Raleigh and reports to the vice president of finance. The IT staff is responsible for SWL's mainframe computer and supports the company's Web site and the inventory, marketing, customer order entry, and accounting systems.

Robert Lansing, SWL's president, believes that IT support is vital to the company's strategic long-range plans and has approved increased IT budgets and expansion of the IT staff. In addition to the mainframe, the company networked personal computers in all offices and many shop floor locations and implemented a company intranet linking all SWL locations.

Even though it could handle its own payroll processing, SWL continues to use BIS for payroll services because BIS does a good job at a reasonable cost, and it relieves SWL of this responsibility. Recently, problems with the payroll system developed, and SWL's payroll department employees had to work overtime to correct errors involving employee deductions.

SWL employees can make two types of voluntary payroll deductions. Starting in 1999, employees could contribute to the newly formed SWL credit union. To enroll or make changes, an employee must complete a deduction form. In 2003, the company gave employees an opportunity to purchase SWL company stock through payroll deductions. Employees enroll in the stock purchase plan or change their deductions by visiting the human resources department, which then sends a weekly list of transactions to SWL's payroll department.

In addition to the credit union and stock purchase deductions, SWL employees soon may have other savings and investment choices. SWL's top management, with strong support from the vice president of human resources, may consider a new Employee Savings and Investment Plan (ESIP) that allows employees to purchase mutual funds, stocks, and other investments through regular payroll deductions. Under this new 401(k) plan, an outside investment firm, Court Street Securities, manages tax-sheltered deductions and services the individual accounts. Each employee maintains direct control over his or her investments using a 24-hour toll-free number or accessing the Court Street Securities Web site. Management expects to make a final decision about the new ESIP in several months.

Request for Information Technology Services

Tina Pham, vice president of human resources, learned that a number of SWL employees had complained about improper paycheck deductions, and she became concerned about employee morale. She decided to discuss the subject with Michael Jeremy, vice president of finance. At their meeting, he listened carefully and promised to look into the matter further.

That afternoon, Mr. Jeremy met with Amy Calico, director of payroll, to ask her about the problem as well as a recent increase in overtime pay in her group. Amy stated that the overtime became necessary because payroll operations recently required more time and effort. She also noted that, because this workload increase came about recently, she lacked the money in her budget to hire any additional people. She did not provide any specific explanation for the payroll deduction errors.

Mr. Jeremy then decided to ask the IT department to investigate the payroll system. He prepared a Request for Information Technology Services, as shown in Figure 2-23, and sent it to the IT department for action. In the request, he mentioned problems with the payroll system and requested help but did not identify the causes of the problems or propose a solution.

Jane Rossman, manager of applications, normally receives systems requests and does an initial review to see whether a preliminary investigation is warranted. After a quick look at Mr. Jeremy's request, Jane decided to contact her boss, Ann Hon, director of information technology. Because SWL does not have a formal systems review committee, Ann normally makes the initial decision on most systems requests. She always consults with other managers if the proposal is significant or could affect their areas. After discussing the proposal, Jane and Ann decided that a preliminary investigation should start right away. Given that the system was eight years old and had never received a major update, it seemed likely that they would find some problems that warranted attention.

FIGURE 2-23 Michael Jeremy's systems request.

Jane assigned Rick Williams, a systems analyst, to conduct a preliminary investigation of the payroll system. Ann sent the e-mail message shown in Figure 2-24 to Mr. Jeremy so he knew that Rick would start the preliminary investigation the following week.

Because the information technology department reports to him, Mr. Jeremy sent the e-mail shown in Figure 2-25 to all SWL departments. Although the message gives few details, it explains that Rick Williams has been authorized to conduct a preliminary investigation and requests everyone's cooperation.

Payroll Department Organization

To begin his investigation, Rick met with Tina Pham, vice president of human resources. She gave Rick copies of job descriptions for all payroll department positions but did not have a current organization chart for that group.

After reviewing the descriptions, Rick visited Amy Calico, director of payroll. She explained how the payroll department was organized. She explained that two people report directly to her: Nelson White, payroll manager, and Nancy Farmer, administrative assistant. Two payroll technicians, Britton Ellis and Debra Williams, report to Nelson White.

Interviews

Rick next decided to interview Michael Jeremy, Amy Calico, and Mike Feiner, director of human resources.

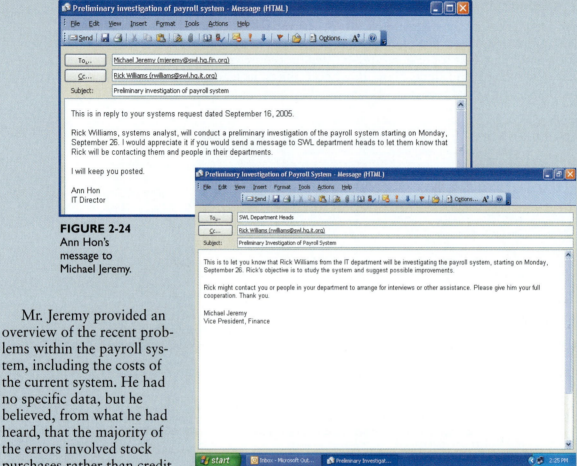

FIGURE 2-24
Ann Hon's
message to
Michael Jeremy.

FIGURE 2-25 Michael Jeremy's message announcing the start of the payroll system investigation.

Mr. Jeremy provided an overview of the recent problems within the payroll system, including the costs of the current system. He had no specific data, but he believed, from what he had heard, that the majority of the errors involved stock purchases rather than credit union deductions.

Later that day, in his meeting with Mike Feiner, Rick found out more about the reported deduction errors. He learned that stock purchase enrollments and changes are handled differently from credit union deductions. For legal reasons, Mike explained, employees must complete a special form for stock purchase plan transactions. When enrolling or making changes, an employee visits the human resources department for a brochure and an information package called a prospectus, which also includes the form required to enroll. At the end of each week, the human resources department prepares a summary of deduction requests and sends it to the payroll department. Payroll clerks then file the changes with the employee's master record.

The next morning, Rick again met with Amy Calico. In the interview, Amy told Rick that some problems with deductions existed, but she did not feel that the payroll clerks were at fault. She suggested that he look elsewhere for the source of the problem. Amy stated that the payroll process generally works well, although it requires a substantial amount of manual effort. She said that if she could hire two additional clerks, it would resolve any remaining problems. During the course of the meeting, Rick began to feel that Amy's opinion might be somewhat biased. As payroll director, she might not want to call attention to problems in her department, and, Rick guessed, it involved other potential issues — such as her wanting more reports and wanting to expand her department. He made a mental note of those possibilities so he could factor them in when considering her comments and assessment of the problem.

CHAPTER CAPSTONE CASE: SoftWear, Limited (continued)

Current Documentation

After completing the three interviews, Rick reviewed his notes and decided to find out more about the actual sequence of operations in the current system. He studied the documentation and found that it provided step-by-step procedures for preparing the payroll. When he asked the payroll clerks about those procedures, he learned that some sections were outdated. The actual sequence of events is shown in Figure 2-26.

Step 1: A new SWL employee completes an employee master sheet and a W-4 form. The human resources department then enters the employee's status and pay rate. Copies of these forms are sent to the payroll department. The payroll department updates the employee master sheet whenever changes are received from the employee or the human resources department. Updates are made with various forms, including forms for credit union and employee stock purchase plan enrollment and changes.

Step 2: On the last day of a weekly pay period, the payroll department prepares and distributes time sheets to all SWL departments. The time sheets list each employee, with codes for various status items such as regular pay, overtime, sick leave, vacation, jury duty, and personal leave.

Step 3: Department heads complete the time sheets on the first business day after the end of a pay period. The sheets then go to the payroll department, where they are reviewed. A payroll clerk enters pay rates and deduction information and forwards the time sheets to the BIS service bureau.

Step 4: BIS enters and processes the time sheet data, prints SWL paychecks, and prepares a payroll register.

Step 5: The checks, time sheets, and payroll register are returned to SWL. The payroll department distributes checks to each department, creates reports for credit union and stock purchase plan deductions, and then transfers necessary funds.

FIGURE 2-26 Sequence of events in payroll processing at SoftWear, Limited.

Rick also discovered that the payroll department never sees a copy of the form that an employee fills out in the human resources department when joining the stock purchase plan or changing deductions. Rick obtained a copy of the SWL stock purchase form from the human resources department and copies of several forms from the payroll department — including employee master sheets, employee time sheets, and credit union deduction forms. Rick put them in a file for later review.

During the preliminary investigation, Rick did not show concern with the detailed information on each form. He would review that information only after management authorized the IT department to continue with the systems analysis phase.

Presentation to Management

After Rick finished his investigation, he analyzed his findings, prepared a preliminary investigation report, and met with Jane and Ann to plan the presentation to management. Ann sent an advance copy of the report to Mr. Jeremy with an e-mail that announced the time and location of the presentation.

Figure 2-27 shows the cover message and the preliminary investigation report. Following the presentation to SWL's top managers and department heads, a question-and-answer session took place. The management group discussed the findings and recommendations and decided that the payroll system needed further analysis. The group also wanted to know if

CHAPTER CAPSTONE CASE: SoftWear, Limited (continued)

the BIS service bureau could handle the ESIP using their current arrangement. Ann replied that no clear answer could be given, and everyone agreed that the project scope should be broadened to include that question.

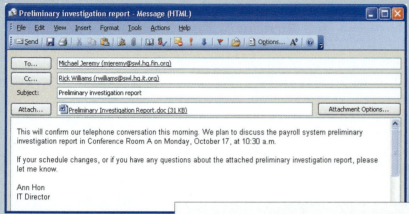

Preliminary investigation report - Message (HTML)

File   Edit   View   Insert   Format   Tools   Actions   Help

Send

To...   Michael Jeremy (mjeremy@swl.hq.fin.org)

Cc...   Rick Williams (rwilliams@swl.hq.it.org)

Subject: Preliminary investigation report

Attach...   Preliminary Investigation Report.doc (31 KB)   Attachment Options...

This will confirm our telephone conversation this morning. We plan to discuss the payroll system preliminary investigation report in Conference Room A on Monday, October 17, at 10:30 a.m.

If your schedule changes, or if you have any questions about the attached preliminary investigation report, please let me know.

Ann Hon
IT Director

Preliminary Investigation Report: SWL Payroll System   **October 7, 2005**

Introduction
The IT department completed a preliminary investigation of the payroll system on October 7. This investigation was the result of a systems request submitted by Michael Jeremy, vice president, finance, on September 16.

Systems Request Summary
Two problems were mentioned in the request: incorrect deductions from employee paychecks, and excessive payroll department overtime to perform manual processing tasks and make corrections.

Preliminary Investigation Findings
1.   The human resources department sends a summary of employee stock purchase deductions to the payroll department. It is likely that data errors occur during this process. Although the errors are corrected, we believe that incorrect payroll information adversely affects employee morale.

2.   The payroll processing arrangement with Business Information Systems (BIS) requires considerable manual effort. BIS does not provide summary reports that SWL needs to verify and apply credit union and stock purchase deductions. Currently, the payroll department handles these tasks manually at the end of each pay period.

3.   Payroll department overtime averages about eight hours per week, plus an additional eight hours at the end of the month, when stock purchase deductions are applied. Total annual overtime is about 512 hours. The average hourly base rate for payroll staff is $16.00, with an overtime rate of $24.00 per hour. The additional expense is about $12,288 per year.

4.   SWL developed its current payroll procedures ten years ago, when the company had only 75 employees. At that time, the only payroll deductions were legally required tax items. Today, the payroll system handles over 450 people and many deduction options that must be verified and applied manually.

Recommendations
The current problems will intensify as SWL continues to grow. At this point, it is unclear whether the current system can be modified to handle tasks that are being done manually. Accordingly, the IT department recommends a full analysis of the current system and possible solutions. The project should focus on two main areas: manual processing at SWL and computer-based payroll processing at BIS.

Time and Cost Estimates
We can perform a study during a two-week period. In addition to the time spent by IT staff, we will conduct about 20 hours of interviews with people outside the IT department. The following is a rough estimate of costs through the systems analysis phase:

Systems analyst	2.0 weeks @ $1,400 per week	$2,800
Other SWL staff	0.5 weeks @ $1,000 per week (average)	500
	Total:	$3,300

If the project continues beyond the systems analysis phase, total cost will depend on what development strategy is followed. If the current system can be modified, we estimate a total project effort of $20,000 to $30,000 over a four-month period. If modification is not feasible, a revised cost estimate will be submitted.

Expected Benefits
A sharp reduction in overtime costs and processing errors will avoid unnecessary expense and improve employee morale. During the systems analysis phase, the IT department will investigate various strategies and solutions to address current problems and strengthen SWL's ability to handle payroll-related IT issues in the future.

FIGURE 2-27   Ann Hon's email to Michael Jeremy, with preliminary investigation report attached.

CHAPTER CAPSTONE CASE: SoftWear, Limited (continued)

SWL Team Tasks

1. You have been assigned to write a formal mission statement for SWL. Start by reviewing SWL's background in Chapter 1, then do Internet research to find mission statements that seem clear, focused, and easy to understand. Pay special attention to Web-based and catalog retail firms to see how they approach the issue. Also keep in mind that SWL, like other firms, has many types of stakeholders who are affected by the company's operations.

2. Review the preliminary investigation report to see whether all four feasibility tests were discussed in the report. Write a brief summary of whether or not the report addressed each feasibility issue, and what comments were made.

3. Review the payroll department organization information on page 84. Using this information, prepare an organization chart for this group. If you have Microsoft Word 2003 or Microsoft Word 2002, you can click the Insert Diagram or Organization Chart button on the Drawing toolbar, then click the Organization Chart button. If you have an older version of Word, you can click Insert – Object – MS Organization Chart.

4. Rick asked you to investigate other firms that offer payroll processing services. Perform an Internet search using the term "payroll processing services." Try your search both with and without placing quotes around the phrase and notice what happens. You can learn more about Internet search techniques in Part 6 of the Systems Analyst's Toolkit. Based on your search results, select an example of a payroll processing firm and write a brief report to Rick. Include the name of the firm, its Web address, the services it offers, and your overall impression of the firm's capability.

PHASE 2 SYSTEMS ANALYSIS

Systems analysis is the second of five phases in the systems development life cycle (SDLC). In the prior phase, systems planning, you conducted a preliminary investigation to learn more about the systems request. Now, in the systems analysis phase, you will use requirements modeling and data and process modeling to represent the new system. Before proceeding to the next phase, systems design, you will consider system development strategies.

PHASE TOPICS

Chapter 3
Requirements Modeling

Chapter 4
Data and Process Modeling

Chapter 5
Development Strategies

DELIVERABLE

System requirements document

TOOLKIT SUPPORT

Primary tools: Communication, financial analysis, and project management tools.
Other tools as required.

CHAPTER 3 Requirements Modeling

CHAPTER 3 is the first of three chapters in the systems analysis phase. This chapter describes the process of gathering facts about a systems project, preparing documentation, and creating models that will be used to design and develop the system.

INTRODUCTION

OBJECTIVES

When you finish this chapter, you will be able to:

- Describe systems analysis phase activities and the end product of the systems analysis phase

- Explain joint application development (JAD) and rapid application development (RAD)

- Understand how systems analysts use a functional decomposition diagram (FDD)

- Describe the Unified Modeling Language (UML) and explain use case diagrams and sequence diagrams

- List and describe system requirements, including outputs, inputs, processes, performance, and controls

- Explain the importance of scalability in system design

- Use fact-finding techniques, including interviews, documentation review, observation, questionnaires, sampling, and research

- Define total cost of ownership (TCO) and explain the concept

- Conduct a successful interview

- Develop effective documentation methods to use during systems development

After an overview of the systems analysis phase, this chapter describes requirements modeling techniques and team-based methods that systems analysts use to visualize and document new systems. The chapter then discusses system requirements and fact-finding techniques, which include interviewing, documentation review, observation, surveys and questionnaires, sampling, and research.

CHAPTER INTRODUCTION CASE: Mountain View College Bookstore

Background: Wendy Lee, manager of college services at Mountain View College, wants a new information system that will improve efficiency and customer service at the three college bookstores.

In this part of the case, Florence Fullerton (systems analyst) and Harry Boston (student intern) are talking about requirements modeling tasks and concepts.

Participants:	Florence and Harry
Location:	Florence's office, Monday morning, October 24, 2005
Project status:	The project has advanced to the systems analysis phase. Now, Florence and Harry will work on modeling, fact-finding, and the documentation they need to build a requirements model for the proposed bookstore information system.
Discussion topics:	Modeling, team-based development strategies, fact-finding techniques, and documentation

Florence: Well, it looks like we're going ahead with the bookstore proposal. I heard from Wendy, the college services manager, and she says that the administration agreed with our recommendation to proceed.

Harry: *So, what do we do next?*

Florence: We need to create a model of the new system, just as you would build a scale model of an airplane. We call this a requirements model, because it will include all the outputs, inputs, processes, and controls for the new system. The model will consist of various diagrams, charts, and documentation.

Harry: *How will we use the model when we're done?*

Florence: We'll study it carefully and discuss it with users who will interact with the system. We'll probably revise the model many times to be sure that it is an accurate and complete picture of user requirements.

Harry: *Who are the users?*

Florence: In this case, users might include bookstore managers and staff, students, faculty members, and people in the college business office. If we want the system to connect with the outside world, external users might include textbook publishers and suppliers of bookstore merchandise.

Harry: *Let's get back to the model. How are we going to build it?*

Florence: Good question. Actually, you and I will coordinate the development, but we'll work with users every step of the way. After all, it's going to be their system, so they should have a major role in building it.

Harry: *What's the best way to involve users in the development process?*

Florence: We have several options: we can follow the traditional SDLC, making sure we get lots of user input and feedback, or we can go a step further by using JAD or RAD techniques. JAD means joint application development, which is a team approach to fact-finding, with lots of user participation. RAD stands for rapid application development, which is like a condensed SDLC.

Harry: *What about the fact-finding you mentioned? How do we do that?*

Florence: First, we'll study any documentation that describes the bookstore's functions. Then we'll conduct more interviews and use a questionnaire or survey, too. We might decide to observe bookstore operations, and sample some of the transactions. Then we'll document everything carefully. Here's a task list to get us started:

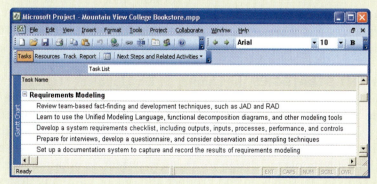

FIGURE 3-1

SYSTEMS ANALYSIS PHASE OVERVIEW

The overall objective of the systems analysis phase is to understand the proposed project, ensure that it will support business requirements, and build a solid foundation for system development. In this phase, you use models and other documentation tools to visualize and describe the proposed system.

Systems Analysis Activities

The systems analysis phase includes the three main activities shown in Figure 3-2: requirements modeling, data and process modeling, and consideration of development strategies.

REQUIREMENTS MODELING This chapter describes **requirements modeling**, which involves fact-finding to describe the current system and identification of the requirements for the new system, such as outputs, inputs, processes, performance, and security. **Outputs** refer to electronic or printed information produced by the system. **Inputs** refer to necessary data that enters the system, either manually or in an automated manner. **Processes** refer to the logical rules that are applied to transform the data into meaningful information. **Performance** refers to system characteristics such as speed, volume, capacity, availability, and reliability. **Security** refers to hardware, software, and procedural controls that safeguard and protect the system and its data from internal or external threats.

Systems Analysis Phase Major Activities

Data and Process Modeling

Requirements Modeling

Development Strategies

FIGURE 3-2 The systems analysis phase consists of requirements modeling, data and process modeling, and consideration of development strategies.

DATA AND PROCESS MODELING In Chapter 4, Data and Process Modeling, you will continue the modeling process by learning how to represent graphically system data and processes using traditional structured analysis techniques. As you learned in Chapter 1, structured analysis identifies the data flowing into a process, the business rules that transform the data, and the resulting output data flow. You also might want to use object modeling as an alternative to data and process modeling. Object modeling is described in Part 5 of the Systems Analyst's Toolkit. Whereas structured analysis treats processes and data as separate components, object-oriented analysis (O-O) combines data and the processes that act on the data into things called objects. These objects represent actual people, things, transactions, and events that affect the system.

DEVELOPMENT STRATEGIES In Chapter 5, Development Strategies, you will consider various development options and prepare for the transition to the systems design phase of the SDLC. You will learn about software trends, acquisition and development alternatives, outsourcing, and formally documenting requirements for the new system.

The deliverable, or end product, of the systems analysis phase is a **system requirements document**, which is an overall design for the new system. In addition, each activity within the systems analysis phase has an end product and one or more milestones. Large systems

projects require considerable effort to coordinate people, tasks, timetables, and budgets. The Systems Analyst's Toolkit describes project management tools that can help monitor and control complex projects.

Systems Analysis Skills

You will need strong analytical and interpersonal skills to build an accurate model of the new system. **Analytical skills** enable you to identify a problem, evaluate the key elements, and develop a useful solution. **Interpersonal skills** are especially valuable to a systems analyst who must work with people at all organizational levels, balance conflicting needs of users, and communicate effectively.

Because information systems affect people throughout the company, you should consider team-oriented strategies as you begin the systems analysis phase.

Team-Oriented Methods and Techniques

Top managers expect the IT department to deliver the best possible information system, at the lowest possible cost, in the shortest possible time. To fulfill these expectations, many IT managers have tried to increase user participation in the development process. Greater user involvement usually results in better communication, faster development times, and more satisfied users.

The traditional model for systems development was an IT department that used structured analysis and consulted users only when their input or approval was needed. Although the IT staff still has a central role, and structured analysis remains a popular method of systems development, many IT managers invite system users to participate actively in various development tasks. A common technique is called **joint application development (JAD)**, which is a team-oriented technique for fact-finding and requirements modeling. Because it is not linked to a specific development methodology, systems developers use JAD whenever group input and interaction are desired.

Another popular user-oriented method is **rapid application development (RAD)**. RAD resembles a condensed version of the entire SDLC, with users involved every step of the way. While JAD typically focuses only on fact-finding and requirements determination, RAD provides a fast-track approach to a full spectrum of system development tasks, including planning, design, construction, and implementation.

JOINT APPLICATION DEVELOPMENT

Joint application development (JAD) is a popular fact-finding technique that brings users into the development process as active participants.

User Involvement

Users have a vital stake in an information system, and they should participate fully in the development process. Until recent years, the IT department usually had sole responsibility for systems development, and users had a relatively passive role. During the development process, the IT staff would collect information from users, define system requirements, and construct the new system. At various stages of the process, the IT staff might ask users to review the design, offer comments, and submit changes.

Today, users typically have a much more active role in systems development. IT professionals now recognize that successful systems must be user-oriented, and users need to be involved, formally or informally, at every stage of system development.

ON THE WEB

For more information about Interpersonal Skills, visit **scsite.com/ sad6e/more**, locate Chapter 3 and then click the Interpersonal Skills link.

ON THE WEB

For more information about JAD, visit **scsite.com/sad6e/ more**, locate Chapter 3 and then click the JAD link.

One popular strategy for user involvement is a JAD team approach, which involves a task force of users, managers, and IT professionals that works together to gather information, discuss business needs, and define the new system requirements.

JAD Participants and Roles

A JAD team, similar to the one shown in Figure 3-3, usually meets over a period of days or weeks in a special conference room or at an off-site location. Either way, JAD participants should be insulated from the distraction of day-to-day operations. The objective is to analyze the existing system, obtain user input and expectations, and document user requirements for the new system.

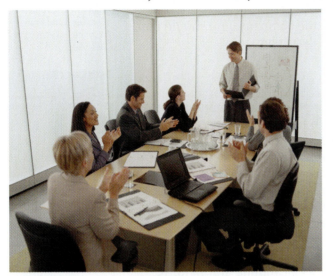

FIGURE 3-3   A JAD team of users, managers, and IT professionals works together to identify and document requirements for a new system.

The JAD group usually has a project leader, who needs strong interpersonal and organizational skills, and one or more members who document and record the results and decisions. Typical JAD participants and their roles are shown in Figure 3-4. IT staff members often serve as JAD project leaders, but that is not always the case. Systems analysts on the JAD team participate in discussions, ask questions, take notes, and provide support to the team. If CASE tools are available, analysts can develop models and enter documentation from the JAD session directly into the CASE tool.

A typical JAD session agenda is shown in Figure 3-5. The JAD process involves intensive effort by all team members. Because of the wide range of input and constant interaction among the participants, many companies believe that a JAD group produces the best possible definition of the new system.

Typical JAD Participants and Roles

JAD PARTICIPANT	ROLE
JAD project leader	Develops an agenda, acts as a facilitator, and leads the JAD session
Top management	Provides enterprise-level authorization and support for the project
Managers	Provide department-level support for the project and understanding of how the project must support business functions and requirements
Users	Provide operational-level input on current operations, desired changes, input and output requirements, user interface issues, and how the project will support day-to-day tasks
Systems analysts and other IT staff members	Provide technical assistance and resources for JAD team members on issues such as security, backup, hardware, software, and network capability
Recorder	Documents results of JAD sessions and works with systems analysts to build system models and develop CASE tool documentation

FIGURE 3-4   Typical JAD participants and roles.

Typical JAD Session Agenda

Project leader	• Introduce all JAD team members • Discuss ground rules, goals, and objectives for the JAD sessions • Explain methods of documentation and use of CASE tools, if any
Top management (sometimes called the project owner or sponsor)	• Explain the reason for the project and express top management authorization and support
Project leader	• Provide overview of the current system and proposed project scope and constraints • Present outline of specific topics and issues to be investigated
Open discussion session, moderated by project leader	• Review the main business processes, tasks, user roles, input, and output • Identify specific areas of agreement or disagreement • Break team into smaller groups to study specific issues and assign group leaders
JAD team members working in smaller group sessions, supported by IT staff	• Discuss and document all system requirements • Develop models and prototypes
Group leaders	• Report on results and assigned tasks and topics • Present issues that should be addressed by the overall JAD team
Open discussion session, moderated by project leader	• Review reports from small group sessions • Reach consensus on main issues • Document all topics
Project leader	• Present overall recap of JAD session • Prepare report that will be sent to JAD team members

FIGURE 3-5 Typical agenda for a JAD session.

JAD Advantages and Disadvantages

Compared with traditional methods, JAD is more expensive and can be cumbersome if the group is too large relative to the size of the project. Many companies find, however, that JAD allows key users to participate effectively in the requirements modeling process. When users participate in the systems development process, they are more likely to feel a sense of ownership in the results, and support for the new system. When properly used, JAD can result in a more accurate statement of system requirements, a better understanding of common goals, and a stronger commitment to the success of the new system.

RAPID APPLICATION DEVELOPMENT

Rapid application development (RAD) is a team-based technique that speeds up information systems development and produces a functioning information system. Like JAD, RAD uses a group approach, but goes much further. While the end product of JAD is a requirements model, the end product of RAD is the new information system. RAD is a complete methodology, with a four-phase life cycle that parallels the traditional SDLC phases. Companies use RAD to reduce cost and development time, and

increase the probability of success. To simplify the system development process, IT vendors offer software that can provide an application development environment, as shown in Figure 3-6.

FIGURE 3-6 Magic Software is an IT vendor that offers a rapid application development tool called eDeveloper.

RAD relies heavily on prototyping and user involvement. The RAD process allows users to examine a working model as early as possible, determine if it meets their needs, and suggest necessary changes. Based on user input, the prototype is modified and the interactive process continues until the system is completely developed and users are satisfied. The project team uses CASE tools to build the prototypes and create a continuous stream of documentation.

RAD Phases and Activities

The RAD model consists of four phases: requirements planning, user design, construction, and cutover, as shown in Figure 3-7. Notice the continuous interaction between the user design and construction phases.

ON THE WEB

For more information about RAD, visit **scsite.com/sad6e/ more**, locate Chapter 3 and then click the RAD link.

REQUIREMENTS PLANNING The **requirements planning phase** combines elements of the systems planning and systems analysis phases of the SDLC. Users, managers, and IT staff members discuss and agree on business needs, project scope, constraints, and system requirements. The requirements planning phase ends when the team agrees on the key issues and obtains management authorization to continue.

USER DESIGN During the **user design phase**, users interact with systems analysts and develop models and prototypes that represent all system processes, outputs, and inputs. The RAD group, or subgroups typically use a combination of JAD techniques and CASE tools to translate user needs into working models. User design is a continuous, interactive process that allows users to understand, modify, and eventually approve a working model of the system that meets their needs.

CONSTRUCTION The **construction phase** focuses on program and application development tasks similar to the SDLC. In RAD, however, users continue to participate and still can suggest changes or improvements as actual screens or reports are developed.

CUTOVER The **cutover phase** resembles the final tasks in the SDLC implementation phase, including data conversion, testing, changeover to the new system, and user training. Compared with traditional methods, the entire process is compressed. As a result, the new system is built, delivered, and placed in operation much sooner.

RAD Objectives

The main objective of all RAD approaches is to cut development time and expense by involving users in every phase of systems development. Because it is a continuous process, RAD allows the development team to make necessary modifications quickly, as

the design evolves. In times of tight corporate budgets, it is especially important to limit the cost of changes that typically occur in a long, drawn-out development schedule.

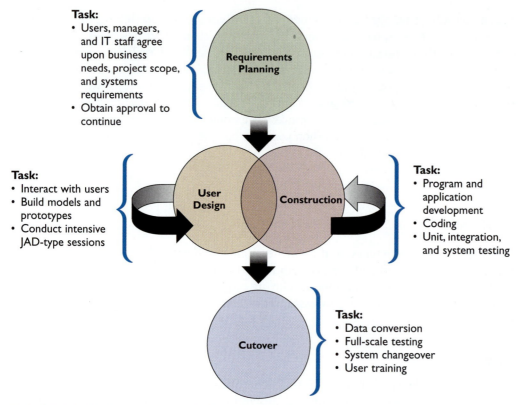

Task:
- Users, managers, and IT staff agree upon business needs, project scope, and systems requirements
- Obtain approval to continue

Task:
- Interact with users
- Build models and prototypes
- Conduct intensive JAD-type sessions

Task:
- Program and application development
- Coding
- Unit, integration, and system testing

Task:
- Data conversion
- Full-scale testing
- System changeover
- User training

Requirements Planning

User Design

Construction

Cutover

FIGURE 3-7 The four phases of the RAD model are requirements planning, user design, construction, and cutover. Notice the continuous interaction between the user design and construction phases.

In addition to user involvement, a successful RAD team must have IT resources, skills, and management support. Because it is a dynamic, user-driven process, RAD is especially valuable when a company needs an information system to support a new business function. By obtaining user input from the beginning, RAD also helps a development team design a system that requires a highly interactive or complex user interface.

RAD Advantages and Disadvantages

RAD has advantages and disadvantages compared with traditional structured analysis methods. The primary advantage is that systems can be developed more quickly with significant cost savings. A disadvantage is that RAD stresses the mechanics of the system itself and does not emphasize the company's strategic business needs. The risk is that a system might work well in the short term, but the corporate and long-term objectives for the system might not be met. Another potential disadvantage is that the accelerated time cycle might allow less time to develop quality, consistency, and design standards. RAD can be an attractive alternative, however, if an organization understands the possible risks.

CASE IN POINT 3.1: NORTH HILLS CONSULTING

Suppose you were employed as a summer intern by North Hills Consulting, which offers a wide range of IT services to clients. North Hills has a Web site that describes the firm and the services it offers. The site includes a monthly feature called "Hot Topic," which reviews current IT trends and developments.

Yesterday, Jane Hall, your supervisor, mentioned that next month's topic would be JAD and RAD, and she asked you to write a draft of the Hot Topic article. Specifically, she wants you to go online and locate at least three references that would be of interest to readers who want to learn more about JAD or RAD. When you have completed your research, she wants you to write a summary of your findings.

MODELING TOOLS AND TECHNIQUES

Models help users, managers, and IT professionals understand the design of a system. Modeling involves graphical methods and non-technical language that represent the system at various stages of development. During requirements modeling, you can use various tools to describe business processes, requirements, and user interaction with the system.

CASE Tools

In Chapter 1 you learned that CASE tools can offer powerful modeling features. For example, the business modeling tutorial shown in Figure 3-8 provides a tool that an analyst can use to document what the business does, why those functions are performed, who carries out the tasks, and how it is done. CASE tool modeling is described in more detail in Part 2 of the Systems Analyst's Toolkit.

Systems analysts use modeling and fact-finding interactively — first they build fact-finding results into models, then they study the models to determine whether additional fact-finding is needed. To help them understand system requirements, systems analysts often use functional decomposition diagrams, which provide a business-oriented overview, and the Unified Modeling Language, which shows how people interact with the system.

> **TOOLKIT TIME**
>
> The CASE Tools in Part 2 of the Systems Analyst's Toolkit can help you document business functions and processes, develop graphical models, and provide an overall framework for information system development. To learn more about these tools, turn to Part 2 of the six-part Toolkit that follows Chapter 10.

Functional Decomposition Diagrams

A **functional decomposition diagram (FDD)** is a top-down representation of a function or process. FDDs also are called **structure charts**. Using an FDD, an analyst can show business functions and break them down into

Business Modeling Tutorial -- Introduction

The Business Modeling provided by System Architect enables you to model the process flows of a business, the functions that are performed, its organizational hierarchy, the systems it has in place, its network architectures, requirements and business rules that are being fulfilled, and how everything fits together. This enables you to understand the basic questions of your business -- the who, what, why, when, where, and how things are being done.

In this tutorial, we will do the following:

- Begin by simply reviewing the current Business Profile of the Chelsea Hotels and Resorts business, to see what the business is currently about. This helps us to understand **what** the business does.

- Review the company's Business Enterprise Direction, to see where we'd like the business to go. We'll take a look at the company's Business Objectives; this helps us to understand **why** functions are enabled, and processes are performed.

- Next we'll learn how to model the process flow of the hotel's Reservation System, using a Process Chart diagram. We will build swimlanes on this diagram, to relate **who** does **what** in the process, and **how** it is done. **It is in this section that you actually begin drawing diagrams with System Architect.** If you are anxious to begin learning how to draw, you can skip the sections above, and go directly to the Introduction to Process Threads and Process Charts section. (You can return to the sections above at a later time.)

- We will build a Process Decomposition diagram and Functional Hierarchy to understand how the functions of the business are enacted by the processes, again answering part of the **how** question.

Next: Defining a Business Profile

FIGURE 3-8 Popkin's System Architect offers a business modeling tutorial.

lower-level functions and processes. Creating an FDD is similar to drawing an organization chart — you start at the top and work your way down. Figure 3-9 shows a four-level FDD of a library system drawn with the Visible Analyst CASE tool. FDDs can be used at several stages of systems development. During requirements modeling, analysts use FDDs to model business functions and show how they are organized into lower-level processes. Those processes translate into program modules during application development.

Unified Modeling Language

The **Unified Modeling Language** (UML) is a widely used method of visualizing and documenting software systems design. UML uses object-oriented design concepts, but it is independent of any specific programming language and can be used to describe business processes and requirements generally.

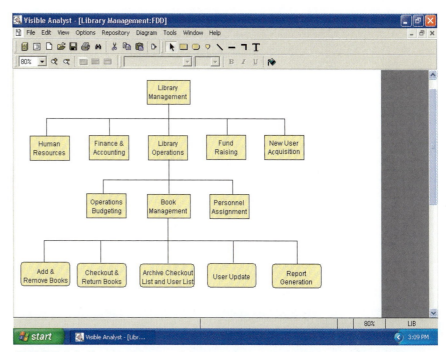

FIGURE 3-9 Four-level functional decomposition diagram (FDD) of a library system.

UML provides various graphical tools, such as use case diagrams and sequence diagrams. During requirements modeling, a systems analyst can utilize the UML to represent the information system from a user's viewpoint. Use case diagrams, sequence diagrams, and other UML concepts are discussed in more detail in Part 5 of the Systems Analyst's Toolkit, along with other object-oriented analysis concepts. A brief description of each technique follows.

USE CASE DIAGRAMS During requirements modeling, systems analysts and users work together to document requirements and model system functions. A **use case diagram** visually represents the interaction between users and the information system. In a use case diagram, the user becomes an **actor**, with a specific role that describes how he or she interacts with the system. Systems analysts can draw use case diagrams freehand or use CASE tools that integrate the use cases into the overall system design.

Figure 3-10 on the next page shows a simple use case diagram for a sales system where the actor is a customer and the use case involves a credit card validation that is performed by the system. Because use cases depict the system through the eyes of a user, common business language can be used to describe the transactions. For example, Figure 3-11 on the next page shows a table that documents the credit card validation use case, and Figure 3-12 on the next page shows a student records system, with several use cases and actors.

TOOLKIT TIME

The Object-Oriented Tools in Part 5 of the Systems Analyst's Toolkit can help you model a system by graphically representing objects within the system and how they interact. To learn more about these tools, turn to Part 5 of the six-part Toolkit that follows Chapter 10.

ON THE WEB

For more information about The Unified Modeling Language, visit **scsite.com/ sad6e/more**, locate Chapter 3 and then click The Unified Modeling Language link.

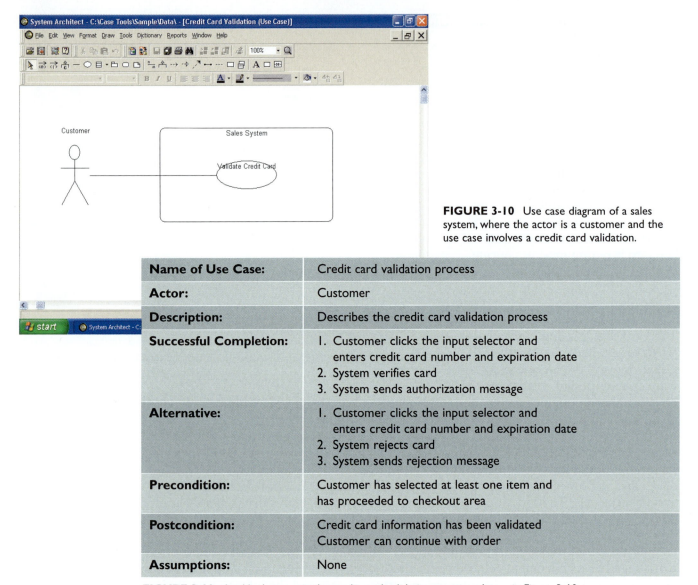

FIGURE 3-10 Use case diagram of a sales system, where the actor is a customer and the use case involves a credit card validation.

Name of Use Case:	Credit card validation process
Actor:	Customer
Description:	Describes the credit card validation process
Successful Completion:	1. Customer clicks the input selector and enters credit card number and expiration date 2. System verifies card 3. System sends authorization message
Alternative:	1. Customer clicks the input selector and enters credit card number and expiration date 2. System rejects card 3. System sends rejection message
Precondition:	Customer has selected at least one item and has proceeded to checkout area
Postcondition:	Credit card information has been validated Customer can continue with order
Assumptions:	None

FIGURE 3-11 A table documents the credit card validation use case shown in Figure 3-10.

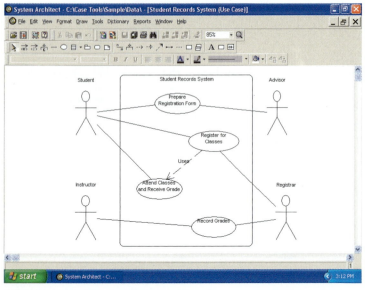

SEQUENCE DIAGRAMS A sequence **diagram** shows the timing of interactions between objects as they occur. A systems analyst might use a sequence diagram to show all possible outcomes, or focus on a single scenario. Figure 3-13 shows a simple sequence diagram of a successful credit card validation. The interaction proceeds from top to bottom along a vertical timeline, while the horizontal arrows represent messages from one object to another.

FIGURE 3-12 Use case diagram of a student records system.

FIGURE 3-13 Sequence diagram of a successful credit card validation showing how the transaction proceeds from top to bottom, along a vertical timeline.

SYSTEM REQUIREMENTS CHECKLIST

During requirements modeling, systems developers must identify and describe all system requirements. A **system requirement** is a characteristic or feature that must be included in an information system to satisfy business requirements and be acceptable to users. System requirements serve as benchmarks to measure the overall acceptability of the finished system.

System requirements fall into five general categories: outputs, inputs, processes, performance, and controls. Typical examples of system requirements for each category are listed below.

Outputs

- The Web site must report online volume statistics every four hours, and hourly during peak periods.

- The inventory system must produce a daily report showing the part number, description, quantity on hand, quantity allocated, quantity available, and unit cost of all sorted by part number.

- The contact management system must generate a daily reminder list for all sales reps.

- The purchasing system must provide suppliers with up-to-date specifications.

- The sales tracking system must produce a daily fast-moving-item report, listing all products that exceed the forecasted sales volume grouped by style, color, size, and reorder status.

- The customer analysis system must produce a quarterly report that identifies changes in ordering patterns or trends with statistical comparisons to the previous four quarters.

Inputs

→ Manufacturing employees must swipe their ID cards into online data collection terminals that record labor costs and calculate production efficiency.

→ The department head must enter overtime hours on a separate screen.

→ Student grades must be entered on machine-scannable forms prepared by the instructor.

→ Each input form must include date, time, product code, customer number, and quantity.

→ Data entry screens must be uniform, except for background color, which can be changed by the user.

→ A data entry person at the medical group must input patient services into the billing system.

Processes

→ The student records system must calculate the GPA at the end of each semester.

→ As the final step in year-end processing, the payroll system must update employee salaries, bonuses, and benefits and produce tax data required by the IRS.

→ The warehouse distribution system must analyze daily orders and create a routing pattern for delivery trucks that maximizes efficiency and reduces unnecessary mileage.

→ The human resources system must interface properly with the existing payroll system.

→ The video rental system must not execute new rental transactions for customers who have overdue tapes.

→ The prescription system must automatically generate an insurance claim form.

Performance

→ The system must support 25 users online simultaneously.

→ Response time must not exceed four seconds.

→ The system must be operational seven days a week, 365 days a year.

→ The accounts receivable system must prepare customer statements by the third business day of the following month.

→ The student records system must produce class lists within five hours after the end of registration.

→ The online inventory control system must flag all low-stock items within one hour after the quantity falls below a predetermined minimum.

Controls

→ The system must provide log-on security at the operating system level and at the application level.

→ An employee record must be added, changed, or deleted only by a member of the human resources department.

→ The system must maintain separate levels of security for users and the system administrator.

➡ All transactions must have audit trails.

➡ The manager of the sales department must approve orders that exceed a customer's credit limit.

➡ The system must create an error log file that includes the error type, description, and time.

FUTURE GROWTH, COSTS, AND BENEFITS

In addition to the system requirements listed above, systems analysts must consider scalability, which determines how a system will handle future growth and demands, and the total cost of ownership, which includes all future operational and support costs.

Scalability

Scalability refers to a system's ability to handle increased business volume and transactions in the future. Because it will have a longer useful life, a scalable system offers a better return on the initial investment.

To evaluate scalability, you need information about projected future volume for all outputs, inputs, and processes. For example, for a Web-based order processing system, you would need to know the estimated number of online customers, the periods of peak online activity, the number and types of data items required for each transaction, and the method of accessing and updating customer files.

Even to print customer statements, you need to know the number of active accounts and have a forecast for one, two, or five years, because that information affects future hardware decisions. In addition, with realistic volume projections, you can provide reliable cost estimates for related expenses, such as postage and online charges.

Similarly, to assure that a Web-based hotel reservation system is sufficiently scalable, you would need to project activity levels for several years of operation. For example, you might forecast the frequency of online queries about room availability and estimate the time required for each query and the average response time. With that information, you could estimate server transaction volume and network requirements.

Transaction volume has a significant impact on operating costs. When volume exceeds a system's limitations, maintenance costs increase sharply. Volume can change dramatically if a company expands or enters a new line of business. For example, a new Internet-based marketing effort might require an additional server and 24-hour technical support.

Data storage also is an important scalability issue. You need to determine how much data storage is required currently and predict future needs based on system activity and growth. Those requirements affect hardware, software, and network bandwidth needed to maintain system performance. You also must consider data retention requirements and determine whether data can be deleted or archived on a specific timetable.

Total Cost of Ownership

In addition to direct costs, systems developers must identify and document indirect expenses that contribute to the **total cost of ownership (TCO)**. TCO is especially important if the development team is assessing several alternatives. After considering the indirect costs, which are not always apparent, a system that seems inexpensive initially might actually turn out to be the most costly choice. One problem is that cost estimates tend to understate indirect costs such as user support and downtime productivity losses. Even if accurate figures are unavailable, systems analysts should try to identify indirect costs and include them in TCO estimates.

🔧 TOOLKIT TIME

The Financial Analysis tools in Part 3 of the Systems Analyst's Toolkit can help you analyze project costs, benefits, and economic feasibility. To learn more about these tools, turn to Part 3 of the six-part Toolkit that follows Chapter 10.

ON THE WEB

For more information about REJ, visit **scsite.com/sad6e/ more**, locate Chapter 3 and then click the REJ link.

Microsoft has developed a method for measuring total costs and benefits, called **Rapid Economic Justification (REJ)**, which is described in Figure 3-14. According to Microsoft, REJ is a framework to help IT professionals analyze and optimize IT investments. Notice that the primary emphasis is on business improvement, rather than operational efficiency. As the Web site points out, the strategic role of IT investments should be included, even when the specific benefits are difficult to quantify.

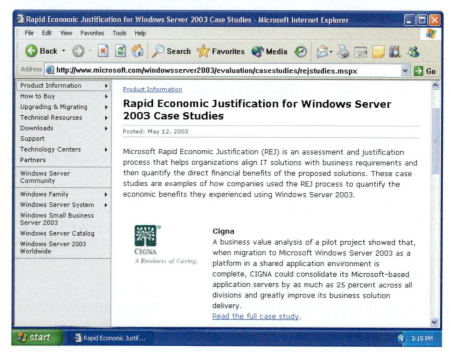

FIGURE 3-14   Microsoft developed Rapid Economic Justification (REJ) as a framework to help IT professionals analyze and optimize IT investments.

FACT-FINDING

Now that you understand the categories of system requirements, scalability, and TCO, the next step is to begin collecting information. Whether you are working on your own or as a member of a JAD team, during requirements modeling you will use various fact-finding techniques, including interviews, document review, observation, surveys and questionnaires, sampling, and research.

Fact-Finding Overview

Although software can help you to gather and analyze facts, no program actually performs fact-finding for you. First, you must identify the information you need. Typically, you begin by asking a series of questions, such as these:

- ➡ What business functions are supported by the current system?
- ➡ What strategic objectives and business requirements must be supported by the new system?
- ➡ What are the benefits and TCO of the proposed system?
- ➡ What transactions will the system process?
- ➡ What information do users and managers need from the system?
- ➡ Must the new system interface with legacy systems?

➡ What procedures could be eliminated by business process reengineering?

➡ What security issues exist?

➡ What risks are acceptable?

➡ What budget and timetable constraints will affect system development?

To obtain answers to these questions, you develop a fact-finding plan, which can involve another series of questions (*who*, *what*, *where*, *when*, and *how*) or use a more structured approach such as the Zachman Framework, which is explained in a following section. Either way, you will develop a strategy, carry out fact-finding techniques, document the results, and prepare a system requirements document, which is presented to management.

Who, What, Where, When, How, and Why?

Fact-finding involves answers to five familiar questions: *who*, *what*, *where*, *when*, and *how*. For each of those questions you also must ask another very important question: *why*. Some examples of these questions are:

1. *Who?* Who performs each of the procedures within the system? Why? Are the correct people performing the activity? Could other people perform the tasks more effectively?

2. *What?* What is being done? What procedures are being followed? Why is that process necessary? Often, procedures are followed for many years and no one knows why. You should question why a procedure is being followed at all.

3. *Where?* Where are operations being performed? Why? Where could they be performed? Could they be performed more efficiently elsewhere?

4. *When?* When is a procedure performed? Why is it being performed at this time? Is this the best time?

5. *How?* How is a procedure performed? Why is it performed in that manner? Could it be performed better, more efficiently, or less expensively in some other manner?

There is a difference between asking what *is* being done and what *could* or *should* be done. The systems analyst first must understand the current situation. Only then can he or she tackle the question of what *should* be done. Figure 3-15 lists the basic questions and when they should be asked. Notice that the first two columns relate to the current system, but the third column focuses on the proposed system.

CURRENT SYSTEM		PROPOSED SYSTEM
Who does it?	Why does this person do it?	Who should do it?
What is done?	Why is it done?	What should be done?
Where is it done?	Why is it done there?	Where should it be done?
When is it done?	Why is it done then?	When should it be done?
How is it done?	Why is it done this way?	How should it be done?

FIGURE 3-15 Sample questions during requirements modeling as the focus shifts from the current system to the proposed system.

ON THE WEB

For more information about The Zachman Framework, visit **scsite.com/sad6e/more**, locate Chapter 3 and then click The Zachman Framework link.

The Zachman Framework

In the 1980s, John Zachman observed how industries such as architecture and construction handled complex projects, and he suggested that the same ideas could be applied to information systems development. His concept, the **Zachman Framework for Enterprise Architecture**, is a model that asks the traditional fact-finding questions in a systems development context, as shown in Figure 3-16. The Zachman Framework is a popular approach, and Popkin Software now includes a CASE tool feature that allows users to view a systems project from the perspective of the Zachman Framework. As the Popkin site explains, a project can be viewed from different perspectives and levels of detail. The Zachman Framework helps managers and users understand the model and assures that overall business goals translate into successful IT projects.

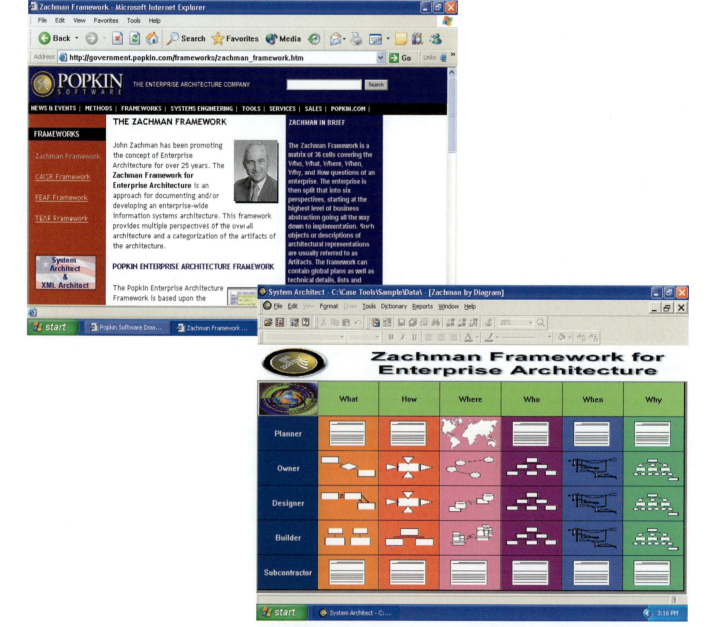

FIGURE 3-16 Popkin Software uses the Zachman Framework for Enterprise Architecture, which asks the traditional fact-finding questions in a systems development context.

INTERVIEWS

Systems analysts spend a great deal of time talking with people, both inside and outside the IT department. Much of that time is spent conducting interviews, which are the most common fact-finding technique. An **interview** is a planned meeting during which you obtain information from another person. You must have the skills needed to plan, conduct, and document interviews successfully.

After you identify the information you need, as described earlier in the chapter, you can begin the interviewing process, which consists of seven steps for each interview:

1. Determine the people to interview.
2. Establish objectives for the interview.
3. Develop interview questions.
4. Prepare for the interview.
5. Conduct the interview.
6. Document the interview.
7. Evaluate the interview.

Step 1: Determine the People to Interview

To get an accurate picture, you must select the right people to interview and ask them the right questions. During the preliminary investigation, you talked mainly to middle managers or department heads. Now, during the systems analysis phase, you might need to interview people from all levels of the organization.

Although you can select your interview candidates from the formal organization charts that you reviewed earlier, you also must consider any informal structures that exist in the organization. Informal structures usually are based on interpersonal relationships and can develop from previous work assignments, physical proximity, unofficial procedures, or personal relationships such as the informal gathering shown in Figure 3-17. In an **informal structure**, some people have more influence or knowledge than appears on an organization chart. Your knowledge of the company's formal and informal structures helps you determine the people to interview during the systems analysis phase.

FIGURE 3-17 An analyst must consider informal structures in the organization when selecting interview candidates.

Should you interview several people at the same time? Group interviews can save time and provide an opportunity to observe interaction among the participants. Group interviews also can present problems. One person might dominate the conversation, even when questions are addressed specifically to others. Organization level also can present a problem, as the presence of senior managers in an interview might prevent lower-level employees from expressing themselves candidly.

Step 2: Establish Objectives for the Interview

After deciding on the people to interview, you must establish objectives for the session. First, you should determine the general areas to be discussed, and then list the facts you want to gather. You also should try to solicit ideas, suggestions, and opinions during the interview.

The objectives of an interview depend on the role of the person being interviewed. Upper-level managers can provide the big picture and help you to understand the system as a whole. Specific details about operations and business processes are best learned from people who actually work with the system on a daily basis.

In the early stages of systems analysis, interviews usually are general. As the fact-finding process continues, however, the interviews focus more on specific topics. Interview objectives also vary at different stages of the investigation. By setting specific objectives, you create a framework that helps you decide what questions to ask and how to phrase the questions.

Step 3: Develop Interview Questions

Creating a standard list of interview questions helps to keep you on track and avoid unnecessary tangents. Also, if you interview several people who perform the same job, a standard question list allows you to compare their answers. Although you have a list of specific questions, you might decide to depart from it because an answer to one question leads to another topic that you want to pursue. That question or topic then should be included in a revised set of questions used to conduct future interviews. If the question proves to be extremely important, you may need to return to a previous interviewee to query him or her on the topic.

The interview should consist of several different kinds of questions: open-ended, closed-ended, or questions with a range of responses. When you phrase your questions, you should avoid **leading questions** that suggest or favor a particular reply. For example, rather than asking, "What advantages do you see in the proposed system?" you might ask, "Do you see any advantages in the proposed system?"

OPEN-ENDED QUESTIONS   Open-ended **questions** encourage spontaneous and unstructured responses. Such questions are useful when you want to understand a larger process or draw out the interviewee's opinions, attitudes, or suggestions. Here are some examples of open-ended questions: What are users saying about the new system? How is this task performed? Why do you perform the task that way? How are the checks reconciled? What added features would you like to have in the new billing system? Also, you can use an open-ended question to probe further by asking: Is there anything else you can tell me about this topic?

CLOSED-ENDED QUESTIONS   Closed-ended **questions** limit or restrict the response. You use closed-ended questions when you want information that is more specific or when you need to verify facts. Examples of closed-ended questions include the following: How many personal computers do you have in this department? Do you review the reports before they are sent out? How many hours of training does a clerk receive? Is the calculation procedure described in the manual? How many customers ordered products from the Web site last month?

RANGE-OF-RESPONSE QUESTIONS   Range-of-response **questions** are closed-ended questions that ask the person to evaluate something by providing limited answers to specific responses or on a numeric scale. This method makes it easier to tabulate the answers and interpret the results. Range-of-response questions might include these: On a scale of 1 to 10, with 1 the lowest and 10 the highest, how effective was your training? How would you rate the severity of the problem: low, medium, or high? Is the system shutdown something that occurs never, sometimes, often, usually, or always?

Step 4: Prepare for the Interview

After setting the objectives and developing the questions, you must prepare for the interview. Careful preparation is essential because an interview is an important meeting and not just a casual chat. When you schedule the interview, suggest a specific day and time and let the interviewee know how long you expect the meeting to last. It is also a good idea to send an e-mail or place a reminder call the day before the interview.

Remember that the interview is an interruption of the other person's routine, so you should limit the interview to no more than one hour. If business pressures force a postponement of the meeting, you should schedule another appointment as soon as it is convenient. Remember to keep department managers informed of your meetings with their staff members. Sending a message to each department manager listing your planned appointments is a good way to keep them informed. Figure 3-18 is an example of such a message.

You should send a list of topics to an interviewee several days before the meeting, especially when detailed information is needed, so the person can prepare for the interview and minimize the need for a follow-up meeting. Figure 3-19 shows a sample message that lists specific questions and confirms the date, time, location, purpose, and anticipated duration of the interview.

If you have questions about documents, ask the interviewee to have samples available at the meeting. Your advance memo should include a list of the documents you want to discuss, if you know what they are. Otherwise, you can make a general request for documents, as the analyst did in her e-mail shown in Figure 3-19.

Two schools of thought exist about the best location for an interview. Some analysts believe that interviews should take place in the interviewee's office, whereas other analysts feel that a neutral location such as a conference room is better.

Supporters of interviews in the interviewee's office believe that is the best location because it makes the interviewee feel comfortable during the meeting. A second

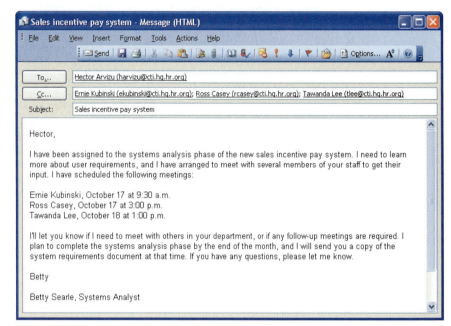

FIGURE 3-18   Sample message to a department head about interviews with people in his group.

FIGURE 3-19   Sample message to confirm a planned meeting and provide advance information about topics to be discussed.

argument in favor of the interviewee's office is that the office is where he or she has the easiest access to supporting material that might be needed during the discussion. If you provide a complete list of topics in advance, however, the interviewee can bring the necessary items to a conference room or other location.

Supporters of neutral locations stress the importance of keeping interruptions to a minimum so both people can concentrate fully. In addition, an interview that is free of interruptions takes less time. If the meeting does take place in the interviewee's office, you should suggest tactfully that all calls be held until the conclusion of the interview.

Step 5: Conduct the Interview

After determining the people to interview, setting your objectives, and preparing the questions, you should develop a specific plan for the meeting. When conducting an interview, you should begin by introducing yourself, describing the project, and explaining your interview objectives.

During the interview, ask questions in the order in which you prepared them, and give the interviewee sufficient time to provide thoughtful answers. Establishing a good rapport with the interviewee is important, especially if this is your first meeting. If the other person feels comfortable and at ease, you probably will receive more complete and candid answers. Your primary responsibility during an interview is to listen carefully to the answers. Analysts sometimes hear only what they expect to hear. You must concentrate on what is said and notice any nonverbal communication that takes place. This process is called **engaged listening**.

After asking a question, allow the person enough time to think about the question and arrive at an answer. Studies have shown that the maximum pause during a conversation is usually three to five seconds. After that interval, one person will begin talking. You will need to be patient and practice your skills in many actual interview situations to be successful.

When you finish asking your questions, summarize the main points covered in the interview and explain the next course of action. For example, mention that you will send a follow-up memo or that the interviewee should get back to you with certain information. When you conclude the interview, thank the person and encourage him or her to contact you with any questions or additional comments. Also, when the interview ends, it is a good idea to ask the interviewee whether he or she can suggest any additional topics that should be discussed.

After an interview, you should summarize the session and seek a confirmation from the other person. By stating your understanding of the discussion, the interviewee can respond and correct you, if necessary. One good approach is to rephrase the interviewee's answers. For example, you can say, "If I understand you correctly, you are saying that ..." and then reiterate the information given by the interviewee.

Step 6: Document the Interview

Although taking notes during an interview has both advantages and disadvantages, the accepted view is that note taking should be kept to a minimum. Although you should write down a few notes to jog your memory after the interview, you should avoid writing everything that is said. Too much writing distracts the other person and makes it harder to establish a good rapport.

After conducting the interview, you must record the information quickly. You should set aside time right after the meeting to record the facts and evaluate the information. For that reason, try not to schedule back-to-back interviews. Studies have shown that 50 percent of a conversation is forgotten within 30 minutes. You, therefore, should use your notes to record the facts immediately so you will not forget them. You can summarize the facts by preparing a narrative describing what took place or by recording the answers you received next to each question on your prepared question list.

Tape recorders are effective tools for an interview; however, many people feel uncomfortable when recorders are present. Before using a recorder, you should discuss its use with the interviewee. Assure the interviewee that you will erase the tape after you transcribe your notes and that you will stop and rewind the tape anytime during the interview at his or her request. If you ask sensitive questions or the interviewee wants to answer a question without being recorded, explain that you will turn off the tape for a period of time during the interview.

Even with a tape recorder in use, you should listen carefully to the interviewee's responses so you can ask good follow-up questions. Otherwise, you might have to return for a second visit to ask the questions you missed the first time. Also, remember that each recorded interview takes twice the amount of time, because you must listen to or view the recorded meeting again after conducting the interview itself.

After the interview, send a memo to the interviewee expressing your appreciation for his or her time and cooperation. In the memo, you should note the date, time, location, purpose of the interview, and the main points you discussed so the interviewee has a written summary and can offer additions or corrections.

Step 7: Evaluate the Interview

In addition to recording the facts obtained in an interview, try to identify any possible biases. For example, an interviewee who tries to protect his or her own area or function might give incomplete answers or refrain from volunteering information. Or, an interviewee with strong opinions about the current or future system might distort the facts. Some interviewees might answer your questions in an attempt to be helpful even though they do not have the necessary experience to provide accurate information.

CASE IN POINT 3.2: DEEP RIVER COLLEGE

Deep River College is a two-year school in Southern California. Twice a year, the fundraising office at Deep River mails requests for donations to the alumni. The staff uses a word processing program and a personal information database to create personalized letters. Data on past contributions and other alumni information, however, is stored manually. The dean, Alexandra Ali, recently submitted a systems request asking the college's IT department to develop a computerized alumni information system. The school does not have a formal systems review committee, and each department has an individual budget for information services.

Eddie Bateman, a systems analyst, performed a preliminary investigation and he concluded that the system met all the feasibility tests. After reading his report, Alexandra asked him to proceed with the systems analysis phase. Eddie has scheduled an interview with her, and he has asked you to help him prepare for the meeting. Specifically, he wants you to list all the topics he should cover during the interview. Eddie also wants you to prepare a list of specific questions that he should ask. Be sure to include open-ended, closed-ended, and range-of-response questions.

Unsuccessful Interviews

No matter how well you prepare for interviews, some are not successful. One of the main reasons could be that you and the interviewee did not get along well. Such a situation can be caused by several factors. For example, a misunderstanding or personality conflict could affect the interview negatively, or the interviewee might be afraid that the new system will eliminate or change his or her job.

In other cases, the interviewee might give only short or incomplete responses to your open-ended questions. If so, you should switch to closed-ended questions or questions with a range of responses, or try rephrasing your open-ended questions into those types of questions. If that still does not help, you should find a tactful way to conclude the meeting.

Continuing an unproductive interview is difficult. The interviewee could be more cooperative later, or you might find the information you seek elsewhere. If failure to obtain specific information will jeopardize the success of the project, inform your supervisor, who can help you decide what action to take. Your supervisor might contact the interviewee's supervisor, ask another systems analyst to interview the person, or find some other way to get the needed information.

CASE IN POINT 3.3: FastPak Overnight Package System

FastPak, the nation's fourth-largest overnight package system, is headquartered in Los Angeles, California. Jesse Evans is a systems analyst on an IT team that is studying ways to update FastPak's package tracking system. Jesse prepared well for her interview with Jason Tanya, FastPak's executive vice president. Mr. Tanya did not ask his assistant to hold his calls during the meeting, however. After several interruptions, Jesse tactfully suggested that she could come back another time, or perhaps that Mr. Tanya might ask his assistant to hold his calls. "No way," he replied. "I'm a very busy man and we'll just have to fit this in as we can, even if it takes all day." Jesse was unprepared for his response. What are her options? Is an analyst always in control of this kind of situation? Why or why not?

Other Fact-Finding Techniques

In addition to interviewing, systems analysts use other fact-finding techniques, including document review, observation, questionnaires and surveys, sampling, and research. Such techniques are used before interviewing begins to obtain a good overview and to help develop better interview questions.

Document Review

Document review can help you understand how the current system is supposed to work. Remember that system documentation sometimes is out of date. Forms can change or be discontinued, and documented procedures often are modified or eliminated. You should obtain copies of actual forms and operating documents currently in use. You also should review blank copies of forms, as well as samples of actual completed forms. You usually can obtain document samples during interviews with the people who perform that procedure. If the system uses a software package, you should review the documentation for that software.

Observation

The **observation** of current operating procedures is another fact-finding technique. Seeing the system in action gives you additional perspective and a better understanding of system procedures. Personal observation also allows you to verify statements made in interviews and determine whether procedures really operate as they are described.

Through observation, you might discover that neither the system documentation nor the interview statements are accurate.

Personal observation also can provide important advantages as the development process continues. For example, recommendations often are better accepted when they are based on personal observation of actual operations. Observation also can provide the knowledge needed to test or install future changes and can help build relationships with the users who will work with the new system.

Plan your observations in advance by preparing a checklist of specific tasks you want to observe and questions you want to ask. Consider the following issues when you prepare your list:

1. Ask sufficient questions to ensure that you have a complete understanding of the present system operation. A primary goal is to identify the methods of handling situations that are not covered by standard operating procedures. For example, what happens in a payroll system if an employee loses a time card? What is the procedure if an employee starts a shift 10 minutes late but then works 20 minutes overtime? Often, the rules for exceptions such as these are not written or formalized; therefore, you must try to document any procedures for handling exceptions.

2. Observe all the steps in a transaction and note the documents, inputs, outputs, and processes involved.

3. Examine each form, record, and report. Determine the purpose each item of information serves.

4. Consider each user who works with the system and the following questions: What information does that person receive from other people? What information does this person generate? How is the information communicated? How often do interruptions occur? How much downtime occurs? How much support does the user require, and who provides it?

5. Talk to the people who receive current reports to see whether the reports are complete, timely, accurate, and in a useful form. Ask whether information can be eliminated or improved and whether people would like to receive additional information.

As you observe people at work, as shown in Figure 3-20, consider a factor called the **Hawthorne Effect**. The name comes from a well-known study performed in the Hawthorne plant of the Western Electric Company in the 1920s. The purpose of the study was to determine how various changes in the work environment would affect employee productivity. The surprising result was that productivity improved during observation whether the conditions were made better or worse. Researchers concluded that productivity seemed to improve whenever the workers knew they were being observed.

Thus, as you observe users, remember that normal operations might not always run as smoothly as your observations indicate. Operations also might run less smoothly because workers might be nervous during

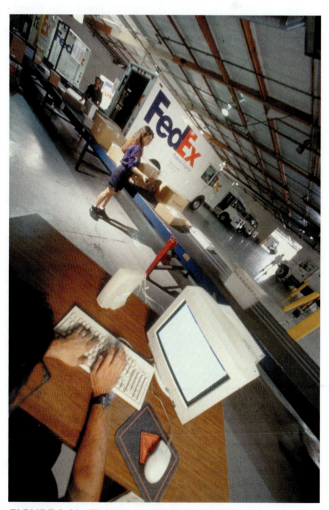

FIGURE 3-20 The Hawthorne study suggested that worker productivity improves during observation. Always consider the Hawthorne Effect when observing the operation of an existing system.

the observation. If possible, meet with workers and their supervisors to discuss your plans and objectives to help establish a good working relationship. In some situations, you might even participate in the work yourself to gain a personal understanding of the task or the environment.

Questionnaires and Surveys

In projects where it is desirable to obtain input from a large number of people, a questionnaire can be a valuable tool. A **questionnaire**, also called a **survey**, is a document containing a number of standard questions that can be sent to many individuals.

Questionnaires can be used to obtain information about a wide range of topics, including workloads, reports received, volumes of transactions handled, job duties, difficulties, and opinions of how the job could be performed better or more efficiently. Figure 3-21 shows a sample questionnaire that includes several different question and response formats.

PURCHASE REQUISITION QUESTIONNAIRE

Pat Kline, Vice President, Finance, has asked us to investigate the purchase requisition process to see if it can be improved. Your input concerning this requisition process will be very valuable. We would greatly appreciate it if you could complete the following questionnaire and return it by March 10 to Dana Juarez in information technology. If you have any questions, please call Dana at x2561.

A.   YOUR OBSERVATIONS
Please answer each question by checking one box.

1.   How many purchase requisitions did you process in the past five working days? _____

2.   What percentage of your time is spent processing requisitions?
[ ] under 20%   [ ] 60–79%
[ ] 21–39%   [ ] 80% or more
[ ] 40–59%

3.   Do you believe too many errors exist on requisitions?
[ ] yes
[ ] no

4.   Out of every 100 requisitions you process, how many contain errors?
[ ] fewer than 5   [ ] 20 to 29
[ ] 5 to 9   [ ] 30 to 39
[ ] 10 to 14   [ ] 40 to 49
[ ] 15 to 19   [ ] 50 or more

5.   What errors do you see most often on requisitions? (Place a 1 next to the most common error, place a 2 next to the second, etc.)
[ ] incorrect charge number   [ ] missing authorization
[ ] missing charge information   [ ] other (please explain) _____
[ ] arithmetic errors
[ ] incorrect discount percent used

B.   YOUR SUGGESTIONS
Please be specific, and give examples if possible.

1.   If the currently used purchase requisition form were to be redesigned, what changes to the form would you recommend?
_____
_____
_____
_____
_____
(If necessary, please attach another sheet)

2.   Would you be interested in meeting with an information technology representative to discuss your ideas further? If so, please complete the following information:

Name _____   Department _____

Telephone _____   E-mail address _____

FIGURE 3-21 Sample questionnaire.

A typical questionnaire starts with a heading, which includes a title, a brief statement of purpose, the name and telephone number of the contact person, the deadline date for completion, and how and where to return the form. The heading usually is followed by general instructions that provide clear guidance on how to answer the questions. Headings also are used to introduce each main section or portion of the survey and include instructions when the type of question or response changes. A long questionnaire might end with a conclusion that thanks the participants and reminds them how to return the form.

What about the issue of anonymity? Should people be asked to sign the questionnaire, or is it better to allow anonymous responses? The answer depends on two questions. First, does an analyst really need to know who the respondents are in order to match or correlate information? For example, it might be important to know what percentage of users need a certain software feature, but specific user names might not be relevant. Second, does the questionnaire include any sensitive or controversial topics? Many people do not want to be identified when answering a question such as "How well has your supervisor explained the system to you?" In such cases, anonymous responses might provide better information.

When designing a questionnaire, the most important rule of all is to make sure that your questions collect the right data in a form that you can use to further your fact-finding. Here are some additional ideas to keep in mind when designing your questionnaire:

- Keep the questionnaire brief and user-friendly.
- Provide clear instructions that will answer all anticipated questions.
- Arrange the questions in a logical order, going from simple to more complex topics.
- Phrase questions to avoid misunderstandings; use simple terms and wording.
- Try not to lead the response or use questions that give clues to expected answers.
- Limit the use of open-ended questions that are difficult to tabulate.
- Limit the use of questions that can raise concerns about job security or other negative issues.
- Include a section at the end of the questionnaire for general comments.
- Test the questionnaire whenever possible on a small test group before finalizing it and distributing to a large group.

A questionnaire can be a traditional paper form, or you can create a **fill-in form** and collect data on the Internet or a company intranet. For example, you can use Microsoft Word, as shown in Figure 3-22 on the next page, to create form fields, including text boxes, check boxes, and drop-down lists where users can click selections. Before you publish the form, you should protect it so users can fill it in but cannot change the layout or design. Forms also can be automated, so if a user answers no to question three, he or she goes directly to question eight, where the form-filling resumes.

Sampling

When studying an information system, you should collect examples of actual documents using a process called **sampling**. The samples might include records, reports, operational logs, data entry documents, complaint summaries, work requests, and various types of forms. Sampling techniques include systematic sampling, stratified sampling, and random sampling.

Suppose you have a list of 200 customers who complained about errors in their statements, and you want to review a representative sample of 20 customers. A **systematic sample** would select every tenth customer for review. If you want to ensure that the sample is balanced geographically, however, you could use a **stratified sample** to select five

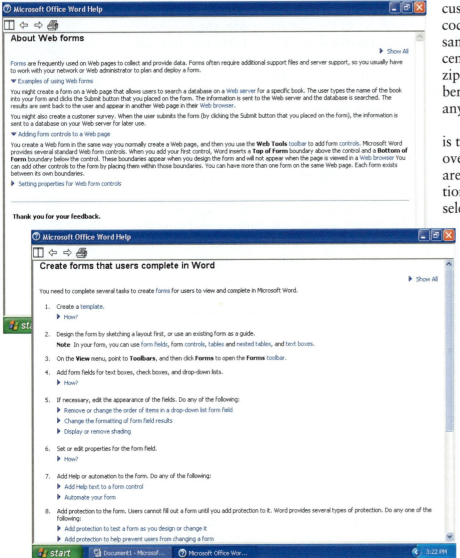

FIGURE 3-22 Microsoft Word enables you to create a fill-in form and collect data on the Internet or a company intranet.

customers from each of four ZIP codes. Another example of stratified sampling is to select a certain percentage of transactions from each zip code, rather than a fixed number. Finally, a **random sample** selects any 20 customers.

The main objective of a sample is to ensure that it represents the overall population accurately. If you are analyzing inventory transactions, for example, you should select a sample of transactions that are typical of actual inventory operations and do not include unusual or unrelated examples. For instance, if a company performs special processing on the last business day of the month, that day is not a good time to sample *typical* daily operations. To be useful, a sample must be large enough to provide a fair representation of the overall data.

You also should consider sampling when using interviews or questionnaires. Rather than interviewing everyone or sending a questionnaire to the entire group, you can use a sample of participants. You must use sound sampling techniques to reflect the overall population and obtain an accurate picture.

ON THE WEB

For more information about Sampling, visit **scsite.com/sad6e/ more**, locate Chapter 3 and then click the Sampling link.

Research

Research is another important fact-finding technique. Your research can include the Internet, IT magazines, and books to obtain background information, technical material, and news about industry trends and developments. In addition, you can attend professional meetings, seminars, and discussions with other IT professionals, which can be very helpful in problem solving.

The Internet is an extremely valuable resource. Part 6 of the Systems Analyst's Toolkit describes a variety of Internet resource tools. Using the Internet, you also can access information from federal and state governments, as well as from publishers, universities, and libraries around the world. Internet **newsgroups** are good resources for exchanging information with other professionals, seeking answers to questions, and monitoring discussions that are of interest to you.

All major hardware and software vendors maintain sites on the Web where you can obtain information about products and services offered by the company and send e-mail with specific questions to company representatives. In addition to contacting specific firms, you can access Web sites maintained by publishers and independent firms that provide links to hundreds of hardware and software vendors, as shown in Figure 3-23. Such sites are one-stop information centers where IT professionals can find information, share ideas, and keep posted on developments in technology.

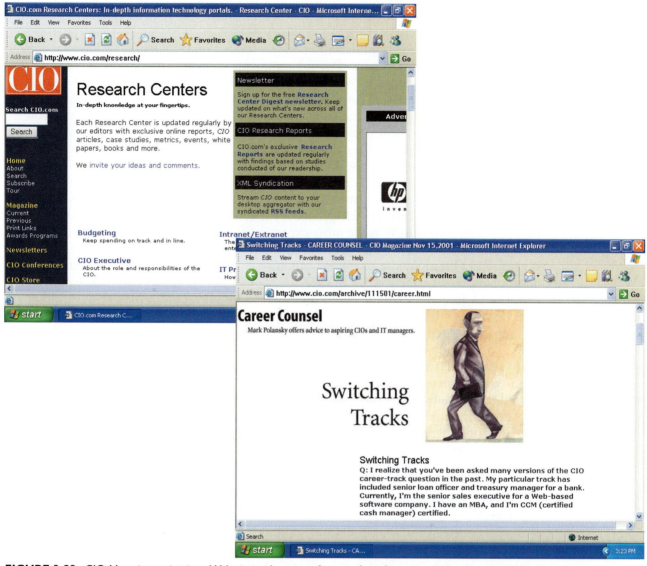

FIGURE 3-23   CIO Magazine maintains a Web site with various features for information technology professionals.

Research also can involve a visit to a physical location, called a **site visit**, where the objective is to observe a system in use at another location. If you are studying your firm's human resources information system, for example, you might want to see how another company's system works. Site visits also are important when considering the purchase of a software package. If the software vendor suggests possible sites to visit, be aware that such sites might constitute a biased sample. A single site visit seldom gives you true pictures, so you should try to visit more than one installation.

Before a site visit, prepare just as you would for an interview. Contact the appropriate manager and explain the purpose of your visit. Decide what questions you will ask and what processes you will observe. During your visit, observe how the system works and note any problems or limitations. You also will want to learn about the support provided by the vendor, the quality of the system documentation, and so on.

Interviews versus Questionnaires

When you seek input from a large group, a questionnaire is a very useful tool. On the other hand, if you require detailed information from only a few people, then you probably should interview each person individually. Is it better to interview or use a questionnaire? Each situation is different, and you must consider the type of information, time constraints, and expense factors.

The interview is more familiar and personal than a questionnaire. People who are unwilling to put critical or controversial comments in writing might talk more freely in person. Moreover, during a face-to-face interview, you can react immediately to anything the interviewee says. If surprising or confusing statements are made, you can pursue the topic with additional questions. In addition, during a personal interview, you can watch for clues to help you determine if responses are knowledgeable and unbiased. Participation in interviews also can affect user attitudes, because people who are asked for their opinions often view the project more favorably.

Interviewing, however, is a costly and time-consuming process. In addition to the meeting itself, both people must prepare, and the interviewer has to do follow-up work. When a number of interviews are planned, the total cost can be quite substantial. The personal interview usually is the most expensive fact-finding technique.

In contrast, a questionnaire gives many people the opportunity to provide input and suggestions. Questionnaire recipients can answer the questions at their convenience and do not have to set aside a block of time for an interview. If the questionnaire allows anonymous responses, people might offer more candid responses than they would in an interview.

Preparing a good questionnaire, however, like a good interview, requires skill and time. If a question is misinterpreted, you cannot clarify the meaning as you can in a face-to-face interview. Furthermore, unless questionnaires are designed well, recipients might view them as intrusive, time-consuming, and impersonal. As an analyst, you should select the technique that will work best in a particular situation.

Another popular method of obtaining input is called **brainstorming**, which refers to a small group discussion of a specific problem, opportunity, or issue. This technique encourages new ideas, allows team participation, and enables participants to build on each other's inputs and thoughts. Brainstorming can be structured or unstructured. In **structured brainstorming**, each participant speaks when it is his or her turn, or passes. In **unstructured brainstorming**, anyone can speak at any time. At some point, the results are recorded and made part of the fact-finding documentation process.

CASE IN POINT 3.4: CYBERSTUFF

Ann Ellis is a systems analyst at CyberStuff, a large company that sells computer hardware and software via telephone, mail order, and the Internet. CyberStuff processes several thousand transactions per week on a three-shift operation and employs 50 full-time and 125 part-time employees. Lately, the billing department has experienced an increase in the number of customer complaints about incorrect bills. During the preliminary investigation, Ann learned that some CyberStuff representatives did not follow established order entry procedures. She feels that with more information, she might find a pattern and identify a solution for the problem.

Ann is not sure how to proceed. She came to you, her supervisor, with two separate questions. First, is a questionnaire the best approach, or would interviews be better? Second, whether she uses interviews, a questionnaire, or both techniques, should she select the participants at random, include an equal number of people from each shift, or use some other approach? As Ann's supervisor, what would you suggest, and why?

DOCUMENTATION

Keeping accurate records of interviews, facts, ideas, and observations is essential to successful systems development. The ability to manage information is the mark of a successful systems analyst and an important skill for all IT professionals.

The Need for Recording the Facts

As you gather information, the importance of a single item can be overlooked or complex system details can be forgotten. The basic rule is to write it down. You should document your work according to the following principles:

- Record information as soon as you obtain it.
- Use the simplest recording method possible.
- Record your findings in such a way that they can be understood by someone else.
- Organize your documentation so related material is located easily.

Often, systems analysts use special forms for describing a system, recording interviews, and summarizing documents. One type of documentation is a narrative list with simple statements about what is occurring, apparent problems, and suggestions for improvement. Other forms of documentation that are described in Chapter 4 include data flow diagrams, flowcharts, sample forms, and screen captures.

Software Tools

Many software programs are available to help you record and document information. Some examples are described here.

CASE TOOLS   You can use CASE tools at every stage of systems development. This chapter contains several examples of CASE tools. Part 2 of the Systems Analyst's Toolkit describes other features and capabilities of CASE tools.

PRODUCTIVITY SOFTWARE   **Productivity software** includes word processing, spreadsheet, database management, and presentation graphics programs. Although Microsoft Office is the best-known set of productivity software programs, other vendors offer products in each of these categories.

Using a word processing program such as Microsoft Word or Corel WordPerfect, you can create reports, summaries, tables, and forms. In addition to standard document preparation, the program can help you organize a presentation with templates, bookmarks, annotations, revision control, and an index. You can consult the program's Help system for more information about those and other features. You also can create fill-in forms to conduct surveys and questionnaires, as described earlier in this chapter.

Spreadsheet software, such as Microsoft Excel or Corel Quattro Pro, can help you track and manage numerical data or financial information. You also can generate graphs and charts that display the data and show possible patterns, and you can use the statistical functions in a spreadsheet to tabulate and analyze questionnaire data. A graphical format often is used in quality control analysis because it highlights problems and their possible causes, and it is effective when presenting results to management. A common tool for showing the distribution of questionnaire or sampling results is a vertical bar chart called a **histogram**. Most spreadsheet programs can create histograms and other charts that can display data you have collected. Figure 3-24 displays a typical histogram that might have resulted from the questionnaire shown in Figure 3-21 on page 114.

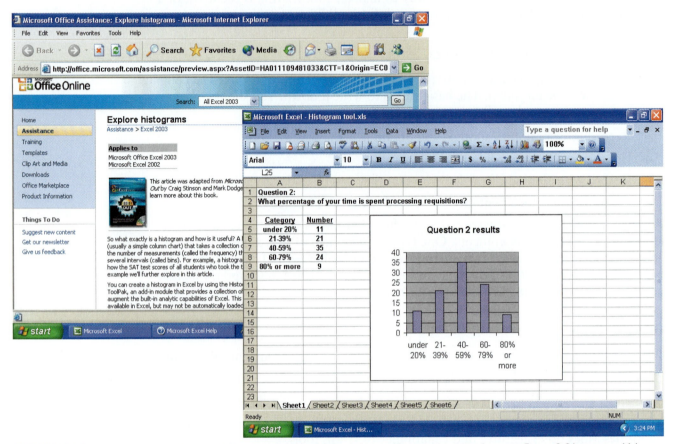

FIGURE 3-24 A histogram using Microsoft Excel displays results from the sample questionnaire shown in Figure 3-21 on page 114.

Database management software allows you to document and organize fact-finding results such as events, observations, and data samples. You can use a database program such as Microsoft Access to manage the details of a complex project, create queries to retrieve specific information, and generate custom reports.

Presentation graphics software, such as Microsoft PowerPoint or Lotus Freelance Graphics, is a powerful tool for organizing and developing your formal presentation. Presentation graphics programs enable you to create organization charts that can be used in a preliminary investigation and later during requirements modeling. These high-quality charts also can be included in written reports and management presentations.

GRAPHIC MODELING SOFTWARE Microsoft Visio is a popular graphic modeling tool that can produce a wide range of charts and diagrams. Visio includes a library of templates, stencils, and shapes. An analyst can use Visio to create many types of visual models, including business processes, flowcharts, network diagrams, organization charts, and Web site maps, such as the one shown in Figure 3-25.

PERSONAL INFORMATION MANAGERS A busy analyst needs to keep track of meetings, interviews, appointments, and deadlines. A **personal information manager** (**PIM**), such as Microsoft Outlook or Lotus Organizer, can help manage those tasks and provide a personal calendar and a to-do list, with priorities and the capability to check off completed items.

In addition to desktop-based organizers, handheld computers are enormously popular. Some handheld computers, also called **personal digital assistants** (**PDAs**), accept handwritten input, while others have small keyboards. These devices can handle calendars, schedules, appointments, telephone lists, and calculations. Examples of PDAs are shown in Figure 3-26.

WIRELESS COMMUNICATION DEVICES Wireless technology is having a major impact on the design and direction of mobile computing. For example, most handheld computers have built-in modems for Web access and wireless capability that allows easy file exchange and synchronization with desktop computers and office networks. As the wireless communications trend continues, vendors offer a wide array of new devices and technologies. To compete in the PDA market, for example, cell phone manufacturers are offering Web-capable phones and devices that combine PDA and cell phone features in a new type of device called a smart phone, which is shown in Figure 3-27 on the next page.

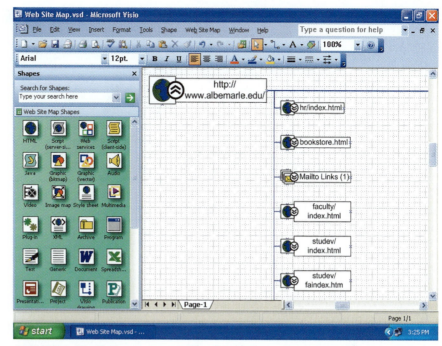

FIGURE 3-25 The Visio screen shows a set of shapes that can be used to create a Web site map.

FIGURE 3-26 Powerful handheld computers can handle calendars, schedules, appointments, telephone lists, and calculations.

FIGURE 3-27 Kyocera's smartphone series combines a digital wireless phone, Web access, and a Palm handheld computer.

PREVIEW OF DATA AND PROCESS MODELING

At the conclusion of requirements modeling, systems developers should have a clear understanding of business processes and system requirements. The next step is to construct a logical model of the system.

Data and process modeling, which is described in Chapter 4, uses a structured analysis approach. Structured analysis is a popular, traditional technique that describes the system in terms of data and the processes that act on that data.

An alternative to structured analysis modeling is object modeling. Object modeling is a methodology that combines data and processes into things called objects that represent actual people, things, transactions, and events. Systems analysts use object models to visualize and document real-world business processes and operations. Object modeling is described in more detail in Part 5 of the Systems Analyst's Toolkit.

IT professionals have differing views about systems development methodologies, and no universally accepted approach exists. By studying both structured analysis and object-oriented methods, you gain valuable knowledge, skills, and perspective. You then can use that information to determine what method, or combination of methods, is best for the different situations you will face in your career.

CHAPTER SUMMARY

The systems analysis phase includes three activities: requirements modeling, data and process modeling, and consideration of development strategies. The main objective is to understand the proposed project, ensure that it will support business requirements, and build a solid foundation for the systems design phase.

During requirements modeling, you identify the business-related requirements for the new information system, including outputs, inputs, processes, performance, and controls. You consider scalability to ensure that the system can support future growth

and expansion. You also estimate total cost of ownership (TCO) to identify all costs, including indirect costs.

Joint application development (JAD) is a popular, team-based approach to fact-finding and requirements modeling. JAD involves an interactive group of users, managers, and IT professionals who participate in requirements modeling and develop a greater commitment to the project and to their common goals.

Rapid application development (RAD) is a team-based technique that speeds up information systems development and produces a functioning information system. RAD is a complete methodology, with a four-phase life cycle that parallels the traditional SDLC phases. Systems analysts use various tools and techniques to model system requirements. Unified Modeling Language (UML) is a widely used method of visualizing and documenting software design through the eyes of the business user. UML tools include use case diagrams and sequence diagrams to represent actors, their roles, and the sequence of transactions that occurs. A functional decomposition diagram (FDD) is used to represent business functions and processes.

The fact-finding process includes interviewing, document review, observation, questionnaires, sampling, and research. Successful interviewing requires good planning and strong interpersonal and communication skills. The systems analyst must decide on the people to interview, set interview objectives, and prepare for, conduct, and analyze interviews. The analyst also might find it helpful to use one or more software tools during fact-finding.

Systems analysts should carefully record and document factual information as it is collected, and various software tools can help an analyst visualize and describe an information system. The chapter concluded with a preview of data and process modeling, which is a structured analysis approach that views the system in terms of data and the processes that act on that data.

Key Terms and Phrases

actor *99*

analytical skills *93*

brainstorming *118*

closed-ended questions *108*

construction phase *96*

cutover phase *96*

document review *112*

engaged listening *110*

fill-in form *115*

functional decomposition diagram (FDD) *98*

Hawthorne Effect *113*

histogram *119*

informal structure *107*

inputs *92*

interpersonal skills *93*

interview *107*

joint application development (JAD) *93*

leading questions *108*

newsgroups *116*

observation *112*

open-ended questions *108*

outputs *92*

performance *92*

personal digital assistants (PDAs) *121*

personal information manager (PIM) *120*

processes *92*

productivity software *119*

questionnaire *114*

random sample *116*

range-of-response questions *108*

rapid application development (RAD) *93*

Rapid Economic Justification (REJ) *104*

requirements modeling *92*

requirements planning phase *96*

research *116*

sampling *115*

scalability *103*

security *92*

sequence diagram *100*

site visit *117*

stratified sample *115*

structured brainstorming *118*

structure charts *98*

survey *114*

system requirement *101*

system requirements document *92*

systematic sample *115*

total cost of ownership (TCO) *103*

Unified Modeling Language (UML) *99*

unstructured brainstorming *118*

use case diagram *99*

user design phase *96*

Zachman Framework for Enterprise
   Architecture *106*

Learn It Online

Instructions: To complete the Learn It Online exercises, start your browser, click the Address bar, and then enter **scsite.com/sad6e/learn**. When the Systems Analysis and Design Learn It Online page is displayed, follow the instructions in the exercises below. Each exercise has instructions for saving your results, either for your own records or for submission to your instructor.

1 Chapter Reinforcement

TF, MC, and SA

Below SAD Chapter 3, click the Chapter Reinforcement link. Print the quiz by clicking Print on the File menu for each page. Answer each question.

2 Flash Cards

Below SAD Chapter 3, click the Flash Cards link and read the instructions. Type 20 (or a number specified by your instructor) in the Number of playing cards text box, type your name in the Enter your Name text box, and then click the Flip Card button. When the flash card is displayed, read the question and then click the ANSWER box arrow to select an answer. Flip through the Flash Cards. If your score is 15 (75%) correct or greater, click Print on the File menu to print your results. If your score is less than 15 (75%) correct, then redo this exercise by clicking the Replay button.

3 Practice Test

Below SAD Chapter 3, click the Practice Test link. Answer each question, enter your first and last name at the bottom of the page, and then click the Grade Test button. When the graded practice test is displayed on your screen, click Print on the File menu to print a hard copy. Continue to take practice tests until you score 80% or better.

4 Who Wants To Be a Computer Genius?

Below SAD Chapter 3, click the Computer Genius link. Read the instructions, enter your first and last name at the bottom of the page, and then click the Play button. When your score is displayed, click the PRINT RESULTS link to print a hard copy.

5 Wheel of Terms

Below SAD Chapter 3, click the Wheel of Terms link. Read the instructions, and then enter your first and last name and your school name. Click the PLAY button. When your score is displayed on the screen, right-click the score and then click Print on the shortcut menu to print a hard copy.

6 Crossword Puzzle Challenge

Below SAD Chapter 3, click the Crossword Puzzle Challenge link. Read the instructions, and then enter your first and last name. Click the SUBMIT button. Work the crossword puzzle. When you are finished, click the Submit button. When the crossword puzzle reappears, click the Print Puzzle button to print a hard copy.

Case-Sim: SCR Associates

Background

SCR Associates is a consulting firm that offers IT solutions and training. SCR needs an information system to manage operations at its new training center. The new system will be called TIMS (Training Information-Management System). As a newly hired systems analyst, you will report to Jesse Baker, systems group manager. You will work on various tasks and practice the skills you learned in this chapter.

Using the Case

The SCR Associates case study is a Web-based simulation that allows you to practice your skills in a real-world environment. The case study transports you to SCR's company intranet, where you can complete 10 work sessions, each aligning with a chapter. As you work on the case, you will receive e-mail and voice mail messages, obtain information from SCR's online libraries, and perform various tasks. The first time you enter the SCR Case, you should go to the Starting page at **scsite.com/sad6e/scr** for detailed instructions.

Preview: Session 3

As you begin the requirements modeling process, you receive specific directions from your supervisor, Jesse Baker. She wants you to conduct a survey of former and prospective students, lead a JAD group session, and draft a list of system requirements based on the results of the JAD session. She also wants to see a functional decomposition diagram showing the main TIMS functions.

To start a work session, you log on to the SCR intranet. When you enter your name and password, an opening screen displays links to the work sessions, and you select Session 3. At this point, you check your e-mail and voice mail messages carefully. Then you begin working on your task list, which includes the following items:

Tasks: Requirements Modeling

1. *Group managers said it was OK for their people to attend a three-day JAD session next week. Send a message to the JAD team members, with a brief explanation of JAD methods and a proposed agenda.*

2. *Design a questionnaire for former and potential students in SCR's training classes. Also, reply to Jesse's message about sampling. Give her a recommendation and reasons.*

3. *Read the JAD session summary in the Data Library and put together a list of system requirements, including outputs, inputs, processes, performance, and controls.*

4. *Draw an FDD of the main functions for TIMS and send it to Jesse.*

FIGURE 3-28 Task list: Session 3.

Chapter Exercises

Review Questions

1. What are the five questions typically used in fact-finding? What additional question can be asked during this process?
2. What is a systems requirement, and how are systems requirements classified?
3. What is JAD, how does it differ from traditional methods of fact-finding, and what are some advantages and potential disadvantages of using JAD?
4. What is total cost of ownership (TCO), and why is it important?
5. What are the three different types of questions? How do those different questions affect the answers given?
6. What are three types of sampling, and why would you use them?
7. What is the Hawthorne Effect? Why is it significant?
8. What is RAD, what are the RAD phases, and what occurs in each phase?
9. To what three different audiences might you have to give a presentation? How would the presentation differ for each? If one presentation is given with all interested parties, to whom should the presentation primarily be addressed?
10. How should you react if your hands shake while you are giving a presentation, or if you are nervous when people are looking at you?

> ⚙ **TOOLKIT TIME**
>
> Answer questions 9 and 10 after you complete the presentations section in Part 1 of the six-part Systems Analyst's Toolkit that follows Chapter 10.

Discussion Topics

1. A group meeting sometimes is suggested as a useful compromise between interviews and questionnaires. In such a group meeting, one systems analyst meets with and asks questions of a number of users at one time. Discuss the advantages and disadvantages of such a group meeting.
2. JAD requires strong interpersonal and communication skills on the part of the systems analyst. Are those skills different from the ones that an analyst needs when conducting one-to-one interviews? Explain your answer.
3. Research the Internet, magazines, or textbooks to find examples of each of the following types of visual aids: bar chart, pie chart, line chart, table, diagram, and bulleted list of key points. How effective do you think each aid is? Find at least one example that you feel could be improved. Discuss its shortcomings and prepare an improved version.
4. Review the presentations section in Part 1 of the Systems Analyst's Toolkit, then attend a speech or presentation and analyze its effectiveness. Consider the speaker's delivery and how he or she organized the material, used visual aids, and handled audience questions. Describe specifically how the speech or presentation was most effective, as well as how it could have been improved.

Projects

1. Design a questionnaire to learn more about the registration process at your school or how customers place orders at a local business. Apply the guidelines you learned in this chapter.
2. Use Microsoft Word or another word processing program to design a simple form, using the program's form-filling feature.
3. Use the Internet to do research about JAD, and present the information to your class.
4. Use the Internet to find a Web site that contains current IT industry news, information, and links. Bookmark the site and print a copy of the initial screen.

Apply Your Knowledge

The Apply Your Knowledge section contains four mini-cases. Each case describes a situation, explains your role in the case, and asks you to respond to questions. You can answer the questions by applying knowledge you learned in the chapter.

1 Elmwood College

Situation:

The school is considering a new system that will speed up the registration process. As a systems analyst, you are asked to develop a plan for fact-finding.

1. List all the possible techniques that you might use.
2. Describe an advantage for each technique.
3. Suppose the development budget is tight. How might that affect the fact-finding process?
4. What are five important questions to use during fact-finding?

2 JAD Session 1

Situation:

You are an IT advisor to a JAD team that is studying a new inventory system. The proposed system will provide more information and faster updates, and automatically monitor fast- or slow-moving items. Some controversy exists about whether to use an on-site or off-site location for the JAD sessions.

1. How would you advise the project leader?
2. Who should be on the JAD team, and what would be their roles as team members?
3. The JAD project leader asked for advice about how to get the first session started. How would you reply?
4. You invited the senior vice president to the opening JAD session, but she says she is quite busy and might not be able to attend unless it is really important. What would you say to her?

3 JAD Session 2

Situation:

The JAD team wants you to draw up a checklist of requirements for the new system.

1. List the five main categories of system requirements.
2. Use your imagination and provide at least one example per category of a system requirement that might be appropriate for an inventory system.
3. The project leader wants you to explain the concept of scalability to the team. How will you do that?
4. Several managers on the team have heard of TCO but are not quite sure what it is. How will you explain it to them?

4 Better Hardware Marketing System

Situation:

Your boss, the IT director, wants you to explain the UML to a group of company managers and users who will serve on a systems development team for the new marketing system.

1. Describe the Unified Modeling Language (UML) and how it can be used during systems development.
2. Explain use case diagrams to the group, and provide a simple example.
3. Explain sequence diagrams to the group, and provide a simple example.
4. During the meeting, a manager asks you to explain why it is desirable to describe the system through the eyes of a user. How would you answer?

Case Studies

Case studies allow you to practice specific skills learned in the chapter. Each chapter contains several case studies that continue throughout the textbook, and a chapter capstone case.

NEW CENTURY HEALTH CLINIC

New Century Health Clinic offers preventive medicine and traditional medical care. In your role as an IT consultant, you will help New Century develop a new information system.

Background

New Century Health Clinic has decided to computerize its office systems. The associates hired you, a local computer consultant, to perform a preliminary investigation. You had several meetings with Dr. Tim Jones to discuss the various office records and accounting systems. Anita Davenport, New Century's office manager, participated in those meetings.

In a report to the associates at the end of your investigation, you recommended conducting a detailed analysis of the patient record system, the patient and insurance billing systems, and the patient scheduling system. You believe that New Century would benefit most from implementing those three systems. Although the systems could be developed independently, you recommended analyzing all three systems together because of the significant interaction among them.

You presented your findings and recommendations at a late afternoon meeting of the associates. After answering several questions, you left the meeting so they could discuss the matter privately. Dr. Jones began the discussion by stating that he was impressed with your knowledge and professionalism, as well as your report and presentation.

Dr. Jones recommended accepting your proposal and hiring you immediately to conduct the systems analysis phase. Dr. Garcia, however, was not as enthusiastic and pointed out that such a study would certainly disrupt office procedures. The staff already had more work than they could handle, she argued, and taking time to answer your questions would only make the situation worse. Dr. Jones countered that the office workload was going to increase in any event, and that it was important to find a long-term solution to the problem. After some additional discussion, Dr. Garcia finally agreed with Dr. Jones's assessment. The next morning, Dr. Jones called you and asked you to go ahead with the systems analysis phase of the project.

Assignments

1. Review the office organization chart you prepared in Chapter 1 for New Century.
2. List the individuals you would like to interview during the systems analysis phase.
3. Prepare a list of objectives for each of the interviews you will conduct.
4. Prepare a list of specific questions for each individual you will interview.
5. Conduct the interviews. (Consult your instructor regarding how to accomplish this. One possibility is through role-playing.)
6. Prepare a written summary of the information gained from each of the interviews. (Your instructor may want you to use a standard set of interview results.)
7. Design a questionnaire that will go to a sample of New Century patients to find out if they were satisfied with current insurance and scheduling procedures. Your questionnaire should follow the suggestions in this chapter. Also, decide what sampling method you will use and explain the reason for your choice.

PERSONAL TRAINER, INC.

Personal Trainer, Inc., owns and operates fitness centers in a dozen Midwestern cities. The centers have done well, and the company is planning an international expansion by opening a new "supercenter" in the Toronto area. Personal Trainer's president, Cassia Umi, hired an IT consultant, Susan Park, to help develop an information system for the new facility. During the project, Susan will work closely with Gray Lewis, who will manage the new operation.

Background

During requirements modeling for the new system, Susan Park met with fitness center managers at several Personal Trainer locations. She conducted a series of interviews, reviewed company records, observed business operations, analyzed the BumbleBee accounting software, and studied a sample of sales and billing transactions. Susan's objective was to develop a list of system requirements for the proposed system. Her fact-finding produced the following information.

Fact-Finding Summary

- A typical center has 300–500 members, with two membership levels: full and limited. Full members have access to all activities. Limited members are restricted to activities they have selected, but they can participate in other activities by paying a usage fee. All members have charge privileges. Charges for merchandise and services are recorded on a charge slip, which is signed by the member. At the end of each day, cash sales and charges are entered into the BumbleBee accounting software, which runs on a computer workstation at each location. Daily cash receipts are deposited in a local bank and credited to the corporate Personal Trainer account. The BumbleBee program produces a daily activity report with a listing of all sales transactions. At the end of the month, the local manager uses BumbleBee to transmit an accounts receivable summary to the Personal Trainer headquarters in Chicago, where member statements are prepared and mailed. Members mail their payments to the Personal Trainer headquarters, where the payment is applied to the member account.

- The BumbleBee program stores basic member information, but does not include information about member preferences, activities, and history.

- Currently, the BumbleBee program produces one local report (the daily activity report) and three reports that are prepared at the headquarters location: a monthly member sales report, an exception report for inactive members and late payers, and a quarterly profit-and-loss report that shows a breakdown of revenue and costs for each separate activity.

During the interviews, Susan received a number of "wish list" comments from local managers and staff members. For example, many managers wanted more analytical features so they could spot trends and experiment with what-if scenarios for special promotions and discounts. Managers also requested better information on "dropouts" who become delinquent in their payments. The most frequent complaint was that managers wanted more frequent information about the profitability of the business activities at their centers.

To enhance their business, managers wanted to offer a computerized activity and wellness log, a personal coach service, and e-mail communication with members.

To manage staff more effectively, managers wanted better ways to manage information about part-time instructors and staff. Several staff members suggested a redesign for the charge slips or — better yet — an automated process to scan a keychain ID card or full-size credit-card.

Assignments

1. List the system requirements for the new system. Review the information that Susan gathered, and assume that she will add her own ideas to achieve more effective outputs, inputs, processes, performance, and controls. Include at least two examples for each category.
2. Are there scalability issues that Susan should consider? What are they?

3. If Susan wants to conduct a survey of current or prospective members to obtain their input, what type of sampling should she use? Why?

4. Draw an FDD that shows the main operations described in the fact statement.

BAXTER COMMUNITY COLLEGE

Baxter Community College is a two-year school in New Jersey. Twice a year, the records office at Baxter mails requests for donations to the alumni. The staff uses a word processing merge file to create personalized letters, but the data on past contributions and other alumni information is stored manually. The registrar, Mary Louise, recently submitted a systems request asking the college's IT department to develop a computerized alumni information system. The school does not have a formal systems review committee, and each department head has an individual budget for routine information services.

Todd Wagner, a systems analyst, was assigned to perform a preliminary investigation. After reading his report, Mary asked him to proceed with the systems analysis phase, saying that a formal presentation was unnecessary. Todd has scheduled an interview tomorrow with her, and he asked you to help him prepare for the meeting.

Assignments

1. Make a list of the topics that you think Todd should cover during the interview.
2. Prepare a list of specific questions that Todd should ask. Include open-ended, closed-ended, and range-of-response questions.
3. Conduct student-to-student interviews, with half the students assuming Todd's role and the other half playing the registrar.
4. Document the information covered during the interviews.

TOWN OF EDEN BAY

The town of Eden Bay owns and maintains a fleet of vehicles. You are a systems analyst reporting to Dawn, the town's IT manager.

Background

In Chapter 2, you learned that the town's maintenance budget has risen sharply in recent years. Based on a preliminary investigation, the town has decided to develop a new information system to manage maintenance information and costs more effectively. The new system will be named RAVE, which stands for Repair Analysis for Vehicular Equipment.

Dawn has asked you to perform additional fact-finding to document the requirements for the new system.

Assignments

1. Review the interview summaries in Chapter 2. For each person (Marie, Martin, Phil, Alice, and Joe), develop three additional questions: an open-ended question, a closed-ended question, and a range-of-response question.
2. Based on what you know so far, list the system requirements for the new system. You can use your imagination if the facts are insufficient. Consider outputs, inputs, processes, performance, and controls. Include at least two examples for each category.
3. You decide to analyze a sample of vehicle records. What sampling methods are available to you? Which one should you use, and why?
4. Dawn thinks it would be a good idea to conduct a JAD session to perform additional fact-finding. Draft a message to the participants, with a brief explanation of JAD methods and a proposed agenda.

CHAPTER CAPSTONE CASE: SoftWear, Limited

SoftWear, Limited (SWL), is a continuing case study that illustrates the knowledge and skills described in each chapter. In this case study, the student acts as a member of the SWL systems development team and performs various tasks.

Background

In Chapter 2, you learned that SWL's vice president of finance, Michael Jeremy, submitted a request for information systems services to investigate problems with the company's payroll system. Jane Rossman, the manager of applications, assigned systems analyst Rick Williams to conduct a preliminary investigation to study the payroll system's problems.

Rick's investigation revealed several problems, including input errors and a need for manual preparation of various reports. The payroll department often is working overtime to correct those errors and produce the required reports.

The IT department recommended conducting an analysis to investigate the problem areas in the payroll system, and Mr. Jeremy approved the study. Now, as the systems analysis phase begins, the next step is requirements modeling.

Human Resources Department Interview

During the preliminary investigation phase, Rick prepared the organization chart of the human resources department shown in Figure 3-29.

FIGURE 3-29 Human resources department organization chart.

Rick learned that some errors occurred in employee stock purchase deductions, so he decided to study that process. He knew that the human resources department initiates stock purchase deductions. He reviewed the organization chart and decided to interview Meredith Rider, manager of human resources administration. Meredith is responsible for completing the personnel records of newly hired employees and sending the forms to the payroll department.

CHAPTER CAPSTONE CASE: SoftWear, Limited (continued)   SWL

Before arranging any interviews, Rick sent the memo shown in Figure 3-30 to the human resources director, Mike Feiner, to keep him posted. Then Rick called Meredith to make an appointment and sent her the confirmation message shown in Figure 3-31 that described the topics and requested copies of related forms.

FIGURE 3-30   Rick Williams's message to Mike Feiner regarding the payroll system investigation.

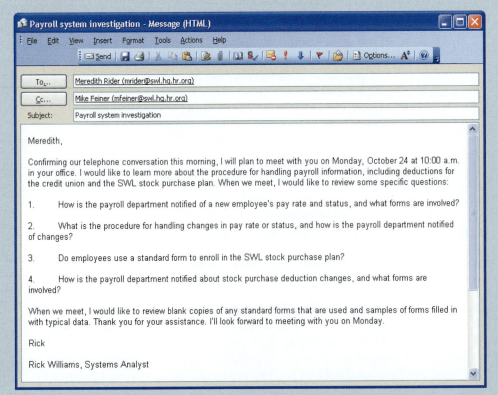

FIGURE 3-31   Rick Williams's message to Meredith Rider regarding preparation for the interview.

CHAPTER CAPSTONE CASE: SoftWear, Limited (continued)   SWL

In the interview, Meredith explained that when employees are hired, they fill in the top portion of a Payroll Master Record Form (Form PR-1) that includes personal data and other required information. The human resources department then completes the form by adding pay rate and other data and sends a copy of the PR-1 form to the payroll department. Meredith showed Rick a blank copy of an online PR-1 form shown in Figure 3-32. She explained that because payroll and personnel information is confidential, she could not give Rick a completed form.

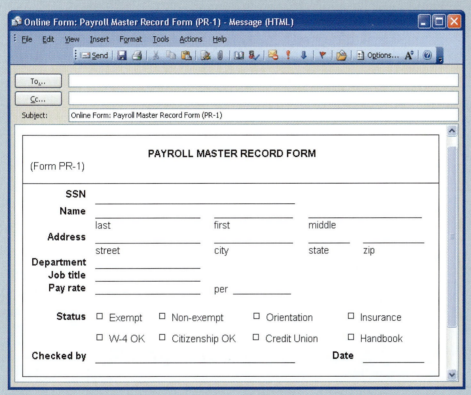

FIGURE 3-32 Payroll Master Record Form (Form PR-1).

When an employee's pay rate or status changes, the human resources department completes the online Payroll Status Change Form (Form PR-2) shown in Figure 3-33 on the next page and sends a copy to the payroll department. The payroll department files that form with the employee's PR-1.

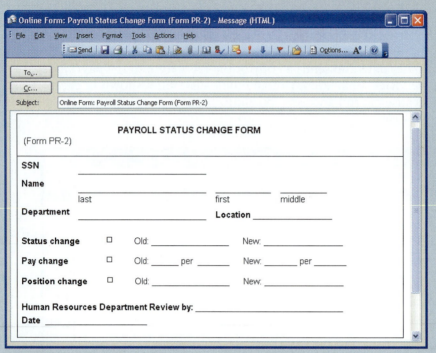

FIGURE 3-33 Payroll Status Change Form (Form PR-2).

Meredith also explained that after completing a 90-day probationary period, employees are allowed to participate in the SWL Credit Union. An employee submits the Payroll Deduction Change Form (Form PR-3) shown in Figure 3-34 to the human resources department, which forwards it to the payroll department.

FIGURE 3-34 Payroll Deduction Change Form (Form PR-3).

CHAPTER CAPSTONE CASE: SoftWear, Limited (continued)   SWL

SWL also has an Employee Stock Purchase Plan. An individual must be employed for 180 days to be eligible for the plan. The employee receives a brochure and prospectus, and then he or she completes the printed Employee Stock Purchase Plan Enrollment and Change Form (Form PR-4) shown in Figure 3-35 to enroll. The human resources department completes the weekly report of all stock plan enrollments and changes on the Employee Stock Purchase Plan Weekly Deduction Summary Report (Form PR-5) shown in Figure 3-36 and then sends a copy to the payroll department. The payroll department records the information on a card that is filed with the employee's master record.

SWL   **EMPLOYEE STOCK PURCHASE PLAN**
Enrollment and Change Form

To be completed by Employee
(Please print clearly)

I, _____ , hereby acknowledge that I have received a brochure and prospectus on the common stock of SoftWear, Limited (SWL) and that I understand the terms and conditions by which SWL stock is offered to employees.

I understand that an account will be established in my name, and stock will be purchased through payroll deductions. I also understand that my ownership rights in SWL stock purchased for this account are subject to the provisions of the Stock Ownership Plan (the Plan), and I agree to the terms thereof.

I understand that I may change or discontinue my contributions at any time, and that I am entitled to a return of my contributions with thirty days written notice.

I wish to contribute a total of $ _____ per week to the Plan. I understand that deductions will be invested monthly on a pro rata basis pursuant to the SWL systems and procedures manual.

_____ SSN _____ Date _____
(Employee signature)

(Form PR-4)

FIGURE 3-35 Employee Stock Purchase Plan Enrollment and Change Form (Form PR-4).

EMPLOYEE STOCK PURCHASE PLAN
Weekly Deduction Summary Report

(Form PR-5)   Week ending:

Code: N= New C = Change	SSN	Employee Name	Deduction Amount

FIGURE 3-36 Employee Stock Purchase Plan Weekly Deduction Summary Report (Form PR-5).

CHAPTER CAPSTONE CASE: SoftWear, Limited (continued)

After the interview with Meredith, Rick sent the follow-up message shown in Figure 3-37 and attached a copy of the interview documentation shown in Figure 3-38.

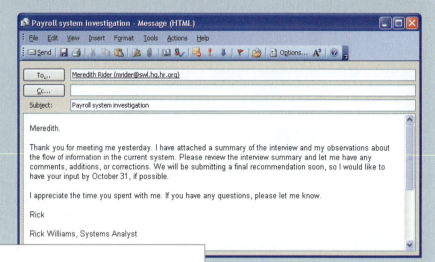

FIGURE 3-37 Follow-up message from Rick Williams to Meredith Rider, with a request for her comments on the interview summary.

Name of System:	Payroll
Date:	October 21 , 2005
Prepared by:	Rick Williams
Title:	Systems Analyst
Purpose:	Interview Summary: Meredith Rider, Manager of Human Resources Administration
Location:	Raleigh

Five basic forms are used by the human resources department that relate to the payroll system:
1. Payroll Master Record Form (Form PR-1)
2. Payroll Status Change Form (Form PR-2)
3. Payroll Deduction Change Form (Form PR-3)
4. Employee Stock Purchase Plan Enrollment and Change Form (Form PR-4)
5. Employee Stock Purchase Plan Weekly Deduction Summary Report (Form PR-5)

When an employee is hired, the following takes place:
1. The human resources department prepares a Payroll Master Record Form (Form PR-1) with employee data, including Social Security number, name, address, telephone, emergency contact, and information about the position, title, and initial pay rate.
2. A copy of this form is sent to the payroll department, where it is filed and maintained.
3. Subsequent pay rate or status changes are submitted by the human resources department to the payroll department on a Payroll Status Change Form (Form PR-2). Payroll then files these change forms with the employee's PR-1 form.

After 90 days of employment, the employee is eligible to join the SWL Credit Union.
1. To enroll, or to make changes in existing deductions, the employee goes to the human resources department and completes a Payroll Deduction Change Form (Form PR-3). The human resources department sends the form to payroll, where it is filed with the employee's Payroll Master Record Form (Form PR-1).

After 180 days of employment, the employee is eligible to enroll in the SWL Stock Purchase Plan.
1. To enroll, an employee completes an Employee Stock Purchase Plan Enrollment and Change Form (Form PR-4).
2. The human resources department prepares an Employee Stock Purchase Plan Weekly Deduction Summary Report Form (Form PR-5) and sends it to the payroll department with copies of the PR-4 forms, which then are filed with the employee's PR-1 form.

Changes in employee status that affect payroll involve the following forms:
1. Pay rate   PR-2
2. Status (exempt vs. nonexempt)   PR-2
3. Federal tax exemptions   PR-3
4. Credit Union deductions   PR-3
5. Employee Stock Purchase Plan deductions   PR-4

When an employee changes Credit Union deductions or federal tax exemptions:
1. The employee completes a Payroll Deduction Change Form (Form PR-3).
2. The form is forwarded to the payroll department.
3. The form is filed with the employee's PR-1 form.

I have identified several problems with the current procedures:
1. Data errors can occur when the human resources staff prepares the weekly summary of employee stock purchase deductions, and no system verification takes place until incorrect deductions are reported.
2. The system performs no verification of employment dates, and it is possible that the 90- and 180-day eligibility periods are applied incorrectly.
3. The filing of the PR-2, PR-3, and PR-4 forms with the Payroll Master Record Forms in the payroll department could lead to problems. If any of the forms are lost or misfiled, incorrect data is entered into the system.

FIGURE 3-38 Documentation of the interview with Meredith Rider.

CHAPTER CAPSTONE CASE: SoftWear, Limited (continued)

Payroll Department Interview

Rick's next interview was with the lead payroll clerk, Nelson White. During the interview, Nelson confirmed that when an employee is hired, a PR-1 form is completed in the human resources department. This form then is forwarded to payroll, where it is filed. He explained that each week the payroll department sends a time sheet to every SWL department manager. The time sheet lists each employee, with space to record regular hours, vacation, sick leave, jury duty, and other codes for accounting purposes.

After each pay period, SWL managers complete their departmental time sheets and return them to the payroll department. Payroll then enters the pay rate and deduction information and delivers the sheets to Business Information Systems (BIS), the service bureau that prepares SWL's payroll.

After the payroll is run, a BIS employee returns the time sheets, paychecks, and the payroll register to SWL. The director of payroll, Amy Calico, sends the paychecks to SWL department heads for distribution to employees.

Nelson uses the weekly payroll register to prepare a report of credit union deductions and a check to the credit union for the total amount deducted. Stock purchases, on the other hand, are processed monthly, based on the stock's closing price on the last business day of the month. Using the weekly payroll registers, Nelson manually prepares a monthly report of employee stock purchases and forwards a copy of the report and a funds transfer authorization to Carolina National Bank, which is SWL's stock transfer agent.

Rick asked Nelson why BIS did not produce a report on employee stock purchase deductions. Nelson replied that although the payroll is run weekly, the stock deductions are invested only once a month. Because the two cycles do not match, the BIS system could not handle the task.

Nelson then referred Rick to the SWL Systems and Procedures Manual page that describes how monthly Employee Stock Purchase Plan investment amounts are calculated, as shown in Figure 3-39. After blanking out the employee's name and Social Security number, Nelson also gave Rick a sample of three monthly deduction registers, as shown in Figure 3-40 on the next page.

Rick began to see why it was taking so much effort to prepare the reports. The process that Nelson described provided much more

---

| SoftWear, Limited | Payroll |
| Systems and Procedures Manual | Page 29 |

VII.   Employee Stock Purchase Plan

The human resources department will notify the payroll department of the weekly deduction that the employee has specified on the Employee Stock Purchase Plan Enrollment and Change Form and send a copy of the Employee Stock Purchase Plan Enrollment and Change Form (Form PR-4) and the Employee Stock Purchase Plan Weekly Deduction Summary Report (Form PR-5) to the payroll department.

Deductions will be made weekly and then invested on a monthly basis. The payroll department will calculate the proper monthly investment amount on a pro rata basis, as follows:

A.   A nominal per diem deduction rate will be established by dividing the weekly deduction by 7, rounded to 3 decimal places.

B.   The monthly Plan investment will be the number of calendar days in the month times the nominal per diem rate, rounded to 2 decimal places. For example:

Weekly deduction: $20.00 / 7 = 2.8571 = $2.857 per diem
Month of January = 31 times 2.857 = 88.567 = $88.57

C.   At the end of each month, the payroll department will prepare a monthly deduction register (Form PR-6) that shows individual employee deductions by a weekly and monthly total.

FIGURE 3-39 Sample page from SWL Systems and Procedures Manual.

detail than the general description that Rick had received during the preliminary investigation from Amy Calico, director of payroll.

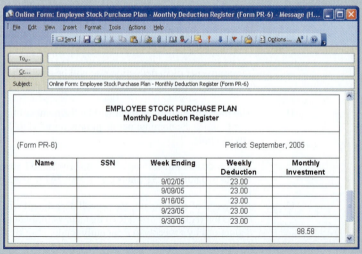

FIGURE 3-40 Sample of the Monthly Deduction Register for the Employee Stock Purchase Plan for July, August, and September 2005, showing the weekly deduction and monthly investment amounts.

BIS Interview

Rick decided that he should talk with someone at the BIS service bureau to find out more about its operations. He learned from Nelson that Linda DeMarco was BIS's customer relations manager, so he scheduled an appointment with her.

When Rick arrived at BIS, Linda greeted him warmly. She explained that she had planned to meet with members of SWL's payroll department within the next month or two to discuss the latest developments. Because Rick now was working on SWL's payroll system, however, this meeting would save her a trip. Rick temporarily abandoned his interview plan and asked Linda what she had in mind.

"The payroll system that your company is using, which we call GAPP, for Generalized Automated Payroll Program, originally was developed here at BIS about eight years ago," Linda began. "In fact, SoftWear, Limited was one of our very first customers. We've worked together for a long time, and we are very committed to your firm. As you know, GAPP was modified and updated many times. But let's face it, even with the patches, GAPP is an antique! Anyway, I have some exciting news. A few months ago, our company decided to develop a new, state-of-the-art payroll system. We are going to call it CHIPS, for Comprehensive High-powered Interactive Payroll System. I am really looking forward to working with your company when you switch over to CHIPS," Linda said.

Rick took a few moments to consider this surprising development. He then asked what would happen with GAPP. Linda stated that GAPP would be available to customers for another year or two, but that BIS would make no further enhancements to that system. Using BIS resources to maintain an obsolete system would not make sense, she explained.

Before this meeting, Rick had hoped that BIS could make some minor changes to solve SWL's payroll problems. He now realized that was impossible, so he decided to learn more about CHIPS.

Rick described the problem with the mismatched deduction cycles and asked if CHIPS would handle that. Linda said that she already had looked into the matter. She pointed out that SWL was their only customer with more than one deduction application cycle. From BIS's point of view, programming CHIPS to handle multiple cycle reports did not make sense. Linda suggested that perhaps a special add-on module could be written, once CHIPS was up and running. BIS could do that kind of job on a contract basis, she added.

Rick then asked when the new system would be available and what the cost would be. Linda stated that current plans were to begin offering CHIPS sometime in the following year. She explained that the system was still in development, and she could not be more specific about timetables and costs. She was sure, however, that the monthly fee for CHIPS would not increase more than 30 percent above the current GAPP charges.

As Rick was preparing to leave, Linda urged him to keep in touch. In the next few months, she explained, plans for CHIPS would become more specific, and she would be able to answer all his questions.

New Developments

When Rick returned from his meeting with Linda, he immediately went to his manager, Jane Rossman. After he described his visit to BIS, Jane telephoned Ann Hon, director of information technology. Within the hour, Jane and Rick held a meeting with Ann in her office. Rick repeated the details of his visit, and Ann asked for his opinion on how the developments at BIS would affect SWL's current systems analysis.

Rick explained that one of the problems — possible input errors when transferring data from the human resources summary list — might be solved easily by developing a new form or procedure. Nevertheless, he saw no obvious solutions for the stock purchase deduction problems, except to change the scope of the payroll project.

Jane, Rick, and Ann then analyzed the situation. They all agreed that because of the upcoming changes at BIS, the current payroll system project would produce very limited results and should be expanded in scope. They totaled the costs of the SWL project to that point and prepared estimates for a detailed investigation of the entire payroll system in order to meet SWL's current and future needs.

Later that week, Ann met with Michael Jeremy, vice president of finance, to discuss the situation and present her proposal to go forward with an expanded analysis. Before she even started, however, Mr. Jeremy filled her in on the latest announcement from SWL's top management: the company had decided to move forward with the new Employee Savings and Investment Plan (ESIP) under consideration. He said that in December, Robert Lansing, SWL's president, would announce a target date of April 1, 2006, for the new ESIP plan. Mr. Jeremy explained that the new plan would be a 401(k) plan with tax advantages for employees.

Facing the new constraints on top of the existing payroll system problems, it looked like SWL would need a new payroll system after all.

The Revised Project

Jane Rossman assigned Carla Moore, a programmer-analyst, to work with Rick Williams on the revised system project. Because they now had to determine the requirements for the complete payroll system, Rick and Carla conducted follow-up interviews with Nelson White and Meredith Rider, as well as Allison Friendly, a human resources representative, and both payroll clerks, Britton Ellis and Debra Williams. During the payroll department interviews, the payroll staff prepared samples of all the existing payroll reports. At the end of the fact-finding process, Rick and Carla decided to prepare the functional decomposition diagram shown in Figure 3-41. The diagram shows the main functions identified during the interviews.

FIGURE 3-41 A functional decomposition diagram (FDD) shows the main functions that were identified during the interviews.

CHAPTER CAPSTONE CASE: SoftWear, Limited (continued)

SWL

The Payroll Register report is shown in Figure 3-42. On the report, each employee is listed on a separate line, along with his or her earnings, deductions, and net pay. BIS creates three copies of this report each week. One copy is sent to Michael Jeremy, and one copy goes to Amy Calico. The third copy is used by the payroll department for determining SWL's obligation for tax withholding and FICA payments and for applying credit union and stock purchase plan deductions. BIS also prints three copies of the Employee Compensation Record shown in Figure 3-43, which shows year-to-date payroll information for each employee.

SWL   **PAYROLL REGISTER**

Week Ending _____   *Page 1*

Employee Data		Earnings			Deductions					Net Pay	
Name	SSN	Regular Pay	Overtime Pay	Total Pay	Federal Tax	State Tax	FICA	Credit Union	Stock Plan	Net Amount	Check Number

FIGURE 3-42 Sample page of SWL Payroll Register report.

SWL   **EMPLOYEE COMPENSATION RECORD**

Name _____   **SSN** _____

Weekly Payroll										Year to Date									
	Earnings			Deductions					Net Pay		Earnings			Deductions					Net Pay
Week Ending	Reg. Pay	OT Pay	Total Pay	Fed. Tax	State Tax	FICA	Credit Union	Stock Plan	Net Pay	Check No.	Reg. Pay	OT Pay	Total Pay	Fed. Tax	State Tax	FICA	Credit Union	Stock Plan	Net Amount
08/05/05	352.00		352.00	45.00	7.40	22.40	10.00	9.20	258.00	011917	10,912.00		10,912.00	1,395.00	229.40	694.40	310.00	285.20	7,998.00
08/12/05	352.00		352.00	45.00	7.40	22.40	10.00	9.20	258.00	016175	11,264.00		11,264.00	1,440.00	236.80	716.80	320.00	294.40	8,256.00
08/19/05	352.00		352.00	45.00	7.40	22.40	10.00	9.20	258.00	020342	11,616.00		11,616.00	1,485.00	244.20	739.20	330.00	303.60	8,514.00
08/26/05	352.00		352.00	45.00	7.40	22.40	10.00	9.20	258.00	030919	11,968.00		11,968.00	1,530.00	251.60	761.60	340.00	312.80	8,772.00

FIGURE 3-43 Sample page of SWL Employee Compensation Record report.

Mr. Jeremy receives a weekly overtime report from BIS that lists every employee who worked overtime that week. When Carla asked him about that report, he stated that he consulted it occasionally but admitted that he did not need the report every week. He also receives an accounting report, but he routinely forwards it to the accounting department. He mentioned that an overall financial summary was more valuable to him.

CHAPTER CAPSTONE CASE: SoftWear, Limited (continued)

Another key output of the payroll system is the payroll paycheck and stub shown in Figure 3-44 that is distributed weekly to employees. In addition to the check itself, the stub lists current and year-to-date totals for regular pay, overtime pay, total pay, deductions, and net pay.

SWL   SOFTWEAR, LIMITED   55-555/5555   No. ____
      999 Technology Plaza   1234567   Date _____
      Raleigh, NC 29991

Pay to the Order of _____ $ _____

_____ Dollars
                        (Not Negotiable)

Carolina Bank
999 Ninth Street
Raleigh, NC 29999   _____
                                1234· 567· 8888

Week Ending ____	This Period	Year-to-Date Totals
EARNINGS		
Regular Pay		
Overtime Pay		
Total Pay		
DEDUCTIONS		
Federal Tax		
State Tax		
FICA		
Credit Union		
Stock Plan		
Net Pay		

FIGURE 3-44   Sample SWL employee paycheck and stub.

SWL Team Tasks

1. When Rick Williams met with Meredith Rider in the human resources department, he asked for copies of actual reports and forms that contained confidential information, but Meredith declined to provide them. Rick has asked you to suggest a reasonable compromise between confidentiality requirements and the need for analysts to review actual records, instead of fictitious data. Think about this, and write a message to Rick with your views.

2. Assume that you were with Rick at the meeting with Linda DeMarco. Review the fact statement, then write an interview summary that documents the main topics that Rick and Linda discussed.

3. Rick asked you to design a questionnaire that would measure employee satisfaction with the current payroll deduction system. Review the sample questionnaire in the chapter, and prepare a draft for Rick. Rick also wants you to suggest various sampling methods so he can make a choice. Include a brief description of various methods, and be sure to include your recommendation and reasons.

4. Rick wants you to interview several employees to learn more about their levels of satisfaction with the current system. Prepare a set of interview questions, and be sure to include at least examples of open-ended, closed-ended, and range-of-response questions. If possible, conduct role-play interviews with other students.

CHAPTER 4

Data and Process Modeling

CHAPTER 4 is the second of three chapters in the systems analysis phase of the SDLC. This chapter discusses data and process modeling techniques that analysts use to show how the system transforms data into useful information. The deliverable, or end product, of data and process modeling is a logical model that will support business operations and meet user needs.

INTRODUCTION

OBJECTIVES

When you finish this chapter, you will be able to:

- Describe data and process modeling concepts and tools, including data flow diagrams, a data dictionary, and process descriptions

- Describe the symbols used in data flow diagrams and explain the rules for their use

- Draw data flow diagrams in a sequence, from general to specific

- Explain how to level and balance a set of data flow diagrams

- Describe how a data dictionary is used and what it contains

- Use process description tools, including structured English, decision tables, and decision trees

- Describe the relationship between logical and physical models

During the requirements modeling process described in Chapter 3, you used fact-finding techniques to investigate the current system and identify user requirements. Now, in Chapter 4, you use data and process modeling techniques to develop a logical model of the proposed system and document the system requirements. A **logical model** shows *what* the system must do, regardless of how it will be implemented physically. Later, in the systems design phase, you build a **physical model** that describes *how* the system will be constructed. Data and process modeling involves three main tools: data flow diagrams, a data dictionary, and process descriptions.

In the final stage of systems analysis, which is explained in Chapter 5, you will learn how to evaluate various development strategies, create a system requirements proposal, and prepare for the systems design phase of the SDLC.

CHAPTER INTRODUCTION CASE: Mountain View College Bookstore

Background: Wendy Lee, manager of college services at Mountain View College, wants a new information system that will improve efficiency and customer service at the three college bookstores.

In this part of the case, Florence Fullerton (systems analyst) and Harry Boston (student intern) are talking about data and process modeling tasks and concepts.

Participants:	Florence and Harry
Location:	Florence's office, Monday afternoon, November 14, 2005
Project status:	Florence and Harry have completed fact-finding for the new system and are ready to develop a requirements model using various diagrams and a data dictionary that will describe and document the proposed system.
Discussion topics:	Data flow diagrams, data dictionaries, and process description tools

Florence:	Hi, Harry. Any questions about the fact-finding we did?
Harry:	*Well, I found out that fact-finding is hard work.*
Florence:	Yes, but it was worth it. Look at what we learned — now we understand how the current system operates, and we know what users expect in the new system. This information will help us build a requirements model that we can present to Wendy and her staff.
Harry:	*What's the next step?*
Florence:	We need to draw a set of data flow diagrams, or DFDs for short.
Harry:	*Do we use a CASE tool to draw the DFDs?*
Florence:	We can draw the initial versions by hand. We'll use a CASE tool to prepare the final version of the diagrams.
Harry:	*What goes into a DFD?*
Florence:	DFDs use four basic symbols that represent processes, data flows, data stores, and entities. You'll learn about these as we go along. I'll also show you how we use techniques called leveling and balancing to develop accurate, consistent DFDs.
Harry:	*Apart from the diagrams, do we need to develop any other documentation?*
Florence:	Yes, we need to create a data dictionary and process descriptions. The data dictionary is an overall storehouse of information about the system, and serves as a central clearinghouse for all documentation. We use process descriptions to explain the logical steps that each process performs. To create these descriptions, we use three tools: structured English statements, decision tables, and decision trees.
Harry:	*Sounds like a lot to do. Where do we begin?*
Florence:	Here's a task list to get us started:

FIGURE 4-1

OVERVIEW OF DATA AND PROCESS MODELING TOOLS

TOOLKIT TIME

The CASE Tools in Part 2 of the Systems Analyst's Toolkit can help you document business functions and processes, develop graphical models, and provide an overall framework for information system development. To learn more about these tools, turn to Part 2 of the six-part Toolkit that follows Chapter 10.

Systems analysts use many graphical techniques to describe an information system. One popular method is to draw a set of data flow diagrams. A **data flow diagram** (DFD) uses various symbols to show how the system transforms input data into useful information. Other graphical tools include entity-relationship diagrams, which are described in Chapter 7 (Data Design); and object models, which are described in Part 5 of the Systems Analyst's Toolkit (Object-Oriented Tools).

DATA FLOW DIAGRAMS

In Part 1 of the Systems Analyst's Toolkit, you learn how to use visual aids to help explain a concept, as shown in Figure 4-2. Similarly, during the systems analysis phase, you learn how to create a visual model of the information system using a set of data flow diagrams.

A data flow diagram (DFD) shows how data moves through an information system but does not show program logic or processing steps. A set of DFDs provides a logical model that shows *what* the system does, not *how* it does it. That distinction is important because focusing on implementation issues at this point would restrict your search for the most effective system design.

ON THE WEB

For more information about Yourdon Symbols, visit **scsite.com/ sad6e/more**, locate Chapter 4 and then click the Yourdon Symbols link.

DFD Symbols

DFDs use four basic symbols that represent processes, data flows, data stores, and entities. Several different versions of DFD symbols exist, but they all serve the same purpose. DFD examples in this textbook use the **Gane and Sarson** symbol set. Another popular symbol set is the **Yourdon** symbol set. Figure 4-3 shows examples of both versions. Symbols are referenced by using all capital letters for the symbol name.

PROCESS SYMBOL A **process** receives input data and produces output that has a different content, form, or both. For instance, the process for calculating pay uses two inputs (pay rate and hours worked) to produce one output (total pay). Processes can be very simple or quite complex. In a typical company, processes might include calculating sales trends, filing online insurance claims, ordering inventory from a supplier's system, or verifying e-mail addresses for Web customers. Processes contain the **business logic**, also called **business rules**, that transform the data and produce the required results.

The symbol for a process is a rectangle with rounded corners. The name of the process appears inside the rectangle. The process name identifies a specific function and consists of a verb (and an adjective, if necessary) followed by a singular noun. Examples of process names are APPLY RENT PAYMENT, CALCULATE COMMISSION, ASSIGN FINAL GRADE, VERIFY ORDER, and FILL ORDER.

Processing details are not shown in a DFD. For example, you might have a process named DEPOSIT PAYMENT. The process symbol

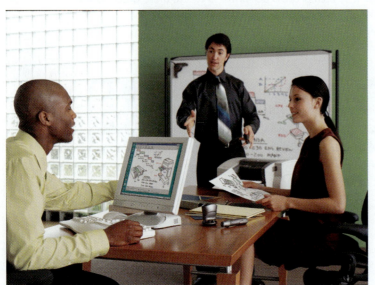

FIGURE 4-2 Systems analysts often use visual aids during presentations.

does not reveal the business logic for the DEPOSIT PAYMENT process. To document the logic, you create a process description, which is explained later in this chapter.

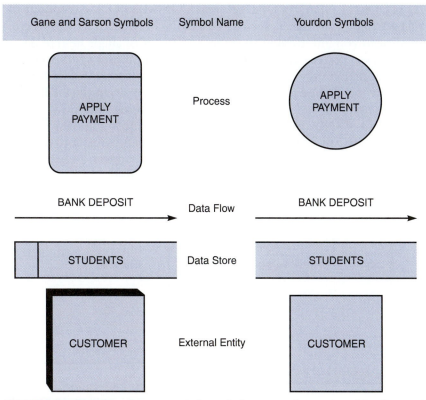

Gane and Sarson Symbols	Symbol Name	Yourdon Symbols
APPLY PAYMENT	Process	APPLY PAYMENT
BANK DEPOSIT →	Data Flow	BANK DEPOSIT →
STUDENTS	Data Store	STUDENTS
CUSTOMER	External Entity	CUSTOMER

FIGURE 4-3 Data flow diagram symbols, symbol names, and examples of the Gane and Sarson and Yourdon symbol sets.

In DFDs, a process symbol can be referred to as a **black box**, because the inputs, outputs, and general functions of the process are known, but the underlying details and logic of the process are hidden. By showing processes as black boxes, an analyst can create DFDs that show how the system functions, but avoid unnecessary detail and clutter. When the analyst wishes to show additional levels of detail, he or she can zoom in on a process symbol and create a more in-depth DFD that shows the process's internal workings — which might reveal even more processes, data flows, and data stores. In this manner, the information system can be modeled as a series of increasingly detailed pictures.

The network router shown in Figure 4-4 is an example of a black box. An observer can see cables that carry data into and out of the router, but the router's internal operations are not revealed — only the results are apparent.

DATA FLOW SYMBOL A **data flow** is a path for data to move from one part of the information system to another. A data flow in a DFD represents one or more data items. For example, a data flow could consist of a single data item (such as a student ID number) or it could include a set of data (such as a class roster with student ID numbers, names, and registration dates for a specific class). Although the DFD does not show the detailed contents of a data flow, that information is included in the data dictionary, which is described later in this chapter.

FIGURE 4-4 A network router is an example of a black box. The cables carry data into and out of the router, but the router's internal operations are hidden inside the case.

The symbol for a data flow is a line with a single or double arrowhead. The data flow name appears above, below, or alongside the line. A data flow name consists of a singular noun and an adjective, if needed. Examples of data flow names are DEPOSIT, INVOICE PAYMENT, STUDENT GRADE, ORDER, and COMMISSION. Exceptions to the singular name rule are data flow names, such as GRADING PARAMETERS, where a singular name could mislead you into thinking a single parameter or single item of data exists.

Figure 4-5 shows correct examples of data flow and process symbol connections. Because a process changes the data's content or form, at least one data flow must enter and one data flow must exit each process symbol, as they do in the CREATE INVOICE process. A process symbol can have more than one outgoing data flow, as shown in the GRADE STUDENT WORK process, or more than one incoming data flow, as shown in the CALCULATE GROSS PAY process. A process also can connect to any other symbol, including another process symbol, as shown by the connection between VERIFY ORDER and ASSEMBLE ORDER in Figure 4-5. A data flow, therefore, *must* have a process symbol on at least one end.

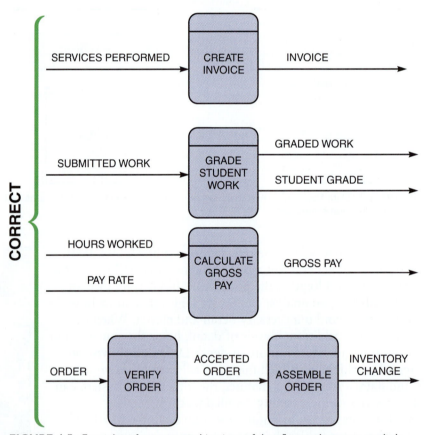

FIGURE 4-5 Examples of correct combinations of data flow and process symbols.

Figure 4-6 shows three data flow and process combinations that you must avoid:

➡ **Spontaneous generation.** The APPLY INSURANCE PREMIUM process, for instance, produces output, but has no input data flow. Because it has no input, the process is called a spontaneous generation process.

➡ **Black hole.** The CALCULATE GROSS PAY is called a black hole process, which is a process that has input, but produces no output.

➡ **Gray hole.** A gray hole is a process that has at least one input and one output, but the input obviously is insufficient to generate the output shown. For example, a date of birth input is not sufficient to produce a final grade output in the CALCULATE GRADE process.

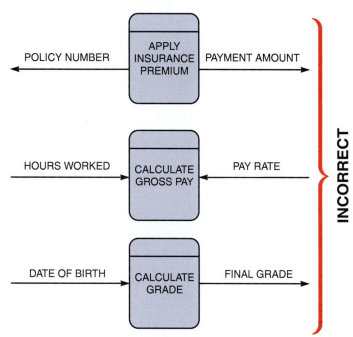

FIGURE 4-6 Examples of incorrect combinations of data flow and process symbols. APPLY INSURANCE PREMIUM has no input and is called a spontaneous generation process. CALCULATE GROSS PAY has no outputs and is called a black hole process. CALCULATE GRADE has an input that is obviously unable to produce the output. This process is called a gray hole.

Spontaneous generation, black holes, and gray holes are impossible logically in a DFD because a process must act on input, shown by an incoming data flow, and produce output, represented by an outgoing data flow.

DATA STORE SYMBOL A **data store** is used in a DFD to represent data that the system stores because one or more processes need to use the data at a later time. For instance, instructors need to store student scores on tests and assignments during the semester so they can assign final grades at the end of the term. Similarly, a company stores employee salary and deduction data during the year in order to print W-2 forms with total earnings and deductions at the end of the year. A DFD does not show the detailed contents of a data store — the specific structure and data elements are defined in the data dictionary, which is discussed later in this chapter.

The physical characteristics of a data store are unimportant because you are concerned only with a logical model. Also, the length of time that the data is stored is unimportant — it can be a matter of seconds while a transaction is processed or a period of months while data is accumulated for year-end processing. What is important is that a process needs access to the data at some later time.

In a DFD, the Gane and Sarson symbol for a data store is a flat rectangle that is open on the right side and closed on the left side. The name of the data store appears between the lines and identifies the data it contains. A data store name is a plural name consisting of a noun and adjectives, if needed. Examples of data store names are STUDENTS, ACCOUNTS RECEIVABLE, PRODUCTS, DAILY PAYMENTS,

PURCHASE ORDERS, OUTSTANDING CHECKS, INSURANCE POLICIES, and EMPLOYEES. Exceptions to the plural name rule are collective nouns that represent multiple occurrences of objects. For example, GRADEBOOK represents a group of students and their scores.

A data store must be connected to a process with a data flow. Figure 4-7 illustrates typical examples of data stores. In each case, the data store has at least one incoming and one outgoing data flow and is connected to a process symbol with a data flow.

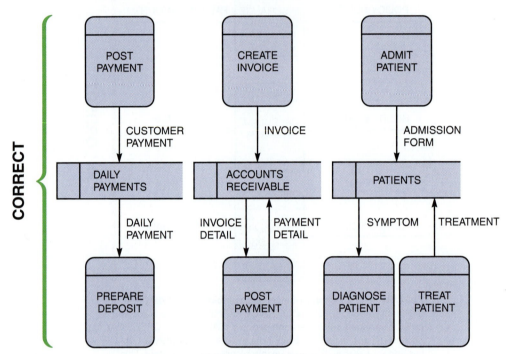

FIGURE 4-7 Examples of correct uses of data store symbols in a data flow diagram.

Violations of the rule that a data store must have at least one incoming and one outgoing data flow are shown in Figure 4-8. In the first example, two data stores are connected incorrectly because no process is between them. Also, COURSES has no incoming data flow and STUDENTS has no outgoing data flow. In the second and third examples, the data stores lack either an outgoing or incoming data flow.

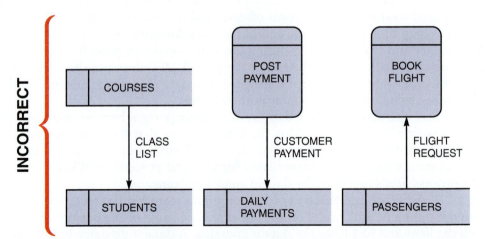

FIGURE 4-8 Examples of incorrect uses of data store symbols: two data stores cannot be connected by a data flow without an intervening process, and each data store should have an outgoing and incoming data flow.

There is an exception to the requirement that a data store must have at least one incoming and one outgoing data flow. In some situations, a data store has no input data flow because it contains fixed reference data that is not updated by the system. For example, consider a data store called TAX TABLE, which contains withholding tax data that a company downloads from the Internal Revenue Service. When the company runs its payroll, the CALCULATE WITHHOLDING process accesses data from this data store. On a DFD, this would be represented as a one-way outgoing data flow from the TAX TABLE data store into the CALCULATE WITHHOLDING process.

ENTITY SYMBOL The symbol for an **entity** is a rectangle, which may be shaded to make it look three-dimensional. The name of the entity appears inside the symbol.

A DFD shows only external entities that provide data to the system or receive output from the system. A DFD shows the boundaries of the system and how the system interfaces with the outside world. For example, a customer entity submits an order to an order processing system. Other examples of entities include a patient who supplies data to a medical records system, a homeowner who receives a bill from a city property tax system, or an accounts payable system that receives data from the company's purchasing system.

DFD entities also are called **terminators**, because they are data origins or final destinations. Systems analysts call an entity that supplies data to the system a **source**, and an entity that receives data from the system a **sink**. An entity name is the singular form of a department, outside organization, other information system, or person. An external entity can be a source or a sink or both, but each entity must be connected to a process by a data flow. Figures 4-9 and 4-10 on the next page show correct and incorrect examples of this rule.

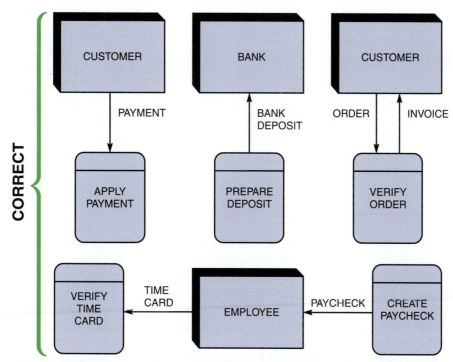

FIGURE 4-9 Examples of correct uses of external entities in a data flow diagram.

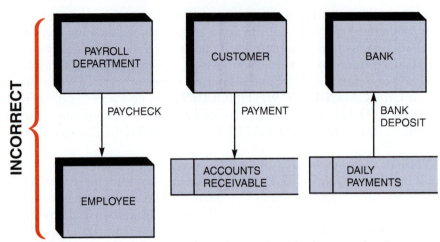

FIGURE 4-10 Examples of incorrect uses of external entities. An external entity must be connected by a data flow to a process, and not directly to a data store or to another external entity.

With an understanding of the proper use of DFD symbols, you are ready to construct diagrams that use these symbols. Figure 4-11 shows a summary of the rules for using DFD symbols.

Data Flow That Connects   *Okay to Use?*

	YES	NO
A process to another process	✓	
A process to an external entity	✓	
A process to a data store	✓	
An entity to another entity		✓
An entity to a data store		✓
A data store to another data store		✓

FIGURE 4-11 Rules for connecting processes, data stores, and entities in a DFD.

CREATING A SET OF DFDS

During requirements modeling, you used interviews, questionnaires, and other techniques to gather facts about the system, and you learned how the various people, departments, data, and processes fit together to support business operations. Now you are ready to create a graphical model of the information system based on your fact-finding results.

To learn how to construct DFDs, you will use examples of three information systems. The first example is a grading system that instructors use to assign final grades based on the scores that students receive during the term. The second example is an order system that a company uses to enter orders and apply payments against a customer's balance. The third example is a manufacturing system that handles a company's production.

You will learn how to create a set of DFDs by performing three main tasks:

Step 1: Draw a context diagram
Step 2: Draw a diagram 0 DFD
Step 3: Draw the lower-level diagrams

Draw a Context Diagram

The first step in constructing a set of DFDs is to draw a context diagram. A **context diagram** is a top-level view of an information system that shows the system's boundaries and scope. To draw a context diagram, you start by placing a single process symbol in the center of the page. The symbol represents the entire information system, and you identify it as process 0. Then you place the entities around the perimeter of the page and use data flows to connect the entities to the central process. You do not show any data stores in a context diagram because data stores are internal to the system.

How do you know which entities and data flows to place in the context diagram? You begin by reviewing the system requirements to identify all external data sources and destinations. During that process, you record the name of the entities, the name and content of the data flows, and the direction of the data flows. If you do that carefully, and you did a good job of fact-finding in the previous stage, you should have no difficulty drawing the context diagram.

CONTEXT DIAGRAM EXAMPLE Figure 4-12 shows the context diagram for a grading system. The GRADING SYSTEM process is at the center of the diagram. The three entities (STUDENT RECORDS SYSTEM, STUDENT, and INSTRUCTOR) are placed around the central process. Interaction among the central process and the entities involves six different data flows. The STUDENT RECORDS SYSTEM entity supplies data through the CLASS ROSTER data flow and receives data through the FINAL GRADE data flow. The STUDENT entity supplies data through the SUBMITTED WORK data flow and receives data through the GRADED WORK data flow. Finally, the INSTRUCTOR entity supplies data through the GRADING PARAMETERS data flow and receives data through the GRADE REPORT data flow.

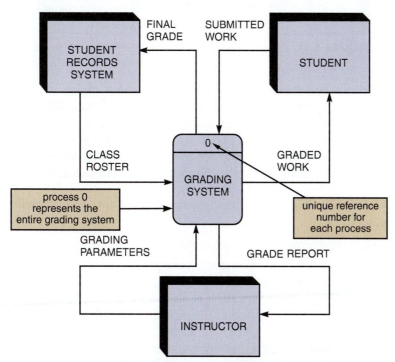

FIGURE 4-12 Context diagram DFD for a grading system.

The context diagram for an order system is shown in Figure 4-13 on the next page. Notice that the ORDER SYSTEM process is at the center of the diagram and five entities surround the process. Three of the entities, SALES REP, BANK, and ACCOUNTING, have single incoming data flows for COMMISSION, BANK DEPOSIT, and

CASH RECEIPTS ENTRY, respectively. The WAREHOUSE entity has one incoming data flow — PICKING LIST — that is, a report that shows the items ordered and their quantity, location, and sequence to pick from the warehouse. The WAREHOUSE entity has one outgoing data flow, COMPLETED ORDER. Finally, the CUSTOMER entity has two outgoing data flows, ORDER and PAYMENT, and two incoming data flows, ORDER REJECT NOTICE and INVOICE.

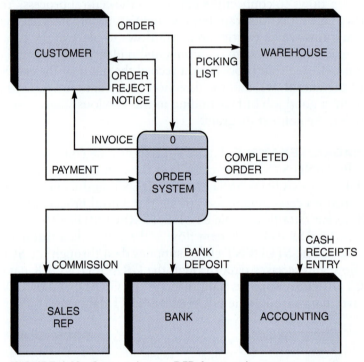

FIGURE 4-13   Context diagram DFD for an order system.

The context diagram for the order system appears more complex than the grading system because it has two more entities and three more data flows. What makes one system more complex than another is the number of components, the number of levels, and the degree of interaction among its processes, entities, data stores, and data flows.

Figure 4-14 shows the context diagram for the manufacturing system that supports the company's production. Notice that the diagram has 13 entities and 18 data flows.

DRAWING GUIDELINES   When you draw a context diagram, and other DFDs, you follow certain guidelines:

1. Draw the context diagram so it fits on one page.

2. Use the name of the information system as the process name in the context diagram. For example, the process names in Figures 4-12 (on the previous page), 4-13, and 4-14 are GRADING SYSTEM, ORDER SYSTEM, and MANUFACTURING SYSTEM. The system name is used as the process name because the context diagram shows the entire information system and its boundaries. For processes in lower-level DFDs, use a verb followed by a descriptive noun, such as UPDATE INVENTORY, CALCULATE OVERTIME, or PRODUCE REPORT.

3. Use unique names within each set of symbols. For instance, the diagram in Figure 4-14 shows only one entity named CUSTOMER and only one data flow named ORDER. Whenever you see the entity CUSTOMER on one of the other manufacturing system DFDs, you know that you are dealing with the same entity. Whenever the ORDER data flow appears, you know that you are dealing with the same data flow. The naming convention also applies to data stores.

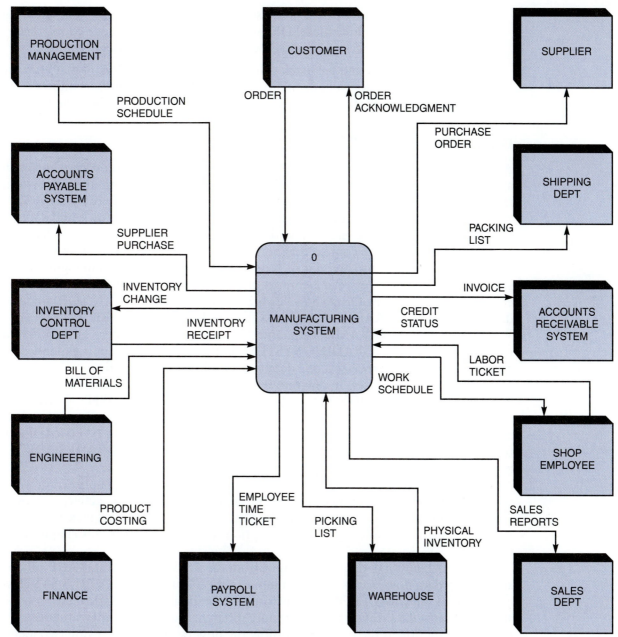

FIGURE 4-14 Context diagram DFD for a manufacturing system.

4. Do not cross lines. One way to achieve that goal is to restrict the number of symbols in any DFD. On lower-level diagrams with multiple processes, you should not have more than nine process symbols. Including more than nine symbols usually is a signal that your diagram is too complex and that you should reconsider your analysis. Another way to avoid crossing lines is to duplicate an entity or data store. When duplicating a symbol on a diagram, make sure to document the duplication to avoid possible confusion. A special notation, such as an asterisk, next to the symbol name and inside the duplicated symbols signifies that they are duplicated on the diagram.

5. Provide a unique name and reference number for each process. Because it is the highest-level DFD, the context diagram contains process 0, which represents the entire information system, but does not show the internal workings. To describe the next level of detail inside process 0, you must create a DFD named diagram 0,

which will reveal additional processes that must be named and numbered. As you continue to create lower-level DFDs, you assign unique names and reference numbers to all processes, until you complete the logical model.

6. Obtain user input and feedback. The main objective is to ensure that your model is accurate and easy to understand. Reviewing models with users allows you to obtain their feedback and approval for the logical design of the system.

Draw a Diagram 0 DFD

A context diagram provides the most general view of an information system and contains a single process symbol, which is like a black box. To show the detail inside the black box, you create DFD diagram 0. **Diagram 0** (the numeral zero, and not the letter O) zooms in on the context diagram and shows major processes, data flows, and data stores. Diagram 0 also repeats the entities and data flows that appear in the context diagram.

When you expand the context diagram into DFD diagram 0, you must retain all the connections that flow into and out of process 0. The grading system in Figure 4-15 shows the relationship between a context diagram and diagram 0. Notice that the three entities (STUDENT RECORDS SYSTEM, STUDENT, and INSTRUCTOR) and the six data flows (FINAL GRADE, CLASS ROSTER, SUBMITTED WORK, GRADED WORK, GRADING PARAMETERS, and GRADE REPORT) appear in both diagrams. In addition, process 0 (GRADING SYSTEM) in the context diagram is expanded in diagram 0 to show four processes, one data store, and five new data flows.

Notice that each process in diagram 0 has a reference number: ESTABLISH GRADEBOOK is 1, ASSIGN FINAL GRADE is 2, GRADE STUDENT WORK is 3, and PRODUCE GRADE REPORT is 4. These reference numbers are important because they identify a series of DFDs. If more detail were needed for ESTABLISH GRADEBOOK, for example, you would draw a diagram 1, because ESTABLISH GRADEBOOK is process 1.

The process numbers do not suggest that the processes are accomplished in a sequential order. Each process always is considered to be available, active, and awaiting data to be processed. If processes must be performed in a specific sequence, you document the information in the process descriptions (discussed later in this chapter), not in the DFD.

The FINAL GRADE data flow output from the ASSIGN FINAL GRADE process is a diverging data flow that becomes an input to the STUDENT RECORDS SYSTEM entity and to the GRADEBOOK data store. A **diverging data flow** is a data flow in which the same data travels to two or more different locations. In that situation, a diverging data flow is the best way to show the flow rather than showing two identical data flows, which could be misleading.

If the same data flows in both directions, you can use a double-headed arrow to connect the symbols. To identify specific data flows into and out of a symbol, however, you use separate data flow symbols with single arrowheads. For example, in Figure 4-15 the separate data flows (SUBMITTED WORK and GRADED WORK) go into and out of the GRADE STUDENT WORK process.

Because diagram 0 is a more detailed or expanded version of process 0 on the context diagram, diagram 0 represents an exploded view of process 0. You also can refer to diagram 0 as a partitioned or decomposed view of process 0. When you explode a DFD, the higher-level diagram is called the **parent diagram**, and the lower-level diagram is referred to as the **child diagram**. The grading system is simple enough that you do not need any additional DFDs to model the system. At that point, the four processes, the one data store, and the 10 data flows can be documented in the data dictionary.

CONTEXT DIAGRAM

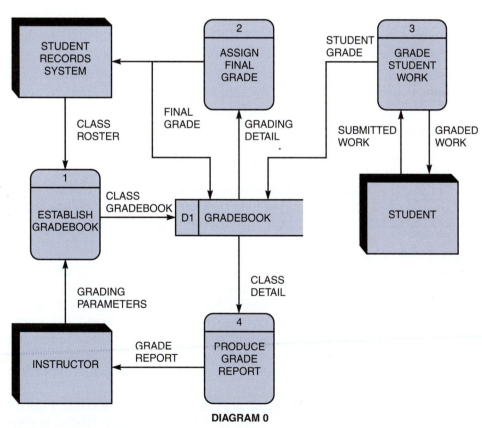

DIAGRAM 0

FIGURE 4-15 Context diagram and diagram 0 for the grading system.

When you create a set of DFDs for a system, you break the processing logic down into smaller units, called functional primitives, that programmers will use to develop code. A **functional primitive** is a process that consists of a single function that is not exploded further. For example, each of the four processes shown in the lower portion of Figure 4-15 on the previous page is a functional primitive. You document the logic for a functional primitive in a process description in the data dictionary. Later, when the logical design is implemented as a physical system, programmers will transform each functional primitive into a unit of program code that carries out the required processing steps. Deciding whether to explode a process further or determine that it is a functional primitive is a matter of experience, judgment, and interaction with programmers who must translate the logical design into code.

Figure 4-16 shows the diagram 0 for the order system. Process 0 on the order system's context diagram is exploded to show three processes (FILL ORDER, CREATE INVOICE, and APPLY PAYMENT), one data store (ACCOUNTS RECEIVABLE), two new data flows (INVOICE DETAIL and PAYMENT DETAIL), and one diverging data flow (INVOICE).

The following walkthrough explains the DFD shown in Figure 4-16:

1. A CUSTOMER submits an ORDER. Depending on the processing logic, the FILL ORDER process either sends an ORDER REJECT NOTICE back to the customer or sends a PICKING LIST to the WAREHOUSE.

2. A COMPLETED ORDER from the WAREHOUSE is input to the CREATE INVOICE process, which outputs an INVOICE to both the CUSTOMER process and the ACCOUNTS RECEIVABLE data store.

3. A CUSTOMER makes a PAYMENT that is processed by APPLY PAYMENT. APPLY PAYMENT requires INVOICE DETAIL input from the ACCOUNTS RECEIVABLE data store along with the PAYMENT. APPLY PAYMENT also outputs PAYMENT DETAIL back to the ACCOUNTS RECEIVABLE data store and outputs COMMISSION to the SALES DEPT, BANK DEPOSIT to the BANK, and CASH RECEIPTS ENTRY to ACCOUNTING.

The walkthrough of diagram 0 illustrates the basic requirements of the order system. To learn more, you would examine the detailed description of each separate process.

Draw the Lower-Level Diagrams

To create lower-level diagrams, you must use leveling and balancing techniques. **Leveling** is the process of drawing a series of increasingly detailed diagrams, until all functional primitives are identified. **Balancing** maintains consistency among a set of DFDs by ensuring that input and output data flows align properly. Leveling and balancing are described in more detail in the following sections.

LEVELING   Leveling uses a series of increasingly detailed DFDs to describe an information system. For example, a system might consist of dozens, or even hundreds, of separate processes. Using leveling, an analyst starts with an overall view, which is a context diagram with a single process symbol. Next, the analyst creates diagram 0, which shows more detail. The analyst continues to create lower-level DFDs until all processes are identified as functional primitives, which represent single processing functions. More complex systems have more processes, and analysts must work through many levels to identify the functional primitives. Leveling also is called **exploding, partitioning,** or **decomposing.**

Figure 4-16 and Figure 4-17 on page 162 provide an example of leveling. Figure 4-16 shows diagram 0 for an order system, with the FILL ORDER process labeled as process 1. Now consider Figure 4-17, which is an exploded view of the FILL ORDER process. Notice that FILL ORDER (process 1) actually consists of three processes: VERIFY ORDER (process 1.1), PREPARE REJECT NOTICE (process 1.2), and ASSEMBLE ORDER (process 1.3).

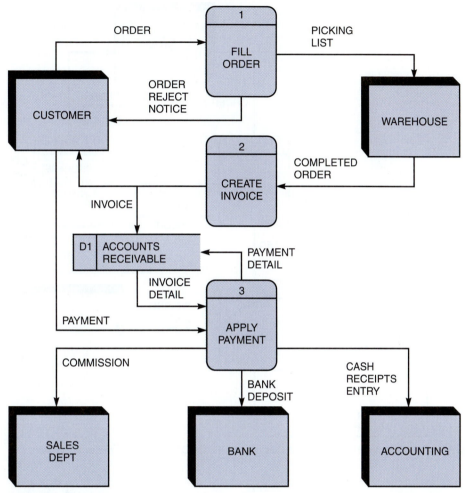

FIGURE 4-16 Diagram 0 DFD for the order system.

As Figure 4-17 shows, all processes are numbered using a decimal notation consisting of the parent's reference number, a decimal point, and a sequence number within the new diagram. In Figure 4-17, the parent process of diagram 1 is process 1, so the processes in diagram 1 have reference numbers of 1.1, 1.2, and 1.3. If process 1.3, ASSEMBLE ORDER, is decomposed further, then it would appear in diagram 1.3 and the processes in diagram 1.3 would be numbered as 1.3.1, 1.3.2, 1.3.3, and so on. This numbering technique makes it easy to integrate and identify all DFDs.

When you compare Figures 4-16 and 4-17, you will notice that Figure 4-17 (the exploded FILL ORDER process) shows two data stores (CUSTOMERS and PRODUCTS) that do not appear on Figure 4-16, which is the parent DFD. Why not? The answer is based on a simple rule: when drawing DFDs, you show a data store only when two or more processes use that data store. The CUSTOMERS and PRODUCTS data stores were internal to the FILL ORDER process, so the analyst did not show them on diagram 0, which is the parent. When you explode the FILL ORDER process into diagram 1 DFD, however, you see that three processes (1.1, 1.2, and 1.3) interact with the two data stores, which now are shown.

Now consider Figure 4-18 on the next page, which shows the same data flows as Figure 4-17, but does not show the CUSTOMER and WAREHOUSE entities. Analysts often use this technique to simplify a DFD and reduce unnecessary clutter. Because the missing symbols appear on the parent DFD, you can refer to that diagram to identify the source or destination of the data flows.

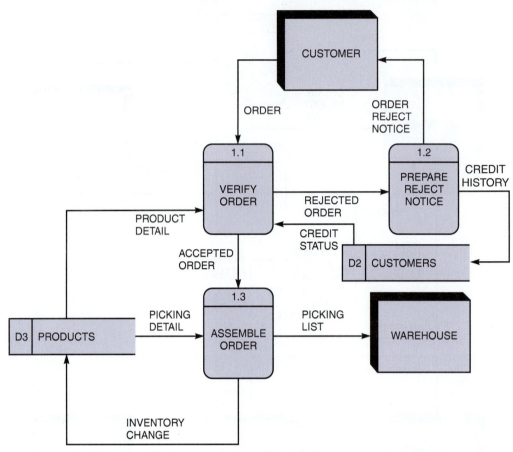

FIGURE 4-17   Diagram 1 DFD shows details of the FILL ORDER process in the order system.

FIGURE 4-18   This diagram does not show the symbols that connect to data flows entering or leaving FILL ORDER on the context diagram.

CASE IN POINT 4.1: Big Ten University

You are the IT director at Big Ten University. As part of a training program, you decide to draw a DFD that includes some obvious mistakes to see whether your newly hired junior analysts can find them. You came up with the diagram 0 DFD shown in Figure 4-19. Based on the rules explained in this chapter, how many problems should the analysts find?

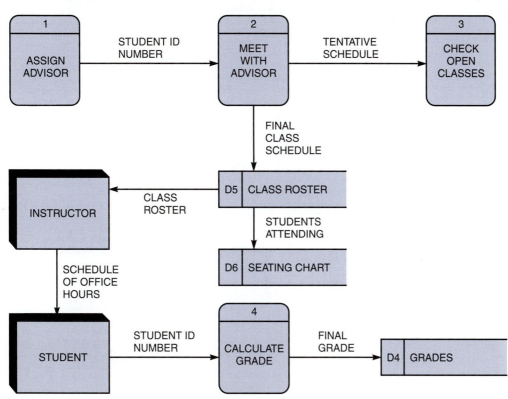

FIGURE 4-19   What are the mistakes in this diagram 0 DFD?

BALANCING   Balancing ensures that the input and output data flows of the parent DFD are maintained on the child DFD. For example, Figure 4-20 shows two DFDs: the order system diagram 0 is shown at the top of the figure, and exploded diagram 3 DFD is shown at the bottom.

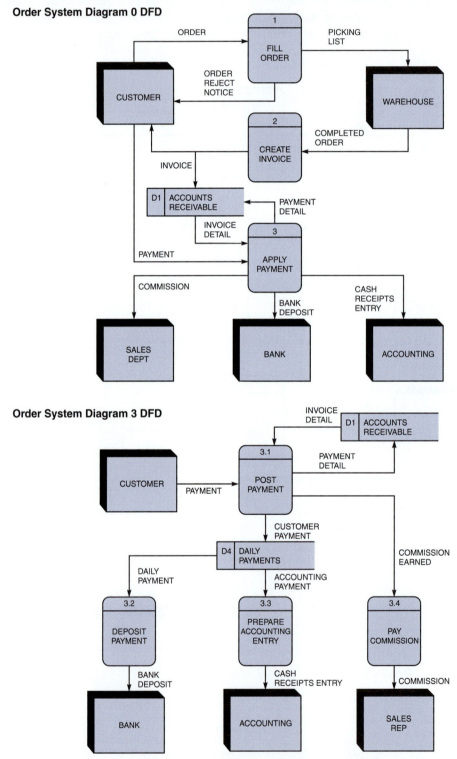

FIGURE 4-20   The order system diagram 0 is shown at the top of the figure, and exploded diagram 3 DFD (for the APPLY PAYMENT process) is shown at the bottom. The two DFDs are balanced, because the child diagram at the bottom has the same input and output flows as the parent process 3 shown at the top.

The two DFDs are balanced, because the child diagram at the bottom has the same input and output flows as the parent process 3 shown at the top. To verify the balancing, notice that the parent process 3, APPLY PAYMENT, has one incoming data flow from an external entity, and three outgoing data flows to external entities. Now examine the child DFD, which is diagram 3. Now, ignore the internal data flows and count the data flows to and from external entities. You will see that the three processes maintain the same one incoming and three outgoing data flows as the parent process.

Another example of balancing is shown in Figures 4-21 and 4-22. The DFDs in these figures were created using Visible Analyst, a popular CASE tool.

Figure 4-21 shows a sample context diagram. The process 0 symbol has two input flows and two output flows. Notice that process 0 can be considered as a black box, with no internal detail shown. In Figure 4-22, process 0 (the parent DFD) is exploded into the next level of detail. Now three processes, two data stores, and four internal data flows are visible. Notice that the details of process 0 are shown inside a dashed line, just as if you could see inside the process.

The DFDs in Figures 4-21 and 4-22 are balanced, because the four data flows into and out of process 0 are maintained on the child DFD. The DFDs also are leveled, because each internal process is numbered to show that it is a child of the parent process.

Now review Figure 4-23 on the next page, which shows diagram 0 for a manufacturing system. Complex manufacturing systems involve many interactive processes and data, as shown in the DFD and the real-life

FIGURE 4-21 Example of a parent DFD diagram, showing process 0 as a black box.

FIGURE 4-22 In the next level of detail, the process 0 black box reveals three processes, two data stores, and four internal data flows — all of which are shown inside the dashed line.

scene shown in Figure 4-24 on the next page. In a large system such as this, each process in diagram 0 can represent an entire system. Using a diagram 0 is just one of dozens of acceptable ways for you to partition a large system into its component systems. As you do so, remember the general rule of thumb that a diagram should have no more than nine process symbols. Figure 4-23 has only four process symbols, so you can imagine how complicated a diagram would be with nine or more processes.

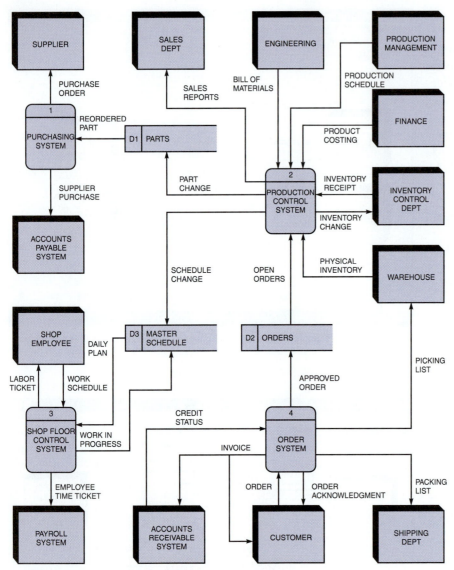

FIGURE 4-23 Diagram 0 for the manufacturing system.

FIGURE 4-24 Complex manufacturing systems require many interactive processes and data sources.

DATA DICTIONARY

A set of DFDs produces a logical model of the system, but the details within those DFDs are documented separately in a data dictionary, which is the second component of structured analysis.

A **data dictionary**, or **data repository**, is a central storehouse of information about the system's data. An analyst uses the data dictionary to collect, document, and organize specific facts about the system, including the contents of data flows, data stores, entities, and processes. The data dictionary also defines and describes all data elements and meaningful combinations of data elements. A **data element**, also called a **data item** or **field**, is the smallest piece of data that has meaning within an information system. Examples of data elements are student grade, salary, Social Security number, account balance, and company name. Data elements are combined into **records**, also called **data structures**. A record is a meaningful combination of related data elements that is included in a data flow or retained in a data store. For example, an auto parts store inventory record might include part number, description, supplier code, minimum and maximum stock levels, cost, and list price.

Figure 4-25 shows a data dictionary and the items that are defined during structured analysis. Significant relationships exist among these items. Notice that the data stores and data flows are based on data structures that are composed of data elements. Data flows are connected to data stores, entities, and processes. Accurately documenting these relationships in a data dictionary is essential so the data dictionary is consistent with the DFDs.

ON THE WEB

For more information about Data Dictionaries, visit **scsite.com/sad6e/ more**, locate Chapter 4 and then click the Data Dictionaries link.

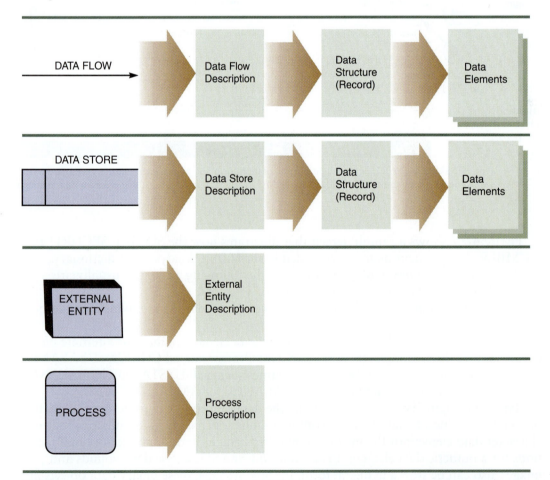

FIGURE 4-25 Contents of the data dictionary, including data flows, data stores, data structures and records, data elements, external entities, and processes.

Documenting the Data Elements

You must document every data element in the data dictionary. Some analysts like to record their notes on online or manual forms. Others prefer to enter the information directly into a CASE tool. Several of the DFDs and data dictionary entries that appear in this chapter were created using a popular CASE tool called Visible Analyst. Although other CASE tools might use other terms or display the information differently, the objective is the same: to provide clear, comprehensive information about the data and processes that make up the system.

Figure 4-26 shows how the analyst used an online documentation form to record information for the SOCIAL SECURITY NUMBER data element. Notice that the figure caption identifies eight specific characteristics for this data element.

1. Online or manual documentation entries often indicate which system is involved. This is not necessary with a CASE tool because all information is stored in one file that is named for the system.
2. The data element has a standard label that provides consistency throughout the data dictionary.
3. The data element can have an alternative name, or alias.
4. This entry indicates that the data element consists of nine numeric characters.
5. Depending on the data element, strict limits might be placed on acceptable values.
6. The data comes from the employee's job application.
7. This entry indicates that only the payroll department has authority to update or change this data.
8. Indicates the individual or department responsible for entering and changing data.

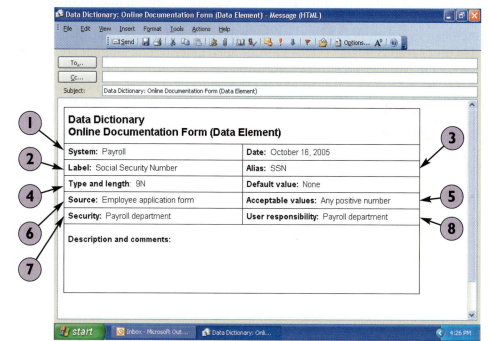

FIGURE 4-26   Using an online documentation form, the analyst has recorded information for a data element named SOCIAL SECURITY NUMBER. Later, the analyst will create a data dictionary entry using a CASE tool.

Figure 4-27 shows a sample screen that illustrates how the SOCIAL SECURITY NUMBER data element might be recorded in the Visible Analyst data dictionary.

Regardless of the terminology or method, the following attributes usually are recorded and described in the data dictionary:

Data element name or label. The data element's standard name, which should be meaningful to users.

Alias. Any name(s) other than the standard data element name; this alternate name is called an **alias.** For example, if you have a data element named CURRENT BALANCE, various users might refer to it by alternate names such as OUTSTANDING BALANCE, CUSTOMER BALANCE, RECEIVABLE BALANCE, or AMOUNT OWED.

Type and length. **Type** refers to whether the data element contains numeric, alphabetic, or character values. **Length** is the maximum number of characters for an alphabetic or character data element or the maximum number of digits and number of decimal positions for a numeric data element. In addition to text and numeric data, sounds and images also can be stored in digital form. In some systems, these binary data objects are

managed and processed just as traditional data elements are. For example, an employee record might include a digitized photo image of the person.

Default value. The value for the data element if a value otherwise is not entered for it. For example, all new customers might have a default value of $500 for the CREDIT LIMIT data element.

Acceptable values. Specification of the data element's **domain**, which is the set of values permitted for the data element; these values either can be specifically listed or referenced in a table, or can be selected from a specified range of values. You also would indicate if a value for the data element is optional. Some data elements have additional **validity rules**. For example, an employee's salary must be within the range defined for the employee's job classification.

Source. The specification for the origination point for the data element's values. The source could be a specific form, a department or outside organization, another information system, or the result of a calculation.

Security. Identification for the individual or department that has access or update privileges for each data element. For example, only a credit manager has the authority to change a credit limit, while sales reps are authorized to access data in a read-only mode.

Responsible user(s). Identification of the user(s) responsible for entering and changing values for the data element.

Description and comments. This part of the documentation allows you to enter additional notes.

FIGURE 4-27 A Visible Analyst screen describes the data element named SOCIAL SECURITY NUMBER. Notice that many of the items were entered from the online form shown in Figure 4-30 on page 171.

Documenting the Data Flows

In addition to documenting each data element, you must document all data flows in the data dictionary. Figure 4-28 on the next page shows a definition for a data flow named COMMISSION. The information on the manual form at the top was entered into the CASE tool data dictionary at the bottom of Figure 4-28.

Although terms can vary, the typical attributes are as follows:

Data flow name or label. The data flow name as it appears on the DFDs.

Description. Describes the data flow and its purpose.

Alternate name(s). Aliases for the DFD data flow name(s).

Origin. The DFD beginning, or source, for the data flow; the origin can be a process, a data store, or an entity.

Destination. The DFD ending point(s) for the data flow; the destination can be a process, a data store, or an entity.

Record. Each data flow represents a group of related data elements called a record or data structure. In most data dictionaries, records are defined separately from the data flows and data stores. When records are defined, more than one data flow or data store can use the same record, if necessary.

Volume and frequency. Describes the expected number of occurrences for the data flow per unit of time. For example, if a company has 300 employees, a TIME CARD data flow would involve 300 transactions and records each week, as employees submit their work hour data.

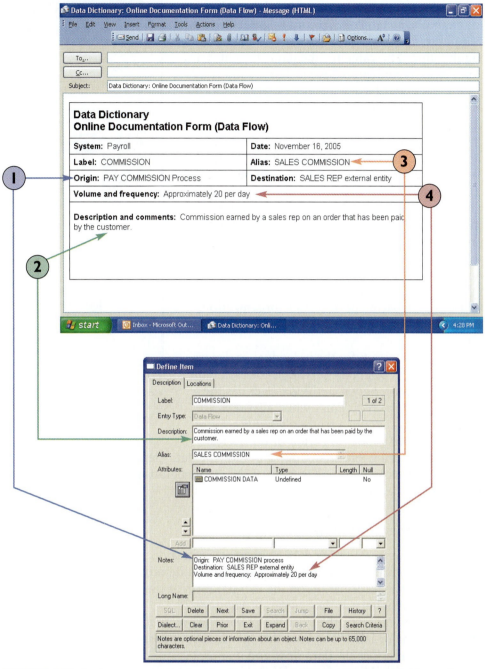

FIGURE 4-28   In the upper screen, an analyst has entered four items of information in an online documentation form. The lower screen shows the same four items entered into a Visible Analyst data dictionary form.

Documenting the Data Stores

You must document every DFD data store in the data dictionary. Figure 4-29 shows the definition of a data store named IN STOCK.

Typical characteristics of a data store are as follows:

Data store name or label. The data store name as it appears on the DFDs.

Description. Describes the data store and its purpose.

Alternate name(s). Aliases for the DFD data store name.

Attributes. Standard DFD names that enter or leave the data store.

Volume and frequency. Describes the estimated number of records in the data store and how frequently they are updated.

Documenting the Processes

You must document every process, as shown in Figure 4-30. Your documentation includes a description of the process's characteristics and, for functional primitives, a process description, which is a model that documents the processing steps and business logic.

Following are typical characteristics of a process:

Process name or label. The process name as it appears on the DFDs.

Description. A brief statement of the process's purpose.

Process number. A reference number that identifies the process and indicates relationships among various levels in the system.

Process description. This section includes the input and output data flows. For functional primitives, the process description also documents the processing steps and business logic. You will learn how to write process descriptions in the next section.

Documenting the Entities

By documenting all entities, the data dictionary can describe all external entities that interact with the system. Figure 4-31 on the next page shows a definition for an external entity named WAREHOUSE.

Typical characteristics of an entity include the following:

Entity name. The entity name as it appears on the DFDs.

Description. Describe the entity and its purpose.

Alternate name(s). Any aliases for the entity name.

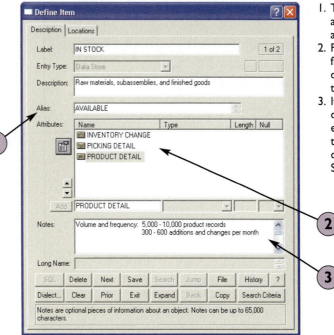

1. This data store has an alternative name, or alias.
2. For consistency, data flow names are standardized throughout the data dictionary.
3. It is important to document these estimates, because they will affect design decisions in subsequent SDLC phases.

FIGURE 4-29   Visible Analyst screen that documents a data store named IN STOCK.

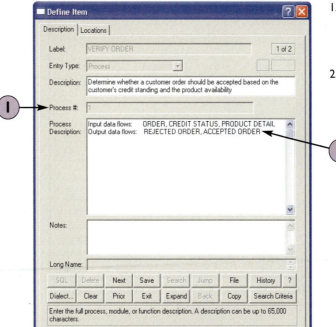

1. The process number identifies this process. Any sub-processes are numbered 1.1, 1.2, 1.3, and so on.
2. These data flows will be described specifically elsewhere in the data dictionary.

FIGURE 4-30   Visible Analyst screen that describes a process named VERIFY ORDER.

1. The external entity also can have an alternative name, or alias, if properly documented.
2. For consistency, these data flow names are standardized throughout the data dictionary.

FIGURE 4-31 Visible Analyst screen that documents an external entity named WAREHOUSE.

1. This data structure is named CREDIT STATUS.
2. The CREDIT STATUS data structure consists of two data elements: CUSTOMER NUMBER and CUSTOMER STATUS CODE.

FIGURE 4-32 Visible Analyst screen that documents a data structure named CREDIT STATUS.

Input data flows. The standard DFD names for the input data flows to the entity.

Output data flows. The standard DFD names for the data flows leaving the entity.

Documenting the Records

A record is a data structure that contains a set of related data elements that are stored and processed together. Data flows and data stores consist of records that you must document in the data dictionary. You define characteristics of each record, as shown in Figure 4-32.

Typical characteristics of a record include the following:

Record or data structure name. The record name as it appears in the related data flow and data store entries in the data dictionary.

Definition or description. A brief definition of the record.

Alternate name(s). Any aliases for the record name.

Attributes. A list of all the data elements included in the record. The data element names must match exactly what you entered in the data dictionary.

Data Dictionary Reports

The data dictionary serves as a central storehouse of documentation for an information system. A data dictionary is created when the system is developed, and is updated constantly as the system is implemented, operated, and maintained. In addition to describing each data element, data flow, data store, record, entity, and process, the data dictionary documents the relationships among these components. You can obtain many valuable reports from a data dictionary, including the following:

➡ An alphabetized list of all data elements by name
➡ A report describing each data element and indicating the user or department that is responsible for data entry, updating, or deletion

➡ A report of all data flows and data stores that use a particular data element

➡ Detailed reports showing all characteristics of data elements, records, data flows, processes, or any other selected item stored in the data dictionary

PROCESS DESCRIPTION TOOLS

A **process description** documents the details of a functional primitive, and represents a specific set of processing steps and business logic. Using a set of process description tools, you create a model that is accurate, complete, and concise. Typical process description tools include structured English, decision tables, and decision trees. When you analyze a functional primitive, you break the processing steps down into smaller units in a process called modular design.

Modular Design

Modular design is based on combinations of three **logical structures**, sometimes called **control structures**, which serve as building blocks for the process. Each logical structure must have a single entry and exit point. The three structures are called sequence, selection, and iteration. A rectangle represents a step or process, a diamond shape represents a condition or decision, and the logic follows the lines in the direction indicated by the arrows.

1. **Sequence.** The completion of steps in sequential order, one after another, as shown in Figure 4-33. One or more of the steps might represent a subprocess that contains additional logical structures.

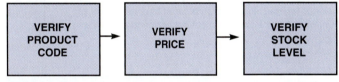

FIGURE 4-33 Sequence structure.

2. **Selection.** The completion of one of two or more process steps based on the results of a test or condition. In the example shown in Figure 4-34, the system tests the input, and if the hours are greater than 40, it performs the CALCULATE OVERTIME PAY process.

3. **Iteration.** The completion of a process step that is repeated until a specific condition changes, as shown in Figure 4-35. An example of iteration is a process that continues to print paychecks until it reaches the end of the payroll file. Iteration also is called **looping**.

Sequence, selection, and iteration structures can be combined in various ways to describe processing logic.

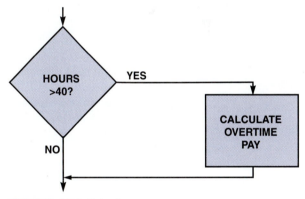

FIGURE 4-34 Selection structure.

Structured English

Structured English is a subset of standard English that describes logical processes clearly and accurately. When you use structured English, you must conform to the following rules:

➡ Use only the three building blocks of sequence, selection, and iteration

➡ Use indentation for readability

FIGURE 4-35 Iteration structure.

FIGURE 4-36 The VERIFY ORDER process description includes logical rules and a structured English version of the policy. Notice the alignment and indentation of the logic statements.

➡ Use a limited vocabulary, including standard terms used in the data dictionary and specific words that describe the processing rules

An example of structured English appears in Figure 4-36, which shows the VERIFY ORDER process that was illustrated earlier. In Figure 4-36, structured English was added to describe the processing logic.

Structured English might look familiar to programming students because it resembles **pseudocode**, which is used in program design. Although the techniques are similar, the primary purpose of structured English is to describe the underlying business logic, while programmers, who are concerned with coding, mainly use pseudocode as a shorthand notation for the actual code.

Figure 4-37 shows another example of structured English. After you study the sales promotion policy, notice that the structured English version describes the processing logic that the system must apply. Following these structured English rules ensures that your process descriptions are understandable to users who must confirm that the process is correct, as well as to other analysts and programmers who must design the information system from your descriptions.

ON THE WEB

For more information about Structured English, visit **scsite.com/sad6e/more**, locate Chapter 4 and then click the Structured English link.

SAMPLE OF A SALES PROMOTION POLICY:

- Preferred customers who order more than $1,000 are entitled to a 5% discount, and an additional 5% discount if they used our charge card.

- Preferred customers who do not order more than $1,000 receive a $25 bonus coupon.

- All other customers receive a $5 bonus coupon.

STRUCTURED ENGLISH VERSION OF THE SALES PROMOTION POLICY:

```
IF customer is a preferred customer, and
        IF customer orders more than $1,000 then
                Apply a 5% discount, and
                        IF customer uses our charge card, then
                                Apply an additional 5% discount
        ELSE
                        Award a $25 bonus coupon
ELSE
        Award a $5 bonus coupon
```

FIGURE 4-37 Sample of a policy with logical rules, and a structured English version of the policy. Notice the alignment and indentation of the logic statements.

Decision Tables

A **decision table** shows a logical structure, with all possible combinations of conditions and resulting actions. Analysts often use decision tables, in addition to structured English, to describe a logical process and ensure that they have not overlooked any logical possibility.

A simple example of a decision table is based on the VERIFY ORDER process shown in Figure 4-38. When documenting a process, it is important to consider every possible outcome to ensure that you have overlooked nothing. From the structured English description shown in Figure 4-38, we know that an accepted order requires that credit status is OK and the product is in stock. Otherwise, the order is rejected. The decision table shown in Figure 4-38 shows all the possibilities. To create the decision table, follow the steps indicated in the figure.

1. Place the name of the process in a heading at the top left.
2. Enter the conditions under the heading, with one condition per line, to represent the customer status and availability of products.
3. Enter all potential combinations of Y/N (for yes and no) for the conditions. Each column represents a numbered possibility called a rule.
4. Place an X in the action entries area for each rule to indicate whether to accept or reject the order.

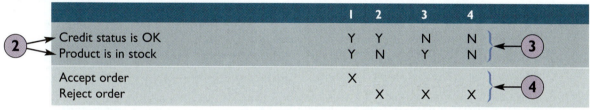

FIGURE 4-38 Example of a simple decision table showing the processing logic of the VERIFY ORDER process.

Because each condition has two possible values, the number of rules doubles each time you add a condition. For example, one condition creates only two rules, two conditions create four rules, three conditions create eight rules, and so on. As shown in Figure 4-39 on the next page, four possible combinations exist, but only one rule — rule 1 — permits an accepted order output.

The first table in Figure 4-39 shows eight rules. Because some rules are duplicates, however, the table can be simplified. To reduce the number of rules, you must look closely at each combination of conditions and actions. If you have rules with three conditions, only one or two of them may control the outcome, and the other conditions do not matter. You can indicate that with dashes (-) as shown in the second table in Figure 4-39. Then you can combine and renumber the rules, as shown in the final table.

In the example, rules 1 and 2 can be combined because credit status is OK, and the waiver is not needed. Rules 3, 4, 7, and 8 also can be combined because the product is not in stock, and credit status does not matter. The result is that instead of eight possibilities, only four logical rules are created that control the VERIFY ORDER process.

In addition to multiple conditions, decision tables can have more than two possible outcomes. An example is presented in the SALES PROMOTION POLICY decision table shown in Figure 4-40 on the next page. The decision table shown here is based on the sales promotion policy described in Figure 4-37. Here three conditions exist: was the customer a preferred customer, did the customer order more than $1,000, and did the customer use our charge card? Based on these three conditions, four possible actions can occur, as shown in the table.

Decision tables often are the best way to describe a complex set of conditions. Many analysts use decision tables because they are easy to construct and understand, and programmers find it easy to work from a decision table when developing code.

ON THE WEB

For more information about Decision Tables, visit **scsite.com/ sad6e/more**, locate Chapter 4 and then click the Decision Tables link.

VERIFY ORDER Process with Credit Waiver (Initial version)

	1	2	3	4	5	6	7	8
Credit status is OK	Y	Y	Y	Y	N	N	N	N
Product is in stock	Y	Y	N	N	Y	Y	N	N
Waiver from credit manager	Y	N	Y	N	Y	N	Y	N
Accept order	X	X			X			
Reject order			X	X		X	X	X

VERIFY ORDER Process with Credit Waiver (With rules marked for combination)

1. Because the product is not in stock, the other conditions do not matter.
2. Because the other conditions are met, the waiver does not matter.

	1	2	3	4	5	6	7	8
Credit status is OK	Y	Y	-	-	N	N	-	-
Product is in stock	Y	Y	N	N	Y	Y	N	N
Waiver from credit manager	-	-	-	-	Y	N	-	-
Accept order	X	X			X			
Reject order			X	X		X	X	X

VERIFY ORDER Process with Credit Waiver (After rule combination and simplification)

	1 (COMBINES PREVIOUS 1, 2)	2 (PREVIOUS 5)	3 (PREVIOUS 6)	4 (COMBINES PREVIOUS 3, 4, 7, 8)
Credit status is OK	Y	N	N	-
Product is in stock	Y	Y	Y	N
Waiver from credit manager	-	Y	N	-
Accept order	X	X		
Reject order			X	X

FIGURE 4-39 A more complex situation is presented in Figure 4-39. In the example, the credit manager can waive the credit status requirement in certain situations. To ensure that all possibilities are covered, notice that the first condition provides an equal number of Ys and Ns, the second condition alternates Y and N pairs, and the third condition alternates single Ys and Ns.

Sales Promotion Policy (Initial version)

	1	2	3	4	5	6	7	8
Preferred customer	Y	Y	Y	Y	N	N	N	N
Ordered more than $1,000	Y	Y	N	N	Y	Y	N	N
Used our charge card	Y	N	Y	N	Y	N	Y	N
5% discount	X	X						
Additional 5% discount	X							
$25 bonus coupon			X					
$5 bonus coupon				X	X	X	X	X

FIGURE 4-40 Sample decision table based on the sales promotion policy described in Figure 4-37 on page 174. This is the initial version of the table, before simplification.

CASE IN POINT 4.2: ROCK SOLID OUTFITTERS (PART 1)

Leah Jones is the IT manager at Rock Solid Outfitters, a medium-sized supplier of outdoor climbing and camping gear. Steve Allen, the marketing director, has asked Leah to develop a special Web-based promotion. As Steve described it to Leah, Rock Solid will provide free shipping for any customer who either completes an online survey form or signs up for the Rock Solid online newsletter. Additionally, if a customer completes the survey *and* signs up for the newsletter, Rock Solid will provide a $10 merchandise credit for orders over $100. Leah has asked you to develop a decision table that will reflect the promotional rules that a programmer will use. She wants you to show all possibilities, then to simplify the results to eliminate any combinations that would be unrealistic or redundant.

Decision Trees

A **decision tree** is a graphical representation of the conditions, actions, and rules found in a decision table. Decision trees show the logic structure in a horizontal form that resembles a tree with the roots at the left and the branches to the right. Like flowcharts, decision trees are useful ways to present the system to management. Decision trees and decision tables provide the same results, but in different forms. In many situations, a graphic is the most effective means of communication, as shown in Figure 4-41.

Figure 4-42 shows the same SALES PROMOTION POLICY conditions and actions shown in Figure 4-40. A decision tree is read from left to right, with the conditions along the various branches and the actions at the far right. Because the example has two conditions with four resulting sets of actions, the example has four terminating branches at the right side of the tree.

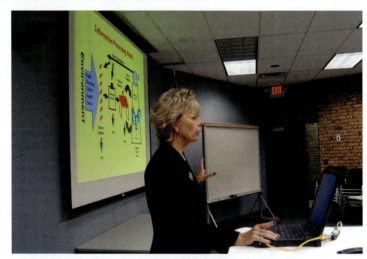

FIGURE 4-41 Analysts and managers often use graphical representations to show the process under consideration.

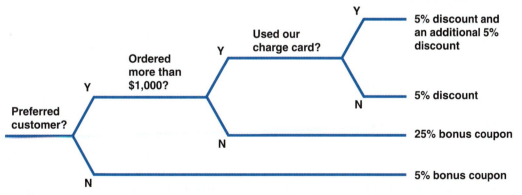

FIGURE 4-42 Sample decision tree. Like a decision table, a decision tree illustrates the action to be taken based on certain conditions, but presents it graphically. This decision tree is based on the sales promotion policy described in Figures 4-37 and 4-40 on pages 174 and 176.

Whether to use a decision table or a decision tree often is a matter of personal preference. A decision table might be a better way to handle complex combinations of conditions. On the other hand, a decision tree is an effective way to describe a relatively simple process.

CASE IN POINT 4.3: ROCK SOLID OUTFITTERS (PART 2)

Leah Jones, the IT manager at Rock Solid Outfitters, thinks you did a good job on the decision table task she assigned to you. Now she wants you to use the same data to develop a decision tree that will show all the possibilities for the Web-based promotion described in Part 1 of the case. She also wants you to discuss the pros and cons of decisions tables versus decision trees.

LOGICAL VERSUS PHYSICAL MODELS

While structured analysis tools are used to develop a logical model for a new information system, such tools also can be used to develop physical models of an information system. A physical model shows how the system's requirements are implemented. During the systems design phase, you create a physical model of the new information system that follows from the logical model and involves operational tasks and techniques.

Sequence of Models

What is the relationship between logical and physical models? Think back to the beginning of the systems analysis phase, when you were trying to understand the existing system. Rather than starting with a logical model, you first studied the physical operations of the existing system to understand how the current tasks were carried out. Many systems analysts create a physical model of the current system and then develop a logical model of the current system before tackling a logical model of the new system. Performing that extra step allows them to understand the current system better.

Four-Model Approach

Many analysts follow a **four-model approach,** which means that they develop a physical model of the current system, a logical model of the current system, a logical model of the new system, and a physical model of the new system. The major benefit of the four-model approach is that it gives you a clear picture of current system functions before you make any modifications or improvements. That is important because mistakes made early in systems development will affect later SDLC phases and can result in unhappy users and additional costs. Taking additional steps to avoid these potentially costly mistakes can prove to be well worth the effort. Another advantage is that the requirements of a new information system often are quite similar to those of the current information system, especially where the proposal is based on new computer technology rather than a large number of new requirements. Adapting the current system logical model to the new system logical model in these cases is a straightforward process.

The only disadvantage of the four-model approach is the added time and cost needed to develop a logical and physical model of the current system. Most projects have very tight schedules that might not allow time to create the current system models. Additionally, users and managers want to see progress on the new system — they are much less concerned about documenting the current system. As a systems analyst, you must stress the importance of careful documentation and resist the pressure to hurry the development process at the risk of creating serious problems later.

CASE IN POINT 4.4: TIP TOP STAFFING

Tip Top Staffing supplies employees to hundreds of IT firms that require specialized skills for specific projects. Systems analysts Lisa Nuevo and Bill Goodman are working on the logical model of Tip Top's billing and records system, using DFDs, a data dictionary, and process descriptions. At some point while working on the logical model of the system, Lisa felt that some improvements should be made in the data forms that Tip Top uses to obtain information about job applicants. Was the subject of improving the forms a physical implementation issue? Is Lisa going off on a tangent by considering how something will be done, instead of sticking to what will be done?

CHAPTER SUMMARY

During data and process modeling, a systems analyst develops graphical models to show how the system transforms data into useful information. The end product of data and process modeling is a logical model that will support business operations and meet user needs. Data and process modeling involves three main tools: data flow diagrams, a data dictionary, and process descriptions.

Data flow diagrams (DFDs) graphically show the movement and transformation of data in the information system. DFDs use four symbols: the process symbol transforms data; the data flow symbol shows data movement; the data store symbol shows data at rest; and the external entity symbol represents someone or something connected to the information system. Various rules and techniques are used to name, number, arrange, and annotate the set of DFDs to make them consistent and understandable.

A set of DFDs is like a pyramid with the context diagram at the top. The context diagram represents the information system's scope and its external connections but not its internal workings. Diagram 0 displays the information system's major processes, data stores, and data flows and is the exploded version of the context diagram's process symbol, which represents the entire information system. Lower-level DFDs show additional detail of the information system through the leveling technique of numbering and partitioning. Leveling continues until you reach the functional primitive processes, which are not decomposed further and are documented with process descriptions. All diagrams must be balanced to ensure their consistency and accuracy.

The data dictionary is the central documentation tool for structured analysis. All data elements, data flows, data stores, processes, entities, and records are documented in the data dictionary. Consolidating documentation in one location allows you to verify the information system's accuracy and consistency more easily and generate a variety of useful reports.

Each functional primitive process is documented using structured English, decision tables, and decision trees. Structured English uses a subset of standard English that defines each process with combinations of the basic building blocks of sequence, selection, and iteration. You also can document the logic by using decision tables or decision trees.

Structured analysis tools can be used to develop a logical model during one systems analysis phase, and a physical model during the systems design phase. Many analysts use a four-model approach, which involves a physical model of the current system, a logical model of the current system, a logical model of the new system, and a physical model of the new system.

Key Terms and Phrases

alias *168*

balancing *160*

black box *149*

black hole *150*

business logic *148*

business rules *148*

child diagram *158*

context diagram *155*

control structures *173*

data dictionary *167*

data element *167*

data flow *149*

data flow diagram (DFD) *148*

data item *167*

data repository *167*

data store *151*

data structures *167*

decision table *175*

decision tree *177*

decomposing *160*

diagram 0 *158*

diverging data flow *158*

domain *169*

entity *153*

exploding *160*

field *167*

four-model approach *178*

functional primitive *159*

Gane and Sarson *148*

gray hole *151*

iteration *173*

length *168*

leveling *160*

logical model *146*

logical structures *173*

looping *173*

modular design *173*

parent diagram *158*

partitioning *160*

physical model *146*

process *148*

process description *173*

pseudocode *174*

records *167*

selection *173*

sequence *173*

sink *153*

source *153*

spontaneous generation *150*

structured English *173*

terminators *153*

type *168*

validity rules *169*

Yourdon *148*

Learn It Online

Instructions: To complete the Learn It Online exercises, start your browser, click the Address bar, and then enter the Web address **scsite.com/sad6e/learn**. When the Systems Analysis and Design Learn It Online page is displayed, follow the instructions in the exercises below. Each exercise has instructions for saving your results, either for your own records or for submission to your instructor.

1   Chapter Reinforcement

TF, MC, and SA

Below SAD Chapter 4, click the Chapter Reinforcement link. Print the quiz by clicking Print on the File menu for each page. Answer each question.

2   Flash Cards

Below SAD Chapter 4, click the Flash Cards link and read the instructions. Type 20 (or a number specified by your instructor) in the Number of playing cards text box, type your name in the Enter your Name text box, and then click the Flip Card button. When the flash card is displayed, read the question and then click the ANSWER box arrow to select an answer. Flip through the Flash Cards. If your score is 15 (75%) correct or greater, click Print on the File menu to print your results. If your score is less than 15 (75%) correct, then redo this exercise by clicking the Replay button.

3   Practice Test

Below SAD Chapter 4, click the Practice Test link. Answer each question, enter your first and last name at the bottom of the page, and then click the Grade Test button. When the graded practice test is displayed on your screen, click Print on the File menu to print a hard copy. Continue to take practice tests until you score 80% or better.

4   Who Wants To Be a Computer Genius?

Below SAD Chapter 4, click the Computer Genius link. Read the instructions, enter your first and last name at the bottom of the page, and then click the Play button. When your score is displayed, click the PRINT RESULTS link to print a hard copy.

5   Wheel of Terms

Below SAD Chapter 4, click the Wheel of Terms link. Read the instructions, and then enter your first and last name and your school name. Click the PLAY button. When your score is displayed on the screen, right-click the score and then click Print on the shortcut menu to print a hard copy.

6   Crossword Puzzle Challenge

Below SAD Chapter 4, click the Crossword Puzzle Challenge link. Read the instructions, and then enter your first and last name. Click the SUBMIT button. Work the crossword puzzle. When you are finished, click the Submit button. When the crossword puzzle is redisplayed, click the Print Puzzle button to print a hard copy.

Case-Sim: SCR Associates

Background

SCR Associates is a consulting firm that offers IT solutions and training. SCR needs an information system to manage operations at its new training center. The new system will be called TIMS (Training Information Management System). As a newly hired systems analyst, you will report to Jesse Baker, systems group man-

ager. You will work on various tasks and practice the skills you learned in this chapter.

Using the Case

The SCR Associates case study is a Web-based simulation that allows you to practice your skills in a real-world environment. The case study transports you to SCR's company intranet, where you can complete 10 work sessions, each aligning with a chapter. As you work on the case, you will receive e-mail and voice mail, obtain information from SCR's online libraries, and perform various tasks. The first time you enter the SCR Case, you should go to the Starting page at **scsite.com/sad6e/scr** for detailed instructions.

Preview: Session 4

You recently completed requirements modeling tasks for the new training information management system (TIMS). Now you are ready to begin data and process modeling, which will produce a logical model of the new system. You will create DFDs, develop a data dictionary, and use decision tables and trees.

To start a work session, you log on to the SCR intranet. When you enter your name and password, an opening screen displays links to the work sessions, and you select Session 4. At this point, you check your e-mail and voice mail messages carefully. Then you begin working on your task list, which includes the following items:

Tasks: Data and Process Modeling

1. *Jesse wants to see a context diagram and a diagram 0 DFD for TIMS.*

2. *Need to review the JAD session summary again! Try to identify four main TIMS functions and draw a lower-level DFD for each process.*

3. *Prepare a reply to Jesse's message about CASE tools. Search the Internet to find two more alternatives.*

4. *Prepare a decision table and a decision tree that show the logical rules described in Jesse's message about fees and discounts.*

FIGURE 4-43   Task list: Session 4.

Chapter Exercises

Review Questions

1. Describe data and process modeling, and name the main data and process modeling techniques.
2. Describe the Gane and Sarson symbols used for processes, data flows, data stores, and entities. Give four examples of typical names for processes, data flows, data stores, and entities.
3. What is the relationship between a context diagram and diagram 0, and which symbol is not used in a context diagram?
4. What is meant by an exploded DFD?
5. Describe a data dictionary and give examples of how and when it is used.
6. Explain the DFD leveling technique.
7. What is a balanced DFD?
8. Describe the steps in creating a decision table.
9. Discuss the pros and cons of decision tables versus decision trees.
10. What is structured English?

Discussion Topics

1. Suppose you were assigned to develop a logical model of the registration system at a school or college. Would you be better off using a top-down approach, or would a bottom-up strategy be better? What would influence your decision?
2. Some systems analysts find it better to start with a decision table, then construct a decision tree. Others believe it is easier to do it in the reverse order. Which do you prefer? Why?
3. A systems analyst attended a week-long workshop on structured analysis. When she returned to her job, she told her boss that structured analysis was not worth the time to learn and use on the job. Her view was that it was too academic and had too much new terminology to be useful in a practical setting. Do you agree or disagree? Defend your position.
4. This chapter describes a black box concept that allows more detail to be shown as a process is exploded. Can the concept be applied in business management generally, or is it limited to information systems design? Provide reasons and examples with your answer.

Projects

1. Draw a context diagram and a diagram 0 DFD that represent the registration system at your school or an imaginary school.
2. On the Internet, locate at least three firms that offer CASE tools. Write e-mail messages to the companies to find out whether they offer demonstration copies or student versions of their products.
3. Suppose that you want to demonstrate a decision table to someone who has never seen one. Think of an example, with two or three conditions, from everyday life. Draw a decision table that captures all possible outcomes.
4. The Yourdon data flow symbols shown on page 149 were designed by Ed Yourdon, a well-known IT author, lecturer, and consultant. Many IT professionals consider him to be one of the most influential men and women in the software field. Learn more about Mr. Yourdon by visiting his Web site at www.yourdon.com, and write a brief review of his accomplishments.

Apply Your Knowledge

The Apply Your Knowledge section contains four mini-cases. Each case describes a situation, explains your role in the case, and asks you to respond to questions. You can answer the questions by applying knowledge you learned in the chapter.

Digital Consulting

Situation:

You are a senior systems analyst at Digital Consulting, a growing IT consulting firm. You are leading the development team for a major client. You need to explain structured analysis to your two newly hired junior analysts (Sara and Mike) before meeting with the client tomorrow afternoon.

1. Describe the rules for creating a context diagram.
2. Make a basic list of dos and don'ts when developing DFDs.
3. Explain the importance of leveling and balancing.
4. Ask Sara and Mike to review the order system context diagram on page 156, and compare it to the order system diagram 0 DFD on page 161. Then ask them to answer the following questions: (a) How many external entities are shown in each diagram? (b) In each diagram, how many data flows connect to the external entities? (c) How many sub-processes are identified in the diagram 0 DFD? (d) Could the data store have been shown in the context diagram? Why or why not?

2 Precision Tools

Situation:

Precision Tools sells a line of high-quality woodworking tools. When customers place orders on the company's Web site, the system checks to see if the items are in stock, issues a status message to the customer, and generates a shipping order to the warehouse, which fills the order. When the order is shipped, the customer is billed. The system also produces various reports.

1. Draw a context diagram for the order system.
2. Draw a diagram 0 DFD for the order system.
3. Name four attributes that you can use to define a process in the order system.
4. Name four attributes that you can use to define an entity in the order system.

3 Claremont School

Situation:

The Claremont School course catalog reads as follows: "To enroll in CIS 288, which is an advanced course, a student must complete two prerequisites — CIS 110 and CIS 286. A student who completes either one of these prerequisites and obtains the instructor's permission, however, will be allowed to take CIS 288."

1. Create a decision table that describes the Claremont School course catalog regarding eligibility for CIS 288. Show all possible rules.
2. Simplify the table you just created. Describe the results.
3. Draw a simplified decision tree to represent the Claremont School catalog. Describe the results.
4. Why might you use a decision tree rather than a decision table?

4 City Bus Lines

Situation:

City Bus Lines is developing an information system that will monitor passenger traffic, peak travel hours, and equipment requirements. The IT manager wants you to document a process called BALANCE that determines whether extra buses currently are needed on a particular route. The BALANCE process automatically assigns additional buses to that route, but *only* if all other routes are operating on schedule. In any case, a supervisor can override the automatic BALANCE process if he or she so desires.

1. Create a decision table that describes the bus transfer process.
2. Draw a decision tree that describes the bus transfer process.
3. Name four attributes that you can use to define a data flow in the bus information system.
4. Name four attributes that you can use to define a data store in the bus information system.

Case Studies

Case studies allow you to practice specific skills learned in the chapter. Each chapter contains several case studies that continue throughout the textbook, and a chapter capstone case.

NEW CENTURY HEALTH CLINIC

New Century Health Clinic offers preventive medicine and traditional medical care. In your role as an IT consultant, you will help New Century develop a new information system.

Background

You began the systems analysis phase at New Century Health Clinic by completing a series of interviews, reviewing existing reports, and observing office operations. (Your instructor may provide you with a sample set of interview summaries.)

As you learned, the doctors, nurses, and physical therapists provide services and perform various medical procedures. All procedures are coded according to Current Procedure Terminology, which is published by the American Medical Association. The procedure codes consist of five numeric digits and a two-digit suffix, and are used for all billing and insurance claims.

From your fact-finding, you determined that seven reports are required at the clinic. The first report is the daily appointment list for each provider. The list shows all scheduled appointment times, patient names, and services to be performed, including the procedure code and description. A second daily report is the call list, which shows the patients who are to be reminded of their next day's appointments. The call list includes the patient name, telephone number, appointment time, and provider name. The third report is the weekly provider report that lists each of the providers and the weekly charges generated, plus a month-to-date (MTD) and a year-to-date (YTD) summary.

The fourth report is the statement — a preprinted form that is produced monthly and mailed in a window envelope. Statement header information includes the statement date, head of household name and address, the previous month's balance, the total household charges MTD, the total payments MTD, and the current balance. The bottom section of the statement lists all activity for the month in date order. For each service performed, a line shows the patient's name, the service date, the procedure code and description, and the charge. The statement also shows the date and amount of all payments and insurance claims. When an insurance payment is received, the source and amount are noted on the form. If the claim is denied or only partially paid, a code is used to explain the reason. A running balance appears at the far right of each activity line.

The associates also require two insurance reports: the weekly Insurance Company Report and the monthly Claim Status Summary. In addition to these six reports, the office staff would like to have mailing labels and computer-generated postcards for sending reminders to patients when it is time to schedule their next appointment. Reminders usually are mailed twice monthly. Now you are ready to organize the facts you gathered and prepare a system requirements document that represents a logical model of the proposed system. Your tools will include DFDs, a data dictionary, and process descriptions.

Assignments

1. Prepare a context diagram for New Century's information system.
2. Prepare a diagram 0 DFD for New Century. Be sure to show numbered processes for handling appointment processing, payment and insurance processing, report processing, and records maintenance. Also, prepare lower-level DFDs for each numbered process.

3. Prepare a list of data stores and data flows needed for the system. Under each data store, list the data elements required.

4. Prepare a data dictionary entry and process description for one of the system's functional primitives.

PERSONAL TRAINER, INC.

Personal Trainer, Inc., owns and operates fitness centers in a dozen midwestern cities. The centers have done well, and the company is planning an international expansion by opening a new "supercenter" in the Toronto area. Personal Trainer's president, Cassia Umi, hired an IT consultant, Susan Park, to help develop an information system for the new facility. During the project, Susan will work closely with Gray Lewis, who will manage the new operation.

Background

Susan Park has completed a preliminary investigation and performed the fact-finding tasks that were described in Chapters 2 and 3. Now, she will use the results to develop a logical model of the proposed information system.

Assignments

Before you perform the following tasks, you should review the information provided in Chapters 2 and 3 of the case.

1. Prepare a context diagram for the new system.
2. Prepare a diagram 0 DFD for the new system.
3. Write a brief memo that explains the importance of leveling a set of DFDs.
4. Write a brief memo that explains the importance of balancing a set of DFDs.

SoftWear, Limited (SWL), is a continuing case study that illustrates the knowledge and skills described in each chapter. In this case study, the student acts as a member of the SWL systems development team and performs various tasks.

Background

Rick Williams, a systems analyst, and Carla Moore, a programmer/analyst, continued their work on the SWL payroll system project. After completing detailed interviews and other fact-finding activities, Rick and Carla now understand how the current system operates and the new requirements desired by users. They are ready to organize and document their findings by preparing a logical model of the payroll system.

Data Flow Diagrams

After they completed the ERD, Rick and Carla felt that they knew more about the entities and how they interacted. Their next task was to prepare an initial version of the context diagram shown in Figure 4-44.

FIGURE 4-44 Initial version of context diagram for SoftWear, Limited's payroll system.

The two analysts knew that the payroll department issues paychecks based on timesheet data submitted by department heads, and that each employee receives a W-2 form at the end of the year. They knew that the human resources department prepares employee status changes, and the payroll department enters the pay data. The diagram also noted the output of state and federal government reports and internal reports to SWL's finance and payroll departments. The credit union and the SWL stock transfer department reports and fund transfers also were included.

Rick and Carla scheduled a meeting for the next day with Amy Calico, director of the payroll department, to discuss the context diagram. At the meeting, Amy made several comments:

➡ The human resources department would be setting up additional ESIP deduction choices for employees under a new 401(k) plan. Human resources also would receive ESIP reports from the payroll system.

➡ The payroll department enters timesheet data received from department heads, who do not interact directly with the system. Rather than showing the department head entity symbol on the context diagram, the input data flow from the payroll department should be expanded and called PAY DETAIL.

➡ State and federal reporting requirements differ, so they should be treated as two separate entities. Also, periodic changes in government tax rates should be shown as inputs to the payroll system.

➡ All accounting reports, except for an overall financial summary, should be distributed to the accounting department instead of to the finance department. The accounting department also should receive a copy of the payroll report.

➡ The bank returns cleared payroll checks to the payroll department once a month. Amy reminded the analysts that the payroll system handles the reconciliation of payroll checks.

After discussing Amy's comments, Rick and Carla prepared the final version of the payroll system context diagram shown in Figure 4-45 on the next page with the suggested changes.

While their conversation with Amy Calico still was fresh in her mind, Carla proposed that they construct the diagram 0 DFD. After going through several draft versions, they completed the diagram 0 shown in Figure 4-46 on page 191. They identified four processes: the check reconciliation subsystem, the pay employee subsystem, the payroll accounting subsystem, and a subsystem that would handle all voluntary deductions, which they called the ESIP deduction subsystem.

Over the next few days, Rick concentrated on partitioning the pay employee subsystem and the ESIP subsystem, while Carla developed the lower-level diagrams for the other two subsystems.

At that point, Rick considered the problem of applying certain deductions on a monthly cycle, even though the deductions were made weekly. To provide flexibility, he decided to use two separate processes, as shown in Figure 4-47 on page 192. When he finished, his diagram 4 DFD contained the two processes EXTRACT DEDUCTION and APPLY DEDUCTION, as well as a local data store, UNAPPLIED DEDUCTIONS. Several local data flows also were included. The first process, EXTRACT DEDUCTION, would deduct the proper amount in each pay period. The deductions would be held in the temporary data store and then applied in the APPLY DEDUCTION process on a weekly or monthly basis, depending on the type of deduction. Rick decided that those processes were functional primitives and he did not need to partition them further. That task completed the logical model of the new SWL payroll system.

Rick and Carla also considered the physical design of the ESIP deduction subsystem that would be completed later. They knew that it would be necessary to add some new forms and to redesign others. They saw that the human resources department would need a new form for enrollments or deduction changes for the credit union, SWL stock purchase plan, or any new ESIP choices that might be offered in the future. The payroll department then could use the form as its official notification. To provide for future expansion and add flexibility, the human resources department also would need a form to notify payroll of any new

CHAPTER CAPSTONE CASE: SoftWear, Limited (continued)   SWL

FIGURE 4-45 Final context diagram for SoftWear, Limited's payroll system.

type of deduction, with a deduction code, the name of the deduction, and the payroll cycle involved. Rick anticipated that the new system would eliminate problems with improper deductions, while adding flexibility and reducing maintenance costs.

FIGURE 4-46 Diagram 0 DFD for SoftWear, Limited's payroll system.

Data Dictionary and Process Descriptions

As they constructed the DFDs for the payroll system, Rick and Carla also developed the data dictionary entries with supporting process descriptions.

CHAPTER CAPSTONE CASE: SoftWear, Limited (continued)

FIGURE 4-47   Diagram 4 DFD for SoftWear, Limited's payroll system shows the detail of process 4, the ESIP DEDUCTION SUBSYSTEM.

Using the Visible Analyst CASE tool, Rick documented the PROCESS 4 ESIP deduction subsystem shown in Figure 4-48. Then he defined the data flow called ESIP REPORT that originates in the APPLY DEDUCTION process and connects to the HUMAN RESOURCES entity, as shown in Figure 4-49. He also documented the ESIP OPTIONS data structure shown in Figure 4-50, which consists of eight data elements, six of which are visible in the figure.

FIGURE 4-48 Data dictionary definition for process 4, the ESIP DEDUCTION SUBSYSTEM.

FIGURE 4-49 Data dictionary definition for the ESIP REPORT data flow.

FIGURE 4-50 Data dictionary definition for the ESIP OPTIONS data structure.

Carla prepared the process description for EXTRACT DEDUCTION as shown in Figure 4-51. Notice that she numbered the process 4.1, because it was exploded from process 4. The two analysts also completed the descriptions for the data element EXTRACTED DEDUCTION as shown in Figure 4-52, and the ESIP ID CODE as shown in Figure 4-53. They spent the next two days documenting the rest of the data flows and entities for the ESIP deduction subsystem, along with data elements and records.

FIGURE 4-51 Data dictionary definition for process 4.1, EXTRACT DEDUCTION.

FIGURE 4-52 Data dictionary definition for the data element EXTRACTED DEDUCTION.

FIGURE 4-53 Data dictionary definition for the data element ESIP ID CODE.

CHAPTER CAPSTONE CASE: SoftWear, Limited (continued) SWL

After completing the documentation of the ESIP deduction subsystem, Carla and Rick met with Amy to review the logical model for the subsystem. After a thorough discussion of all proposed changes and processing, Amy approved the model.

Rick and Carla continued their analysis and documentation of the payroll system over the next several days. As they completed a model of a portion of the information system, they would meet with the appropriate users at SWL to review the model, obtain user input, make necessary adjustments to the model, and obtain the users' approval. After Rick and Carla finished the complete payroll information system logical model, they turned their attention to completing the rest of the system requirements document.

SWL Team Tasks

Suppose that you are working with Rick and Carla when a new systems request comes in. SWL's vice president of marketing, Amy Neal, wants to change the catalog mailing program and provide a reward for customers who use the Internet.

Amy's plan specifies that customers will remain on SWL's mailing list if they either requested a catalog, ordered from SWL in the last two years, or signed the guest register on SWL's new Web site. To encourage Internet visitors, customers who register on the Web site also will receive a special discount certificate.

To document the requirements, Rick wants you to design a decision table. Initially, it appears to have eight rules, but you notice that some of those rules are duplicates, or might not be realistic combinations.

1. Design the decision table with all possibilities.
2. Simplify the table by combining rules where appropriate.
3. Draw a decision tree that reflects Amy Neal's policy.
4. Create a set of structured English statements that accurately describes the policy.

CHAPTER 5 Development Strategies

CHAPTER 5 is the final chapter in the systems analysis phase of the SDLC. This chapter describes software trends, acquisition and development strategies, traditional versus Web-based development, outsourcing versus in-house development, the system requirements document, prototyping, and preparing for the transition to the next SDLC phase — systems design.

INTRODUCTION

OBJECTIVES

When you finish this chapter, you will be able to:

- Describe software trends, including the concept of software as a service
- Explain software acquisition alternatives, including traditional versus Web-based software development strategies
- Describe software outsourcing options, including offshore outsourcing and the role of service providers
- Explain advantages and disadvantages of developing software in-house versus other alternatives
- Explain cost-benefit analysis and financial analysis tools
- Explain the differences between a request for proposal (RFP) and a request for quotation (RFQ)
- Describe the contents of the system requirements document
- Explain the transition from systems analysis to systems design, and the difference between logical and physical design
- Explain the transition to systems design and the importance of prototyping
- Discuss guidelines for systems design

The main objective of the systems analysis phase is to build a logical model of the new information system. In Chapters 3 and 4, you learned about requirements modeling and data and process modeling. Chapter 5 describes the remaining activities in the systems analysis phase, which include evaluation of alternative solutions, preparation of the system requirements document, and presentation of the system requirements document to management. The chapter also describes the transition to systems design, prototyping, and systems design guidelines.

CHAPTER INTRODUCTION CASE: Mountain View College Bookstore

Background: Wendy Lee, manager of college services at Mountain View College, wants a new information system that will improve efficiency and customer service at the three college bookstores.

In this part of the case, Florence Fullerton (systems analyst) and Harry Boston (student intern) are talking about development strategies for the new system.

Participants:	Florence and Harry
Location:	Florence's office, Tuesday morning, November 22, 2005
Project status:	Florence and Harry have developed a requirements model that includes data flow diagrams, a data dictionary, and process descriptions. Now they are ready to discuss development strategies for the new bookstore system.
Discussion topics:	Web-based versus traditional development, cost-benefit analysis, steps in purchasing a software package, transition from systems analysis to systems design, and systems design guidelines

Florence: Good morning, Harry. Are you ready for the next step?

Harry: *Sure. Now that we have a logical model of the bookstore system, what comes next?*

Florence: We're at a transition point between the logical design, which describes what the new system will do, and the physical design phase, which describes how it will be done, including the user interface and physical components. Before we start the physical design, we have to study various systems development options and make a recommendation to Wendy.

Harry: *What are the options?*

Florence: Well, some large organizations use Web-based systems hosted by outside vendors who supply and maintain the software. In a sense, the customer rents the application. I checked with our IT director, and she feels we're not ready for that approach. She wants us to implement a system on the college LAN, and then migrate to a Web-based system later. That brings us to the next set of questions.

Harry: *Such as?*

Florence: We need to consider our role in the development process. We have several choices. We can build the system ourselves, which is called in-house development. Or we can purchase a software package, which might need some degree of modification to meet our needs. Or we could consider various outsourcing options, including hiring an IT consultant to help with development tasks. Either way, we need to do a cost-benefit study and come up with a recommendation.

Harry: *What about the transition from logical to physical design that you mentioned?*

Florence: The idea is to take our logical design, which is similar to an architect's proposal, and translate it into a physical design, which is more like a working blueprint. If we decide to develop the system in-house, we'll probably build a prototype, or working model of the system. If we decide to purchase a package, we'll follow a series of steps that will help us select the best product. We'll also talk about systems design guidelines.

Harry: *When you mention the idea of a blueprint, it sounds like we're getting ready to pick up our tools and go to work.*

Florence: We sure are. Here's a task list to get us started:

FIGURE 5-1

DEVELOPMENT STRATEGIES OVERVIEW

Just a few years ago, a typical company either developed software itself, purchased a software package (which might need some modification), or hired consultants or outside resources to perform the work. Today, that company has many more choices, including application service providers, Web-hosted software options, and firms that offer a variety of enterprise-wide software solutions.

Selecting the best development path is an important decision that requires companies to consider three key topics: the impact of the Internet, software outsourcing options, and in-house software development alternatives. These topics are reviewed in the following sections.

THE IMPACT OF THE INTERNET

The Internet has triggered enormous changes in business methods and operations, and software acquisition is no exception. This section examines a trend that views software as a service, the changing marketplace for software, and how Web-based development compares to traditional methods.

Software as a Service

The **Software and Information Industry Association (SIIA)** is an industry group that focuses on the digital economy. SIIA believes that the concept of *software as a service* is redefining the way that companies develop and deploy their information systems. In a recent report, SIIA stated that many observers expect traditional packaged applications to be replaced by Web-based services that remove the responsibility for installation, maintenance, and upgrades from a company's in-house staff. The SIIA publication noted that the acquisition of software as a *service* rather than a *product* will have a major impact on the software industry. Because of the importance of this issue, SIIA has established an industry-wide working group called the Software as a Service Initiative, as shown in Figure 5-2.

Many software industry leaders, including Microsoft, believe that the concept of *software as a service* represents a new way of looking at software acquisition and use, as shown in Figure 5-3.

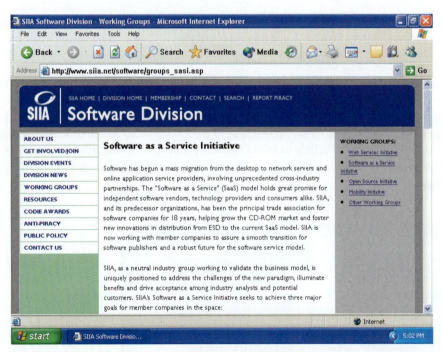

FIGURE 5-2 The Software and Information Industry Association (SIIA) is an industry group that focuses on the digital economy. SIIA predicts a shift from traditional in-house software services to outside service providers.

The Changing Software Marketplace

In the traditional model, software vendors develop and sell application packages to customers. Typically, customers purchase licenses that give them the right to use the software under the terms of the license agreement. Although this model still accounts for most software acquisition, a new model, which views software as a service, is changing the picture. In addition to traditional vendors, the marketplace now includes many forms of outsourcing, including application service providers and firms that offer Internet business services. Although there is no industry-wide agreement on definitions, it is important for a systems analyst to understand emerging concepts and marketplace trends.

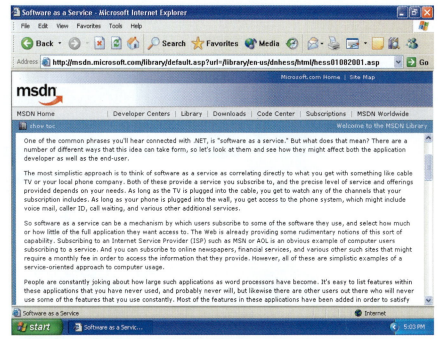

FIGURE 5-3   Microsoft believes that *software as a service* represents a new model for hosting commerce, business, and knowledge management application services.

The Impact of the Internet on Systems Development

As a systems analyst, you must consider whether development will take place in a Web-centric framework, or in a traditional environment. As Internet-based systems become more popular, developers will focus on **Web-based application development**, where the Web becomes an integral part of the application, rather than just a communication channel. In Chapter 1, you learned that two major Web-based development environments are IBM's **WebSphere** and Microsoft's **.NET**, which are shown in Figure 5-4 on the next page.

Before you select a development approach, you should consider some differences between traditional and Web-based systems. Building the application in a Web-based environment might involve different risks and benefits, compared to a traditional environment. The following sections list some characteristics of traditional versus Web-based development.

TRADITIONAL DEVELOPMENT   In a traditional systems development environment:

- Systems design is influenced by compatibility issues, including existing hardware and software platforms and legacy system requirements.
- Systems are designed to run on local and wide-area company networks.
- Systems often utilize Internet links and resources, but Web-based features are treated as enhancements rather than core elements of the design.
- Development typically follows one of three main paths: in-house development, purchase of a software package with possible modification, or use of outside consultants.
- Scalability can be affected by telecommunications limitations and local network constraints.

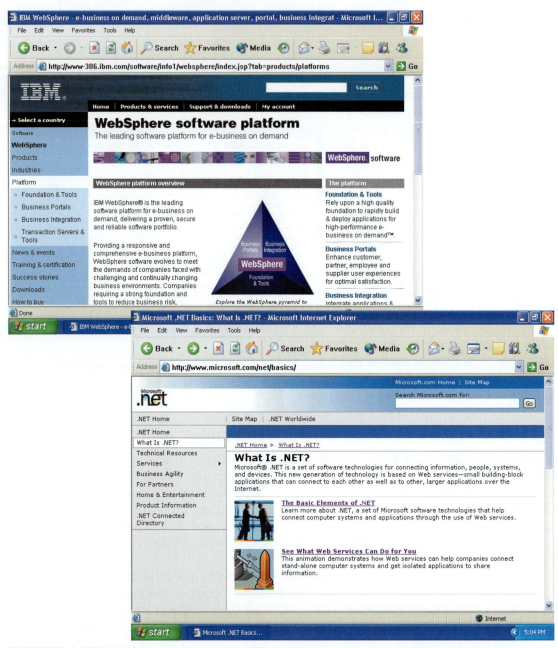

FIGURE 5-4 IBM's WebSphere and Microsoft's .NET are Web-based software development environments.

- Many applications require substantial desktop computing power and resources.
- Security issues usually are less complex than with Web-based systems, because the system operates on a private telecommunication network, rather than the Internet.

WEB-BASED DEVELOPMENT In a Web-based systems development environment:

- Systems are developed and delivered in an Internet-based framework such as .NET or WebSphere.
- Internet-based development treats the Web *as* the platform, rather than just a communication channel.

- Web-based systems are easily scalable, and can run on multiple hardware environments.

- Large firms tend to deploy Web-based systems as enterprise-wide software solutions for applications such as customer relationship management, order processing, and materials management.

- Web-based software treats the software application as a service that is less dependent on desktop computing power and resources.

- When companies acquire Web-based software as a *service* rather than a *product* they purchase, they can limit in-house involvement to a minimum and have the vendor install, configure, and maintain the system by paying agreed-upon fees.

- Web-based software usually requires additional layers, called **middleware**, to communicate with existing software and legacy systems.

OUTSOURCING

Outsourcing is the transfer of information systems development, operation, or maintenance to an outside firm that provides these services, for a fee, on a temporary or long-term basis. Outsourcing can refer to relatively minor programming tasks, the rental of software from a service provider, the outsourcing of a basic business process (often called **business process outsourcing**, or **BPO**), or the handling of a company's entire IT function. Numerous firms and organizations offer information about outsourcing topics and issues. For example, The Outsourcing Center, shown in Figure 5-5, provides free research, case studies, database directories, market intelligence, and updates on trends and best practices in outsourcing as a strategic business solution.

ON THE WEB

For more information about Outsourcing, visit **scsite.com/sad6e/more**, locate Chapter 5 and then click the Outsourcing link.

The Growth of Outsourcing

Traditionally, firms outsourced IT tasks as a way of controlling costs and dealing with rapid technological change. While those reasons still are valid, outsourcing has become part of an overall IT strategy for many organizations. The outsourcing trend also has affected software vendors, who have adjusted their marketing accordingly. For example, Oracle Corporation now offers a service called **On Demand**, which provides E-business applications on a fixed fee basis, as shown in Figure 5-6 on the next page. Oracle also cites data that shows that businesses spend up to 80 percent of their IT budgets maintaining existing software and systems, which forces IT managers "... to spend time managing tedious upgrades instead of revenue-generating IT projects."

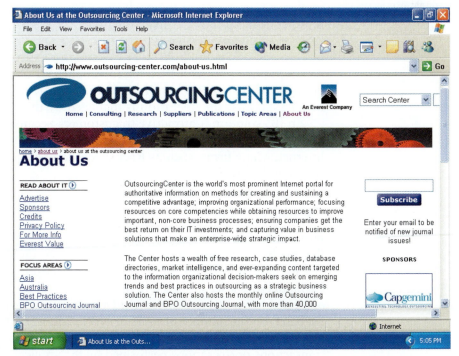

FIGURE 5-5 The Outsourcing Center is dedicated to providing information about outsource trends and practices.

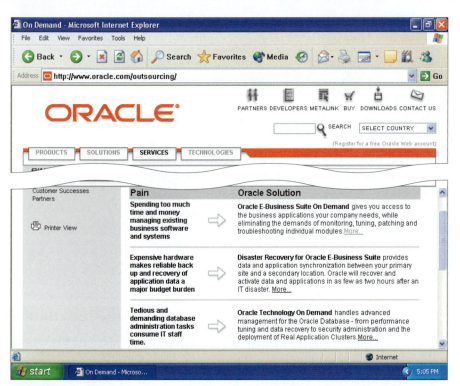

FIGURE 5-6 Oracle Corporation offers a fixed-fee outsourcing plan called On Demand.

A firm that offers outsourcing solutions is called a **service provider**. Some service providers concentrate on specific software applications; others offer business services such as order processing and customer billing. Still others offer enterprise-wide software solutions that integrate and manage functions such as accounting, manufacturing, and inventory control.

Two popular outsourcing options involve application service providers and firms that offer Internet business services. These terms are explained in the following sections.

APPLICATION SERVICE PROVIDERS An **application service provider** (**ASP**) is a firm that delivers a software application, or access to an application, by charging a usage or subscription fee. An ASP provides more than a license to use the software; it *rents* an operational package to the customer. ASPs typically provide commercially available software such as databases and accounting packages. If a company uses an ASP to supply a data management package, for example, the company does not have to design, develop, implement, or maintain the package. ASPs represent a rapidly growing trend, using the Internet as the primary delivery channel.

INTERNET BUSINESS SERVICES Some firms offer **Internet business services (IBS)**, which provide powerful Web-based support for transactions such as order processing, billing, and customer relationship management. Another term for IBS is **managed hosting**, because the operation is managed by the outside firm, or host.

An IBS solution is attractive to customers because it offers online data center support, mainframe computing power for mission-critical functions, and universal access via the Internet. Many firms, such as Rackspace, compete in the managed hosting market, as shown in Figure 5-7.

Outsourcing Fees

Firms that offer software as a service, rather than a product, have developed fee structures that are based on how the application is used by customers during a specific time period. Several models exist, including fixed fee, subscription, and usage or transaction. A **fixed fee model** uses a set fee based on a specified level of service and user support. An example of a fixed fee model is Oracle's On Demand service. A **subscription model** has a variable fee based on the number of users or workstations that have access to the application. Finally, a **usage model** or **transaction model** charges a variable fee based on the volume of transactions or operations performed by the application.

When a company considers outsourcing, it should estimate usage characteristics to determine which fee structure would be most desirable, and then attempt to negotiate a service provider contract based on that model.

ON THE WEB

For more information about Application Service Providers, visit **scsite.com/ sad6e/more**, locate Chapter 5 and then click the Application Service Providers link.

Outsourcing Issues and Concerns

When a company decides to outsource IT functions, it takes an important step that can affect the firm's resources, operations, and profitability. Mission-critical IT systems should be outsourced only if the result is a cost-attractive, reliable, business solution that fits the company's long-term business strategy and involves an acceptable level of risk. Moving IT work overseas raises even more issues, including potential concerns about control, culture, communication, and security.

In addition to long-term strategic consequences, outsourcing also can affect day-to-day company operations and can raise some concerns. For example, a company must turn over sensitive data to an external service provider and trust the provider to maintain security, confidentiality, and quality. In addition, before outsourcing, a company must review carefully issues relating to insurance, potential liability, licensing and information ownership, warranties, and disaster recovery.

FIGURE 5-7 Rackspace Corporation offers multi-platform managed hosting and IBS services.

Most importantly, a company considering outsourcing must realize that the solution can be only as good as the outsourcing firm that provides the service. A dynamic economy can give rise to business failures and uncertainty about the future. In this climate, it is especially important to review the history and financial condition of an outsourcing firm before making a commitment.

Mergers and acquisitions also can affect outsourcing clients. For example, after their merger, Compaq and Hewlett-Packard restructured and streamlined the products and services offered by the new company. Even with large, financially healthy firms such as these, a merger or acquisition can have some impact on clients and customers. If stability is important, an outsourcing client should consider these issues.

Outsourcing can be especially attractive to a company whose volume fluctuates widely, such as a defense contractor. In other situations, a company might decide to outsource application development tasks to an IT consulting firm if the company lacks the time or expertise to handle the work on its own. Outsourcing relieves a company of the responsibility of adding IT staff in busy times and downsizing when the workload lightens. A major disadvantage of outsourcing is that it raises employee concerns about job security. Talented IT people usually prefer positions where the firm is committed to in-house IT development — if they do not feel secure, they might decide to work directly for the service provider.

Offshore Outsourcing

Offshore outsourcing, or **global outsourcing,** refers to the practice of shifting IT development, support, and operations to other countries. In a trend similar to the outflow of manufacturing jobs over a several-decade period, many firms are sending IT work overseas at an increasing rate. For example, an April 2003 article in *CIO* magazine cited Dartmouth professor Matthew Slaughter's view that IT work will move offshore even faster than manufacturing, because it is easier to ship work across telephone lines and put consultants on airplanes than it is to ship bulky raw materials, build factories, and deal with tariffs and transportation issues. According to an August 2003 report in *ComputerWorld* magazine, Gartner, a leading IT research and consulting firm, predicts that by 2005 one in 10 IT jobs at U.S. IT companies and one in 20 at non-IT companies will move offshore.

The main reason for offshore outsourcing is the same as domestic outsourcing: lower bottom-line costs. Offshore outsourcing, however, involves some additional issues and concerns. For example, workers, customers, and shareholders in some companies have protested this trend, and have raised public awareness of possible economic impacts. Even more important, offshore outsourcing involves unique concerns regarding project control, security issues, disparate cultures, and effective communication with critical functions that might be located halfway around the globe. To address these issues, managers must take specific steps, such as the ones suggested by Information Disciplines, Inc., as shown in Figure 5-8. Before a firm chooses an offshore strategy, it should analyze carefully the benefits and potential risks.

Offshore Software Development Contracts

A MANAGER'S GUIDE TO SEVEN ESSENTIAL REQUIREMENTS

1. Make sure the low labor cost is really lower.

2. Assess the programmers' skills realistically.

3. Have solid specifications.

4. Make sure the project plan is very, very detailed.

5. Make sure status reporting is unambiguous.

6. Don't overlook language skills.

7. Look at work samples.

A final word

Nothing in the above advice is much different than for a critical project done in-house or through a local contractor. But when you're dealing with people you don't know, who come from a different culture, and whom you don't see regularly, the penalties for not following these common-sense disciplines are that much higher.

Source: Information Disciplines, Inc.
idinews.com/offshore.html

FIGURE 5-8 Information Disciplines, Inc., an IT consulting firm, raises some interesting issues with regard to offshore software development contracts.

CASE IN POINT 5.1: TURNKEY SERVICES

Turnkey Services is an application service provider that offers payroll and tax preparation services for hundreds of businesses in the Midwest. The firm is considering a major expansion into accounting and financial services, and is looking into the possibility of supporting this move by hiring IT subcontractors in several foreign countries. Peter Belmont, Turnkey's president, has asked you to help him reach a decision. Specifically, he wants you to cite the pros and cons of offshore outsourcing. He expects you to perform Internet research on this topic, and he wants you to present your views at a meeting of Turnkey managers next week.

IN-HOUSE SOFTWARE DEVELOPMENT OPTIONS

In addition to numerous outsourcing options, a company can choose to develop its own systems, or purchase, possibly customize, and implement a software package. These development alternatives are shown in Figure 5-9. Although many factors influence this decision, the most important consideration is total cost of ownership (TCO), which was explained in Chapter 3. In addition to these options, companies also develop user applications designed around commercial software packages, such as Microsoft Office 2003, to improve user productivity and efficiency.

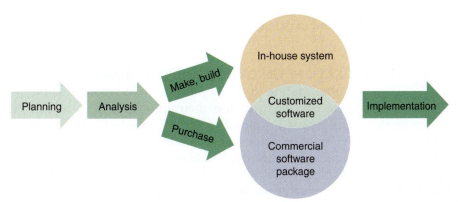

FIGURE 5-9 Instead of outsourcing, a company can choose to develop a system in-house, or purchase and possibly customize a commercial package.

Make or Buy Decision

The choice between developing versus purchasing software often is called a **make or buy**, or **build or buy** decision. The company's IT department makes, builds, and develops **in-house software**. A **software package** is obtained from a vendor or application service provider.

The package might be a standard commercial program or a customized package designed specifically for the purchaser. Companies that develop software for sale are called **software vendors**. A firm that enhances a commercial package by adding custom features and configuring it for a particular industry is called a **value-added reseller** (VAR).

Software packages are available for every type of business activity. A software package that can be used by many different types of organizations is called a **horizontal application**. An accounting package is a good example of a horizontal application because it can be utilized by many different businesses, or separate divisions that exist in large, diversified companies.

ON THE WEB

For more information about Value-Added Resellers, visit **scsite.com/sad6e/ more**, locate Chapter 5 and then click the Value-Added Resellers link.

612-333921 © Masterfile (Royalty-Free Div.) www.masterfile.com

FIGURE 5-10 Hotel chains require vertical applications to support reservation systems and information needs that are unique to the hotel industry.

In contrast, a software package developed to handle information requirements for a specific type of business is called a **vertical application**. For example, organizations with special system requirements include colleges, banks, hospitals, insurance companies, construction companies, real estate firms, and airlines. A hotel chain might require a vertical application for its guest reservation system, as shown in Figure 5-10, and use horizontal applications for basic business needs, such as payroll processing and accounts payable.

Of the in-house software acquisition options — developing a system, buying a software package, or customizing a software package — each has advantages, disadvantages, and cost considerations, as shown in Figure 5-11. These software acquisition options are described in detail in the following sections.

Developing Software In-House

With an enormous variety of software packages available to handle horizontal and vertical business operations, why would a firm choose to develop its own software? Typically, companies choose in-house development to satisfy unique business requirements, to minimize changes in business procedures and policies, to meet constraints of existing systems and existing technology, and to develop internal resources and capabilities.

SATISFY UNIQUE BUSINESS REQUIREMENTS Companies often decide to develop software in-house because no commercially available software package can meet their unique business requirements. A college, for example, needs a course scheduling system based on curriculum requirements, student demand, classroom space, and available instructors. A package delivery company needs a system to identify the best combination of routes and loading patterns for the company's fleet of delivery trucks. If existing software packages cannot handle those requirements, then in-house developed software might be the only choice.

REASONS FOR IN-HOUSE DEVELOPMENT	REASONS FOR PURCHASING A SOFTWARE PACKAGE
Satisfy unique business requirements	Lower costs
Minimize changes in business procedures and policies	Requires less time to implement
Meet constraints of existing systems	Proven reliability and performance benchmarks
Meet constraints of existing technology	Requires less technical development staff
Develop internal resources and capabilities	Future upgrades provided by the vendor
Satisfy unique security requirements	Obtain input from other companies

FIGURE 5-11 Companies consider various factors when comparing in-house development to the purchase of a software package.

MINIMIZE CHANGES IN BUSINESS PROCEDURES AND POLICIES A company also might choose to develop its own software if available packages will require changes in current business operations or processes. Installing a new software package almost always requires some degree of change in how a company does business; however, if the installation of a purchased package will be too disruptive, the organization might decide to develop its own software instead.

MEET CONSTRAINTS OF EXISTING SYSTEMS Any new software installed must work with existing systems. For example, if a new budgeting system must interface with an existing accounting system, finding a software package that works correctly with the existing accounting system might prove difficult. If so, a company could develop its own software to ensure that the new system will interface with the old system.

MEET CONSTRAINTS OF EXISTING TECHNOLOGY Another reason to develop software in-house is that the new system must work with existing hardware and legacy systems. That could require a custom design not commercially available. Some companies have older microcomputer workstations that cannot handle graphics-intensive software or high-speed Internet access. In that situation, the company either must upgrade the environment or must develop in-house software that can operate within the constraints of the existing hardware. As a systems analyst, you addressed the issue of technical feasibility during the preliminary investigation. Now, in the systems analysis phase, you must examine the advantages and disadvantages of in-house software development to decide whether it is justifiable.

DEVELOP INTERNAL RESOURCES AND CAPABILITIES By designing a system in-house, companies can develop and train an IT staff that understands the organization's business functions and information support needs. Many firms feel that in-house IT resources and capabilities provide a competitive advantage because an in-house team can respond quickly when business problems or opportunities arise. For example, if a company lacks internal resources, it must depend on an outside firm for vital business support. Also, outsourcing options might be attractive, but a series of short-term solutions would not necessarily translate into lower TCO over the long term. Top managers often feel more comfortable with an internal IT team to provide overall guidance and long-term stability.

Purchasing a Software Package

If a company decides not to outsource, a commercially available software package might be an attractive alternative to developing its own software. Advantages of purchasing a software package over developing software in-house include lower costs, less time to implement a system, proven reliability and performance benchmarks, less technical development staff, future upgrades that are provided by the vendor, and the ability to obtain input from other companies who already have implemented the software.

LOWER COSTS Because many companies use software packages, software vendors spread the development costs over many customers. Compared to software developed in-house, a software package almost always is less expensive, particularly in terms of initial investment.

REQUIRES LESS TIME TO IMPLEMENT When you purchase a package, it already has been designed, programmed, tested, and documented. The in-house time normally spent on those tasks, therefore, is eliminated. Of course, you still must install the software and integrate it into your systems environment, which can take a significant amount of time.

PROVEN RELIABILITY AND PERFORMANCE BENCHMARKS If the package has been on the market for any length of time, any major problems probably have been detected already and corrected by the vendor. If the product is popular, it almost certainly has been rated and evaluated by independent reviewers.

REQUIRES LESS TECHNICAL DEVELOPMENT STAFF Companies that use commercial software packages often are able to reduce the number of programmers and systems analysts on the IT staff. Using commercial software also means that the IT staff can concentrate on systems whose requirements cannot be satisfied by software packages.

FUTURE UPGRADES PROVIDED BY THE VENDOR Software vendors regularly upgrade software packages by adding improvements and enhancements to create a new version or release. A new release of a software package, for example, can include drivers to support a new laser printer or a new type of data storage technology. In many cases, the vendor receives input and suggestions from current users when planning future upgrades.

INPUT FROM OTHER COMPANIES Using a commercial software package means that you can contact users in other companies to obtain their input and impressions. You might be able to try the package or make a site visit to observe the system in operation before making a final decision.

Customizing a Software Package

If the standard version of a software product does not satisfy a company's requirements, the firm can consider adapting the package to meet its needs. Three ways to customize a software package are:

1. You can purchase a basic package that vendors will customize to suit your needs. Many vendors offer basic packages in a standard version with add-on components that are configured individually. A vendor offers options when the standard application will not satisfy all customers. A human resources information system is a typical example, because each company handles employee compensation and benefits differently. If you need assistance in making a determination, firms such as Ideas International offer services to help you select and configure a system, as shown in Figure 5-12.

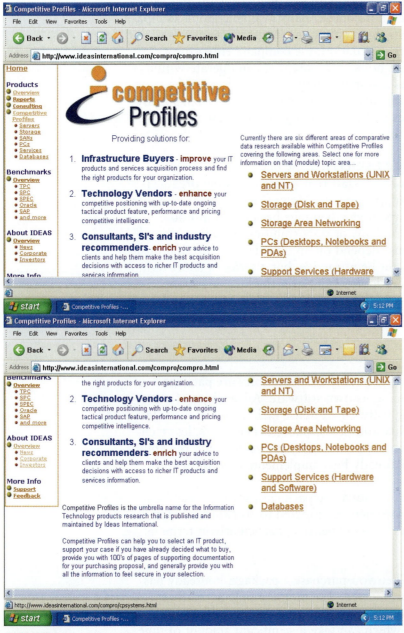

FIGURE 5-12 Firms such as Ideas International offer services to help customers select and configure a system.

2. You can negotiate directly with the software vendor to make enhancements to meet your needs by paying for the changes.

3. You can purchase the package and make your own modifications, if this is permissible under the terms of the software license. A disadvantage of this approach is that systems analysts and programmers might be unfamiliar with the software and will need time to learn the package and make the modifications correctly.

Additionally, some advantages of purchasing a standard package can be lost if the product must be customized. If the vendor does the customizing, the modified package probably will cost more and take longer to obtain. Another issue is future support: although vendors regularly upgrade their standard software packages, they might not upgrade a customized version. In addition, if the modifications are done by the company purchasing the software, when a new release of the package becomes available, the company might have to modify the new version.

Creating User Applications

Business requirements sometimes can be fulfilled by a user application, rather than a formal information system or commercial package. User applications are examples of user productivity systems, which were discussed in Chapter 1 on page 14.

A **user application** utilizes standard business software, such as Microsoft Word or Microsoft Excel, which has been configured in a specific manner to enhance user productivity. For example, to help a sales rep respond rapidly to customer price requests, an IT support person can set up a form letter with links to a spreadsheet that calculates incentives and discounts. In addition to configuring the software, the IT staff can create a **user interface**, which includes screens, commands, controls, and features that enable users to interact more effectively with the application. User interface design is described in Chapter 6.

In some situations, user applications offer a simple, low-cost solution. Most IT departments have a backlog of projects, and IT solutions for individuals or small groups do not always receive a high priority. At the same time, application software is more powerful, flexible, and user-friendly than ever. Companies such as Microsoft and Corel offer software suites and integrated applications that can exchange data with programs that include tutorials, wizards, and Help features to guide less experienced users who know what they need to do but do not know how to make it happen.

Many companies empower lower-level employees by providing more access to data and more powerful data management tools. The main objective is to allow lower-level employees more access to the data they require to perform their jobs, with no intervention from the IT department. This can be accomplished by creating effective user interfaces for company-wide applications such as accounting, inventory, and sales systems. Another technique is to customize standard productivity software, such as Microsoft Word or Microsoft Excel, to create user applications. In either case, empowerment makes the IT department more productive because it can spend less time responding to the daily concerns and data needs of users and more time on high-impact systems development projects that support strategic business goals.

Empowerment reduces costs and makes good business sense, but companies that adopt this approach must provide the technical support that empowered users require. In most large and medium-sized companies, a **help desk**, or **information center** (**IC**), within the IT department is responsible for providing user support. The IC staff offers services such as hotline assistance, training, and guidance to users who need technical help.

Once they learn an application, many users can perform tasks that once required a programmer. Some user applications have powerful **screen generators** and **report generators** that allow users to design their own data entry forms and reports. For example, as shown in Figure 5-13 on the next page, Microsoft Access includes

FIGURE 5-13 Microsoft Access includes Form Wizard and Report Wizard tools that ask a series of questions, and then create the form or report.

Form Wizard and Report Wizard tools that ask a series of questions, and then create a screen form or report. Those design tools allow users to design specific input and output views that meet their operational needs — with little or no assistance required from the IT staff.

Users typically require spreadsheets, database management programs, and other software packages to meet their information needs. If user applications access corporate data, you must provide appropriate controls to ensure data security and integrity. For example, some files should be hidden totally from view; others should have **read-only properties** so users can view, but not change, the data. For security reasons, companies usually restrict user applications to PC-based systems within a user's department.

ROLE OF THE SYSTEMS ANALYST

At this point in the systems development process, the company must decide whether to use an outsourcing option, develop software in-house, acquire a software package, develop user applications, or select some combination of these solutions. The decision will affect the remaining SDLC phases and your involvement as a systems analyst. The decision to develop software in-house, for example, will require more participation from the systems analyst than outsourcing or choosing a commercial package. Management usually makes a determination after receiving written recommendations from the IT staff and a formal presentation, which is described later in this chapter.

Even a single system can use a mix of software alternatives. For example, a company might purchase a standard software package to process its payroll, and then develop its own software to handle the interface between the payroll package and the company's in-house manufacturing cost analysis system.

The evaluation and selection of alternatives is not a simple process. The objective is to obtain the product with the lowest total cost of ownership, but actual cost and performance can be difficult to forecast. With a large number of choices, how do you select the best alternative?

When selecting hardware and software, systems analysts often work as an **evaluation and selection team**. A team approach ensures that critical factors are not overlooked and that a sound choice is made. The evaluation and selection team also must include users, who will participate in the selection process and feel a sense of ownership in the new system.

The primary objective of the evaluation and selection team is to eliminate system alternatives that will not meet requirements, rank the alternatives that are feasible, and present the viable alternatives to management for a final decision. The process begins with a careful study of the costs and benefits of each alternative, as explained in the following section.

ANALYZING COST AND BENEFITS

In Chapter 2, you learned that economic feasibility is one of the four feasibility measurements that are made during the preliminary investigation of a systems request. Now, at the end of the systems analysis phase of the SDLC, you must apply financial analysis tools and techniques to evaluate development strategies and decide how the project will move forward. Part 3 of the Systems Analyst's Toolkit describes three popular tools, which are payback analysis, return on investment (ROI), and net present value (NPV). These tools, and others, can be used to determine total cost of ownership (TCO), which was described in Chapter 3 on page 103. At this stage, you will identify specific systems development strategies and choose a course of action. For example, a company might find that its total cost of ownership will be higher if it develops a system in-house, compared to outsourcing the project or using an ASP.

Figure 5-14 on the next page shows how Compaq, an IT solution provider, addresses TCO questions and issues. Compaq states that it is interested in more than just TCO — the company's main objective is to provide its customers with a TCO that is among the industry's lowest, providing the highest value IT solution. Notice that the site offers a TCO snapshot tool, which can be downloaded.

ON THE WEB

For more information about Financial Analysis Tools, visit **scsite.com/ sad6e/more**, locate Chapter 5 and then click the Financial Analysis Tools link.

Financial Analysis Tools

Part 3 of the Systems Analyst's Toolkit explains how to use three main cost analysis tools: payback analysis, return on investment (ROI), and net present value (NPV). **Payback analysis** determines how long it takes an information system to pay for itself through reduced costs and increased benefits. **Return on investment (ROI)** is a percentage rate that compares the total net benefits (the return) received from a project to the total costs (the investment) of the project. The **net present value (NPV)** of a project is the total value of the benefits minus the total value of the costs, with both costs and benefits adjusted to reflect the point in time at which they occur.

CASE IN POINT 5.2: STERLING ASSOCIATES

Joan Sterling is CEO and principal stockholder of Sterling Associates, which specializes in advising clients on IT projects and information systems development. Joan is creating a brochure for prospective new clients. She wants you to develop a section that describes payback analysis, ROI, and NPV in simple terms, and mentions the pros and cons of each financial analysis tool. She suggested that you start by reviewing the material in Part 3 of the Systems Analyst's Toolkit.

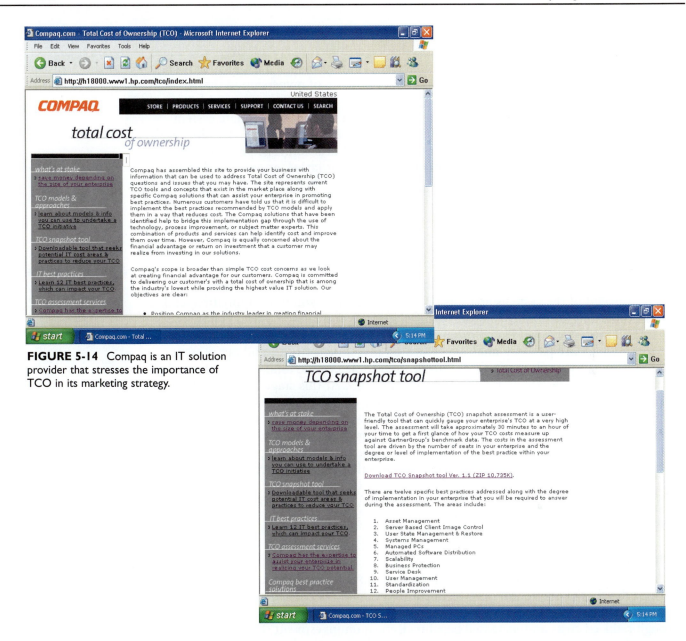

FIGURE 5-14 Compaq is an IT solution provider that stresses the importance of TCO in its marketing strategy.

Cost-Benefit Analysis Checklist

Companies use all three financial analysis tools to evaluate various development strategies. The best way to apply the tools is to develop a cost-benefit checklist with the following steps:

- → List each development strategy being considered.
- → Identify all costs and benefits for each alternative. Be sure to indicate when costs will be incurred and benefits realized.
- → Consider future growth and the need for scalability.
- → Include support costs for hardware and software.
- → Analyze various software licensing options, including fixed fees and formulas based on the number of users or transactions.
- → Apply the financial analysis tools to each alternative.
- → Study the results and prepare a report to management.

THE SOFTWARE ACQUISITION PROCESS

Although each situation is different, the following section describes a typical example of the issues and tasks involved in software acquisition.

Step 1: Evaluate the Information System Requirements

Based on your analysis of the system requirements, you must identify the system's key features; consider network and Web-related issues; estimate volume and future growth; specify any hardware, software, or personnel constraints; and prepare a request for proposal or quotation.

IDENTIFY KEY FEATURES Whether you are considering in-house development or outsourcing options, you must develop a clear, detailed list of features that can serve as an overall specification for the system. Using the data you gathered during fact-finding, which was discussed in Chapter 3, you must list all system requirements and critical features. This information will be included in the system requirements document, which is the end product of the SDLC systems analysis phase.

CONSIDER NETWORK AND WEB-RELATED ISSUES As you evaluate the system requirements, you must consider network and Web-related issues. You must decide whether the system will run on a network, the Internet, or a company intranet, and build these requirements into the design. Also, you must determine whether the system will exchange data with vendor or customer systems, and ensure that the system will be compatible.

ESTIMATE VOLUME AND FUTURE GROWTH You need to know the current volume of transactions and forecast future growth. Figure 5-15 shows volume estimates for an order processing system. In addition to current levels, the figure displays two forecasts, one based on the existing order processing procedures and another that assumes a new Web site is operational.

Online Order Processing System Estimated Activity During Next 12-Month Period

	CURRENT LEVEL	FUTURE GROWTH BASED ON EXISTING ORDER PROCESSING PROCEDURES	FUTURE GROWTH ASSUMING NEW WEB SITE IS OPERATIONAL
Customers	36,500	40,150	63,875
Daily Orders	1,435	1,579	2,811
Daily Order Lines	7,715	7,893	12,556
Sales Reps	29	32	12
Order Processing Support Staff	2	4	3
Products	600	650	900

FIGURE 5-15 Volume estimate for an order processing system showing current activity levels and two forecasts: one based on the existing order processing procedures and another that assumes a new Web site is operational.

A comparison of the two forecasts shows that the Web site will generate substantially more new customers, process almost 80 percent more orders, and require 60 percent fewer sales reps. If you are considering in-house development, you must make sure that your software and hardware can handle future transaction volumes and data storage requirements. Conversely, if you are considering outsourcing, volume and usage data is essential to analyze ASP fee structures and develop cost estimates for outsourcing options.

SPECIFY HARDWARE, SOFTWARE, OR PERSONNEL CONSTRAINTS You must determine whether existing hardware, software, or personnel issues will affect the acquisition decision. For example, if the firm has a large number of legacy systems or if an ERP strategy has been adopted, these factors will have an impact on the decision. Also, you must investigate the company's policy regarding outsourcing IT functions, and whether outsourcing is part of a long-term strategy. With regard to personnel issues, you must define in-house staffing requirements to develop, acquire, implement, and maintain the system — and determine whether the company is willing to commit to those staffing levels versus an outsourcing option.

PREPARE A REQUEST FOR PROPOSAL OR QUOTATION To obtain the information you need to make a decision, you should prepare a request for proposal or a request for quotation. The two documents are similar but used in different situations, based on whether or not you have selected a specific software product.

A **request for proposal (RFP)** is a document that describes your company, lists the IT services or products you need, and specifies the features you require. An RFP helps assure that your organization's business needs will be met. An RFP also spells out the service and support levels you require. Based on the RFP, vendors can decide if they have a product

REQUEST FOR PROPOSAL
ACCOUNTS PAYABLE SYSTEM

Features		Standard Feature	Comments
1.	Interface to general ledger	✔	
2.	Matching to receiving documents	✔	
3.	Matching to purchase documents	✔	
4.	Automatic check printing	✔	
5.	Recurring payments		Planned For Next Release
6.	Flexible payment selection	✔	
7.	Checking statement reconciliation		Will Do On Custom Basis
8.	Consolidated check preparation	✔	
9.	Duplicate invoice check		No Plans For This Feature
10.	Manual check processing	✔	

Reports

1.	Vendor listing	✔	By Vendor Name
2.	Invoice register	✔	
3.	Check register	✔	
4.	Cash requirements	✔	Weekly And Monthly
5.	Detail aging	✔	30, 60, 90, 120 + Days
6.	Form 1099 reports		Planned For Next Release
7.	Account distribution	✔	
8.	Bank statement reconciliation		Will Do On Custom Basis

FIGURE 5-16 An RFP requires a vendor to indicate whether its product supports specific features and reports. Although the package in Figure 5-16 does not offer all the features requested in the RFP, the vendor plans to provide some of the features in future versions. Information on pricing and terms appears in another section of the document.

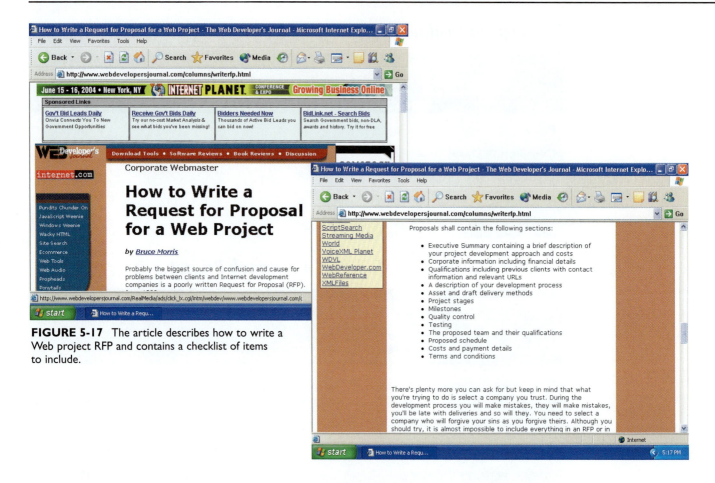

FIGURE 5-17   The article describes how to write a Web project RFP and contains a checklist of items to include.

that will meet your needs. RFPs vary in size and complexity, just like the systems they describe. An RFP for a large system can contain dozens of pages with unique requirements and features. You can use an RFP to designate some features as essential and others as desirable. An RFP also requests specific pricing and payment terms.

Figure 5-16 shows an example of a page from an RFP. Notice that the vendor has indicated whether the required features and reports are standard and has provided explanatory comments.

Figure 5-17 shows an article that describes how to write a Web project RFP and contains a checklist of items to include. The article suggests that in addition to stating the project's objectives and specifications, you should describe your company, provide a timetable, and identify the resources you will provide for the project. Notice that the list includes milestones, quality control, and testing, as well as detailed cost figures and payment terms.

When you evaluate several responses to an RFP, you might find it helpful to use an evaluation model. An **evaluation model** is a technique that uses a common yardstick to measure and compare vendor ratings.

Figure 5-18 on the next page shows two evaluation models for a network project. The evaluation model at the top of the figure simply lists the key elements and each vendor's score. The model at the bottom of the figure adds a weight factor. In this example each element receives a rating based on its relative importance. Although the initial scores are the same in both models, notice that vendor A has the highest point total in the top example, but vendor C emerges as the best in the weighted model.

Unweighted Evaluation Model for a Network Project

Instructions: Rate each vendor on a scale from 1(low) to 10 (high), then add vendor scores to calculate total points.			
	VENDOR A	**VENDOR B**	**VENDOR C**
Price	6	5	9
Completion Date	2	5	8
Layout/Design	8	8	5
References	10	6	3
TOTAL POINTS	26	24	25

Weighted Evaluation Model for a Network Project

Instructions: Rate each vendor on a scale from 1(low) to 10 (high), then multiply the vendor's score by the weight factor. Add vendor scores to calculate total points.				
	WEIGHT FACTOR	**VENDOR A**	**VENDOR B**	**VENDOR C**
Price	25	6 * 25 = 150	5 * 25 = 125	9 * 25 = 225
Completion Date	25	2 * 25 = 50	5 * 25 = 125	8 * 25 = 200
Layout/Design	35	8 * 35 = 280	8 * 35 = 280	5 * 35 = 175
References	15	10 * 15 = 150	6 * 15 = 90	3 * 15 = 45
TOTAL POINTS	100	630	620	645

FIGURE 5-18 The three vendors have the same initial ratings, but the two evaluation models produce different results. In the unweighted model at the top of the figure, vendor A has the highest total points. However, after applying weight factors, vendor C is the winner, as shown in the model at the bottom of the figure.

Evaluation models can be used throughout the SDLC, and you will find them a valuable tool. You can use a spreadsheet program to build an evaluation model, experiment with different weighting factors, and graph the results.

A **request for quotation** (**RFQ**) is more specific than an RFP. When you use an RFQ, you already know the specific product or service you want and you need to obtain price quotations or bids. RFQs can involve outright purchase or a variety of leasing options and can include maintenance or technical support terms. Many vendors provide convenient RFQ forms on their Web sites, as shown in Figure 5-19. RFPs and RFQs have the same objective: to obtain vendor replies that are clear, comparable, and responsive so you can make a well-informed selection decision.

In today's fast-paced IT marketplace, traditional methods for obtaining RFPs often are too slow. The ASPstreet.com Web site shown in Figure 5-20 offers an online meeting place where customers can post RFPs and vendors can reply with solutions and bids.

Step 2: Identify Potential Vendors or Outsourcing Options

The next step is to identify potential vendors or outsourcing providers. The Internet is a primary marketplace for all IT products and services, and you can find descriptive information on the Web about all major products and acquisition alternatives.

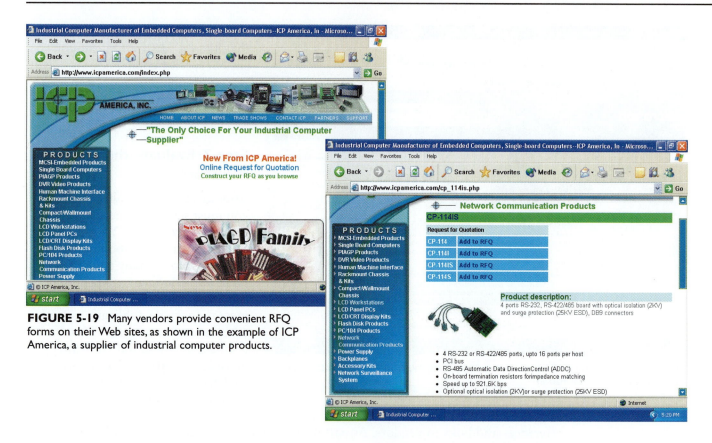

FIGURE 5-19 Many vendors provide convenient RFQ forms on their Web sites, as shown in the example of ICP America, a supplier of industrial computer products.

If you need to locate vertical applications for specific industries, you can research industry trade journals or Web sites to find reviews for industry-specific software. Industry trade groups often can direct you to companies that offer specific software solutions.

Another approach is to work with a consulting firm. Many IT consultants offer specialized services that help companies select software packages. A major advantage of using a consultant is that you can tap into broad experience that is difficult for any one company to acquire. Consultants can be located by contacting professional organizations or industry sources, or simply by searching the Internet. Using a consultant involves additional expense but can prevent even more costly mistakes.

Another valuable resource is the Internet bulletin board system that contains thousands of forums, called **newsgroups**, that cover every imaginable topic. Newsgroups are excellent sources of information and good places to exchange ideas with other analysts and IT professionals. You

FIGURE 5-20 The ASPstreet.com Web site offers an online meeting place where customers can post RFPs and vendors can reply with solutions and bids.

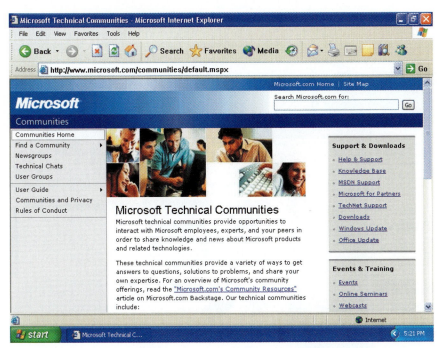

FIGURE 5-21 Microsoft Communities include newsgroups and chat sessions where users can exchange information.

can search the Web for newsgroups that interest you, or you can visit the sites of specific companies, such as Microsoft, that provide a framework for newsgroups and chat sessions, as shown in Figure 5-21.

Step 3: Evaluate the Alternatives

After identifying the alternatives, you must select the one that best fits the company's needs. You should obtain information about the options from as many sources as possible, including vendor presentations and literature, product documentation, trade publications, and companies that perform software testing and evaluation. To learn more about particular software packages, search the Internet using keywords that describe the application. Web sites maintained by consultants and software publishers often include product references and links to vendors. As part of the evaluation process, you should try to obtain information from existing users, test the application, and benchmark the package.

EXISTING USERS You can contact existing users to obtain feedback and learn about their experiences. For large-scale software packages, ASPs and vendors typically supply user references. User references are important because you need to know whether the software package has worked well for companies like yours. Be aware that some vendors limit their reference lists to satisfied clients, so you can expect mostly positive feedback from those firms.

APPLICATION TESTING If a software package is one of the options, find out if it is possible for users in your organization to try the product. For horizontal applications or a small system, using a demonstration copy to enter a few sample transactions could be an acceptable test. For vertical applications or large systems, a team of IT staff and users might need several days or weeks to perform tests.

ON THE WEB

For more information about Benchmark Tests, visit **scsite.com/ sad6e/more**, locate Chapter 5 and then click the Benchmark Tests link.

BENCHMARKING To determine whether a package can handle a certain transaction volume efficiently, you can perform a benchmark test. A **benchmark** measures the time a package takes to process a certain number of transactions. For example, a benchmark test can measure the time needed to post 1,000 sales transactions.

If you use benchmarks, remember that a benchmark test is conducted in a controlled environment, which might not resemble the actual day-to-day situation at your company. Although benchmarking cannot predict your specific results, benchmark testing is a good way to measure relative performance of two or more competing products in a standard environment.

Many IT publications publish regular reviews of individual packages, including benchmark tests, and often have annual surveys covering various categories of software. Some of the publications shown in Figure 5-22 also offer online versions and additional Web-based features, search capability, and IT links.

You also can obtain information from independent firms that benchmark various software packages and sell comparative analyses of the results, as shown in Figure 5-23 on the next page. The Transaction Processing Performance Council (TPC) is an example of a non-profit organization that publishes standards and reports for its members and the general public, while InfoSizing is an IT consulting firm that offers analysis of performance benchmarks.

Finally, you should match each package against the RFP features and rank the choices. If some features are more important than others, give them a higher weight using an evaluation model similar to the one shown in Figure 5-18 on page 216.

Step 4: Perform Cost-Benefit Analysis

Review the suggestions in this chapter and in Part 3 of the Systems Analyst's Toolkit, and develop a spreadsheet to identify and calculate TCO for

FIGURE 5-22 Many IT publications provide specialized information, reviews of individual software packages, and benchmark tests. These reviews are important to the systems analyst because they can provide an unbiased opinion of the package.

each option you are considering. Be sure to include all costs, using the volume forecasts you prepared. If you are considering outsourcing options, carefully study the alternative fee structure models described earlier. If possible, prepare charts to show the results graphically, and build in what-if capability so you can gauge the impact if one or more variables change.

If you are considering a software package, be sure to consider acquisition options. When you purchase software, what you are buying is a **software license** that gives you the right to use the software under certain terms and conditions. For example, the license could allow you to use the software only on a single computer, a specified number of computers, a network, or an entire site, depending on the terms of the agreement. Other license restrictions could prohibit you from making the software available to others or modifying the program. For desktop applications, software license terms and conditions usually cannot be modified. For large-scale systems, license agreement terms often can be negotiated.

Also consider user support issues, which can account for a significant part of TCO. If you select an outsourcing alternative, the arrangement probably will include certain technical support and maintenance. If you choose in-house development, you must consider the cost of providing these services on your own. If you purchase a software package, consider a supplemental **maintenance agreement**, which offers additional support and assistance from the vendor. The agreement might provide full support for a period of time or list specific charges for particular services. Some software packages provide free technical support for a period of time. Afterward, support is offered with a charge per occurrence, or per minute or hour of technical support time. Some software vendors contact registered owners whenever a new release is available and usually offer the new release at a reduced price.

> **TOOLKIT TIME**
>
> The Financial Analysis tools in Part 3 of the Systems Analyst's Toolkit can help you analyze project costs, benefits, and economic feasibility. To learn more about these tools, turn to Part 3 of the six-part Toolkit that follows Chapter 10.

Step 5: Prepare a Recommendation

You should prepare a recommendation that evaluates and describes the alternatives, together with the costs, benefits, advantages, and disadvantages of each option. At this point, you may be required to submit a formal system requirements document

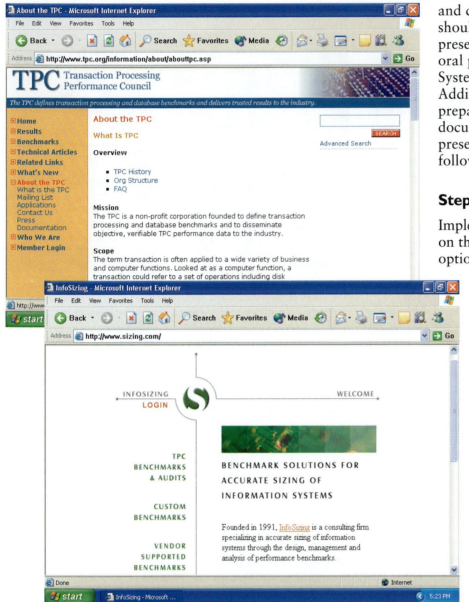

FIGURE 5-23 The Transaction Processing Performance Council is a non-profit organization that publishes standards and reports for its members and the general public, while InfoSizing is an IT consulting firm that offers analysis of performance benchmarks.

and deliver a presentation. You should review the suggestions for presenting written proposals and oral presentations in Part 1 of the Systems Analyst's Toolkit. Additional suggestions about preparing the system requirements document and the management presentation are contained in the following section.

Step 6: Implement the Solution

Implementation tasks will depend on the solution selected. In-house options will require more time and effort than outsourcing alternatives. For large systems or network installations, the process can require considerable time and effort. Your installation strategy should be planned well in advance, especially if any disruption of normal business operations is expected. If the software package is customized, then the task will be more complex and difficult.

Before the new software becomes operational, you must complete all implementation steps, including loading, configuring, and testing the software; training users; and converting data files to the new system's format. Chapter 9 will discuss implementation strategies and techniques in more detail.

CASE IN POINT 5.3: DOUG'S SPORTING GOODS

Doug's Sporting Goods sells hiking and camping supplies. The company has grown considerably in the last two years. Doug Sawyer, the company's founder and president, wants to develop a customer order entry system and hired your IT consulting firm to advise him about software alternatives. Doug is leaning toward in-house development because he does not want to depend on outside vendors and suppliers for technical support and upgrades. Doug also says that he is not interested in selling on the Web, but that could change in the future.

Doug wants to meet with you tomorrow to make a decision. What will you say to Doug at the meeting?

COMPLETION OF SYSTEMS ANALYSIS TASKS

To complete the systems analysis phase, you must prepare the system requirements document and your presentation to management.

System Requirements Document

The **system requirements document,** or **software requirements specification,** contains the requirements for the new system, describes the alternatives that were considered, and makes a specific recommendation to management. This important document is the starting point for measuring the performance, accuracy, and completeness of the finished system before entering the systems design phase.

The system requirements document is like a contract that identifies what the system developers must deliver to users. Recall that system requirements are identified during the fact-finding process, and a system requirements checklist is created at that time. Various examples of system requirements are listed on pages 213–216. You should write the system requirements document in language that users can understand so they can offer input, suggest improvements, and approve the final version.

Because the system requirements document can be lengthy, you should format and organize it so it is easy to read and use. The system requirements document should include a cover page and a detailed table of contents. You also can add an index and a glossary of terms to make the document easier to use. The content of the system requirements document will depend on the company and the complexity of the system.

Presentation to Management

The presentation to management at the end of the systems analysis phase is one of the most critical milestones in the systems development process. At this point, managers make key decisions that affect the future development of the system.

Prior to the management presentation, you might give two other presentations: one to the principal individuals in the IT department to keep them posted, and another presentation to users to answer their questions and invite feedback. The system requirements document is the basis for all three presentations, and you should distribute the document (or a summary) in advance so the recipients can review it.

When preparing your presentation, you should review the suggestions in Part 1 of the Systems Analyst's Toolkit, which will help you design and deliver a successful presentation. If you plan a slide presentation, you should review the Toolkit guidelines for effective presentations. In addition to the techniques found in the Toolkit, also keep the following suggestions in mind:

- Begin your presentation with a brief overview of the purpose and primary objectives of the system project, the objectives of this presentation, and what decisions need to be made.

- Summarize the primary viable alternatives. For each alternative, describe the costs, advantages, and disadvantages.

- Explain why the evaluation and selection team chose the recommended alternative.

- Allow time for discussion and for questions and answers.

- Obtain a final decision from management or agree on a timetable for the next step in the process.

The object of the management presentation is to obtain approval for the development of the system and to gain management's full support, including necessary financial resources. Management probably will choose one of five alternatives: develop an in-house system, modify a current system, purchase or customize a software package, perform additional systems analysis work, or stop all further work. Depending on their decision, your next task as a systems analyst will be one of the following:

1. Implement an outsourcing alternative. If outsourcing is selected, you will work with representatives of the service provider to achieve a smooth transition to the new environment.

2. Develop an in-house system. Begin the systems design phase for the new system, which is described in Chapters 6, 7, and 8.

3. Purchase or customize a software package. Negotiate the purchase terms with the software vendor for management approval. Then, if the package will be used without modification, you can begin planning the systems implementation phase. If you must make modifications to the package, your next step is to start the systems design phase. If the vendor will make the modifications, then your next step is to start planning the testing and documentation of the modifications as part of the systems implementation phase, which is described in Chapter 9.

4. Perform additional systems analysis work. Management might want you to investigate certain alternatives further, explore alternatives not examined, develop a prototype, reduce the project scope because of cost constraints, or expand the project scope based on new developments. If necessary, you will perform the additional work and schedule a follow-up presentation.

5. Stop all further work. The decision might be based on your recommendation, a shift in priorities or costs, or for other reasons. Whatever the reason, if that is management's decision, then you have no additional tasks for the project other than to file all your research in a logical location so it can be retrieved if the project is reopened in the future.

After the presentation and management decision, you will begin a transition to the systems design phase of the SDLC. If you are developing an in-house system or modifying a package, you will build a model of the proposed system and start designing the system's output, input, files, and data structures. The following sections describe several tools and techniques that can assist you in that process, including prototyping, CASE tools, and alternative graphical tools.

THE TRANSITION TO SYSTEMS DESIGN

If management decides to develop the system in-house, then the transition to the systems design phase begins. In a smaller company, you might be assigned full responsibility for the design tasks. In a large IT group, you might work as a member of the design team even though you had not participated in the earlier SDLC phases. The following sections discuss preparation for systems design and the relationship between analysis and design tasks.

The chapter concludes with a list of systems design guidelines, and a description of prototyping methods and tools.

Preparing for Systems Design Tasks

When systems design begins, it is essential to have an accurate and understandable system requirements document. Your document contains the design for the new system and is the starting point for the systems design phase. Errors, omissions, ambiguities, and other problems will affect the quality of the finished product. As you proceed to the design phase, you must be certain that you performed a thorough and accurate systems analysis and communicated the results in your system requirements document.

The Relationship between Logical and Physical Design

You develop the logical design of an information system during the systems analysis phase of the SDLC. The **logical design** defines the functions and features of the system and the relationships among its components. The logical design includes the output that must be produced by the system, the input needed by the system, and the processes that must be performed by the system without regard to how tasks will be accomplished *physically*.

As previously discussed, a logical design defines *what* must take place, not *how* it is to be accomplished. Logical designs do not address the actual methods of implementation. The logical design for a customer records system, for example, describes the data that must be entered for each customer, specifies that records must be displayed in customer number order, and explains what information to produce for a customer status report. Specifications for the actual input, or entry, of data, the sorting method, the physical process of creating the report, and the exact format of the report are not part of the logical design.

In contrast to the logical design, the **physical design** of an information system is a plan for the actual implementation of the system. You develop the physical design during the systems design phase of the SDLC. The physical design is built on the system's logical design and describes a specific implementation, much like a working blueprint describes the actual construction of a building.

In a typical system, the physical design describes the actual processes of entering, verifying, and storing data; the physical layout of data files; the sorting procedures; the exact format of reports; and so on. Whereas logical design is concerned with *what* the system must accomplish, physical design is concerned with *how* the system will meet those requirements.

Because logical and physical designs are related so closely, good systems design is impossible without careful, accurate systems analysis. In fact, the design phase typically cannot begin until the analysis work is complete. Although some overlap is possible, it usually is better to complete the analysis phase before moving on to systems design; however, each situation is different. For example, you might return to fact-finding if you discover that you overlooked an important issue, if users have significant new needs, or if legal or governmental requirements change.

SYSTEMS DESIGN GUIDELINES

The systems analyst must understand the logical design of the system before beginning the physical design of any one component. The first step is to review the system requirements document, which is especially important if you did not work on the previous phase or if a substantial amount of time has passed since the analysis phase was completed. After you review the system requirements, you are ready to start the actual design process. What should you do first, and why?

The best place to begin is with data design, which defines the physical data structures, elements, and relationships. When data design is complete, you move to the user interface, which affects the interaction between the user and the system. As you develop the user interface, you will work on specific input and output design tasks. Then you will work on the architecture that will translate the design into code modules.

STEP	ACTIVITY	DESCRIPTION
1	**Review system requirements.**	Become familiar with the logical design.
2	**Design the system.**	
	• User interface	Design an overall user interface, including screens, commands, controls, and features that enable users to interact with an application.
	• Input processes	Determine how data will be input to the system and design necessary source documents.
	• Input and output	Design the physical layout for each input and output formats and reports screen and printed report.
	• Data	Determine how data will be organized, stored, maintained, updated, accessed, and used.
	• System architecture	Determine processing strategies and methods, client/server interaction, network configuration, and Internet/intranet interface issues.
3	**Present the system design.**	Create the systems design specification document, in which you describe the proposed system design, the anticipated benefits of the system, and the estimated development and implementation costs.

FIGURE 5-24 The systems design phase of the SDLC consists of three main steps.

Because the components of a system are interdependent, the design phase is not a series of clearly defined steps. Although you might start with one component, it is not unusual to work on several components at the same time. For example, making a decision to change a report format might require other changes in data design or input screens.

The final step in systems design is to prepare a systems design specification and present your results to management. Those tasks and other systems design activities are listed and described in Figure 5-24.

Systems Design Objectives

The goal of **systems design** is to build a system that is effective, reliable, and maintainable.

→ To be effective, the system must satisfy the defined requirements and constraints. The system also must be accepted by users who use it to support the organization's business objectives.

→ A system is reliable if it adequately handles errors, such as input errors, processing errors, hardware failures, or human mistakes. Ideally, *all* errors can be prevented. Unfortunately, no system is completely foolproof, whether it is a payroll system, a telephone switching system, an Internet access system, or a space shuttle navigation system. A more realistic approach to building a reliable system is to plan for errors, detect them as early as possible, allow for their correction, and prevent them from damaging the system itself.

→ A system is maintainable if it is well designed, flexible, and developed with future modifications in mind. No matter how well a system is designed and implemented, at some point it will need to be modified. Modifications will be necessary to correct problems, to adapt to changing user requirements, to enhance the system, or to take advantage of changing technology. Your systems design must be capable of handling future modifications or the system soon will be outdated and fail to meet requirements.

As shown in Figure 5-25, design considerations involve users, data, and architecture.

SYSTEMS DESIGN CONSIDERATIONS

User Considerations

- Consider points where users interact with the system
- Anticipate future user, system, and organizational needs

Data Considerations

- Enter data where and when it occurs
- Verify data where it is input
- Use automated data entry methods whenever possible
- Control access for data entry
- Report every instance of entry and change of data
- Enter data only once

Architecture Considerations

- Use a modular design
- Design independent modules that perform a single function

FIGURE 5-25 Good design results in systems that are effective, reliable, and maintainable. Design considerations involve users, data, and architecture.

USER CONSIDERATIONS Of the many issues you must consider during systems design, your most important goal is to make the system acceptable to users, or user-friendly. Throughout the design process, the essential factor to consider is how decisions will affect users. Always remember that you are designing the system for the users, and keep these basic points in mind:

Carefully consider any point where users receive output from, or provide input to, the system. Above all, the user interface must be easy to learn and use. Input processes should be well documented, easy to follow, intuitive, and forgiving of errors. Output should be attractive and easy to understand, with an appropriate level of detail.

Anticipate future needs of the users, the system, and the organization. Suppose that an employee master file contains a one-character field to indicate each employee's category. The field currently has two valid values: *F* indicates a full-time employee, and *P* indicates a part-time employee. Depending on the field value, either FULL-TIME or PART-TIME will print as the value on various reports. While those two values could be programmed, or **hard-coded**, into the report programs, designing a separate table with category codes and captions is a better choice. The hard-coded solution is straightforward, but if the organization adds another value, such as *X* for FLEXTIME, a programmer would have to change all the report programs. If a separate table for codes and captions is used, it can be changed easily without requiring modifications to the reports.

Provide flexibility. Suppose that a user wants a screen display of all customer balances that exceed $5,000 in an accounts receivable system. How should you design that feature? The program could be coded to check customer balances against a fixed value of 5000, which is a simple solution for both the programmer and the user because no extra keystrokes are required to produce the display. That approach, however, is inflexible. For instance, if a user later needs a list of customers whose balances exceed $7,500 rather than $5,000, the existing system cannot provide the information. To accommodate the request, the programmer would have to change and retest the program and rewrite new documentation.

On the other hand, you could design the program to produce a report of all customers whose balance exceeds a specific amount entered by the user. For example, if a user wants to display customers with balances of more than $7,500, he or she can enter the number 7500 in a parameter query. A **parameter** is a value that the user enters whenever the query is run, which provides flexibility, enables users to access information easily, and costs less.

A good systems design can combine both approaches. For example, you could design the program to accept a variable amount entered by the user but start with a default value of 5,000. A **default** is a value that the system displays automatically. Users can press the ENTER key to accept the default value, or enter another value.

Often the best design strategy is to come up with several alternatives, so users can decide what will work best for them. Again, always remember to design the system with the users in mind.

CASE IN POINT 5.4: DOWNTOWN!

Downtown! is a rapidly growing Web-based retailer with about 100 management and technical support employees at its headquarters office in Florida. Mary Estrada, the firm's IT manager, is planning a new information system that will give users better access to sales and marketing data and trends. She has a concern, however: She knows that users often request reports but use only a small portion of the data. In many offices she sees inboxes filled with printed reports gathering dust. Mary asked for your opinion: What if new system users could design most of their own reports without assistance from the IT staff, by using a powerful, user-friendly report writer program? Do you think they would request as many reports or the same types of reports? What are the pros and cons of giving users total control over output?

DATA CONSIDERATIONS Data entry and storage considerations are important parts of the systems design. Here are some guidelines to follow:

Data should be entered into the system where and when it occurs because delays cause data errors. For example, employees in the receiving department should enter data about incoming shipments when the shipments arrive, and sales clerks should enter data about new orders when they take the orders.

Data should be verified when it is entered, to catch errors immediately. The input design should specify a data type such as alphabetic, numeric, or alphanumeric and a range of acceptable values for each data entry item. If an incorrect data value is entered, the system should recognize and flag it immediately. The system also should allow corrections at any time. Some errors, for example, are corrected easiest right at entry while the original source documents are at hand or the customer is on the telephone. Other errors may need further investigation, so users must be able to correct errors at a later time.

Automated methods of data entry should be used whenever possible. Receiving department employees in many companies, for example, use scanners to capture data about merchandise received. Automated data entry methods, such as the scanner shown in Figure 5-26, reduce input errors and improve employee productivity.

Access for data entry should be controlled and all entries or changes to critical data values should be reported. Dollar fields and many volume fields are considered critical data fields. Examples of critical volumes include the number of checks processed, the number of medical prescriptions dispensed, or the number of insurance premium payments received. Reports that trace the entry of and changes to critical data values are called **audit trails** and are essential in every system.

Every instance of entry and change to data should be logged. For example, the system should record when a customer's credit limit was established, and by whom, which is necessary to construct the history of a transaction.

Data should be entered into a system only once. If input data for a payroll system also is needed for a human resources system, you should design a program interface between the systems so data can be transferred automatically.

Data duplication should be avoided. In an inventory file, for example, the suppliers' addresses should not be stored with every part record. Otherwise, the address of a vendor who supplies 100 different parts is repeated 100 times in the data file. Additionally, if the vendor's address changes, all 100 parts records must be updated. Data duplication also can produce inconsistencies. If those 100 stored addresses for the vendor are not identical, how would a user know which version is correct? In Chapter 7, you will learn about data design and a technique called normalization, which is a set of rules that can help you identify and avoid data design problems when you create a database.

ARCHITECTURE CONSIDERATIONS In addition to the issues affecting users and data, you should consider the following suggestions:

Use a modular design. In a modular design, you create individual processing components, called modules, which connect to a higher-level program or process. In a traditional, structured design, each module represents a specific process or subprocess shown on a DFD and documented in a process description. If you are using an object-oriented design, as described in Part 5 of the Systems Analyst's Toolkit, object classes are represented by code modules. You will learn more about modular design in Chapter 8, which describes application architecture.

Design modules that perform a single function are easier to understand, implement, and maintain. Independent modules also provide greater flexibility because they can be developed and tested individually, and then combined at a later point in the development process. Modular design is helpful especially when developing large-scale systems, because separate teams of analysts and programmers can work on different areas of the project and then integrate the modules to create a finished system.

FIGURE 5-26 Automated data entry methods, such as the RFID scanner shown above, reduce input errors and improve employee productivity.

Design Trade-Offs

You will find that design goals often conflict with each other. In the systems design phase, you constantly must analyze alternatives and weigh trade-offs. To make a system easier to use, for example, programming requirements might be more complex. Making a system more flexible might increase maintenance requirements. Meeting one user's requirements could make it harder to satisfy another user's needs.

Most design trade-off decisions that you will face come down to the basic conflict of quality versus cost. Although every project has budget and financial constraints, you should avoid decisions that achieve short-term savings but might mean higher costs later. For example, if you try to reduce implementation costs by cutting back on system testing or user training, you can create higher operational costs in the future. If necessary, you should document and explain the situations carefully to management and discuss the possible risks. Each trade-off must be considered individually, and the final result must be acceptable to users, the systems staff, and company management.

PROTOTYPING

Prototyping produces an early, rapidly constructed working version of the proposed information system, called a **prototype**. Prototyping, which involves a repetitive sequence of analysis, design, modeling, and testing, is a common technique that can be used to design anything from a new home to a computer network. For example, engineers use a prototype to evaluate an aircraft design before production begins, as shown in the wind tunnel testing in Figure 5-27.

User input and feedback is essential at every stage of the systems development process. Prototyping allows users to examine a model that accurately represents system outputs, inputs, interfaces, and processes. Users can "test-drive" the model in a risk-free environment and either approve it or request changes. In some situations, the prototype evolves into the final version of the information system; in other cases, the prototype is intended only to validate user requirements and is discarded afterward.

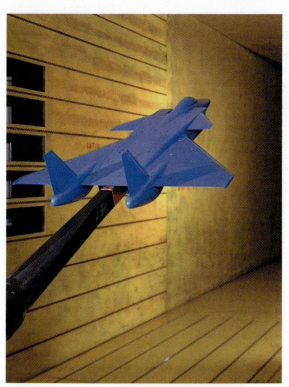

FIGURE 5-27 Wind tunnel testing is a typical example of prototyping.

Prototyping Methods

Systems analysts use two different prototyping methods: system prototyping and design prototyping. **System prototyping** produces a full-featured, working model of the information system. As Figure 5-28 shows, a system prototype is ready for the implementation phase of the SDLC. System prototyping is important especially in rapid application development (RAD), which is described in Chapter 3. Using RAD methods, a team of users, managers, and IT staff members works together to develop a model of the information system that evolves into the completed system. The RAD team defines, analyzes, designs, and tests prototypes using a highly interactive process, which is shown in Figure 3-7 on page 97.

FIGURE 5-28 The end product of system prototyping is a working model of the information system, ready for implementation.

Systems analysts also use prototyping to verify user requirements, after which the prototype is discarded and implementation continues, as shown in Figure 5-29. The approach is called **design prototyping**, or **throwaway prototyping**. In this case, the prototyping objectives are more limited, but no less important. The end product of design prototyping is a user-approved model that documents and benchmarks the features of the finished system.

Design prototyping makes it possible to capture user input and approval while continuing to develop the system within the framework of the SDLC. Systems analysts typically use design prototyping as they construct outputs, inputs, and user interfaces, as discussed in Chapter 6.

FIGURE 5-29 The end product of design prototyping is a user-approved model that documents and benchmarks the features of the finished system.

Whenever possible, you should allow users to experiment with a prototype and provide feedback on how well it meets their needs. This approach can increase development costs, but the expense will be offset by lower costs during subsequent SDLC phases. Prototyping offers many benefits, including the following:

→ Users and systems developers can avoid misunderstandings.

→ System developers can create accurate specifications for the finished system based on the prototype.

→ Managers can evaluate a working model more effectively than a paper specification.

→ Systems analysts can use a prototype to develop testing and training procedures before the finished system is available.

→ Prototyping reduces the risk and potential financial exposure that occur when a finished system fails to support business needs.

Although most systems analysts believe that the advantages of prototyping far outweigh any disadvantages, you should consider the following potential problems:

→ The rapid pace of development can create quality problems, which are not discovered until the finished system is operational.

→ Other system requirements, such as reliability and maintainability, cannot be tested adequately using a prototype.

→ In very complex systems, the prototype becomes unwieldy and difficult to manage.

Prototyping Tools

Systems analysts can use powerful tools to develop prototypes. Most prototyping is done using CASE tools, application generators, report generators, screen generators, and fourth-generation languages (4GLs). In a **fourth-generation language** (4GL), the commands tend to resemble natural statements that people use. For example, a 4GL statement might be PRINT ALL PRODUCTS WHERE CODE = IN STOCK AND STATUS = OK.

In combination, the tools provide a framework for rapid, efficient software development, called a **fourth-generation environment**, as shown in Figure 5-30 on the next page.

Part 2 of the Systems Analyst's Toolkit describes CASE tools in more detail and explains how systems analysts can use them to speed the development process, reduce costs, and avoid design errors. In a fourth-generation environment, the development tools are highly interactive. For example, systems analysts use CASE tools to create a series of diagrams and definitions, which generate a data dictionary automatically. The data dictionary organizes and documents all data elements and interacts with application, screen, and report generators to produce a system prototype.

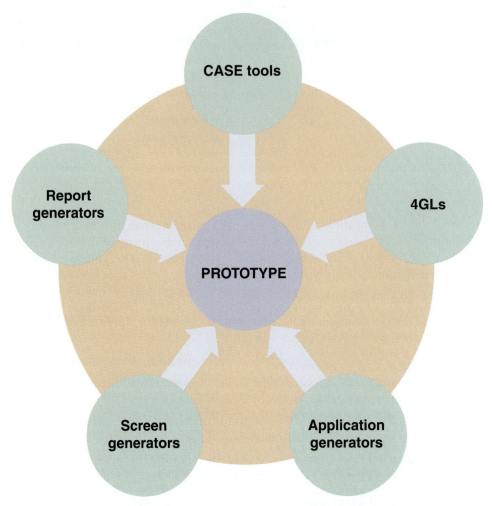

FIGURE 5-30 A fourth-generation environment provides a framework for rapid, efficient software development.

Limitations of Prototypes

The final version of the system typically demands higher-level performance than the prototype can provide. A prototype is a functioning system, but it is less efficient than a fully developed system. Because it is a model, rather than a completed system, the prototype will have slower processing speeds and response times. The prototype also might lack security requirements, exception and error handling procedures, and other required functions. Despite those limitations, systems developers can upgrade the prototype into the final information system by adding the necessary capability. Otherwise, the prototype is discarded and the remaining SDLC phases are completed.

Even when it does not evolve into the finished system, a prototype helps to ensure that the final product will meet all requirements. Satisfying system requirements is the ultimate goal of systems development, and prototyping is an extremely valuable tool during the process.

Other Modeling Tools

As you proceed from logical design to physical design, you continue to use DFDs, object modeling tools, and CASE tools. You also should know about systems flowcharts, which are another method of describing the physical design of a system.

ON THE WEB

For more information about ANSI, visit **scsite.com/sad6e/ more**, locate Chapter 5 and then click the ANSI link.

A **systems flowchart** is a modeling tool that uses various symbols to identify input and output operations, represent data or files, and show media such as disks, documents, and reports. Some systems analysts still use systems flowcharts, but you are more likely to see them as documentation on legacy systems. Most systems flowcharts use a standard set of symbols developed by the **American National Standards Institute** (**ANSI**), as shown in Figure 5-31. Notice that a symbol's shape indicates its meaning.

Figure 5-32 shows an example of a flowchart that uses ANSI symbols. The figure shows how customer payments are processed and posted in an accounting system. Lines with arrowheads indicate the flow of data, just as they do in data flow diagrams.

In Figure 5-32, the flowchart shows three major processing steps that are completed in sequence:

➡ The first process (symbol 2) verifies an online customer payment (symbol 1) by reading from the accounts receivable file (symbol 3), reporting the validity of the online payment, and posting valid payments to the daily payments file (symbol 4).

➡ The second process (symbol 5) sorts the daily payments into accounting code sequence and then creates the sorted daily payments file (symbol 6).

➡ The third process (symbol 7) reads the sorted daily payments, prepares the accounting entries, and produces the cash receipts report (symbol 8).

CHAPTER SUMMARY

This chapter describes system development strategies, the preparation and presentation of the system requirements document, and the transition to the systems design phase of the SDLC.

An important trend that views software as a service, rather than a product, has created new software acquisition options. Systems analysts must consider Web-based development environments such as .NET and WebSphere, and various outsourcing options, including application service providers and Internet business services. Application service providers (ASPs) charge subscription fees for providing application software packages. Internet business services (IBSs) offer powerful Web-based servers, software hosting, and IT support services to customers.

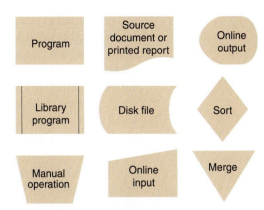

FIGURE 5-31 Examples of ANSI symbols. Notice that the shape of an ANSI symbol indicates its meaning.

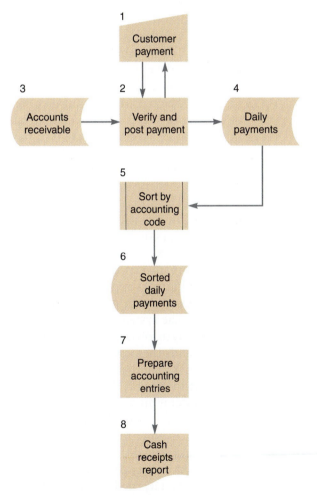

FIGURE 5-32 An example of a flowchart that uses ANSI symbols. The figure shows how customer payments are processed and posted in an accounting system. Notice that symbols 1, 3, 4, 6, and 8 represent data or files stored in a specific form or physical media, while symbols 2, 5, and 7 represent programs.

Traditional systems must function in various hardware and software environments, be compatible with legacy systems, and operate within the constraints of company networks and desktop computing capability. Such systems utilize Internet links and resources as enhancements. In contrast, Internet-based systems treat the Web *as* the platform, rather than just a communication channel. Many large companies use Web-based systems to handle enterprise-wide applications. Compared to traditional systems, Web-based systems are more scalable, less dependent on specific hardware and software, and more adaptable to outsourcing the operation and support of a software application.

If a company chooses to handle its own software development needs, it can create in-house systems, or purchase (and possibly customize) commercially available software packages from a software vendor or value-added reseller (VAR).

Compared with developing an in-house system, an existing commercial software package can be an attractive alternative, because a package generally costs less, takes less time to implement, has a proven track record, and is upgraded frequently. In-house development or customizing a software package might be the best choice when a standard software package cannot meet specific business requirements or constraints. In addition to customizing software packages, companies can create user applications based on standard software that has been specially configured to enhance user productivity.

The systems analyst's role in the software development process depends on the specific development strategy. In-house development requires much more involvement than outsourcing or choosing a commercial package.

The most important factor in choosing a development strategy is total cost of ownership (TCO). Financial analysis tools include payback analysis, which determines how long it takes for a system to pay for itself through reduced costs and increased benefits; return on investment (ROI), which compares a project's total return to its total costs; and net present value (NPV), which analyzes the value of a project by adjusting costs and benefits to reflect the time that they occur.

The process of acquiring software involves a series of steps: evaluate the system requirements, consider network and Web-related issues, identify potential software vendors or outsourcing options, evaluate the alternatives, perform cost-benefit analysis, prepare a recommendation, and implement the solution. During software acquisition, a company can use a request for proposal (RFP) or a request for quotation (RFQ). An RFP invites vendors to respond to a list of system requirements and features; an RFQ seeks bids for a specific product or service.

The system requirements document is the deliverable, or end product, of the systems analysis phase. The document details all system requirements and constraints, recommends the best solution, and provides cost and time estimates for future development work. The system requirements document is the basis for the management presentation. At this point, the firm might decide to develop an in-house system, modify the current system, purchase or customize a software package, perform additional systems analysis work, or stop all further work.

As you prepared for the transition from the systems analysis to systems activities, you learned that a prototype is a working model of the proposed system that you can use to verify the system requirements with users or as a basis for the new system.

You learned that a set of interactive tools, called a fourth-generation environment, can help you construct the prototype. A fourth-generation environment includes screen generators, report writers, application or code generators, and fourth-generation languages, all of which interact with a data dictionary developed with CASE tools. You also learned that systems flowcharts sometimes can represent the physical model of an information system. Finally, you reviewed a set of systems design guidelines and suggestions, including user considerations, data considerations, and processing considerations.

Key Terms and Phrases

American National Standards Institute (ANSI) *231*

application service provider (ASP) *202*

audit trails *226*

benchmark *218*

build or buy *205*

business process outsourcing (BPO) *201*

default *226*

design prototyping *228*

evaluation and selection team *211*

evaluation model *215*

fixed fee model *202*

fourth-generation environment *229*

fourth-generation language (4GL) *229*

global outsourcing *204*

hard-coded *225*

help desk *209*

horizontal application *205*

in-house software *205*

information center (IC) *209*

Internet business services (IBS) *202*

logical design *223*

maintenance agreement *219*

make or buy *205*

managed hosting *202*

middleware *201*

.NET *199*

net present value (NPV) *211*

newsgroups *217*

offshore outsourcing *204*

On Demand *201*

outsourcing *201*

parameter *226*

payback analysis *211*

physical design *223*

prototype *228*

prototyping *228*

read-only properties *210*

report generators *209*

request for proposal (RFP) *214*

request for quotation (RFQ) *216*

return on investment (ROI) *211*

screen generators *209*

service provider *202*

Software and Information Industry Association (SIIA) *198*

software license *219*

software package *205*

software requirements specification *221*

software vendors *205*

subscription model *202*

system prototyping *228*

system requirements document *221*

systems design *224*

systems flowchart *231*

throwaway prototyping *228*

transaction model *202*

usage model *202*

user application *209*

user interface *209*

value-added reseller (VAR) *205*

vertical application *206*

Web-based application development *199*

WebSphere *199*

Learn It Online

Instructions: To complete the Learn It Online exercises, start your browser, click the Address bar, and then enter **scsite.com/sad6e/learn**. When the Systems Analysis and Design Learn It Online page is displayed, follow the instructions in the exercises below. Each exercise has instructions for saving your results, either for your own records or for submission to your instructor.

1 Chapter Reinforcement

TF, MC, and SA

Below SAD Chapter 5, click the Chapter Reinforcement link. Print the quiz by clicking Print on the File menu for each page. Answer each question.

2 Flash Cards

Below SAD Chapter 5, click the Flash Cards link and read the instructions. Type 20 (or a number specified by your instructor) in the Number of playing cards text box, type your name in the Enter your Name text box, and then click the Flip Card button. When the flash card is displayed, read the question and then click the ANSWER box arrow to select an answer. Flip through the Flash Cards. If your score is 15 (75%) correct or greater, click Print on the File menu to print your results. If your score is less than 15 (75%) correct, then redo this exercise by clicking the Replay button.

3 Practice Test

Below SAD Chapter 5, click the Practice Test link. Answer each question, enter your first and last name at the bottom of the page, and then click the Grade Test button. When the graded practice test is displayed on your screen, click Print on the File menu to print a hard copy. Continue to take practice tests until you score 80% or better.

4 Who Wants To Be a Computer Genius?

Below SAD Chapter 5, click the Computer Genius link. Read the instructions, enter your first and last name at the bottom of the page, and then click the Play button. When your score is displayed, click the PRINT RESULTS link to print a hard copy.

5 Wheel of Terms

Below SAD Chapter 5, click the Wheel of Terms link. Read the instructions, and then enter your first and last name and your school name. Click the PLAY button. When your score is displayed on the screen, right-click the score and then click Print on the shortcut menu to print a hard copy.

6 Crossword Puzzle Challenge

Below SAD Chapter 5, click the Crossword Puzzle Challenge link. Read the instructions, and then enter your first and last name. Click the SUBMIT button. Work the crossword puzzle. When you are finished, click the Submit button. When the crossword puzzle is redisplayed, click the Print Puzzle button to print a hard copy.

Case-Sim: SCR Associates

Background

SCR Associates is a consulting firm that offers IT solutions and training. SCR needs an information system to manage operations at its new training center. The new system will be called TIMS (Training Information Management System). As a newly hired systems analyst, you will report to Jesse Baker, systems group manager. You will work on various tasks and practice the skills you learned in this chapter.

Using the Case

The SCR Associates case study is a Web-based simulation that allows you to practice your skills in a real-world environment. The case study transports you to SCR's company intranet, where you can complete 10 work sessions, each aligning with a chapter. As you work on the case, you will receive e-mail and voice mail messages, obtain information from SCR's online libraries, and perform various tasks. The first time you enter the SCR Case, you should go to the Starting page at **scsite.com/sad6e/scr** for detailed instructions.

Preview: Session 5

As you consider various development strategies for the TIMS system, you receive specific directions from your supervisor, Jesse Baker. She wants you to determine whether vertical software packages exist, and she wants you to explore outsourcing options for the new system. She also expects you to conduct a cost-benefit analysis of developing TIMS in-house, and she wants your input on outsourcing and prototyping.

To start a work session, you log on to the SCR intranet. When you enter your name and password, an opening screen displays links to the work sessions, and you select Session 5. At this point, you check your e-mail and voice mail messages carefully. Then you begin working on your task list, which includes the following items:

Tasks: Development Strategies

1. Determine whether vertical software packages exist for training operations management. Search the Internet and draft a message describing the results.

2. Investigate the possibility of outsourcing the TIMS system. List the options, together with advantages and disadvantages of each.

3. Perform three tasks to analyze in-house development of TIMS:
   - (a) Visit the SCR Data Library and review the questionnaire summary and cost-benefit summary;
   - (b) Organize this data into a spreadsheet with columns for years 0, 1, 2, and 3, and rows for the items. Be sure to group developmental costs, operational costs, and revenues separately;
   - (c) Use the spreadsheet data to calculate payback, ROI, and NPV for the TIMS project.

4. Jesse wants my thoughts on how we can use prototyping for TIMS. She also wants me to prepare a system requirements document and a management presentation.

FIGURE 5-33 Task list: Session 5.

Chapter Exercises

Review Questions

1. Describe the trend that views software as a service rather than a product. What effect has this trend had on software acquisition options?
2. Explain the difference between horizontal application software and vertical application software.
3. What is the most common reason for a company to choose to develop its own information system? Give two other reasons why a company might choose the in-house approach.
4. What is an RFP, and how does it differ from an RFQ?
5. What is the purpose of a benchmark test?
6. Explain software licenses and maintenance agreements.
7. What decisions might management reach at the end of the systems analysis phase, and what would be the next step in each case?
8. What is a prototype, and how do systems developers use prototyping?
9. What is a fourth-generation environment?
10. Explain the relationship between logical and physical design.

Discussion Topics

1. As more companies outsource systems development, will there be less need for in-house systems analysts? Why or why not?
2. Suppose you tried to explain the concept of throwaway prototyping to a manager, and she responded by asking, "So, is throwaway prototyping a waste of time and money?" How would you reply?
3. Select a specific type of vertical application software to investigate. Visit local computer stores and use the Internet to determine what software packages are available. Describe the common features of those packages and the features that distinguish one product from another.
4. Select a specific type of horizontal application software to investigate. Visit local computer stores and use the Internet to determine what software packages are available. Describe the common features of those packages and the features that distinguish one product from another.

Projects

1. The text mentions several firms and organizations that offer IT benchmarking. Locate another benchmarking firm on the Internet, and write a description of the services it offers.
2. Turn to Part 3 of the Systems Analyst's Toolkit and review the concept of net present value (NPV). Determine the NPV for the following: An information system will cost $95,000 to implement over a one-year period and will produce no savings during that year. When the system goes online, the company will save $30,000 during the first year of operation. For the next four years, the savings will be $20,000 per year. Assuming a 12 percent discount rate, what is the NPV of the system?
3. Visit the IT department at your school or at a local company and determine whether the information systems were developed in-house or purchased as software packages. If packages were acquired, determine what customizing was done, if any. Write a brief memo describing the results of your visit.
4. To create user applications as described in this chapter, systems analysts often use macros. Microsoft defines a macro as "a series of commands and instructions that you group together as a single command to accomplish a task automatically." Learn more about macros by using the Help feature in Microsoft Word, and identify three tasks that might be performed by macros.

Apply Your Knowledge

The Apply Your Knowledge section contains four mini-cases. Each case describes a situation, explains your role in the case, and asks you to respond to questions. You can answer the questions by applying knowledge you learned in the chapter.

1 Top Sail Realty

Situation:

Top Sail Realty is one of the largest time-sharing and rental brokers for vacation cottages along the North Carolina coast. After 10 successful years of matching up owners and renters, Top Sail decided to acquire a computerized reservation and booking system. Top Sail's owner read an article about software packages, and she asked you, as an IT consultant, for your advice.

1. Should Top Sail implement a Web-based system? Why or why not?
2. What software acquisition options are available to Top Sail?
3. Do you consider the reservations system to be a horizontal or a vertical application? Give reasons for your answer.
4. When you evaluate software packages, what steps will you follow?

2 One Way Movers, Inc.

Situation:

As IT manager at One Way, you scheduled a management presentation next week. You prepared and distributed a systems requirement document, and you anticipate some intense questioning at the meeting.

1. When planning your presentation, what are some techniques you will use?
2. Based on the suggestions in the Systems Analyst's Toolkit, what visual aids can you use during your presentation?
3. In deciding on your proposal, what options does management have?
4. If management decides to purchase or customize a software package, what steps will you take?

3 **Tangible Investments Corporation**

Situation:

Tangible Investments Corporation needs a new customer billing system. As project leader, you decided to create a prototype that users can evaluate before the final design is implemented. You plan to use a traditional structured analysis methodology. To prepare for your meeting with top management tomorrow, you need to review the following topics.

1. Explain the main purpose of prototyping.
2. Explain why a prototype might or might not evolve into the final version of the system.
3. Describe the tools typically used in developing prototypes.
4. List three advantages and three disadvantages of prototyping.

4 **IT Flash Magazine**

Situation:

You are a staff writer at IT Flash Magazine, a popular online newsletter aimed at IT professionals. Your editor has asked you to prepare a special report for next week's edition. Specifically, she wants you to research the subject of software outsourcing, and other significant trends that might affect software development in the future. If possible, she wants you to cite specific sources for your information, including IT employment statistics and employment forecasts from the Bureau of Labor Statistics.

1. Search for information about software outsourcing generally, using the search techniques described in Part 6 of the Systems Analyst's Toolkit.
2. Visit the Bureau of Labor Statistics site at bls.gov and search for information about employment trends affecting systems analysts, computer programmers, and software engineers.
3. Does the Bureau of Labor Statistics offer any comments or insights into the subject of outsourcing generally? What conclusions does it reach?
4. In your report, comment on whether the offshore outsourcing of IT jobs is just another step in the progression that began with manufacturing jobs, or represents a whole new trend. Be sure to cite Web research sources and your own reasons.

Case Studies

Case studies allow you to practice specific skills learned in the chapter. Each chapter contains several case studies that continue throughout the textbook, and a chapter capstone case.

NEW CENTURY HEALTH CLINIC

New Century Health Clinic offers preventive medicine and traditional medical care. In your role as an IT consultant, you will help New Century develop a new information system.

Background

Based on your earlier recommendations, New Century decided to continue the systems development process for a new information system that would improve operations, decrease costs, and provide better service to patients.

Now, at the end of the systems analysis phase, you are ready to prepare a system requirements document and give a presentation to the New Century associates. Many of the proposed system's advantages were described during the fact-finding process. Those include smoother operation, better efficiency, and more user-friendly procedures for patients and New Century staff.

You also must examine tangible costs and benefits to determine the economic feasibility of several alternatives. If New Century decides to go ahead with the development process, the main options are to develop the system in-house or purchase a vertical package and configure it to meet New Century's needs. You have studied those choices and put together some preliminary figures.

You know that New Century's current workload requires three hours of office staff overtime per week at a base rate of $8.50 per hour. In addition, based on current projections, New Century will need to add another full-time clerical position in about six months. Neither the overtime nor the additional job will be needed if New Century implements the new system. The current manual system also causes an average of three errors per day, and each error takes about 20 minutes to correct. The new system should eliminate those errors.

Based on your research, you estimate by working full-time you could complete the project in about 12 weeks. Your consulting rate, which New Century agreed to, is $30 per hour. If you design the new system as a database application, you can expect to spend about $2,500 for a networked commercial package. After the system is operational and the staff is trained, New Century should be able to handle routine maintenance tasks without your assistance.

As an alternative to in-house development, a vertical software package is available for about $9,000. The vendor offers a lease-purchase package of $3,000 down, followed by two annual installments of $3,000 each. If New Century buys the package, it would take you about four weeks to install, configure, and test it, working full-time. The vendor provides free support during the first year of operation, but then New Century must sign a technical support agreement at an annual cost of $500. Although the package contains many of the features that New Century wants, most of the reports are pre-designed and it would be difficult to modify their layouts.

No matter which approach is selected, New Century probably will need you to provide about 10 hours of initial training and support each week for the first three months of operation. After the new system is operational, it will need routine maintenance, file backups, and updating. These tasks will require about four hours per week and can be performed by a clinic staff member. In both cases, the necessary hardware and network installation will cost about $5,000.

In your view, the useful life of the system will be about five years, including the year in which the system becomes operational.

Assignments

You scheduled a presentation to New Century in one week, and you must submit a system requirements document during the presentation. Prepare both the written documentation and the presentation. (To give a successful presentation, you will need to learn the skills described in Part 1 of the Systems Analyst's Toolkit.) Your oral and written presentation must include the following tasks:

1. Provide an overview of the proposed system, including costs and benefits, with an explanation of the various cost-and-benefit types and categories.
2. Develop an economic feasibility analysis, using payback analysis, ROI, and present value (assume a discount rate of 10 percent).
3. Prepare a context diagram and diagram 0 for the new system.
4. Provide a brief explanation of the various alternatives that should be investigated if development continues, including in-house development and any other possible strategies.

You may wish to include other material to help your audience understand the new system and make a decision on the next step.

Presentation Rules

The following presentation rules should be considered:

- Use suitable visual aids.
- Use presentation software, if possible.
- Distribute handouts before, during, or after the presentation.
- Follow the guidelines in Part 1 of the Systems Analyst's Toolkit.
- Keep your presentation to 30 minutes, including 5 minutes for questions.

Rules for the System Requirements Document

Consider the following rules while preparing the system requirements document:

- Follow the guidelines in Part 1 of the Systems Analyst's Toolkit.
- Include charts, graphs, or other helpful visual information in the document.
- Spell check and carefully proofread the entire document.

PERSONAL TRAINER, INC.

Personal Trainer, Inc., owns and operates fitness centers in a dozen Midwestern cities. The centers have done well, and the company is planning an international expansion by opening a new "supercenter" in the Toronto area. Personal Trainer's president, Cassia Umi, hired an IT consultant, Susan Park, to help develop an information system for the new facility. During the project, Susan will work closely with Gray Lewis, who will manage the new operation.

Background

During data and process modeling, Susan Park developed a logical model of the proposed system. She drew an entity-relationship diagram and constructed a set of leveled and balanced DFDs. Now Susan is ready to consider various development strategies for the new system. She will investigate traditional and Web-based approaches and weigh the advantages and disadvantages of in-house development versus other alternatives. As she moves ahead to the systems design phase, she will review design guidelines, consider the use of prototypes, and analyze the possible use of codes.

Before You Begin . . .

Review the facts presented in the Personal Trainer case study in Chapters 2, 3, and 4. Use that information to complete the following tasks.

Assignments

1. Should the new system be designed as a Web-based system? Why or why not? What are some specific issues and options that Susan should consider in making a decision?

2. Assume that Cassia Umi, Personal Trainer's president, has asked Susan to prepare a system requirements document and deliver a presentation to the management team. What should be the main elements of the system requirements document? Also, based on the suggestions in Part 1 of the Systems Analyst's Toolkit, what visual aids should Susan use during her presentation?

3. Should Susan use a prototype during systems design? What options does she have, and how would you advise her?

4. Susan wants to prepare a presentation that will calculate the total cost of ownership for the system. What financial analysis tools are available to her, and what are the advantages (and possible disadvantages) of each tool?

CUTTING EDGE

Part 4 of the Systems Analyst's Toolkit discusses **software change control**, which is the process of managing and controlling changes after management approves the system requirements document. You should review the material about this topic now, before completing the Cutting Edge case study.

Background

Cutting Edge is a company that develops and sells accounting software tailored to specific businesses and industries. Product manager Michelle Kellogg is leading a development team working on a specialized package for building contractors. The systems analysis phase was completed on March 6. The package is scheduled for release on August 1.

On April 1, Michelle received a request from Cutting Edge's CEO for a new feature to be added to the package. She asked Michelle to analyze the change and determine its impact on the project.

Michelle reviewed the results at a meeting on April 15. Adding the new feature to the package now increases the development cost by $28,000 and delays the release date by one month. Michelle also evaluated a second alternative: develop the package without the requested change and add the feature in a follow-up release, which requires two additional months to complete and costs $66,000.

Assignments

1. Because the project is in the systems design phase and no programming has been started, why would incorporating the requested change add one month and $28,000 to the project?

2. If the change were delayed until after the initial release of the package, why would it require two additional months and $66,000 more to implement a new version with the desired feature?

3. What are the advantages and disadvantages of each alternative?

4. Suppose you are Michelle and you must recommend action on the change request. What factors would you consider, and what would you recommend?

CHAPTER CAPSTONE CASE: SoftWear, Limited

SoftWear, Limited (SWL), is a continuing case study that illustrates the knowledge and skills described in each chapter. In this case study, the student acts as a member of the SWL systems development team and performs various tasks.

Background

Systems analyst Rick Williams and programmer/analyst Carla Moore continued to work on a logical model of the payroll system. Meanwhile, the information systems department recently purchased and installed Visible Analyst, a CASE toolkit that supports logical and physical modeling. Rick and Carla traveled to Massachusetts to attend a one-week workshop to learn how to use the package.

After returning from their trip, Rick and Carla decided to create the logical model for the payroll system with Visible Analyst. They felt that the time spent now would pay off in later phases of the project. Rick and Carla used the manual DFDs they created in Chapter 4 to create computerized DFDs using Visible Analyst. Now all related items for the new system are stored in the CASE tool.

Over the next month, Rick and Carla looked at various alternatives and spent their time evaluating the potential solutions. They determined that the best solution was to purchase a payroll package, but the ESIP processing was so unique that none of the available software packages would handle SWL's specific requirements. They concluded that SWL should purchase a payroll package and develop the ESIP system in-house. Jane Rossman and Ann Hon agreed with their recommendation.

The systems analysts completed work on the logical model, alternative evaluations, and cost and time estimates and then prepared the system requirements document for the payroll system. The document was printed and distributed and a management presentation was scheduled at the end of the following week.

At this point, the IT team members were confident that they had done a good job. They had worked closely with SWL users throughout the development process and received user approval on important portions of the document as it was being prepared. They developed visual aids, rehearsed the presentation, and then tried to anticipate questions that management might ask.

Carla gave the management presentation. She recommended that SWL purchase a payroll package sold by Pacific Software Solutions and that ESIP processing be developed in-house to interface with the payroll package.

During the presentation, Carla and Rick answered questions on several points, including the economic analysis they had done. Michael Jeremy, vice president of finance, was especially interested in the method they used to calculate payback analysis, return on investment, and net present value for the new system.

Robert Lansing, SWL's president, arrived for the last part of the presentation. When the presentation ended, he asked the top managers how they felt about the project, and they indicated support for the proposal made by the IT department. The next step was to negotiate a contract with Pacific Software Solutions and for Rick and Carla to begin systems design for the ESIP processing component.

CHAPTER CAPSTONE CASE: SoftWear, Limited (continued)   SWL

SWL Team Tasks

1. Although the presentation was successful, Rick and Carla both feel that the IT department should have a checklist to serve as a suggested model for IT staff people who must prepare management presentations. They asked you to suggest a list of dos and don'ts for presentations.

2. Rick and Carla also want you to review the DFDs that they prepared to see whether you have any suggestions for improvement. If you have access to a copier, make a copy of the DFDs shown in Chapter 4 and then write your notes directly on the diagrams. Otherwise, you can present a brief memo listing your comments.

3. Michael Jeremy, vice president of finance, was interested in the financial analysis tools that Rick and Carla used in the presentation. Rick has asked you to write a memo to Mr. Jeremy explaining each tool, with a specific description of how it is used, and what results can be obtained. To do this, you might need to review the material in Part 3 of the Systems Analyst's Toolkit.

4. Although SWL decided to develop the ESIP system in-house, Ann Hon, director of information technology, has requested a report on the trend toward outsourcing software development. Perform Internet research to get up-to-date information about this topic, and prepare a memo for Ms. Hon. Be sure to cite your sources of information, and any Web sites you might want her to visit.

PHASE 3 SYSTEMS DESIGN

Systems Design is the third of five phases in the systems development life cycle (SDLC). In the previous phase, systems analysis, you developed a logical model of the system and considered various development strategies. Now you are ready to begin the physical design of the system that will meet the specifications described in the system requirements document. Systems design tasks include output and user interface design, data design, and system architecture.

PHASE TOPICS

Chapter 6
Output and User
Interface Design

Chapter 7
Data Design

Chapter 8
System Architecture

DELIVERABLE

System Design Specification

TOOLKIT SUPPORT

Primary tools: Communications, CASE, and project management tools. Other tools as required.

CHAPTER 6 Output and User Interface Design

CHAPTER 6 is the first of three chapters in the systems design phase of the SDLC. This chapter explains how to design the desired system output, and how to construct an effective user interface that includes suitable input screens and procedures. The chapter stresses the importance of user feedback and involvement in all design decisions.

INTRODUCTION

Output and user interface design is the first task in the systems design phase of the SDLC. Output design focuses on user needs for screen and printed forms of output, while user interface design stresses user interaction with the computer, including input design and procedures.

This chapter begins with a discussion of output design, including printed reports and other system outputs. The chapter then covers user interface design concepts, including functions, layout, usability; and input procedures, controls, and formats.

OBJECTIVES

When you finish this chapter, you will be able to:

- Discuss output design issues and various types of output
- Design various types of reports, and suggest output controls and security
- Explain the concept of user interface design and human-computer interaction, including the basic principles of user-centered design
- List specific guidelines for user interface design
- Describe user interface techniques, including screen elements and controls
- Explain input design concepts, techniques, and methods
- Describe guidelines for data entry screen design
- Use validation checks for reducing input errors
- Design effective source documents and input controls

CHAPTER INTRODUCTION CASE: Mountain View College Bookstore

Background: Wendy Lee, manager of college services at Mountain View College, wants a new information system that will improve efficiency and customer service at the three college bookstores.

In this part of the case, Florence Fullerton (systems analyst) and Harry Boston (student intern) are talking about output and user interface design issues.

Participants:	Florence and Harry
Location:	Mountain View College Cafeteria, Thursday afternoon, December 8, 2005
Project status:	Florence and Harry have examined development strategies for the new bookstore system. After performing cost-benefit analysis, they recommended in-house development of the new bookstore system. Now they are ready to begin the systems design phase by working on output and user interface design for the new system.
Discussion topics:	Output design issues, and user interface concepts and principles

Florence: Hi, Harry. Ready to start work on output and user interface design?

Harry: *Sure. I guess we start with output, because that's the most important issue to users.*

Florence: Right. We'll deal with on-screen and printed output. The other big issue with users is how they interact with the system. The user interface involves human-computer interaction. As you know, we've come a long way from character-based screens. We'll create a graphical interface to make it easy for users to learn and work with the new system. The object is to design everything from a user's point of view.

Harry: *How do we do that?*

Florence: Well, many sources of information about effective design concepts and principles are available. IBM's user bill of rights is a good example. We'll study those, and then ask our own users for their input and suggestions.

Harry: *What about input and data entry?*

Florence: Good question. You've heard the old saying, "garbage in, garbage out." User interface principles apply to user input generally, but repetitive data entry deserves special attention. We need to create screen forms that are logical and easy to understand, as well as data entry validation checks. We also need to review any source documents that will be filled in manually.

Harry: *Anything else?*

Florence: Yes. The bookstore system probably will have some confidential data regarding budgets and markup policies, so we'll have to consider output control and security. If you're ready, here's a task list to get us started:

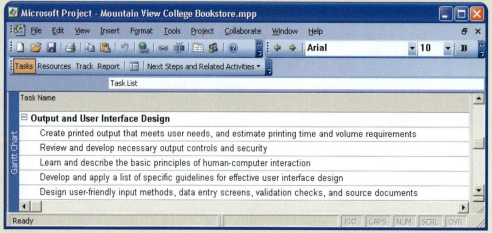

FIGURE 6-1

OUTPUT DESIGN

Before designing output, ask yourself several questions:

→ What is the purpose of the output?

→ Who wants the information, why is it needed, and how will it be used?

→ What specific information will be included?

→ Will the output be printed, viewed on-screen, or both? What type of device will the output go to?

→ When will the information be provided, and how often must it be updated?

→ Do security or confidentiality issues exist?

The design process should not begin until you have answered those questions. Some of the information probably was gathered during the systems analysis phase. To complete your understanding, you should meet with users to find out exactly what kind of output is needed. You can use prototypes and mock-ups to obtain feedback throughout the design process. Your answers will affect your output design strategies, as you will see in the next section.

Types of Output

Although most system output is printed in reports or displayed on screens, new technology has had an enormous impact on how people communicate and obtain information. The change especially is true in business information systems that require significant user interaction.

Figure 6-2 shows that, in addition to printed and screen output, information is delivered to users by means of the Internet, e-mail, audio output, automated facsimile systems, computer output microfilm, computer to laser disk, and other specialized methods. The type of output and the technology needed usually are decided during the systems analysis phase, based on user requirements. Now, in the systems design phase, you must design the actual reports, screen forms, and other output delivery methods.

INTERNET-BASED INFORMATION DELIVERY Millions of firms use the Internet to reach new customers and markets around the world. To support the explosive growth in e-commerce, Web designers must provide user-friendly screen interfaces that display output and accept input from customers. For example, a business can link its inventory system to its Web site so the output from the inventory system is displayed as an online catalog. Customers visiting the site can review the items, obtain current prices, and check product availability. Another example of Web-based output is a system that provides customized responses to product or technical questions. When a user enters a product inquiry or requests technical support, the system responds with appropriate information from an on-site knowledge base.

E-MAIL E-mail has become an essential means of internal and external business communication. Employees send and receive e-mail on local or wide area networks, including the Internet. Companies send new product information to customers via e-mail, and financial services companies use e-mail messages to confirm online stock trades. Employees use e-mail to exchange documents, data, and schedules and to share business-related information they need to perform their jobs. In many firms, e-mail has virtually replaced traditional memos and printed correspondence.

ON THE WEB

For more information about E-Mail, visit **scsite.com/sad6e/ more**, locate Chapter 6 and then click the E-Mail link.

Information Delivery Method	Description
Audio	Audio output consists of speech or sounds that can be stored digitally and reproduced as audible information.
Automated facsimile	Automated facsimile systems allow users to request and receive specific information by facsimile.
Computer output microfilm (COM)	Computer output microfilm (COM) records information as images on microfilm rolls or microfiche sheets.
Computer output to laser disk (COLD)	When many paper documents must be stored and accessed, computer output to laser disk (COLD) technology can be used to scan the documents and store the digital images on a high-density laser disk medium.
E-mail	E-mail, or electronic messaging systems, supports internal and external business communications using local or wide area networks, including the Internet.
Internet-based	The Internet has profoundly affected business communications and changed the way business is conducted. Companies today depend on Web-based information delivery to support business operations, to manage the enterprise, and to provide an information infrastructure.
Mobile devices	Messages and data can be transmitted to a wide array of mobile devices, including handheld computers, cell phones, and similar products that combine computing power, multimedia capability, and Internet access.
Other specialized devices	Diverse business operations require specialized applications, including point-of-sale terminals, ATMs, special-purpose printers, plotters, digital photos, and visual displays on machines and appliances.
Printer	Prints text and graphics on various types of paper.
Screen	Displays text and graphics on a computer workstation or handheld device.

FIGURE 6-2 Common information delivery methods.

AUDIO **Audio output** can be attached to an e-mail message or inserted as an audio clip in a Microsoft Word document, as shown in Figure 6-3 on the next page. In addition, many firms use automated systems to handle voice transactions and provide information to customers. For example, using a telephone keypad, a customer can confirm an airline seat assignment, check a credit card balance, or determine the current price of a mutual fund.

AUTOMATED FACSIMILE SYSTEMS Some firms use **automated facsimile**, sometimes called **faxback** systems, to allow a customer to request a fax using e-mail, via the company Web site, or by telephone. The response is transmitted in a matter of seconds back to the user's fax machine. A computer firm, for example, might allow customers to request technical updates, information on new device drivers, or product assistance via fax. That type of automated output is available 24 hours a day and provides an immediate response to a customer.

COMPUTER OUTPUT MICROFILM (COM) Computer output microfilm (COM) systems, such as microfilm and microfiche, capture an image of a document and produce film output. Users then can retrieve, view, and print the images. **Microfilm** records the images on a roll of film, and **microfiche** records images using a small sheet of film. COM systems are especially important where it is necessary to show a signature, date stamp, or other visual feature of a document.

COMPUTER OUTPUT TO LASER DISK (COLD) **Computer output to laser disk** (COLD) is another way to store images of paper documents. Using COLD technology, a paper document is scanned, and the digital image is stored on a high-density laser disk medium. COLD technology also enables rapid information retrieval of formatted

information. For example, if an insurance company stores thousands of paper application forms, special software can treat the document as data and extract information from a particular column or area on the form.

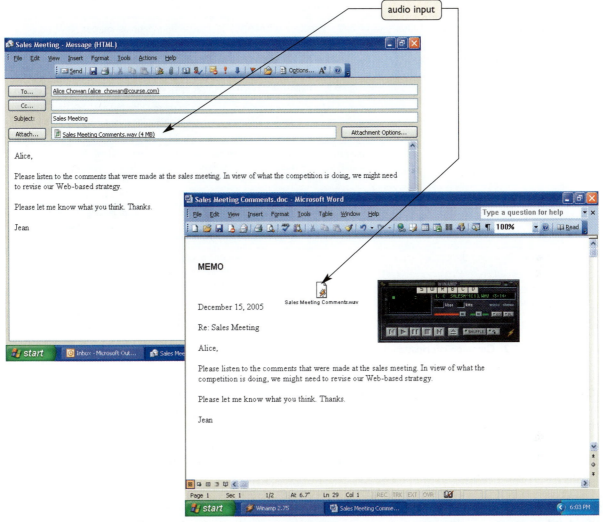

FIGURE 6-3 Audio output can be attached to an e-mail message (upper screen) or inserted as an audio clip in a Microsoft Word document (lower screen). Either way, the recipient can double-click the link or icon and a media player opens the file.

SPECIALIZED FORMS OF OUTPUT An incredibly diverse marketplace requires a variety of specialized output. Consider the following examples:

- Retail point-of-sale terminals that handle computer-based credit card transactions, print receipts, and update inventory records.

- Automatic teller machines (ATMs) that process bank transactions and print deposit and withdrawal slips.

- Special-purpose printers that produce labels, photos, driver's licenses and, in some states, lottery tickets.

- Plotters that produce high-quality images such as blueprints, maps, and electronic circuit diagrams.

- Digitized photos that companies can print on employee identification cards.

- Programmable devices such as television sets, VCRs, and microwave ovens that display visual output.

In today's interconnected world, output from one system often becomes input into another system. For example, within a company, production data from the manufacturing system becomes input to the inventory system. The same company might transmit employee W-2 tax data to the IRS system electronically. A company employee might use tax preparation software to file a tax return electronically, receive a refund deposited directly into his or her bank account, and see the deposit reflected on the bank's information system.

Although digital technology has opened new horizons in business communications, printed output still is a common type of output, and specific considerations apply to it. For those reasons, printed output is discussed in its own section, which follows.

PRINTED AND SCREEN OUTPUT

Although many organizations strive to reduce the flow of paper and printed reports, few firms have been able to eliminate printed output totally. Because they are portable, printed reports are convenient, and even necessary in some situations. Many users find it handy to view screen output, then print the information they need for a discussion or business meeting. Printed output also is used in **turnaround documents**, which are output documents that are later entered back into the same or another information system. In some areas, your telephone or utility bill, for example, might be a turnaround document printed by the company's billing system. When you return the required portion of the bill with your check, the bill is scanned into the company's accounts receivable system to record the payment accurately.

Reports

Whether printed or viewed on-screen, reports should be attractive and easy to understand. Systems analysts should realize managers sometimes judge an entire project by the quality of the reports they receive.

To be useful, a report must include the information that a user needs. From a user's point of view, a report with too little information is of no value. Too much information, however, can make a report confusing and difficult to understand. When designing reports, the essential goal is to match the report to the user's specific information needs. Depending on their job functions, users might need one or more of the reports described below.

DETAIL REPORTS A **detail report** produces one or more lines of output for each record processed. Each line of output printed is called a **detail line**. Figure 6-4 on the next page shows a simple detail report of employee hours for a chain of retail stores. Notice that one detail line prints for each employee. All the fields in the record do not have to be printed, nor do the fields have to be printed in the sequence in which they appear in the record. An employee paycheck that has multiple output lines for a single record is another example of a detail report.

A well-designed detail report should provide totals for numeric fields. Notice that the report shown in Figure 6-4 lacks subtotals and grand totals for regular hours, overtime hours, and total hours. Figure 6-5 on the next page shows the same report with subtotals and grand totals added. In the example, the STORE NUMBER field is called a **control field** because it controls the output.

When the value of a control field changes, a control break occurs. A **control break** usually causes specific actions, such as printing subtotals for a group of records. That type of detail report is called a **control break report**. To produce a control break report, the records must be arranged, or sorted, in control field order. The sorting can be done by the report program itself, or in a previous procedure.

ON THE WEB

For more information about Printed Output, visit **scsite.com/ sad6e/more**, locate Chapter 6 and then click the Printed Output link.

STORE NUMBER	EMPLOYEE NAME	POSITION	REGULAR HOURS	OVERTIME HOURS	TOTAL HOURS
8	Andres, Marguerite	Clerk	20.0	0.0	20.0
8	Bogema, Michelle	Clerk	12.5	0.0	12.5
8	Davenport, Kim	Asst Mgr	40.0	5.0	45.0
8	Lemka, Susan	Clerk	32.7	0.0	32.7
8	Linquist, Linda	Clerk	16.0	0.0	16.0
8	Ramirez, Rudy	Manager	40.0	8.5	48.5
8	Ullery, Ruth	Clerk	20.0	0.0	20.0
11	Byrum, Cheri	Clerk	15.0	0.0	15.0
11	Byrum, Mary	Clerk	15.0	0.0	15.0
11	Deal, JoAnn	Clerk	4.8	0.0	4.8
11	Gadzinski, Barbara	Manager	40.0	10.0	50.0
11	Huyhn, Loc	Clerk	20.0	0.0	20.0
11	Schuller, Monica	Clerk	10.0	0.0	10.0
11	Stites, Carol	Clerk	40.0	12.0	52.0
11	Thompson, Mary Kay	Asst Mgr	40.0	1.5	41.5
17	De Martini, Jennifer	Clerk	40.0	8.4	48.4
17	Haff, Lisa	Manager	40.0	0.0	40.0
17	Rittenbery, Sandra	Clerk	40.0	11.0	51.0
17	Wyer, Elizabeth	Clerk	20.0	0.0	20.0
17	Zeigler, Cecille	Clerk	32.0	0.0	32.0

EMPLOYEE HOURS
WEEK ENDING DATE: 6/24/05
PAGE 1

detail lines

FIGURE 6-4   A detail report with one printed line per employee.

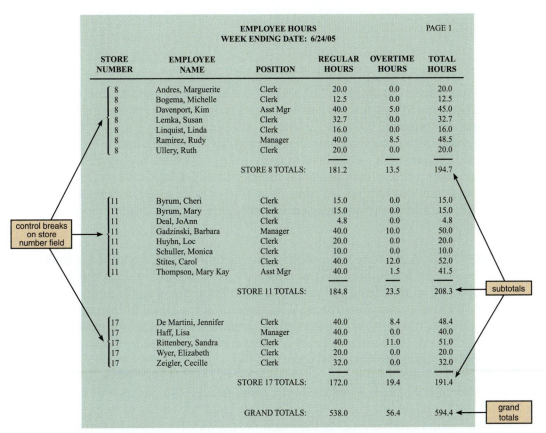

FIGURE 6-5   This detail report contains the same data as Figure 6-4, but provides much more information. Control breaks are used to separate the data for each store, with subtotals and grand totals for numeric fields.

Because it contains one or more lines for each record, a detail report can be quite lengthy. Consider, for example, a large auto parts business. If the firm stocks 3,000 parts,

then the detail report would include 3,000 detail lines on approximately 50 printed pages. A user who wants to locate any part in short supply has to examine 3,000 detail lines to find the critical items. A much better alternative is to produce an exception report.

EXCEPTION REPORTS An **exception report** displays only those records that meet a specific condition or conditions. Exception reports are useful when the user wants information only on records that might require action, but does not need to know the details. For example, a credit manager might use an exception report to identify only those customers with past due accounts, or a customer service manager might want a report on all packages that were not delivered within a specified time period. Figure 6-6 shows an exception report that includes information only for those employees who worked overtime, instead of listing information for all employees.

STORE NUMBER	POSITION	EMPLOYEE NAME	OVERTIME HOURS
		OVERTIME REPORT	PAGE 1
		WEEK ENDING DATE: 6/24/05	
8	Asst Mgr	Davenport, Kim	5.0
	Manager	Ramirez, Rudy	8.5
		STORE 8 TOTALS:	13.5
11	Manager	Gadzinski, Barbara	10.0
	Clerk	Stites, Carol	12.0
	Asst Mgr	Thompson, Mary Kay	1.5
		STORE 11 TOTALS:	23.5
17	Clerk	De Martini, Jennifer	8.4
	Clerk	Rittenbery, Sandra	11.0
		STORE 17 TOTALS:	19.4
		GRAND TOTAL:	56.4

FIGURE 6-6 An exception report that shows information *only* for employees who worked overtime.

SUMMARY REPORTS Upper-level managers often want to see total figures and do not need supporting details. A sales manager, for example, might want to know total sales for each sales representative, but not want a detail report listing every sale made by them. In that case, a **summary report** is appropriate. Similarly, a personnel manager might need to know the total regular and overtime hours worked by employees in each store but might not be interested in the number of hours worked by each employee. For the personnel manager, a summary report such as the one shown in Figure 6-7 on the next page would be useful. Generally, reports used by individuals at higher levels in the organization include less detail than reports used by lower-level employees.

User Involvement in Report Design

Printed reports are an important way of delivering information to users, so recipients should approve all report designs in advance. To avoid problems, you should submit each design for approval as you complete it, rather than waiting until you finish all report designs.

STORE NUMBER					REGULAR HOURS	OVERTIME HOURS	TOTAL HOURS

EMPLOYEE HOURS SUMMARY
WEEK ENDING DATE: 6/24/05

PAGE 1

STORE NUMBER	REGULAR HOURS	OVERTIME HOURS	TOTAL HOURS
8	181.2	13.5	194.7
11	184.8	23.5	208.3
17	172.0	19.4	191.4
TOTALS:	538.0	56.4	594.4

FIGURE 6-7 A summary report lists subtotals and grand totals.

When designing a report, you should prepare a sample report, which is called a **mock-up,** or prototype, for users to review. The sample should include typical field values and contain enough records to show all the design features. Depending on the type of printed output, you can use a word processor, a report generator, or a printer spacing chart to create mock-up reports.

Report Design Principles

Printed reports must be attractive, professional, and easy to read. Good report design, like any other aspect of the user interface, requires effort and attention to detail. To produce a well-designed report, the analyst must consider several topics, including report headers and footers, page headers and footers, column headings and alignment, column spacing, field order, and grouping of detail lines. Figure 6-8 shows an example of those design features.

REPORT HEADERS AND FOOTERS Every report should have a report header and a report footer. The **report header,** which appears at the beginning of the report, identifies the report, and contains the report title, date, and other necessary information. The **report footer,** which appears at the end of the report, can include grand totals for numeric fields and other end-of-report information, as shown in Figure 6-8.

PAGE HEADERS AND FOOTERS Every page should include a **page header,** which appears at the top of the page and includes the column headings that identify the data. The headings should be short but descriptive. Avoid abbreviations unless you know that users will understand them clearly. Either a page header or a **page footer,** which appears at the bottom of the page, is used to display the report title and the page number.

COLUMN HEADING ALIGNMENT Figure 6-9 shows several column heading alignment options. In Example 1, the left-justified column headings do not work well with numeric fields because the amount 1.25 would print past the right edge of the AMOUNT heading. In Example 2, the right-justified headings cause a problem with alphanumeric fields, because none of the characters in a short name would print under any part of the NAME heading. Centering headings over *maximum* field widths, as shown in Example 3, is not ideal when many of the actual values are shorter than the maximum width. Many designers prefer Example 4, where headings are left-justified over alphanumeric fields and right-justified over numeric fields.

COLUMN SPACING You should space columns of information carefully. A crowded report is hard to read, and large gaps between columns make it difficult for the eye to follow a line. Columns should stretch across the report, with uniform spacing and

suitable margins at top, bottom, right, and left. Some report designers use landscape orientation when working with a large number of columns; others prefer to break the information into more than one report. In some cases, a smaller point size will solve the problem, but the report must remain readable and acceptable to users.

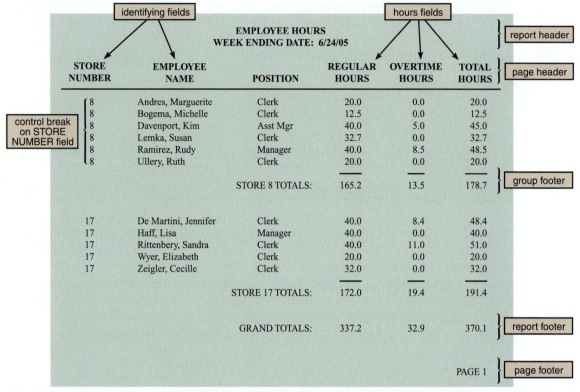

FIGURE 6-8 The Employee Hours report is a detail report with control breaks, subtotals, and grand totals. Notice that a report header identifies the report, a page header contains column headings, a group footer contains subtotals for each store, a report footer contains grand totals, and a page footer identifies the page number.

	NAME		NUMBER	AMOUNT
Example 1: Column headings are left-justified over maximum field widths.	NAME XXXXXXXXXXXXXXXXXXXXXXXXX		NUMBER ZZZ9	AMOUNT ZZZ,ZZ9.99
Example 2: Column headings are right-justified over maximum field widths.		NAME XXXXXXXXXXXXXXXXXXXXXXXXX	NUMBER ZZZ9	AMOUNT ZZZ,ZZ9.99
Example 3: Column headings are centered over maximum field widths.	NAME XXXXXXXXXXXXXXXXXXXXXXXXX		NUMBER ZZZ9	AMOUNT ZZZ,ZZ9.99
Example 4: Column headings are left-justified over alphanumeric fields and right-justified over numeric fields.	NAME XXXXXXXXXXXXXXXXXXXXXXXXX		NUMBER ZZZ9	AMOUNT ZZZ,ZZ9.99

FIGURE 6-9 Four different column heading alignment options.

FIELD ORDER Fields should be displayed and grouped in a logical order. The report shown in Figure 6-8, for example, shows the detail lines printed in alphabetical order within store number, so the store number is in the left column, followed by the employee

name. The employee position relates to the employee's name, so the items are adjacent. The three hours fields also are placed together.

GROUPING DETAIL LINES   Often, it is meaningful to arrange detail lines in groups, based on a control field. For example, using the department number as a control field, individual employees can be grouped by department. You can print a **group header** above the first detail line and a **group footer** after the last detail line in a group, as shown in Figure 6-8 on the previous page. In a group footer, you can include a subtotal, an average, or a count of the records in that group.

Report Design Issues

Revisit the Employee Hours report shown in Figure 6-8. Although the report follows many of the design guidelines discussed, you still could improve it. Too much detail is on the page, forcing users to search for the information they need. Can you see any material that you could eliminate?

If most employees do not work overtime, then overtime hours should stand out. You can do that by not printing 0.0 when overtime hours are zero. Repeating the store number for each employee also is unnecessary, because the employees are grouped by store number. Another way to avoid repeating the store number is to use a group header to identify each store, and eliminate the STORE NUMBER field altogether. Finally, most of the employees in a store are clerks. The manager and assistant manager titles would stand out better if the word Clerk were not printed for all clerical employees. Those changes have been made in Figure 6-10, and the EMPLOYEE NAME and POSITION columns were exchanged to avoid a large gap between names and the REGULAR HOURS column.

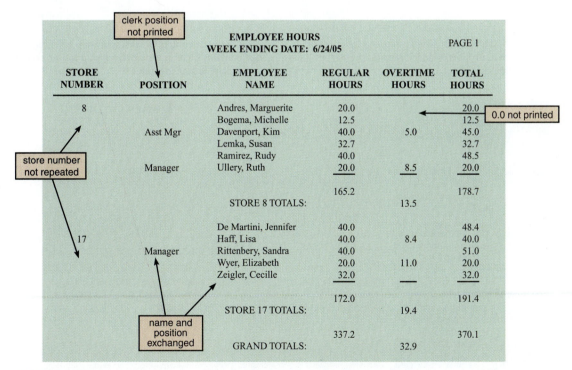

FIGURE 6-10   An improved version of the Employee Hours report shown in Figure 6-6 on page 253.

Good design standards produce reports that are uniform and consistent. When a system produces multiple reports, each report should share common design elements. For example, the date and page numbers should print in the same place on each report

page. Abbreviations used in reports should be consistent. When indicating a numeric value, it is confusing for one report to use #, another *NO*, and a third *NUM*. Items in a report also should be consistent. If one report prints inventory location as shelf number followed by bin number, then printing bin number followed by shelf number on another report creates confusion.

Most of the design principles for plain paper reports also apply to reports on preprinted forms, except that heading information usually is preprinted for reports such as invoices and monthly statements. The same functional and aesthetic design principles also apply to preprinted forms. You should make column headings short but descriptive and avoid nonstandard abbreviations. Use reasonable spacing between columns for better readability. The order and placement of printed fields should be logical, and totals should be identified clearly.

When designing a preprinted form, you should contact the form's vendor for advice on paper sizes, type styles and sizes, paper and ink colors, field placement, and other important form details. Your goal is to design a form that is attractive, readable, and useful, at a reasonable price. After a report design is approved, you should document the design by creating a **report analysis form**, which contains information about the fields, data types and lengths, report frequency and distribution, and other comments.

Designing Character-Based Reports

Although the vast majority of reports are designed in a graphical environment where the report designer can use various type styles, fonts, and images to produce an attractive layout, many systems still produce one or more **character-based reports** that use a character set with fixed, rather than proportional, spacing. Printing character-based reports on high-speed impact printers is a fast, inexpensive method for producing large-scale reports, such as payroll or inventory reports at a business, or registration rosters at a school. This is especially true if multiple copies are required.

When report designers create or modify a character-based report, they use a traditional tool that still works well, called a printer spacing chart. A **printer spacing chart** is a grid of rows and columns where you indicate print positions and field sizes.

CASE IN POINT 6.1: LAZY EDDIE

Lynn Jennings is the IT manager at Lazy Eddie, a chain that specializes in beanbag chairs and recliners. She asked Jan Lauten, a senior systems analyst, to review the large number of printed reports that are distributed to Lazy Eddie's 35 store managers. "Jan, I just can't believe that our people really read all of those reports," Lynn said. "We constantly add new reports, and we never seem to eliminate the old ones. Sometimes I think all we're doing is keeping the paper companies in business!" Jan replied, "I agree, but what can we do? The managers say they want the reports, but I always see them stacked on top of file cabinets. I've never seen anyone read a report."

"I have an idea," Lynn said. "I want you to come up with a procedure that requires users to review and justify their information needs to see if they really use the reports we send them. You could design a form that asks if the information still is required, and why. Try to get users to decide if a report is worth the cost of producing it. Do you think you can do it?"

"Sure I can," Jan replied. When Jan returned to her office, she wondered where to begin. What advice would you give to Jan?

Printing Volume and Time Requirements

Technological advances have resulted in printers that are faster, better, and less expensive than their predecessors. Powerful laser printers are the standard for business printing because they offer speed, excellent quality, and graphical output. Impact printers still are used for multiple form output and certain high-speed applications.

Although printed output is necessary in many situations, a high volume of reports can significantly increase a system's TCO (total cost of ownership). Paper is expensive to purchase, print, store, and dispose of, and printed information is outdated quickly. Printed output can include a three-page document for one user, or a 500-page inventory report for another.

As a systems analyst, you must determine if printing resources can handle the system's requirements. Although technology advances have made high-speed printing relatively inexpensive, every printer has specific capacities and limitations. Efficient printing operations, timely delivery of finished reports, and accurate forecasts of paper and storage needs all depend on accurate estimates of print volumes and times.

LENGTH CALCULATIONS

After completing a report design, it is important to estimate the length of the printed output. For example, consider the Employee Hours report shown previously in Figure 6-8 on page 255. Assume that the company has a total of 380 employees in six stores. The paper will have 66 lines per page. Six lines are reserved for the top and bottom margins, leaving 60 printed lines per page. In the report, every page begins with six lines of heading information (report heading and page heading), leaving 54 lines per page for printing employee detail lines, store (group) footing lines, and grand total footing lines.

For the total 380 employees, 380 detail lines will print. Each of the six stores has three footing lines, for a total of 18 store footing lines. Finally, the grand total requires three additional lines. The complete report will include 401 detail and total lines. At 54 lines per page, the report will require 7.4 pages. Therefore, the final estimate for the paper requirements for the weekly report is eight printed pages per week. Figure 6-11 shows those volume calculations.

CALCULATING THE LENGTH OF THE REPORT

	66	total lines available per page of stock paper
-	6	lines reserved for top and bottom margins
-	6	lines per page for 2 title lines, 1 blank line, 2 column heading lines, and 1 hyphen line
	54	available detail lines per page
	3	lines per store for 1 line with hyphens, 1 line of store totals, and 1 blank line
×	6	stores
	18	store footing lines
+	3	lines per report for 2 lines with hyphens and 1 line of grand totals
	21	footing lines
+	380	detail lines
	401	report lines
÷	54	lines per page
	7.4	**printed pages**

FIGURE 6-11 Report volume calculations for the Employee Hours report shown in Figure 6-8 on page 255.

TIME CALCULATIONS You also can estimate the time required to print the report. Laser printers are rated in **ppm** (**pages per minute**). For example, at 16 ppm, a laser printer would print a single copy of the eight-page Employee Hours report in about 30 seconds.

Companies also use high-speed **line printers**, which are impact printers commonly used for internal reports such as payroll or inventory reports that were referred to in the discussion of character-based reports. Impact printers can use multi-part forms to produce more than one copy, which is an advantage to firms that require several copies of the same report.

If the Employee Hours report were printed on a line printer with a speed of 2,000 lines per minute, you would divide

401 lines by 2,000 lines per minute, for a total time of .20 minutes, or 12 seconds of printing time.

Figure 6-12 shows the paper requirements and printer time calculations for a much larger report. The example dramatically shows the value of volume and time estimates. Imagine the problems that might occur when the report is printed for the first time if no one estimated that it would take nearly 19 hours to print 38,889 pages.

Both of the time calculation examples are for reports printed on plain paper. If special forms are used, the calculation process is similar, but you must add a time factor for loading and unloading the forms.

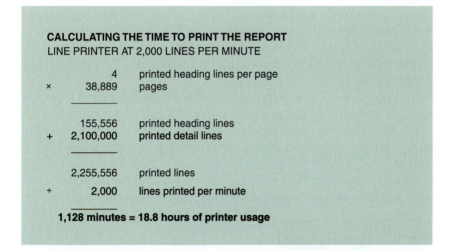

CALCULATING THE LENGTH OF THE REPORT

	66	total lines available per page of stock paper
-	6	lines reserved for top and bottom margins
-	6	lines per page for 2 page heading lines, 1 blank line, 2 column heading lines, and 1 blank line
	54	available detail lines per page
	2,100,000	detail lines
÷	54	detail lines per page

38,889 printed pages

CALCULATING THE TIME TO PRINT THE REPORT
LINE PRINTER AT 2,000 LINES PER MINUTE

	4	printed heading lines per page
×	38,889	pages
	155,556	printed heading lines
+	2,100,000	printed detail lines
	2,255,556	printed lines
÷	2,000	lines printed per minute

1,128 minutes = 18.8 hours of printer usage

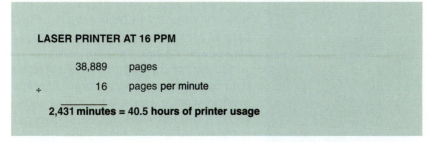

LASER PRINTER AT 16 PPM

	38,889	pages
÷	16	pages per minute

2,431 minutes = 40.5 hours of printer usage

FIGURE 6-12 Report volume calculations for a monthly report for 2,100,000 customer accounts.

ON THE WEB

For more information about Output Control and Security, visit **scsite.com/sad6e/more**, locate Chapter 6 and then click the Output Control and Security link.

Output Control and Security

Output must be accurate, complete, current, and secure. Companies use various **output control** methods to maintain output integrity and security. For example, every report should include an appropriate title, report number or code, printing date, and time period covered. Reports should have pages that are numbered consecutively, identified as *Page nn of nn*, and the end of the report should be labeled clearly. Control totals and record counts should be reconciled against input totals and counts. Reports should be selected at random for a thorough check of correctness and completeness. All processing errors or interruptions must be logged so they can be analyzed.

Output security protects privacy rights and shields the organization's proprietary data from theft or unauthorized access. To ensure output security, you must perform several important tasks. First, limit the number of printed copies and use a tracking procedure to account for each copy. When printed output is distributed from a central location, you should use specific procedures to ensure that the output is delivered to authorized recipients only. That is especially true when reports contain sensitive information, such as payroll data. All sensitive reports should be stored in secure areas. All pages of confidential reports should be labeled appropriately.

FIGURE 6-13 To maintain output security, it is important to shred sensitive material.

As shown in Figure 6-13, it is important to shred sensitive reports, out-of-date reports, and output from aborted print runs. Blank check forms must be stored in a secure location and be inventoried regularly to verify that no forms are missing. If signature stamps are used, they must be stored in a secure location away from the forms storage location.

In most organizations, the IT department is responsible for output control and security measures. Systems analysts must be concerned with security issues as they design, implement, and support information systems. Whenever possible, security should be designed into the system by using passwords, shielding sensitive data, and controlling user access. Physical security always will be necessary, especially in the case of printed output that is tangible and can be viewed and handled easily.

As part of the trend toward enterprise-wide data management, many companies have installed diskless workstations, which offer security advantages. A **diskless workstation**, shown in Figure 6-14, is a network terminal that supports a full-featured user interface, but limits the printing or copying of data, except to certain network resources that can be monitored and controlled more easily.

FIGURE 6-14 A diskless workstation supports a full-featured user interface, but can limit the printing or copying of data.

USER INTERFACE DESIGN

ON THE WEB

For more information about User Interface Design, visit **scsite.com/sad6e/more**, locate Chapter 6 and then click the User Interface Design link.

Although output design involves a separate set of physical design issues, it is an integral part of a larger concept called a user interface (UI). A **user interface** (UI) describes how users interact with a computer system, and consists of all the hardware, software, screens, menus, functions, output, and features that affect two-way communications between the user and the computer.

Figure 6-15 suggests an interesting viewpoint that interface designers should keep in mind: industry leader IBM believes that the best interfaces are the ones that users do not even notice — they make sense because they do what users expect them to do.

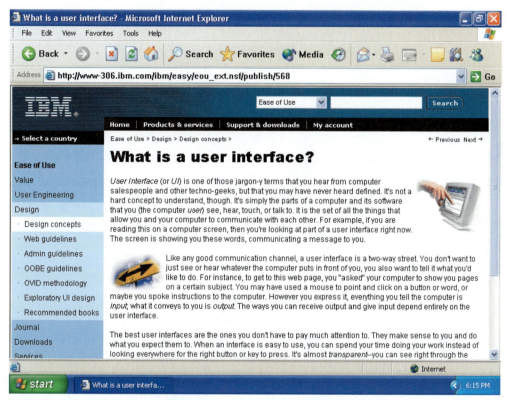

FIGURE 6-15   IBM and Microsoft devote a great deal of effort to make user interfaces simple and easy to learn.

Evolution of the User Interface

When developing older systems, analysts typically designed all the printed and screen output first, then worked on the inputs necessary to produce the results. Often, the user interface mainly consisted of **process-control** screens that allowed the user to send commands to the system. That approach worked well with traditional systems that simply transformed input data into structured output.

As information management evolved from centralized data processing to dynamic, enterprise-wide systems, the primary focus also shifted — from the IT department to the users themselves. The IT group became a supplier of information technology, rather than a supplier of information. Today, the main focus is on users within and outside the company, how they communicate with the information system, and how the system supports the firm's business operations. Figure 6-16 on the next page compares a traditional, processing-centered information system to a modern, user-centered system. Notice that the IT department, which was the main interface for user information requests, has become a system facilitator that maintains and supports the system for its users.

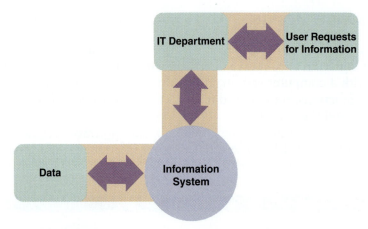

Traditional, Processing-Centered Information System Model

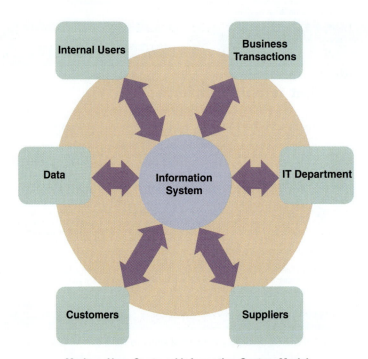

Modern, User-Centered Information System Model

FIGURE 6-16 Compare the traditional, processing-centered system at the top of the figure to the modern, user-centered information system at the bottom. Notice the change in the role of the IT department.

In a **user-centered** system, the distinction blurs between input, output, and the interface itself. Most users work with a varied mix of input, screen output, and data queries as they perform their day-to-day job functions. Because all those tasks require interaction with the computer system, the user interface is a vital element in the systems design phase. Ergosoft laboratories is one of many firms that offer consulting services and software solutions to help companies develop successful user interfaces, as shown in Figure 6-17.

User interface design requires an understanding of human-computer interaction and user-centered design principles, which are discussed in the next section. Input and output design topics are covered later in this chapter.

FIGURE 6-17 Ergosoft laboratories is an example of a firm that offers consulting services and software solutions to help companies develop successful user interfaces.

Human-Computer Interaction

A user interface is based on basic principles of human-computer interaction. **Human-computer interaction** (HCI) describes the relationship between computers and people who use them to perform business-related tasks, as shown in Figure 6-18 on the next page. HCI concepts apply to everything from PC desktops to global networks. In its broadest sense, a user interface includes all the communications and instructions necessary to enter input to the system and to obtain output in the form of screen displays or printed reports.

As a systems analyst, you will design user interfaces for in-house developed software and customize interfaces for various commercial packages and user productivity

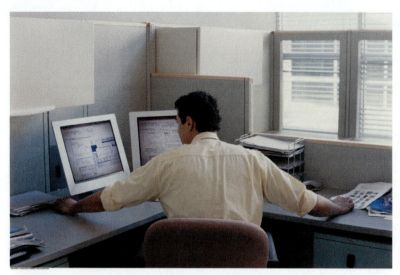

FIGURE 6-18 A user interface is based on basic principles of human-computer interaction, which describes the relationship between computers and people who use them to perform business-related tasks.

applications. Your main objective is to create a user-friendly design that is easy to learn and use.

Industry leaders Microsoft and IBM both devote considerable resources to user interface research, as shown in Figure 6-19. At its Redmond labs, Microsoft usability engineers observe participants through one-way mirrors. On its Almaden Research Center Web site, IBM traces the history and evolution of the human-computer interface — beginning with users typing complex commands in green text on a black screen, through the introduction of the **graphical user interface (GUI)** with graphical objects and pointing devices, up to current times where interface designers strive to translate user behavior, needs, and desires into a transparent interface.

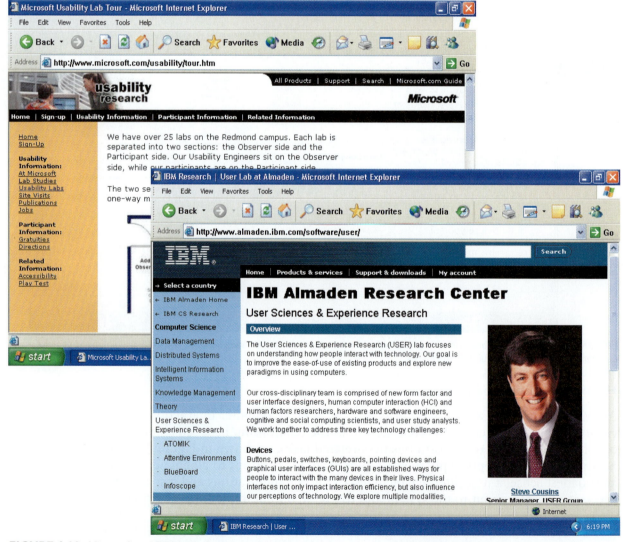

FIGURE 6-19 Microsoft and IBM both devote considerable resources to user interface research.

CASE IN POINT 6.2: Casual Observer Software

Casual Observer Software's main product is a program that monitors and analyzes user keystrokes and mouse clicks to learn more about the way employees use their computer systems. The problem is that some users feel this is an unwarranted intrusion into their privacy, and they prefer not to be observed. Some even fear that the data would be used for other reasons, including performance appraisal. You are a consultant who has been hired by a client firm that is trying to decide whether or not to use this software.

Before you advise the client, go back and review the Microsoft usability lab shown in Figure 6-19, where the users being studied in the Redmond labs were willing participants. Then, refer to Chapter 3, Requirements Modeling, page 113, and consider the Hawthorne Effect, which suggests that employees might behave differently when they know they are being observed. Finally, think about the ethical issues that might be involved in this situation. What will you advise your client, and why?

IBM believes that the user interface evolution will lead to computers that truly are *consumer products* that are simple and natural for the general population to use. This will occur, in IBM's view, because computers will function in a friendlier, more predictable way — much like a telephone or fax machine. Most important, the interface will be based on the perspective of a user rather than a computer engineer, programmer, or systems analyst. To understand the magnitude of this shift in thinking, consider the powerful statement shown in Figure 6-20 on the next page, where IBM usability expert Dr. Clare-Marie Karat states that "in this new computer age, the customer is not only right, the customer has rights."

The user rights cited by Dr. Karat include the following 10 items:

ON THE WEB

For more information about Human-Computer Interaction, visit **scsite.com/ sad6e/more**, locate Chapter 6 and then click the Human-Computer Interaction link.

- ➡ Perspective: The user always is right. If there is a problem with the use of the system, the system is the problem, not the user.

- ➡ Installation: The user has the right to install and uninstall software and hardware systems easily without negative consequences.

- ➡ Compliance: The user has the right to a system that performs exactly as promised.

- ➡ Instruction: The user has the right to easy-to-use instructions (user guides, online or contextual help, and error messages) for understanding and utilizing a system to achieve desired goals and recover efficiently and gracefully from problem situations.

- ➡ Control: The user has the right to be in control of the system and to be able to get the system to respond to a request for attention.

- ➡ Feedback: The user has the right to a system that provides clear, understandable, and accurate information regarding the task it is performing and the progress toward completion.

- ➡ Dependencies: The user has the right to be informed clearly about all systems requirements for successfully using software or hardware.

- ➡ Scope: The user has the right to know the limits of the system's capabilities.

- ➡ Assistance: The user has the right to communicate with the technology provider and receive a thoughtful and helpful response when raising concerns.

- ➡ Usability: The user should be the master of software and hardware technology, not vice versa. Products should be natural and intuitive to use.

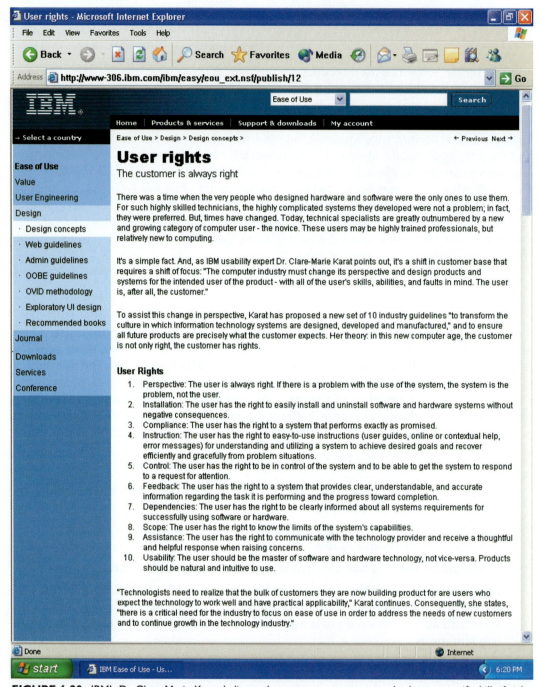

FIGURE 6-20   IBM's Dr. Clare-Marie Karat believes that users are customers who have a specific bill of rights.

Basic Principles of User-Centered Design

Although IT professionals have different views about interface design, most would agree that good design depends on eight basic principles, which are described below.

UNDERSTAND THE UNDERLYING BUSINESS FUNCTIONS   The interface designer must understand the underlying business functions and how the system supports individual, departmental, and enterprise goals. The overall objective is to design an interface that helps users to perform their jobs. A good starting point might be to analyze a functional decomposition diagram (FDD). As you learned in Chapter 3, an FDD is a graphical representation of business functions that starts with major functions, and then breaks them down into several levels of detail. An FDD can provide a checklist of user tasks that you must include in the interface design.

MAXIMIZE GRAPHICAL EFFECTIVENESS Studies show that people learn better visually. The immense popularity of Microsoft Windows is largely the result of a graphical user interface that is easy to learn and use. Now that GUIs have become universal in application packages, users expect in-house software also to have GUIs. A well-designed GUI can help users learn a new system rapidly, and work with the system effectively. Also, in a GUI environment, a user can display and work with multiple windows on a single screen and transfer data between programs. Because GUIs are used for data entry as well as for process control, they must follow the guidelines for data entry screen design discussed later in this chapter.

PROFILE THE SYSTEM'S USERS A systems analyst should understand user experience, knowledge, and skill levels. If a wide range of capability exists, the interface should be flexible enough to accommodate novices as well as experienced users.

THINK LIKE A USER To develop a user-centered interface, the designer must learn to think like a user and see the system through a user's eyes. The interface should use terms and metaphors that are familiar to users. Users are likely to have real-world experience with many other machines and devices that provide feedback, such as automobiles, ATM machines, and microwave ovens. Based on that experience, users will expect useful, understandable feedback from a computer system.

USE PROTOTYPING From a user's viewpoint, the interface is the most critical part of the system design because it is where he or she interacts with the system — perhaps for many hours each day. It is essential to construct models and prototypes for user approval. An interface designer should obtain as much feedback as possible, as early as possible. You can present initial screen designs to users in the form of a **storyboard**, which is a sketch that shows the general screen layout and design. The storyboard can be created with software, or drawn freehand. Users must test all aspects of the interface design and provide feedback to the designers. User input can be obtained in interviews, via questionnaires, and by observation. Interface designers also can obtain data, called **usability metrics**, by using software that can record and measure user interaction with the system.

DESIGN A COMPREHENSIVE INTERFACE The user interface should include all tasks, commands, and communications between users and the information system. The screen in Figure 6-21 shows the main options for a student registration system. Each screen option leads to another screen, with more options. The objective is to offer a reasonable number of choices that a user easily can comprehend. Too many options on one screen can confuse a user — but too few options increase the number of submenu levels and complicate the navigation process. Often, an effective strategy is to present the most common choice as a default, but allow the user to select other options.

CONTINUE THE FEEDBACK PROCESS Even after the system is operational, it is important to monitor system usage and solicit user suggestions. You can

FIGURE 6-21 The screen displays the main options for a school's student registration system.

TOOLKIT TIME

The Communication Tools in Part 1 of the Systems Analyst's Toolkit can help you communicate effectively with users. To learn more about these tools, turn to Part 1 of the six-part Toolkit that follows Chapter 10.

determine if system features are being used as intended by observing and surveying users. Sometimes, full-scale operations highlight problems that were not apparent when the prototype was tested. Based on user feedback, Help screens might need revision and design changes to allow the system to reach its full potential.

DOCUMENT THE INTERFACE DESIGN   You should document all screen designs for later use by programmers. If you are using a CASE tool or screen generator, number the screen designs and save them in a hierarchy similar to a menu tree. User-approved sketches and storyboards also can be used to document the user interface.

By applying basic user-centered design principles, a systems analyst can plan, design, and deliver a successful user interface.

Guidelines for User Interface Design

It is important to design a user interface that is easy to use, attractive, and efficient. When you create a user interface, you should follow eight basic guidelines. These guidelines also apply to data entry screen design, which is discussed later in this chapter.

1. Focus on basic objectives.
2. Build an interface that is easy to learn and use.
3. Provide features that promote efficiency.
4. Make it easy for users to obtain help or correct errors.
5. Minimize input data problems.
6. Provide feedback to users.
7. Create an attractive layout and design.
8. Use familiar terms and images.

Good user interface design is based on a combination of ergonomics, aesthetics, and interface technology. **Ergonomics** describes how people work, learn, and interact with computers; **aesthetics** focuses on how an interface can be made attractive and easy to use; and **interface technology** provides the operational structure required to carry out the design objectives. As shown in Figure 6-22, Cognetics Corporation sums it up by saying that an interface must be effective, efficient, engaging, error tolerant, and easy to learn.

The following sections provide examples of the basic user interface design guidelines. As mentioned earlier, many of the specific points also apply to data entry screen design, which is discussed on page 279.

FIGURE 6-22 Cognetics Corporation believes that an interface must be effective, efficient, engaging, error tolerant, and easy to learn.

FOCUS ON BASIC OBJECTIVES

- ➡ Facilitate the system design objectives, rather than calling attention to the interface.
- ➡ Create a design that is easy to learn and remember.
- ➡ Design the interface to improve user efficiency and productivity.
- ➡ Write commands, actions, and system responses that are consistent and predictable.
- ➡ Minimize data entry problems.
- ➡ Allow users to correct errors easily.
- ➡ Create a logical and attractive layout.

BUILD AN INTERFACE THAT IS EASY TO LEARN AND USE

- ➡ Label clearly all controls, buttons, and icons.
- ➡ Select only those images that users can understand easily, if you use images to identify icons or controls. Also, provide on-screen instructions that are logical, concise, and clear. For example, the top screen in Figure 6-23 shows three control buttons, but only the printer image has an obvious meaning. In the bottom screen, notice the difference in two messages: the first provides little or no information; the second one is easy to understand.
- ➡ Show all commands in a list of menu items, but dim any commands that are not currently available.
- ➡ Make it easy to navigate or return to any level in the menu structure.

PROVIDE FEATURES THAT PROMOTE EFFICIENCY

- ➡ Organize tasks, commands, and functions in groups that resemble actual business operations. You should group functions and submenu items in a multilevel menu hierarchy, or tree, that is logical and reflects how users typically perform the tasks. Figure 6-24 on the next page shows an example of a menu hierarchy for an order tracking system.
- ➡ Create alphabetical menu lists or place the selections used frequently at the top of the menu list. No universally accepted approach to menu item placement exists. The best strategy is to design a prototype and obtain feedback from users. Some applications, such as Microsoft Word, even allow menus to show recently used commands first. Some users might accept that design, but others might find it distracting.
- ➡ Provide shortcuts so experienced users can avoid multiple menu levels. You can create shortcuts using hot keys that allow a user to press the ALT key + the underlined letter of a command.

FIGURE 6-23 In the example shown at the top of the figure, only one of the control buttons has an obvious meaning. In the bottom screen, the first message is hard to understand, but the bottom message is unmistakable.

➡ Use default values if the majority of values in a field are the same. For example, if 90 percent of the firm's customers live in Albuquerque, use *Albuquerque* as the default value in the City field.

➡ Use a duplicate value function that enables users to insert the value from the same field in the previous record.

➡ Provide a fast-find feature that displays a list of possible values as soon as users enter the first few letters.

➡ Use a natural language feature that allows users to type commands or requests in normal English phrases. For example, Microsoft Office products allow users to request Help by typing a question into a dialog box. The software then uses natural language technology to retrieve a list of topics that match the request. Most users like natural language features because they do not have to memorize a series of complex commands and syntax. According to the American Association for Artificial Intelligence (AAAI), whose Web site is shown in Figure 6-25, the value of being able to communicate with computers in everyday "natural" language cannot be overstated. Natural language technology is used in speech recognition systems, text-to-speech synthesizers, automated voice response systems, Web search engines, text editors, and language instruction materials.

Customer Order Tracking System

FIGURE 6-24 Tasks, commands, and functions should be organized in logical groups, such as this menu hierarchy for a customer order tracking system.

MAKE IT EASY FOR USERS TO OBTAIN HELP OR CORRECT ERRORS

➡ Ensure that Help is always available. Help screens should provide information about menu choices, procedures, shortcuts, and errors.

➡ Provide user-selected Help and context-sensitive Help. **User-selected** Help displays information when the user requests it. By making appropriate choices through the menus and submenus, the user eventually reaches a screen with the desired information. Figure 6-26 shows the main Help screen for the student registration system. **Context-sensitive** Help offers assistance for the task in progress. Figure 6-27 shows a Help dialog box that is displayed if a user requests Help while entering data into the ADVISOR ASSIGNED field. Clicking the Close button returns the user to the current task.

➡ Provide a direct route for users to return to the point from where Help was requested. Title every Help screen to identify the topic, and keep Help text simple and concise. Insert blank lines between paragraphs to make Help easier to read, and provide examples where appropriate.

➡ Include contact information, such as a telephone extension or e-mail address if a department or Help desk is responsible for assisting users.

➡ Require user confirmation before data deletion (*Are you sure?*) and provide a method of recovering data that is deleted inadvertently. Build in safeguards that prevent critical data from being changed or erased.

➡ Provide an Undo key or a menu choice that allows the user to eradicate the results of the most recent command or action.

➡ When a user-entered command contains an error, highlight the erroneous part and allow the user to make the correction without retyping the entire command.

➡ Use hypertext links to assist users as they navigate through Help topics.

MINIMIZE INPUT DATA PROBLEMS

➡ Provide data validation checks. More information on data validation techniques is provided in the section on input design later in this chapter.

➡ Display event-driven messages and reminders. Just as context-sensitive Help is important to users, it is desirable to display an appropriate message when it is time for the user to perform a certain task. For example, when exiting the system, a message might ask users if they want a printed report of the data entered during the recent session.

➡ Establish a list of predefined values that users can click to select. Predefined values prevent spelling errors, avoid inappropriate data in a field, and make the user's job easier — the input screen displays a list of acceptable values and the user simply points and clicks the choice.

➡ Build in rules that enforce data integrity. For example, if the user tries to enter an order for a new customer, the customer must be added before the system will accept the order data.

➡ Use **input masks**, which are templates or patterns that make it easier for users to enter data. Microsoft Access 2003 provides standard input masks for fields such as dates, telephone numbers, ZIP codes, and Social Security

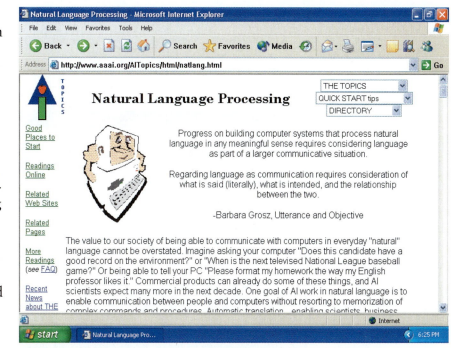

FIGURE 6-25 The American Association for Artificial Intelligence (AAAI) sees natural language processing as a key element of the communication process between users and their computers.

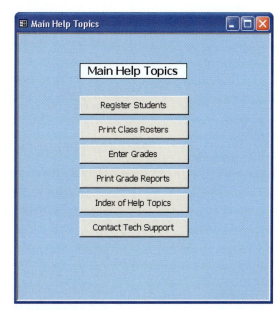

FIGURE 6-26 The main Help screen for the student registration system.

FIGURE 6-27 A context-sensitive dialog box that is displayed if a user requests help while entering data into the ADVISOR ASSIGNED field. Clicking the Close button returns the user to the task.

numbers. In addition, you can create custom input masks for any type of data, as shown in Figure 6-28. Notice that a mask can manipulate the input data and apply a specific format. For example, if a user enters text in lowercase letters, the input mask >*LLLLLLLL* will convert the data automatically to uppercase letters.

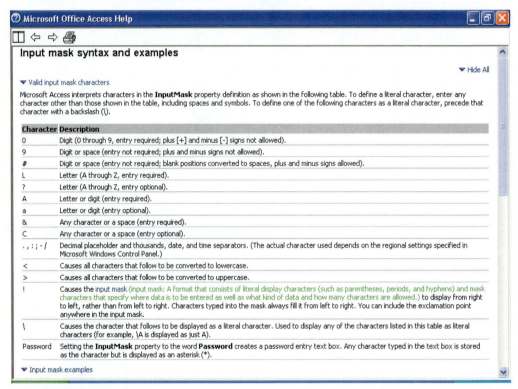

FIGURE 6-28 You can create custom input masks for any type of data or field values, as shown in this example using Microsoft Access 2003.

PROVIDE FEEDBACK TO USERS

➡ Display messages at a logical place on the screen, and be consistent.

➡ Alert users to lengthy processing times or delays. Give users an on-screen progress report, especially if the delay is lengthy.

➡ Allow messages to remain on the screen long enough for users to read them. In some cases, the screen should display messages until the user takes some action.

➡ Let the user know whether the task or operation was successful or not. For example, use messages such as *Update completed, All transactions have been posted*, or *ID Number not found*.

➡ Provide a text explanation if you use an icon or image on a control button. This helps the user to identify the control button when moving the mouse pointer over the icon or image.

➡ Use messages that are specific, understandable, and professional. Avoid messages that are cute, cryptic, or vague, such as: *ERROR — You have entered an unacceptable value*, or *Error DE4-16*. Better examples are: *Enter a number between 1 and 5; Customer number must be numeric. Please re-enter a numeric value*; or *Call the Accounting Department, Ext. 239 for assistance.*

CREATE AN ATTRACTIVE LAYOUT AND DESIGN

- Use appropriate colors to highlight different areas of the screen; avoid gaudy and bright colors.

- Use special effects sparingly. For example, animation and sound might be effective in some situations, but too many special effects can be distracting and annoying to a user, especially if he or she must view them repeatedly.

- Use hyperlinks that allow users to jump to related topics.

- Group related objects and information. Visualize the screen the way a user will see it, and simulate the tasks that the user will perform.

- Screen density is important. Keep screen displays uncluttered, with enough white space to create an attractive, readable design.

- Display titles, messages, and instructions in a consistent manner and in the same general locations on all screens.

- Use consistent terminology. For example, do not use the terms *delete*, *cancel*, and *erase* to indicate the same action. Similarly, the same sound always should signal the same event.

- Ensure that commands always will have the same effect. For example, if the *BACK* control button returns a user to the prior screen, the *BACK* command always should perform that function throughout the application.

- Ensure that similar mouse actions will produce the same results throughout the application. The results of pointing, clicking, and double-clicking should be consistent and predictable.

- When the user enters data that completely fills the field, do not move automatically to the next field. Instead, require the user to confirm the entry by pressing the ENTER key or TAB key at the end of every fill-in field.

USE FAMILIAR TERMS AND IMAGES

- Remember that users are accustomed to a pattern of *red = stop, yellow = caution*, and *green = go*. Stick to that pattern and use it when appropriate to reinforce on-screen instructions.

- Provide a keystroke alternative for each menu command, with easy-to-remember letters, such as File, Exit, and Help.

- Use familiar commands if possible, such as Cut, Copy, and Paste.

- Provide a Windows look and feel in your interface design if users are familiar with Windows-based applications.

- Avoid complex terms and technical jargon; instead, select terms that come from everyday business processes and the vocabulary of a typical user.

User Interface Controls

The designer can include many control features, such as menu bars, toolbars, dialog boxes, text boxes, toggle buttons, list boxes, scroll bars, drop-down list boxes, option buttons, check boxes, command buttons, spin bars, and calendar controls, among others. Figure 6-29 on the next page shows a data entry screen for the student registration system. The screen design uses several features that are described in the following section.

The **menu bar** at the top of the screen displays the main menu options. Some software packages allow you to create customized menu bars and toolbars. You can add a shortcut feature that lets a user select a menu command either by clicking the desired choice or by

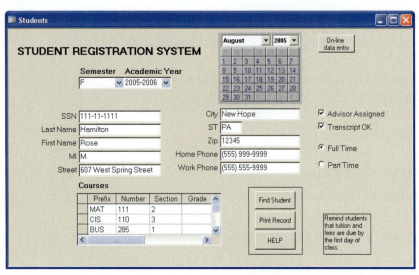

FIGURE 6-29 A data entry screen for the student registration system. This screen uses several design features that are described in the text.

pressing the ALT key + the underlined letter. Some forms also use a **toolbar** that contains icons or buttons that represent shortcuts for executing common commands.

A **command button** initiates an action such as printing a form or requesting Help. For example, when a user clicks the Find Student command button in Figure 6-29, a dialog box opens with instructions, as shown in Figure 6-30.

Other design features include dialog boxes, text boxes, toggle buttons, list boxes, scroll bars, drop-down list boxes, option or radio buttons, check boxes, and calendar controls. These features are described as follows:

➡ A **dialog box** allows a user to enter information about a task that the system will perform.

➡ A **text box** can display messages or provide a place for a user to enter data.

➡ A **toggle button** is used to represent on or off status — clicking the toggle button switches to the other status.

➡ A **list box** displays a list of choices that the user can select. If the list does not fit in the box, a **scroll bar** allows the user to move through the available choices.

➡ A **drop-down list box** displays the current selection; when the user clicks the arrow, a list of the available choices displays.

➡ An **option button**, or **radio button**, represents one choice in a set of options. The user can select only one option at a time, and selected options show a black dot.

➡ A **check box** is used to select one or more choices from a group. Selected options are represented by a checkmark or an X.

➡ A **calendar control** allows the user to select a date that the system will use as a field value.

Screen design requires a sense of aesthetics as well as technical skills. You should design screens that are attractive, easy to use, and workable. You also should obtain user feedback early and often as the design process continues.

The opening screen is especially important because it introduces the application and allows users to view the main options. When designing an opening screen, you can use a main form that functions as a switchboard. A **switchboard** uses command buttons that enable users to navigate the system and select from groups of related tasks. Figure 6-31 shows the switchboard and a data entry screen for a project management system. Notice the drop-down list box that allows users to enter a status code simply by clicking a selection.

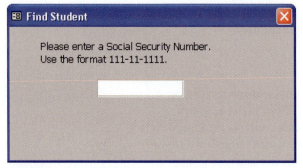

FIGURE 6-30 When a user clicks the Find Student command button, a dialog box is displayed with instructions.

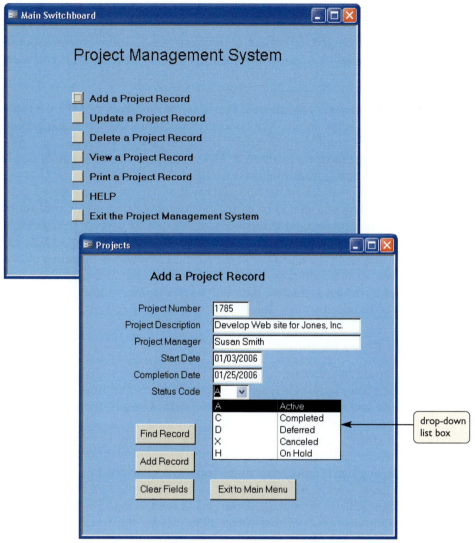

FIGURE 6-31   An example of a switchboard and data entry screen for a project management system.

CASE IN POINT 6.3: TRUSTWORTHY INSURANCE COMPANY

Trustworthy Insurance maintains its headquarters in a large midwestern city. Right now, a debate is raging in the IT department. Several analysts want to use standard, company-wide desktop screen layouts and icons. Others want to allow users to set up their screens any way they choose. Those who argue for standardization point out that Trustworthy employs a number of part-time employees, who fill in for employees on vacation. Without a standard interface, these people would have to reorient to every workstation, and the proponents of standardization claim that would reduce productivity and increase costs. Those opposed to standardization believe that employees are most productive when they have control over their workplace, including the ability to design an interface they feel is attractive, even if no one else does.

   You are on a committee that was charged with resolving this issue, and yours is the tie-breaking vote. What will you decide, and why?

INPUT DESIGN

Input technology has changed dramatically in recent years. Today, many input devices and techniques are available, as shown in Figure 6-32. Businesses use the new technology to speed up the input process, reduce costs, and capture data in new forms, such as the digital signature shown in Figure 6-33 on page 278.

No matter how data enters an information system, the quality of the output is only as good as the quality of the input. The concept, sometimes known as **garbage in, garbage out** (GIGO), is familiar to IT professionals, who know that the best time to avoid problems is when the data is entered. The main objective of input design is to ensure the quality, accuracy, and timeliness of input data.

During input design, you determine how data will be captured and entered into the system. **Data capture** uses an automated or manually operated device to identify source data and convert it into computer-readable form. Examples of data capture devices include credit card scanners and bar code readers. **Data entry** is the process of manually entering data into the information system, usually in the form of keystrokes or mouse clicks.

Input design has six main objectives: select a suitable input and data entry method, reduce input volume, design attractive data entry screens, use validation checks to reduce input errors, design required source documents, and develop effective input controls.

Input and Data Entry Methods

Input processes should be efficient, timely, and logical. Systems analysts apply business process engineering techniques when studying transactions and business operations to determine how and when data should enter the system. Usually, the first decision is whether to use batch or online input methods. Each method has advantages and disadvantages, and the systems analyst must consider the following factors:

BATCH INPUT Using **batch input**, data entry usually is performed on a specified time schedule, such as daily, weekly, monthly, or longer. For example, batch input occurs when a payroll department collects time cards at the end of the week and enters the data as a **batch**. Another example is a school that enters all grades for the academic term in a batch.

ONLINE INPUT Although batch input is used in specific situations, most business activity requires **online data entry**. The online method offers major advantages, including the immediate validation and availability of data. A popular online input method is **source data automation**, which combines online data entry and automated data capture using input devices such as **RFID tags** or **magnetic data strips**. Source data automation is fast and accurate, and minimizes human involvement in the translation process.

Many large companies use a combination of source data automation and a powerful communication network to manage global operations instantly. Some common examples of source data automation are:

→ Businesses that use point-of-sale (POS) terminals equipped with bar code scanners and magnetic swipe scanners to input credit card data.

→ Automatic teller machines (ATMs) that read data strips on bank cards.

→ Factory employees who use magnetic ID cards to clock on and off specific jobs so the company can track production costs accurately.

→ Hospitals that imprint bar codes on patient identification bracelets and use portable scanners when gathering data on patient treatment and medication.

→ Retail stores that use portable bar code scanners to log new shipments and update inventory data.

→ Libraries that use handheld scanners to read optical strips on books.

Input Device	Description
Biological feedback device	Device that creates a digital image of biological data such as fingerprints, retina patterns, or facial characteristics.
Data collection device	Fixed or portable devices that can read data on-site; fixed devices include ATMs and warehouse inventory control points; portable devices include terminals used by package delivery drivers, some of which can capture and store a signature digitally.
Digital camera	Device that records photographs in digital form rather than using traditional film; the resulting data file can be stored, displayed, or manipulated by the computer.
Electronic whiteboard	Electronic version of a standard whiteboard that can capture and store text or graphics that are written or drawn on the board. An electronic whiteboard also functions as a touch screen that can display computer-based images and data.
Graphic input device	Includes light pens, digitizers, and graphics tablets that allow drawings to be translated into digital form that can be processed by a computer.
Handheld computer stylus	Device that allows users to form characters on the screen of a handheld computer. Handwriting recognition software can translate the characters into computer-readable input.
Input devices for physically challenged users	These devices include on-screen keyboard displays that allow a user to point to and click a character, and actuating technology that uses head-mounted pointers, foot pedals, and breath-sensitive controls, among others.
Internet workstation	Enables the user to provide input to Web-based intranet or Internet recipients; can be integrated with information system output or personal computer applications.
Keyboard	Most common input device.
MICR (magnetic ink character recognition)	Technology used primarily in the banking industry to read magnetic ink characters printed on checks.
Microphone	A microphone converts sound waves into digital information that can be stored, transmitted, attached to e-mail and documents, and manipulated in other ways.
Mouse	Pointing device that allows the user to move the insertion point to a specific location on the screen and select options. In addition to control buttons, a mouse can include a wheel that allows the user to scroll the viewing screen. A mouse can be wired or wireless, and digital versions offer additional precision and control. A trackball is a stationary version of a mouse. Instead of moving the device itself, the user rotates the ball.
Pointing stick	Pressure-sensitive pointing device located between the keys on a notebook computer. A pointing stick resembles a button or pencil eraser.
Radio frequency identification (RFID)	RFID technology uses high-frequency radio waves to track physical objects. RFID can be used to track items in a wide range of information systems, including supply chain management, inventory control, and point-of-sale. RFID also can be used to monitor the movement of people or objects in a security management system.
Scanner/optical recognition	Devices that read printed bar codes, characters, or images.
Telephone	Technology that allows users to press telephone buttons or speak selected words to choose options in a system, such as electronic funds transfer, shop-at-home purchases, or registration for college courses.
Terminal	Device that might be dumb (screen and keyboard only) or intelligent (screen, keyboard, independent processing).
Touch screen	Sensors that allow users to interface with the computer and select options by touching specific locations on the screen. Touch pads also are used as pointing devices on notebook computers.
Video input	Video camera input, in digital form, that can be stored and replayed later.
Voice input device	Device that allows users to enter data and issue commands using spoken words; also can be used in connection with telephone input, so a user can press, or say, a number to select a processing option.
Wireless input	Wireless input devices are wireless versions of traditional scanners, bar code readers, data collection devices, or pointing devices. Wireless input provides portability and ease of use.

FIGURE 6-32 Common types of input devices.

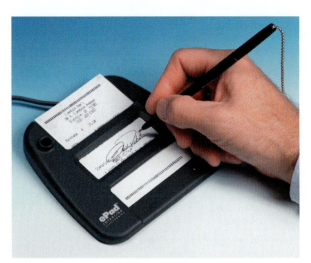

FIGURE 6-33 When a customer's signature is stored in digital form, it becomes input to the information system.

TRADEOFFS Although online input offers many advantages, it does have some disadvantages. For example, unless source data automation is used, manual data entry is slower and more expensive than batch input because it is performed at the time the transaction occurs and often done when computer demand is at its highest.

The decision to use batch or online input depends on business requirements. For example, hotel reservations must be entered and processed immediately, but hotels can enter their monthly performance figures in a batch. In fact, some input occurs naturally in batches. A cable TV provider, for example, receives customer payments in batches when the mail arrives.

Input Volume

To reduce input volume, you must reduce the number of data items required for each transaction. Data capture and data entry require time and effort, so when you reduce input volume, you avoid unnecessary labor costs, get the data into the system more quickly, and decrease the number of errors. The following guidelines will help reduce input volume:

1. Input necessary data only. Do not input a data item unless it is needed by the system. A completed order form, for example, might contain the name of the clerk who took the order. If that data is not needed by the system, the user should not enter it.

2. Do not input data that the user can retrieve from system files or calculate from other data. In the order system example shown in Figure 6-34, the system generates an order number and logs the current date and time. Then the user enters a customer ID. If the entry is valid, the system displays the customer name so the user can verify it. The user then enters the item and quantity. Note that the description, price, extended price, total price, sales tax, and grand total are retrieved automatically or calculated by the system.

3. Do not input constant data. If orders are in batches with the same date, then a user should enter the order date only once for the first order in the batch. If orders are entered online, then the user can retrieve the order date automatically using the current system date.

4. Use codes. Code are shorter than the data they represent, and coded input can reduce data entry time. For example, in the order system example in Figure 6-34, the Customer ID and Item fields are codes. You will learn more about various types of codes in Chapter 7, Data Design.

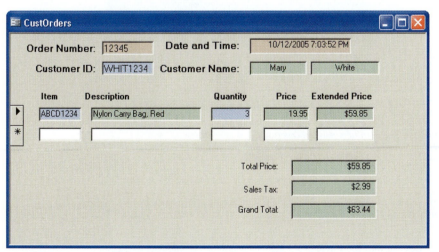

FIGURE 6-34 In this data screen for customer orders, the system generates an order number and logs the current date and time. The user enters a customer ID. If the entry is valid, the system displays the customer name so the user can verify it. The user then enters the item and quantity. Note that the description, price, extended price, total price, sales tax, and grand total are retrieved automatically or calculated by the system.

Designing Data Entry Screens

Some users work with many features of the user interface; others spend most of their time entering data. This section discusses interface guidelines and concepts that primarily relate to repetitive data entry. Notice that many of the guidelines are based on general principles of interface design discussed in this chapter.

The most effective method of online data entry is **form filling**, in which a blank form that duplicates or resembles the source document is completed on the screen. The user enters the data and then moves to the next field. The following guidelines will help you design data entry screens that are easy to learn and use.

1. Restrict user access to screen locations where data is entered. For example, when the screen in Figure 6-34 appears, the system should position the insertion point in the first data entry location. After the operator enters a Customer ID, the insertion point should move automatically to the entry location for the next field (Item). A user should be able to position the insertion point only in places where data is entered on the form.

2. Provide a descriptive caption for every field, and show the user where to enter the data and the required or maximum field size. Typically, white boxes show the location and length of each field. Other methods used to indicate field locations are video highlighting, underscores, special symbols, or a combination of these features.

3. Display a sample format if a user must enter values in a field in a specific format. For example, provide an on-screen instruction to let users know that the date format is MMDDYY, and provide an example if the user must enter **separators**, such as slashes. It is better to use an input mask, so users simply can enter 112705 to represent November 27, 2005.

4. Require an ending keystroke for every field. Pressing the ENTER key or the TAB key should signify the end of a field entry. Avoid a design that moves automatically to the next item when the field is full. The latter approach requires an ending keystroke *only* when the data entered is less than the maximum field length. It is confusing to use two different data entry procedures.

5. Do not require users to type leading zeroes for numeric fields. For example, if a three-digit project number is 045, the operator should be able to type 45 instead of 045 before pressing the ENTER key. An exception to that rule might occur when entering a date, where a leading zero is needed to identify single-digit months or days, such as 06-04-2005.

6. Do not require users to type trailing zeroes for numbers that include decimals. For example, when a user types a value of 98, the system should interpret the value as 98.00 if the field has been formatted to include numbers with two decimal places. The decimal point is needed *only* to indicate nonzero decimal places, such as 98.76.

7. Display default values so operators can press the ENTER key to accept the suggested value. If the default value is not appropriate, the operator can change it.

8. Use a default value when a field value will be constant for successive records or throughout the data entry session. For example, if records are input in order by date, the date used in the first transaction should be used as the default date until a new date is entered, at which time the new date becomes the default value.

9. Display a list of acceptable values for fields, and provide meaningful error messages if the user enters an unacceptable value. An even better method, which was described in the user interface design section, is to provide a drop-down list box containing acceptable values that allows the user to select a value by clicking.

FIGURE 6-35   This is an enhanced version of the data entry screen shown in Figure 6-34. The new version has command buttons that provide flexibility and allow the user to perform various functions.

10. Provide a way to leave the data entry screen at any time without entering the current record. This feature is available in the screen shown in Figure 6-35, which is an enhanced version of the data entry screen shown in Figure 6-34 on page 278. Notice that the new version has command buttons that provide flexibility and allow the user to perform various functions. For example, clicking the Cancel Order Without Entering button cancels the current order and moves the insertion point back to the beginning of the form.

11. Provide users with an opportunity to confirm the accuracy of input data before entering it by displaying a message such as, *Add this record? (Y/N)*. A positive response *(Y)* adds the record, clears the entry fields, and positions the insertion point in the first field so the user can input another record. If the response is negative *(N)*, the current record is not added and the user can correct the errors.

12. Provide a means for users to move among fields on the form in a standard order or in any order they choose. For example, when a user opens the form shown in Figure 6-35, the insertion point automatically will be in the first field. After the user fills in each field and confirms the entry, the insertion point moves to the next field, in a predetermined order. In a graphical user interface (GUI), the user can override the standard field order and select field locations using the mouse or arrow keys.

13. Design the screen form layout to match the layout of the source document. If the source document fields start at the top of the form and run down in a column, the input screen should use the same design.

14. Allow users to add, change, delete, and view records. Figure 6-35 shows a screen that can be used for entering orders, finding items, and finding customers. After the operator enters a customer identification code, the order form displays current values for all appropriate fields. Then the operator can view the data, make changes, enter the order, or cancel without ordering. Messages such as: *Apply these changes? (Y/N)* or *Delete this record? (Y/N)* should require users to confirm the actions. Highlighting the letter N as a default response will avoid problems if the user presses the ENTER key by mistake.

15. Provide a method to allow users to search for specific information, as shown in Figure 6-35.

Input Errors

Reducing the number of input errors improves data quality. One way to reduce input errors is to eliminate unnecessary data entry, as discussed earlier in the chapter. For example, a user cannot misspell a customer name if it is not entered, or is entered automatically based on the user entering the customer ID. Similarly, an outdated item price cannot be used if the item price is retrieved from a master file instead of being entered manually.

The best defense against incorrect data is to identify and correct errors before they enter the system by using data validation checks. A **data validation check** improves input quality by testing the data and rejecting any entry that fails to meet specified conditions. You can design at least eight types of data validation checks into the input process.

1. A **sequence check** is used when the data must be in some predetermined sequence. If the user must enter work orders in numerical sequence, for example, then an out-of-sequence order number indicates an error, or if the user must enter transactions chronologically, then a transaction with an out-of-sequence date indicates an error.

2. An **existence check** is used for mandatory data items. For example, if an employee record requires a Social Security number, an existence check would not allow the user to save the record until he or she enters a suitable value in the Social Security number field.

3. A **data type check** tests to ensure that a data item fits the required data type. For example, a numeric field must have only numbers or numeric symbols, and an alphabetic field can contain only the characters A through Z (or a through z).

4. A **range check** tests data items to verify that they fall between a specified minimum and maximum value. The daily hours worked by an employee, for example, must fall within the range of 0 to 24. When the validation check involves a minimum or a maximum value, but not both, it is called a **limit check**. Checking that a payment amount is greater than zero, but not specifying a maximum value, is an example of a limit check.

5. A **reasonableness check** identifies values that are questionable, but not necessarily wrong. For example, input payment values of $.05 and $5,000,000.00 both pass a simple limit check for a payment value greater than zero, and yet both values could be errors. Similarly, a daily hours worked value of 24 passes a 0 to 24 range check; however, the value seems unusual, and the system should verify it using a reasonableness check.

6. A **validity check** is used for data items that must have certain values. For example, if an inventory system has 20 valid item classes, then any input item that does not match one of the valid classes will fail the check. Verifying that a customer number on an order matches a customer number in the customer file is another type of validity check. Because the value entered must refer to another value, that type of check also is called **referential integrity**, which is explained in Chapter 7, Data Design. Another validity check might verify that a new customer number does *not* match a number already stored in the customer master file.

7. A **combination check** is performed on two or more fields to ensure that they are consistent or reasonable when considered together. Even though all the fields involved in a combination check might pass their individual validation checks, the combination of the field values might be inconsistent or unreasonable. For example, if an order input for 30 units of a particular item has an input discount rate applicable only for purchases of 100 or more units, then the combination is invalid; either the input order quantity or the input discount rate is incorrect.

8. **Batch controls** are totals used to verify batch input. Batch controls might check data items such as record counts and numeric field totals. For example, before entering a batch of orders, a user might calculate the total number of orders and the sum of all the order quantities. When the batch of orders is entered, the order system also calculates the same two totals. If the system totals do not match the input totals, then a data entry error has occurred. Unlike the other validation checks, batch controls do not identify specific errors. For example, if the sum of all the order quantities does not match the batch control total, you know only that one or

FIGURE 6-36 Examples of caption techniques for source documents.

more orders in that batch were entered incorrectly or not input. The batch control totals often are called **hash totals**, because they are not meaningful numbers themselves, but are useful for comparison purposes.

Source Documents

A **source document** is a form used to request and collect input data, trigger or authorize an input action, and provide a record of the original transaction. During the input design stage, you develop source documents that are easy to complete and inexpensive.

Consider a time when you struggled to complete a poorly designed form. You might have encountered insufficient space, confusing instructions, or poor organization, all symptoms of incorrect **form layout**. Good form layout makes the form easy to complete and provides enough space, both vertically and horizontally, for users to enter the data. A form should indicate data entry positions clearly using blank lines or boxes and descriptive captions. Figure 6-36 shows several techniques for using line and boxed captions in source documents, and an example of check boxes, which are effective when a user must select choices from a list.

The placement of information on a form also is important. Source documents typically include most of the zones shown in Figure 6-37. The **heading zone** usually contains the company name or logo and the title and number of the form. The **control zone** contains codes, identification information, numbers, and dates that are used for storing completed forms. The **instruction zone** contains instructions for completing the form. The main part of the form, called the **body zone**, usually takes up at least half of the space on the form and contains captions and areas for entering variable data. If totals are included on the form, they appear in the **totals zone**. Finally, the **authorization zone** contains any required signatures.

Information should flow on a form from left to right and top to bottom to match the way users read documents naturally. That layout makes the form easy to use for the individual who completes the form, and for users who enter data into the system using the completed form. You can review samples of source document design that appear in the SWL case study on pages 297–298.

Layout and design also are important on Web-based forms. Consider the online subscription application for *InfoWorld* shown in Figure 6-38. Notice that the Web-based form uses option buttons, a drop-down list box, and text boxes to make it easier for the subscriber to fill out.

A major challenge of Web-based form design is that most people read and interact differently with on-screen information compared to paper forms. In the view of Dr. Jakob Nielsen, a pioneer in Web usability design, users simply do not read on the Web, as shown in Figure 6-39 on the next page. Dr. Nielsen believes that users *scan* a page, picking out individual words and sentences. As a result, Web designers must use **scannable text** to capture and hold a user's attention. On his site, Dr. Nielson offers several suggestions for creating scannable text. Also notice that Dr. Nielsen employs various usability metrics to measure user responses, comprehension, and recall.

Input Control

Input control includes the necessary measures to ensure that input data is correct, complete, and secure. You must focus on input control during every phase of input design, starting with source documents that promote data accuracy and quality. When a batch input method is used, the computer can produce an input log file that identifies and documents the data entered.

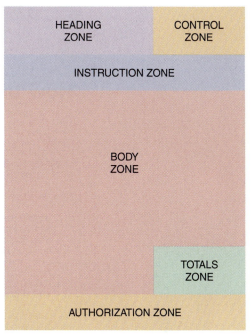

FIGURE 6-37 Source document zones.

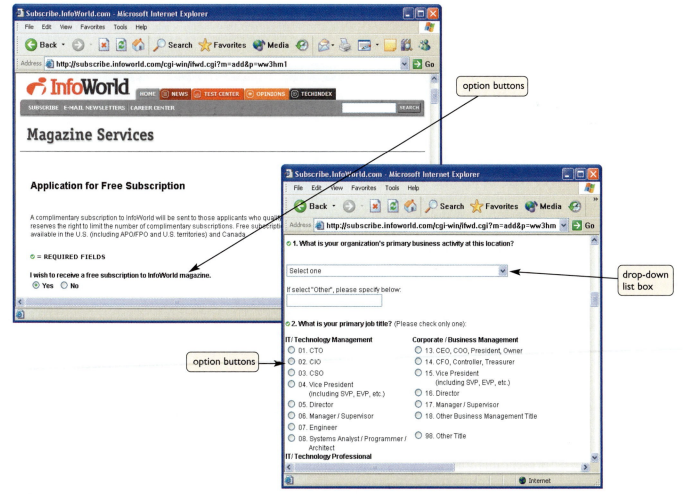

FIGURE 6-38 Notice that the Web-based subscription form for *InfoWorld* uses various features to make it easier for the subscriber to complete the form.

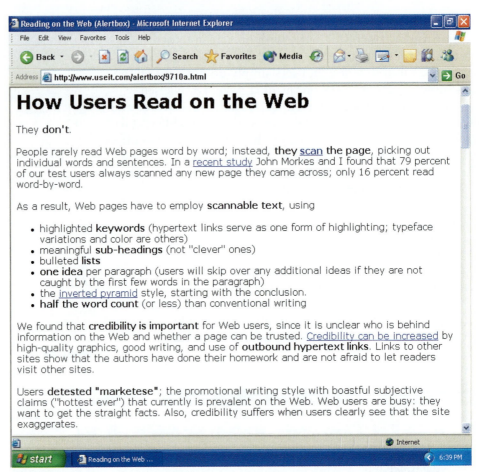

FIGURE 6-39   Dr. Jakob Nielsen believes that users scan Web material rather than reading it. He suggests that Web designers must use scannable text and employ usability metrics to measure the results.

Every piece of information should be traceable back to the input data that produced it. That means that you must provide an **audit trail** that records the source of each data item and when it entered the system. In addition to recording the original source, an audit trail must show how and when data is accessed or changed, and by whom. All those actions must be logged in an audit trail file and monitored carefully.

A company must have procedures for handling source documents to ensure that data is not lost before it enters the system. All source documents that originate from outside the organization should be logged when they are received. Whenever source documents pass between departments, the transfer should be recorded.

Data security policies and procedures protect data from loss or damage, which is a vital goal in every organization. If the safeguards are not 100 percent effective, data recovery utilities should be able to restore lost or damaged data. Once data is entered, the company should store source documents in a safe location for some specified length of time. The company should have a **records retention policy** that meets all legal requirements and business needs.

Audit trail files and reports should be stored and saved. Then, if a data file is damaged, you can use the information to reconstruct the lost data. Data security also involves protecting data from unauthorized access. System sign-on procedures should prevent unauthorized individuals from entering the system, and users should change their passwords regularly. Having several levels of access also is advisable. For example, a data entry person might be allowed to *view* a credit limit, but not *change* it. Sensitive data can be **encrypted,** or coded, in a process called **encryption,** so only users with decoding software can read it.

CASE IN POINT 6.4: BOOLEAN TOYS

When should a systems analyst decide a design issue, and when should users be allowed to select what works best for them? The field of ergonomics is concerned with improving the work environment and studying how users interact with their environment.

Suppose you are a systems analyst studying the order processing system at Boolean Toys, a fast-growing developer of software for preschool children. You know that many data entry users have complained about the input screens. Some users would prefer to rearrange the order of the fields; others would like to change the background color on their screens; still others want shortcuts that would allow them to avoid a series of introductory screens.

What if Boolean's users could customize their own data entry screens without assistance from the IT staff by using a menu-driven utility program? What would be the pros and cons of such an approach?

CHAPTER SUMMARY

The purpose of systems design is to create a physical model of the system that satisfies the logical design requirements that were defined during the systems analysis phase. The chapter began with a discussion of output design issues and a description of various types of output, such as Web-based information delivery, audio output, automated facsimile and faxback systems, e-mail, and other specialized forms of output.

You learned about various types of printed reports, including detail, exception, and summary reports. The chapter also described the features and sections of reports, including control fields, control breaks, report headers and footers, page headers and footers, and group headers and footers. Examples of report design were presented, along with suggestions about designing character-based reports. You learned how to estimate printing volume and time. Also, you learned about output control and the various measures you can take to achieve adequate output control to ensure that information is correct, complete, and secure.

You learned about human-computer interaction concepts and graphical user interfaces (GUIs), which use graphical objects and techniques that allow users to communicate with the system. User-centered design principles require an analyst to understand the business functions, maximize graphical effectiveness, profile the system's users, think like a user, use prototyping, design a comprehensive interface, continue the feedback process, and document the interface design.

The chapter listed several interface design guidelines, which suggested that you focus on basic objectives, make the interface easy to learn and use, provide features that promote efficiency, make it easy for users to obtain Help and correct errors, minimize input data problems, provide feedback to users, create an attractive layout and design, and use familiar terms and images.

You learned that an interface can include various controls, including menu bars, toolbars, drop-down list boxes, dialog boxes, toggle buttons, list boxes, option buttons, check boxes, command buttons, and spin bars. Controls are placed on a main switchboard, which is like a graphical version of a main menu.

During input design, you learned about batch and online input methods. Input design includes selecting appropriate input media and methods, developing efficient input procedures, reducing input volume, and avoiding input errors. In carrying out those tasks, the systems analyst must consider three key procedures: data capture, data entry, and input methods. Data capture involves identifying and recording source data. Data entry involves converting source data into a computer-readable form and entering it into the system. A wide variety of input media is available, including optical, voice, and magnetic recognition devices; special-purpose terminals; and graphical input devices.

An effective way to reduce input errors is to reduce input volume. You also can reduce errors by using well-designed data entry screens and by using data validation checks that verify data sequence, existence, range and limit, reasonableness, validity, combination, and batch controls.

You learned about source document design and the various zones in a source document, including the heading zone, the control zone, the instruction zone, the body zone, the totals zone, and the authorization zone. Finally, you learned about input control, including audit trails, data security, privacy issues, and records retention policies.

Key Terms and Phrases

Learn It Online

Instructions: To complete the Learn It Online exercises, start your browser, click the Address bar, and then enter the Web address **scsite.com/sad6e/learn**. When the Systems Analysis and Design Learn It Online page is displayed, follow the instructions in the exercises below. Each exercise has instructions for saving your results, either for your own records or for submission to your instructor.

1 Chapter Reinforcement

TF, MC, and SA

Below SAD Chapter 6, click the Chapter Reinforcement link. Print the quiz by clicking Print on the File menu for each page. Answer each question.

2 Flash Cards

Below SAD Chapter 6, click the Flash Cards link and read the instructions. Type 20 (or a number specified by your instructor) in the Number of playing cards text box, type your name in the Enter your Name text box, and then click the Flip Card button. When the flash card is displayed, read the question and then click the ANSWER box arrow to select an answer. Flip through the Flash Cards. If your score is 15 (75%) correct or greater, click Print on the File menu to print your results. If your score is less than 15 (75%) correct, then redo this exercise by clicking the Replay button.

3 Practice Test

Below SAD Chapter 6, click the Practice Test link. Answer each question, enter your first and last name at the bottom of the page, and then click the Grade Test button. When the graded practice test is displayed on your screen, click Print on the File menu to print a hard copy. Continue to take practice tests until you score 80% or better.

4 Who Wants To Be a Computer Genius?

Below SAD Chapter 6, click the Computer Genius link. Read the instructions, enter your first and last name at the bottom of the page, and then click the Play button. When your score is displayed, click the PRINT RESULTS link to print a hard copy.

5 Wheel of Terms

Below SAD Chapter 6, click the Wheel of Terms link. Read the instructions, and then enter your first and last name and your school name. Click the PLAY button. When your score is displayed on the screen, right-click the score and then click Print on the shortcut menu to print a hard copy.

6 Crossword Puzzle Challenge

Below SAD Chapter 6, click the Crossword Puzzle Challenge link. Read the instructions, and then enter your first and last name. Click the SUBMIT button. Work the crossword puzzle. When you are finished, click the Submit button. When the crossword puzzle is redisplayed, click the Print Puzzle button to print a hard copy.

Case-Sim: SCR Associates

Background

SCR Associates is a consulting firm that offers IT solutions and training. SCR needs an information system to manage operations at its new training center. The new system will be called TIMS (Training Information Management System). As a newly hired systems analyst, you will report to Jesse Baker, systems group manager. You will work on various tasks and practice the skills you learned in this chapter.

Using the Case

The SCR Associates case study is a Web-based simulation that allows you to practice your skills in a real-world environment. The case study transports you to SCR's company intranet, where you can complete 10 work sessions, each aligning with a chapter. As you work on the case, you will receive e-mail and voice mail messages, obtain information from SCR's online libraries, and perform various tasks. The first time you enter the SCR Case, you should go to the Starting page at **scsite.com/sad6e/scr** for detailed instructions.

Preview: Session 6

Now that the overall data design is complete, Jesse Baker wants you to work on output and user interface design. You will consider user needs, and apply principles of human-computer interaction to build a user-centered interface that is easy to learn and use. You also will consider data validation checks, source documents, forms, and reports.

To start a work session, you log on to the SCR intranet. When you enter your name and password, an opening screen displays links to the work sessions, and you select Session 6. At this point, you check your e-mail and voice mail messages carefully. Then you begin working on your task list, which includes the following items:

Tasks: Output and User Interface Design

1. *Create a detail report that will display all SCR courses in alphabetical order, with the course name and the instructor name in a group header; the Social Security number, name, and telephone number of each current student in the detail section; and the student count in a group footer.*

2. *Create a switchboard design with control buttons that lead to students, instructors, courses, course schedules, and course rosters. Allow a user to add, update, or delete records in each area. Jesse wants to see storyboards that show the proposed screens.*

3. *Suggest data validation checks for data entry screens.*

4. *Create a source document for an SCR mail-in registration form. Also need a design for a Web-based course registration form.*

FIGURE 6-40 Task list: Session 6.

Chapter Exercises

Review Questions

1. List and describe various types of output, including technology-based forms of information delivery.
2. Define detail reports, exception reports, and summary reports. Explain the concept of a control field and how it is used to produce a control-break report.
3. Explain the concept of human-computer interaction (HCI).
4. Describe eight principles for a user-centered interface design.
5. Explain each of the data validation checks mentioned in this chapter.
6. Describe six types of user interface controls, and provide an example of how you could use each type in a data entry screen.
7. Explain the concept of a GUI and a switchboard. How does a GUI design differ from a character-based screen design?
8. Explain batch and online input methods. Define source data automation and provide an example.
9. What are five principles of source document design?
10. Provide four guidelines for reducing input volume.

Discussion Topics

1. Some systems analysts maintain that source documents are unnecessary. They say that all input can be entered directly into the system, without wasting time in an intermediate step. Do you agree? Can you think of any situations where source documents are essential?
2. Some systems analysts argue, "Give users what they ask for. If they want lots of reports and reams of data, then that is what you should provide. Otherwise, they will feel that you are trying to tell them how to do their jobs." Others say, "Systems analysts should let users know what information can be obtained from the system. If you listen to users, you'll never get anywhere, because they really don't know what they want and don't understand information systems." What do you think of these arguments?
3. Suppose your network support company employs 75 technicians who travel constantly and work at customer sites. Your task is to design an information system that provides technical data and information to the field team. What types of output and information delivery would you suggest for the system?
4. A user interface can be quite restrictive. For example, the interface design might not allow a user to exit to a Windows desktop or to log on to the Internet. Should a user interface include such restrictions? Why or why not?

Projects

1. Visit the administrative office at your school or a local company. Ask to see examples of output documents, such as computer-printed invoices, form letters, or class rosters. Analyze the design and appearance of each document, and try to identify at least one possible improvement for each.
2. Search the Web to find an example of an attractive user interface. Document your research and discuss it with your class.
3. Examine various application software packages to find examples of good (or bad) user interface design. Document your research and discuss it with your class.
4. Search your own files or review other sources to find good (or bad) examples of source document design. Document your research and discuss it with your class.

Apply Your Knowledge

The Apply Your Knowledge section contains four mini-cases. Each case describes a situation, explains your role in the case, and asks you to respond to questions. You can answer the questions by applying knowledge you learned in the chapter.

1   North Shore Boat Sales

Situation:

North Shore Boat Sales sells new and used boats and operates a Web-based boat brokerage business in Toronto. The company has grown, and North Shore needs a new information system to manage the inventory, the brokerage operation, and information about prospective buyers and sellers. Dan Robeson, the owner, asked you to design samples of computer screens and reports that the new system might produce.

1. Design a switchboard that includes the main information management functions that North Shore might require. Create a storyboard with a design layout that allows customers to perform the following functions: obtain information about new boats, obtain information about used boats, send an e-mail to North Shore, learn more about the company, or review links to other marine-related sites.

2. Prospective buyers might want to search for boats by type, size, price range, or manufacturer. Develop a screen design that would permit those choices.

3. Suggest reports that might be useful to North Shore's management.

4. Suggest the general layout for a Web-based source document that prospective sellers could use to describe their boats. The information should include boat type (sail or power), manufacturer, year, length, type of engine, hull color, and asking price.

2   Terrier News

Situation:

Terrier News is a monthly newsletter devoted to various breeds of terriers and topics of interest to terrier owners and breeders. Annie West, the editor and publisher, asked you to help her design a system to enter and manage the hundreds of classified ads that Terrier News publishes. Some ads are for dogs wanted; some are for dogs for sale; and some offer products and services.

1. Design a suitable source document for ads that are telephoned or mailed in.

2. Explain user-centered design principles in a brief memo to Annie.

3. Suggest at least four user interface design guidelines that could be used for the new system.

4. Suggest several types of controls that might be used on the switchboard you plan to design. Explain why you chose each control, and create a storyboard that shows the switchboard layout.

3 **Sky-High Internet Services**

Situation:

Sky-High Internet Services is a leading Internet service provider in a metropolitan area. The new customer billing system has caused an increase in complaints. Tammy Jones, the office manager, asked you to investigate the situation. After interviewing data entry operators and observing the online data input process, you are fairly certain that most errors occur when data is entered.

1. Write a brief memo to Tammy explaining the importance of data validation during the input process.
2. Suggest at least three specific data validation checks that might help reduce input errors.
3. Would a batch input system offer any advantages? Write a brief memo to Tammy stating your views.
4. Suppose that Sky-High is predicting 25 percent annual growth, on a current base of 90,000 customers. If the growth pattern holds, how many customers will Sky-High have in three years? If it takes about 12 minutes to enter a new customer into the system, how many additional data entry operators will be needed to handle the growth next year? Assume that an operator works about 2,000 hours per year. Also assume a 30-percent annual attrition rate for existing customers.

4 **Castle Point Antique Auction**

Situation:

Castle Point Antique Auction operates a successful Web site that offers an auction forum for buyers and sellers of fine antiques. Monica Creighton, the owner, asked you to help her design some new documents and reports.

1. Suggest the general layout for a Web-based source document that prospective bidders would submit. The information should include user ID, password, name, address, telephone, e-mail address, item number, bid offered, and method of payment (money order, check, American Express, MasterCard, or Visa).
2. Suggest the general layout for a Web-based source document that prospective sellers could use to describe their antiques. The information should include the user ID, password, item, dimensions, origin, condition, and asking price.
3. Write a brief memo to Monica explaining the difference between detail reports, exception reports, and summary reports. Suggest at least one example of each type of report that she might want to consider.
4. Suppose Castle Point wants to print a catalog of current items. How long would it take to print a list of 2,500 items, at five items per page, on a laser printer rated at 20 ppm?

Case Studies

Case studies allow you to practice specific skills learned in the chapter. Each chapter contains several case studies that continue throughout the textbook, and a chapter capstone case.

NEW CENTURY HEALTH CLINIC

The associates at New Century Health Clinic approved your recommendations for a new computer system. Your next step is to develop a design for the new system, including output and user interface issues.

Background

To complete the output and user interface design for the new information system at New Century, you should review the DFDs and object-oriented diagrams you prepared previously, and the rest of the documentation from the systems analysis phase. Perform the following tasks.

Assignments

1. Dr. Jones has asked you to create a monthly Claim Status Summary report. He wants you to include the insurance company number, the patient number and name, the procedure date, the procedure code and description, the fee, the date the claim was filed, the amount of the claim, the amount of reimbursement, and the amount remaining unpaid. He wants you to group the data by insurance company number, with subtotals by company and grand totals for each numeric field. When you design the report, make sure to include printer spacing charts, a mock-up report, and a report analysis form.

2. Design the daily appointment list and a monthly statement using a printer spacing chart or graph paper. Include a mock-up report and a report analysis form for each report.

3. Determine the data required for a new patient. Design an input source document that will be used to capture the data and a data entry screen to input the information.

4. What data validation checks would the clinic need for the new patient data entry screen? Write a brief memo with your recommendations.

PERSONAL TRAINER, INC.

Personal Trainer, Inc., owns and operates fitness centers in a dozen midwestern cities. The centers have done well, and the company is planning an international expansion by opening a new "supercenter" in the Toronto area. Personal Trainer's president, Cassia Umi, hired an IT consultant, Susan Park, to help develop an information system for the new facility. During the project, Susan will work closely with Gray Lewis, who will manage the new operation.

Background

Following the decision to use an in-house team to develop a design prototype, Susan began to work on the physical design for Personal Trainer's new information system. At this stage, she is ready to begin working with Gray on the output and user interface design. Together, Susan and Gray will seek to develop a user-centered design that is easy to learn and use. Personal Trainer users will include managers, fitness instructors, support staff, and members themselves.

Assignments

1. Create a detail report that will display all Personal Trainer courses in alphabetical order, with the course name and the instructor name in a group header; the Social Security number, name, and telephone number of each current student in the detail section; and the student count in a group footer.

2. Create a switchboard design with control buttons that lead to members, fitness instructors, activities and services, schedules, and fitness class rosters. Allow a user to add, update, or delete records in each area.

3. Suggest context-sensitive and specific Help for the switchboard and lower-level menus and forms. Prepare storyboards that show the proposed screens. Also suggest at least six types of data validation checks for data entry screens.

4. Design a mail-in source document that members can use to register for fitness classes. Also design a Web-based registration form.

VIDEO SUPERSTORE

Video Superstore has hired you to design two online data entry screens. Based on what you know about the operation of a video rental store, complete the following assignments.

Assignments

1. Design a weekly operations summary report that will include overall data on rentals, new customers, late charges, and anything else you think a store manager might want to review. Be sure to include numeric activity and dollar totals.

2. Design a data entry screen for entering new members.

3. Design a video rental input screen. In addition to the video data, the video rental form must include the following fields: Member Number, Name, and Date.

4. Suggest at least three data validation checks that might help reduce input errors for the video rental system.

CHAPTER CAPSTONE CASE: SoftWear, Limited

SoftWear, Limited (SWL), is a continuing case study that illustrates the knowledge and skills described in each chapter. In this case study, the student acts as a member of the SWL systems development team and performs various tasks.

Background

SoftWear, Limited, decided to use the payroll package developed by Pacific Software Solutions and customize it by adding its own ESIP system to handle SWL's Employee Savings and Investment Plan.

Because most of the payroll requirements would be handled by Pacific's payroll package, the IT team decided that Carla Moore would work on the new ESIP modules, and Rick Williams would concentrate on the rest of the payroll system. A new systems analyst, Becky Evans, was assigned to help Rick with the payroll package.

Pacific Software Solutions offered free training for new customers, so Rick and Becky attended a three-day train-the-trainer workshop at Pacific's site in Los Angeles. When they returned, they began developing a one-day training session for SWL users, including people from the accounting, payroll, and human resources departments. The initial training would include the features and processing functions of the new payroll package that was scheduled to arrive the following week.

Carla's first task was to work on the ESIP outputs. She had to design several reports: the ESIP Deduction Register, the ESIP Payment Summary, and the checks that SWL sends to the credit union and the stock purchase plan. Carla also needed to develop an ESIP Accounting Summary as a data file to be loaded into the accounting system.

Carla learned that standard SWL company checks were used to make the payments to the credit union and stock purchase department. In addition, the output entry to the accounting system had been specified by the accounting department in a standard format for all entries into that system.

To prepare the new ESIP Deduction Register, Carla reviewed the documentation from the systems analysis phase to make sure that she understood the logical design and the available data fields.

Carla decided to use a monthly format because accounting would apply some deductions on a monthly cycle. She started her design with a standard SWL report heading. Then she added a control heading and footing for each employee's Social Security number. The total of employee deductions would be compared with the transferred ESIP funds to make sure that they matched. After preparing a rough layout, Carla used a report generator (Microsoft Access) to create the design shown in Figure 6-41. Then she prepared the mock-up report shown in Figure 6-42 on the next page, using test data for the month of May 2005.

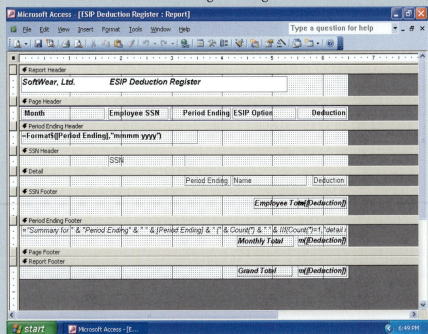

FIGURE 6-41 The layout for the ESIP Deduction Register that Carla created. Notice that SSN is a control break field. An SSN header introduces the group of detail records, and an SSN footer includes subtotals for the group.

CHAPTER CAPSTONE CASE: SoftWear, Limited (continued)

During the systems analysis phase, Carla learned that the accounting department required a control report to show the ESIP deduction amounts that were not yet applied. The control report is used to verify the amount of the checks or fund transfers SWL makes to the credit union and stock purchase plan. The accounting department needs the control

SoftWear, Ltd.	*ESIP Deduction Register*			
Month	**Employee SSN**	**Period Ending**	**ESIP Option**	**Deduction**
May 2005				
	111-11-1111			
		5/6/2005	Stock Purchase Plan	$15.00
		5/6/2005	Credit Union	$20.00
		5/13/2005	Credit Union	$25.00
		5/13/2005	Stock Purchase Plan	$15.00
		5/20/2005	Stock Purchase Plan	$15.00
		5/20/2005	Credit Union	$20.00
		5/27/2005	Stock Purchase Plan	$15.00
		5/27/2005	Credit Union	$20.00
			Employee Total	*$145.00*
	222-22-2222			
		5/6/2005	Stock Purchase Plan	$10.00
		5/6/2005	Credit Union	$30.00
		5/13/2005	Stock Purchase Plan	$10.00
		5/13/2005	Credit Union	$30.00
		5/20/2005	Stock Purchase Plan	$10.00
		5/20/2005	Credit Union	$30.00
		5/27/2005	Credit Union	$30.00
		5/27/2005	Stock Purchase Plan	$10.00
			Employee Total	*$160.00*
	333-33-3333			
		5/6/2005	ESIP: Option 1	$9.99
		5/13/2005	ESIP: Option 1	$9.99
		5/20/2005	ESIP: Option 1	$9.99
		5/27/2005	ESIP: Option 1	$9.99
			Employee Total	*$39.96*
Summary for Period Ending 5/27/2005 (20 detail records)				
			Monthly Total	*$344.96*
			Grand Total	*$344.96*

FIGURE 6-42   Mock-up for the ESIP Deduction Register.

CHAPTER CAPSTONE CASE: SoftWear, Limited (continued)

report to verify the accounting system outputs and balance the ESIP deduction totals against the payroll system's Payroll Register report.

Figure 6-43 shows a mock-up of the ESIP Payment Summary report. Carla met with Buddy Goodson, director of accounting, to review the design. Buddy was pleased with the report and felt it would be acceptable to the company's outside auditors. Buddy met with the auditing firm later that week and secured the team's approval.

As Carla turned her attention to the user interface for the ESIP system, she realized that she would need to develop two new source documents: an ESIP Option Form and an ESIP Deduction Authorization Form. She also planned to design a main switchboard and all necessary screen forms.

SoftWear, Ltd. ESIP Payment Summary Report

Last Deduction Period in Month: 5/27/2005

ESIP Code	Name	Deduction
CREDUN	Credit Union	$205.00
ESIP01	ESIP: Option 1	$39.96
SWLSTK	Stock Purchase Plan	$100.00
	Grand Total:	$344.96

FIGURE 6-43 Mock-up of the ESIP Payment Summary Report.

Carla started by designing the ESIP Option Form that could be used for adding new ESIP options and modifying existing ones when authorized by the vice president of human resources. She included an ESIP ID code, an ESIP option name, and other information as shown in Figure 6-44. For each field, she established a range of acceptable values.

SWL Employee Saving and Investment Plan
ESIP Option Form   ESIP ID _____

INSTRUCTIONS: Recommendations must be reviewed by SWL's legal counsel before submission.

ESIP Option Name: _____
Description: _____
Deduction Cycle: _____
Application Cycle: _____
Minimum Service: _____
Minimum Deduction Amount: $_____
Maximum Deduction Percentage: %_____

Approval: _____ Date: _____
(Vice President - Human Resources)

FIGURE 6-44 The ESIP Option Form for adding new ESIP options and modifying existing ones.

CHAPTER CAPSTONE CASE: SoftWear, Limited (continued)

Next, Carla worked on a data entry screen based on the ESIP Option Form. Using SWL's existing screen design standards, she quickly developed the screen shown in Figure 6-45. Carla decided that she could make the screen more useful if users could view data on existing options. Her design allowed users to add, delete, save, clear, or find a record by clicking the appropriate command button.

Instead of waiting until all input design was finished, Carla decided to create mock-ups to show Tina Pham, vice president of human resources, and Mike Feiner, director of human resources. Figure 6-46 shows the two mock-ups. Carla reasoned that if any comments or suggestions were offered, they also would apply to other input screens.

FIGURE 6-45 Data entry screen for adding and changing ESIP options.

FIGURE 6-46 Carla's mock-up screens with actual data to obtain user approval.

CHAPTER CAPSTONE CASE: SoftWear, Limited (continued) SWL

The ESIP Deduction Authorization Form was more complicated than the ESIP Option Form because it required more data and signatures. It took several hours for Carla to design the form shown in Figure 6-47. She divided the form into three sections: the employee completes the information in the top section; human resources completes the middle section; and payroll representatives complete the bottom section.

FIGURE 6-47 The ESIP Deduction Authorization Form.

Carla designed a data entry screen based on the ESIP Deduction Authorization Form shown in Figure 6-47 and made the screen consistent with the other ESIP screen designs. Now a user could add, delete, save, clear, or find a record by clicking the appropriate command buttons. Carla also provided instructions to the operator for exiting from the system.

CHAPTER CAPSTONE CASE: SoftWear, Limited (continued)

Carla decided to create a series of mock-ups to show users how the new ESIP deduction screen would work. Figure 6-48 shows the screen after the user has entered an employee's Social Security number. In Figure 6-49, the system has retrieved the employee's name, Sean R. Fitzpatrick, so the user can verify it against the source document. Figure 6-50 shows that the user has entered the stock purchase plan code, SWLSTK, and the system has supplied the name. Finally, the user enters the $10.00 deduction and the current date.

The users approved the new design, with one suggestion — the system date should be added automatically as the entry date. Carla made the change and designed the switchboard shown in Figure 6-51. The switchboard layout was based on comments that users made during the design process. Now that she had a working model, Carla went back to the users to show them the complete package.

FIGURE 6-48 Data entry screen for ESIP deductions. Here, the user has entered an employee Social Security number and is about to press the ENTER key. Notice that the form has several command buttons, including a STOP button that exits the program.

FIGURE 6-49 After the user presses the ENTER key, the system retrieves the employee name and displays it so the user can verify it. Notice that the user must check a box to verify that the form has been signed properly.

FIGURE 6-50 The user has entered an employee stock purchase deduction of $10.00 and is ready to save the record.

CHAPTER CAPSTONE CASE: SoftWear, Limited

FIGURE 6-51   The ESIP switchboard includes option buttons and command buttons to select various processing choices.

SWL Team Tasks

1. An interesting issue came up at a recent meeting with SWL users. It seems that some users want to modify the data entry screens they use. For example, several users would prefer to rearrange the order of the fields; others would like to change the background color on their screens; still others want shortcuts that would allow them to avoid a series of introductory screens. What if SWL users could customize their own data entry screens without assistance from the IT staff by using a menu-driven design feature? Carla asked you to think about this and let her know the pros and cons of user-driven screen design.

2. Carla Moore also wants employees to have an online information request form that they can use to learn more about ESIP options and request up-to-date balances for their ESIP accounts. Follow the guidelines and suggestions in this chapter, and design an online screen form for Carla.

3. In addition to being available online, Carla wants the information request form to be available as a paper source document, which can be used by employees who do not have easy access to the online form. Follow the guidelines and suggestions in this chapter, and design a paper source document for Carla.

4. Carla wants an update on usability, how users read on the Web. Review the material in this chapter, along with Figure 6-20 on page 266 and Figure 6-39 on page 284. Visit these Web sites, and any others that provide more information on this topic. Summarize the results of your research in a memo to Carla.

CHAPTER 7 Data Design

CHAPTER 7 is the second of three chapters in the systems design phase of the SDLC. In this chapter, you will focus on data design skills that are necessary to construct the physical model of the information system.

INTRODUCTION

OBJECTIVES

When you finish this chapter, you will be able to:

- Explain data design concepts and data structures
- Describe file processing systems and various types of files
- Understand database systems and define the components of a database management system (DBMS)
- Describe Web-based data design
- Explain data design terminology, including entities, fields, common fields, records, files, tables, and key fields
- Describe data relationships, draw an entity-relationship diagram, define cardinality, and use cardinality notation
- Explain the concept of normalization
- Explain the importance of codes and describe various coding schemes
- Describe relational and object-oriented database models
- Explain data warehousing and data mining
- Differentiate between logical and physical storage and records
- Explain data control measures

In the systems analysis phase, you created data flow diagrams and identified data elements, data flows, and data stores to build a logical design for the information system. In this part of the systems design phase, you will develop a physical plan for data organization, storage, and retrieval.

This chapter begins with a review of data design concepts and terminology, then discusses file-based systems and database systems, including Web-based databases. You will learn how to create entity-relationship diagrams that show the relationships among data elements, and you will learn how to use normalization concepts to build an effective data design. You also will learn about codes that can be used to represent data items. The chapter concludes with a discussion of data storage and access, including strategic tools such as data warehousing and data mining, physical design issues, logical and physical records, data storage formats, and data control.

CHAPTER INTRODUCTION CASE: Mountain View College Bookstore

Background: Wendy Lee, manager of college services at Mountain View College, wants a new information system that will improve efficiency and customer service at the three college bookstores.

In this part of the case, Florence Fullerton (systems analyst) and Harry Boston (student intern) are talking about data design issues.

Participants:	Florence and Harry
Location:	Mountain View College Cafeteria, Monday morning, December 19, 2005
Project status:	Florence and Harry have completed their output and user interface design tasks and are ready to continue the systems design phase by working on data design for the new system.
Discussion topics:	Data design terms and concepts, cardinality, relational databases, normalization, Web-based design, codes, and physical design issues

Florence: Good morning, Harry. Now that we have a logical model of the bookstore information system, we're ready for the next step. We have to select an overall data design strategy. I think we should start by looking at a relational database, rather than a file processing design.

Harry: *What are the pros and cons?*

Florence: Well, in some situations file processing systems are better, especially when you have to process large numbers of records in a sequence. But in our case, I think a relational database would be more powerful and flexible.

Harry: *I know what a database is, but what do you mean by the term relational?*

Florence: In a relational database, all the entities — the individual people, places, events, and transactions — are stored in separate locations called tables, which are related or linked together. That means you have to enter an item of data only once, and you can access all the data items just as if they were all stored in a single location.

Harry: *That makes sense. How do we decide what data goes where?*

Florence: We'll start by creating an entity-relationship diagram. Then we'll develop a set of table designs that follow a set of rules called normalization.

Harry: *I've heard that term before. Aren't there several different levels of normalization, called normal forms?*

Florence: Yes, and we want our data to be in what's called third normal form, which is what most business-related systems use. We also will consider using various codes to represent data items.

Harry: *I know that we decided to build the system to run on the college network and then migrate to a Web-based system in the future. But shouldn't we use a design that will make it easy to migrate to the Web?*

Florence: Yes, and a relational database will be the most flexible approach.

Harry: *Sounds good. Any other issues?*

Florence: Well, we need to consider some physical design issues, too. Here's a task list to get us started:

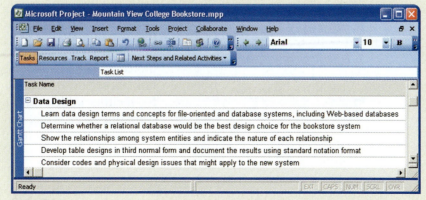

FIGURE 7-1

DATA DESIGN CONCEPTS

Before constructing an information system, a systems analyst must understand basic data design concepts, including data structures and the characteristics of file processing and database systems, including Web-based database design.

Data Structures

A **data structure** is a framework for organizing and storing data in an information system. Data structures consist of files or tables that are linked in various ways. Each **file** or **table** contains data about people, places, things, or events that interact with the information system. For example, one file or table might contain data about customers, and other files or tables might store data about products, orders, suppliers, or employees. Depending on how the system's files and tables are organized and linked, an information system is called either a file processing system or a database management system.

A **file processing system**, also called **a file-oriented system**, stores and manages data in one or more separate files. Examples of two file processing systems are shown in Figure 7-2. The figure shows an auto repair shop with a Job Records system that uses a JOB data file, and an Employee Records system that uses a MECHANIC data file. In the example shown, the Job Records system uses a file that contains all the data necessary to answer inquiries and generate reports about work performed at the shop. Similarly, the Employee Records system uses a file that stores all the data necessary to answer inquiries and generate reports about shop employees. A major disadvantage of file-oriented systems is that the same data is stored in more than one place. For example, notice that three items of information (Mechanic No, Name, and Pay Rate) are stored in both data files.

Now consider Figure 7-3, which shows how the same auto repair shop might use a database system instead of a file-oriented system. A **database system** consists of linked tables that form one overall data structure. Compared to file processing, a database system offers much greater flexibility and efficiency. For example, in the file processing designs shown in Figure 7-2, the two files are unrelated — but in the database design in Figure 7-3, the tables are linked by the Mechanic No field. This link allows information to be accessed from either table as if the two tables were one large table, making it unnecessary to store duplicate information in both tables.

File processing systems still exist to handle specific applications, but most information systems today are designed

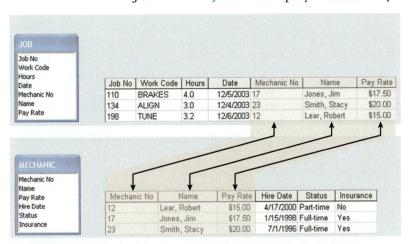

FIGURE 7-2 Example of an auto repair shop that uses two separate file-oriented systems: a Job Records system (with a JOB data file) and an Employee Records system (with a MECHANIC data file). Notice that three items of information must be duplicated in both data files.

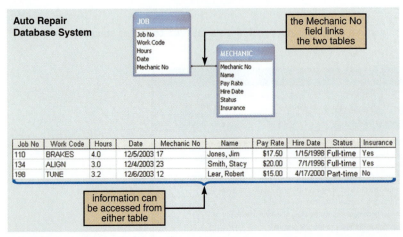

FIGURE 7-3 Example of a database design for the auto repair shop that links two data tables and avoids duplication. Notice that the Mechanic No field provides a link between the two tables, and information can be accessed from either table.

as databases. The pros and cons of file processing compared with database systems are discussed in the following section.

Overview of File Processing

Companies mainly use file processing to handle large volumes of structured data on a regular basis. Many older systems utilized file processing designs because that approach was well suited to mainframe hardware and batch input. Although less common today, file processing can be more efficient and cost less than a DBMS in certain situations. For example, consider a credit card company that posts thousands of daily transactions from a TRANSACTION file to customer balances stored in a CUSTOMER file, as shown in Figure 7-4. For that relatively simple process, file processing is highly effective.

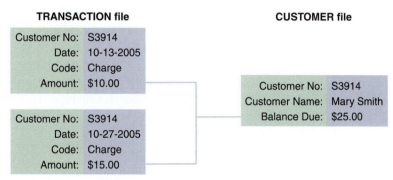

FIGURE 7-4 A credit card company might use a file processing system to post daily sales transactions from a TRANSACTION file to the CUSTOMER file.

In a typical file processing environment, a company might have three departments, each with its own information system and data files. Three potential problems exist in a file processing environment. The first problem is **data redundancy**, which means that data common to two or more information systems is stored in several places. Data redundancy requires more storage space, and maintaining and updating data in several locations is expensive.

Secondly, **data integrity** problems can occur if updates are not applied in every file. Changing the data in only one of the systems will cause inconsistent data and result in incorrect information in the second system.

The third problem is the **rigid data structure** of a typical file processing environment. Businesses must make decisions based on company-wide data, and managers often require information from multiple business units and departments. In a file processing environment, that means retrieving information from independent, file-based systems, which is slow and inefficient.

A file-oriented information system can contain various types of files, including master files, table files, transaction files, work files, security files, and history files.

- A **master file** stores relatively permanent data about an entity. For example, a PRODUCT master file contains one logical record for each product the company sells. The quantity field in each record might change daily, but other data, such as the product's code, name, and description, would not change. As another example, a school might maintain master files for courses, students, and faculty members.

- A **table file** contains reference data used by the information system. As with master files, table files are relatively static and are not updated by the information system. Examples of table files include tax tables and postage rate tables.

- A **transaction file** stores records that contain day-to-day business and operational data. A transaction file is an input file that updates a master file; after the update is completed, the transaction file has served its purpose. Unless they are saved for security or backup reasons, transaction files are temporary files. An example of a transaction file is a charges and payments file that updates a customer balance file.

- A **work file**, also called a **scratch file**, is a temporary file created by an information system for a single task. Most often a work file is created by one process in the information system and used by another process within the same system. Work files can contain copies of master file records or various other records that are needed temporarily. Examples of work files include sorted files and report files that hold output reports until they are printed.

- A **security file** is created and saved for backup and recovery purposes. Examples of security files include audit trail files and backups of master, table, and transaction files. New security files must be created regularly to replace outdated files.

- A **history file** is a file created for historical or archiving purposes. For example, students who have not registered for any course in the last two semesters might be deleted from the active student master file and added to an inactive student file, which is a history file that can be used for queries or reports. If an inactive student registers again, his or her data record is deleted from the inactive student file and added back to the active student master file.

Overview of Database Systems

A properly designed database system offers a solution to the problems of file processing. A database provides an overall framework that avoids data redundancy and supports a real-time, dynamic environment, two potential problems of a file processing system.

In a file processing environment, data files are designed to fit individual business systems. In contrast, in a database environment, several systems can be built around a single database. Figure 7-5 shows a database environment with a database serving five separate information systems.

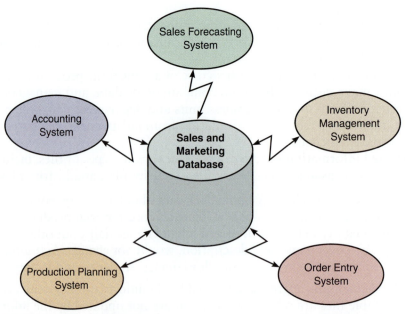

FIGURE 7-5 A typical database environment might consist of a database serving five separate business systems.

A **database management system** (DBMS) is a collection of tools, features, and interfaces that enables users to add, update, manage, access, and analyze the contents of a set of data. From a user's point of view, the main advantage of a DBMS is that it offers timely, interactive, and flexible data access. Specific DBMS advantages include the following:

- **Scalability**, which means that a system can be expanded, modified, or downsized easily to meet the rapidly changing needs of a business enterprise. For example, if a company decides to add data about secondary suppliers of material it uses, a new table can be added to the relational database and linked with a common field.

- Better support for client/server systems. In a **client/server** system, processing is distributed throughout the organization. Client/server systems require the power and flexibility of a database design. You will learn more about client/server systems in Chapter 8.

- Economy of scale. Database design allows better utilization of hardware. If a company maintains an enterprise-wide database, processing is less expensive using a powerful mainframe server instead of using several smaller computers. The inherent efficiency of high-volume processing on larger computers is called **economy of scale**.

- Flexible data sharing. Data can be shared across the enterprise, allowing more users to access more data. A database can be highly flexible, allowing users to view the same information in different ways. Users are empowered because they have access to the information they need to do their jobs.

- Enterprise-wide application. Typically, a DBMS is managed by a person called a **database administrator** (DBA), who assesses overall requirements and maintains the database for the benefit of the entire organization rather than a single department or user. Database systems can support enterprise-wide applications more effectively than file processing systems.

- Stronger standards. Effective database administration helps ensure that standards for data names, formats, and documentation are followed uniformly throughout the organization.

- Controlled redundancy. Redundancy means storing data in more than one place, which can result in inconsistency and data errors. Because the data is stored in a set of related tables, data items do not need to be duplicated in multiple locations. Even where some duplication is desirable for performance reasons, or disaster recovery, the database approach allows control of the redundancy.

- Better security. The DBA can define authorization procedures to ensure that only legitimate users can access the database and can allow different users to have different levels of access. Most DBMSs provide sophisticated security support.

- Increased programmer productivity. Programmers do not have to create the underlying file structure for a database. That allows them to concentrate on logical design and, therefore, a new database application can be developed more quickly than a file-oriented system.

- Data independence. Systems that interact with a DBMS are relatively independent of how the physical data is maintained. That design provides the DBA flexibility to alter data structures without modifying information systems that use the data.

Database Tradeoffs

Although a DBMS has many advantages, some design tradeoffs exist. Because DBMSs are powerful, they require more expensive hardware, software, and data networks capable of supporting a multi-user environment. In addition, a DBMS is more complex than a file processing system; therefore, the learning curve for systems analysts, database administrators, and users usually is steeper, which increases TCO (Total Cost of Ownership). Finally, procedures for security, backup, and recovery are more complicated and critical in a database environment. When a company maintains all vital data resources in a database, a DBMS failure seriously disrupts business operations.

Although the trend is toward enterprise-wide database design, many companies still use a combination of centralized DBMSs and smaller, department-level data management systems. Why is this so? Most large businesses view data as a company-wide resource that must be accessible to users throughout the company. At the same time, other factors encourage a decentralized design, including network expense; a reluctance to move away from smaller, more flexible systems; and a realization that enterprise-wide DBMSs can be highly complex and expensive to maintain. The compromise, in many cases, is a client/server design, where processing is shared among several computers. Client/server systems are described in detail in Chapter 8. As with many design decisions, the best solution depends on the individual circumstances.

DBMS COMPONENTS

A DBMS provides an interface between a database and users who need to access the data. Although users are concerned primarily with an easy-to-use interface and support for their business requirements, a systems analyst must understand all of the components of a DBMS. In addition to interfaces for users, database administrators, and related systems, a DBMS also has a data manipulation language, a schema and subschemas, and a physical data repository, as shown in Figure 7-6.

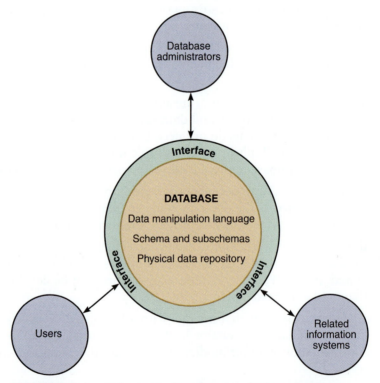

FIGURE 7-6 In addition to interfaces for users, database administrators, and related information systems, a DBMS also has a data manipulation language, a schema and subschemas, and a physical data repository.

Interfaces for Users, Database Administrators, and Related Systems

When users, database administrators, and related information systems request data and services, the DBMS processes the request, manipulates the data, and provides a response.

USERS   Users typically work with predefined queries and switchboard commands, but also use query languages to access stored data. A **query language** allows a user to specify a task without specifying how the task will be accomplished. Some query languages use natural language commands that resemble ordinary English sentences. With a **query by example (QBE)** language, the user provides an example of the data requested. Many database programs also generate **SQL** (**structured query language**), which is a language that allows PC client workstations to communicate with servers and mainframe computers. Figure 7-7 on the next page shows a QBE request for all Cool Vanilla or Electric Blue 2005 PT Cruisers with roof racks. The QBE request generates the SQL commands shown at the bottom of Figure 7-7.

DATABASE ADMINISTRATORS   A DBA is responsible for DBMS management and support. DBAs are concerned with data security and integrity, preventing unauthorized access, providing backup and recovery, audit trails, maintaining the database, and supporting user needs. Most DBMSs provide utility programs to assist the DBA in creating and updating data structures, collecting and reporting patterns of database usage, and detecting and reporting database irregularities.

RELATED INFORMATION SYSTEMS   A DBMS can support several related information systems that provide input to, and require specific data from, the DBMS. Unlike a user interface, no human intervention is required for two-way communication between the DBMS and the related systems.

Data Manipulation Language

A **data manipulation language (DML)** controls database operations, including storing, retrieving, updating, and deleting data. Most commercial DBMSs, such as Oracle and IBM's DB/2, use a DML. Some database products, such as Microsoft Access, also provide an easy-to-use graphical environment that enables users to control operations with menu-driven commands.

Schema

The complete definition of a database, including descriptions of all fields, tables, and relationships, is called a **schema**. You also can define one or more subschemas. A **subschema** is a view of the database used by one or more systems or users. A subschema defines only those portions of the database that a particular system or user needs or is allowed to access. For example, to protect individual privacy, you might not want to allow a project management system to retrieve employee pay rates. In that case, the project management system subschema would not include the pay rate field. Database designers also use subschemas to restrict the level of access permitted. For example, specific users, systems, or locations might be permitted to create, retrieve, update, or delete data, depending on their needs and the company's security policies.

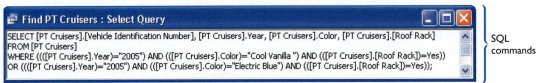

FIGURE 7-7 Using QBE, a user can request a list of all Cool Vanilla or Electric Blue 2005 PT Cruisers with roof racks. The QBE request generates the SQL commands shown.

Physical Data Repository

In Chapter 4, you learned about a data dictionary, which describes all data elements included in the logical design. At this stage of the systems development process, the data dictionary is transformed into a physical data repository, which also contains the schema and subschemas. The physical repository might be centralized, or it might be distributed at several locations. In addition, the stored data might be managed by a single DBMS, or several systems. To resolve potential database connectivity and access problems, companies use ODBC-compliant software that enables communication among various systems and DBMSs. **ODBC**, which stands for **open database connectivity**, is an industry-standard protocol that makes it possible for software from different vendors to interact and exchange data. ODBC uses SQL statements that the DBMS understands and can execute, similar to the ones shown in Figure 7-7. Another common standard is called **JDBC**, or **Java database connectivity**. JDBC enables Java applications to exchange data with any database that uses SQL statements and is JDBC-compliant.

You will learn more about physical design issues in Chapter 8, which discusses system architecture, and in Chapter 9, which discusses system implementation and data conversion.

WEB-BASED DATABASE DESIGN

The concept of Web-based systems was discussed in Chapter 5, Development Strategies. In this chapter, you will revisit this concept and examine the main components of a Web-based database system. The following sections discuss the characteristics of Web-based design, Internet terminology, connecting a database to the Web, and data security on the Web.

Characteristics of Web-Based Design

Figure 7-8 lists some major characteristics of Web-based database design. In a Web-based design, the Internet serves as the front end, or interface, for the database management system. Internet technology provides enormous power and flexibility, because the system is not tied to any specific combination of hardware and software. Access to the database requires only a Web browser and an Internet connection. Web-based systems are popular because they offer ease of access, cost-effectiveness, and worldwide connectivity — all of which are vital to companies that must compete in a global economy.

Web-Based Database Design Characteristics

CHARACTERISTIC	EXPLANATION
Global access	The Internet enables worldwide access, using existing infrastructure and standard telecommunications protocols.
Ease of use	Web browsers provide a familiar interface that is user-friendly and easily learned.
Multiple platforms	Web-based design is not dependent on a specific combination of hardware or software. All that is required is a browser and an Internet connection.
Cost effectiveness	Initial investment is relatively low, because the Internet serves as the communication network. Users require only a browser, and Web-based systems do not require powerful workstations. Flexibility is high, because numerous outsourcing options exist for development, hosting, maintenance, and system support.
Security issues	Security is a universal issue, but Internet connectivity raises special concerns. These can be addressed with a combination of good design, software that can protect the system and detect intrusion, stringent rules for passwords and user identification, and vigilant users and managers.
Adaptability issues	The Internet offers many advantages in terms of access, connectivity, and flexibility. Migrating a traditional database design to the Web, however, can require design modification, additional software, and some added expense.

FIGURE 7-8 Web-based design characteristics include global access, ease of use, multiple platforms, cost effectiveness, security issues, and adaptability issues. In a Web-based design, the Internet serves as the front end, or interface, for the database management system. Access to the database requires only a Web browser and an Internet connection.

Internet Terminology

To understand Web-based data design, it is helpful to review some basic Internet terms and concepts. To access information on the Internet, a person uses a **Web browser**, which is an application that enables the user to navigate, or browse, the Internet and display Web pages on his or her local computer. A **Web page** is a text document written in **HTML**, which stands for **Hypertext Markup Language**. HTML uses formatting codes called **tags**, which specify how the text and visual elements will be displayed in a Web browser. Web pages are stored on a **Web server**, which is a computer that receives requests and makes Web pages available to users. Together, the Web server and the Web pages are referred to as a **Web site**.

In addition to maintaining a Web site, many companies use intranets and extranets to support business operations and communications. An **intranet** is a private, company-owned

ON THE WEB

For more information about HTML, visit **scsite.com/sad6e/ more**, locate Chapter 7 and then click the HTML link.

network to provide Web-based access to internal users. An **extranet** is an extension of a company intranet that allows access by external users, such as customers and suppliers. Extranets are typical examples of B2B (business-to-business) data sharing and EDI (electronic data interchange), which were discussed in Chapter 1. Because intranets and extranets use the same **protocols**, or data transmission standards, as the Internet, they are called **Web-centric**.

The Internet and company intranets/extranets are forms of client/server architecture. In a client/server design, tasks are divided between **clients**, which are workstations that users interact with, and **servers**, which are computers that supply data, processing, and services to the client workstations. Client/server architecture is discussed in more detail in Chapter 8, System Architecture.

Connecting a Database to the Web

To access data in a Web-based system, the database must be connected to the Internet or intranet. The database and the Internet speak two different languages, however. Databases are created and managed by using various languages and commands that have nothing to do with HTML, which is the language of the Web. The objective is to connect the database to the Web and enable data to be viewed and updated.

To bridge the gap, it is necessary to use **middleware**, which is software that integrates different applications and allows them to exchange data. Middleware can interpret client requests in HTML form and translate the requests into commands that the database can execute. When the database responds to the commands, middleware translates the results into HTML pages that can be displayed by the user's browser, as shown in Figure 7-9. Notice that the four steps in the process can take place using the Internet or a company intranet as the communications channel.

FIGURE 7-9   When a client workstation requests a Web page (1), the Web server uses middleware to generate a data query to the database server (2). The database server responds (3) and middleware translates the retrieved data into an HTML page that can be sent by the Web server and displayed by the user's browser (4).

A popular example of middleware is Macromedia's ColdFusion, which is shown in Figure 7-10. Middleware is discussed in more detail in Chapter 8.

Data Security

Web-based data must be secure, yet easily accessible to authorized users. To achieve this goal, well-designed systems provide security at three levels: the database itself, the Web server, and the telecommunication links that connect the components of the system.

Data security is discussed in this chapter, in Chapter 8, System Architecture, and in Chapter 10, System Operations, Support, and Security.

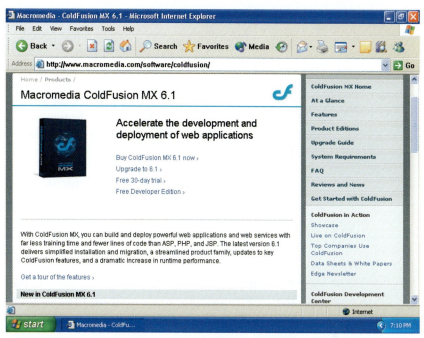

FIGURE 7-10 A popular example of middleware is Macromedia's ColdFusion. The latest version is called ColdFusion MX. Notice that the customer can combine ColdFusion's ease of use with IBM's WebSphere, which is a framework for Web-based application development and hosting.

DATA DESIGN TERMINOLOGY

Using the concepts discussed in the previous section, a systems analyst can select a design approach and begin to construct the system. The first step is to understand data design terminology.

Definitions

Figure 7-11 shows a CUSTOMER entity, which is represented by a table, or file, with eight fields and three records. Notice that the Customer ID field serves as the primary key. These terms are defined in the following sections.

ENTITY An **entity** is a person, place, thing, or event for which data is collected and maintained. For example, an online sales system may include entities named CUSTOMER, ORDER, PRODUCT, and SUPPLIER. When you prepared DFDs during the systems analysis phase, you identified various entities and data stores. Now you will consider the relationships among the entities.

CUSTOMER Table or File

FIGURE 7-11 The CUSTOMER entity is represented by a table or file with eight fields, three records, and a primary key.

TABLE OR FILE Data is organized into tables or files. A table, or file, contains a set of related records that store data about a specific entity. Tables and files are shown as two-dimensional structures that consist of vertical columns and horizontal rows. Each column represents a field, or characteristic of the entity, and each row represents a record, which is an individual instance, or occurrence of the entity. For example, the CUSTOMER table in Figure 7-11 on the previous page has eight columns, or fields, that describe the entity and three rows, or records, each representing a specific customer.

Although they can have different meanings in a specific context, the terms *table* and *file* often can be used interchangeably.

FIELD A **field**, also called an **attribute**, is a single characteristic or fact about an entity. In the example shown in Figure 7-11, the CUSTOMER entity has eight fields that store the Customer ID, First Name, Last Name, Address, City, State, Zip, and E-mail Address.

A **common field** is an attribute that appears in more than one entity. Common fields can be used to link entities in various types of relationships.

RECORD A **record**, also called a **tuple** (rhymes with couple), is a set of related fields that describes one instance, or occurrence of an entity, such as one customer, one order, or one product. A record might have one or dozens of fields, depending on what information is needed.

Key Fields

During the systems design phase, you use **key fields** to organize, access, and maintain data structures. The four types of keys are primary keys, candidate keys, foreign keys, and secondary keys.

PRIMARY KEY A **primary key** is a field or combination of fields that uniquely and minimally identifies a particular member of an entity. For example, in a customer table the customer number is a unique primary key because no two customers can have the same customer number. That key also is minimal because it contains no information beyond what is needed to identify the customer. In Figure 7-11, Customer ID is an example of a primary key based on a single field.

A primary key also can be composed of two or more fields. For example, if a student registers for three courses, his or her student number will appear in three records in the registration system. If one of those courses has 20 students, 20 separate records will exist for that course number — one record for each student who registered.

In the registration file, neither the student number nor the course ID is unique, so neither field can be a primary key. To identify a specific student in a specific course, the primary key must be a combination of student number and course ID. In that case, the primary key is called a **combination key**. A combination key also can be called a **composite key**, a **concatenated key**, or a **multi-valued key**.

Figure 7-12 shows four different tables. The first three tables have single-field primary keys. Notice that in the fourth table, however, the primary key is a combination of two fields: STUDENT-NUMBER and COURSE-ID.

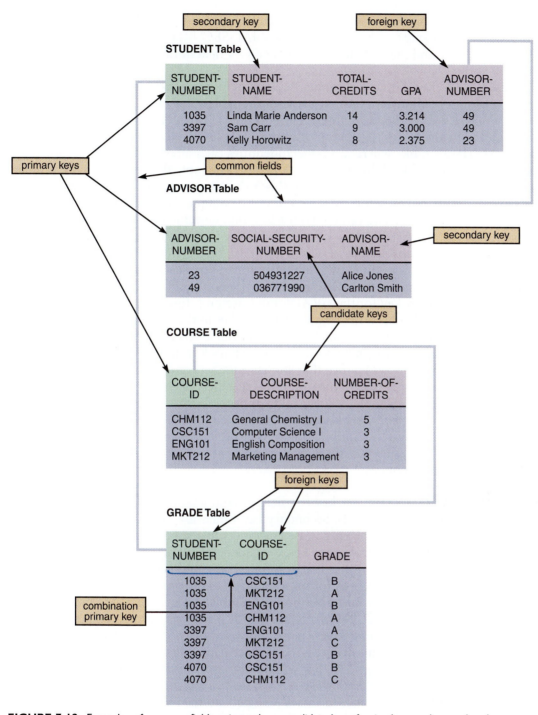

FIGURE 7-12 Examples of common fields, primary keys, candidate keys, foreign keys, and secondary keys.

CANDIDATE KEY Sometimes you have a choice of fields or field combinations to use as the primary key. Any field that could serve as a primary key is called a **candidate key**. For example, if every employee has a unique employee number, then you could use either the employee number or the Social Security number as a primary key. Because you can designate only one field as a primary key, you should select the field that contains the least amount of data and is the easiest to use. Any field that is not a primary key or a candidate key is called a **nonkey field**.

The primary keys shown in Figure 7-12 on the previous page also are candidate keys. Two other candidate keys exist: the SOCIAL-SECURITY-NUMBER field in the ADVISOR table and the COURSE-DESCRIPTION field in the COURSE table.

FOREIGN KEY Recall that a common field exists in more than one table and can be used to form a relationship, or link, between the tables. For example, in Figure 7-12, the ADVISOR-NUMBER field appears in both the STUDENT table and the ADVISOR table and joins the tables together. Notice that ADVISOR-NUMBER is a primary key in the ADVISOR table, where it uniquely identifies each advisor, and is a foreign key in the STUDENT table. A **foreign key** is a field in one table that must match a primary key value in another table in order to establish the relationship between the two tables.

Unlike a primary key, a foreign key need not be unique. For example, Carlton Smith has advisor number 49. The value 49 must be a unique value in the ADVISOR table because it is the primary key, but 49 can appear any number of times in the STUDENT table, where the advisor number serves as a foreign key.

Figure 7-12 also shows how two foreign keys can serve as a composite primary key in another table. Consider the GRADE table at the bottom of the figure. The two fields that form the primary key for the GRADE table are both foreign keys: the STUDENT-NUMBER field, which must match a student number in the STUDENT table, and the COURSE-ID field, which must match one of the course IDs in the COURSE table.

How can these two foreign keys serve as a primary key in the GRADE table? When you study the table, you will notice that student numbers and course IDs can appear any number of times, but the *combination* of a specific student and a specific course occurs only once. For example, student 1035 appears four times and course CSC151 appears three times — but there is only *one* combined instance of student 1035 *and* course CSC151. Because the combination of the specific student (1035) and the specific course (CSC151) is unique, it assures that the grade (B) will be assigned to the proper student in the proper course.

SECONDARY KEY A **secondary key** is a field or combination of fields that can be used to access or retrieve records. Secondary key values are not unique. For example, if you need to access records for only those customers in a specific ZIP code, you would use the ZIP code field as a secondary key. Secondary keys also can be used to sort or display records in a certain order. For example, you could use the GPA field in a STUDENT file to display records for all students in grade point order.

The need for a secondary key arises because a table can have only one primary key. In a CUSTOMER file, the CUSTOMER-NUMBER is the primary key, so it must be unique. You might know a customer's name, however, but not the customer's number. For example, you might want to access a customer named James Morgan in the table shown in Figure 7-11 on page 313, but you do not know his customer number. If you search the table using the CUSTOMER-NAME field as a secondary key, you can retrieve the records for all customers named James Morgan and then select the correct one.

In Figure 7-12, student name and advisor names are identified as secondary keys, but other fields also could be used. For example, to find all students who have a particular advisor, you could use the ADVISOR-NUMBER field in the STUDENT file as a secondary key.

Referential Integrity

Validity checks can help avoid data input errors. One type of validity check, called **referential integrity**, is a set of rules that avoids data inconsistency and quality problems. In a relational database, referential integrity means that a foreign key value cannot be entered in one table unless it matches an existing primary key in another table. For example, referential integrity would prevent you from entering a customer order

 ON THE WEB

For more information about Referential Integrity, visit **scsite.com/sad6e/more**, locate Chapter 7 and then click the Referential Integrity link.

in an order table unless that customer already exists in the customer table. Without referential integrity, you might have an order called an **orphan**, because it had no related customer.

In the example shown in Figure 7-12 on page 315, referential integrity will not allow a user to enter an advisor number (foreign key value) in the STUDENT table unless a valid advisor number (primary key value) already exists in the ADVISOR table.

Referential integrity also can prevent the deletion of a record if the record has a primary key that matches foreign keys in another table. For example, suppose that an advisor resigns to accept a position at another school. You cannot delete the advisor from the ADVISOR table while records in the STUDENT file still refer to that advisor number. Otherwise, the STUDENT records would be orphans. To avoid the problem, students must be reassigned to other advisors by changing the value in the ADVISOR-NUMBER field; then the advisor record can be deleted.

When creating a relational database, you can build referential integrity into the design. Figure 7-13 shows a Microsoft Access screen that identifies a common field and allows the user to enforce referential integrity rules.

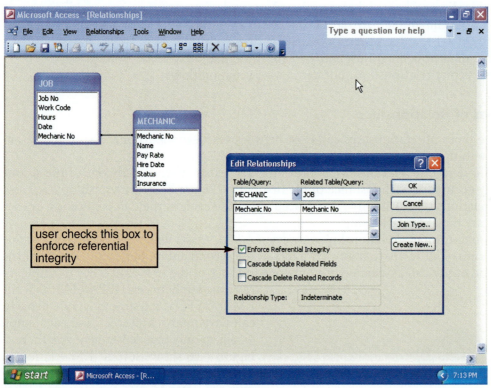

FIGURE 7-13 Microsoft Access allows a user to specify that referential integrity rules will be enforced in a relational database design.

ENTITY-RELATIONSHIP DIAGRAMS

Recall that an entity is a person, place, thing, or event for which data is collected and maintained. For example, entities might be customers, sales regions, products, or orders. An information system must recognize the relationships among entities. For example, a *customer* entity can have several instances of an *order* entity, and an *employee* entity can have one instance, or none, of a *spouse* entity.

ON THE WEB

For more information about Entity-Relationship Diagrams, visit **scsite.com/sad6e/ more**, locate Chapter 7 and then click the Entity-Relationship Diagrams link.

An **entity-relationship diagram** (ERD) is a model that shows the logical relationships and interaction among system entities. An ERD provides an overall view of the system and a blueprint for creating the physical data structures.

Drawing an ERD

The first step is to list the entities that you identified during the systems analysis phase and to consider the nature of the relationships that link them. At this stage, you can use a simplified method to show the relationships between entities.

Although there are different ways to draw ERDs, a popular method is to represent entities as rectangles and relationships as diamond shapes. The entity rectangles are labeled with singular nouns, and the relationship diamonds are labeled with verbs, usually in a top-to-bottom and left-to-right fashion. For example, in Figure 7-14, a doctor entity *treats* a patient entity. Unlike data flow diagrams, entity-relationship diagrams depict relationships, not data or information flows.

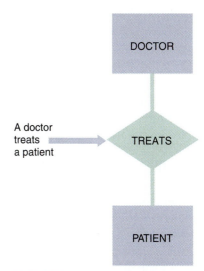

FIGURE 7-14 In an entity-relationship diagram, entities are labeled with singular nouns and relationships are labeled with verbs. The relationship is interpreted as a simple English sentence.

Types of Relationships

Three types of relationships can exist between entities: one-to-one, one-to-many, and many-to-many.

A **one-to-one relationship**, abbreviated **1:1**, exists when exactly one of the second entity occurs for each instance of the first entity. Figure 7-15 shows examples of several 1:1 relationships. A number 1 is placed alongside each of the two connecting lines to indicate the 1:1 relationship.

A **one-to-many relationship**, abbreviated **1:M**, exists when one occurrence of the first entity can relate to many instances of the second entity, but each instance of the second entity can associate with only one instance of the first entity. For example, the relationship between DEPARTMENT and EMPLOYEE is one-to-many: one department can have many employees, but each employee works in only one department at a time. Figure 7-16 shows several 1:M relationships. The line connecting the *many* entity is labeled with the letter M, and the number 1 labels the other connecting line. How many is *many*? The first 1:M relationship shown in Figure 7-16 shows the entities INDIVIDUAL and AUTOMOBILE. One individual might own five automobiles, or one, or none. Thus, *many* can mean any number, including zero.

A **many-to-many relationship**, abbreviated **M:N**, exists when one instance of the first entity can relate to many instances of the second entity, and one instance of the second entity can relate to many instances of the first entity. The relationship between STUDENT and CLASS, for example, is

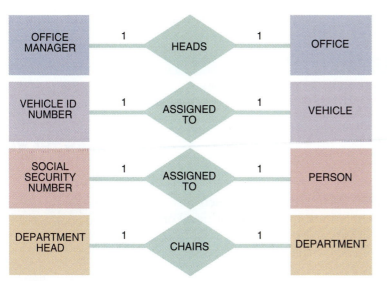

FIGURE 7-15 Examples of one-to-one (1:1) relationships.

many-to-many — one student can take many classes, and one class can have many students enrolled. Figure 7-17 shows several M:N entity-relationships. One of the connecting lines is labeled with the letter M, and the letter N labels the other connection.

Notice that an M:N relationship is different from 1:1 or 1:M relationships because the event or transaction that links the two entities is actually a third entity, called an **associative entity** that has its own characteristics. In the first example in Figure 7-17, the ENROLLS IN symbol represents a REGISTRATION entity that records each instance of a specific student enrolling in a specific course. Similarly, the RESERVES SEAT ON symbol represents a RESERVATION entity that records each instance of a specific passenger reserving a seat on a specific flight. In the third example, the LISTS symbol represents an ORDER-LINE entity that records each instance of a specific product listed in a specific customer order.

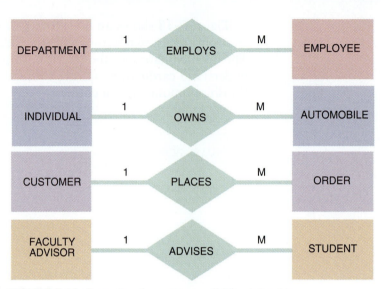

FIGURE 7-16 Examples of one-to-many (1:M) relationships.

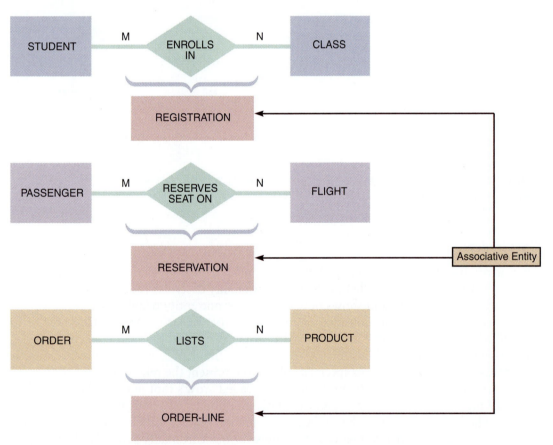

FIGURE 7-17 Examples of many-to-many (M:N) relationships. Notice that the event or transaction that links the two entities is an associative entity with its own set of attributes and characteristics.

Figure 7-18 shows an ERD for a sales system. Notice the various entities and relationships shown in the figure, including the associative entity named ORDER-LINE. The detailed nature of these relationships is called cardinality. As an analyst, you must understand cardinality in order to create a data design that accurately reflects all relationships among system entities.

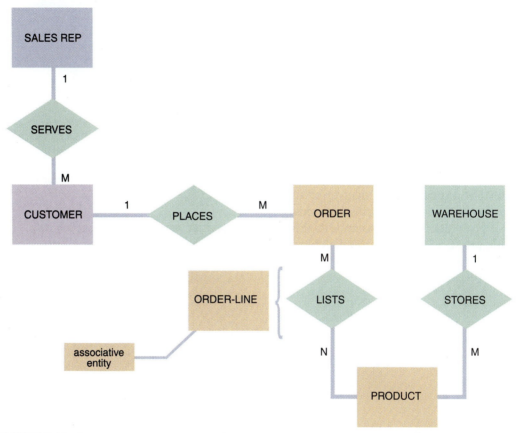

FIGURE 7-18 An entity-relationship diagram for SALES REP, CUSTOMER, ORDER, PRODUCT, and WAREHOUSE. Notice that the ORDER and PRODUCT entities are joined by an associative entity named ORDER-LINE.

Cardinality

ON THE WEB

For more information about Cardinality, visit scsite.com/sad6e/more, locate Chapter 7 and then click the Cardinality link.

After an analyst draws an initial ERD, he or she must define the relationships in more detail by using a technique called cardinality. **Cardinality** describes the numeric relationship between two entities and shows how instances of one entity relate to instances of another entity. For example, consider the relationship between two entities: CUSTOMER and ORDER. One customer can have one order, many orders, or none, but each order must have one and only one customer. An analyst can model this interaction by adding **cardinality notation,** which uses special symbols to represent the relationship.

A common method of cardinality notation is called **crow's foot notation** because of the shapes, which include circles, bars, and symbols, that indicate various possibilities. A single bar indicates one, a double bar indicates one and only one, a circle indicates zero, and a crow's foot indicates many. Figure 7-19 shows various cardinality symbols, their meanings, and the UML representations of the relationships. As you learned in Chapter 3, the **Unified Modeling Language (UML)** is a widely used method of visualizing and documenting software systems design.

In Figure 7-20, four examples of cardinality notation are shown. In the first example, one and only one CUSTOMER can place anywhere from zero to many of the ORDER entity. In the second example, one and only one ORDER can include one ITEM ORDERED or many. In the third example, one and only one EMPLOYEE can have one SPOUSE or none. In the fourth example, one EMPLOYEE, or many employees, or none, can be assigned to one PROJECT, or many projects, or none.

Most CASE products support the drawing of ERDs from entities in the data repository. Figure 7-21 shows part of a library system ERD drawn using the Visible Analyst CASE tool. Notice that crow's foot notation is used to show the nature of the relationships, which are described in both directions.

Now that you understand database elements and their relationships, you can start designing tables. The first step is the normalization of your table designs, which is described next.

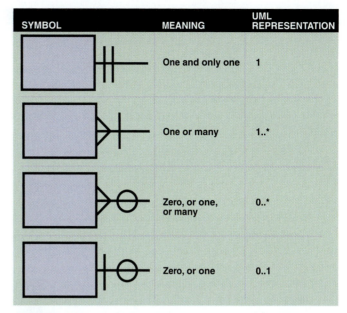

SYMBOL	MEANING	UML REPRESENTATION
	One and only one	1
	One or many	1..*
	Zero, or one, or many	0..*
	Zero, or one	0..1

FIGURE 7-19   Crow's foot notation is a common method of indicating cardinality. The four examples show how you can use various symbols to describe the relationships between entities.

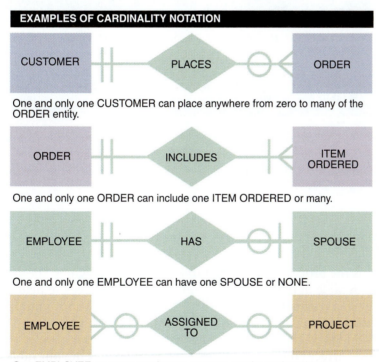

EXAMPLES OF CARDINALITY NOTATION

CUSTOMER — PLACES — ORDER

One and only one CUSTOMER can place anywhere from zero to many of the ORDER entity.

ORDER — INCLUDES — ITEM ORDERED

One and only one ORDER can include one ITEM ORDERED or many.

EMPLOYEE — HAS — SPOUSE

One and only one EMPLOYEE can have one SPOUSE or NONE.

EMPLOYEE — ASSIGNED TO — PROJECT

One EMPLOYEE, or many employees, or none, can be assigned to one PROJECT, or many projects, or none.

FIGURE 7-20   In the first example of cardinality notation, one and only one CUSTOMER can place anywhere from zero to many of the ORDER entity. In the second example, one and only one ORDER can include one ITEM ORDERED or many. In the third example, one and only one EMPLOYEE can have one SPOUSE or none. In the fourth example, one EMPLOYEE, or many employees, or none, can be assigned to one PROJECT, or many projects, or none.

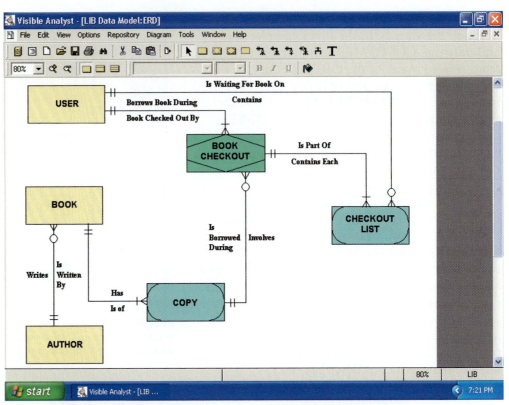

FIGURE 7-21 An ERD for a library system drawn with Visible Analyst. Notice that crow's foot notation has been used and relationships are described in both directions.

CASE IN POINT 7.1: TOPTEXT PUBLISHING

TopText Publishing is a textbook publishing company. Many authors write more than one book for TopText, and some books are written by more than one author. You have been asked to draw an ERD that shows this relationship, and to include cardinality notation.

NORMALIZATION

ON THE WEB

For more information about Normalization, visit **scsite.com/ sad6e/more**, locate Chapter 7 and then click the Normalization link.

Normalization is the process of creating table designs by assigning specific fields or attributes to each table in the database. A **table design** specifies the fields and identifies the primary key in a particular table or file. Working with a set of initial table designs, you use normalization to develop an overall database design that is simple, flexible, and free of data redundancy. Normalization involves applying a set of rules that can help you identify and correct inherent problems and complexities in your table designs.

The normalization process typically involves four stages: unnormalized design, first normal form, second normal form, and third normal form. The three normal forms constitute a progression in which third normal form represents the best design. Most business-related databases must be designed in third normal form.

Standard Notation Format

Designing tables is easier if you use a **standard notation format** to show a table's structure, fields, and primary key. The standard notation format in the following examples starts with the name of the table, followed by a parenthetical expression that contains the field names separated by commas. The primary key field(s) is underlined, like this:

NAME (<u>FIELD 1</u>, FIELD 2, FIELD 3)

Repeating Groups and Unnormalized Designs

During data design, you must be able to recognize a repeating group of fields. A **repeating group** is a set of one or more fields that can occur any number of times in a single record, with each occurrence having different values.

Repeating groups often occur in manual documents prepared by users. For example, consider a school registration form with the student's information at the top of the form, followed by a list of courses the student is taking. If you were to design a table based on this registration form, the courses would represent a repeating group of values for each student.

An example of a repeating group is shown in Figure 7-22. The first two records in the ORDER table contain multiple products, which represent a repeating group of fields. Notice that in addition to the order number and date, the records with multiple products contain repetitions of the product number, description, and number ordered. You can think of a repeating group as a set of child (subsidiary) records contained within the parent (main) record.

RECORD#	ORDER-NUM	ORDER-DATE	PRODUCT-NUM	PRODUCT-DESC	NUM-ORDERED
1	40311	03112005	304	All-purpose gadget	7
			633	Assembly	1
			684	Super gizmo	4
2	40312	03112005	128	Steel widget	12
			304	All-purpose gadget	3
3	40313	03122005	304	All-purpose gadget	144

FIGURE 7-22 In the ORDER table design, records 1 and 2 have repeating groups because they contain several products. ORDER-NUM is the primary key for the ORDER table, and PRODUCT-NUM serves as a primary key for the repeating group. Because it contains a repeating group, the ORDER table design is unnormalized.

A table design that contains a repeating group is called **unnormalized**. The standard notation method for representing an unnormalized design is to enclose the repeating group of fields within a second set of parentheses. An example of an unnormalized table would look like this:

NAME (<u>FIELD 1</u>, FIELD 2, FIELD 3, (REPEATING FIELD 1, REPEATING FIELD 2))

Now review the unnormalized ORDER table design shown in Figure 7-22. Following the notation guidelines, you can describe the design as follows:

ORDER (<u>ORDER-NUM</u>, ORDER-DATE, (<u>PRODUCT-NUM</u>, PRODUCT-DESC, NUM-ORDERED))

The notation indicates that the ORDER table design contains five fields, which are listed within the outer parentheses. The ORDER-NUM field is underlined to show that it is the primary key. The PRODUCT-NUM, PRODUCT-DESC, and NUM-ORDERED fields are enclosed within an inner set of parentheses to indicate that they are fields within a repeating group. Notice that PRODUCT-NUM also is underlined because it acts as the primary key of the repeating group. If a customer orders three different products in one order, then the fields PRODUCT-NUM, PRODUCT-DESC, and NUM-ORDERED repeat three times, as shown in Figure 7-22 on the previous page.

First Normal Form

A table is in **first normal form** (1NF) if it does not contain a repeating group. To convert an unnormalized design to 1NF, you must expand the table's primary key to include the primary key of the repeating group.

For example, in the ORDER table shown in Figure 7-22, the repeating group consists of three fields: PRODUCT-NUM, PRODUCT-DESC, and NUM-ORDERED. Of the three fields, only PRODUCT-NUM can be a primary key because it uniquely identifies each instance of the repeating group. The product description cannot be a primary key because it might or might not be unique. For example, a company might sell a large number of parts with the same descriptive name, such as *washer*, relying on a coded part number to identify uniquely each washer size.

When you expand the primary key of ORDER table to include PRODUCT-NUM, you eliminate the repeating group and the ORDER table is now in 1NF, as shown:

> ORDER (<u>ORDER-NUM</u>, ORDER-DATE, <u>PRODUCT-NUM</u>, PRODUCT-DESC, NUM-ORDERED)

Figure 7-23 shows the ORDER table in 1NF. Notice that when you eliminate the repeating group, additional records emerge — one for each combination of a specific order and a specific product. The result is more records, but a greatly simplified design. In the new version, the repeating group for order number 40311 has become three separate records, and the repeating group for order number 40312 has become two separate records. Therefore, when a table is in 1NF, each record stores data about a single instance of a specific order and a specific product.

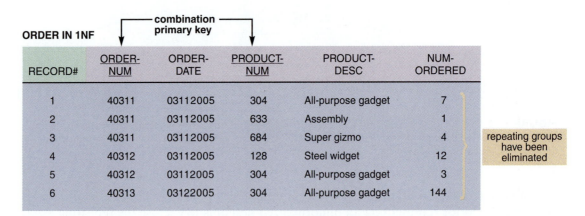

FIGURE 7-23 The ORDER table as it appears in 1NF. The repeating groups have been eliminated. Notice that the repeating group for order 40311 has become three separate records, and the repeating group for order 40312 has become two separate records. The 1NF primary key is a combination of ORDER-NUM and PRODUCT-NUM, which uniquely identifies each record.

Also notice that the 1NF design shown in Figure 7-23 has a combination primary key. The primary key of the 1NF design cannot be the ORDER-NUM field alone, because the order number does not uniquely identify each product in a multiple-item order. Similarly, PRODUCT-NUM cannot be the primary key, because it appears more than once if several orders include the same product. Because each record must reflect a specific product in a

specific order, you need *both* fields, ORDER-NUM and PRODUCT-NUM, to identify a single record uniquely. Therefore, the primary key is the *combination* of two fields: ORDER-NUM and PRODUCT-NUM.

Second Normal Form

To understand second normal form (2NF), you must understand the concept of functional dependence. For example, field X is **functionally dependent** on field Y if the value of field X depends on the value of field Y. For example, in Figure 7-23, the ORDER-DATE value is functionally dependent on the ORDER-NUM, because for a particular order number, there can be only one value for that order's date. In contrast, a product description is not dependent on the order number. For a particular order number, there might be several product descriptions — one for each item ordered.

A table design is in **second normal form** (**2NF**) if it is in 1NF *and* if all fields that are not part of the primary key are functionally dependent on the *entire* primary key. If any field in a 1NF table depends on only one of the fields in a combination primary key, then the table is not in 2NF.

Notice that if a 1NF design has a primary key that consists of only one field, the problem of partial dependence does not arise — because the entire primary key is a single field. Therefore, a 1NF table with a single-field primary key is automatically in 2NF.

Now reexamine the 1NF design for the ORDER table shown in Figure 7-23:

ORDER (<u>ORDER-NUM</u>, ORDER-DATE, <u>PRODUCT-NUM</u>, PRODUCT-DESC, NUM-ORDERED)

Recall that the primary key is the combination of the order number and the product number. The NUM-ORDERED field depends on the *entire* primary key, because NUM-ORDERED refers to a specific product number *and* a specific order number. In contrast, the ORDER-DATE field depends on the order number, which is only a part of the primary key. Similarly, the PRODUCT-DESC field depends on the product number, which also is only a part of the primary key. Because some fields are not dependent on the *entire* primary key, the design is not in 2NF.

A standard process exists for converting a table from 1NF to 2NF. The objective is to break the original table into two or more new tables and reassign the fields so that each nonkey field will depend on the entire primary key in its table. To accomplish this, you follow these steps:

1. First, create and name a separate table for each field in the existing primary key. For example, in Figure 7-23, the ORDER table's primary key has two fields, ORDER-NUM and PRODUCT-NUM, so you must create two tables. The ellipsis (…) indicates that fields will be assigned later. The result is:

    ORDER (<u>ORDER-NUM</u>,…)

    PRODUCT (<u>PRODUCT-NUM</u>,…)

2. Next, create a new table for each possible combination of the original primary key fields. In the Figure 7-23 example, you would create and name a new table with a combination primary key of ORDER-NUM and PRODUCT-NUM. This table describes individual lines in an order, so it is named ORDER-LINE, as shown:

    ORDER-LINE (<u>ORDER-NUM</u>, <u>PRODUCT-NUM</u>,…)

3. Finally, study the three tables and place each field with its appropriate primary key, which is the minimal key on which it functionally depends. When you finish placing all the fields, remove any table that did not have any additional fields

assigned to it. The remaining tables are the 2NF version of your original table. In the Figure 7-23 example, the three tables would be shown as:

ORDER (<u>ORDER-NUM</u>, ORDER-DATE)

PRODUCT (<u>PRODUCT-NUM</u>, PRODUCT-DESC)

ORDER-LINE (<u>ORDER-NUM</u>, <u>PRODUCT-NUM</u>, NUM-ORDERED)

Figure 7-24 shows the 2NF table designs. By following the steps, you have converted the original 1NF table into three 2NF tables.

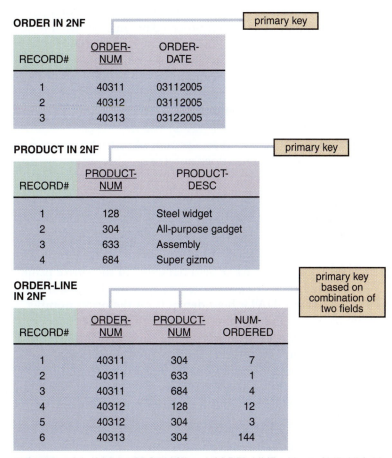

FIGURE 7-24 ORDER, PRODUCT, and ORDER-LINE tables in 2NF. All fields are functionally dependent on the primary key.

Why is it important to move from 1NF to 2NF? Four kinds of problems are found with 1NF designs that do not exist in 2NF:

- Consider the work necessary to change a particular product's description. Suppose 500 current orders exist for product number 304. Changing the product description involves modifying 500 records for product number 304. Updating all 500 records would be cumbersome and expensive.

- 1NF tables can contain inconsistent data. Because someone must enter the product description in each record, nothing prevents product number 304 from having different product descriptions in different records. In fact, if product number 304 appears in a large number of order records, some of the matching product descriptions might be inaccurate or improperly spelled. Even the presence or absence of a hyphen in the orders for *All-purpose gadget* would create consistency problems. If a data entry person must enter a term such as *IO1 Queue Controller* numerous times, it certainly is possible that some inconsistency will result.

- Adding a new product is a problem. Because the primary key must include an order number and a product number, you need values for both fields in order to add a record. What value do you use for the order number when you want to add a new product that has not been ordered by any customer? You could use a dummy order number, and then replace it with a real order number when the product is ordered to solve the problem, but that solution also creates difficulties.

- Deleting a product is a problem. If all the related records are deleted once an order is filled and paid for, what happens if you delete the only record that contains product number 633? The information about that product number and its description is lost.

Has the 2NF design eliminated all potential problems? To change a product description, now you can change just one PRODUCT record. Multiple, inconsistent values for the product description are impossible because the description appears in only one location. To add a new product, you simply create a new PRODUCT record, instead of creating a dummy order record. When you remove the last ORDER-LINE record for a particular product number, you do not lose that product number and its description because the PRODUCT record still exists. The four potential problems are eliminated, and the three 2NF designs are superior to both the original unnormalized table and the 1NF design.

Third Normal Form

A popular rule of thumb is that a design is in 3NF if every nonkey field depends on *the key, the whole key, and nothing but the key.* As you will see, a 3NF design avoids redundancy and data integrity problems that still can exist in 2NF designs.

Consider the following CUSTOMER table design, as shown in Figure 7-25:

CUSTOMER (<u>CUSTOMER-NUM</u>, CUSTOMER-NAME, ADDRESS, SALES-REP-NUM, SALES-REP-NAME)

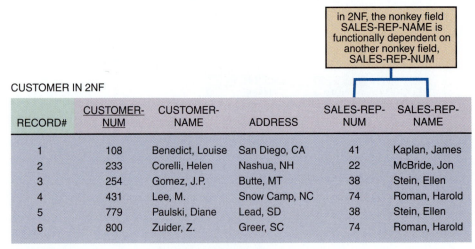

CUSTOMER IN 2NF

RECORD#	CUSTOMER- NUM	CUSTOMER- NAME	ADDRESS	SALES-REP- NUM	SALES-REP- NAME
1	108	Benedict, Louise	San Diego, CA	41	Kaplan, James
2	233	Corelli, Helen	Nashua, NH	22	McBride, Jon
3	254	Gomez, J.P.	Butte, MT	38	Stein, Ellen
4	431	Lee, M.	Snow Camp, NC	74	Roman, Harold
5	779	Paulski, Diane	Lead, SD	38	Stein, Ellen
6	800	Zuider, Z.	Greer, SC	74	Roman, Harold

in 2NF, the nonkey field SALES-REP-NAME is functionally dependent on another nonkey field, SALES-REP-NUM

FIGURE 7-25 2NF design for the CUSTOMER table.

The table is in 1NF because it has no repeating groups. The design also is in 2NF because the primary key is a single field. But the table still has four potential problems similar to the four 1NF problems described earlier. Changing the name of a sales rep still requires changing every record in which that sales rep name appears. Nothing about the design prohibits a particular sales rep from having different names in different records. In addition, because the sales rep name is included in the CUSTOMER

table, you must create a dummy CUSTOMER record to add a new sales rep who has not yet been assigned any customers. Finally, if you delete all the records for customers of sales rep number 22, you will lose that sales rep's number and name.

Those potential problems are caused because the design is not in 3NF. A table design is in **third normal form** (**3NF**) if it is in 2NF and if no nonkey field is dependent on another nonkey field. Remember that a nonkey field is a field that is not a candidate key for the primary key. The CUSTOMER example in Figure 7-25 on the previous page is not in 3NF because one nonkey field, SALES-REP-NAME, depends on another nonkey field, SALES-REP-NUM.

To convert the table to 3NF, you must remove all fields from the 2NF table that depend on another nonkey field and place them in a new table that uses the nonkey field as a primary key. In the CUSTOMER example, the SALES-REP-NAME field depends on another field, SALES-REP-NUM, which is not part of the primary key. Therefore, to reach 3NF, you must remove SALES-REP-NAME and place it into a new table that uses SALES-REP-NUM as the primary key. As shown in Figure 7-26, the third normal form produces two separate tables:

CUSTOMER (<u>CUSTOMER-NUM</u>, CUSTOMER-NAME, ADDRESS, SALES-REP-NUM)

SALES-REP (<u>SALES-REP-NUM</u>, SALES-REP-NAME)

CUSTOMER IN 3NF

RECORD#	CUSTOMER-NUM	CUSTOMER-NAME	ADDRESS	SALES-REP-NUM
1	108	Benedict, Louise	San Diego, CA	41
2	233	Corelli, Helen	Nashua, NH	22
3	254	Gomez, J.P.	Butte, MT	38
4	431	Lee, M.	Snow Camp, NC	74
5	779	Paulski, Diane	Lead, SD	38
6	800	Zuider, Z.	Greer, SC	74

in 3NF, no nonkey field is dependent on another nonkey field

SALES-REP IN 3NF

RECORD#	SALES-REP-NUM	SALES-REP-NAME
1	22	McBride, Jon
2	38	Stein, Ellen
3	41	Kaplan, James
4	74	Roman, Harold

FIGURE 7-26   When the CUSTOMER table is transformed from 2NF to 3NF, the result is two tables: CUSTOMER and SALES-REP.

A Normalization Example

To show the normalization process, consider the familiar situation in Figure 7-27, which depicts several entities in a school advising system: ADVISOR, COURSE, and STUDENT. The relationships among the three entities are shown in the ERD in Figure 7-28. The following sections discuss normalization rules for these three entities.

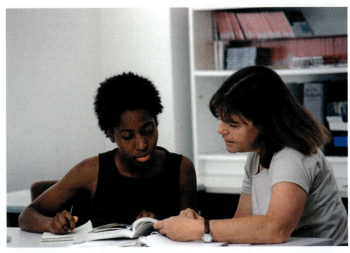

FIGURE 7-27 A faculty advisor, who represents an entity, can advise many students, each of whom can register for one or many courses.

Before you start the normalization process, you notice that the STUDENT table contains fields that relate to the ADVISOR and COURSE entities, so you decide to begin with the initial design for the STUDENT table, which is shown in Figure 7-29 on the next page. Notice that the table design includes the student number, student name, total credits taken, grade point average (GPA), advisor number, advisor name, and, for every course the student has taken, the course number, course description, number of credits, and grade received.

The STUDENT table in Figure 7-29 is unnormalized, because it has a repeating group. The STUDENT table design can be written as:

STUDENT (<u>STUDENT-NUMBER</u>, STUDENT-NAME, TOTAL-CREDITS, GPA, ADVISOR-NUMBER, ADVISOR-NAME, (<u>COURSE-NUMBER</u>, COURSE-DESC, NUM-CREDITS, GRADE))

To convert the STUDENT record to 1NF, you must expand the primary key to include the key of the repeating group, producing:

STUDENT (<u>STUDENT-NUMBER</u>, STUDENT-NAME, TOTAL-CREDITS, GPA, ADVISOR-NUMBER, ADVISOR-NAME, <u>COURSE-NUMBER</u>, COURSE-DESC, NUM-CREDITS, GRADE)

Figure 7-30 on the next page shows the 1NF version of the sample STUDENT data. Do any of the fields in the 1NF STUDENT record depend on only a portion of the primary key? The student name, total credits, GPA, advisor number, and advisor name all relate only to the student number and have no relationship to the course number. The course description depends on the course number, but not on the student number. Only the GRADE field depends on the entire primary key.

FIGURE 7-28 An initial entity-relationship diagram for ADVISOR, STUDENT, and COURSE.

STUDENT

STUDENT-NUMBER	STUDENT-NAME	TOTAL-CREDITS	GPA	ADVISOR-NUMBER	ADVISOR-NAME	COURSE-NUMBER	COURSE-DESC	NUM-CREDITS	GRADE
1035	Linda	47	3.647	49	Smith	CSC151	Computer Science I	4	B
						MKT212	Marketing Management	3	A
						ENG101	English Composition	3	B
						CHM112	General Chemistry I	4	A
						BUS105	Introduction to Business	2	A
3397	Sam	29	3.000	49	Smith	ENG101	English Composition	3	A
						MKT212	Marketing Management	3	C
						CSC151	Computer Science I	4	B
4070	Kelly	14	2.214	23	Jones	CSC151	Computer Science I	4	B
						CHM112	General Chemistry I	4	C
						ENG101	English Composition	3	C
						BUS105	Introduction to Business	2	C

repeating groups

FIGURE 7-29 The STUDENT table is unnormalized because it contains a repeating group that represents the courses each student has taken.

STUDENT

STUDENT-NUMBER	STUDENT-NAME	TOTAL-CREDITS	GPA	ADVISOR-NUMBER	ADVISOR-NAME	COURSE-NUMBER	COURSE-DESC	NUM-CREDITS	GRADE
1035	Linda	47	3.647	49	Smith	CSC151	Computer Science I	4	B
1035	Linda	47	3.647	49	Smith	MKT212	Marketing Management	3	A
1035	Linda	47	3.647	49	Smith	ENG101	English Composition	3	B
1035	Linda	47	3.647	49	Smith	CHM112	General Chemistry I	4	A
1035	Linda	47	3.647	49	Smith	BUS105	Introduction to Business	2	A
3397	Sam	29	3.000	49	Smith	ENG101	English Composition	3	A
3397	Sam	29	3.000	49	Smith	MKT212	Marketing Management	3	C
3397	Sam	29	3.000	49	Smith	CSC151	Computer Science I	4	B
4070	Kelly	14	2.214	23	Jones	CSC151	Computer Science I	4	B
4070	Kelly	14	2.214	23	Jones	CHM112	General Chemistry I	4	C
4070	Kelly	14	2.214	23	Jones	ENG101	English Composition	3	C
4070	Kelly	14	2.214	23	Jones	BUS105	Introduction to Business	2	C

FIGURE 7-30 The STUDENT table in 1NF. Notice that the primary key has been expanded to include STUDENT-NUMBER and COURSE-NUMBER. Also, the repeating group has been eliminated.

Following the 1NF – 2NF conversion process described earlier, you would create a new table for each field and combination of fields in the primary key, and place the other fields with their appropriate key. The result is:

STUDENT (<u>STUDENT-NUMBER</u>, STUDENT-NAME, TOTAL-CREDITS, GPA, ADVISOR-NUMBER, ADVISOR-NAME)

COURSE (<u>COURSE-NUMBER</u>, COURSE-DESC, NUM-CREDITS)

GRADE (<u>STUDENT-NUMBER</u>, <u>COURSE-NUMBER</u>, GRADE)

You now have converted the original 1NF STUDENT table to three tables, all in 2NF. In each table, every nonkey field depends on the entire primary key.

Figure 7-31 on the next page shows the 2NF STUDENT, COURSE, and GRADE designs and sample data. Are all three tables in 3NF? The COURSE and GRADE are in 3NF. STUDENT is not in 3NF, however, because the ADVISOR-NAME field depends on the ADVISOR-NUMBER field, which is not part of the STUDENT primary key. To convert STUDENT to 3NF, you remove the ADVISOR-NAME field from the STUDENT table and place it into a table with ADVISOR-NUMBER as the primary key.

Figure 7-32 on the next page shows the 3NF versions of the sample data for STUDENT, ADVISOR, COURSE, and GRADE. The final 3NF design is:

STUDENT (<u>STUDENT-NUMBER</u>, STUDENT NAME, TOTAL-CREDITS, GPA, ADVISOR-NUMBER)

ADVISOR (<u>ADVISOR-NUMBER</u>, ADVISOR-NAME)

COURSE (<u>COURSE-NUMBER</u>, COURSE-DESC, NUM-CREDITS)

GRADE (<u>STUDENT-NUMBER</u>, <u>COURSE-NUMBER</u>, GRADE)

Figure 7-33 on page 333 shows the complete ERD after normalization. Now there are four entities: STUDENT, ADVISOR, COURSE, and GRADE, which is an associative entity. If you go back to Figure 7-28 (on page 329), which was drawn before you identified GRADE as an entity, you can see that the M:N relationship between STUDENT and COURSE has been converted into two 1:M relationships: one relationship between STUDENT and GRADE and the other relationship between COURSE and GRADE.

To create 3NF designs, you must understand the nature of first, second, and third normal forms. In your work as a systems analyst, you will encounter designs that are much more complex than the examples in this chapter. You also should know that normal forms beyond 3NF exist, but they rarely are used in business-oriented systems.

CASE IN POINT 7.2: CYBERTOYS

You handle administrative support for CyberToys, a small chain that sells computer hardware and software and specializes in personal service. The company has four stores located at malls and is planning more. Each store has a manager, a technician, and between one and four sales reps.

Joan Jamison, the owner, wants a personnel records database, and she asked you to review a table that she designed. She suggested fields for store number, location, store telephone, manager name, and manager home telephone. She also wants fields for technician name and technician home telephone and fields for up to four sales rep names and sales rep home telephones.

Draw Joan's suggested design and analyze it using the normalization concepts you learned in the chapter. What do you think of Joan's design and why? What would you propose?

STUDENT

STUDENT-NUMBER	STUDENT-NAME	TOTAL-CREDITS	GPA	ADVISOR-NUMBER	ADVISOR-NAME
1035	Linda	47	3.647	49	Smith
3397	Sam	29	3.000	49	Smith
4070	Kelly	14	2.214	23	Jones

primary key

COURSE

COURSE-NUMBER	COURSE-DESC	NUM-CREDITS
BUS105	Introduction to Business	2
CHM112	General Chemistry I	4
CSC151	Computer Science I	4
ENG101	English Composition	3
MKT212	Marketing Management	3

primary key

GRADE

primary key based on combination of two fields

STUDENT-NUMBER	COURSE-NUMBER	GRADE
1035	CSC151	B
1035	MKT212	A
1035	ENG101	B
1035	CHM112	A
1035	BUS105	A
3397	ENG101	A
3397	MKT212	C
3397	CSC151	B
4070	CSC151	B
4070	CHM112	C
4070	ENG101	C
4070	BUS105	C

FIGURE 7-31 STUDENT, COURSE, and GRADE tables in 2NF. Notice that all fields are functionally dependent on the entire primary key of their respective tables.

STUDENT

STUDENT-NUMBER	STUDENT-NAME	TOTAL-CREDITS	GPA	ADVISOR-NUMBER
1035	Linda	47	3.647	49
3397	Sam	29	3.000	49
4070	Kelly	14	2.214	23

in 3NF, no nonkey field is dependent on another nonkey field

ADVISOR

ADVISOR-NUMBER	ADVISOR-NAME
23	Jones
49	Smith

COURSE

COURSE-NUMBER	COURSE-DESC	NUM-CREDITS
BUS105	Introduction to Business	2
CHM112	General Chemistry I	4
CSC151	Computer Science I	4
ENG101	English Composition	3
MKT212	Marketing Management	3

GRADE

STUDENT-NUMBER	COURSE-NUMBER	GRADE
1035	CSC151	B
1035	MKT212	A
1035	ENG101	B
1035	CHM112	A
1035	BUS105	A
3397	ENG101	A
3397	MKT212	C
3397	CSC151	B
4070	CSC151	B
4070	CHM112	C
4070	ENG101	C
4070	BUS105	C

FIGURE 7-32 STUDENT, ADVISOR, COURSE, and GRADE tables in 3NF. When the STUDENT table is transformed from 2NF to 3NF, the result is two tables: STUDENT and ADVISOR.

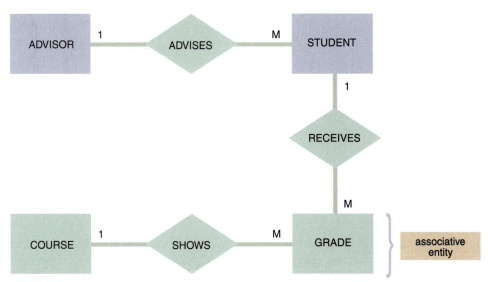

FIGURE 7-33 The entity-relationship diagram for STUDENT, ADVISOR, and COURSE after normalization. The GRADE entity was identified during the normalization process. GRADE is an associative entity that links the STUDENT and COURSE tables.

USING CODES DURING DATA DESIGN

A **code** is a set of letters or numbers that represents a data item. Codes can be used to simplify output, input, and data formats. During the data design process, you review existing codes and develop new ones that will be used to store and access data efficiently.

Overview of Codes

Because codes often are used to represent data, you encounter them constantly in your everyday life. Student numbers, for example, are unique codes to identify students in a school registration system. Three students with the name John Turner might be enrolled at your school, but only one is student number 268960.

Your ZIP code is another common example. A ZIP code contains multiple items of information compressed into nine digits. The first digit identifies one of ten geographical areas of the United States. The combination of the next three digits identifies a major city or major distribution point. The fifth digit identifies an individual post office, an area within a city, or a specific delivery unit. The last four digits identify a post office box or a specific street address.

For example, consider the ZIP code 27906-2624 shown in Figure 7-34. The first digit, 2, indicates a broad geographical area in the eastern United States. The digits, 790, indicate Elizabeth City, North Carolina. The fifth digit, 6, identifies the post office that services the College of the Albemarle. The last four digits, 2624, identify the post office box for the college.

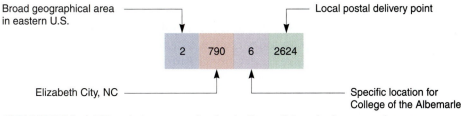

FIGURE 7-34 A ZIP code is an example of a significant digit code that uses subgroups to provide information.

As you can imagine, codes serve many useful purposes. Because codes often are shorter than the data they represent, they save storage space and costs, reduce data transmission time, and decrease data entry time. For example, ZIP codes are used to classify and sort mail efficiently. Codes also can be used to reveal or conceal information. The last two digits of a seven-digit part number, for example, can represent the supplier number. The coded wholesale price on a retail price tag is known to salespeople but generally not to customers.

Finally, codes can reduce data input errors in situations when the coded data is easier to remember and enter than the original source data, when only certain valid codes are allowed, and when something within the code itself can provide immediate verification that the entry is correct.

Types of Codes

Companies use many different coding methods. Because information system users must work with coded data, the codes should be easy to learn and apply. If you plan to create new codes or change existing ones, you first should obtain comments and feedback from users. The following section describes eight common coding methods.

1. **Sequence codes** are numbers or letters assigned in a specific order. Sequence codes contain no additional information other than an indication of order of entry into the system. For example, a human resource system issues consecutive employee numbers to identify employees. Because the codes are assigned in the order in which employees are hired, you can use the code to see that employee number 584 was hired after employee number 433. The code, however, does not indicate the starting date of either person's employment.

2. **Block sequence codes** use blocks of numbers for different classifications. College course numbers usually are assigned using a block sequence code. 100-level courses, such as Chemistry 110 and Mathematics 125, are freshman-level courses, whereas course numbers in the 200s indicate sophomore-level courses. Within a particular block, the sequence of numbers can have some additional meaning, such as when English 151 is the prerequisite for English 152.

3. **Alphabetic codes** use alphabet letters to distinguish one item from another based on a category, an abbreviation, or an easy-to-remember value, called a mnemonic code. Many classification codes fit more than one of the following definitions:

   a. **Category codes** identify a group of related items. For example, a local department store uses a two-character category code to identify the department in which a product is sold: GN for gardening supplies, HW for hardware, and EL for electronics.

   b. **Abbreviation codes** are alphabetic abbreviations. For example, standard state codes include NY for New York, ME for Maine, and MN for Minnesota. Some abbreviation codes are called **mnemonic codes** because they use a specific combination of letters that are easy to remember. Many three-character airport codes such as those pictured in Figure 7-35 are mnemonic codes: LAX represents Los Angeles International Airport, DFW is Dallas/Ft. Worth Airport, and JFK is John F. Kennedy International Airport. Some airport codes are not mnemonic, such as ORD, which designates Chicago O'Hare International Airport, or HPN, which identifies the White Plains, New York Airport.

4. **Significant digit codes** distinguish items by using a series of subgroups of digits. ZIP codes, for example, are significant digit codes. Other such codes include inventory location codes that consist of a two-digit warehouse code, followed by a one-digit floor number code, a two-digit section code, a one-digit aisle number, and a two-digit bin number code. Figure 7-36 illustrates the inventory location code 11205327. What looks like a large eight-digit number is actually five separate numbers, each of which has significance.

5. **Derivation codes** combine data from different item attributes, or characteristics, to build the code. Most magazine subscription codes are derivation codes. One popular magazine's subscriber code consists of the subscriber's five-digit ZIP code, followed by the first, third, and fourth letters of the subscriber's last name, the last two digits of the subscriber's house number, and the first, third, and fourth letters of the subscriber's street name. The magazine's subscriber code for one particular subscriber is shown in Figure 7-37.

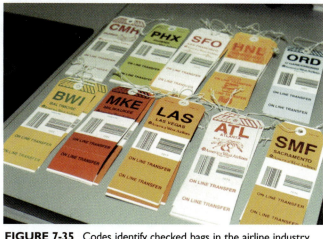

FIGURE 7-35 Codes identify checked bags in the airline industry. Codes are machine-readable using the bar code that is printed when the bag is checked. Airline employees recognize the unique three-character code that identifies the destination. A bar code reader scans a code that also represents the employee number who checked in the bag, the passenger's name, and other pertinent information.

6. **Cipher codes** use a keyword to encode a number. A retail store, for example, might use a 10-letter word, such as CAMPGROUND, to code wholesale prices, where the letter C represents 1, A represents 2, and so on. Thus, the code, GRAND, indicates that the store paid $562.90 for the item.

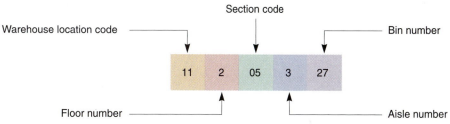

FIGURE 7-36 Sample of a code that uses significant digits to pinpoint the location of an inventory item.

7. **Action codes** indicate what action is to be taken with an associated item. For example, a student records program might prompt a user to enter or click an action code such as *D* (to display a record), *A* (to add a record), and *X* (to exit the program).

Developing a Code

Devising a code with too many features makes it difficult to remember, decipher, and verify. Keep the following suggestions in mind when developing a code:

1. Keep codes concise. Do not create codes that are longer than necessary. For example, if you need a code to identify each of 250 customers, you will not need a six-digit code.

2. Allow for expansion. A coding scheme must allow for reasonable growth in the number of assigned codes. If the company currently has eight warehouses, you should not use a one-digit code for the warehouse number. If three more warehouses are

FIGURE 7-37 A magazine subscriber code is derived from various parts of the name and address.

added, the code must be increased to two digits or changed to a character code in order to identify each location. The rule also applies to using a single letter as a character code; you might need more than 26 codes in the future.

3. Keep codes stable. Changes in codes can cause consistency problems and require data updates. During the changeover period, you will have to change all the stored occurrences of a particular code and all documents containing the old code, as users switch to the new code. Usually, both the old and new codes are used for an interim period, and special procedures are required to handle the two codes. For example, when area codes change, you can use either area code for a certain time period.

4. Make codes unique. Codes used for identification purposes must be unique to have meaning. If the code HW can indicate hardware or houseware, the code is not very useful.

5. Use **sortable** codes. If products with three-digit codes in the 100s or the 300s are of one type, while products with codes in the 200s are a different type, a simple sort will not group all the products of one type together. In addition, be careful that single-digit character codes will sort properly with double-digit codes — in some cases you must add a leading zero (01, 02, 03, and so on) to ensure that codes sort correctly.

6. Avoid confusing codes. Do not code some part numbers with two letters, a hyphen, and one digit, and others with one letter, a hyphen, and two digits. Avoid allowing both letters and numbers to occupy the same positions within a code because some of those are easily confused. It is easy to confuse the number zero (0) and the uppercase letter O, or the number one (1) with the lowercase letter L (l) or uppercase letter I. For example, the five-character code 5Z081 easily can be misread as 5ZO8I, or 52081, or even totally incorrectly as S2OBI.

7. Make codes meaningful. Codes must be easy to remember, useful for users, convenient to use, and easy to encode and interpret. Using SW as a code for the southwest sales region, for example, has far more meaning than the code 14. Using ENG as the code for the English department is easier to interpret and remember than either XVA or 132.

8. Use a code for a single purpose. Do not use a single code to classify two or more unrelated attributes. For example, if you use a single code to identify the combination of an employee's department *and* the employee's insurance plan type, users will have difficulty identifying all the subscribers of a particular plan, or all the workers in a particular department, or both. A separate code for each separate characteristic makes much more sense.

9. Keep codes consistent. For example, if the payroll system already is using two-digit codes for departments, do not create a new, different coding scheme for the personnel system. If the two systems already are using different coding schemes, you should try to convince the users to adopt a consistent coding scheme.

CASE IN POINT 7.3: DotCom Tools

DotCom Tools operates a small business that specializes in hard-to-find woodworking tools. The firm advertises in various woodworking magazines, and currently accepts mail and telephone orders. DotCom is planning a Web site that will be the firm's primary sales channel. The site will feature an online catalog, powerful search capabilities, and links to woodworking information and resources.

DotCom has asked you, an IT consultant, whether a set of codes would be advantageous and if so, what codes you would suggest. Provide at least two choices for a customer code and at least two choices for a product code. Be sure to describe your choices and provide some specific examples. Also include an explanation of why you selected these particular codes and what advantages they might offer.

STEPS IN DATABASE DESIGN

After normalizing your table designs and considering the use of codes, you are ready to create the database. The following steps can be used to create database and file designs. To highlight the steps, consider another familiar situation shown in Figure 7-38, which involves an information system for a video rental store.

1. *Create an initial ERD.* Start by reviewing DFDs and class diagrams to identify system entities. In addition, consider any data stores shown on DFDs to determine whether they might represent entities. Next, create a draft of the ERD. Carefully analyze each relationship to determine if it is 1:1, 1:M, or M:N. Figure 7-39 shows the initial ERD for the entities MEMBER and VIDEO in the video rental system.

2. *Assign all data elements to entities.* Verify that every data element in the data dictionary is associated logically with an entity. For the video rental system, the initial table designs with all data elements are listed under the ERD in Figure 7-39.

3. *Create 3NF designs for all tables, taking care to identify all primary, secondary, and foreign keys.* Generate the final ERD that will include new entities identified during normalization. Figure 7-40 on the next page shows the final ERD and the normalized designs. Notice that a new associative entity, RENTAL, was identified during normalization and the M:N relationship became two 1:M relationships.

FIGURE 7-38 A video rental involves several entities, including members and videos. In the store's information system, each entity is represented by a table that contains various fields.

```
MEMBER (MEMBER-NUMBER, NAME, ADDRESS, CITY, STATE, ZIP, HOME-TELEPHONE,
    WORK-TELEPHONE, CREDIT-CARD-CODE, CREDIT-CARD-NUMBER, (VIDEO-ID, TITLE,
    DATE-RENTED, DATE-RETURNED))
VIDEO (VIDEO-ID, TITLE)
```

FIGURE 7-39 The initial entity-relationship diagram and table designs for the video rental system. Notice that the MEMBER table contains a repeating group.

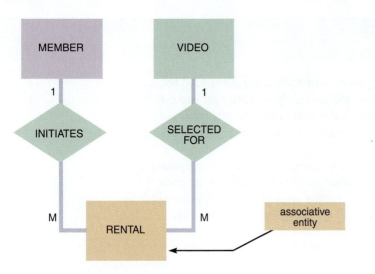

MEMBER (<u>MEMBER-NUMBER</u>, NAME, ADDRESS, CITY, STATE, ZIP, HOME-TELEPHONE,
WORK-TELEPHONE, CREDIT-CARD-CODE, CREDIT-CARD-NUMBER)
VIDEO (<u>VIDEO-ID</u>, TITLE)
RENTAL (<u>MEMBER-NUMBER</u>, <u>VIDEO-ID</u>, DATE-RENTED, DATE-RETURNED)

FIGURE 7-40 The final entity-relationship diagram and normalized table designs for the video rental system. RENTAL has been identified as an associative entity that links the MEMBER and VIDEO tables.

4. *Verify all data dictionary entries.* Make sure that the data dictionary entries for all data stores, records, and data elements are documented completely and correctly. Also be sure that all codes that were developed or identified during the data design process are documented in the data dictionary.

After creating your final ERD and normalized table designs, you can transform them into a database. Your next step will be to consider the design and characteristics of various database models.

DATABASE MODELS

The two most popular database models are relational and object-oriented. Other models exist, but they are less common and generally are found on older, mainframe-based systems.

Relational databases can run on many platforms, including personal computers, and are well suited to client/server computing because they are so powerful and flexible. Object-oriented databases are modular, cost-effective, and a logical extension of the object-oriented analysis process.

Relational Databases

Earlier in this chapter, you learned that a relational database uses common fields, which are attributes that appear in more than one table, to establish relationships between the tables and form an overall data structure. This type of design, called a **relational model**, was introduced during the 1970s and became popular because it was flexible and powerful. Three decades later, the relational design still is the predominant model.

Figure 7-41 represents a relational database design for a company that performs on-site computer service. Figure 7-42 shows the tables, primary keys, and common fields in the relational database.

The design in Figure 7-42 uses many of the concepts described earlier in this chapter and demonstrates the power of a relational model. Separate tables exist for CUSTOMER, TECHNICIAN, SERVICE-CALL, SERVICE-PARTS-DETAIL, SERVICE-LABOR-DETAIL, PARTS, and LABOR-CODE tables. Notice that all the tables use a single field as a primary key, except the SERVICE-LABOR-DETAIL and

FIGURE 7-41 A relational database design for a computer service company uses common fields to link the tables and form an overall data structure. Notice the one-to-many notation symbols, and the primary keys, which are shown in bold.

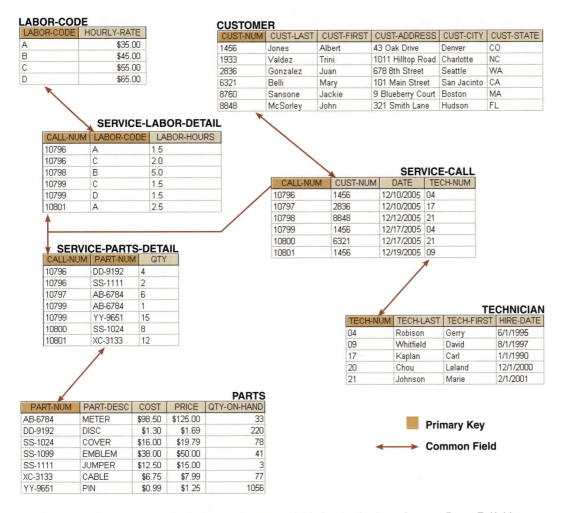

FIGURE 7-42 The tables, primary keys, and common fields for the database shown in Figure 7-41. Notice that the relational design avoids redundancy and that all tables are in 3NF (all nonkey fields are functionally dependent on the primary key, the whole key, and nothing but the key).

SERVICE-PARTS-DETAIL tables, in which the primary key requires a combination of two fields to identify each record uniquely.

Because all the tables are linked, a user can request data that meets specific conditions. To visualize how a relational DBMS handles complex queries, refer to Figure 7-42 and consider the following three examples. Suppose a user wants to see:

1. All customers who received service after 12/15/2005.

2. All service calls on which technician Marie Johnson put in more than four hours of labor.

3. The number and description of all parts sold to customers who live in Washington.

In the first example, the DBMS looks in the SERVICE-CALL table and finds three records with a date later than 12/15/2005. Then, using CUSTOMER-NUM, which is a foreign key in the SERVICE-CALL table, the DBMS seeks matching primary key values in the CUSTOMER table to identify customers Albert Jones and Mary Belli.

In the second example, the DBMS locates Marie Johnson in the TECHNICIAN table and extracts her technician number, which is a primary key. Using her TECH-NUM value of 21, the DBMS identifies Marie's two service calls by seeking matching values of

21 in the TECH-NUM field in the SERVICE-CALL table. Next, the DBMS uses the CALL-NUM values of 10798 and 10800 to check for matching records with more than four hours in the SERVICE-LABOR-DETAIL table. In the example, only service call 10798 meets all the requirements.

In the third example, the DBMS first locates all records with the value *WA* in the CUST-STATE field in the CUSTOMER table. The process identifies customer 2836, Juan Gonzalez. Using the value 2836, which is a primary key value in the CUSTOMER table, the DBMS seeks matching values in the CUST-NUM field in the SERVICE-CALL table. After locating service call 10797, the DBMS seeks matching values in the PART-NUM field of the SERVICE-PARTS-DETAIL table. Then using the value AB-6784, the DBMS seeks the matching primary key value in the PARTS table and obtains the description from the PART-DESC field. The results indicate that six meters with part number AB-6784 were sold to Washington customers. Because it uses a relational model, the DBMS in Figure 7-42 on the previous page is very powerful and flexible.

New entities and attributes can be added at any time without restructuring the entire database. If the company wants to add new parts, new service codes, new customers, or new technicians, it can do so without affecting existing data or relationships. Updating information also is simple in a relational design. For example, suppose customer Trini Valdez changes her address from 1011 Hilltop Road to 23 Down Lane. Even though she is listed on 18 separate service calls, only one change is needed in the CUSTOMER table. Because a common field links the CUSTOMER and SERVICE-CALL tables, it is not necessary to make a change in 18 individual records.

TOOLKIT TIME

The Object-Oriented Tools in Part 5 of the Systems Analyst's Toolkit can help you model a system by graphically representing objects within the system and how they interact. To learn more about these tools, turn to Part 5 of the six-part Toolkit that follows Chapter 10.

Object-Oriented Databases

Ten years ago, virtually all information systems were designed and implemented as relational databases or file processing systems. As object-oriented analysis became popular during the late 1990s, some analysts began to describe systems in terms of objects. Part 5 of the Systems Analyst's Toolkit describes object-oriented analysis and design concepts that will add to your overall understanding of data design.

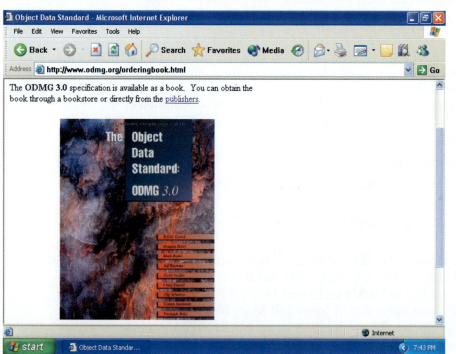

Today, many systems developers are using **object-oriented database** (**OODB**) design as a natural extension of the object-oriented analysis process. Some IT professionals believe that OODBs will have a major impact and might eventually replace the relational approach. Most object-oriented developers support the **Object Data Standard**, which is a design standard set forth by the **Object Database Management Group** (**ODMG**), as shown in Figure 7-43.

Each object in an OODB has a unique **object identifier**, which is similar to a primary key in a relational database. The identifier allows the object to interact with other objects and form

FIGURE 7-43 Many object-oriented developers support OODB design standards promulgated by the Object Data Management Group (ODMG).

relationships, as shown in Figure 7-44. Programmers use object-oriented languages, such as C++, to describe and implement object-to-object relationships that resemble the relationships found in a traditional ERD.

DATA STORAGE AND ACCESS

Data storage and access involve strategic business tools, such as data warehousing and data mining software, as well as logical and physical storage issues, selection of data storage formats, and special considerations regarding storage of date fields.

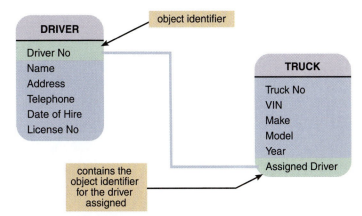

FIGURE 7-44 Objects have object identifiers that enable them to communicate and interact.

Strategic Tools for Data Storage and Access

Companies use data warehousing and data mining as strategic tools to help manage the huge quantities of data they need for business operations and decisions. A large number of software vendors compete for business in this fast-growing IT sector.

DATA WAREHOUSING Large firms maintain many databases, which might or might not be linked together into an overall structure. To provide rapid access to this information, companies use software packages that organize and store data in special configurations called data warehouses. A **data warehouse** is an integrated collection of data that can include seemingly unrelated information, no matter where it is stored in the company. Because it can link various information systems and databases, a data warehouse provides an enterprise-wide view to support management analysis and decision making.

A data warehouse allows users to specify certain **dimensions**, or characteristics. By selecting values for each characteristic, a user can obtain multidimensional information from the stored data. For example, in a typical company, most data is generated by transaction-based systems, such as order processing systems, inventory systems, and payroll systems. If a user wants to identify the customer on sales order 34071, he or she can retrieve the data easily from the order processing system by entering an order number.

On the other hand, suppose that a user wants to see May 2005 sales results for Sally Brown, the sales rep assigned to Jo-Mar Industries. The data is stored in two different systems: the sales information system and the human resources information system, as shown in Figure 7-45 on the next page. Without a data warehouse, it would be difficult for a user to extract data that spans several information systems and time frames. Rather than accessing separate systems, a data warehouse stores transaction data in a format that allows users to retrieve and analyze the data easily.

DATA MINING Data mining software looks for meaningful patterns and relationships among data. For example, data mining software could help a consumer products firm identify potential customers based on their prior purchases. Many firms, including the industry leaders in Figure 7-46 on the next page, offer data mining services and research.

The enormous growth in e-commerce has focused attention on data mining as a tool to analyze Web visitor behavior and traffic trends. In a recent article in *New Architect*, a Web-based magazine, Dan R. Greening noted that Web hosts typically possess a lot of information about visitors, but most of it is of little value. His article notes that smart marketers and business analysts are using data mining techniques, which he describes as "machine learning algorithms that find buried patterns in databases, and report or act on those findings."

FIGURE 7-45 A data warehouse stores data from several systems. By selecting data dimensions, a user can retrieve specific information without having to know how or where the data is stored.

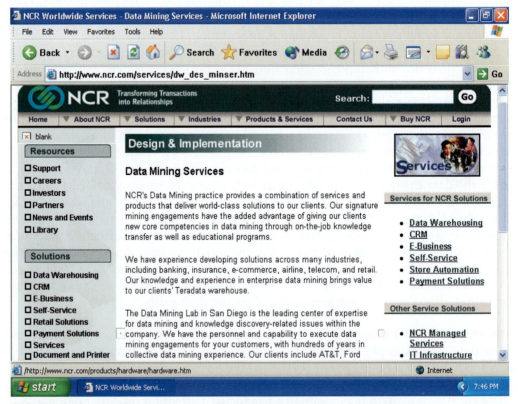

FIGURE 7-46 Many IT industry leaders offer data mining services and research.

The author stresses privacy concerns, and suggests that Web hosts use a clear privacy statement for visitors. He concludes by saying that "The great advantage of Web marketing is that you can measure visitor interactions more effectively than in brick-and-mortar stores or direct mail. Data mining works best when you have clear, measurable goals." Some of the goals he suggests are:

- Increase average pages viewed per session
- Increase number of referred customers
- Reduce **clicks to close,** which means average page views to accomplish a purchase or obtain desired information
- Increase checkouts per visit
- Increase average profit per checkout

Because it can detect patterns and trends in large amounts of data, data mining is a valuable tool for managers who must make management decisions involving complex issues.

Logical and Physical Storage

It is important to understand the difference between logical storage and physical storage. **Logical storage** refers to information as seen through a user's eyes, regardless of how or where that information actually is organized or stored. In contrast, **physical storage** is strictly hardware-related, because it involves the process of reading and writing binary data to physical media such as a hard drive or CD-ROM. For example, portions of a document might be stored in different physical locations on a hard drive, but the user sees the document as a single logical entity on his or her computer screen.

LOGICAL STORAGE The basic elements of logical data are alphabetic or numeric **characters,** such as the letter *A* or the number *9*. A group of characters forms a field, which describes a single characteristic, or attribute, of a person, place, thing, or event. A field also is called a **data element** or a **data item.**

Each instance of a field has a specific value. For example, CUSTOMER NUMBER is a field. One customer number might have a three-character value of *823* and another customer number might have a four-character value of *6467*. When designing fields, you should provide space for the largest values that can be anticipated, without allocating unnecessarily large storage capacities that will not be used.

A **logical record** is a set of field values that describes a single person, place, thing, or event. For example, a logical customer record contains specific field values for a single customer, including the customer's number, name, address, telephone number, credit limit, and so on. Application programs see a logical record as a group of related fields, regardless of how or where the data is stored physically.

The term, record, usually refers to a logical record. Whenever an application program issues a read or write command, the operating system supplies one logical record to the program or accepts one logical record from the program. The physical data might be stored on one or more servers, in the same building or thousands of miles away, but all the application program sees is the logical record — the physical storage location is irrelevant.

PHYSICAL STORAGE Physical storage involves a **physical record,** or **block,** which is the smallest data unit that can be handled by the operating system. The system reads or writes one physical record at a time. When the system *reads* a physical record, it loads the data from storage into a **buffer,** which is a segment of computer memory. The physical storage location can be local, remote, or Web-based. Similarly, when the system *writes* a physical record, all data in the memory buffer is saved physically to a storage location.

Consider Figure 7-47 and notice that a physical record can contain many logical records. The actual number of logical records in a physical record is determined by the **blocking factor**. For example, a blocking factor of two means that each physical record will consist of two logical records. Notice that the figure shows a data file with fields, logical records, and physical records that use a blocking factor of two. Some database programs, such as Microsoft Access, automatically write a physical record each time that a logical record is created or updated.

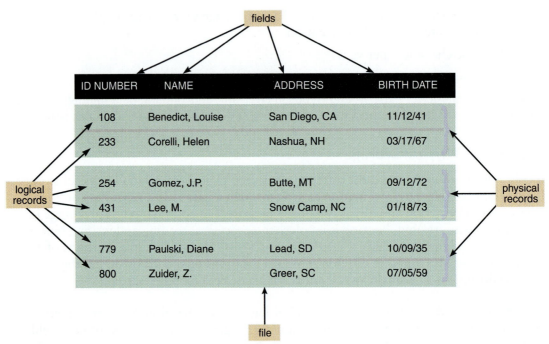

ID NUMBER	NAME	ADDRESS	BIRTH DATE
108	Benedict, Louise	San Diego, CA	11/12/41
233	Corelli, Helen	Nashua, NH	03/17/67
254	Gomez, J.P.	Butte, MT	09/12/72
431	Lee, M.	Snow Camp, NC	01/18/73
779	Paulski, Diane	Lead, SD	10/09/35
800	Zuider, Z.	Greer, SC	07/05/59

FIGURE 7-47 A data file consists of physical records, or blocks, that contain logical records. Each logical record is a set of related field values.

Data Storage Formats

On a computer, all data is stored in the form of **binary digits** that have only two possible values: zero (0) or one (1). A computer recognizes binary digits as electrical or optical signals that it can read, write, store, and understand. Each binary digit is called a **bit**, and each group of eight bits is called a **byte**. A single bit can have two possible values (0 or 1), two bits can have four possible values (00, 01, 10, or 11), three bits can have eight possible values (000, 001, 010, 011, 100, 101, 110, or 111), and so on. Following this binary pattern, an eight-bit byte can represent 256 possible values.

Computers use four primary data storage formats: EBCDIC, ASCII, Unicode, and binary. The following sections describe these formats and how they are used.

EBCDIC AND ASCII EBCDIC, which stands for **Extended Binary Coded Decimal Interchange Code**, is a data storage method used on most mainframe computers. **ASCII** is an acronym for **American Standard Code for Information Interchange**, which is used on most minicomputers and personal computers. EBCDIC and ASCII require one byte of storage for each character, numeric digit, or symbol. For example, the ASCII code for the number *1212* would require four bytes of storage, and the ASCII code for the name *Alexandra* would require nine bytes of storage.

UNICODE Unicode is a relatively recent coding method that represents characters as integers. Unlike EBCDIC and ASCII, which use eight bits for each character, Unicode uses 16 bits per character, which allows it to represent more than 65,000 unique characters. That is important as software design becomes global, and large firms require multilingual computer operations. For example, consider the challenge of offering multinational versions of a program that will be sold in Asia, Europe, and North America. For this reason, many IT experts believe that Unicode will become a dominant coding format in the future. The Unicode Consortium maintains standards and support for Unicode, as shown in Figure 7-48.

Traditionally, software firms developed an initial product in English. When they needed an international version, they would translate the program into one or more languages. This process was expensive and slow, and introduced a significant error factor. Unicode offers a different approach: to **internationalize** the software at the outset by creating separate files for source code versus language-specific information that easily can be translated or reformatted for multinational use. Today, most international software products, such as Microsoft Office, use and support Unicode standards.

BINARY A binary storage format offers more efficient storage of numeric data, compared to character-based format, which requires one byte per alphanumeric character. For example, an **integer format** requires only two bytes to store numbers from –32,768 to 32,767, and a **long integer format** can store numbers from –2,147,483,648 to 2,147,483,647 using only four bytes of storage. Other binary formats exist for efficient storage of exceedingly long numbers.

Selecting a Data Storage Format

In many cases, a user can select a specific data storage format. For example, when using Microsoft Office, you can store documents, spreadsheets, and databases in Unicode-compatible form by using the font called **Arial Unicode MS**. Depending on your system, however, you might have to install the font initially to make it accessible.

How should you select a data storage format? The best answer is it depends on the situation. While Unicode has many advantages, it also has some disadvantages. In fact, because of size and typographical design issues, Microsoft recommends that you use Unicode only when you *must* deal with multilingual data. When choosing numeric data formats, you should use a format that will be

FIGURE 7-48 Unicode is an international coding format that represents characters as integers, using 16 bits per character. The Unicode Consortium maintains standards and support for Unicode.

adequate for all possible current and future data. For example, if you are sure that the highest numeric value in a database field will be 10, you could use a **byte format** that can handle numbers from 0 – 255 in a single byte of storage. In this case, it would be unnecessary and wasteful to use a storage format such as long integer that requires, but would not use, four bytes of storage.

Date Fields

What is the best way to store date fields? Based on industry-wide experience with Y2K issues, most date formats now are based on the model established by the **International Organization for Standardization (ISO)**, which requires a format of four digits for the year, two for the month, and two for the day (YYYYMMDD). A date stored in that format can be sorted easily and used in comparisons. If a date in ISO form is larger than another date in the same form, then the first date is later. For example, 20050815 is later than 20050131, just as August 15, 2005, is later than January 31, 2005.

But, what if dates must be used in calculations? For example, if a manufacturing order placed on June 23 takes three weeks to complete, when will the order be ready? If a payment due on August 13 is not paid until April 27 of the following year, exactly how late is the payment and how much interest is owed? Absolute dates are easier to use in such calculations.

An **absolute date** is the total number of days from some specific base date. To calculate the number of days between two absolute dates, you subtract one date from the other. For example, if the base date is January 1, 1900, then August 27, 2006 has an absolute date value of 38956. Similarly, May 13, 2005 has an absolute date of 38485. If you subtract the earlier date value from the later one, the result is 471 days. You can use a spreadsheet to determine and display absolute dates easily, as shown in Figure 7-49.

FIGURE 7-49 Microsoft Excel utilizes absolute dates that can be used in calculations, starting with January 1, 1900, which has a numeric value of 1. In the example shown, August 27, 2006 is displayed in number format as 38956, and May 13, 2005 is displayed as 38485. The difference between the dates is 471 days.

The best method for storing date fields depends on how the specific date will be printed, displayed, or used in a calculation. To determine the best format, you must consider how the date will be used most often, and whether date calculations will be required.

CASE IN POINT 7.4: SoccerMom

SoccerMom Company sells a patented seat that spectators can take to youth soccer games. The seat folds so it is small enough to fit in the glove box of most vehicles. The company operates a factory in Kansas and also contracts its manufacturing projects to small firms in Canada and Mexico.

An unusual problem has occurred for this small multinational company: people are getting confused about dates in internal memos, purchase orders, and e-mail. Towson Hopkins handles all IT functions for SoccerMom. When he designed the company's database, he was not aware that the format for dates in Canada and Mexico was different from the format used in the United States. For example, in Canada and Mexico, the notation 2/1/06 indicates January 2, 2006, whereas in the United States the same notation indicates February 1, 2006. Although it seems like a small point, the date confusion has resulted in several order cancellations.

Towson has asked for your advice. You could suggest writing a simple program to convert the dates automatically or designing a switchboard command that would allow users to select a date format as data is entered. You realize, however, that SoccerMom might want to do business in other countries in the future. What would be the best course of action? Should SoccerMom adapt to the standard of each country, or should it maintain a single international format? What are the arguments for each option?

DATA CONTROL

Just as it is important to secure the physical part of the system, as shown in Figure 7-50, file and database control must include all measures necessary to ensure that data storage is correct, complete, and secure. File and database control also is related to input and output techniques discussed earlier.

A well-designed DBMS must provide built-in control and security features, including subschemas, passwords, encryption, audit trail files, and backup and recovery procedures to maintain data. Your main responsibility is to ensure that the DBMS features are used properly.

Earlier in this chapter, you learned that a subschema can be used to provide a limited view of the database to a specific user, or level of users. Limiting access to files and databases is the most common way of protecting stored data. Users must furnish a proper **user ID** and **password** to access a file or database. Different privileges, also called **permissions,** can be associated with different users, so some employees can be limited to read-only access, while other users might be allowed to update or delete data. For highly sensitive data, additional access codes can be

FIGURE 7-50 System security involves the physical controls shown here and a range of software controls, including access codes, data encryption, passwords, and audit trails.

established that restrict specific records or fields within records. Stored data also can be encrypted to prevent unauthorized access. **Encryption** is the process of converting readable data into unreadable characters to prevent unauthorized access to the data.

All system files and databases must be backed up regularly and a series of **backup** copies must be retained for a specified period of time. In the event of a file catastrophe, **recovery procedures** can be used to restore the file or database to its current state at the time of the last backup. **Audit log files**, which record details of all accesses and changes to the file or database, can be used to recover changes made since the last backup. You also can include **audit fields**, which are special fields within data records to provide additional control or security information. Typical audit fields include the date the record was created or modified, the name of the user who performed the action, and the number of times the record has been accessed.

CHAPTER SUMMARY

In this chapter, you continued your study of the systems design phase of the SDLC. You learned that files and tables contain data about people, places, things, or events that affect the information system. File processing systems, also called file-oriented systems, manage data stored in separate files, including master files, table files, transaction files, work files, security files, and history files.

A database consists of linked tables that form an overall data structure. A database management system (DBMS) is a collection of tools, features, and interfaces that enable users to add, update, manage, access, and analyze data in a database.

DBMS designs are more powerful and flexible than traditional file-oriented systems. A database environment offers scalability, support for organization-wide access, economy of scale, data sharing among user groups, balancing of conflicting user requirements, enforcement of standards, controlled redundancy, effective security, flexibility, better programmer productivity, and data independence. Large-scale databases are complex and require extensive security and backup/recovery features.

DBMS components include interfaces for users, database administrators, and related systems; a data manipulation language; a schema; and a physical data repository. Other data management techniques include data warehousing, which stores data in an easily accessible form for user access, and data mining, which looks for meaningful patterns and relationships among data.

In an information system, an entity is a person, place, thing, or event for which data is collected and maintained. A field, or attribute, is a single characteristic of an entity. A record, or tuple, is a set of related fields that describes one instance of an entity. Records are grouped into files (in a file-oriented system) and tables (in a database environment).

A primary key is the field or field combination that uniquely and minimally identifies a specific record; a candidate key is any field that could serve as a primary key. A foreign key is a field or field combination that must match the primary key of another file or table. A secondary key is a field or field combination used as the basis for sorting or retrieving records.

An entity-relationship diagram (ERD) is a graphic representation of all system entities and the relationships among them. The ERD is based on entities and data stores in DFDs prepared during the systems analysis phase. The three basic relationships represented in an ERD are one-to-one (1:1), one-to-many (1:M), and many-to-many (M:N). In a M:N relationship, the two entities are linked by an associative entity.

The relationship between two entities also is referred to as cardinality. A common form of cardinality notation is called crow's foot notation, which uses various symbols to describe the characteristics of the relationship.

Normalization is a process for avoiding problems in data design. A first normal form (1NF) record has no repeating groups. A record is in second normal form (2NF) if it is in 1NF and all nonkey fields depend on the entire primary key. A record is in third normal form (3NF) if it is in 2NF and if no field depends on a nonkey field.

Data design tasks include creating an initial ERD; assigning data elements to an entity; normalizing all table designs; and completing the data dictionary entries for files, records, and data elements. Files and database tables should be sized to estimate the amount of storage space they will require.

You learned that a code is a set of letters or numbers used to represent data in a system. By using codes, you can speed up data entry, reduce data storage space, and reduce transmission time. Codes also can be used to reveal or to conceal information. The main types of codes are sequence codes, block sequence codes, classification codes, alphabetic codes (including category codes, abbreviation codes, and mnemonic codes), significant digit codes, derivation codes, cipher codes, and action codes.

The most common database models are relational and object-oriented. The relational model is powerful and flexible, and provides the best support for client/server architecture. Object-oriented database (OODB) design is becoming more popular as a natural extension of the object-oriented analysis process. Each object in an OODB has a unique object identifier, which is similar to a primary key in a relational database and allows the object to interact with other objects and form relationships.

Logical storage is information seen through a user's eyes, regardless of how or where that information actually is organized or stored. Physical storage is hardware-related and involves reading and writing blocks of binary data to physical media. A logical record is a related set of field values that describes a single person, place, thing, or event. A physical record consists of one or more logical records, depending on the blocking factor. Data storage formats include EBCDIC, ASCII, Unicode, and binary. Dates can be stored in several formats, including ISO and absolute format.

File and database control measures include limiting access to the data, data encryption, backup/recovery procedures, audit-trail files, and internal audit fields.

Key Terms and Phrases

Learn It Online

Instructions: To complete the Learn It Online exercises, start your browser, click the Address bar, and then enter the Web address **scsite.com/sad6e/learn**. When the Systems Analysis and Design Learn It Online page is displayed, follow the instructions in the exercises below. Each exercise has instructions for saving your results, either for your own records or for submission to your instructor.

1 Chapter Reinforcement

TF, MC, and SA

Below SAD Chapter 7, click the Chapter Reinforcement link. Print the quiz by clicking Print on the File menu for each page. Answer each question.

2 Flash Cards

Below SAD Chapter 7, click the Flash Cards link and read the instructions. Type 20 (or a number specified by your instructor) in the Number of playing cards text box, type your name in the Enter your Name text box, and then click the Flip Card button. When the flash card is displayed, read the question and then click the ANSWER box arrow to select an answer. Flip through the Flash Cards. If your score is 15 (75%) correct or greater, click Print on the File menu to print your results. If your score is less than 15 (75%) correct, then redo this exercise by clicking the Replay button.

3 Practice Test

Below SAD Chapter 7, click the Practice Test link. Answer each question, enter your first and last name at the bottom of the page, and then click the Grade Test button. When the graded practice test is displayed on your screen, click Print on the File menu to print a hard copy. Continue to take practice tests until you score 80% or better.

4 Who Wants To Be a Computer Genius?

Below SAD Chapter 7, click the Computer Genius link. Read the instructions, enter your first and last name at the bottom of the page, and then click the Play button. When your score is displayed, click the PRINT RESULTS link to print a hard copy.

5 Wheel of Terms

Below SAD Chapter 7, click the Wheel of Terms link. Read the instructions, and then enter your first and last name and your school name. Click the PLAY button. When your score is displayed on the screen, right-click the score and then click Print on the shortcut menu to print a hard copy.

6 Crossword Puzzle Challenge

Below SAD Chapter 7, click the Crossword Puzzle Challenge link. Read the instructions, and then enter your first and last name. Click the SUBMIT button. Work the crossword puzzle. When you are finished, click the Submit button. When the crossword puzzle is redisplayed, click the Print Puzzle button to print a hard copy.

Case-Sim: SCR Associates

Background

SCR Associates is a consulting firm that offers IT solutions and training. SCR needs an information system to manage operations at its new training center. The new system will be called TIMS (Training Information Management System). As a newly hired systems analyst, you will report to Jesse Baker, systems group manager. You will work on various tasks and practice the skills you learned in this chapter.

Using the Case

The SCR Associates case study is a Web-based simulation that allows you to practice your skills in a real-world environment. The case study transports you to SCR's company intranet, where you can complete 10 work sessions, each aligning with a chapter. As you work on the case, you will receive e-mail and voice mail messages, obtain information from SCR's online libraries, and perform various tasks. The first time you enter the SCR Case, you should go to the Starting page at **scsite.com/sad6e/scr** for detailed instructions.

Preview: Session 7

Your supervisor, Jesse Baker, has asked you to begin working on data design tasks for the new information system, which will be implemented as a relational database. You will need to identify the entities, draw an ERD, design tables, and add sample data to each table.

To start a work session, you log on to the SCR intranet. When you enter your name and password, an opening screen displays links to the work sessions, and you select Session 7. At this point, you check your e-mail and voice mail messages carefully. Then you begin working on your task list, which includes the following items:

Tasks: Data Design

1. *List all the entities that interact with the TIMS system. Start by reviewing the data library, previous e-mail messages, DFDs, and other documentation.*

2. *Draw an ERD that shows cardinality relationships among the entities. Send the diagram to Jesse.*

3. *For each entity, Jesse wants to see table designs in 3NF. Use standard notation format to show the primary key and the other fields in each table.*

4. *Jesse wants to use sample data to populate fields for at least three records in each table. Better get started on this right away.*

FIGURE 7-51   Task list: Session 7.

Chapter Exercises

Review Questions

1. Explain the main differences between a file processing system and a database system.
2. What is a DBMS? Briefly describe the components of a DBMS.
3. Describe a primary key, candidate key, secondary key, foreign key, and common field.
4. What are entity-relationship diagrams and how are they used? What symbol is used to represent an entity in an ERD? What symbol is used for a relationship? What is cardinality, and what symbols do you use in the crow's foot notation method?
5. What are data warehousing and data mining? Are the terms related?
6. What is the criterion for a table design to be in first normal form? How do you convert an unnormalized design to 1NF?
7. What are the criteria for a table design to be in second normal form? How do you convert a 1NF design to 2NF?
8. What are the criteria for a table design to be in third normal form? How do you convert a 2NF design to 3NF?
9. Explain the difference between a logical record and a physical record.
10. How would a specific date, such as May 1, 2005, be represented as an absolute date?

Discussion Topics

1. Are there ethical issues to consider when planning a database? For example, should sensitive personal data (such as medical information) be stored in the same DBMS that manages employee salary and benefits data? Why or why not?
2. Suggest three typical business situations where referential integrity avoids data problems.
3. Consider an automobile dealership with three locations. Data fields exist for stock number, vehicle identification number, make, model, year, color, and invoice cost. Identify the possible candidate keys, the likely primary key, a probable foreign key, and potential secondary keys.
4. In the example shown in Figures 7-25 and 7-26 on pages 327 and 328, the 2NF customer table was converted to two 3NF tables. Verify that the four potential problems identified for 2NF tables were eliminated in the 3NF design.

Projects

1. Search the Internet to find information about data storage formats. Also do research on international date formats. Determine whether the date format used in the United States is the most common format.
2. Visit the IT department at your school or at a local business and determine whether the organization uses file processing systems, DBMSs, or both. Write a brief memo with your conclusions.
3. Use Microsoft Access or similar database software to create a DBMS for the imaginary company called TopText Publishing, which is described in Case In Point 7.1 on page 322. Add several sample records to each table and report to the class on your progress.
4. Visit the bookstore at your school or a bookstore in your area. Interview the manager or store employees to learn how the operation works and what entities are involved in bookstore operations. Remember that an entity is a person, place, thing, or event that affects the information system. Draw an ERD, including cardinality that describes the bookstore operations.

Apply Your Knowledge

The Apply Your Knowledge section contains four mini-cases. Each case describes a situation, explains your role in the case, and asks you to respond to questions. You can answer the questions by applying knowledge you learned in the chapter.

1 Pick and Shovel Construction Company

Situation:

Pick and Shovel Construction Company is a multi-state building contractor specializing in medium-priced town homes. C. T. Scott, the owner, is in your office for the third time today to see how the new relational database project is coming along. Unfortunately, someone mentioned to C. T. that the delay had something to do with achieving "normalization."

"Why is all this normalization stuff so important?" he asks. "The old system worked OK most of the time, and now you are telling me that we need all these special rules. Why is this necessary?"

1. How should you respond to C. T.? Write him a brief memo with your views.
2. Assume that the Pick and Shovel's main entities are its customers, employees, projects, and equipment. A customer can hire the company for more than one project, and employees sometimes work on more than one project at a time. Equipment, however, is assigned only to one project. Draw an ERD showing those entities.
3. Add cardinality notation to your ERD.
4. Create 3NF table designs.

2 Puppy Palace

Situation:

Puppy Palace works with TV and movie producers who need dogs that can perform special tricks, such as headstands, somersaults, ladder climbs, and various dog-and-pony tricks. Puppy Palace has about 16 dogs and a list of 50 tricks from which to choose. Each dog can perform one or more tricks, and many tricks can be performed by more than one dog. When a dog learns a new trick, the trainer assigns a skill level. Some customers insist on using dogs that score a 10, which is the highest skill level. As an IT consultant, you have been asked to suggest 3NF table designs. You are fairly certain that a M:N relationship exists between dogs and tricks.

1. Draw an ERD for the Puppy Palace information system.
2. Indicate cardinality.
3. Identify all fields you plan to include in the dogs and tricks tables. For example, in the dogs table, you might want breed, size, age, name, and so on. In the tricks table, you might want the trick name and description. You will need to assign a primary key in each table. *Hint:* Before you begin, review some database design samples in this chapter. You might spot a similar situation that requires an associative entity that you can use as a pattern. In addition, remember that numeric values work well in primary key fields.
4. Create 3NF table designs.

Mayville Public Library

Situation:

Mayville is a rural village with a population of 900. Until now, Mayville was served by a bookmobile from a larger town. The Mayville Village Council has authorized funds for a small public library, and you have volunteered to set up an information system for the library. Assume that the library will have multiple copies of certain books.

1. Draw an ERD for the Mayville library system.
2. Indicate cardinality.
3. Identify all fields you plan to include in the tables.
4. Create 3NF table designs.

Western Wear Outfitters

Situation:

Western Wear is a mail-order firm that offers an extensive selection of casual clothing for men and women. Western Wear plans to launch a new Web site, and the company wants to develop a new set of product codes. Currently, 650 different products exist, with the possibility of adding more in the future. Many products come in various sizes, styles, and colors. The marketing manager asked you to develop an individualized product code that can identify a specific item and its characteristics. Your initial reaction is that it can be done, but the code might be fairly complex. Back in your office, you give the matter some thought.

1. Design a code scheme that will meet the marketing manager's stated requirements.
2. Write a brief memo to the marketing manager suggesting at least one alternative to the code she proposed, and state your reasons.
3. Suggest a code scheme that will identify each Western Wear customer.
4. Suggest a code scheme that will identify each specific order.

Case Studies

Case studies allow you to practice specific skills learned in the chapter. Each chapter contains several case studies that continue throughout the textbook, and a chapter capstone case.

NEW CENTURY HEALTH CLINIC

New Century Health Clinic offers preventive medicine and traditional medical care. In your role as an IT consultant, you will help New Century develop a new information system.

Background

After completing the user interface, input, and output design for the new information system at New Century, you will consider data design issues. Begin by studying the DFDs and object-oriented diagrams you prepared previously and the rest of the documentation from the systems analysis phase. Perform the following tasks:

Assignments

1. Create an initial entity-relationship diagram for the New Century Health Clinic system.
2. Normalize your table designs.
3. If you identified any new entities during normalization, create a final entity-relationship diagram for the system.
4. Write a memo for your documentation file that contains your recommendation about whether a file processing or a database environment should be used. Attach copies of your ERD(s) and normalized designs.

PERSONAL TRAINER, INC.

Personal Trainer, Inc., owns and operates fitness centers in a dozen midwestern cities. The centers have done well, and the company is planning an international expansion by opening a new "supercenter" in the Toronto area. Personal Trainer's president, Cassia Umi, hired an IT consultant, Susan Park, to help develop an information system for the new facility. During the project, Susan will work closely with Gray Lewis, who will manage the new operation.

Background

After evaluating various development strategies, Susan prepared a system requirements document and submitted her recommendations to Cassia Umi, Personal Trainer's president. During her presentation, Susan discussed several development strategies, including in-house development and outsourcing. She did not feel that a commercial software package would meet Personal Trainer's needs.

Based on her research, Susan felt it would be premature to select a development strategy at this time. Instead, she recommended to Cassia that an in-house team should develop a design prototype, using a relational database as a model. Susan said that the prototype would have two main objectives: it would represent a user-approved model of the new system, and it would identify all systems entities and the relationships among them. Susan explained that it would be better to design the basic system first, and then address other issues, including Web enhancements and implementation options. She proposed a three-step plan: data design, user interface design, and application architecture. She explained that systems analysts refer to this as the systems design phase of a development project.

Cassia agreed with Susan's recommendation, and asked her to go forward with the plan.

Assignments

1. Review the Personal Trainer fact-finding summary in Chapter 3 and draw an ERD with cardinality notation. Assume that system entities include members, activities and services, and fitness instructors.

2. Design tables in 3NF. As you create the database, include various codes for at least three of the fields.

3. Use sample data to populate the fields for at least three records in each table.

4. Recommend a date format for the new system. Should Personal Trainer adopt a single international standard, or should the format be determined by the country in which the center is located? Write a message to Susan with your recommendation.

5. Convert the table designs to 3NF.

FASTFLIGHT AIRLINES

FastFlight Airlines is a small air carrier operating in three northeastern states. FastFlight is computerizing its passenger reservation system. The data items must include reservation number, flight number, flight date, origin, destination, departure time, arrival time, passenger name, and seat number. For example, flight number 303 leaves Augusta, Maine, daily at 9:23 a.m. and arrives in Nashua, New Hampshire, at 10:17 a.m. A typical reservation number might be AXQ1001, for passenger Lisa Lane, in seat 4A, on flight 303 on 11/12/2005.

Assignments

1. Create an ERD for the reservations system.

2. Create 3NF table designs for the system.

3. For each of the entities identified, design tables and identify the possible candidate keys, the primary key, a probable foreign key, and potential secondary keys.

4. Use sample data to populate the fields for three records.

CHAPTER CAPSTONE CASE: SoftWear, Limited

SoftWear, Limited (SWL), is a continuing case study that illustrates the knowledge and skills described in each chapter. In this case study, the student acts as a member of the SWL systems development team and performs various tasks.

Background

Work continued on the ESIP system. Rick said that the system would be a client/server design that could support SWL's current and future business requirements. He also said that Ann Hon wanted to use the ESIP system as a prototype for developing other SWL systems in the future. Ann said that the new design would have to be powerful, flexible, and scalable. With that in mind, the team decided that a DBMS strategy was the best solution for SWL's future information systems requirements.

ERDs and Normalization

Rick asked Tom and Becky to draw an entity-relationship diagram with normalized designs. Tom and Becky used the Visible Analyst, a CASE tool, to produce the diagram shown in Figure 7-52. Rick noticed that only two entities were shown: EMPLOYEE and DEDUCTION. Rick suggested that the ESIP-OPTION and HUMAN RESOURCES entities should be added. Tom and Becky agreed. The second version of their ERD is shown in Figure 7-53.

With the ERD completed, Tom turned to the design of the EMPLOYEE table. He suggested the following design:

EMPLOYEE (<u>SSN</u>, EMPLOYEE-NAME, HIRE-DATE)

"The table obviously is in 1NF, because it has no repeating groups," Tom said. "It's also in 2NF, because it has a single field as the primary key. And I'm sure it's in 3NF, because the

FIGURE 7-52 The initial ERD shows two entities: EMPLOYEE and DEDUCTION. Notice that crow's foot notation indicates that one and only one employee can authorize anywhere from zero to many deductions.

CHAPTER CAPSTONE CASE: SoftWear, Limited (continued) **SWL**

employee name and the hire date both depend on the Social Security number." Everyone agreed that this was the correct design. Tom and Becky turned their attention to designing the ESIP-OPTION table and later suggested the following design:

ESIP-OPTION (<u>OPTION-CODE</u>, OPTION-NAME, DESCRIPTION, DEDUCTION-CYCLE, APPLICATION-CYCLE, MIN-SERVICE, MIN-DEDUCTION, MAX-DEDUCTION)

The design appeared to meet the test for 3NF. Although seven fields existed in addition to the primary key, each field seemed to depend on the entire primary key. Finally, Becky proposed the following design for the DEDUCTION record:

DEDUCTION (<u>SSN</u>, <u>ESIP-OPTION</u>, <u>DATE</u>, EMPLOYEE-NAME, AMOUNT)

This time, Rick felt that the table was in 1NF, but not in 2NF because the EMPLOYEE-NAME field was dependent on only a part of the key rather than the entire key. Becky agreed with him and suggested that the EMPLOYEE-NAME field could be removed and accessed using the EMPLOYEE table. The SSN field could be used as a foreign key to match values in the EMPLOYEE table's primary key. To put the table into 2NF, she revised the DEDUCTION table design as follows:

DEDUCTION (<u>SSN</u>, <u>ESIP-OPTION</u>, <u>DATE</u>, AMOUNT)

With that change, everyone agreed that the table also was in 3NF because the AMOUNT field depended on the entire primary key. The next step was to work on a system design to interface with the payroll system and provide support for SWL's long-term information technology goals.

While Rick, Tom, and Becky were working on ERDs and normalization, Pacific Software delivered the payroll package that SWL ordered. Tom was assigned to work on installing and configuring the package and training users on the new payroll system.

Meanwhile, Rick felt that SWL should get more information about client/server design. With Ann Hon's approval, he contacted several IT consulting firms that advertised their client/server design expertise on the Internet. Rick and Becky met with three firms and recommended that SWL work with True Blue Systems, a consulting group with a local office in Raleigh, not far from SWL's headquarters. In addition to the design for the ESIP system, Rick suggested that the agenda should include a general discussion about a future SWL intranet with support for Web standards, and the possibility that employees could access their ESIP accounts from home via the Internet.

FIGURE 7-53 Second version of the ERD. Now, the DEDUCTION entity has relationships to two other entities: EMPLOYEE and ESIP-OPTION.

CHAPTER CAPSTONE CASE: SoftWear, Limited (continued)

SWL Team Tasks

1. Rick asked you to help him put together a brief progress update for Michael Jeremy and several other top managers. Specifically, Rick wants you to explain the concept of normalization without using a lot of technical jargon. Rick wants you to summarize the concept using plain English and simple examples.

2. At SWL, each employee is assigned to a specific department. Employees from several departments often are assigned to special project teams, however, when a new product is launched or for major marketing events. Carla wants to develop a project management system to track the projects, employees assigned, and accumulated project hours. She believes that employees and projects are in a M:N relationship. She showed you an initial design where all data is stored in a single table:

    PROJECT DATA (<u>PROJECT-NUMBER</u>, PROJECT-NAME, START-DATE, PROJECT-STATUS, (<u>EMPLOYEE-NUMBER</u>, EMPLOYEE-NAME, JOB-TITLE, DEPT-NUMBER, DEPT-NAME, PROJECT-HOURS))

    How would you describe Carla's design?

3. Carla wants you to create an ERD, including cardinality, for the project management system. She says that you probably will need to add an associative entity.

4. After you create the ERD in the previous step, design a table for each entity, in third normal form.

CHAPTER 8 System Architecture

CHAPTER 8 is the final chapter in the systems design phase of the SDLC. This chapter describes system architecture, which translates the logical design of an information system into a physical blueprint, or architecture. As you plan the system architecture, you will learn about servers, clients, processing methods, networks, and related issues.

INTRODUCTION

OBJECTIVES

When you finish this chapter, you will be able to:

- Provide a checklist of issues to consider when selecting a system architecture
- Describe servers, server-based processing, clients, and client-based processing
- Explain client/server architecture, including tiers, cost-benefit issues, and performance considerations
- Describe the impact of the Internet on system architecture
- Explain the difference between online and batch processing
- Define network topology, and provide examples of hierarchical, star, bus, and ring network models
- Explain network protocols and licensing issues
- Explain system management tools and techniques, including performance measurement, fault management, backup, and disaster recovery
- Describe the system design specification and explain the contents of each section

At this point in the SDLC, your objective is to determine an overall architecture to implement the information system. An information system requires hardware, software, data, procedures, and people to accomplish a specific set of functions. An effective system combines those elements into an **architecture**, or design, that is flexible, cost-effective, technically sound, and able to support the information needs of the business.

System architecture translates the logical design of an information system into a physical structure that includes hardware, software, network support, processing methods, and security. The end product of the systems design phase is the system design specification. If this document is approved, the next step is systems implementation.

CHAPTER INTRODUCTION CASE: Mountain View College Bookstore

Background: Wendy Lee, manager of college services at Mountain View College, wants a new information system that will improve efficiency and customer service at the three college bookstores.

In this part of the case, Florence Fullerton (systems analyst) and Harry Boston (student intern) are talking about system architecture issues.

Participants:	Florence and Harry
Location:	Mountain View College cafeteria, Wednesday afternoon, January 4, 2006
Project status:	The team has completed data design tasks and user interface, output, and input design work. The last step in the systems design phase is to consider a system architecture for the bookstore system.
Discussion topics:	System architecture checklist, client/server architecture, processing methods, network issues, and system management tools

Florence:	Hi, Harry. Did you enjoy the holiday break?
Harry:	*I sure did. Now I'm ready to get back to work.*
Florence:	Good. As the last step in the systems design phase of the SDLC, we need to study the physical structure, or architecture, of the bookstore system. Our checklist includes enterprise resource planning, total cost of ownership, scalability, Web integration, legacy systems, processing methods, and security issues that could affect the system design.
Harry:	*Where do we start?*
Florence:	Well, the bookstore interfaces with many publishers and vendors, so we'll consider supply chain management, which is part of enterprise resource planning, or ERP for short.
Harry:	*What happens after we finish the checklist?*
Florence:	Then we'll define a client/server architecture. As I see it, the bookstore client workstations will share the processing with a server in the IT department. Also, we may need to look at middleware software to connect the new system with existing legacy systems, such as the college accounting system.
Harry:	*Anything else?*
Florence:	Yes. We need to select a network plan, or topology, so we'll know how to plan the physical cabling and connections – or possibly use wireless technology. Finally, we'll tackle some of the system management issues, including performance, backup, and disaster recovery. When we're done, we'll submit a system design specification for approval.
Harry:	*Sounds good to me.*
Florence:	Good. Here's a task list to get us started.

FIGURE 8-1

SYSTEM ARCHITECTURE CHECKLIST

Just as an architect begins a project with a list of the owner's requirements, a systems analyst must approach system architecture with an overall checklist. Before making a decision, the analyst must consider seven specific issues that will affect the architecture choice:

→ Enterprise resource planning (ERP)

→ Initial and total cost of ownership (TCO)

→ Scalability

→ Web integration

→ Legacy system interface requirements

→ Processing options

→ Security issues

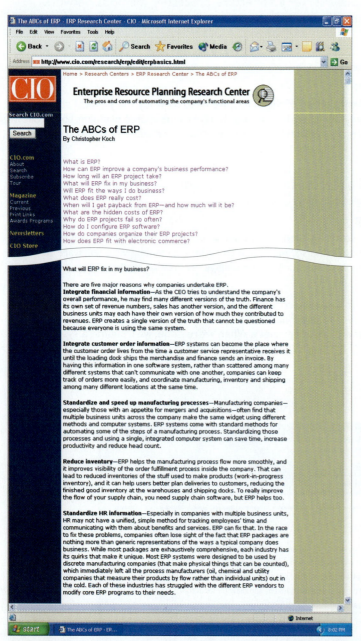

FIGURE 8-2 The *CIO* article suggests five major reasons why companies undertake ERP.

Enterprise Resource Planning

Many companies use **enterprise resource planning (ERP)** software, which was described in Chapter 1. The objective of ERP is to establish a company-wide strategy for using IT resources. ERP defines a specific architecture, including standards for data, processing, network, and user interface design. A main advantage of ERP is that it describes a specific hardware and software **environment**, also called a **platform**, that ensures connectivity and easy integration of future systems, including in-house software and commercial packages.

In an article in *CIO* magazine, Christopher Koch suggested five major reasons why companies undertake ERP, as shown in Figure 8-2: integrate financial information, integrate customer order information, standardize and speed up manufacturing processes, reduce inventory, and standardize human resources information.

Many companies are extending ERP systems to suppliers and customers in a process called **supply chain management**. In a totally integrated supply chain, a customer order could cause a production planning system to schedule a work order, which in turn triggers a call for certain parts from one or more suppliers. In a dynamic, highly competitive economy, ERP can help companies achieve faster response, better customer service, and lower operating costs. Industry leaders Microsoft and SAP are major competitors in the ERP and supply chain management market, as shown in Figure 8-3, and it is interesting to note Microsoft's prediction that RFID will have a major impact on supply chain management. In Chapter 1, you learned that RFID technology allows companies to track inventory items by using small devices that respond to radio frequency signals.

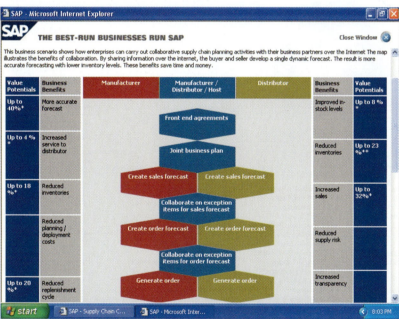

FIGURE 8-3   Microsoft and SAP are major competitors in the ERP and supply chain management market.

CASE IN POINT 8.1:   ABC SYSTEMS

You are a systems analyst at ABC Systems, a fast-growing IT consulting firm that provides a wide range of services to companies that want to establish e-commerce operations. During the last 18 months, ABC acquired two smaller firms and set up a new division that specializes in supply chain management. Aligning ABC's internal systems was quite a challenge, and top management was not especially happy with the integration cost or the timetable. To avoid future problems, you have decided to suggest an ERP strategy, and you plan to present your views at the staff meeting tomorrow. ABC's management team is very informal and prefers a loose, flexible style of management. How will you persuade them that ERP is the way to go?

Initial Cost and TCO

You learned earlier about the importance of considering economic feasibility and TCO during systems planning and analysis. Now, during the final design stage, you make decisions that will have a major impact on the initial costs and TCO for the new system. At this point, you should review all previous cost estimates and ask the following questions:

→ If in-house development was selected as the best alternative initially, is it still the best choice? Is the necessary technical expertise available, and does the original cost estimate appear realistic?

→ If a specific package was chosen initially, is it still the best choice? Are newer versions or competitive products available? Have any changes occurred in pricing or support?

→ Have any new types of outsourcing become available?

→ Have any economic, governmental, or regulatory events occurred that could affect the proposed project?

→ Have any significant technical developments occurred that could affect the proposed project?

→ Have any major assumptions changed since the company made the build versus buy decision?

→ Are there any merger or acquisition issues to consider, whereby the company might require compatibility with a specific environment?

→ Have any new trends occurred in the marketplace? Are new products or technologies on the verge of being introduced?

→ Have you updated the original TCO estimate? If so, are there any significant differences?

The answers to these questions might affect the initial cost and TCO for the proposed system. You should reanalyze system requirements and alternatives now, before proceeding to design the system architecture. To ensure that all costs are considered, you might want to review a comprehensive chart of accounts suggested by GartnerGroup, as shown in Figure 8-4. Notice that increased complexity has a direct impact on TCO.

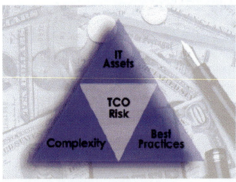

TCO Analyst

A White Paper on GartnerGroup's
Next Generation Total Cost of Ownership Methodology

TCO Analyst White Paper

Figure 5. GartnerGroup TCO Chart of Accounts

1. Capital	3. Technical Support	Technical Support (Cont'd)
Hardware	Tier 1 Help Desk	Technical Training
Software	Documentation	IS Network Learning
IS Allocated	Data Extract	Software Distribution
Network	Configuration Review	NOS Maintenance
Desktop	Application Consulting	Disk Management
Server	Vendor Liaison	Security/Virus
2. Administration	Standards Development	NOS Configuration
Asset Management	End-User Training	NOS Performance Management
Security	Product Introduction	4. End-User Operations
Legal	Product Review	Data Management
P&P Enforcement	Newsletter	Applications Development
Formal Audit	User Group	Formal Learning
Informal Audit	IS Desktop Learning	Casual Learning
Client Purchasing	Planning	"Futz" Factor
Installation	Utilization Review	Client-Peer Support
Capacity Planning	Install/Move/Upgrade	Network Costs
Adds, Moves and Changes	Service/PM (outsourced)	Network-Peer Support
Upgrades	Install Network	Misdiagnosis
Server Purchasing	Tier 2 Support	Peer Training
Security Administration	Tier 3 Support	Supplies
NOS Administration		

Figure 8. The Impact of Complexity on TCO

Source: GartnerGroup

FIGURE 8-4 GartnerGroup suggests a comprehensive checklist that includes all possible elements of TCO.

Scalability

Scalability, also called **extensibility,** refers to a system's ability to expand, change, or downsize easily to meet the changing needs of a business enterprise. Scalability is especially important in implementing systems that are volume-related, such as transaction processing systems. A scalable system is necessary to support a dynamic, growing business. For example, a scalable network could handle anywhere from a few dozen nodes to thousands of nodes; a scalable DBMS could support the acquisition of a new sales division. When investing large amounts of money in a project, management is especially concerned about scalability issues that could affect the system's life expectancy.

ON THE WEB

For more information about TCO, visit **scsite.com/sad6e/more**, locate Chapter 8, and then click the TCO link.

Web Integration

An information system includes **application programs,** also called **applications,** that handle the input, manage the processing logic, and provide the required output. The systems analyst must know if a new application will be part of an e-commerce strategy and the degree of integration with other Web-based components. As you learned earlier, a **Web-centric** architecture follows Internet design protocols and enables a company to integrate the new application into its e-commerce strategy. Even where e-commerce is not involved, a Web-centric application can run on the Internet or a company intranet or extranet. A Web-based application avoids many of the connectivity and compatibility problems that typically arise when different hardware environments are involved. In a Web-based environment, a firm's external business partners can use standard Web browsers to import and export data.

An example of Web integration is shown in Figure 8-5. Notice that IBM uses the term e-marketplaces to describe Internet-based solutions that allow customers and suppliers to automate procurement processes and achieve substantial benefits.

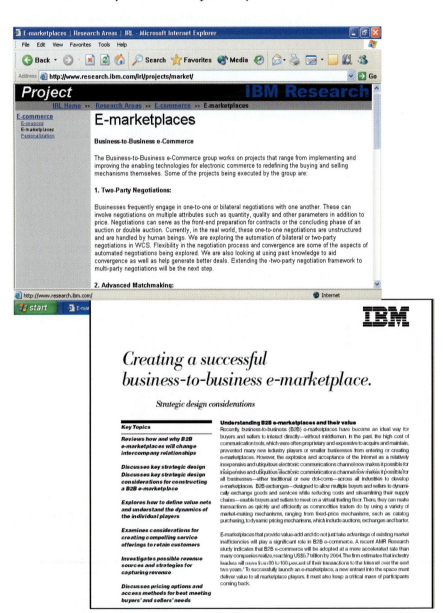

FIGURE 8-5 IBM uses the term e-marketplaces to describe Internet-based solutions that allow customers and suppliers to automate procurement processes and achieve substantial benefits.

Legacy System Interface Requirements

The new system might have to interface with one or more **legacy systems,** which are older systems that typically run on mainframe computers. When considering physical design, a systems analyst must determine how the new application will communicate with existing legacy systems. For example, a new marketing information system might need to report sales data to a mainframe-based accounting system and obtain product cost data from a legacy manufacturing system.

Interfacing a new system with a legacy system involves analysis of data formats and compatibility. In some cases, a company will need to convert legacy file data, which can be an expensive and time-consuming process. Finally, to select the best architecture, the analyst must know if the new application eventually will replace the legacy system.

Processing Options

In planning the architecture, designers also must consider how the system will process data — online or in batches. For example, a high-capacity transaction processing system, such as an order entry system, requires more network, processing, and data storage resources than a monthly billing system that handles data in batches. Also, if the system must operate online, 24 hours a day and seven days a week (typically known as **24/7**), provision must be made for backup and speedy recovery in the event of system failure.

The characteristics of online and batch processing methods are described later in this chapter, with examples of each type.

Security Issues

Security is a concern at every stage of system development. As the logical and physical design is translated into specific hardware and software, the systems analyst must consider security issues that relate to system design specifications and determine how the company will address them, as shown in Figure 8-6. This chapter discusses security issues that arise when data or processing is performed at various locations, rather than at a centralized facility. In certain mission-critical systems, those security issues could have a major impact on system architecture and design.

Web-based systems introduce additional security concerns, as critical data must be protected in the Internet environment. E-commerce applications raise many other security concerns as firms seek to reassure customers that their personal data is safe and secure. After the systems design phase of the SDLC, security issues are absolutely critical once the system becomes operational. System security is discussed in detail in Chapter 10, Systems Operation, Support, and Security.

FIGURE 8-6 Login names and passwords are an important part of system security.

PLANNING THE ARCHITECTURE

Every information system involves three main functions: data storage and access methods, application programs to handle the processing logic, and an interface that allows users to interact with the system. Depending on the architecture, the three functions are performed on a server, on a client, or are divided between the server and the client. As you plan the system design, you must determine where the functions will be carried out and the advantages and disadvantages of each design approach. This section discusses server and client characteristics and how each design alternative handles system functions.

Servers

A **server** is a computer that supplies data, processing services, or other support to one or more computers, called **clients**. A system design where the server performs all the processing is described as **mainframe architecture,** and a server that supports a large number of clients at various locations is called a **centralized system**.

Although the actual server does not have to be a mainframe, the terms mainframe architecture and centralized system typically describe a multiuser environment where the server is significantly more powerful than the clients. A systems analyst should know the history of mainframe architecture to understand the server's role in modern system design.

BACKGROUND In the 1960s, mainframe architecture was the only system design available. In addition to centralized data processing, early systems performed all data input and output at a central location, often called a **data processing center**. Physical data was delivered or transmitted in some manner to the data processing center, where it was entered into the system. Users in the organization had no input or output capability, except for printed reports that were distributed by a corporate IT department.

SERVER-BASED PROCESSING As network technology advanced and became affordable, companies installed terminals at remote locations, so that users could enter and access data from anywhere in the organization, regardless of where the centralized computer was located. A **terminal** included a keyboard and display screen to handle input and output, but lacked independent processing capability. In a centralized design, as shown in Figure 8-7, the remote user's keystrokes are transmitted from his or her terminal to the mainframe, which responds by sending screen output back to the user's screen.

A main advantage of server-based processing is that various types of terminals can communicate with the mainframe, and the design is not tied to a specific hardware platform. A disadvantage is that server-based processing typically uses character-based terminals that provide a limited interface for users. In a server-based system, all data storage, access, and application programs are located on the mainframe.

Today, mainframe architecture still is used in industries that require large amounts of data processing that can be done in batches at a central location. For example, a credit card company might run monthly statements in a batch, or a bank might use mainframe servers to update customer balances each night. In a blend of old and new technology, an Internet-based retail operation might use centralized data management at a customer service center to support and manage its online sales activity, as shown in Figure 8-8.

As server technology evolved, terminals also changed dramatically. Instead of simple input–output devices, a company might use a mix of PCs, handheld computers, and other specialized hardware that allows users to interact with a centralized server. In most companies, workstations that use powerful GUIs have replaced character-based terminals.

FIGURE 8-7 In a centralized design, the remote user's keystrokes are transmitted to the mainframe, which responds by sending screen output back to the user's screen.

FIGURE 8-8 Internet-based retail operations use customer service centers to support and manage online sales activity.

Clients

As PC technology exploded in the 1980s, microcomputers quickly appeared on corporate desktops. Users found that they could run their own word processing, spreadsheet, and database applications, without assistance from the IT group, in a mode called stand-alone computing. Before long, most companies linked the stand-alone computers into networks that enabled the clients to exchange data and perform local processing.

STAND-ALONE COMPUTING When an individual user works in **stand-alone** mode, the workstation performs all the functions of a server by storing, accessing, and processing data, as well as providing a user interface. Although stand-alone PCs improved employee productivity and allowed users to perform tasks that previously required IT department assistance, stand-alone computing was inefficient and expensive. Even worse, maintaining data on individual workstations raised major concerns about data security, integrity, and consistency. Without a central storage location, it was impossible to protect and back up valuable business data, and companies were exposed to enormous risks. In some cases, users who were frustrated by a lack of support and services from the IT department created and managed their own databases. In addition to security concerns, this led to data inconsistency and unreliability.

LOCAL AND WIDE AREA NETWORKS Most companies resolved the problems of stand-alone computing by joining clients into a **local area network (LAN)** that allows sharing of data and hardware resources, as shown in Figure 8-9. One or more LANs, in turn, can connect to a centralized mainframe. Advances in data communication technology made it possible to create powerful networks that could use satellite links, high-speed fiber-optic lines, or the Internet to share data.

FIGURE 8-9 A LAN allows sharing of data and hardware, such as printers and scanners.

ON THE WEB

For more information about Local and Wide Area Networks, visit **scsite.com/sad6e/ more**, locate Chapter 8, and then click the Local and Wide Area Networks link.

A **wide area network (WAN)** spans long distances and can connect LANs that are continents apart, as shown in Figure 8-10. When a user accesses data on a LAN or WAN, the network is **transparent** because a user sees the data as if it were stored on his or her own workstation. Company-wide systems that connect one or more LANs or WANs are called **distributed systems**. The capabilities of a distributed system depend

FIGURE 8-10 A WAN can connect many LANs and link users who are continents apart.

on the power and capacity of the underlying data communication network. Compared to mainframe architecture, distributed systems increase concerns about data security and integrity because many individual clients require access to perform processing.

CLIENT-BASED PROCESSING   In a typical LAN, clients share data stored on a local server that supports a group of users or a department. As LANs became popular, the most common LAN configuration was a file server design, as shown in Figure 8-11. In a **file server** design, also called a **file sharing architecture**, an individual LAN client has a copy of the application program installed locally, while the data is stored on a central file server. The client requests a copy of the data file and the server responds by transmitting the entire data file to the client. After performing the processing locally, the client returns the data file to the central file server where it is stored. File sharing designs are efficient only if the number of networked users is low and the transmitted data file sizes are relatively small. Because the entire data file is sent to each requesting client, a file server design requires significant network resources.

Client
- Handles user interface
- Sends data request to server
- Receives data files from server
- Runs application program locally to process data
- Sends data file back to server

File Server
- Receives data requests from client
- Sends data files to client
- Stores data files
- Manages multiuser access
- Generates a substantial amount of LAN traffic

FIGURE 8-11   Example of a LAN file server design. The server stores and manages the data, while the clients run the application program and perform all the processing.

CLIENT/SERVER ARCHITECTURE

Today's interconnected world requires an information architecture that spans the entire enterprise. Whether you are dealing with a departmental network or a multinational corporation, as a systems analyst you will work with a distributed computing strategy called client/server architecture.

Overview

Although no standard definition exists, the term **client/server architecture** generally refers to systems that divide processing between one or more networked clients and a central server. In a typical client/server system, the client handles the entire user interface,

ON THE WEB

For more information about Client/Server Architecture, visit **scsite.com/sad6e/ more**, locate Chapter 8, and then click the Client/Server Architecture link.

including data entry, data query, and screen presentation logic. The server stores the data and provides data access and database management functions. Application logic is divided in some manner between the server and the clients. In a client/server interaction, the client submits a request for information from the server, which carries out the operation and responds to the client. As shown in Figure 8-12, the data file is not transferred from the server to the client — only the request and the result are transmitted across the network. To fulfill a request from a client, the server might contact other servers for data or processing support, but that process is transparent to the client. The analogy can be made to a restaurant where the customer gives an order to a server, who relays the request to a cook, who actually prepares the meal.

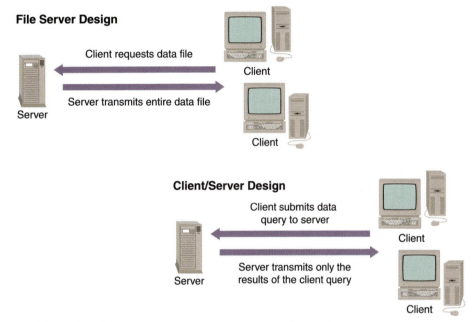

FIGURE 8-12 A file server design compared to a client/server design.

Characteristics of Client/Server Versus Mainframe Systems		
Characteristics	**Client/Server**	**Mainframe**
Basic architecture	Very flexible	Very rigid
Application development	Flexible Fast Object-oriented	Highly structured Slow Traditional
User environment	PC-based GUI Empowers the user Improves productivity	Uses terminals Text interface Constrains the user Limited options
Security and control features	Decentralized Difficult to control	Centralized Easier to control
Processing options	Can be shared and configured in any form desired	Cannot be modified
Data storage options	Can be distributed to place data closer to users	All data is stored centrally
Hardware/software integration	Very flexible Multivendor model	Very rigid Single proprietary vendor

FIGURE 8-13 Characteristics of client/server and mainframe systems.

Figure 8-13 lists some major differences between client/server and traditional mainframe systems. Many early client/server systems did not produce expected savings because few clear standards existed, and development costs often were higher than anticipated. Implementation was expensive because clients needed powerful hardware and software to handle shared processing tasks. In addition, many companies had an installed base of mainframe data, called **legacy data**, which was difficult to access and transport to a client/server environment.

As large-scale networks grew more powerful, client/server systems became more cost-effective. Many companies invested in client/server systems to achieve a unique combination of computing power, flexibility, and support for changing business operations. Today, client/server architecture is the

dominant form of systems design, using Internet protocols and network models such as the ones described on pages 387 – 390. As businesses form new alliances with customers and suppliers, the client/server concept continues to expand to include clients and servers outside the organization.

Client/Server Design Styles

Client/server designs can take many forms, depending on the type of server and the relationship between the server and the clients. Figure 8-14 shows the client/server interaction for a database server, a transaction server, an object server, and a Web server. Notice that in each case, the processing is divided between the server and the clients. The nature of the communication depends on the type of server: a database server processes individual SQL commands, a transaction server handles a set of SQL commands, an object server exchanges object messages with clients, and a Web server sends and receives Internet-based communications.

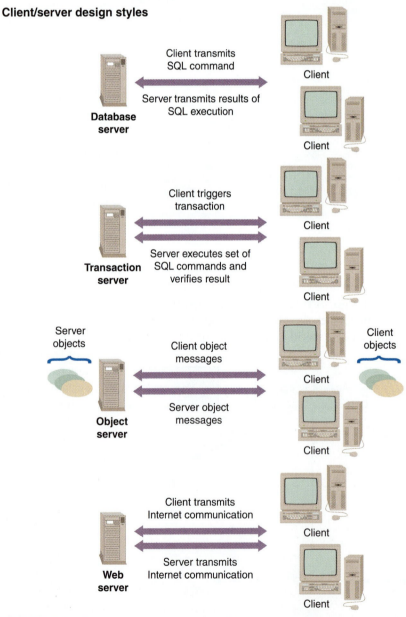

FIGURE 8-14   Client/server interaction for a database server, a transaction server, an object server, and a Web server.

Types of Clients: Fat and Thin

Client/server designs can be based on fat or thin clients. A **fat client**, also called a **thick client**, design locates all or most of the application processing logic at the client. A **thin client** design locates all or most of the processing logic at the server. What are the advantages and disadvantages of each design? Most IT experts agree that thin client designs provide better performance, because program code resides on the server, near the data. In contrast, a fat client handles more of the processing and must access and update the data more often. Compared with maintaining a central server, fat client TCO also is higher, because of initial hardware and software requirements and the ongoing expense of supporting and updating remote client computers. A fat client design, however, is simpler and less expensive to develop, because the architecture resembles traditional file server designs where all processing is performed at the client. Figure 8-15 compares the characteristics of fat and thin clients.

Characteristic	Fat Client	Thin Client
Network traffic	Higher, because the fat client must communicate more often with the server to access data and update processing results	Lower, because most interaction between code and data takes place at the server
Performance	Slower, because more network traffic is required	Faster, because less network traffic is required
Initial cost	Higher, because more powerful hardware is required	Lower, because workstation hardware requirements are not as stringent
Maintenance cost	Higher, because more program code resides on the client	Lower, because most program code resides on the central server
Ease of development	Easier, because systems resemble traditional file-server designs where all processing was performed at the client	More difficult, because developers must optimize the division of processing logic

FIGURE 8-15 Characteristic of fat and thin clients.

Client/Server Tiers

Early client/server designs were called two-tier designs. In a **two-tier** design, the user interface resides on the client, all data resides on the server, and the application logic can run either on the server or on the client, or be divided between the client and the server.

More recently, another form of client/server design, called a three-tier design, has become popular. In a **three-tier** design, the user interface runs on the client and the data is stored on the server, just as with a two-tier design. A three-tier design also has a middle layer between the client and server that processes the client requests and translates them into data access commands that can be understood and carried out by the server, as shown in Figure 8-16. You can think of the middle layer as an **application server**, because it provides the **application logic**, or **business logic**, required by the system. Three-tier designs also are called **n-tier** designs, to indicate that some designs use more than one intermediate layer.

The advantage of the application logic layer is that a three-tier design enhances overall performance by reducing the data server's workload. The

FIGURE 8-16 Characteristics of two-tier versus three-tier client/server design.

separate application logic layer also relieves clients of complex processing tasks. Because it can run on a mini-computer that is much more powerful than the typical client workstations, the middle layer is more efficient and cost-effective in large-scale systems. Figure 8-17 shows where the data, the application logic, and the user interface are located on various types of architecture. In a client/server system, the tiers communicate using software called middleware, which is described in the following section.

Architecture		Data	Application Logic	User Interface
Central data processing center	Server	X	X	X
	Client			
Central server with remote terminals	Server	X	X	
	Client			X
Stand-alone client	Server			
	Client	X	X	X
Two-tier client/server	Server	X	X	
	Client		X	X
Three-tier client/server	Data server	X		
	Application server		X	
	Client			X

FIGURE 8-17   The table shows where the data, the application logic, and the user interface are located on various types of architecture.

Middleware

In an n-tier system, special utility software called **middleware** enables the tiers to communicate and pass data back and forth. Some IT professionals refer to middleware as the glue that holds clients and servers together.

Middleware provides a transparent interface that enables system designers to integrate dissimilar software and hardware. For example, middleware can link a departmental database to a Web server, which can be accessed by client computers via the Internet or a company intranet. Middleware also can integrate legacy systems and Web-based applications, as shown in Figure 8-18 on the next page. For example, when a user enters a customer number on a Web-based inquiry form, the middleware accesses a legacy accounting system and returns the results.

Cost-Benefit Issues

To support business requirements, information systems need to be scalable, powerful, and flexible. For most companies, client/server systems offer the best combination of features to meet those needs. Whether a business is expanding or downsizing, client/server systems enable the firm to scale the system in a rapidly changing environment. As the size of the business changes, it is easier to adjust the number of clients and the processing functions they perform than it is to alter the capability of a large-scale central server.

Client/server computing also allows companies to transfer applications from expensive mainframes to less expensive client platforms. In addition, using common languages such as SQL, clients and servers can communicate across multiple platforms. That difference is important because many businesses have substantial investments in a variety of hardware and software environments.

Finally, compared to file server designs, client/server systems reduce network load and improve response times. For example, consider a user at a company headquarters who wants information about total sales figures. In a file server design, the system might need to transmit three separate sales transaction files from three regional offices in order to provide sales data that the client would process; in a client/server system, the server locates the data, performs the necessary processing, and responds immediately to the client's request. The data retrieval and processing functions are transparent to the client because they are done on the server, not the client.

FIGURE 8-18   Middleware connects dissimilar applications and enables them to communicate and exchange data. Middleware also can integrate legacy systems and Web-based applications.

Client/Server Performance Issues

While it provides many important advantages over file-based systems, client/server architecture does involve performance issues that relate to the separation of server-based data and networked clients that must access the data.

Consider the difference between client/server design and a centralized environment, where a server-based program issues a command that is executed by the server's own CPU. Processing speed is enhanced because program instructions and data both travel on an internal system bus, which moves data more efficiently than an external network.

In contrast to the centralized system, a client/server design separates applications and data. Networked clients submit data requests to the server, which responds by sending data back to the clients. When the number of clients and the demand for services increases beyond a certain level, network capacity becomes a constraint, and system performance declines dramatically.

In the Web site article shown in Figure 8-19, IBM states that most client/server systems run into a wall at some point. The article goes on to state, "… the old mind set of 'open the file and read one record at a time' has gotten many client-server projects and tools into far too much trouble. And it gets very expensive when a business learns this lesson when trying to go from 60 to 90 users, only to find out that the wall is somewhere in between."

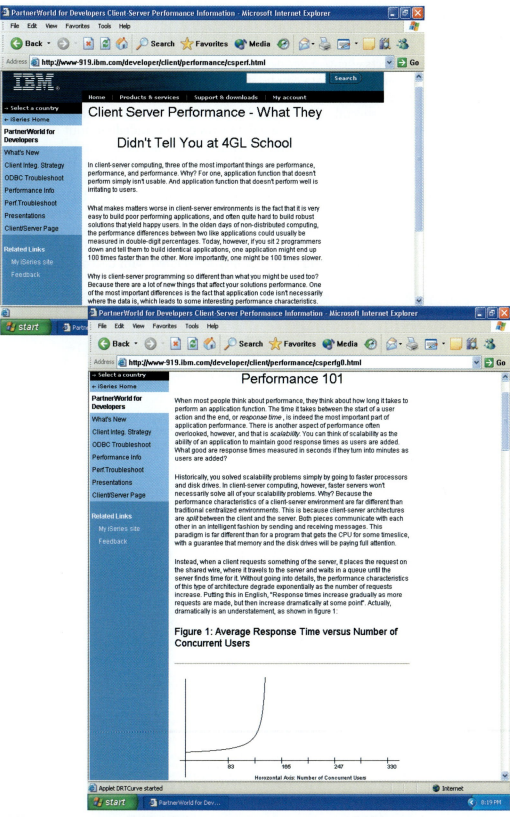

FIGURE 8-19 According to IBM, client-server performance issues are far different than in a centralized environment. Response times increase gradually as more requests are made, but then increase dramatically at some point.

What is the answer to enhancing client/server performance? According to IBM, client/server systems must be designed so the client contacts the server only when necessary and makes as few trips as possible.

Another issue that affects client/server performance is data storage. Just as processing can be done at various places, data can be stored in more than one location using a **distributed database management system (DDBMS)**.

Using a DDBMS offers several advantages: data stored closer to users can reduce network traffic; the system is scalable, so new data sites can be added without reworking the system design; and with data stored in various locations, the system is less likely to experience a catastrophic failure. A potential disadvantage of distributed data storage involves data security. It can be more difficult to maintain controls and standards when data is stored in various locations. In addition, the architecture of a DDBMS is more complex and difficult to manage. As shown in Figure 8-20, Sybase is a leading software vendor that offers products to support distributed data management systems. As the Sybase document points out, companies want it both ways — they want the control that comes with centralization *and* the flexibility associated with decentralization.

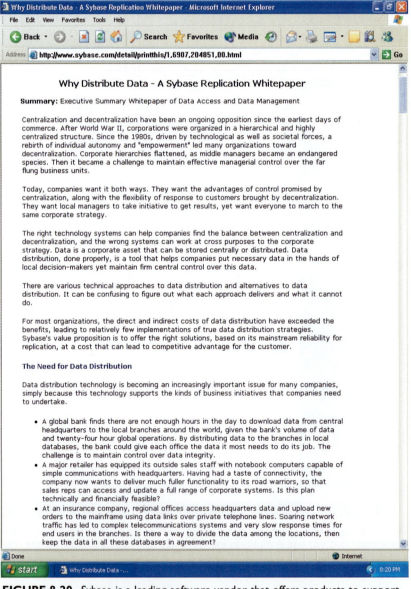

FIGURE 8-20 Sybase is a leading software vendor that offers products to support distributed data management systems.

INTERNET-BASED ARCHITECTURE

The Internet has had an enormous impact on system architecture. The Internet has become more than a communication channel — many IT observers see it as a fundamentally different environment for system development.

Recall that in a traditional client-server system, the client handles the user interface, as shown in Figure 8-16 on page 374, and the server (or servers in a multi-tier system) handles the data and application logic. In a sense, part of the system runs on the client, part on the server. In contrast, in an Internet-based architecture, in addition to data and application logic, the entire user interface is provided by the Web server in the form of HTML coded documents that are interpreted and displayed by the client's browser. Shifting the responsibility for the interface from the client to the server simplifies the process of data transmission and results in lower hardware costs and complexities.

E-business trends are reshaping the corporate landscape as firms, large and small, learn how to harness the power of the Web and build efficient, reliable, and cost-effective business solutions. To support this trend, systems analysts must suggest e-commerce strategies that apply available technology and meet their company's business requirements. The following sections will discuss several e-commerce strategies, including in-house development, packaged solutions and e-business service providers, and corporate portals.

Developing E-Commerce Solutions In-House

In Chapter 5, you learned how to analyze advantages and disadvantages of in-house development versus purchasing a software package. The same basic principles apply to system design.

If you decide to proceed with an in-house solution, you must have an overall plan to help achieve your goals. How should you begin? Figure 8-21 offers guidelines for companies developing e-commerce strategies. An in-house solution usually requires a greater initial investment, but provides more flexibility for a company that must adapt quickly in a dynamic e-commerce environment. By working in-house, a company has more freedom to integrate with customers and suppliers and is less dependent on vendor-specific solutions.

For smaller companies, the decision about in-house development is even more critical, because it will require financial resources and management attention that many small companies would be unable or unwilling to commit. In this regard, consider the interesting examples shown in Figure 8-22 on the next page, which is a site maintained by MasterCard Business Solutions. In the first scenario, a small business with 10 employees wants to sell its products on the Web and elects an in-house development strategy. The first year cost in this example was $3,696. Compare this to the firm in the second example. In this case, a young couple wants to expand a hobby into a Web-based business. By using a prepackaged Web-based service from a national computer services company, they were able to implement their site for a much smaller investment.

Guidelines for In-house E-commerce Site Development
Analyze the company's business needs and develop a clear statement of your goals. Consider the experience of other companies with similar projects.
Obtain input from users who understand the business and technology issues involved in the project. Plan for future growth, but aim for ease of use.
Determine whether the IT staff has the necessary skills and experience to implement the project. Consider training, additional resources, and the use of consultants if necessary.
Consider integration requirements for existing legacy systems or enterprise resource planning. Select a physical infrastructure carefully, so it will support the application, now and later.
Develop the project in modular form so users can test and approve the functional elements as you go along.
Connect the application to existing in-house systems and verify interactivity.
Test every aspect of the site exhaustively. Consider a preliminary rollout to a pilot group to obtain feedback before a full launch.

FIGURE 8-21 Guidelines for companies developing e-commerce strategies.

FIGURE 8-22 A comparison of an in-house versus a packaged solution.

After presenting the two scenarios in Figure 8-22, the MasterCard site went on to point out that both companies ended up with well-designed, secure sites where customers could place orders using a credit card. But Company A paid over four times as much as Company B, even without counting the significant staff time Company A spent in developing the site in-house. MasterCard pointed out that Company A, however, did gain a number of advantages, including the following:

- A Web site that was unique, with a look and feel consistent with the company's other marketing efforts.

- Complete control over the organization of the site, the number of pages, and the size of the files.

- A much more scalable structure to handle increases in sales and product offerings in the future.

➡ More flexibility to change the site as the company changes.

➡ The opportunity to integrate its Web-based business systems with other information systems, creating the potential for more savings and better customer service.

Finally, it should be noted that neither of the companies in the examples chose to host their e-commerce sites internally. Although internal hosting has some advantages, such as greater control and security, the expense would be much greater, especially for a small- to medium-sized firm.

CASE IN POINT 8.2: SMALL POTATOES, INC.

Small Potatoes is a family-operated seed business that has grown rapidly. Small Potatoes specializes in supplying home gardeners with the finest seeds and gardening supplies. Until now, the firm has done all its business by placing ads in gardening and health magazines, and taking orders using a toll-free telephone number.

Now, the family has decided to establish a Web site and sell online, but there is some disagreement about the best way to proceed. Some say it would be better to develop the site on their own, and Betty Lou Jones, a recent computer science graduate, believes she can handle the task. Others, including Sam Jones, Betty's grandfather, feel it would be better to outsource the site and focus on the business itself. Suppose the family asked for your opinion. What would you say? What additional questions would you ask?

Packaged Solutions and E-Commerce Service Providers

As the examples in Figure 8-22 show, if a small company is reluctant to take on the challenge and complexity of developing an Internet commerce site in-house, an alternative can be a packaged solution or an e-commerce service provider. This is true even for medium- to large- sized firms. Many vendors, including Microsoft, offer turnkey systems for companies that want to get an e-business up and running quickly, as shown in Figure 8-23.

For large-scale systems that must integrate with existing applications, packaged solutions might be less attractive. Another alternative is to use an application service provider (ASP). As explained in Chapter 5, an ASP provides applications, or access to applications, by charging a usage or subscription fee. Today, many ASPs offer full-scale Internet business services for companies that decide to outsource those functions. A Web-focused ASP, such as Intershop, can develop, maintain, and host

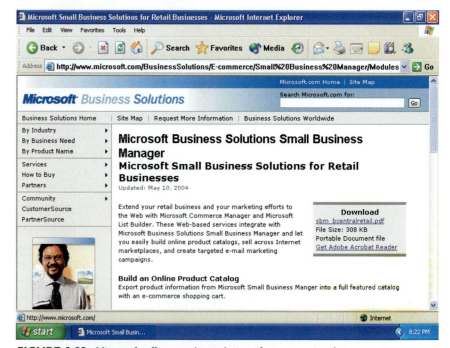

FIGURE 8-23 Microsoft offers turnkey solutions for companies that want to get an e-business up and running quickly.

a Web site, as shown in Figure 8-24. As with packaged solutions, a company must consider whether the advantage of lower initial cost outweighs the disadvantage of reduced flexibility later on.

A systems analyst confronts a bewildering array of products and strategies when implementing Internet-based systems. A good starting point might be to consider the experience of other companies in the same industry. Many firms, including Sun Microsystems, offer success stories and case studies of successful systems development, as shown in Figure 8-25. Although each situation is different, this type of research can provide valuable information about a vendor's products and services.

Corporate Portals

A **portal** is an entrance to a multifunction Web site. After entering a portal, a user can navigate to a destination using various tools and features provided by the portal designer. A **corporate portal** can provide access for customers, employees, suppliers,

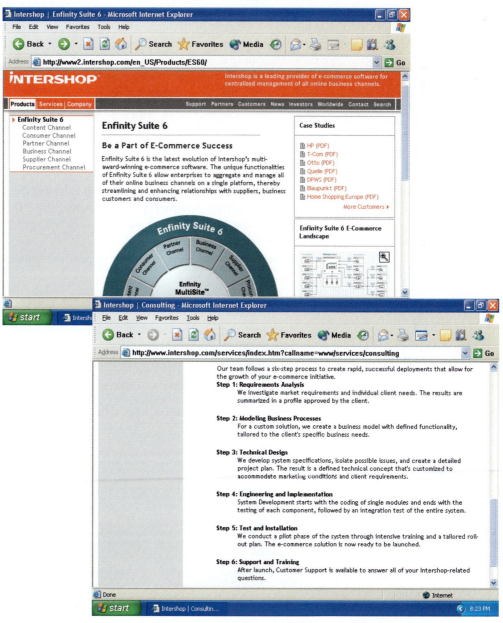

FIGURE 8-24 A Web-focused ASP, such as Intershop, can develop, maintain, and host a Web site.

and the public. In a Web-based system, portal design provides an important link between the user and the system, and poor design can weaken system effectiveness and value. Figure 8-26 shows Oracle Corporation's site, which describes multifunction portals that can improve productivity, communications, and decision making. Notice Oracle's statement that portals provide a personalized view of the content and applications users need to do their jobs.

Another industry leader, SAP, offers a product called SAP Enterprise Portal, which is shown in Figure 8-27 on the next page. According to the company, SAP Enterprise Portal allows a firm quickly and effectively to integrate SAP solutions, third-party applications, legacy systems, databases, unstructured documents, internal and external Web content, and collaboration tools.

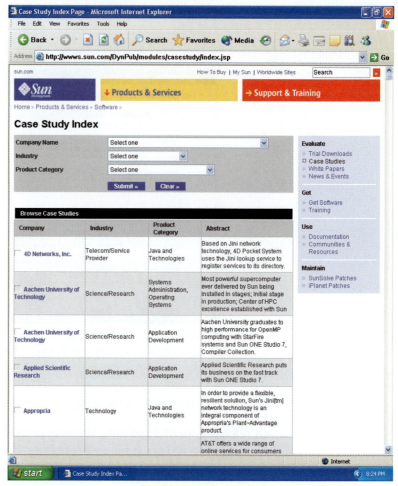

FIGURE 8-25   Success stories and case studies can provide valuable information about a vendor's products and services.

FIGURE 8-26   Oracle Corporation offers multifunction portals that can improve productivity, communications, and decision making.

FIGURE 8-27 SAP offers a product called Enterprise Portal, which gives users a single view that spans the enterprise.

PROCESSING METHODS

In selecting an architecture, the systems analyst must determine whether the system will be an online system, a batch processing system, or a combination of the two.

Online Processing

Early computer systems relied mainly on batch processing, but the vast majority of systems today use online processing. An **online system** handles transactions when and where they occur and provides output directly to users. Because it is interactive, online processing avoids delays and allows a constant dialog between the user and the system.

An airline reservations system is a familiar example of online processing. When an online customer views the screen shown in Figure 8-28, he or she can enter the origin, destination, travel dates, and travel times. The system searches a database and responds by displaying available flights, times, and prices. The customer can make a reservation, enter a name, address, credit card information, and other required data and the system creates the reservation, assigns a seat, and updates the flight database immediately.

Online processing also can be used with file-oriented systems. Figure 8-29 shows what happens when a customer

FIGURE 8-28 A Web-based airline reservations system is an example of online processing on the Internet.

uses an ATM to inquire about an account balance. After the ATM verifies the customer's card and password, the customer enters the request (Step 1). Then, the system accesses the account master file using the account number as the primary key and retrieves the customer's record (Step 2). The system verifies the account number and displays the balance (Step 3). Data is retrieved and the system transmits the current balance to the ATM, which prints it for the customer. Online processing systems have four typical characteristics:

1. The system processes transactions completely when and where they occur.

2. Users interact directly with the information system.

3. Users can access data randomly.

4. The information system must be available whenever necessary to support business functions.

ATM QUERY PROCESS

Step 1: Customer enters his or her account number and requests an account balance

Step 2: Retrieves current account balance

Step 3: Verifies bank account number and displays balance on ATM screen

FIGURE 8-29 When a customer requests a balance, the ATM system verifies the account number, submits the query, retrieves the current balance, and displays the balance on the ATM screen.

Batch Processing

In a **batch processing** system, data is collected and processed in groups, or batches. Although online processing is used for interactive business systems that require immediate data input and output, batch processing can handle other situations more efficiently. For example, batch processing typically is used for large amounts of data that must be processed on a routine schedule, such as paychecks or credit card transactions.

In batch processing, input transactions are grouped into a single file and processed together. For example, when a firm produces customer statements at the end of the month, a batch application might process many thousands of records in one run of the program. A batch processing system has several main characteristics: collect, group, and process transactions periodically; the IT operations group can run batch programs on a predetermined schedule, without user involvement, during regular business hours, at night, or on weekends; and batch programs require significantly fewer network resources than online systems.

CASE IN POINT 8.3: R/Way Trucking Company

You are the new IT manager at R/Way, a small but rapidly growing trucking company headquartered in Cleveland, Ohio. The company slogan is "Ship It R/Way — State-of-the-Art in Trucking and Customer Service." R/Way's information system currently consists of a file server and three workstations where freight clerks enter data, track shipments, and prepare freight bills. To perform their work, the clerks obtain data from the server and use database and spreadsheet programs stored on their PCs to process the data.

Unfortunately, your predecessor did not design a relational database. Instead, data is stored in several files, including one for shippers, one for customers, and one for shipments. The system worked well for several years, but cannot handle current volume or support online links for R/Way shippers and customers. The company president is willing to make changes, but he is reluctant to spend money on major IT improvements unless you can convince him that they are necessary.

What would you recommend and why?

Combined Online and Batch Processing

FIGURE 8-30 Retail point-of-sale terminals provide customer sales support and transaction processing capability.

Even an online system can use batch processing to perform certain routine tasks. Online processing also can be used with file-oriented systems. Figure 8-30 shows a familiar **point-of-sale (POS)** terminal, and Figure 8-31 shows how a retail chain uses POS terminals to drive online and batch processing methods. Notice that the system uses online processing to handle data entry and inventory updates, while reports and accounting entries are performed in a batch.

The retail store system illustrates both online processing and batch processing of data. During business hours, the salesperson enters a sale on a point-of-sale (POS) terminal, which is part of an information system that handles daily sales transactions and maintains the online inventory file. When the salesperson enters the transaction, online processing occurs. The system performs calculations, updates the inventory file, and produces output on the POS terminal in the form of a screen display and a printed receipt. At the same time, each sales transaction creates input data for day-end batch processing.

POINT OF SALE (POS) PROCESSING

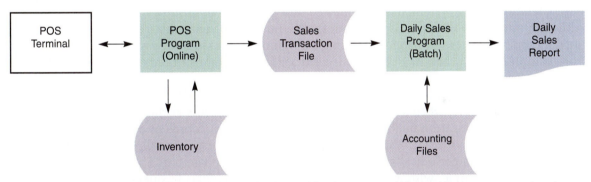

FIGURE 8-31 Many retailers use a combination of online and batch processing. When a salesperson enters the sale on the POS terminal, the online system retrieves data from the item file, updates the quantity in stock, and produces a sales transaction record. At the end of the day, a batch processing program produces a daily sales report and updates the accounting system.

When the store closes, the system uses the sales transactions to produce the daily sales report and related accounting entries using batch processing. Performing the processing online before all sales transactions are completed does not make sense. In that situation, a batch method provides better routine transaction processing, while an online approach supports point-of-sale processing, which must be done as it occurs.

In the retail store example, both online and batch processing are integral parts of the information system. Online processing offers an inherent advantage because data is entered and validated as it occurs, so the stored data is available sooner and always is up-to-date. Online processing is more expensive, however, and the effect of computer system downtime or slowdown while transactions are processed causes far more disruption than in batch processing. In addition, backup and recovery for online processing are more difficult. In many situations, batch processing is cost-effective, less vulnerable to system disruption, and less intrusive to normal operations. Many information systems will continue to use a combination of online and batch processing for some time to come.

NETWORK MODELS

A network allows the sharing of hardware, software, and data resources in order to reduce expenses and provide more capability to users. When planning a network design, you must consider network terms and concepts, including the OSI model, network modeling tools, network topology, network protocols, licensing issues, and wireless networks, which are covered in this section. You also must consider system performance, security, and interruption issues, which are covered later in this chapter.

The OSI Reference Model

Based on the discussion of system architecture earlier in this chapter, you already understand basic network terms such as client, server, LAN, WAN, file server design, client/server architecture, tiers, and middleware.

Before you study network topology, you should have a basic understanding of the **OSI (open system interconnection) model**, which describes how data actually moves from an application on one computer to an application on another networked computer. The OSI model consists of seven layers. Each layer performs a specific function, as follows:

- Application layer: provides network services requested by a local workstation.
- Presentation layer: assures that data is uniformly structured and formatted for network transmission.
- Session layer: defines control structures that manage the communications link between computers.
- Transport layer: provides reliable data flow and error recovery.
- Network layer: defines network addresses and determines how data is routed over the network.
- Data link layer: defines specific methods of transmitting data over the physical layer, such as defining the start and end of a data block.
- Physical layer: contains physical components that carry data, such as cabling and connecters.

In the OSI model, data proceeds down through the layers on the transmitting computer, then up through the layers on the receiving computer. Along the way, data may pass through one or more network routers that control the path from one network address to another.

It is important to understand that OSI is a logical model and is not tied to any specific physical environment or hardware. As a conceptual model, OSI offers a set of design standards that can promote interoperability among networks and products that are based on the OSI model.

Network Modeling Tools

As you translate the OSI logical model into a physical model of the networked system, you can use software tools, such as Microsoft Visio, which is a multipurpose drawing tool, to represent the physical structure and network components. Visio offers a wide variety of drawing types, styles, templates, and shapes. For example, Visio supplies templates for basic network designs, plus manufacturer-specific symbols for firms such as Cisco, IBM, Bay Systems, and Hewlett-Packard, among others.

Visio is an example of a CASE tool that can help you plan, analyze, design, and implement an information system. Visio can be used to create a simple network model, either by using drag-and-drop shapes displayed on the left of the screen, or by using provided

ON THE WEB

For more information about The OSI Reference Model, visit **scsite.com/sad6e/ more**, locate Chapter 8, and then click The OSI Reference Model link.

TOOLKIT TIME

The CASE Tools in Part 2 of the Systems Analyst's Toolkit can help you document business functions and processes, develop graphical models, and provide an overall framework for information system development. To learn more about these tools, turn to Part 2 of the six-part Toolkit that follows Chapter 10.

wizards to walk through a step-by-step network design process. Figure 8-32 shows an example of a simple network model created using the drag-and-drop feature.

Network Topology

The way a network is configured is called the **network topology**. LAN and WAN networks typically are arranged in four patterns: hierarchical, star, bus, and ring. The concepts are the same regardless of the size of the network, but the physical implementation is different for a large-scale WAN that spans an entire business enterprise compared with a small LAN in a single department. The four topologies are described in the following sections.

FIGURE 8-32 Microsoft Visio can be used to create a simple network drawing using drag-and-drop shapes displayed on the left of the screen.

HIERARCHICAL NETWORK In a **hierarchical network**, as shown in Figure 8-33, one computer (typically a mainframe) controls the entire network. Satellite computers or servers control lower levels of processing and network devices. An example of a hierarchical network might be a retail chain, with a central computer that stores data about sales activity and inventory levels and local computers that

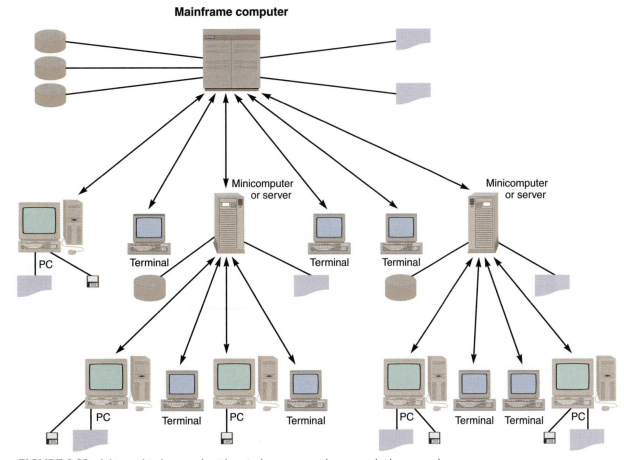

FIGURE 8-33 A hierarchical network with a single computer that controls the network.

handle store-level operations. The stores transmit data to the central computer, which analyzes sales trends, determines optimum stock levels, and coordinates a supply chain management system. In this situation, a hierarchical network works well, because it mirrors the actual operational flow in the organization. One disadvantage of a hierarchical network is that if a business adds additional processing levels, the network becomes more complex and expensive to operate and maintain.

STAR NETWORK A **star network** has a central computer with network devices connected to it. At the center of the star, which is called the **hub**, the central computer manages the network. A star configuration, as shown in Figure 8-34, often is used when network control is important, because all traffic must flow into and out of the hub. The central computer in a star network does not have to serve as the primary data storage location; it can serve as a network coordinator that enables the other devices to transmit and receive stored data from each other. While a star network provides efficiency and close control, a major disadvantage of this design is that the entire network depends on the central computer. In most large star networks, backup systems are available in case of a failure in the central computer.

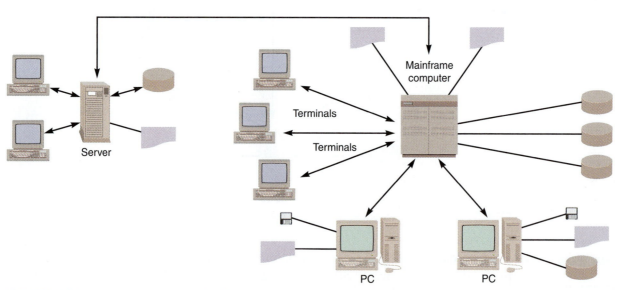

FIGURE 8-34 A star network with a central computer and connected workstations.

BUS NETWORK In a **bus network**, as shown in Figure 8-35 on the next page, a single communication path connects the mainframe computer, server, workstations, and peripheral devices. Information is transmitted in either direction from any workstation to another workstation, and any message can be directed to a specific device. An advantage of the bus network is that devices can be attached or detached from the network at any point without disturbing the rest of the network. In addition, a failure in one workstation on the network does not necessarily affect other workstations on the network. One disadvantage of a bus network is that performance can decline as more users and devices are added, because all message traffic must flow along the central bus. This does not occur in the treelike structure of a hierarchical network or the hub-and-spoke design of a star network, where network traffic in one path does not affect traffic elsewhere on the network.

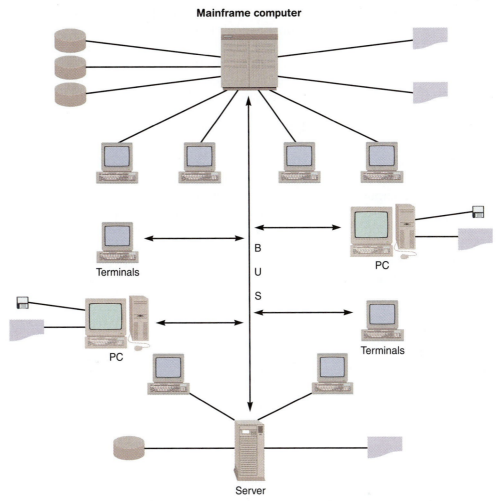

Mainframe computer

Terminals

PC

B
U
S

PC

Terminals

Server

FIGURE 8-35   A bus network with all devices connected to a single communication path.

ON THE WEB

For more information
about Network
Protocols, visit
**scsite.com/sad6e/
more**, locate
Chapter 8, and then
click the Network
Protocols link.

RING NETWORK   A **ring network**, as shown in Figure 8-36, resembles a circle of computers that communicate with each other. A ring network often is used when processing is performed at local sites rather than at a central location. For example, users accessing computers in the accounting, personnel, and shipping departments perform the processing for individual functions and then use the ring network to exchange data with other computers on the network. Data flows in only one direction in a ring network. One disadvantage of a ring network is that if a network device (such as a PC or a printer) fails, the devices downstream from the failed device cannot communicate with the network.

Network Protocols and Licensing Issues

In all cases, the network must use a **protocol**, which is a set of standards that govern network data transmission. A popular network protocol is **Transmission Control Protocol/Internet Protocol (TCP/IP)**. Originally developed by the U.S. Department of Defense to permit interconnection of military computers, today TCP/IP is the backbone of the Internet. Other network protocols include NetBIOS, which is a popular protocol for LANs, and IPX, which is a protocol used by Novell Corporation for its NetWare products.

TCP/IP actually consists of many individual protocols that control the handling of files, mail, and addresses, among others. A familiar example of a TCP/IP protocol is the

file transfer protocol (FTP), which provides a reliable means of copying files from one computer to another over a TCP/IP network, such as the Internet or an intranet.

When considering a network design, it is important to take into account software licensing restrictions. Various types of individual and site licenses are available from software vendors. Some vendors limit the number of users or the number of computers that can access the program simultaneously. You also must carefully investigate the capabilities of network software to ensure that it can handle the anticipated system traffic.

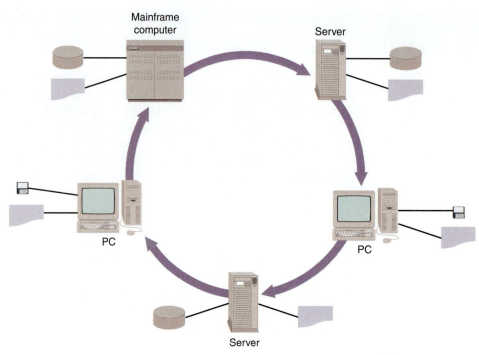

FIGURE 8-36 A ring network with a set of computers that send and receive data flowing in one direction.

Wireless Networks

Although a LAN can provide enormous flexibility, a significant cost element involves the initial expense of cabling and the inevitable wiring changes that occur in a dynamic organization. Many companies find wireless technology to be an attractive alternative. A **wireless local area network**, or **WLAN**, is relatively inexpensive to install and is well-suited to workgroups and users who are not anchored to a specific desk or location.

Wireless networks are based on various standards and protocols that are evolving constantly. The most popular of these is called the **802.11 network standard**, which is a family of specifications developed by the **Institute of Electrical and Electronics Engineers (IEEE)** for wireless LANs. A popular version of this standard, **802.11b**, also known as **802.11 High Rate**, or **Wi-Fi**, has a nominal transmission rate of 11 million bits per second within a 100-meter range.

With the growing popularity of wireless networks, many firms and organizations exist to offer products, services, and information. One of these is the Wi-Fi Alliance, which maintains a Web site at www.wi-fi.org. According to the site, the Alliance is a nonprofit international association formed in 1999 to certify interoperability of wireless network products based on IEEE 802.11 specification. Currently the Wi-Fi Alliance has over 200 member companies from around the world, and over 1,250 products have received Wi-Fi certification. The stated goal of the Wi-Fi Alliance is to enhance the user experience through product interoperability.

Although they have many advantages, wireless networks pose special concerns with regard to system security. These issues are discussed in detail in Chapter 10, System Operation, Support, and Security.

CASE IN POINT 8.4:   SPIDER IT SERVICES

Spider IT Services specializes in custom network design and installation. Firms hire Spider to do an overall analysis of their network needs, including a detailed cost-benefit study. Recently, a problem arose. One of Spider's clients complained that the relatively new network was too slow and lacked sufficient capacity. Reviewing the case, Spider's top management realized that the rapidly growing client had simply outgrown the network much earlier than anticipated.

Could this problem have been avoided? Note that IBM, in the article shown in Figure 8-19 on page 377, commented that performance can "degrade exponentially" in certain kinds of network situations. Consider the IBM article and other material in this chapter, and offer your views.

SYSTEM MANAGEMENT AND SUPPORT

The information system design must include provision for system management and support tools to monitor system performance and deal with system interruptions — from fault management to disaster recovery.

Performance Management

ON THE WEB

For more information about Backup and Disaster Recovery, visit **scsite.com/sad6e/ more**, locate Chapter 8, and then click the Backup and Disaster Recovery link.

Performance management tools are designed to collect information about system resources and activity levels. A performance management tool can monitor system usage, capacity, and trends. Performance management also can include fine-tuning the network configuration or software settings to optimize performance.

In the e-business era, slow performance can be as devastating as no performance at all. Customers expect reliable, fast responses from a Web-based system 24 hours a day, seven days a week. To help meet that need, firms such as NetScout Systems offer comprehensive performance management packages, as shown in Figure 8-37. A NetScout product called nGenius offers detailed, system-wide views of applications, users, and response times.

The NetScout Web site mentions studies that show network delays cost the industry more revenue than actual stoppages, because they occur so frequently and are difficult to detect. NetScout's conclusion is that network delays and application bottlenecks profoundly affect revenues, productivity, customer satisfaction, and communication, and make a company less competitive and profitable.

Fault Management, Backup, and Disaster Recovery

No matter how well it is designed, every system will experience some problems, such as hardware failures, software errors, user mistakes,

FIGURE 8-37   A performance management tool can monitor system usage, capacity, and trends. A NetScout product called nGenius offers detailed, system-wide views of applications, users, and response times.

and power outages. Unfortunately, hackers and cyber-vandalism represent a new threat that you also must consider. As part of the systems design, you must anticipate those problems and plan for ways to deal with them.

The best strategy is to prevent problems before they can affect the system. For example, you learned earlier that data validation, audit trail files, security measures, and other control features help ensure that data is entered and processed correctly. You must provide additional means, however, to deal with system faults and interruptions.

FAULT MANAGEMENT A system administrator's main concern is to detect and resolve operational problems as quickly as possible. That task, often called **fault management**, includes monitoring the system for signs of trouble, logging all system failures, diagnosing the problem, and applying corrective action. The more complex the system, the more difficult it can be to analyze symptoms and isolate a cause. In addition to addressing the immediate problem, it is important to evaluate performance patterns and trends. Automated tools are available to assist system administrators in that task, such as the OpManager software offered by AdventNet, which is shown in Figure 8-38. According to AdventNet, its fault management software can improve productivity through automated notification of problems, identify root causes and fix problems quickly, eliminate fire-fighting and manage IT services proactively, and prevent service outages and response time bottlenecks.

BACKUP AND DISASTER RECOVERY Every system design must include provisions for data backup and recovery. **Backup** refers to copying data continuously, or at prescribed intervals. **Recovery** procedures involve restoring the data and restarting the system after an interruption. An overall backup and recovery plan often is called a **disaster recovery plan**.

The tragic events of September 11, 2001, and increased concern about global terrorism have forced many companies to reassess their plans for backup and disaster recovery. Unfortunately, IT professionals who are responsible for backup and disaster recovery

FIGURE 8-38 Fault management includes monitoring the system for signs of trouble, logging all system failures, diagnosing the problem, and applying corrective action. OpManager software, offered by AdventNet, can assist system administrators by evaluating network performance and problems.

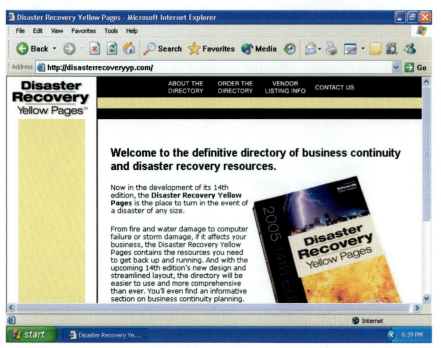

FIGURE 8-39 The Disaster Recovery Yellow Pages site offers a wide range of products and services of interest to IT professionals who are responsible for backup and disaster recovery planning.

planning must prepare for the worst-case scenario in order to protect their company's investment and business continuity. The heightened focus on disaster recovery has spawned a whole new industry, as indicated in Figure 8-39, which shows a site called Disaster Recovery Yellow Pages.

Backup and recovery planning depends on the type of system involved. The simplest example is a batch processing system, which presents few backup and recovery problems. In this type of system, the batch transaction file and the previous version of the master file are saved as backup files in case the new master file is damaged or the update program execution is interrupted. Any problems are corrected by executing the update program again with the transaction file and the previous master file as inputs.

With online systems, you either must perform backups when the system is inactive, or must continuously back up the data during system operation. Most large systems use streaming tape devices that constantly record all processing activity as it occurs. If processing is interrupted, data is recovered by restoring files from the backup media. Another common strategy is to use a **RAID** (**redundant array of independent disks**) system, which mirrors the data while processing continues. RAID systems are called **fault-tolerant,** because a failure of any one disk does not disable the system.

Experienced IT professionals often note that the three most important types of insurance are backup, backup, and more backup. As shown in Figure 8-40, firms such as NovaStor offer a wide variety of backup software and strategies for small- and medium-sized companies.

Many companies are using Web-based data backup services such as the ones shown in Figure 8-41. Firms such as Rocky Mountain Software and industry leader IBM offer Web-based, automated, data storage and retrieval solutions. Using the Internet as a backup solution is a cost-effective, flexible, and reliable strategy.

Another approach to online system backup uses a special file called a **log file,** or **journal file,** which contains a copy of each record as it

FIGURE 8-40 Firms such as NovaStor offer a wide variety of backup software and strategies.

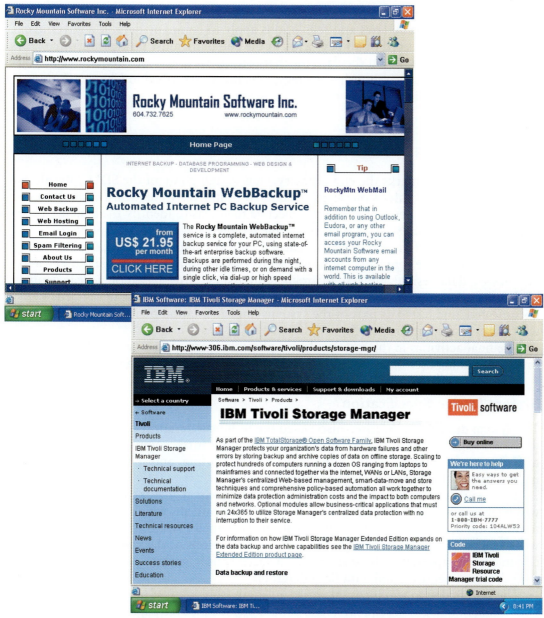

FIGURE 8-41 Using the Internet as a backup solution is a cost-effective, flexible, and reliable strategy.

appears before and after modification. If data is damaged, the most recent backup is used to recover, or restore, the data file. Then, a special transaction recovery program processes the log file to bring the data file forward to its state at the time the damage occurred. The total recovery time can take many hours for large-scale databases and data files with large numbers of records and transactions. Logging functions are included in most large-scale DBMSs.

In a worst-case scenario, business insurance can help offset expenditures due to system failure and business losses. Those policies can be expensive and require a high deductible amount, however, which must be borne by the company, not the insurer. Many IT professionals feel that the combination of Y2K, events of September 11, 2001, and global concern about terrorism has raised the awareness level throughout the corporate world, and that will make it easier to obtain top management support for prevention and recovery efforts.

Apart from backup and recovery procedures necessary to sustain business operations, **file retention** laws and regulations apply to company data. If a government rule specifies that a record of all payments to the company must be kept for three years, then your design must retain the data for that period. To satisfy that requirement, you can implement a data warehousing strategy, which was described in Chapter 7, to provide easy, cost-effective access to the data.

SYSTEMS DESIGN COMPLETION

System architecture marks the end of the systems design phase of the SDLC. Recall that back in the systems analysis phase, all functional primitives were identified and documented with process descriptions. The objective then was to identify the system's functions and determine *what* each logical module would do, without attempting to determine *how* that function would be carried out. Moving from analysis to design tasks, the development process continued with consideration of output and user interface design, data design, and system architecture issues. Now, based on a clear definition of system requirements and design, software applications can be developed, documented, and tested as part of the systems implementation phase of the SDLC, which is described in Chapter 9.

The final activities in the systems design phase are preparing a system design specification, obtaining user approval, and delivering a presentation to management.

System Design Specification

The **system design specification**, also called the **technical design specification** or the **detailed design specification**, is a document that presents the complete design for the new information system, along with detailed costs, staffing, and scheduling for completing the next SDLC phase — systems implementation.

The system design specification is the baseline against which the operational system will be measured. Unlike the system requirements document, which is written for users to understand, the system design specification is oriented toward the programmers who will use it to create the necessary programs. Some sections of the system requirements document are repeated in the system design specification, such as process descriptions, data dictionary entries, and data flow diagrams.

The system design specification varies in length, so you must organize it carefully and number all pages in sequence. You should include a cover page, a detailed table of contents, and an index. The contents of the system design specification depend on company standards and the complexity of the system. A typical system design specification uses a structure similar to Figure 8-42, which is described in the following sections.

1. *Executive Summary.* The management summary provides a brief overview of the project for company managers and executives. It outlines the development efforts to date, provides a current status report, summarizes current project costs and costs for the remaining phases, reviews the overall benefits of the new system, presents the systems development phase schedule, and highlights any issues that management will need to address.

2. *System Components.* This section contains the complete design for the new system, including the user interface, outputs, inputs, files, databases, and network specifications. You should include source documents, report and screen layouts, DFDs, and all other relevant documentation. You also should include the requirements for all support processing, such as backup and recovery, startup processing, and file retention. If the purchase of a software package is part of the strategy, you must include any interface information required between the package and the

system you are developing. If you use a CASE design tool, you can print design diagrams and most other documentation directly from the tool.

3. *System Environment*. This section describes the constraints, or conditions, affecting the system, including any requirements that involve operations, hardware, systems software, or security. Examples of operational constraints include transaction volumes that must be supported, data storage requirements, processing schedules, reporting deadlines, and online response times.

4. *Implementation Requirements*. In this section, you specify startup processing, initial data entry or acquisition, user training requirements, and software test plans.

5. *Time and Cost Estimates*. This section provides detailed schedules, cost estimates, and staffing requirements for the systems development phase and revised projections for the remainder of the SDLC. You also present total costs-to-date for the project and compare those costs with your prior estimates.

6. *Appendices*. Supplemental material can be included in appendices at the end of the system design specification. In this section, you might include copies of documents from the first three phases if they would provide a helpful reference for readers.

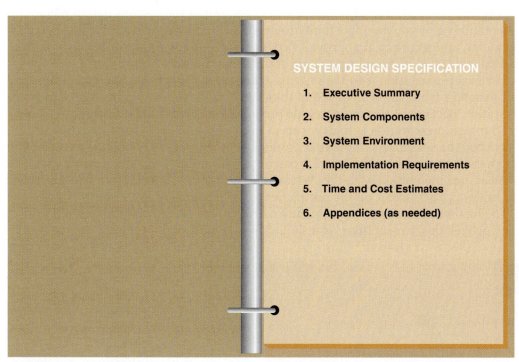

FIGURE 8-42   The organization of a typical system design specification.

User Approval

Users must review and approve the interface design, report and menu designs, data entry screens, source documents, and other areas of the system that affect them. The review and approval process continues throughout the systems design phase. When you complete the design for a report, you should meet with users to review the prototype, adjust the design if necessary, and obtain written approval. Chapter 6 of the textbook contains many suggestions regarding how to create attractive, effective report designs.

Securing approvals from users throughout the design phase is very important. That approach ensures that you do not have a major task of obtaining approvals at the end, it keeps the users involved with the system's development, and it gives you feedback

🔧 TOOLKIT TIME

The Communication Tools in Part 1 of the Systems Analyst's Toolkit can help you develop better reports and presentations. To learn more about these tools, turn to Part 1 of the six-part Toolkit that follows Chapter 10.

about whether or not you are on target. Some sections of the system design specification might not interest users, but anything that does affect them should be approved as early as possible.

Other IT department members also need to review the system design specification. IT management will be concerned with staffing, costs, hardware and systems software requirements, network impact, and the effect on the operating environment when the new system is added. The programming team will want to get ready for its role, and the operations group will be interested in processing support, report distribution, network loads, integration with other systems, and any hardware or software issues for which they need to prepare. You must be a good communicator to keep people up-to-date, obtain their input and suggestions, and obtain necessary approvals.

When the system design specification is complete, you distribute the document to a target group of users, IT department personnel, and company management. You should distribute the document at least one week before your presentation to allow the recipients enough time to review the material.

Presentations

Usually, you will give several presentations at the end of the systems design phase. The presentations give you an opportunity to explain the system, answer questions, consider comments, and secure final approval. Part 1 of the Systems Analyst's Toolkit can provide valuable guidelines and tips about oral presentations.

The first presentation is to the systems analysts, programmers, and technical support staff members who will be involved in future project phases or operational support for the system. Because of the audience, the presentation is technically oriented.

Your next presentation is to department managers and users from departments affected by the system. As in the first presentation, your primary objective is to obtain support and approval for the systems design. This is not a technical presentation; it is aimed at user interaction with the system and management's interest in budgets, schedules, staffing, and impact on the production environment.

The final presentation is for company management, as shown in Figure 8-43. By the time you give this presentation, you should have obtained all necessary approvals from prior presentations, and you should have the support of users and the IT department. Just like the management presentation at the end of the systems analysis phase, this presentation has a key objective: to obtain management's approval and support for the next development step — systems implementation — including a solid commitment for financial and other resources needed.

Based on the presentation and the data you submitted, management might reach one of three decisions: proceed with systems development, perform additional work on the systems design phase, or terminate the project. The next chapter discusses systems implementation, which is the fourth SDLC phase.

FIGURE 8-43 The presentation to management seeks approval and support for systems implementation, including a solid commitment for financial and other resources needed.

CHAPTER SUMMARY

An information system combines hardware, software, data, procedures, and people into a system architecture. The architecture translates the system's logical design into a physical structure that includes hardware, software, and processing methods. The software consists of application programs, also called applications, that handle the input, manage the processing logic, and provide the required output.

Before selecting an architecture, the analyst must consider enterprise resource planning, initial cost and TCO, scalability, Web integration, legacy interface requirements, processing options, and security issues.

Enterprise resource planning (ERP) establishes an enterprise-wide strategy for IT resources and specific standards for data, processing, network, and user interface design. Companies can extend ERP systems to suppliers and customers in a process called supply chain management. A systems analyst must assess initial cost and TCO and ensure that the design is scalable. Scalability means that a system can be expanded, modified, or downsized easily to meet business needs. The analyst also must consider if the system will be Web-centric and follow Internet design protocols, and if it must interface with existing systems, called legacy systems. System security is an important concern throughout the design process, especially for e-commerce applications that involve credit card and personal data. Processing options affect system design and resources required.

An architecture requires servers and clients. Servers are computers that supply data, processing services, or other support to one or more computers called clients. In mainframe architecture, the server performs all processing, and terminals communicate with the centralized system. Clients can be connected in distributed systems to form local area networks (LANs) or wide area networks (WANs). A typical LAN design involves file server design, where the client requests a copy of a data file and the server responds by transmitting the entire file to the client.

Client/server architecture divides processing between one or more clients and a central server. In a typical client/server system, the client handles the entire user interface, including data entry, data query, and screen presentation logic. The server stores the data and provides data access and database management functions. Application logic is divided in some manner between the server and the clients. In a typical client/server interaction, the client submits a request for information from the server, which carries out the operation and responds to the client. Compared to file server designs, client/server systems are more scalable and flexible.

A fat, or thick, client design places all or most of the application processing logic at the client. A thin client design places all or most of the processing logic at the server. Thin client designs provide better performance, because program code resides on the server, near the data. In contrast, a fat client handles more of the processing, and must access and update the data more often. Compared with maintaining a central server, fat client TCO also is higher, because of initial hardware and software requirements and the ongoing expense of maintaining and updating remote client computers. The fat client design is simpler to develop, because the architecture resembles traditional file server designs where all processing is performed at the client.

Client/server designs can be two-tier or three-tier (also called n-tier). In a two-tier design, the user interface resides on the client, all data resides on the server, and the application logic can run either on the server or on the client, or be divided between the client and the server. In a three-tier design, the user interface runs on the client and the data is stored on the server, just as with a two-tier design. A three-tier design also has a middle layer between the client and server that processes the client requests and translates them into data access commands that can be understood and carried out by the server.

The middle layer is called an application server, because it provides the application logic, or business logic. Middleware is software that connects dissimilar applications and enables them to communicate and pass data. In planning the system design, a systems analyst also must consider cost-benefit and performance issues.

The Internet has had an enormous impact on system architecture. In implementing a design, an analyst should consider e-commerce strategies, the availability of packaged solutions, and corporate portals, which are entrances to a multifunction Web site.

The primary processing methods are online and batch processing. Users interact directly with online systems that continuously process their transactions when and where they occur and continuously update files and databases. In contrast, batch systems process transactions in groups and execute them on a predetermined schedule. Many online systems also use batch processing to perform routine tasks, such as handling reports and accounting entries.

Networks allow the sharing of hardware, software, and data resources in order to reduce expenses and provide more capability to users. The network is represented by a seven-layer logical model called the OSI (open system interconnection) model. Various OSI layers handle specific functions as data flows down from the sending computer and up into the receiving computer.

The way a network is configured is called the network topology. Networks typically are arranged in four patterns: hierarchical, star, bus, and ring. A single mainframe computer usually controls a hierarchical network, a star network connects workstations to a central computer, a bus network connects workstations in a single-line communication path, and a ring network connects workstations in a circular communication path. Wireless networks, or WLANs, are becoming more common, especially in situations where the additional flexibility of wireless is important.

CASE tools can be used to model and document system architecture and network design. System management and support involves performance management, fault management, backup and disaster recovery, and file retention policies.

The system design specification presents the complete systems design for an information system and is the basis for the presentations that complete the systems design phase. Following the presentations, the project either progresses to the systems development phase, requires additional systems design work, or is terminated.

Key Terms and Phrases

24/7 *368*

802.11b *391*

802.11 High Rate *391*

802.11 network standard *391*

applications *367*

application logic *374*

application programs *367*

application server *374*

architecture *362*

backup *393*

batch processing *385*

bus network *389*

business logic *374*

centralized system *369*

client/server architecture *371*

clients *369*

corporate portal *382*

data processing center *369*

detailed design specification *396*

disaster recovery plan *393*

distributed database management
  system (DDBMS) *378*

distributed systems *370*

enterprise resource planning (ERP) *364*

environment *364*

extensibility *367*

fat client *374*

fault management *393*

fault-tolerant *394*

file retention *396*

file server *371*

file sharing architecture *371*

file transfer protocol (FTP) *391*

hierarchical network *388*

hub *389*

Institute of Electrical and Electronics
  Engineers (IEEE) *391*

journal file *394*

legacy data *372*

legacy systems *367*

local area network (LAN) *370*

log file *394*

mainframe architecture *369*

middleware *375*

network topology *388*

n-tier *374*

online system *384*

open database connectivity (ODBC) *410*

OSI (open system interconnection) model *387*

platform *364*

point-of-sale (POS) *386*

portal *382*

protocol *390*

RAID (redundant array of
  independent disks) *394*

recovery *393*

ring network *390*

scalability *367*

server *369*

stand-alone *370*

star network *389*

supply chain management *364*

system architecture *362*

system design specification *396*

technical design specification *396*

terminal *369*

thick client *374*

thin client *374*

three-tier *374*

Transmission Control Protocol/Internet
  Protocol (TCP/IP) *390*

transparent *370*

two-tier *374*

Web-centric *367*

Wi-Fi *391*

wide area network (WAN) *370*

wireless local area network (WLAN) *391*

Learn It Online

Instructions: To complete the Learn It Online exercises, start your browser, click the Address bar, and then enter the Web address **scsite.com/sad6e/learn**. When the Systems Analysis and Design Learn It Online page is displayed, follow the instructions in the exercises below. Each exercise has instructions for saving your results, either for your own records or for submission to your instructor.

1   Chapter Reinforcement

TF, MC, and SA

Below SAD Chapter 8, click the Chapter Reinforcement link. Print the quiz by clicking Print on the File menu for each page. Answer each question.

2   Flash Cards

Below SAD Chapter 8, click the Flash Cards link and read the instructions. Type 20 (or a number specified by your instructor) in the Number of playing cards text box, type your name in the Enter your Name text box, and then click the Flip Card button. When the flash card is displayed, read the question and then click the ANSWER box arrow to select an answer. Flip through the Flash Cards. If your score is 15 (75%) correct or greater, click Print on the File menu to print your results. If your score is less than 15 (75%) correct, then redo this exercise by clicking the Replay button.

3   Practice Test

Below SAD Chapter 8, click the Practice Test link. Answer each question, enter your first and last name at the bottom of the page, and then click the Grade Test button. When the graded practice test is displayed on your screen, click Print on the File menu to print a hard copy. Continue to take practice tests until you score 80% or better.

4   Who Wants To Be a Computer Genius?

Below SAD Chapter 8, click the Computer Genius link. Read the instructions, enter your first and last name at the bottom of the page, and then click the Play button. When your score is displayed, click the PRINT RESULTS link to print a hard copy.

5   Wheel of Terms

Below SAD Chapter 8, click the Wheel of Terms link. Read the instructions, and then enter your first and last name and your school name. Click the PLAY button. When your score is displayed on the screen, right-click the score and then click Print on the shortcut menu to print a hard copy.

6   Crossword Puzzle Challenge

Below SAD Chapter 8, click the Crossword Puzzle Challenge link. Read the instructions, and then enter your first and last name. Click the SUBMIT button. Work the crossword puzzle. When you are finished, click the Submit button. When the crossword puzzle is redisplayed, click the Print Puzzle button to print a hard copy.

Case-Sim: SCR Associates

Background

SCR Associates is a consulting firm that offers IT solutions and training. SCR needs an information system to manage operations at its new training center. The new system will be called TIMS (Training Information Management System). As a newly hired systems analyst, you will report to Jesse Baker, systems group manager. You will work on various tasks and practice the skills you learned in this chapter.

Using the Case

The SCR Associates case study is a Web-based simulation that allows you to practice your skills in a real-world environment. The case study transports you to SCR's company intranet, where you can complete 10 work sessions, each aligning with a chapter. As you work on the case, you will receive e-mail and voice mail messages, obtain information from SCR's online libraries, and perform various tasks. The first time you enter the SCR Case, you should go to the Starting page at **scsite.com/sad6e/scr** for detailed instructions.

Preview: Session 8

Your supervisor, Jesse Baker, wants you to be familiar with the main issues that a systems analyst should consider when selecting an architecture, including enterprise resource planning, initial costs and TCO, scalability, Web integration, legacy interface requirements, processing options, and security issues.

To start a work session, you log on to the SCR intranet. When you enter your name and password, an opening screen displays links to the work sessions, and you select Session 8. At this point, you check your e-mail and voice mail messages carefully. Then you begin working on your task list, which includes the following items:

Tasks: System Architecture Tasks

1. Jesse wants me to recommend a vendor who offers an ERP strategy. I need to review the SAP and Oracle Web sites, and at least two others that offer ERP solutions, and reply to her with the results and the reasons for my recommendations.

2. Visit SCR's data library to review SCR's network configuration and then send Jesse a recommendation for the TIMS system architecture. She wants me to suggest an overall client/server design, number of tiers, and network topology. She also asked me to comment on these issues: legacy data, Web-centricity, scalability, security, and batch processing that might be needed. Jesse said it was OK to make reasonable assumptions in my proposal to her.

3. Search the Internet for a network monitoring product. Describe its features, specifications, and price. Also do research on the Internet to learn more about TCO, and develop a TCO checklist that includes the five most important elements of TCO, because of their magnitude or potential impact on TIMS.

4. Prepare a system design specification as Jesse requested.

FIGURE 8-44 Task list: Session 8.

Chapter Exercises

Review Questions

1. Define the term system architecture. Define the term scalability, and explain why it is important to consider scalability in system design.
2. When selecting an architecture, what items should a systems analyst consider as part of the overall design checklist?
3. What is enterprise resource planning (ERP) and why is it important? What is supply chain management?
4. Explain the term server and provide an example of server-based processing; explain the term client and provide an example of client-based processing.
5. Describe client/server architecture, including fat and thin clients, client/server tiers, and middleware.
6. Describe the impact of the Internet on system architecture. Include examples.
7. Explain the difference between online processing and batch processing and provide an example of each type.
8. Explain the difference between a LAN and a WAN, define the term topology, and draw a sketch of each network model.
9. Explain system management and support tools and concepts, including performance management, fault management, backup and disaster recovery, and file retention.
10. List the sections of a system design specification, and describe the contents.

Discussion Topics

1. Information technology has advanced dramatically in recent years. At the same time, enormous changes in the business world have occurred as companies reflect global competition and more pressure for quality, speed, and customer service. Did the new technology inspire the business changes, or was it the other way around? Explain your answer.
2. Internet-based sales have shown explosive growth in recent years. Actually, business-to-business, or B2B, Internet volume is increasing even more rapidly than business-to-consumer, or B2C volume. How does B2B interaction differ from consumer-based Internet marketing, and why might this be so?
3. This chapter described seven guidelines that a systems analyst might use when considering an architecture. In your view, are all the items of equal weight and importance, or should some be ranked higher? Justify your position.
4. One manager states, "When a new system is proposed, I want a written report, not an oral presentation. I only want to see the facts about costs, benefits, and schedules. Systems analysts shouldn't attempt to sell a system in an oral presentation." Do you agree with that point of view? Explain your position.

Projects

1. Visit the IT department at your school or a local company to determine what type of network it is using. Draw a sketch of the network configuration.
2. Perform research on the Internet or visit a local computer store to find out more about network performance monitoring products. Write a brief memo with your results.
3. Perform research on the Internet to identify an ASP that offers Web-based business solutions, and write a brief memo describing the firm and its services.
4. Perform research on the Internet to find out more about fat and thin client hardware and costs. Submit your results, with examples.

Apply Your Knowledge

The Apply Your Knowledge section contains four mini-cases. Each case describes a situation, explains your role in the case, and asks you to respond to questions. You can answer the questions by applying knowledge you learned in the chapter.

1   Digital Dynamics

Situation:

After three years as a successful Web design firm in Southern California, Digital Dynamics has decided to add two new business ventures: a group that specializes in supplying qualified employees to high-tech firms and a training division that offers online courses in advanced Web design and e-commerce skills. As a senior systems analyst, you have been asked to study the situation and make recommendations.

1. Should Digital Dynamics adopt ERP? What specific advantages would ERP offer?
2. How could the concept of supply chain management apply to a company's service-based division? Provide some specific suggestions.
3. Should Digital Dynamics use separate portals for employees, customers, and suppliers? If you follow the example of Oracle Corporation in the textbook, what type of portal design would you suggest?
4. Is the experience of other companies relevant? Use the Internet to locate examples of Web-based firms that offer personnel services and technical training. How would you evaluate the Web sites you visited? What specific features impressed you favorably or unfavorably?

2   R/Way Trucking

Situation:

As you learned earlier in this chapter, R/Way is a small but rapidly growing trucking company headquartered in Cleveland, Ohio. R/Way's information system currently consists of a file server and three workstations where freight clerks enter data, track shipments, and prepare freight bills. To perform their work, the clerks obtain data from a file server and use database and spreadsheet programs stored on stand-alone PCs to process the data. At your meeting yesterday, R/Way's president approved your recommendation to create a relational database to handle R/Way operations and provide links for R/Way shippers and customers.

1. Review the concept of supply chain management. Although R/Way offers services rather than products, could that concept apply to the design of R/Way's new system? If so, how?
2. What would be the advantages of selecting an Internet-based architecture for R/Way's system?
3. Should R/Way's new system be based on file-server or client/server architecture? Why?
4. What would be the pros and cons of selecting in-house development versus a packaged solution for the R/Way system?

3 Nothing But Net

Situation:

Nothing But Net is an IT consulting firm that specializes in e-commerce solutions. As a newly hired systems analyst, you have been asked to research some current topics.

1. Obtain at least two estimates of how much consumers are projected to spend on Internet purchases during the next three years. Are the estimates similar? If not, which forecast do you believe, and why?

2. Many of Nothing But Net's customers are startup firms that must fight hard to attract investment capital, and many traditional lending institutions are skeptical of new Web-based firms. Perform research to determine the mortality rate of new e-commerce firms that use the Web as their primary marketing channel, and write a brief memo that describes the results of your research.

3. Some IT professionals predict that traditional companies will increase their Internet marketing efforts, making it even harder for new Web-based firms to compete. Perform research to find out more about the topic and share your results with the class.

4. Suppose you were asked to draft a sales brochure for Nothing But Net. List all the services in which potential customers might be interested.

4 Aunt Ann's Kitchen

Situation:

Aunt Ann's Kitchen offers a line of specialty food products to institutional customers and restaurant chains. The firm prides itself on using only the finest ingredients and preparation methods. The owner, Ann Rose, hired you as an IT consultant to help her plan the system architecture for a new sales and marketing system. She asked you to start with the following questions:

1. What opportunities do you see for building supply chain management features into the new system?

2. What client/server design features might increase network performance for the new system?

3. What are the advantages of developing a Web-centric design for the new system?

4. What security concerns exist and how could you resolve them?

Case Studies

Case studies allow you to practice specific skills learned in the chapter. Each chapter contains several case studies that continue throughout the textbook, and a chapter capstone case.

NEW CENTURY HEALTH CLINIC

New Century Health Clinic offers preventive medicine and traditional medical care. In your role as an IT consultant, you will help New Century develop a new information system.

Background

The New Century clinic associates accepted your interface, output, input, and data designs and your recommendation to install a server and four personal computers as clients on a local area network. The network will include a tape backup unit and Internet access via a modem that can exchange data with insurance companies. A high-speed laser printer and an impact printer for multipart forms will be accessible by any of the four PCs. Now you will determine system architecture for the New Century system.

When you created ERDs and record designs for New Century during the data design process in Chapter 8, you considered whether to use a file-processing or database approach. As you know, each strategy has advantages and disadvantages, depending on the specific hardware and software environment and business requirements. At this point, you must decide which way to proceed, and Dr. Jones will accept your recommendation (with your instructor's approval). You should start by reviewing the DFDs and object-oriented diagrams that you prepared in the systems analysis phase, and the ERDs and table designs that you created in the systems design phase. Then, review the system architecture checklist at the beginning of this chapter.

Assignments

1. What would be the advantages of selecting an Internet-based architecture for the New Century system?
2. Should the New Century system be based on file-server or client/server architecture? Why?
3. Could the New Century system use both online and batch processing? How?
4. Prepare an outline for a system design specification and describe the contents of each section.

PERSONAL TRAINER, INC.

Personal Trainer, Inc., owns and operates fitness centers in a dozen Midwestern cities. The centers have done well, and the company is planning an international expansion by opening a new "supercenter" in the Toronto area. Personal Trainer's president, Cassia Umi, hired an IT consultant, Susan Park, to help develop an information system for the new facility. During the project, Susan will work closely with Gray Lewis, who will manage the new operation.

Background

Susan and Gray finished their work on the user interface, input, and output design. They developed a user-centered design that would be easy to learn and use. Now Susan turned her attention to the architecture for the new system.

Susan wanted to consider enterprise resource planning, total cost of ownership, scalability, Web integration, legacy systems, processing methods, and security issues. She also needed to select a network plan, or topology, that would dictate the physical cabling and network connections, or consider a wireless network.

Finally, she planned to consider system management issues, including performance, fault detection, backup, and disaster recovery. When all these tasks were completed, she would submit a system design specification for approval.

Assignments

1. Would an ERP strategy work well for Personal Trainer? Investigate ERP strategies and products available from Internet vendors and submit a recommendation based on your research.

2. If Susan chooses a client/server architecture, what issues must she consider? Prepare a checklist for her that includes the main topics and issues she should consider.

3. What are your recommendations for backup and disaster recovery for the new system?

4. Prepare an outline for a system design specification and describe the contents of each section.

CHAPTER CAPSTONE CASE: SoftWear, Limited   **SWL**

SoftWear, Limited (SWL), is a continuing case study that illustrates the knowledge and skills described in each chapter. In this case study, the student acts as a member of the SWL systems development team and performs various tasks.

Background

Jane Rossman, manager of applications, and Rick Williams, systems analyst, had several meetings with True Blue Systems, the consulting firm hired to assist SWL in implementing the new ESIP system. Michael Jeremy, SWL's finance vice president, requested that True Blue also make recommendations about a possible SWL intranet to link all SWL locations and support client/server architecture.

The initial report from True Blue indicated that the new ESIP system should be designed as a DBMS so it could interface with the new mainframe payroll package. True Blue suggested that the ESIP system be implemented on a server in the payroll department and developed as a Microsoft Access application. They felt that this approach provided a relational database environment, client/server capability, and SQL command output to communicate with the mainframe. Figure 8-45 shows the proposed design of the system.

Jane Rossman met with Ann Hon to review True Blue's report and get her approval for training IT staff members. Jane had some prior experience in Access application development, but Rick had none, so Jane suggested that Rick and Becky Evans, another systems analyst, should attend a one-week workshop. Ann agreed.

Ann, Jane, and Rick met with Michael Jeremy to get his approval before proceeding further. He asked them to develop a specific budget and timetable including all necessary hardware, software, and training costs. They had most of the information, but they needed some help from True Blue to estimate the cost of network implementation, installation, and physical cabling.

The first phase of the project would use a local area network to link the various headquarter departments to the mainframe. A second phase, proposed by True Blue, would connect all SWL locations to a wide area network, with the possibility that employees could access their individual ESIP accounts over the internal network or from outside the company using the Internet.

A week later, Ann received a memo from Michael Jeremy that said he had approved the project and that she should start work immediately.

System Architecture

The ESIP development team included Jane, Rick, and Becky. The group discovered that the Microsoft Access application consists of interactive objects such as tables, queries, forms, reports, macros, and code modules.

FIGURE 8-45 Diagram of the proposed ESIP system.

They decided to begin by reviewing the entity-relationship diagrams they prepared previously to determine the overall structure of the DBMS design. Then they identified the tables, reviewed the relationships among them, and analyzed the record designs they had developed.

They also reviewed output requirements, input screen designs, processing considerations, backup and recovery procedures, and controls that must be built into the new system.

As recommended by True Blue Systems, the new ESIP system would be implemented as a client/server design, with the data stored on the payroll department server, which would be linked to clients in the payroll and human resources department.

Planning the System

In their first meeting, Jane asked the team to define all the tasks that the new system would perform, including a list of all reports and other required output. Jane explained that ESIP data would be stored on the server, but the application logic and objects such as forms, queries, and reports would be located on client workstations. Separating the objects from the data would provide better security and reduce the network loads, she explained.

Security Issues

In their next planning session, Jane asked the group to consider all security issues affecting the new system design. Because the system contains payroll data, it is important to control user access and updates. The team decided to use the security features in Access for control, including passwords and user and workgroup accounts for employees authorized to use the ESIP application. Each user would be assigned a permission level that grants access only to certain objects.

Jane explained her plan for system security by saying, "We'll create a comprehensive security plan later that will cover all the operational security issues for the new system. Meanwhile, let's go back to the department heads, Michael Jeremy and Tina Pham, to get their input on what the security levels should be." She added that "Users will be allowed to create and modify certain forms and reports, but most other actions will be permitted only by authorized IT department members."

Creating the Database Objects

Before creating the database objects, the team reviewed the ERDs and verified that the records designs were in 3NF. In addition, they verified that the new payroll system permitted cross-platform access because the ESIP system required data from the payroll master file. They discovered that the payroll package used a standard data format called **open database connectivity (ODBC)** that supported links to the Access database. After planning the system, they started creating the objects.

Planning the User Interface

From earlier interviews, the IT team knew that users in the payroll and human resources departments wanted an interface that would be easy to learn and simple to operate. Jane asked Becky to start designing a main form, or switchboard, that would display automatically when the ESIP application started. All ESIP screen forms would use buttons, menus, and icons as shown in Figure 8-46.

Becky created a prototype of the input screens to show to users. After securing user approval, the screen designs were added to the system specification document for the ESIP system.

CHAPTER CAPSTONE CASE: SoftWear, Limited (continued)

Using Visual Basic and Macros

Because she was a programmer before her assignment as a systems analyst, Becky wanted to know if they would be using Visual Basic as a program development language. Jane told her that they would write many of the procedures in Visual Basic because it allows more powerful data manipulation than macros and makes it easier to customize error messages. They would use macros, however, to speed up the development process and handle simple tasks such as opening and closing forms and running reports.

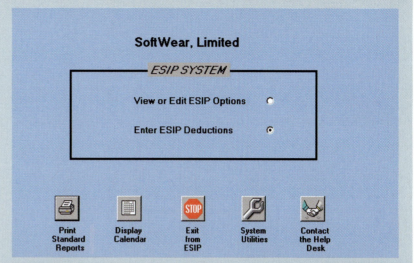

FIGURE 8-46 Sample of a main switchboard that displays when the ESIP system starts.

Completing the Systems Design Phase

The IT team completed the systems design phase by writing the documentation and designing backup and recovery, file retention, and start-up procedures. The final step was to develop a system design specification for the ESIP system.

Rick and Becky showed a draft of the system design specification to Jane and Ann. After incorporating their changes, they e-mailed copies to a distribution list of users, IT staff members, and managers. Their presentations to users and IT staff members went well, and at the management presentation, they received final approval to implement the ESIP system.

SWL Team Tasks

1. Rick Williams asked you to suggest software products that can provide network management features suitable for a network with 25–50 users. You can use the Internet to research the topic.

2. In the Background section of the SWL case, you learned that True Blue Systems had recommended a local area network to link the various headquarters departments to the SWL mainframe. Should a wireless network have been considered? Your task is to research wireless network products and submit a recommendation for a WLAN installation, supported by an explanation of wireless advantages and possible limitations. Be sure to consider flexibility, scalability, and security issues.

3. Assume that the recommendation you made in the preceding task was accepted. Now you have been asked to develop a specific budget for a WLAN that would consist of 50 workstations. You need to research the TCO of this project, including the cost of hardware, software, installation, and maintenance. You can make reasonable assumptions where you might not have specific facts, but you should state those assumptions clearly.

4. Rick also wants you to start thinking about security issues for a company-wide security policy he will be developing later. He asked you to think about a fundamental question, and let him know your views. The question is "Who is ultimately responsible for security — users, management, or the IT department?" Write a brief memo to Rick explaining your views, and your reasoning.

PHASE 4 SYSTEMS IMPLEMENTATION

Systems Implementation is the fourth of five phases in the systems development life cycle (SDLC). In the previous phase, systems design, you developed a physical model that included data design, user interface, input and output design, and system architecture. Now you will begin systems implementation tasks, including application development, testing, documentation, training, data conversion, system changeover, and post-implementation evaluation of the results. At the conclusion of the systems implementation phase, users will be working with the system on a day-to-day basis, and you will focus on system operation, security, and support, which is the final phase in the SDLC.

PHASE TOPIC

Chapter 9
Systems Implementation

DELIVERABLE

A completely functioning
information system.

TOOLKIT SUPPORT

Primary tools: Communications,
CASE, and project management
tools. Other tools as required.

CHAPTER 9 Systems Implementation

CHAPTER 9 describes the systems implementation phase of the SDLC. This chapter describes application development, installation, and evaluation.

INTRODUCTION

OBJECTIVES

When you finish this chapter, you will be able to:

- Explain the importance of software quality assurance and software engineering
- Describe the application development process
- Draw a structure chart showing top-down design, modular design, cohesion, and coupling
- Explain the coding process and how code is generated
- Explain unit testing, integration testing, and system testing
- Differentiate between program, system, operations, and user documentation
- List the main steps in system installation and evaluation
- Develop an overall training plan with specific objectives for each group of participants, compare in-house and outside training providers, and describe effective training techniques
- Describe the data conversion process
- Identify and describe changeover methods
- Explain post-implementation evaluation
- Describe the final report to management

During systems implementation, you will learn about application development, testing, documentation, training, data conversion, system changeover, and post-implementation evaluation of the results.

In the systems implementation phase, the system design specification serves as a blueprint for constructing the new system. The initial task is application development, which requires systems analysts and programmers to work together to construct the necessary programs and code modules. Before a changeover can occur, the system must be tested and documented carefully, users must be trained, and existing data must be converted. After the new system is operational, a formal evaluation of the results takes place as part of a final report to management.

CHAPTER INTRODUCTION CASE: Mountain View College Bookstore

Background: Wendy Lee, manager of college services at Mountain View College, wants a new information system that will improve efficiency and customer service at the three college bookstores.

In this part of the case, Florence Fullerton (systems analyst) and Harry Boston (student intern) are talking about implementation tasks for the new system.

Participants:	Wendy, Florence, and Harry
Location:	Wendy Lee's office, Monday morning, February 6, 2006
Project status:	The system design specification was approved, and Florence and Harry are ready to implement the new bookstore information system.
Discussion topics:	Implementation tasks, including quality assurance, structure charts, testing, training, data conversion process, system changeover, and post-implementation evaluation

Florence:	Good morning, Wendy. We're ready to start the implementation process, and I'd like to go over our plans. Harry will be assisting me, so I asked him to join us.
Wendy:	*I'm glad you did. I met Harry during the interviews several months ago.*
Harry:	Hi, Wendy, good to see you again.
Florence:	OK, let's get started. First of all, we'll focus on quality assurance right from the start. We're also looking at a structured approach called software engineering to guide us.
Wendy:	*Sounds good. What are the major tasks on your list?*
Florence:	Well, the biggest task is to translate the physical design model into actual program code and produce a functioning system that we can test. In that process, we'll develop structure charts that the programmers in the IT department can use as blueprints, and I'll work with them every step of the way. Harry will help me coordinate with the people actually writing the code.
Harry:	It will be great to see all the design work finally turn into a functioning system.
Florence:	It sure will. Anyway, we'll proceed to do several types of testing, and we'll document everything we do. When we're ready, we'll put the new system into what's called a test environment until we're ready to go online with the operational environment.
Wendy:	*What about training?*
Florence:	Good question. We'll consider several kinds of training — we'll see what's available or we might do our own.
Wendy:	*Then what?*
Florence:	The final steps will be data conversion and system changeover. After the new system is up and running, we'll schedule a formal evaluation and submit a final report. Here's a task list to get us started.

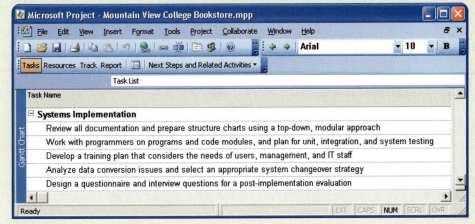

FIGURE 9-1

ON THE WEB

For more information about Software Engineering, visit **scsite.com/sad6e/ more**, locate Chapter 9 and then click the Software Engineering link.

SOFTWARE QUALITY ASSURANCE

In today's competitive business environment, companies are intensely concerned with the quality of their products and services. A successful organization constantly must improve quality in every area, including its information systems. Top management must provide the leadership, encouragement, and support needed for high-quality IT resources.

No matter how carefully a system is designed and implemented, problems can occur, especially in a complex system. Rigorous testing catches errors in the implementation stage, but it is much less expensive to correct mistakes earlier in the development process. The main objective of **quality assurance** is to avoid problems or to detect them as soon as possible. Poor quality can result from inaccurate requirements, design problems, coding errors, faulty documentation, and ineffective testing.

In an effort to achieve high standards of quality, software systems developers should consider software engineering concepts, internationally recognized quality standards, and careful project management techniques.

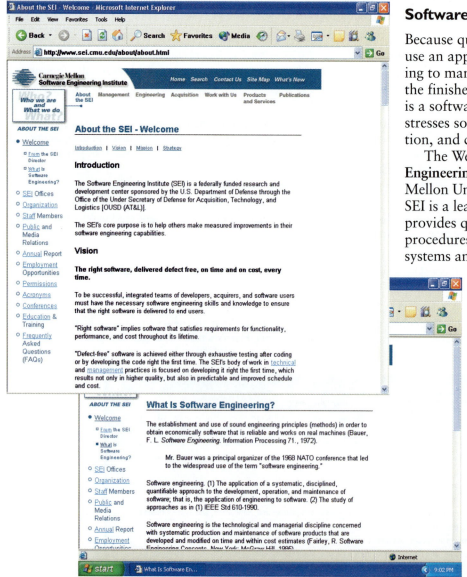

Software Engineering

Because quality is so important, you can use an approach called software engineering to manage and improve the quality of the finished system. **Software engineering** is a software development process that stresses solid design, accurate documentation, and careful testing.

The Web site for the **Software Engineering Institute (SEI)** at Carnegie Mellon University is shown in Figure 9-2. SEI is a leader in software engineering and provides quality standards and suggested procedures for software developers and systems analysts. SEI's primary objective is to find better, faster, and less expensive methods of software development. To achieve that goal, SEI designed a set of software development standards called the **Capability Maturity Model (CMM)**®, which has been used successfully by thousands of organizations around the globe. The purpose of the model, which was introduced in 1991, was to improve software quality, reduce development time, and cut costs. More recently, SEI established a new model, called **Capability Maturity Model Integration (CMMI)**®, that integrates software and systems development into a much larger framework called **process improvement**.

FIGURE 9-2 The Software Engineering Institute (SEI) provides leadership in software engineering that improves the quality of systems that depend on software.

According to SEI, "The quality of a product is largely determined by the quality of the process that is used to develop and maintain it." By seeing software as part of a larger process, rather than as an end in itself, the CMMI® extends the original CMM® concept into what SEI calls "... the next generation model." An excellent CMMI® tutorial is available at www.sei.cmu.edu/cmmi/presentations/euro-sepg-tutorial/sld001.htm.

The CMMI® tracks an organization's processes, using five maturity levels, from Level 1, which is referred to as unpredictable, poorly controlled, and reactive, to Level 5, in which the optimal result is process improvement. The five CMM® levels are shown in Figure 9-3.

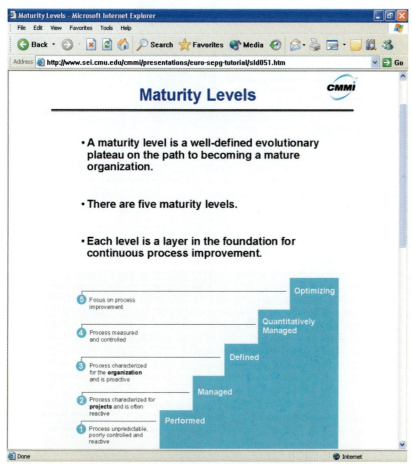

FIGURE 9-3 The CMMI® includes five maturity levels, from Level 1, which is referred to as unpredictable, poorly controlled, and reactive, to Level 5, in which the optimal result is process improvement.

TOOLKIT TIME

The Project Management tools in Part 4 of the Systems Analyst's Toolkit can help you plan, manage, and control complex information systems projects. To learn more about these tools, turn to Part 4 of the six-part Toolkit that follows Chapter 10.

International Organization for Standardization (ISO)

You learned in Chapter 7 that the International Organization for Standardization (ISO) is a worldwide body that establishes quality standards for products and services, as shown in Figure 9-4 on the next page. ISO standards include everything from internationally recognized symbols, such as those shown in Figure 9-5 on the next page, to the ISBN numbering system that identifies this textbook. In addition, ISO seeks to offer a global consensus of what constitutes good management practices — practices that can help firms deliver consistently high-quality products and services.

Because software is so important to a company's success, many firms seek assurance that software systems, either purchased or developed in-house, will meet rigid quality standards. In 1991, ISO established a set of guidelines called ISO 9000-3, which provided a quality assurance framework for developing and maintaining software. A company can

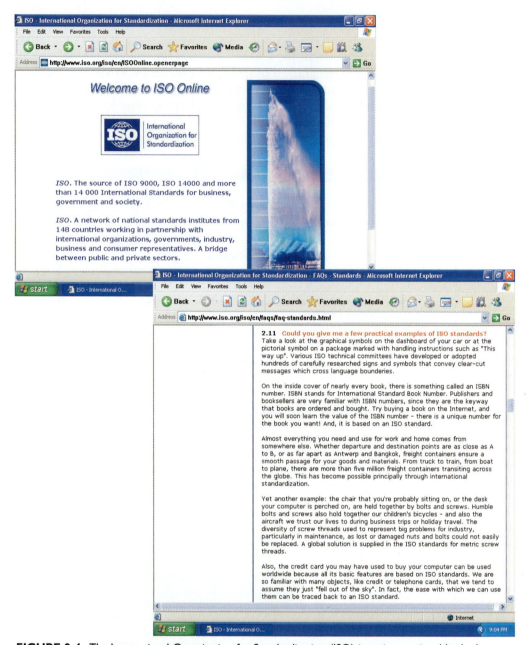

FIGURE 9-4 The International Organization for Standardization (ISO) is an international body that establishes quality standards for products and services, including software development.

ON THE WEB

For more information about ISO, visit **scsite.com/sad6e/ more**, locate Chapter 9 and then click the ISO link.

FIGURE 9-5 ISO standards include internationally recognized symbols.

specify ISO 9000-3 standards when it purchases software from a supplier or use ISO guidelines for in-house software development to ensure that the final result measures up to ISO standards. ISO requires a specific development plan, which outlines a step-by-step process for transforming user requirements into a finished product. ISO standards can be quite detailed. For example, ISO requires that a software supplier document all testing and maintain records of test results. If problems are found, they must be resolved, and any modules affected must be retested. Additionally, software and hardware specifications of all test equipment must be documented and included in the test records.

OVERVIEW OF APPLICATION DEVELOPMENT

Application development is the process of constructing the programs and code modules that serve as the building blocks of the information system. In Chapter 1, you learned that structured analysis and object-oriented (O-O) analysis are two popular systems analysis methods. Whether an application is implemented as a structured or object-oriented design, the objective is to translate the logical design into program and code modules that will function properly.

Creation of the System Design

At this point, it might be helpful to review the tasks involved in the creation of the system design.

- In Chapter 3, you learned about requirements modeling and how to use functional decomposition diagrams (FDDs) to break complex business operations down into smaller units, or functions.

- In Chapter 4, you learned about structured data and process modeling, and you created data flow diagrams (DFDs). You also developed process descriptions for functional primitive processes that documented the business logic and processing requirements.

- In Chapter 5, you selected a development strategy.

- In Chapter 6, you planned the system's output and designed the user interface.

- In Chapter 7, you worked with data design issues, analyzed relationships between system entities, and constructed entity-relationship diagrams (ERDs).

- In Chapter 8, you considered an overall system architecture.

- If you used object-oriented analysis, you learned about object modeling in several chapters, and in Part 5 of the Systems Analyst's Toolkit, where you saw how an information system can be represented by objects that contain both data and processes, called methods, which act on the data.

Taken together, this set of tasks produced an overall design and a plan for physical implementation.

Application Development Steps

Whether you used structured or object-oriented (O-O) analysis, you now are ready to translate the design into a functioning application. Building a new system requires careful planning. After an overall strategy is established, individual modules must be designed, coded, tested, and documented. A **module** consists of related program code organized into small units that are easy to understand and maintain. After the modules are developed and tested individually, more testing takes place, along with thorough documentation of the entire system, as shown in Figure 9-6.

When you create modules, you start by reviewing documentation from prior SDLC phases and creating a set of program designs. At this point, you will learn whether your ongoing documentation efforts were adequate. If you built a documentation file early in the development process, and added to it regularly,

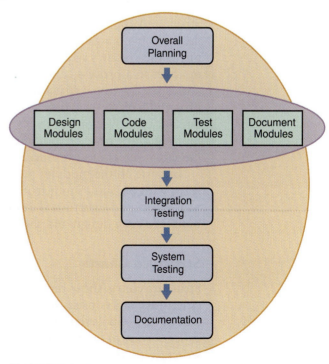

FIGURE 9-6 The main steps in application development.

ON THE WEB

For more information about Application Development, visit **scsite.com/sad6e/more**, locate Chapter 9 and then click the Application Development link.

you now have a valuable repository of information about the system. In addition to the system design specification, you will refer to DFDs, process descriptions, ERDs, and anything else that describes the functions that a program or module must perform and its relationship to other programs and modules.

Some documentation, such as screen layouts, report layouts, source documents, and data dictionary entries, must be reviewed regardless of whether you used a structured or object-oriented analysis method. If you used an object-oriented approach, however, you also will review your object model, including use case diagrams, class diagrams, object-relationship diagrams, sequence diagrams, and state-transition diagrams.

After the design is created, coding can begin. Although programmers typically perform the actual coding, IT managers usually assign systems analysts to work with them as part of a team effort. The module then is tested as a unit, and all necessary documentation is prepared and checked.

Project Management

Regardless of whether structured analysis or object-oriented design methods are used, even a modest-sized project might have hundreds or even thousands of modules. For this reason, application development can become quite complex and difficult to manage. At this stage, project management is especially important. Users and managers are looking forward to the new system, and it is very important to set realistic schedules, meet project deadlines, control costs, and maintain quality. To achieve these goals, the systems analyst or project manager should use project management tools and techniques similar to those described in Part 4 of the Systems Analyst's Toolkit to monitor and control the development effort.

The following sections describe the application development process. Structured development techniques and tools are discussed first, followed by object-oriented development methods.

STRUCTURED APPLICATION DEVELOPMENT

Structured application development usually involves a **top-down approach,** which proceeds from a general design to a detailed structure. After a systems analyst documents the system's requirements, he or she breaks the system down into subsystems and modules in a process called **partitioning.** This approach also is called **modular design** and is similar to constructing a leveled set of DFDs. By assigning modules to different programmers, several development areas can proceed at the same time. As explained in Part 4 of the Systems Analyst's Toolkit, you can use project management software to monitor work on each module, forecast overall development time, estimate required human and technical resources, and calculate a critical path for the project.

Because all the modules must work together properly, an analyst must proceed carefully, with constant input from programmers and IT management to achieve a sound, well-integrated structure. The analyst also must ensure that integration capability is built into each design and thoroughly tested.

Structure Charts

Structure charts show the program modules and the relationships among them. A **structure chart** consists of rectangles that represent the program modules, with arrows and other symbols that provide additional information. Typically, a higher-level module, called a **control module,** directs lower-level modules, called **subordinate modules.** In a structure chart, symbols represent various actions or conditions. Structure chart symbols represent modules, data couples, control couples, conditions, and loops.

MODULE A rectangle represents a module, as shown in Figure 9-7. Vertical lines at the edges of a rectangle indicate that module 1.3 is a library module. A **library module** is reusable code and can be invoked from more than one point in the chart.

DATA COUPLE An arrow with an empty circle represents a data couple. A **data couple** shows data that one module passes to another. In the data couple example shown in Figure 9-8, the Look Up Customer Name module exchanges data with the Maintain Customer Data module.

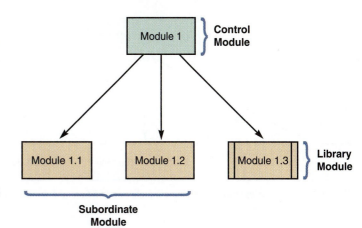

FIGURE 9-7 An example of structure chart modules.

CONTROL COUPLE An arrow with a filled circle represents a control couple. A **control couple** shows a message, also called a **flag**, which one module sends to another. In the example shown in Figure 9-9, the Update Customer File module sends an Account Overdue flag back to the Maintain Customer Data module. A module uses a flag to signal a specific condition or action to another module.

CONDITION A line with a diamond on one end represents a condition. A **condition** line indicates that a control module determines which subordinate modules will be invoked, depending on a specific condition. In the example shown in Figure 9-10 on the next page, Sort Inventory Parts is a control module with a condition line that triggers one of the three subordinate modules.

LOOP A curved arrow represents a loop. A **loop** indicates that one or more modules are repeated. In the example shown in Figure 9-11 on the next page, the Get Student Grades and Calculate GPA modules are repeated.

Cohesion and Coupling

Cohesion and coupling are important tools for evaluating the overall design. As explained in the following sections, it is desirable to have modules that are highly cohesive and loosely coupled.

Cohesion measures a module's scope and processing characteristics. A module that performs a single function or task has a high degree of cohesion, which is desirable. Because it focuses on a single task, a cohesive module is much easier to code and reuse. For example, a module named Verify Customer Number is more cohesive than a module named Calculate And Print Statements. If you notice the word *and* in a module name, you know that more than one task is involved. If a module must perform multiple tasks, more complex coding is required and the module will be more difficult to create and maintain.

FIGURE 9-8 An example of a structure chart data couple.

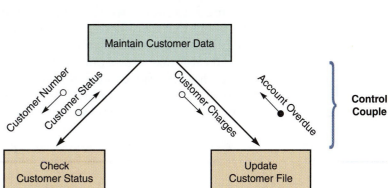

FIGURE 9-9 An example of a structure chart control couple.

Another way to understand cohesion is to remember what you did during data and process modeling. To create a leveled set of DFDs, you identified processes, and then broke the processes down into functional primitives that performed a single task. Now, during application development, you must translate those functional primitives into

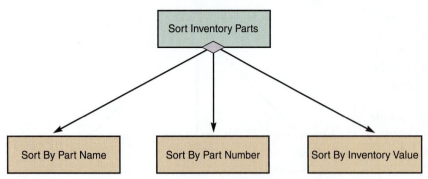

FIGURE 9-10 An example of a structure chart condition and condition lines.

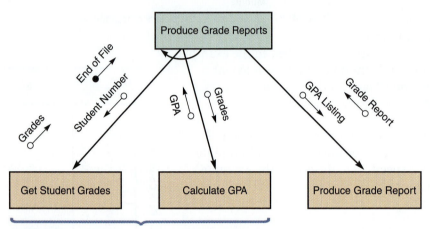

The curved arrow indicates that these modules are repeated.

FIGURE 9-11 An example of a structure chart loop.

cohesive modules. If you need to make a module more cohesive, you can split it into separate units, each of which performs a single function. In the example shown in Figure 9-12, the task called Check Customer Status actually consists of two separate tasks: Check Customer Number and Check Customer Credit Limit. Notice that Example A is less cohesive than Example B, because it combines the two tasks into a single module, while Example B treats them as separate modules. By treating the tasks as separate modules, you achieve more cohesion and better program quality.

Coupling describes the relationships and interdependence among modules. Modules that are independent are **loosely coupled**, which is desirable. Loosely coupled modules are easier to maintain and modify, because the logic in one module does not affect other modules. If a programmer needs to update a loosely coupled module, he or she can accomplish the task in a single location. If modules are **tightly coupled**, one module refers to internal logic contained in another module. For example, a Calculate GPA module might refer to an internal variable, such as Student Status, contained in another module called Update Student Status. In that case, a logic error in the second module affects the first module's processing sequence.

Figure 9-13 shows two examples of coupling. In the tightly coupled example on the right, notice that the subordinate module, Calculate Current Charges, depends on a status flag that it receives from the control module, Update Customer Balance. A **status flag** is an indicator that allows one module to send a message to another module. Passing status flags down from a control module generally is regarded as poor design, because logic problems in the control module can affect logic and coding in the subordinate module. In contrast, the loosely coupled modules on the left are logically independent. Rather

FIGURE 9-12 An example of structure chart cohesion.

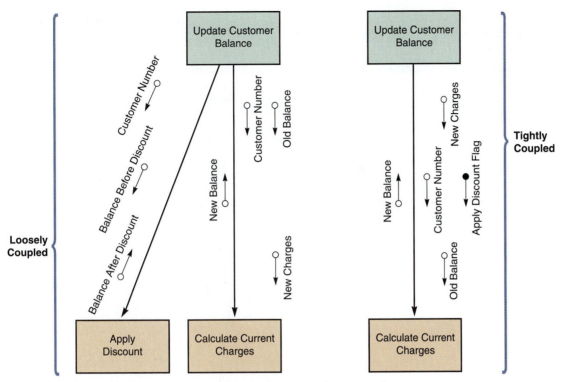

FIGURE 9-13 An example of loosely coupled and tightly coupled structure charts.

than passing a flag down to the subordinate module, the control module allows the Apply Discount module to handle discount processing independently. Logic errors, if any, are confined to the Apply Discount module, where they can be detected and resolved more easily.

Structure Chart Examples

Several of the structure chart samples in this section are based on material found in Chapter 4. For example, Figure 9-14 shows the initial design for a structure chart based on the sales promotion policy that was described in structured English in Figure 4-37 on page 175. The module named Process Sales Promotion Actions is a control module with four subordinate modules. Data couples and control couples have not yet been added. Notice the loop symbol, which represents repetitive processing.

FIGURE 9-14 Initial design for a structure chart based on the sales promotion policy that was described in structured English in Figure 4-37 on page 175.

In another example, Figure 9-15 shows a structure chart based on a Grading System DFD that was described in Figure 4-15 on page 159. Notice that each subordinate module exchanges data with a higher-level control module. Each module appears to perform a single task and is cohesive. The modules are independent and loosely coupled.

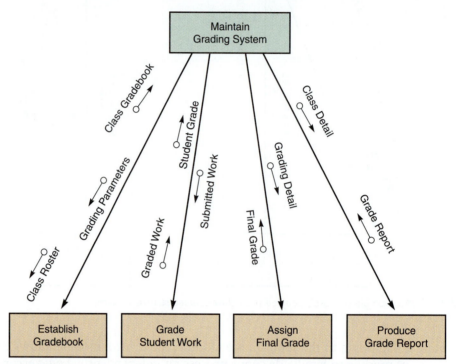

FIGURE 9-15 A structure chart based on the Grading System DFD described in Figure 4-15 on page 159.

Drawing a Structure Chart

If you used a structured analysis method, your structure charts will be based on the DFDs you created during data and process modeling.

Typically, you follow four steps when you create a structure chart. You review DFDs to identify the processes and methods, identify the program modules and determine control-subordinate relationships, add symbols for couples and loops, and analyze the structure chart to ensure that it is consistent with your system documentation.

STEP 1: REVIEW THE DFDS Your first step is to review all DFDs for accuracy and completeness, especially if changes have occurred since the systems analysis phase. For example, Figure 9-16 shows a DFD for the order system you studied in Chapter 4. If object models also were developed, you should analyze them to identify the objects, the methods that each object must perform, and the relationships among the objects. A method is similar to a functional primitive, and requires code to implement the necessary actions.

STEP 2: IDENTIFY MODULES AND RELATIONSHIPS Working from the logical model, you transform functional primitives or object methods into program modules. When analyzing a set of DFDs, remember that each DFD level represents a processing level. If you are using DFDs, you would work your way down from the context diagram to the lower-level diagrams, identifying control modules and subordinate modules, until you reach functional primitives. If more cohesion is desired, you can divide processes

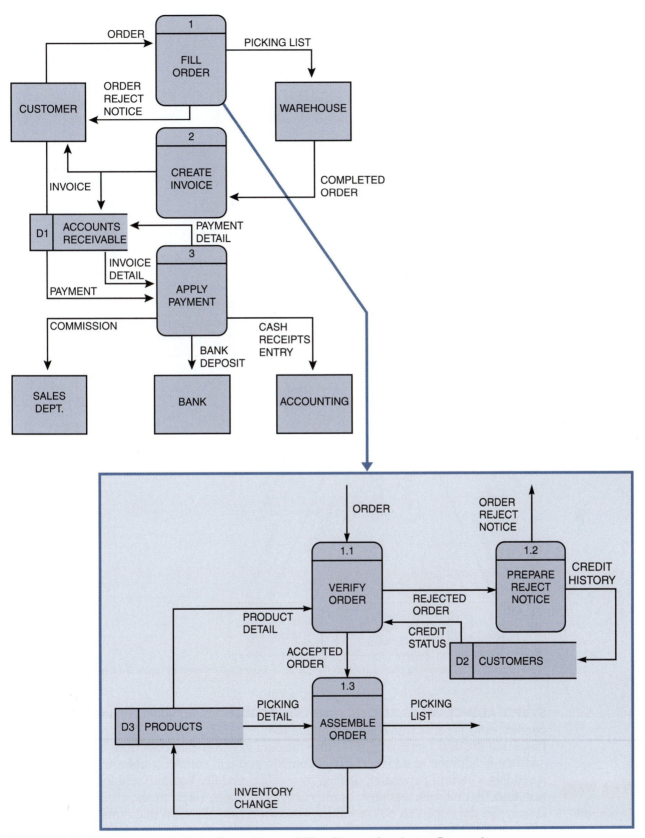

FIGURE 9-16 DFDs for a sample Order System. The top DFD is Diagram 0; under it is Diagram 1.

into smaller modules that handle a single task. Figure 9-17 shows a structure chart based on the DFDs in Figure 9-16 on the previous page. Notice how the chart relates to the various DFD levels.

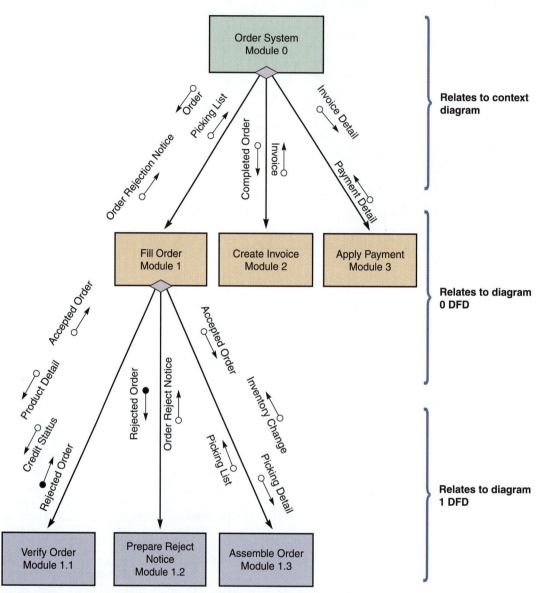

FIGURE 9-17   A structure chart based on the Order System DFDs shown in Figure 9-16 on page 425.

STEP 3: ADD COUPLES, LOOPS, AND CONDITIONS   Next, you add couples, loops, and conditions to the structure chart. If you are working with DFDs, you can review the data flows and the data dictionary to identify the data elements that pass from one module to another. In addition to adding the data couples, you add control couples where a module is sending a control parameter, or flag, to another module. You also add loops and condition lines that indicate repetitive or alternative processing steps, as shown in Figure 9-17. If you also developed an object model, you can review the class diagrams and object relationship diagrams to be sure that you understand the interaction among the objects.

STEP 4: ANALYZE THE STRUCTURE CHART AND THE DATA DICTIONARY   At this point, the structure chart is ready for careful analysis. You should check each process, data element, or object method to ensure that the chart reflects all previous documentation and that the logic is correct. You also should determine that modules are strongly cohesive and loosely coupled. Often, you must draw several versions of the chart. Some CASE tools can help you analyze the chart and identify problem areas.

Other Structured Development Tools

In addition to structure charts, other structured development tools include program flowcharts and pseudocode.

PROGRAM FLOWCHARTS

Program flowcharts graphically represent the logic and interaction between program modules using a series of symbols connected by arrows. Using program flowcharts, programmers can break large systems into subsystems that are easier to understand and code. Figure 9-18 illustrates a program flowchart for calculating sales commissions. Notice that each diamond-shaped symbol represents a specific decision that determines the actions the program will perform next.

PSEUDOCODE   Pseudocode is a technique for representing program logic. Pseudocode is similar to structured English, which was explained in Chapter 4. Pseudocode is not language-specific, so you can use it to describe a software module in plain English without requiring strict syntax rules. Using pseudocode, a systems analyst or a programmer can describe program actions they can implement in any programming

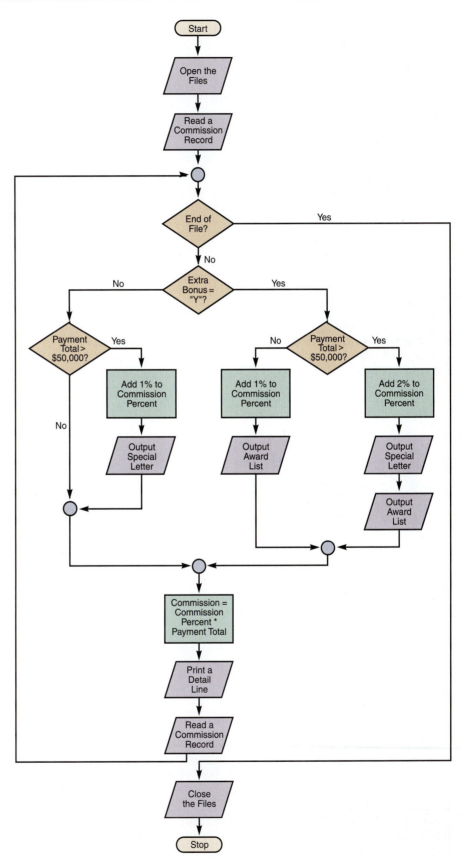

FIGURE 9-18   A program flowchart shows the logic needed to calculate commissions and perform related tasks, modified as shown.

```
Open the files
Read a COMMISSION record
Do until end of file
        If EXTRA BONUS equals Y
                If PAYMENT TOTAL is greater than $50,000
                        Add 2% to COMMISSION PERCENT
                        Output SPECIAL LETTER
                        Output AWARD LIST
                Else
                        Add 1% to COMMISSION PERCENT
                        Output AWARD LIST
                ENDIF
        Else
                If PAYMENT TOTAL is greater than $50,000
                        Add 1% to COMMISSION PERCENT
                        Output SPECIAL LETTER
                ENDIF
        ENDIF
        Calculate COMMISSION = COMMISSION PERCENT times PAYMENT TOTAL
        Print a detail line
        Read a COMMISSION record
ENDDO
Close the files
End the program
```

FIGURE 9-19 An example of pseudocode that documents the logical steps in the sales commission flowchart shown in Figure 9-18 on the previous page.

language. Figure 9-19 illustrates the pseudocode used to document the sales commission module.

If a programmer believes that changes are needed in the design, he or she contacts the systems analyst to review the suggested revisions. For example, a programmer notices that certain information is duplicated in a report design. If the changes could affect users, the analyst must inform them in advance and document all modifications and user approvals in the system design specification.

OBJECT-ORIENTED APPLICATION DEVELOPMENT

When you studied the object-oriented methods described in Part 5 of the Systems Analyst's Toolkit, you learned that O-O analysis makes it easier to translate an object model directly into an object-oriented programming language. Although many structured design concepts also apply to object-oriented methodology, there are some differences.

Object-Oriented Application Development Compared to Structured Development

When implementing a structured design, a structure chart is used to describe the interaction between program modules, as explained earlier. In contrast, when implementing an object-oriented design, relationships between objects already exist. Because object interaction is defined during the O-O analysis process, the application's structure is represented by the object model itself.

As Part 5 of the Systems Analyst's Toolkit explains, objects contain both data and program logic, called methods. Individual object instances belong to classes of objects with similar characteristics. The relationship and interaction among classes are described using a class diagram, such as the one shown in Figure 9-20. A class diagram includes the class **attributes**, which describe the characteristics of objects in the class, and **methods**, which represent program logic. For example, the Customer class describes customer objects. Customer attributes include Number, Name, Address, and so on. Methods for the Customer class include Place order, Modify order, and Pay invoice, among others. The Customer class can exchange messages with the Order class.

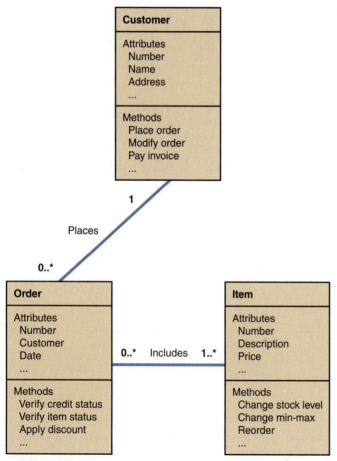

FIGURE 9-20 A simplified class diagram for a customer order processing system.

In addition to class diagrams, programmers get an overview of object interaction by using object relationship diagrams that were developed during the O-O analysis process. For example, Figure 9-21 shows an object relationship diagram for a fitness center. Notice the model shows the objects and how they interact to perform business functions and transactions.

FIGURE 9-21 An object-relationship diagram for a fitness center.

Implementation of Object-Oriented Designs

When a programmer translates an object-oriented design into an application, he or she analyzes the classes, attributes, methods, and messages that are documented in the object model. During this process, the programmer makes necessary revisions and updates to class diagrams, sequence diagrams, state transition diagrams, and activity diagrams.

The programmer's main objective is to translate object methods into program code modules and determine what event or message will trigger the execution of each module. To accomplish the task, the programmer analyzes sequence diagrams and state transition diagrams that show the events and messages that trigger changes to an object. O-O applications are called event-driven, because each event, transaction, or message triggers a corresponding action. The programmer can represent the program steps in pseudocode initially, or use CASE tools and code generators to create object-oriented code directly from the object model.

CODING

Coding is the process of turning program logic into specific instructions that the computer system can execute. Working from a specific design, a programmer uses a programming language to transform program logic into code statements. An individual programmer might create a small program, while larger programs typically are divided into modules that several individuals or groups can work on simultaneously.

Programming Environments

Each IT department has its own programming environment and standards. Visual C++, Visual Basic, and SQL are examples of commonly used programming languages, and many commercial packages use a proprietary set of commands. As more companies use Internet applications and protocols, HTML, Java, and other Web-centric languages will be used extensively. Also, as you learned earlier, industry giants such as IBM's WebSphere and Microsoft's .NET are **integrated development environments (IDEs)** that are designed to allow easy integration of system components with less time spent on developing code for interactive modules.

> **TOOLKIT TIME**
>
> The CASE tools in Part 2 of the Systems Analyst's Toolkit can help you understand IDEs. To learn more about these tools, turn to Part 2 of the six-part Toolkit that follows Chapter 10.

FIGURE 9-22 First, a programmer uses keystrokes and mouse actions to create the Microsoft Access macro shown in the top screen. The macro opens a customer order form and produces a beep sound. Access converts the macro to the editable code shown in the bottom screen — complete with commands, comments, and error-handling procedures.

Generating Code

You learned in earlier chapters that systems analysts use application generators, report writers, screen generators, fourth-generation languages, and other CASE tools that produce code directly from program design specifications. Some commercial applications can generate editable program code directly from macros, keystrokes, or mouse actions. Figure 9-22 shows an example of a Visual Basic code module in Microsoft Access that opens a customer order form and produces a beep sound. A macro automatically generated the code, and the macro itself was created by a series of keystrokes and mouse actions. Notice that the code module shown in Figure 9-22 includes program commands, comments, and error-handling procedures.

TESTING THE SYSTEM

After coding, a programmer must test each program to make sure it functions correctly. Later, programs are tested in groups, and finally the development team must test the entire system. The first step is to compile the program using a CASE tool or a language compiler. This process detects **syntax errors**, which are language grammar errors. The programmer corrects the errors until the program executes properly.

Next, the programmer desk checks the program. **Desk checking** is the process of reviewing the program code to spot **logic errors**, which produce incorrect results. This process can be performed by the person who wrote the program or by other programmers. Many organizations require a more formal type of desk checking called a **structured walkthrough**, or **code review**.

Typically, a group of three to five IT staff members participate in code review. The group usually consists of project team members and might include other programmers and analysts who did not work on the project. The objective is to have a peer group identify errors, apply quality standards, and verify that the program meets the requirements of the system design specification. Errors found during a structured walkthrough are easier to fix while coding is still in the developmental stages.

In addition to analyzing logic and program code, the project team usually holds a session with users called a **design walkthrough**, to review the interface with a cross-section of people who will work with the new system and assure that all necessary features have been included. This is a continuation of the modeling and prototyping effort that began early in the systems development process.

The next step in application development is to initiate a sequence of unit testing, integration testing, and system testing, as shown in Figure 9-23.

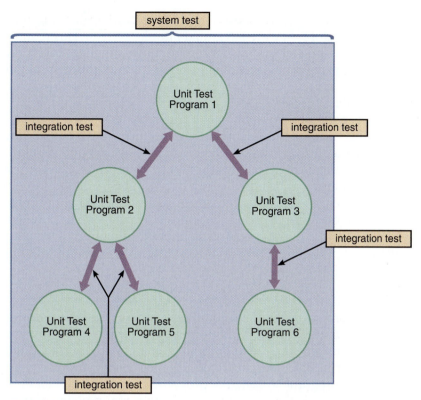

FIGURE 9-23   The first step in testing is unit testing, followed by integration testing, and then system testing.

CASE IN POINT 9.1:   YOUR MOVE, INC.

You work for April Olivia, the IT manager at Your Move, Inc., a large retailer specializing in games of all kinds. The company is in the final stages of developing a new inventory management system, and April wants you to handle the testing.

"Be sure you put lots of errors into the test data," she said. "Users are bound to make mistakes, and we need to design built-in safeguards that will catch the mistakes, and either fix them automatically, or alert the user to the problem."

Of course, April's comment makes a lot of sense, but you've never done this before and you wonder how to proceed. Should you try to invent every possible data error? How will you know that you've thought of every situation that could occur? Consider the problem, develop an approach, and write up your plan in a brief memo.

Unit Testing

The testing of an individual program or module is called **unit testing**. The objective is to identify and eliminate execution errors that could cause the program to terminate abnormally, and logic errors that could have been missed during desk checking.

Test data should contain both correct data and erroneous data and should test all possible situations that could occur. For example, for a field that allows a range of numeric values, the test data should contain minimum values, maximum values, values outside the acceptable range, and alphanumeric characters. During testing, programmers can use software tools to determine the location and potential causes of program errors.

During unit testing, programmers must test programs that interact with other programs and files individually, before they are integrated into the system. This requires a technique called stub testing. In **stub testing**, the programmer simulates each program outcome or result and displays a message to indicate whether or not the program executed successfully. Each stub represents an entry or exit point that will be linked later to another program or data file.

To obtain an independent analysis, someone other than the programmer who wrote the program usually creates the test data and reviews the results. Systems analysts frequently create test data during the systems design phase as part of an overall test plan. A **test plan** consists of detailed procedures that specify how and when the testing will be performed, who will participate, and what test data will be used. A comprehensive test plan should include scenarios for every possible situation the program could encounter.

Regardless of who creates the test plan, the project manager or a designated analyst also reviews the final test results. Some organizations also require users to approve final unit test results.

Integration Testing

ON THE WEB

For more information about System Testing, visit **scsite.com/ sad6e/more**, locate Chapter 9 and then click the System Testing link.

Testing two or more programs that depend on each other is called **integration testing**, or **link testing**. For example, consider an information system with a program that checks and validates customer credit status, and a separate program that updates data in the customer master file. The output from the validation program becomes input to the master file update program. Testing the programs independently does not guarantee that the data passed between them is correct. Only by performing integration testing for this pair of programs can you make sure that the programs work together properly. Figure 9-23 on the previous page shows integration testing for several groups of programs. Notice that a program can have membership in two or more groups.

Systems analysts usually develop the data they use in integration testing. As is the case with all forms of testing, integration test data must consider both normal and unusual situations. For example, integration testing might include passing typical records between two programs, followed by blank records, to simulate an unusual event or an operational problem. You should use test data that simulates actual conditions because you are testing the interface that links the programs. A testing sequence should not move to the integration test stage unless it has performed properly in all unit tests.

System Testing

After completing integration testing, you must perform **system testing**, which involves the entire information system, as shown in Figure 9-23. A system test includes all typical processing situations and is intended to assure users, developers, and managers that the program meets all specifications and that all necessary features have been included.

During a system test, users enter data, including samples of actual, or live, data, perform queries, and produce reports to simulate actual operating conditions. All processing options and outputs are verified by users and the IT project development team to ensure that the system functions correctly. Commercial software packages must undergo system testing similar to that of in-house developed systems, although unit and integration testing usually are not performed. Regardless of how the system was developed, system testing has the following major objectives:

- ➡ Perform a final test of all programs
- ➡ Verify that the system will handle all input data properly, both valid and invalid

- Ensure that the IT staff has the documentation and instructions needed to operate the system properly and that backup and restart capabilities of the system are adequate (the details of creating this sort of documentation are discussed later in this chapter)

- Demonstrate that users can interact with the system successfully

- Verify that all system components are integrated properly and that actual processing situations will be handled correctly

- Confirm that the information system can handle predicted volumes of data in a timely and efficient manner

Successful completion of system testing is the key to user and management approval, which is why system tests sometimes are called **acceptance tests**. Final acceptance tests, however, are performed during systems installation and evaluation, which is described later in this chapter.

How much testing is necessary? The answer depends on the situation and requires good judgment and input from other IT staff members, users, and management, as shown in Figure 9-24. Unfortunately, IT project managers often are pressured to finish testing quickly and hand the system over to users. Common reasons for premature or rushed testing are demands from users, tight systems development budgets, and demands from top management to finish projects early. Those pressures hinder the testing process and often have detrimental effects on the final product.

You should regard thorough testing as a cost-effective means of providing a quality product. Every error caught during testing eliminates potential expenses and operational problems. No system, however, is 100 percent error-free. Often, errors go undetected until the system becomes operational. Errors that affect the integrity or accuracy of data must be corrected immediately. Minor errors, such as typographical errors in screen titles, can be corrected later.

Some users want a system that is a completely finished product, while others realize that minor changes can be treated as maintenance items after the system is operational. In the final analysis, you must decide whether or not to postpone system installation if problems are discovered. If conflicting views exist, management will decide whether or not to install the system after a full discussion of the options.

FIGURE 9-24 System testing requires good judgment and input from other IT staff members, users, and IT management.

CASE IN POINT 9.2: WEBTEST, INC.

As a new systems analyst, you suspect that testing Web-based systems probably involves a different set of tools and techniques, compared to testing traditional LAN-based systems. Because you've always wanted to run your own IT company, you have decided to launch a startup firm called WebTest, Inc., that would offer consulting services specifically aimed at testing the performance, integrity, efficiency, and security of Internet-based systems.

Your idea is to identify and purchase various Web site testing tools that currently are available, then use these tools as a Web site testing consultant. No one in your area offers this type of consulting service, so you have high hopes.

Now, you need to perform Internet research to learn more about Web testing software that is available. Review the Internet Resources Tools section, which is Part 6 of the six-part Systems Analyst's Toolkit that follows Chapter 10, and use a search engine to develop a list of at least four products that you might want to use. For each product, write up a brief description of its overall purpose, its features and benefits, its cost, and how it would fit into your business game plan.

DOCUMENTATION

Documentation describes an information system and helps the users, managers, and IT staff who must interact with it. Accurate documentation can reduce system downtime, cut costs, and speed up maintenance tasks. Figure 9-25 shows an example of software that can automate the documentation process and help software developers generate accurate, comprehensive reference material.

Documentation is essential for successful system operation and maintenance. In addition to supporting a system's users, accurate documentation is essential for IT staff members who must modify the system, add a new feature, or perform maintenance. Documentation includes program documentation, system documentation, operations documentation, and user documentation.

Program Documentation

Program documentation describes the inputs, outputs, and processing logic for all program modules. The program documentation process starts in the systems analysis phase and continues during systems implementation. Systems analysts prepare overall documentation, such as process descriptions and report layouts, early in the SDLC. This documentation guides programmers, who construct modules that are well supported by internal and external comments and descriptions that can be understood and maintained easily. A systems analyst usually verifies that program documentation is complete and accurate.

System Documentation

System documentation describes the system's functions and how they are implemented. System documentation includes data dictionary entries, data flow diagrams, object models, screen layouts, source documents, and the systems request that initiated the project. System documentation is necessary reference material for the programmers and analysts who must support and maintain the system.

Most of the system documentation is prepared during the systems analysis and systems design phases. During the systems implementation phase, an analyst must review prior documentation to verify that it is complete, accurate, and up-to-date, including any changes made during the implementation process. For example, if a screen or

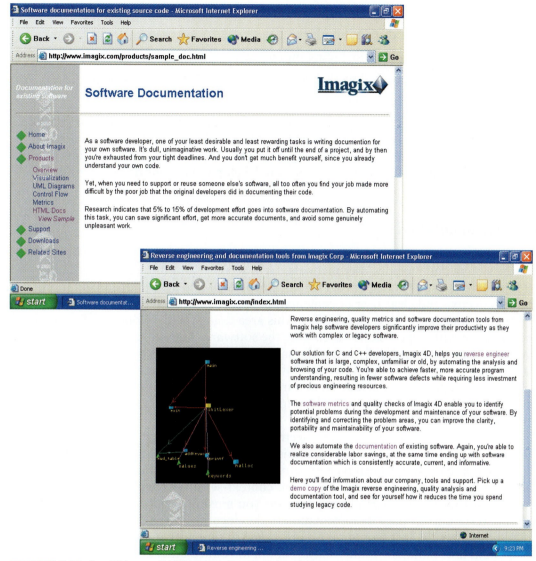

FIGURE 9-25   In addition to CASE tools, software such as Imagix can automate the task of software documentation.

report has been modified, the analyst must update the documentation. Updates to the system documentation should be made in a timely manner to prevent oversights.

Operations Documentation

If the information system environment involves a minicomputer, a mainframe, or centralized servers, the analyst must prepare documentation for the IT group that supports centralized operations. A mainframe installation might require the scheduling of batch jobs and the distribution of printed reports. In this type of environment, the IT operations staff serves as the first point of contact when users experience problems with the system.

Operations documentation contains all the information needed for processing and distributing online and printed output. Typical operations documentation includes the following information:

➡ Program, systems analyst, programmer, and system identification

➡ Scheduling information for printed output, such as report run frequency and deadlines

ON THE WEB

For more information about Documentation, visit **scsite.com/ sad6e/more**, locate Chapter 9 and then click the Documentation link.

- → Input files and where they originate; and output files and destinations
- → E-mail and report distribution lists
- → Special forms required, including online forms
- → Error and informational messages to operators and restart procedures
- → Special instructions, such as security requirements

Operations documentation should be clear, concise, and available online if possible. If the IT department has an operations group, you should review the documentation with them, early and often, to identify any problems. If you keep the operations group informed at every phase of the SDLC, you can develop operations documentation as you go along.

User Documentation

User documentation consists of instructions and information to users who will interact with the system and includes user manuals, Help screens, and tutorials. Programmers or systems analysts usually create program documentation and system documentation. To produce effective and clear user documentation — and hence have a successful project — you need someone with expert skills in this area doing the development, just as you need someone with expert skills developing the software. The skill set required to develop documentation usually is not the same as that to develop a system. This is particularly true as you move into the world of online documentation, which needs to coordinate with print documentation and intranet and Internet information. Technical writing requires specialized skills, and competent technical writers are valuable members of the IT team.

Just as you cannot throw a system together in several days, you cannot add documentation at the end. That is a common misconception and often proves fatal to a project. While that has always been true of software user documentation, this is an even more critical issue now that online Help and context-sensitive Help so often are needed. Context-sensitive Help is part of the program. You must put coded callouts in the text that link to the correct page of information in the documentation. To try to go back and add this after the fact would take a great deal of time; depending on the project size, it could take months! Additionally, it could introduce other coding errors — and it all has to be tested as well.

Systems analysts usually are responsible for preparing documentation to help users learn the system. In larger companies, a technical support team that includes technical writers might assist in the preparation of user documentation and training materials. Regardless of the delivery method, user documentation must be clear, understandable, and readily accessible to users at all levels.

User documentation includes the following:

- → A system overview that clearly describes all major system features, capabilities, and limitations
- → Description of source document content, preparation, processing, and samples
- → Overview of menu and data entry screen options, contents, and processing instructions
- → Examples of reports that are produced regularly or available at the user's request, including samples
- → Security and audit trail information
- → Explanation of responsibility for specific input, output, or processing requirements

→ Procedures for requesting changes and reporting problems

→ Examples of exceptions and error situations

→ Frequently asked questions (FAQs)

→ Explanation of how to get help and procedures for updating the user manual

Most users prefer **online documentation,** which provides immediate Help when they have questions or encounter problems. Many users are accustomed to context-sensitive Help screens, hints and tips, hypertext, on-screen demos, and other user-friendly features commonly found in popular software packages; they expect the same kind of support for in-house developed software.

If the system will include online documentation, that fact needs to be identified as one of the system requirements. If the documentation will be created by someone other than the analysts who are developing the system, that person or group needs to be involved as early as possible to become familiar with the software and begin developing the required documentation and support material. In addition, system developers must determine whether the documentation will be available from within the program, or as a separate entity in the form of a tutorial, slide presentation, reference manual, or Web site. If necessary, links should be created within the program that will take the user to the appropriate documentation.

Effective online documentation is an important productivity tool because it empowers users and reduces the time that IT staff members must spend in providing telephone, e-mail, or face-to-face assistance. Interactive tutorials are especially popular with users who like to learn by doing. Many software packages provide tutorials, as shown in Figure 9-26.

FIGURE 9-26 Interactive tutorials are especially popular with users who like to learn by doing.

In addition to program-based assistance, the Internet offers an entirely new level of comprehensive, immediate support. Many programs include links to Web sites, intranet sites, and Internet-based technical support, as shown in Figure 9-27. The sites usually include up-to-date information, tips, and FAQs.

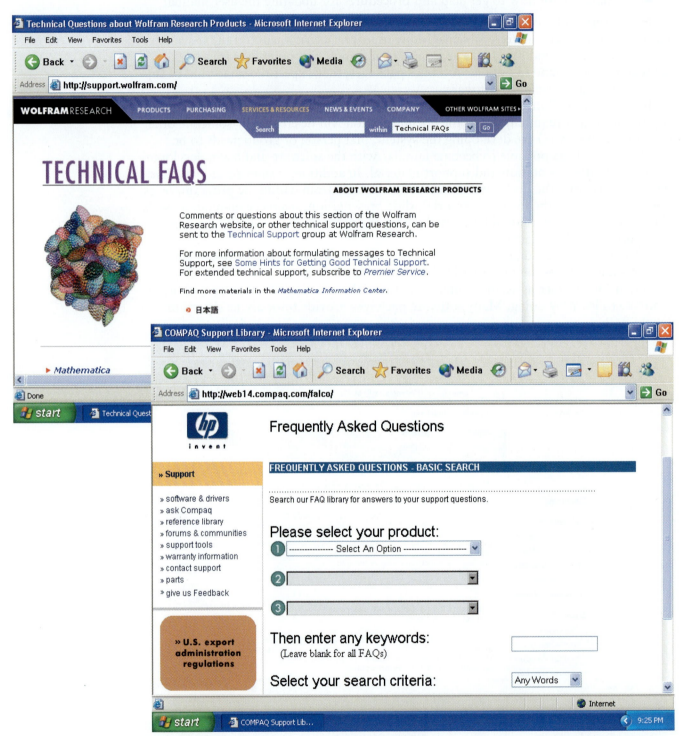

FIGURE 9-27 Many vendors provide technical support sites that offer up-to-date information, tips, and frequently asked questions (FAQs).

Although online documentation is essential, written documentation material also is valuable, especially in training users and for reference purposes. A sample page from a user manual is shown in Figure 9-28. Systems analysts or technical writers usually prepare the manual, but many companies invite users to review the material and participate in the development process.

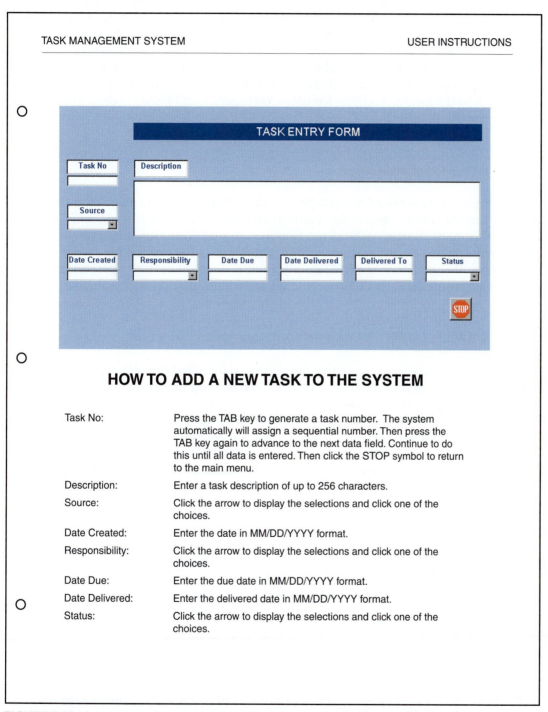

FIGURE 9-28 A sample page from a user manual. The instructions explain how to add a new task to the system.

No matter what form of user documentation your system will require, you must keep in mind that it can take a good deal of time to develop. The time between finishing software coding and the time when a complete package — including documentation — can be released to users is entirely dependent on how well the documentation is thought out in advance. If the completion of your project includes providing user documentation, this issue needs to be addressed from the very beginning of the project. Determining what the user documentation requirements are and ascertaining who will complete the documents is critical to a timely release of the project.

Neglecting user documentation issues until after all the program is complete often leads to one of two things: 1) the documentation will be thrown together as quickly as possible just to get it out the door on time, and it more than likely will be inadequate; or 2) it will be done correctly, and the product release will be delayed considerably.

User training typically is scheduled when the system is installed; the training sessions offer an ideal opportunity to distribute the user manual and explain the procedures for updating it in the future. Training for users, managers, and IT staff is described later in this chapter.

MANAGEMENT APPROVAL

After system testing is complete, you present the results to management. You should describe the test results, update the status of all required documentation, and summarize input from users who participated in system testing. You also must provide detailed time schedules, cost estimates, and staffing requirements for making the system fully operational. If system testing produced no technical, economical, or operational problems, management determines a schedule for system installation and evaluation.

SYSTEM INSTALLATION AND EVALUATION

The following sections describe system installation and evaluation tasks that are performed for every information systems project, whether you develop the application in-house or purchase it as a commercial package.

The new system now is ready to go to work. Your earlier design activities produced the overall architecture and processing strategy, and you consulted users at every stage of development. You developed and tested programs individually, in groups, and as a complete system. You prepared the necessary documentation and checked it for accuracy, including support material for IT staff and users. Now, you will carry out the remaining steps in systems implementation:

- Prepare a separate operational and test environment
- Provide training for users, managers, and IT staff
- Perform data conversion and system changeover
- Carry out a post-implementation evaluation of the system
- Present a final report to management

OPERATIONAL AND TEST ENVIRONMENTS

You learned earlier that an environment, or platform, is a specific combination of hardware and software. The environment for the actual system operation is called the **operational environment** or **production environment**. The environment that analysts and programmers use to develop and maintain programs is called the **test environment**. A separate test environment is necessary to maintain system security and integrity and protect the operational environment. Typically, the test environment resides on a limited-access workstation or server located in the IT department.

Access to the operational environment is limited to users and must strictly be controlled. Systems analysts and programmers should not have access to the operational environment except to correct a system problem or to make authorized modifications or enhancements. Otherwise, IT department members have no reason to access the day-to-day operational system.

The test environment for an information system contains copies of all programs, procedures, and test data files. Before making any changes to an operational system, you must verify them in the test environment and obtain user approval. Figure 9-29 shows the differences between test environments and operational environments.

An effective testing process is essential, whether you are examining an information system or a batch of computer chips. Every experienced systems analyst can tell you a story about an apparently innocent program change that was introduced without being tested properly. In those stories, the innocent change invariably ends up causing some unexpected and unwanted changes to the program. After any modification, you should repeat the same acceptance tests you ran when the system was developed. By restricting access to the operational area and performing all tests in a separate environment, you can protect the system and avoid problems that could damage data or interrupt operations.

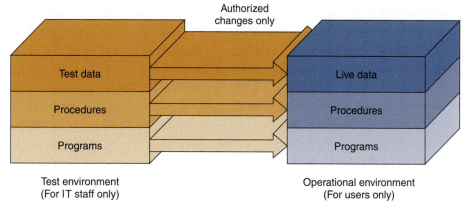

FIGURE 9-29 The test environment versus the operational environment. Notice that access to the test environment is limited to IT staff, while the operational environment is restricted to users.

The operational environment includes hardware and software configurations and settings, system utilities, telecommunications resources, and any other components that might affect system performance. Because network capability is critically important in a client/server environment, you must verify connectivity, specifications, and performance before installing any applications. You should check all communications features in the test environment carefully, and then check them again after loading the applications into the operational environment. Your documentation should identify all network specifications and settings, including technical and operational requirements for communications hardware and software. If you have to build or upgrade network resources to support the new system, you must test the platform rigorously before system installation begins.

TRAINING

No system can be successful without proper training, whether it involves software, hardware, or manufacturing, as shown in Figure 9-30. A successful information system requires training for users, managers, and IT staff members. The entire systems development effort can depend on whether or not people understand the system and know how to use it effectively.

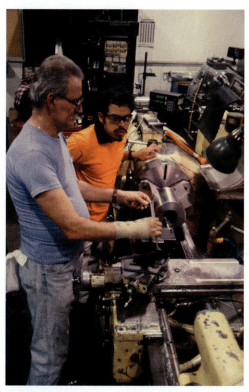

FIGURE 9-30 In any situation, training must fit the needs of users and help them carry out their job functions.

ON THE WEB

For more information about Training, visit **scsite.com/sad6e/ more**, locate Chapter 9 and then click the Training link.

Training Plan

You should start to consider a **training plan** early in the systems development process. As you create documentation, you should think about how to use the material in future training sessions. When you implement the system, it is essential to provide the right training for the right people at the right time. The first step is to identify who should receive training and what training is needed. You must look carefully at the organization, how the system will support business operations, and who will be involved or affected. Figure 9-31 shows specific training topics for users, managers, and IT staff. Notice that each group needs a mix of general background and detailed information to understand and use the system.

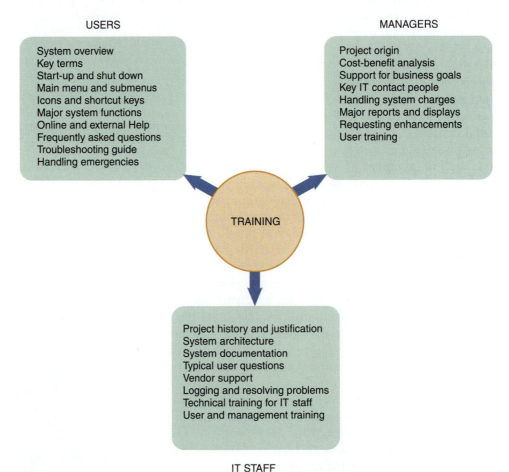

USERS

System overview
Key terms
Start-up and shut down
Main menu and submenus
Icons and shortcut keys
Major system functions
Online and external Help
Frequently asked questions
Troubleshooting guide
Handling emergencies

MANAGERS

Project origin
Cost-benefit analysis
Support for business goals
Key IT contact people
Handling system charges
Major reports and displays
Requesting enhancements
User training

TRAINING

Project history and justification
System architecture
System documentation
Typical user questions
Vendor support
Logging and resolving problems
Technical training for IT staff
User and management training

IT STAFF

FIGURE 9-31 Examples of training topics for three different groups. Users, managers, and IT staff members have different training needs.

As shown in Figure 9-31, the three main groups for training are users, managers, and IT staff. A manager does not need to understand every submenu or feature, but he or she does need a system overview to ensure that users are being trained properly and are using the system correctly. Similarly, users need to know how to perform their day-to-day job functions, but do not need to know how the company allocates system operational charges among user departments. IT staff people probably need the most information. To support the new system, they must have a clear understanding of how the system functions, how it supports business requirements, and the skills that users need to operate the system and perform their tasks.

After you identify the objectives, you must determine how the company will provide training. The main choices are to obtain training from vendors, outside training firms, or use IT staff and other in-house resources.

Vendor Training

If the system includes the purchase of software or hardware, then vendor-supplied training is one of the features you should include in the RFPs (requests for proposal) and RFQs (requests for quotation) that you send to potential vendors.

Many hardware and software vendors offer training programs free or at a nominal cost for the products they sell. In other cases, the company might negotiate the price for training, depending on their relationship with the vendor and the prospect of future purchases. The training usually is conducted at the vendor's site by experienced trainers who provide valuable hands-on experience. If a large number of people need training, you might be able to arrange classes at your location.

Vendor training, as shown in Figure 9-32, often gives the best return on your training dollars because it is focused on products that the vendor developed. The scope of vendor training, however, usually is limited to a standard version of the vendor's software or hardware. You might have to supplement the training in-house, especially if your IT staff customized the package.

FIGURE 9-32 Users must be trained on the new system. Training sessions might be one-on-one or group situations such as the one shown here. Many vendors provide product training as part of an overall service to customers.

Outside Training Resources

You also can look into an independent training firm to provide in-house hardware or software training. If vendor training is not practical and your organization does not have the internal resources to perform the training, you might find that outside training consultants are a desirable alternative.

The rapid expansion of information technology has produced tremendous growth in the computer-training field. Many training consultants, institutes, and firms are available that provide either standardized or customized training packages. IT industry leaders, such as IBM and Hewlett-Packard, offer a wide variety of training solutions, as shown in Figure 9-33.

If you decide to investigate outside training resources, you can contact a training provider and obtain references from clients. You also can seek

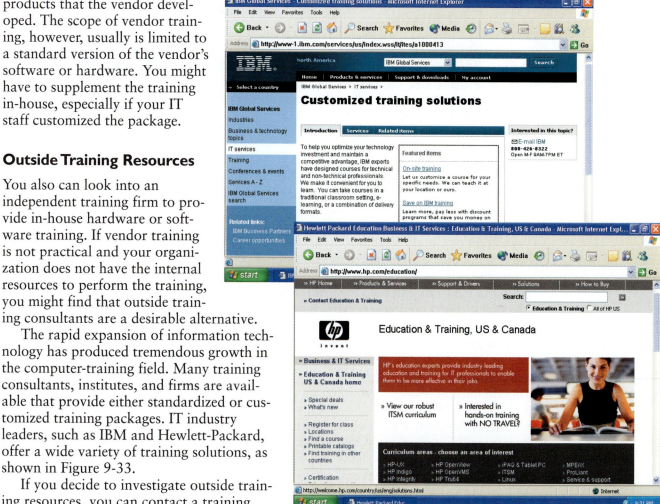

FIGURE 9-33 IT industry leaders, such as IBM and Hewlett-Packard, offer a wide variety of training solutions.

assistance from nonprofit sources with an interest in training, including universities, industry associations, and information management organizations. For example, Figure 9-34 shows the Web site for the **Center for the Application of Information Technologies (CAIT)** that describes a variety of IT education and training resources.

FIGURE 9-34   The Center for the Application of Information Technologies (CAIT) uses its Web site to present information technology education and training and describes the organization's mission.

In-House Training

The IT staff and user departments often share responsibility for developing and conducting training programs for internally developed software. If your organization has a help desk, the staff might be able to handle user training.

Multimedia is an effective training method. Presentation software, such as Microsoft PowerPoint or Corel Presentations, allows you to design training sessions that combine slides, animation, and sound. You also can use programs that capture actual keystrokes and mouse actions, and then replay the screens as a demonstration for users. If your firm has a media or graphic arts group, they can help you prepare training aids such as videotapes, charts, and other instructional materials. When developing a training program, you should keep the following guidelines in mind.

Train people in groups, with separate training programs for distinct groups. Group training makes the most efficient use of time and training facilities. In addition, if the group is small, trainees can learn from the questions and problems of others. A training program must address the job interests and skills of a wide range of participants. For example, IT staff personnel and users require very different information. Problems often arise when some participants have technical backgrounds and others do not. A single program will not meet everyone's needs.

Select the most effective place to conduct the training. Training employees at your company's location offers several advantages. Employees incur no travel expense, they can respond to local emergencies that require immediate attention, and training can take place in the actual environment where the system will operate. You can encounter some disadvantages, however. Employees who are distracted by telephone calls and other duties will not get the full benefit of the training. In addition, using the organization's computer facilities for training can disrupt normal operations and limit the amount of actual hands-on training.

Provide for learning by hearing, seeing, and doing. Some people learn best from lectures, discussions, and question-and-answer sessions. Others learn best from viewing demonstrations or from reading documentation and other material. Most people learn best from hands-on experience. You should provide training that supports each type of learning.

Prepare effective training materials, including interactive tutorials. User-friendly training materials contribute to training effectiveness and provide a valuable resource for users. You can prepare the material in various forms, including traditional training manuals, printed handouts, or online material. The main goal is to deliver user-friendly, cost-effective training. Regardless of the instructional method, the training lessons should include step-by-step instructions for using all the features of the information system.

Most people learn best when they participate actively in the training process. A **tutorial** is a series of online interactive lessons that present material and provide a dialog with users. Figure 9-35 shows a sample tutorial lesson for a sales prospect management system. In Lesson 1, the user learns how to enter and exit the system. In Lesson 2, which is shown in Figure 9-36 on the next page, the user learns how to add a sales prospect and return to the main menu.

FIGURE 9-35 A sample tutorial for a sales prospect management system. In the first lesson, the user learns how to enter and exit the system.

A training package also should include a reference section that summarizes all options and commands, and a listing of all error messages and what action the user should take when a problem occurs. More sophisticated tutorials might offer interactive sessions where users practice various tasks and get feedback on their progress. Even if you lack the resources to develop interactive tutorials, you can design a series of dialog boxes that respond with Help information and suggestions when users select various menu topics.

Rely on previous trainees. After one group of users has been trained, they can assist others. Users often learn more quickly from co-workers who share common experience and job responsibilities. Using a **train-the-trainer** strategy, you can select knowledgeable users who then conduct sessions for others. When utilizing train-the-trainer techniques, the initial training must include not only the use of the application or system, but some instruction on how to present the materials effectively.

Sales Prospect Management System
Lesson 2: Adding a Sales Prospect

- Start your computer and enter the Sales Prospect Management System as explained in Lesson 1. Click the Add a Prospect button on the main switchboard. The blank form shown below displays.

Add a Sales Prospect

First Name	Prospect ID	Dial Phone Number
Last Name	Title	Contact Via E-mail
Company	Work Phone	Generate Memo
Dear	Work Extension	
Address	Fax Number	Add Another Prospect
City		Return to Main Menu
State/Province		HELP
Postal Code		
Country		
E-mail Address		
Referred By		
Notes		

- Enter the data into the fields as shown on the screen below. The system will add the Prospect ID automatically. Press the ENTER key to move to the next field.

Add a Sales Prospect

Field	Value	Field	Value	
First Name	Samuel	Prospect ID	10343	Dial Phone Number
Last Name	Rose	Title	Tech Support Manager	Contact Via E-mail
Company	Last Resort Systems, Inc.	Work Phone	(555) 123-4567	Generate Memo
Dear	Sam	Work Extension	2219	
Address	1303 Van Buren Drive	Fax Number	(555) 123-9999	Add Another Prospect
City	Annapolis			Return to Main Menu
State/Province	MD			HELP
Postal Code	21403-9999			
Country	US			
E-mail Address	sam_rose@lrs.com			
Referred By	Emma Nell			
Notes	Sam's company might be merging with SuperSystems. This would be a great time to get our foot in the door.			

- When you have entered all the data, compare your screen to the one shown above. If it matches, you have entered a sales prospect successfully. Click the Return to Main Menu button. You now are ready for Lesson 3, Updating Prospect Data.

FIGURE 9-36 A second sample lesson in the online tutorial.

When training is complete, many organizations conduct a full-scale test, or **simulation**, which is a dress rehearsal for users and IT support staff. Organizations include all procedures, such as those that they execute only at the end of a month, quarter, or year, in the simulation. As questions or problems arise, the participants consult the system documentation, Help screens, or each other to determine appropriate answers or actions. This full-scale test provides valuable experience and builds confidence for everyone involved with the new system.

DATA CONVERSION

Data conversion is an important part of the system installation process. During **data conversion**, existing data is loaded into the new system. Depending on the system, data conversion can be done before, during, or after the operational environment is complete. You should develop a data conversion plan as early as possible, and the conversion process should be tested when the test environment is developed.

ON THE WEB

For more information about Data Conversion, visit **scsite.com/sad6e/ more**, locate Chapter 9 and then click the Data Conversion link.

Data Conversion Strategies

When a new system replaces an existing system, you should automate the data conversion process, if possible. The old system might be capable of **exporting** data in an acceptable format for the new system or in a standard format, such as ASCII or ODBC. **ODBC** (**Open Database Connectivity**) is an industry-standard protocol that allows DBMSs from various vendors to interact and exchange data. Most database vendors provide ODBC drivers, which are a form of middleware. As you learned in Chapter 8, middleware connects dissimilar applications and enables them to communicate.

If a standard format is not available, you must develop a program to extract the data and convert it to an acceptable format. Data conversion is more difficult when the new system replaces a manual system, because all data must be entered manually unless it can be scanned. Even when you can automate data conversion, a new system often requires additional data items, which might require manual entry.

Data Conversion Security and Controls

You should maintain strict input controls during the conversion process, when data is extremely vulnerable. You must ensure that all system control measures are in place and operational to protect data from unauthorized access and to help prevent erroneous input.

Even with careful data conversion and input controls, some errors will occur. For example, duplicate customer records or inconsistent part numbers might have been tolerated by the old system, but will cause the new system to crash. Most organizations require that users verify all data, correct all errors, and supply every missing data item during conversion. Although the process can be time-consuming and expensive, it is essential that the new system be loaded with accurate, error-free data.

SYSTEM CHANGEOVER

System changeover is the process of putting the new information system online and retiring the old system. Changeover can be rapid or slow, depending on the method. The four changeover methods are direct cutover, parallel operation, pilot operation, and phased operation. Direct cutover is similar to throwing a switch that instantly changes over from the old system to the new. Parallel operation requires that both systems run simultaneously for a specified period, resulting in the slowest method. The other methods,

FIGURE 9-37 The four system changeover methods.

pilot and phased operation, fall somewhere between direct cutover and parallel operation. Figure 9-37 illustrates the four system changeover methods.

Direct Cutover

The **direct cutover** approach causes the changeover from the old system to the new system to occur immediately when the new system becomes operational. Direct cutover usually is the least expensive changeover method because the IT group has to operate and maintain only one system at a time.

Direct cutover, however, involves more risk than other changeover methods. Regardless of how thoroughly and carefully you conduct testing and training, some difficulties can arise when the system goes into operation. Problems can result from data situations that were not tested or anticipated or from errors caused by users or operators. A system also can encounter difficulties because live data typically occurs in much larger volumes than test data.

Although initial implementation problems are a concern with all four changeover methods, they are most significant when the direct cutover approach is used. Detecting minor errors also is more difficult with direct cutover because users cannot verify current output by comparing it to output from the old system. Major errors can cause a system process to terminate abnormally, and with the direct cutover method, you cannot revert to the old system as a backup option.

Companies often choose the direct cutover method for implementing commercial software packages because they feel that commercial packages involve less risk of total system failure. Commercial software is certainly not risk-free, but the software vendor usually maintains an extensive knowledge base and can supply reliable, prompt fixes for most problems.

For systems developed in-house, most organizations use direct cutover only for noncritical situations. Direct cutover might be the only choice, however, if the operating environment cannot support both the old and new systems or if the old and new systems are incompatible.

Timing is very important when using a direct cutover strategy. Most systems operate on weekly, monthly, quarterly, and yearly cycles. For example, consider a payroll system that produces output on a weekly basis. Some employees are paid twice a month, however, so the system also operates semimonthly. Monthly, quarterly, and annual reports also require the system to produce output at the end of every month, quarter, and year. When a cyclical information system is implemented in the middle of any cycle, complete processing for the full cycle requires information from both the old and the new systems. To minimize the need to require information from two different systems, cyclical information systems usually are converted using the direct cutover method at the beginning of a quarter, calendar year, or fiscal year.

Parallel Operation

The **parallel operation** changeover method requires that both the old and the new information systems operate fully for a specified period. Data is input into both systems, and output generated by the new system is compared with the equivalent output from the old system. When users, management, and the IT group are satisfied that the new system operates correctly, the old system is terminated.

The most obvious advantage of parallel operation is lower risk. If the new system does not work correctly, the company can use the old system as a backup until appropriate changes are made. It is much easier to verify that the new system is working properly under parallel operation than under direct cutover, because the output from both systems is compared and verified during parallel operation.

Parallel operation, however, does have some disadvantages. First, it is the most costly changeover method. Because both the old and the new systems are in full operation, the company pays for both systems during the parallel period. Users must work in both systems and the company might need temporary employees to handle the extra workload. In addition, running both systems might place a burden on the operating environment and cause processing delays.

Parallel operation is not practical if the old and new systems are incompatible technically, or if the operating environment cannot support both systems. Parallel operation also is inappropriate when the two systems perform different functions or if the new system involves a new method of business operations. For example, until a company installs new data scanners in a factory, it is impractical to launch a new production tracking system that requires that technology.

Pilot Operation

The **pilot operation** changeover method involves implementing the complete new system at a selected location of the company. A new sales reporting system, for instance, might be implemented in only one branch office, or a new payroll system might be installed in only one department. In these examples, the group that uses the new system first is called the **pilot site**. During pilot operation, the old system continues to operate for the entire organization, including the pilot site. After the system proves successful at the pilot site, it is implemented in the rest of the organization, usually using the direct cutover method. Therefore, pilot operation is a combination of parallel operation and direct cutover methods.

Restricting the implementation to a pilot site reduces the risk of system failure, compared with a direct cutover method. Operating both systems for only the pilot site is less expensive than a parallel operation for the entire company. In addition, if you later use a parallel approach to complete the implementation, the changeover period can be much shorter if the system proves successful at the pilot site.

Phased Operation

The **phased operation** changeover method allows you to implement the new system in stages, or modules. For example, instead of implementing a new manufacturing system all at once, you first might install the materials management subsystem, then the production control subsystem, then the job cost subsystem, and so on. You can implement each subsystem by using any of the other three changeover methods.

Analysts sometimes confuse phased and pilot operation methods. Both methods combine direct cutover and parallel operation to reduce risks and costs. With phased operation, however, you give a part of the system to all users, while pilot operation provides the entire system, but to only some users.

One advantage of a phased approach is that the risk of errors or failures is limited to the implemented module only. For instance, if a new production control subsystem fails to operate properly, that failure might not affect the new purchasing subsystem or the existing shop floor control subsystem.

Phased operation is less expensive than full parallel operation because you have to work with only one part of the system at a time. A phased approach is not possible, however, if the system cannot be separated easily into logical modules or segments. In addition, if the system involves a large number of separate phases, phased operation can cost more than a pilot approach.

Figure 9-38 shows that each changeover method has risk and cost factors. As a systems analyst, you must weigh the advantages and disadvantages of each method and recommend the best choice in a given situation. The final changeover decision will be based on input from the IT staff, users, and management — and the choice must reflect the nature of the business and the degree of acceptable risk.

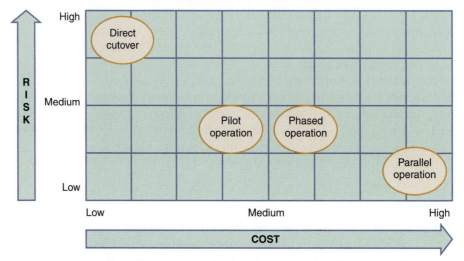

FIGURE 9-38   Relative risk and cost characteristics of the four changeover methods.

CASE IN POINT 9.3:   GLOBAL COOLING

You are a systems analyst at Global Cooling, a leading manufacturer of air conditioning units. You are leading a team that is developing a new production scheduling system. The project is now in the application development stage. Unit testing has been completed, and you are in the final stages of integration testing. Your supervisor, Ella Pham, is eager to implement the new application ahead of schedule and asked if you could trim system testing from two weeks to three days, and use a direct cutover method instead of the parallel changeover method that originally was planned. Write a brief memo expressing your views.

POST-IMPLEMENTATION TASKS

Once the new system is operational, you must perform two additional tasks: prepare a post-implementation evaluation and deliver a final report to management.

Post-Implementation Evaluation

A **post-implementation evaluation** assesses the overall quality of the information system. The evaluation verifies that the new system meets specified requirements, complies with user objectives, and produces the anticipated benefits. In addition, by providing feedback to the development team, the evaluation also helps improve IT development practices for future projects.

A post-implementation evaluation should examine all aspects of the development effort and the end product — the developed information system. A typical evaluation includes feedback for the following areas:

- Accuracy, completeness, and timeliness of information system output
- User satisfaction
- System reliability and maintainability
- Adequacy of system controls and security measures
- Hardware efficiency and platform performance
- Effectiveness of database implementation
- Performance of the IT team
- Completeness and quality of documentation
- Quality and effectiveness of training
- Accuracy of cost-benefit estimates and development schedules

You can apply the same fact-finding techniques in a post-implementation evaluation that you used to determine the system requirements during the systems analysis phase. When evaluating a system, you should:

- Interview members of management and key users
- Observe users and computer operations personnel actually working with the new information system
- Read all documentation and training materials
- Examine all source documents, output reports, and screen displays
- Use questionnaires to gather information and opinions from a large number of users
- Analyze maintenance and help desk logs

Figure 9-39 on the next page shows the first page of a sample user evaluation form for the new information system where users evaluate 18 separate elements on a numerical scale, so the results can be tabulated easily. Following that section, the form provides space for open-ended comments and suggestions.

Whenever possible, people who were not directly involved in developing the system should conduct the post-implementation evaluation. IT staff and users usually perform the evaluation, although some firms use an internal audit group or independent auditors to ensure the accuracy and completeness of the evaluation.

When should post-implementation evaluation occur? Is it better to wait until the new system has been in operation for one month, six months, one year, or longer? Users can forget details of the developmental effort if too much time elapses before the evaluation. After several months or a year, for instance, users might not remember whether they learned a procedure through training, from user documentation, or by experimenting with the system on their own.

Users also might forget their impressions of IT team members over time. An important purpose of the post-implementation evaluation is to improve the quality of IT department functions, including interaction with users, training, and documentation. Consequently, the evaluation team should perform the assessment while users are able to recall specific incidents, successes, and problems so they can offer suggestions for improvement. Post-implementation evaluation primarily is concerned with assessing the quality of the new system. If the team performs the evaluation too soon after

USER EVALUATION FORM

System: Evaluator: Date:

Please evaluate the information system project by circling the one number for each factor that best represents your assessment.

	Unsatisfactory		Acceptable		Excellent

SYSTEM OUTPUT

1. Accuracy of information	1	2	3	4	5	6
2. Completeness of information	1	2	3	4	5	6
3. Ease of use	1	2	3	4	5	6
4. Timeliness of information	1	2	3	4	5	6

USER INTERFACE

5. Clarity of instructions	1	2	3	4	5	6
6. Quality of Help messages	1	2	3	4	5	6
7. Ease of use	1	2	3	4	5	6
8. Appropriateness of options	1	2	3	4	5	6
9. Clarity of error messages	1	2	3	4	5	6
10. Prevention of input errors	1	2	3	4	5	6

INFORMATION TECHNOLOGY STAFF

11. Cooperation	1	2	3	4	5	6
12. Availability	1	2	3	4	5	6
13. Knowledge	1	2	3	4	5	6
14. Reporting of progress	1	2	3	4	5	6
15. Communication skills	1	2	3	4	5	6

TRAINING

16. Completeness	1	2	3	4	5	6
17. Appropriateness	1	2	3	4	5	6
18. Schedule	1	2	3	4	5	6

FIGURE 9-39 Sample user evaluation form. The numerical scale allows easy tabulation of results. Following this section, the form provides space for open-ended comments and suggestions.

implementation, users will not have enough time to learn the new system and appreciate its strengths and weaknesses. Although many IT professionals recommend conducting the evaluation after at least six months of system operation, pressure to finish the project sooner usually results in an earlier evaluation in order to allow the IT department to move on to other tasks.

Ideally, conducting a post-implementation evaluation should be standard practice for all information systems projects. Sometimes, evaluations are skipped because users are eager to work with the new system, or because IT staff members have more pressing priorities. In some organizations, management might not recognize the importance and benefits of a post-implementation evaluation. The evaluations are extremely important, however, because they enable the development team and the IT department to learn what worked and what did not work. Otherwise, developers might commit the same errors in another system.

CASE IN POINT 9.4: YORKTOWN INDUSTRIES

Cindy Winslow liked her new job as lead systems analyst at Yorktown Industries. She was pleased that her development team completed the new human resources system ahead of schedule and under budget. Cindy looked forward to receiving the post-implementation evaluation because she was confident that both the system and the development team would receive high marks from users and managers.

After the system operated for one month, Cindy received a call from her supervisor, Ted Haines. Ted told her that she would have to handle the evaluation, even though she headed the development effort. Cindy told Ted that she did not feel comfortable evaluating her own team's work. She explained that someone who was not involved in its development should do an independent evaluation. Ted responded that he had full confidence in Cindy's ability to be objective. He explained that no one else was available and he needed the evaluation quickly so he could move forward with the next stage in the corporate development plan.

Cindy was troubled about the situation and she called you, a professional acquaintance, for your advice. What would you tell her and why?

Final Report to Management

At the end of each SDLC phase, you submit a report to management, and the systems implementation phase is no exception. Your report should include the following:

- ⇒ Final versions of all system documentation
- ⇒ Planned modifications and enhancements to the system that have been identified
- ⇒ Recap of all systems development costs and schedules
- ⇒ Comparison of actual costs and schedules to the original estimates
- ⇒ Post-implementation evaluation, if it has been performed

The final report to management marks the end of systems development work. In the next chapter, you will study the role of a systems analyst during systems operation, security, and support, which is the final phase of the SDLC.

> **🔧 TOOLKIT TIME**
>
> The Communication tools in Part I of the Systems Analyst's Toolkit can help you develop better reports and presentations. To learn more about these tools, turn to Part I of the six-part Toolkit that follows Chapter 10.

CHAPTER SUMMARY

The systems implementation phase consists of application development, testing, installation, and evaluation of the new system. During application development, analysts determine the overall design strategy and work with programmers to complete design, coding, testing, and documentation. Quality assurance is essential during the implementation phase. Many companies utilize software engineering concepts and quality standards established by the International Organization for Standardization (ISO).

During application development, large systems can be broken down into subsystems and modules that represent a particular transaction or process described in a DFD or object model. When structured analysis methods are used, programmers and systems analysts create structure charts, program flowcharts, and pseudocode to represent program modules logically. If an object-oriented approach was used, the development team will review the object model, including use case diagrams, class diagrams, object-relationship diagrams, sequence diagrams, and state-transition diagrams.

A structure chart consists of symbols that represent program modules, data couples, control couples, conditions, and loops. A rectangle represents a program module, which consists of program code that accomplishes a specific function. An arrow with an empty circle represents a data couple, which shows data that one module passes to another. An arrow with a filled circle represents a control couple, which shows a message, also called a flag, which one module sends to another. A line with a diamond on one end represents a condition, which indicates a control module that determines which subordinate modules are invoked, depending on a specific condition. A curved arrow represents a loop, which indicates that one or more modules are repeated.

Cohesion measures a module's scope and processing characteristics. A module that performs a single function or task has a high degree of cohesion, which is desirable. Coupling measures relationships and interdependence among modules. Modules that are relatively independent are loosely coupled, which is desirable.

Typically, you follow four steps when you create a structure chart. You review DFDs and object models to identify the processes and methods, identify the program modules and determine control-subordinate relationships, add symbols for couples and loops, and analyze the structure chart to ensure that it is consistent with your system documentation.

Programmers perform desk checking, code review, and unit testing tasks during application development. Systems analysts design the initial test plans, which include test steps and test data for integration testing and system testing. Integration testing is necessary for programs that interact. The final step is system testing for the completed system. System testing includes users in the testing process.

In addition to system documentation, analysts and technical writers also prepare operations documentation and user documentation. Operations documentation provides instructions and information to the IT operations group. User documentation consists of instructions and information for users who interact with the system and includes user manuals, Help screens, and tutorials.

During the installation process, you establish an operational, or production, environment for the new information system that is completely separate from the test environment. The operational environment contains live data and is accessible only by authorized users. All future changes to the system must be verified in the test environment before they are applied to the operational environment.

Everyone who interacts with the new information system should receive training appropriate to his or her role and skills. The IT department usually is responsible for training. Software or hardware vendors or professional training organizations also can provide training. When you develop a training program, remember the following guidelines: train people in groups; utilize people already trained to help train others; develop separate programs for distinct employee groups; and provide for learning by using discussions, demonstrations, documentation, training manuals, and interactive tutorials.

Data conversion often is necessary when installing a new information system. When a new system replaces a computerized system, you should automate the data conversion process if possible. The old system might be capable of exporting data in a format that the new system can use, or you might have to extract the data and convert it to an acceptable format. Data conversion from a manual system often requires labor-intensive data entry or scanning. Even when data conversion can be automated, a new system often requires additional data items, which might require manual entry. Strict input controls are important during the conversion process to protect data integrity and quality. Typically, data is verified, corrected, and updated during the conversion process.

System changeover is the process of putting the new system into operation. Four changeover methods exist: direct cutover, parallel operation, pilot operation, and phased operation.

With direct cutover, the old system stops and the new system starts simultaneously; direct cutover is the least expensive, but the riskiest changeover method. With parallel operation, users operate both the old and new information systems for some period of time; parallel operation is the most expensive and least risky of the changeover methods. Pilot operation and phased operation represent compromises between direct cutover and parallel operation; both methods are less risky than direct cutover and less costly than parallel operation. With pilot operation, a specified group within the organization uses the new system for a period of time, while the old system continues to operate for the rest of the users. After the system proves successful at the pilot site, it is implemented throughout the organization. With phased operation, you implement the system in the entire organization, but only one module at a time, until the entire system is operational.

A post-implementation evaluation assesses and reports on the quality of the new system and the work done by the project team. Although it is best if people who were not involved in the systems development effort perform the evaluation, that is not always possible. The evaluation should be conducted early so users have a fresh recollection of the development effort, but not before users have experience using the new system.

The final report to management includes the final system documentation, describes any future system enhancements that already have been identified, and details the project costs. The report represents the end of the development effort and the beginning of the new system's operational life.

Key Terms and Phrases

acceptance tests *433*

application development *419*

attributes *428*

Capability Maturity Model (CMM)® *416*

Capability Maturity Model Integration (CMMI)® *416*

Center for the Application of Information Technologies (CAIT) *444*

code review *430*

coding *429*

cohesion *421*

condition *421*

control couple *421*

control module *420*

coupling *422*

data conversion *447*

data couple *421*

design walkthrough *430*

desk checking *430*

direct cutover *448*

documentation *434*

exporting *447*

flag *421*

integrated development environments (IDEs) *429*

integration testing *432*

library module *421*

link testing *432*

logic errors *430*

loop *421*

loosely coupled *422*

methods *428*

modular design *420*

module *419*

ODBC (Open Database Connectivity) *447*

online documentation *437*

operational environment *440*

operations documentation *435*

parallel operation *448*

partitioning *420*

phased operation *449*

pilot operation *449*

pilot site *449*

post-implementation evaluation *450*

process improvement *416*

production environment *440*

program documentation *434*

pseudocode *427*

quality assurance *416*

simulation *447*

Software Engineering Institute (SEI) *416*

software engineering *416*

status flag *422*

structure chart *420*

structured walkthrough *430*

stub testing *432*

subordinate modules *420*

syntax errors *430*

system changeover *447*

system documentation *434*

system testing *432*

test data *431*

test environment *440*

test plan *432*

tightly coupled *422*

top-down approach *420*

training plan *442*

train-the-trainer *446*

tutorial *445*

unit testing *431*

user documentation *436*

Learn It Online

Instructions: To complete the Learn It Online exercises, start your browser, click the Address bar, and then enter the Web address **scsite.com/sad6e/learn**. When the Systems Analysis and Design Learn It Online page is displayed, follow the instructions in the exercises below. Each exercise has instructions for saving your results, either for your own records or for submission to your instructor.

1 Chapter Reinforcement

TF, MC, and SA

Below SAD Chapter 9, click the Chapter Reinforcement link. Print the quiz by clicking Print on the File menu for each page. Answer each question.

2 Flash Cards

Below SAD Chapter 9, click the Flash Cards link and read the instructions. Type 20 (or a number specified by your instructor) in the Number of playing cards text box, type your name in the Enter your Name text box, and then click the Flip Card button. When the flash card is displayed, read the question and then click the ANSWER box arrow to select an answer. Flip through the Flash Cards. If your score is 15 (75%) correct or greater, click Print on the File menu to print your results. If your score is less than 15 (75%) correct, then redo this exercise by clicking the Replay button.

3 Practice Test

Below SAD Chapter 9, click the Practice Test link. Answer each question, enter your first and last name at the bottom of the page, and then click the Grade Test button. When the graded practice test is displayed on your screen, click Print on the File menu to print a hard copy. Continue to take practice tests until you score 80% or better.

4 Who Wants To Be a Computer Genius?

Below SAD Chapter 9, click the Computer Genius link. Read the instructions, enter your first and last name at the bottom of the page, and then click the Play button. When your score is displayed, click the PRINT RESULTS link to print a hard copy.

5 Wheel of Terms

Below SAD Chapter 9, click the Wheel of Terms link. Read the instructions, and then enter your first and last name and your school name. Click the PLAY button. When your score is displayed on the screen, right-click the score and then click Print on the shortcut menu to print a hard copy.

6 Crossword Puzzle Challenge

Below SAD Chapter 9, click the Crossword Puzzle Challenge link. Read the instructions, and then enter your first and last name. Click the SUBMIT button. Work the crossword puzzle. When you are finished, click the Submit button. When the crossword puzzle is redisplayed, click the Print Puzzle button to print a hard copy.

Case-Sim: SCR Associates

Background

SCR Associates is a consulting firm that offers IT solutions and training. SCR needs an information system to manage operations at its new training center. The new system will be called TIMS (Training Information Management System). As a newly hired systems analyst, you will report to Jesse Baker, systems group manager. You will work on various tasks and practice the skills you learned in this chapter.

Using the Case

The SCR Associates case study is a Web-based simulation that allows you to practice your skills in a real-world environment. The case study transports you to SCR's company intranet, where you can complete 10 work sessions, each aligning with a chapter. As you work on the case, you will receive e-mail and voice mail messages, obtain information from SCR's online libraries, and perform various tasks. The first time you enter the SCR Case, you should go to the Starting page at **scsite.com/sad6e/scr** for detailed instructions.

Preview: Session 9

You assisted your supervisor, Jesse Baker, in planning an architecture for the new TIMS system. Now she wants you to work on system implementation tasks and issues. Specifically, she wants you to develop a structure chart, testing and training plans, implementation guidelines, and a post-implementation review.

To start a work session, you log on to the SCR intranet. When you enter your name and password, an opening screen displays links to the work sessions, and you select Session 9. At this point, you check your e-mail and voice mail messages carefully. Then you begin working on your task list, which includes the following items:

Tasks: Systems Implementation

1. Jesse wants to see a structure chart. She said to use program modules based on the processes we identified earlier. She wants the modules to be cohesive and loosely coupled.

2. Need to develop a testing plan that includes unit testing, integration testing, and system testing as Jesse requested in her message. Also, draft a reminder to all IT staff members about the importance of careful documentation.

3. Jesse says it's important for SCR support staff and users to understand the difference between the test environment and the operational environment. Draft a message that explains the installation process and provides guidelines for all concerned. Also need to develop a training plan for TIMS, using Jesse's message as a guide. List the groups that should receive training, the topics that should be covered, and training methods we might use.

4. Jesse wants me to recommend a data conversion plan and a changeover method for TIMS. She also wants to see a plan for post-implementation review of TIMS. She wants suggestions on fact-gathering methods, a list of topics to cover, the best time to conduct the review, and who should perform it.

FIGURE 9-40   Task list: Session 9.

Chapter Exercises

Review Questions

1. Where does systems implementation fit in the SDLC, what tasks typically are performed during systems implementation, and why is quality assurance so important?
2. Describe top-down design and modular design.
3. Describe structure charts and symbols, and define cohesion and coupling.
4. Define unit testing, integration testing, and system testing.
5. What types of documentation does a systems analyst prepare, and what would be included in each type?
6. What is the purpose of an operational environment and a test environment?
7. Who must receive training before a new information system is implemented?
8. List and describe the four system changeover methods. Which of the system changeover methods generally is the most expensive? Why? Which of the system changeover methods generally is the riskiest? Why?
9. Who should be responsible for performing a post-implementation evaluation?
10. List the information usually included in the final report to management.

Discussion Topics

1. A supervisor states, "Integration testing is a waste of time. If each program is tested adequately, integration testing is not needed. Instead, we should move on to system testing as soon as possible. If modules don't interact properly, we'll handle it then." Do you agree or disagree with this comment? Justify your position.
2. Suppose you are a systems analyst developing a detailed test plan. Explain the testing strategies you will use in your plan. Will you use live or simulated data?
3. Using the Internet, locate an example of training for a software or hardware product. Write a brief summary of the training, the product, the type of training offered, and the cost of training (if available). Discuss your findings with the class.
4. Suppose that you designed a tutorial to train a person in the use of specific software or hardware, such as a Web browser. What specific information would you want to know about the recipient of the training? How would that information affect the design of the training material?

Projects

1. In this chapter, you learned about the importance of testing. Design a generic test plan that describes the testing for an imaginary system.
2. Design a generic post-implementation evaluation form. The form should consist of questions that you could use to evaluate any information system. The form should evaluate the training received and any problems associated with the program.
3. Create a one-page questionnaire to distribute to users in a post-implementation evaluation of a recent information system project. Include at least 10 questions that cover the important information you want to obtain.
4. On the Internet, locate an example of an online tutorial and reference material for a software product. Are the instructions and lesson steps clear and effective? Does the training assume that the user is an expert or a novice? What are your suggestions for improving the material?

Apply Your Knowledge

The Apply Your Knowledge section contains four mini-cases. Each case describes a situation, explains your role in the case, and asks you to respond to questions. You can answer the questions by applying knowledge you learned in the chapter.

1 Sand and Surf Retailers

Situation:

Sand and Surf Retailers recently acquired several smaller companies to expand its chain of clothing outlets. To establish consistency for the current organization and future acquisitions, Sand and Surf decided to develop an in-house application called SPS (Standard Purchasing System). The SPS system would standardize purchasing practices for each Sand and Surf subsidiary and manage all purchasing information. System testing will be completed by the end of the week.

1. What types of documentation are needed for this application?
2. During application development, what steps should the IT staff follow to develop a structure chart?
3. What suggestions do you have for Help screens and online tutorials?
4. What types of testing should be performed? What types of test data should be used?

2 Albatross Airfreight

Situation:

Albatross Airfreight specializes in shipping cargo via air across North America. In an effort to modernize, the company has begun to computerize manual business processes. The new IT infrastructure includes a computer system that tracks cargo from departure point to destination. At this point, the new system is ready for implementation. Systems analysts are modularizing the system, and programmers are ready to start coding the first modules.

1. What issues should systems analysts and programmers discuss before they proceed with the project?
2. As a systems analyst on this project, how would you describe your primary responsibilities, and how could you contribute to the quality of the finished product?
3. As a programmer, how would you describe your primary responsibilities, and how could you contribute to the quality of the finished product?
4. Will the use of structure charts be beneficial during this stage of development? Discuss the advantages of structure charts compared with program flowcharts and pseudocode.

3 Victorian Creations

Situation:

Victorian Creations is a growing business that specializes in the reproduction of furniture from the Victorian era. Since 1998, sales have increased steadily. The original accounting system was a package from Peachtree Software, which initially ran on a stand-alone PC and later on a LAN. Now, the firm is preparing to install a powerful, scalable accounting package that can support the company's current and future operations. You have been asked to develop a training plan for users.

1. Who should receive training on the new software, and what topics should the training cover?
2. Investigate an accounting package such as Peachtree to learn if the product can convert data from other accounting programs.
3. What changeover strategy would you suggest for the new accounting system? Explain your answer.
4. When should a post-implementation review be scheduled? Explain your answer.

4 Calico Prints

Situation:

Calico Prints creates a wide range of fabrics and wallpapers. Recently the company updated its payroll software as an in-house development project. Users and IT staff members have completed a comprehensive training curriculum. The system has been in the operational environment for approximately six weeks, and no major problems have occurred. You are responsible for the post-implementation evaluation.

1. What are some techniques you might use to obtain an accurate evaluation?
2. What are some specific questions you would include in a questionnaire? Who should receive the questionnaire?
3. Are there general guidelines that apply to the timing of a post-implementation evaluation? What are they?
4. In your view, should the company schedule a post-implementation evaluation for the payroll system at this time? Give specific reasons for your answer.

Case Studies

Case studies allow you to practice specific skills learned in the chapter. Each chapter contains several case studies that continue throughout the textbook, and a chapter capstone case.

NEW CENTURY HEALTH CLINIC

New Century Health Clinic offers preventive medicine and traditional medical care. In your role as an IT consultant, you will help New Century develop a new information system.

Background

You completed the systems design for the insurance system at New Century Health Clinic. The associates at the clinic have approved the design specification, and you hired two programmers, Bill Miller and Celia Goldring, to assist you with the programming and testing of the insurance system.

For Assignments 3 and 4, assume that a server and six client workstations have been purchased, installed, and networked in the clinic offices. You now are ready to begin installation and evaluation of the system.

Assignments

1. Plan the testing required for the system. You should consider unit, integration, and system testing in your test plan and determine who should participate in the testing. Also design the test data that you will use. Prepare a structure chart that shows the main program functions for the New Century system.

2. You have asked Anita Davenport, New Century's office manager, to contribute to the user manual for the insurance system. She suggested that you include a section of frequently asked questions (FAQs), which you also could include in the online documentation. Prepare 10 FAQs and answers for use in the printed user manual and context-sensitive Help screens. Also identify the specific people who will require training on the new system. Describe the type and level of training you recommend for each person or group.

3. Recommend a changeover method for New Century's system and justify your recommendation. If you suggest phased operation or pilot operation, specify the order in which you would implement the modules or how you would select a pilot workstation or location.

4. Should the associates perform a post-implementation evaluation? If an assessment is done, who should perform it? What options are available and which would you recommend?

PERSONAL TRAINER, INC.

Personal Trainer, Inc., owns and operates fitness centers in a dozen Midwestern cities. The centers have done well, and the company is planning an international expansion by opening a new "supercenter" in the Toronto area. Personal Trainer's president, Cassia Umi, hired an IT consultant, Susan Park, to help develop an information system for the new facility. During the project, Susan will work closely with Gray Lewis, who will manage the new operation.

Background

Susan finished work on system architecture issues, and her system design specification was approved. Now she is ready to address system implementation tasks, including quality assurance, structure charts, testing, training, data conversion, system changeover, and post-implementation evaluation.

Assignments

1. Identify the specific groups of people who need training on the new system. For each group, describe the type of training you would recommend and list the topics you would cover.

2. Suggest a changeover method for the new billing system and provide specific reasons to support your choice. If you recommend phased operation, specify the order in which you would implement the modules. If your recommendation is for pilot operation, specify the department or area you would select as the pilot site and justify your choice.

3. Develop a data conversion plan that specifies which data items must be entered, the order in which the data should be entered, and which data items are the most time-critical.

4. You decide to perform a post-implementation evaluation to assess the quality of the system. Who would you involve in the process? What investigative techniques would you use and why?

FANCIFUL CRYSTAL

Fanciful Crystal has produced fine crystal products for many years. The company once dominated the global market, but sales have declined recently. Last year, Fanciful Crystal rushed to implement a new Web-based system to boost sagging sales. Unfortunately, the online system was not tested thoroughly and experienced start-up problems. For example, customers complained about order mix-ups and overcharges for deliveries. You are a new system analyst with the company, and your supervisor asked you to investigate the problems.

1. Based on what you know about e-commerce, how would you have tested a new Web-based system?

2. Should ISO standards have been considered? Explain your answer.

3. What should Fanciful Crystal do in the future to avoid similar problems when developing new systems?

4. Three months after the system changeover, you perform a post-implementation evaluation. Prepare three evaluation forms for the new information system: one for users, one for managers, and one for the IT operations staff.

CHAPTER CAPSTONE CASE: SoftWear, Limited

SoftWear, Limited (SWL), is a continuing case study that illustrates the knowledge and skills described in each chapter. In this case study, the student acts as a member of the SWL systems development team and performs various tasks.

Background

The ESIP development team of Jane Rossman, Tom Adams, and Becky Evans started work on the ESIP system, which they would develop as a Microsoft Access application in a client/server environment. Jane and Tom scheduled additional meetings with the consulting firm, True Blue Systems, while Becky started designing the main switchboard and the data input screens.

The ESIP system design included a server to interact with various SWL client workstations and an interface to the new payroll package from Pacific Software. The payroll package was implemented successfully on SWL's mainframe, and several payroll cycles were completed without any processing problems.

When the ESIP development team met on Monday morning, the members studied the overview that True Blue submitted, shown in Figure 9-41. Jane said they would use a top-down design approach. Their first step was to partition the system and break it down into a set of modules on a structure chart. Each module would represent a program or function to be performed by one or more macros or Visual Basic procedures.

FIGURE 9-41 The ESIP system plan as submitted by True Blue Systems.

The team reviewed the documentation carefully, using the DFDs they prepared during the systems analysis phase. The team determined that the ESIP system needed to perform five main tasks: extract the ESIP deductions during payroll processing; apply the extracted deductions to specific ESIP options; update employee deduction selections; update ESIP option choices; and handle fund transfers to internal and external ESIP entities. To accomplish those tasks, the system would need a variety of reports, controls, query and display capabilities, input screens, security provisions, and other features.

CHAPTER CAPSTONE CASE: SoftWear, Limited (continued)

Of the five main ESIP processes, only the extracting of payroll deductions would be done on SWL's mainframe. Jane said they would need to develop an interface program to control the extraction processing, but all the other functions would run on the ESIP server and clients. By afternoon, they had produced the structure chart shown in Figure 9-42.

FIGURE 9-42 Structure chart for the ESIP system.

After studying the tasks and requirements, Jane estimated the time needed to design, code, unit test, and document each module. She also estimated the time needed for integration and system testing, completing the ESIP system documentation, and receiving management approval. Jane used Microsoft Project software to create a Gantt chart, which is explained in the Systems Analyst's Toolkit, to manage and track the project and show the individual assignments. The chart indicated that many tasks could be performed concurrently and displayed the critical path. The development team agreed that they would meet daily to review their progress and discuss any problems.

Mainframe Interface

Jane's next step was to meet with Rick Williams, who was familiar with the new payroll package, to discuss the ESIP deduction extraction program that executes when the mainframe runs the weekly payroll. Jane learned that the new payroll package was developed as a database application, and she could write the extract module in Visual Basic.

Working together, Jane and Becky prepared a design, wrote the commands, and unit tested the ESIP program modules with test files they created. They used stubs to indicate inputs and outputs to files with which the extraction program would interact. After verifying the results, Jane created a procedure for downloading the deduction file from the mainframe to the ESIP server in the payroll department. She tested the download procedure and updated the documentation.

CHAPTER CAPSTONE CASE: SoftWear, Limited (continued)   SWL

ESIP Server

The team started developing the Access database application that would handle the other ESIP functions. The plan was for Becky to finish the basic switchboard and screen designs, then add features that users had requested, including custom menus and icons for frequently used functions. Becky also would design all the reports documented in the data dictionary.

Meanwhile, Jane and Tom worked on the other modules. Their first task was to examine the ERDs developed in the systems design phase to ensure that the entities and normalized record designs still were valid. Then they would start creating individual objects, including tables, queries, macros, and code modules, using the application design tools in Access.

Jane and Tom defined the data tables, identified primary keys, and linked the tables into a relational structure as shown in Figure 9-43. They used online Access Help to make sure that they were using the correct field types, sizes, and names, and that the tables would work properly with the input screens created by Becky. Jane and Tom used an agreed-upon naming convention for all objects to ensure consistency among the systems.

After they designed and loaded the tables with test data, Jane and Tom developed queries that would allow users to retrieve, display, update, and delete records. Some queries affected only individual records, such as ESIP options, while they designed other queries for specific reports, such as the ESIP Deduction Register query shown in Figure 9-44, which displays deductions first in date order, then by employee SSN. This query also produces SQL commands shown in the lower screen that will be transmitted to the ESIP server.

Jane and Tom also developed macros that performed specific actions when certain events occurred. They tested each macro by stepping through it to make

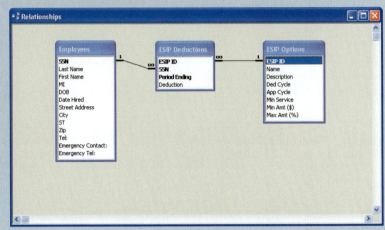

FIGURE 9-43 Relational structure for the ESIP system tables. Notice that the field or fields that comprise the primary key are shown in bold. Common fields link the tables, and referential integrity is indicated by the 1 (one) and ∞ (many) symbols.

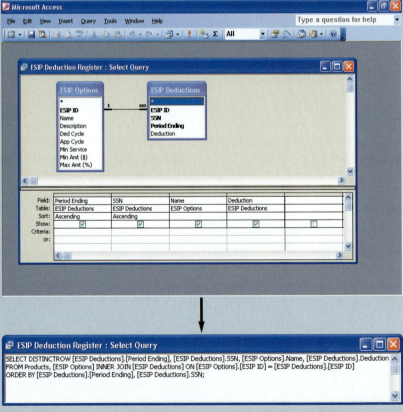

FIGURE 9-44 Example of a query that will provide data for the ESIP Deduction Register. Notice that the query sorts deductions by date, then by employee SSN. The query also produces SQL commands shown in the lower screen that will be transmitted to the ESIP server.

sure the commands executed properly. The macros later would be linked to various buttons and menus that Becky was designing into her switchboard and input screens. To save coding time, Tom converted several macros to Visual Basic in order to work on additional features and capabilities.

Jane and Tom also completed work on various security features, including password protection and several levels of permission required to view, modify, or delete specific objects. Later, when the system became operational, management would authorize specific permission levels, and Jane would designate a system administrator to maintain security and system policies.

Completing Application Development

In three weeks, the ESIP development team finished unit testing. Becky tested the switchboard, macros, queries, screen forms, menus, submenus, and code modules to ensure that they functioned correctly. Next, they linked the modules and performed integration testing. The testing ran smoothly, and they encountered no significant problems.

After integration testing, the analysts asked several principal users to participate in system testing. During this process, some minor screen changes were suggested and implemented after checking with users who would be affected by those changes. In addition, it turned out that one of the reports did not include a federally required Employer Identification Number (EIN). Because the reports had been designed using the Access report generator, the development team easily implemented this change.

The team members prepared user documentation as they completed each task. To produce a clear, understandable user manual, they decided to ask Amy Calico, SWL's payroll director, to review their notes and help them write a draft for current and future users. They wanted to explain the system in nontechnical terms, with adequate illustrations, screen shots, and a set of frequently asked questions. Jane said that the entire manual could be put online after SWL's intranet was developed.

Installation of the ESIP System

After a successful period of parallel operation, SWL fully implemented the payroll package purchased from Pacific Software and was ready to start installation of the ESIP system. In preparation, the IT development team of Jane Rossman, Tom Adams, and Becky Evans confirmed that SWL's existing network could handle the additional traffic generated by the new system. True Blue Systems, the outside consulting firm, noted in its report that the network might need to be upgraded in the future, especially if SWL expanded the number of networked applications and users.

Tom's first task was to install the ESIP application on the server in the payroll department and to verify that the system could communicate properly with SWL's mainframe. Then, he installed and tested a new high-speed tape cartridge backup system for the ESIP system.

Next, Tom loaded the ESIP application on a client PC in the human resources department. He checked all hardware and system software settings and used several test files to ensure that the client communicated with the ESIP server in the payroll department.

Meanwhile, Becky Evans and Rick Williams worked together on the interface between the ESIP system and the mainframe. They previously created a module called an extract program that directed the mainframe payroll system to capture the ESIP payroll deductions, store them in a file, and transmit the file back to the ESIP system. They already tested the interface using stubs to represent actual input and output files. Next, they would use a test data file with examples of every possible combination of permissible deductions and several improper deductions that testing should detect.

CHAPTER CAPSTONE CASE: SoftWear, Limited (continued)   SWL

As soon as Rick confirmed that the payroll package was ready for the interface test, Tom set up the ESIP server and sent the test file to the mainframe. Then, he ran the module that sent processing commands to the payroll system. Everyone was pleased to see that the mainframe handled the test data properly and generated an extracted deduction file, which it downloaded to the ESIP server.

Becky and Rick were ready to conduct hands-on training with the payroll group, so they arranged an early morning session with Amy Calico, Nelson White, Britton Ellis, and Debra Williams. Becky walked them through the steps, which were described clearly in the user manual, and then answered several questions. The payroll employees seemed pleased with the explanation and commented on how much easier the new system would be for them to use.

Next, Becky went to see Mike Feiner, director of human resources. Mike would be the only person allowed to add, change, or delete any of the ESIP options. Based on written authorization from Tina Pham, vice president of human resources, Mike would have a special password and permission level to allow him to perform those actions. Becky described to Mike how the system worked and then showed him how to enter, modify, and delete a test option she prepared. For security reasons, the special documentation for those functions would not be printed in the user manual itself, but would be retained in the IT department files.

Becky and Tom met again with the payroll group to show users how to enter the deduction authorizations for individual employees. Although the new payroll system was operational, the company still handled ESIP deductions manually. Using the ESIP server and another networked payroll PC, the payroll clerks were able to enter actual payroll data during a three-day test period. The built-in edit and validation features detected the errors that the team purposely inserted as test data and even identified several invalid authorizations that they had not noticed previously. The group produced printed reports and asked other payroll department members to review and verify the output.

Jane Rossman had a last-minute idea: perhaps they should send a notice to all SWL employees describing the new ESIP system. The flyer also could remind employees how to select options and invite their questions or comments. Michael Jeremy, vice president of finance, thought that Jane's idea was excellent.

Up to that point, the company had made no final decision about the changeover method for the new system. Because the ESIP system replaced a series of manual processing steps, the main question was whether they should run the manual system in parallel operation for a specified period. Managers in the payroll, human resources, and accounting departments all wanted the new system operational as soon as possible, and Jane decided to use a direct cutover method, although not everyone agreed with the decision. In any case, the cutover was scheduled for Friday, May 5, 2006, when the first weekly payroll in May was processed.

Starting on Monday, April 24, the IT team met again with each of the users and reviewed a final checklist. No problems appeared, and the system was ready to interface with the mainframe and handle live data in an operational environment. On Friday morning, May 5, the payroll department ran the ESIP module that sent the processing commands to the payroll system. Later that morning, during the weekly processing cycle, the payroll package created a file with the extracted deductions and passed it back to the ESIP server.

With the ESIP system using real input data, IT department members visited each of the recently trained users to make sure they were experiencing no difficulties. They received good reports — users in the payroll and human resources departments seemed pleased with the new system. They were able to access the ESIP data, enter new deductions, and had no problems with screen output or printed reports.

The direct cutover to the ESIP system occurred without major problems. By the end of June, the system had completed nine weekly payroll cycles, produced all required reports

CHAPTER CAPSTONE CASE: SoftWear, Limited (continued)   SWL

and outputs, and properly handled the monthly transfer of funds to the credit union and the SWL stock purchase plan.

During the first part of July, the IT department conducted a post-implementation evaluation with a team that consisted of two people: Katie Barnes, a systems analyst who had not been involved in the ESIP system development, and Ben Mancuso, a member of the finance department designated by Michael Jeremy. The evaluation team reviewed system operations, conducted interviews, and asked users to complete a brief questionnaire. The results were favorable, and it appeared that users were very satisfied with the new ESIP system. When the evaluation was completed in mid-July, Ann Hon sent the

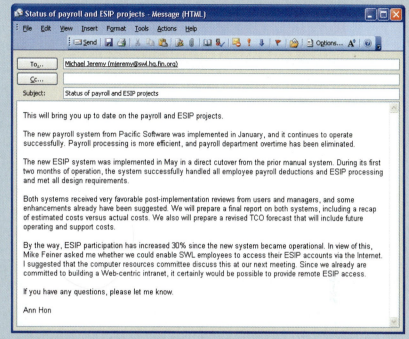

FIGURE 9-45 E-mail message from Ann Hon to Michael Jeremy regarding the payroll and ESIP systems.

e-mail message shown in Figure 9-45 to Michael Jeremy. The systems development effort for the ESIP system was completed successfully.

SWL Team Tasks

1. Rick has asked you to help him develop a recommendation for future software testing. One of his concerns is that in systems testing, it is virtually impossible to simulate every system transaction and function. Specifically, Rick wants you to suggest some guidelines that will produce the most reliable test results. He suggested that you should consider who should be involved in the testing, what types of transactions should be tested, and when the testing should be done. Based on what you already have learned about the ESIP system in earlier chapters, what would you recommend? Write a brief memo to Rick with your suggestions.

2. Rick also wants you to prepare a list of interview questions for users and design a brief questionnaire that measures the effectiveness of the new system. Develop the interview questions and questionnaire by following the guidelines suggested in this chapter and in Chapter 3, which discusses fact-finding techniques.

3. Assume that you had been asked to help develop the ESIP database shown in Figure 9-43 on page 466. Use Microsoft Access to create a database with three tables: Employees, ESIP Options, and ESIP Deductions, using the fields and primary keys shown in Figure 9-43. Populate your tables with at least five sample records. Then add the relationships between the tables, using referential integrity. Finally, design and test a query similar to the one in Figure 9-44 on page 466. When you are done, submit your database for review.

4. On page 468, you learned that Jane was under pressure from SWL managers to get the ESIP system up and running. You also learned that not everyone on the IT staff agreed with her decision to use a direct cutover method. What are some of the disadvantages of direct cutover? What other methods might have been used? What would you have done?

PHASE 5

SYSTEMS OPERATION, SUPPORT, AND SECURITY

PHASE TOPIC

Chapter 10
Systems Operation, Support, and Security

DELIVERABLE

An operational information system that is maintained, supported, and secured properly.

TOOLKIT SUPPORT

Primary tools: Communications, CASE, financial analysis, and project management tools. Other tools as required.

Systems Operation, Support, and Security is the final phase in the systems development life cycle (SDLC). In the previous phase, systems implementation, you worked on application development, testing, installation, and evaluation. Now, in the systems operation, support, and security phase, you will be supporting a functioning information system. You continuously will assess and improve the system, and you will be alert to any signs of obsolescence that might signal the end of the system's useful life. You will also address multi-level security issues and take appropriate steps to protect the system and maintain the integrity of its data.

CHAPTER 10 Systems Operation, Support, and Security

CHAPTER 10 describes systems operation, support, and security tasks that begin after the system becomes operational and continue throughout the useful life of the system. In addition to user support, this chapter discusses maintenance, security, and performance measurement issues.

INTRODUCTION

OBJECTIVES

When you finish this chapter, you will be able to:

- Explain how the systems operation, support, and security phase relates to the rest of the system development process
- Describe user support activities, including user training and help desks
- Discuss the four main types of system maintenance: corrective, adaptive, perfective, and preventive
- Explain various techniques for managing systems operation and support
- Describe techniques for managing system performance, including workload measurement and capacity planning
- Assess system security at five levels: physical security, network security, application security, file security, and user security
- List factors indicating that a system has reached the end of its useful life
- Assess future challenges for IT professionals as technology reshapes the workplace

Now that the system is operational, the real key question is whether or not the system meets user expectations, supports business objectives, and is secure. Systems must be maintained and improved continuously to meet changing business demands, and users constantly require assistance.

In addition to performing maintenance, a systems analyst is like an internal consultant who provides guidance, support, and training. Successful, robust systems often need the most support because users want to learn the features, try all the capabilities, and discover how the system can help them perform their business functions. In most organizations, more than half of all IT department effort goes into supporting existing systems and making them more valuable to users.

This chapter begins with a discussion of systems support, including user training and help desks. You will study the four main types of maintenance: corrective, adaptive, perfective, and preventive. You also will learn how the IT group uses maintenance teams, configuration management, and maintenance releases, and you will examine system performance issues, and maintenance tools. You will analyze the security system at each of the five security levels: physical security, network security, application security, file security, and user security. Finally, you will learn how to recognize system obsolescence.

CHAPTER INTRODUCTION CASE: Mountain View College Bookstore

Background: Wendy Lee, manager of college services at Mountain View College, wants a new information system that will improve efficiency and customer service at the three college bookstores.

In this part of the case, Florence Fullerton (systems analyst) and Harry Boston (student intern) are talking about operation, support, and security issues for the new system.

Participants:	Florence and Harry
Location:	Florence's office, Friday afternoon, March 31, 2006
Project status:	Florence and Harry successfully have implemented the bookstore information system. Now they will discuss strategies for supporting and maintaining the new system.
Discussion topics:	Support activities, user training, system maintenance, and techniques for managing systems operation, enhancing system performance and security, and detecting factors indicating system obsolescence

Florence:	Well, we finally made it. The system is up and running and the users seem satisfied. Now we focus on supporting the system and assuring that it delivers its full potential.
Harry:	*How do we do that?*
Florence:	First, we need to set up specific procedures for handling system support and maintenance. We'll set up a help desk that will offer user training, answer technical questions, and enhance user productivity.
Harry:	*Sounds good. I'll set up a training package for new users who missed the initial training sessions.*
Florence:	Yes, and be prepared for a variety of maintenance requests.
Harry:	*Really? What do you mean?*
Florence:	Well, there are four types of maintenance. Users typically ask for help that requires corrective maintenance to fix problems or adaptive maintenance to add new features. We, as IT staff, will be responsible for perfective maintenance, which makes the system more efficient, and preventive maintenance to avoid problems.
Harry:	*Anything else for us to do?*
Florence:	Yes, we'll need a system for managing maintenance requests from users. Also, we'll need to handle configuration management, maintenance releases, and version control. These tools will help us keep the system current and reduce unnecessary maintenance costs.
Harry:	*What about keeping tabs on system performance issues?*
Florence:	That's important, along with capacity planning to be sure the system can handle future growth.
Harry:	*What about the security of the system?*
Florence:	That's an excellent point. We'll look at physical security, network security, application security, file security, and user security.
Harry:	*Sounds like we'll be busy for quite a while.*
Florence:	Well, that depends on the system itself and user expectations. Every system has a useful life, including this one. We'll do everything we can to get a good return on the initial investment, but we'll also watch for signs of obsolescence — at that point it's time to begin the SDLC all over again. Let's get started. Here are some tasks we can work on:

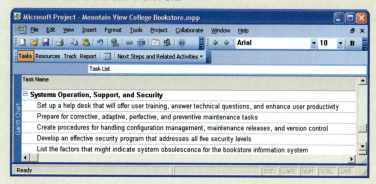

FIGURE 10-1

OVERVIEW OF SYSTEMS SUPPORT AND MAINTENANCE

The systems operation, support, and security phase begins when a system becomes operational and continues until the system reaches the end of its useful life. Throughout the development process, the objective has been to create an information system that is efficient, easy to use, and affordable. After delivering the system, the analyst has two other important tasks: he or she must support users and provide necessary maintenance to keep the system operating properly.

USER SUPPORT ACTIVITIES

Companies provide user support in many forms, including user training and a help desk to provide technical support and assistance.

User Training

In Chapter 9, you learned about initial training that is performed when a new system is introduced. Additionally, new employees must be trained on the company's information systems. For example, a firm that produces electronic assemblies must train its new employees, as shown in Figure 10-2.

If significant changes take place in the existing system or if a new version is released, the IT department might develop a **user training package**. Depending on the nature of the changes, the package could include online support via e-mail, a special Web site, a revision to the user guide, a training manual supplement, or formal training sessions. Training users about system changes is similar to initial training. The main objective is to show users how the system can help them perform their jobs.

FIGURE 10-2 Whether a company is training manufacturing technicians, data entry personnel, or customer service representatives, employees need high-quality instruction to perform their jobs efficiently.

Help Desks

As systems and data structures become more complex, users need constant support and guidance. To make data more accessible and to empower users, many IT departments create help desks. A **help desk** is a centralized resource staffed by IT professionals that provides users with the support they need to do their jobs. A help desk has three main objectives: show people how to use system resources more effectively, provide answers to technical or operational questions, and make users more productive by teaching them how to meet their own information needs. A help desk often is called an **information center** (**IC**) because it is the first place users turn when they need information or assistance.

A help desk does not replace traditional IT maintenance and support activities. Instead, help desks enhance productivity and improve utilization of a company's information resources.

Help desk representatives need strong interpersonal and technical skills plus a solid understanding of the business, because they interact with users in many departments. A help desk should document carefully all inquiries, support tasks, and activity levels. The

ON THE WEB

For more information about Help Desks, visit **scsite.com/ sad6e/more**, locate Chapter 10, and then click the Help Desks link.

information can identify trends and common problems and can help build a technical support knowledge base.

During a typical day, the help desk staff member shown in Figure 10-3 might have to perform the following tasks:

→ Show a user how to create a data query or report that displays specific business information

→ Resolve network access or password problems

→ Demonstrate an advanced feature of a system or a commercial package

→ Help a user recover damaged data

→ Offer tips for better operation

→ Explain an undocumented software feature

→ Show a user how to write a macro

→ Explain how to access the company's intranet or the Internet

→ Assist a user in developing a simple database to track time spent on various projects

→ Answer questions about software licensing and upgrades

→ Provide information about system specifications and the cost of new hardware or software

→ Recommend a system solution that integrates data from different locations to solve a business problem

→ Provide hardware support by installing or reconfiguring devices such as scanners, printers, network cards, CD-ROM drives, backup devices, and sound systems

→ Enable users to maintain data consistency and integrity among a desktop computer, a notebook computer, and a handheld computer

FIGURE 10-3 A help desk, also called an information center (IC), provides guidance and assistance to system users. When a user contacts a help desk, the response should be prompt and effective.

In addition to functioning as a valuable link between IT staff and users, the help desk is a central contact point for all IT maintenance activities. The help desk is where users report system problems, ask for maintenance, or submit new systems requests. A help desk can utilize many types of automated support, just as outside vendors do, including e-mail responses, on-demand fax capability, an online knowledge base, frequently asked questions (FAQs), discussion groups, bulletin boards, and automated voice mail.

Online Chat Support

Interactive support also can be delivered in the form of an online chat. For example, as shown in Figure 10-4 on the next page, Hewlett-Packard offers a pre-sales consulting feature that enables a customer to chat interactively with a product sales specialist.

Online chat rooms also can facilitate interactive support. For example, BlackBoard, Inc., is a company that sells software that many colleges use to deliver Internet-based courses. As shown in Figure 10-5 on the next page, Blackboard provides a chat room called a **Virtual Classroom**, which is an open room where students can ask questions and interact online with an instructor.

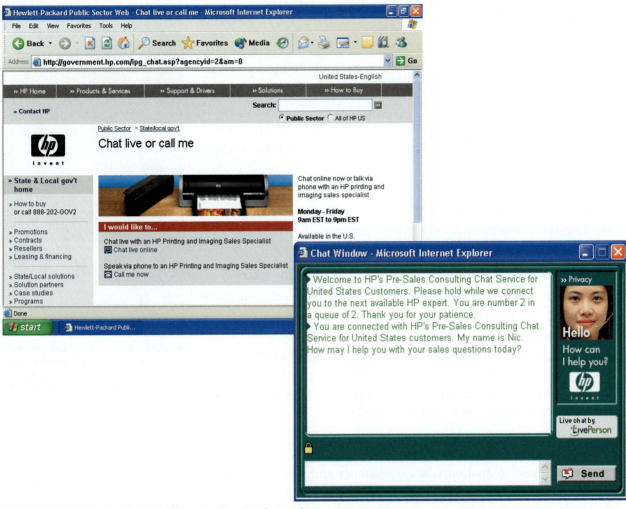

FIGURE 10-4   Hewlett-Packard offers an online chat feature for prospective customers.

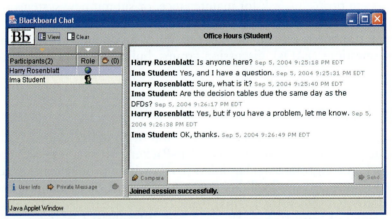

FIGURE 10-5   A Blackboard Virtual Classroom allows students to ask questions and interact online with an instructor.

MAINTENANCE ACTIVITIES

The systems operation, support, and security phase is an important component of TCO (total cost of ownership) because ongoing maintenance expenses can determine the economic life of a system. Computer systems must be maintained carefully by

trained professionals, just as the carrier-based aircraft shown in Figure 10-6 must be serviced by skilled technicians. In both cases, the quality of the maintenance will directly affect the company's return on its initial investment.

Figure 10-7 shows a typical pattern of operational and maintenance expenses during the useful life of a system. **Operational costs** include items such as supplies, equipment rental, and software leases. Notice that the lower area shown in Figure 10-7 represents fixed operational expenses, while the upper area represents maintenance expenses.

Maintenance expenses vary significantly during the system's operational life and include spending to support maintenance activities. **Maintenance activities** include changing programs, procedures, or documentation to ensure correct system performance; adapting the system to changing requirements; and making the system operate more efficiently. Those needs are met by corrective, adaptive, perfective, and preventive maintenance.

FIGURE 10-6 Regardless of the type of system, high-quality maintenance must be performed by trained professionals.

Although some overlap exists, four types of maintenance tasks can be identified, as shown by the examples in Figure 10-8 on the next page. **Corrective maintenance** is performed to fix errors, **adaptive maintenance** adds new capability and enhancements, **perfective maintenance** improves efficiency, and **preventive maintenance** reduces the possibility of future system failure. Some analysts use the term maintenance to describe only corrective maintenance that fixes problems. It is helpful, however, to view the maintenance concept more broadly and differentiate among the different types of tasks.

Maintenance expenses usually are high when a system is implemented because problems must be detected, investigated, and resolved by corrective maintenance. Once the system becomes stable, costs usually remain low and involve minor adaptive maintenance. Eventually, both adaptive and perfective maintenance activities increase in a dynamic business environment.

TOOLKIT TIME

The Financial Analysis tools in Part 3 of the Systems Analyst's Toolkit can help you analyze and manage maintenance costs, and determine when a system is reaching the end of its useful life. To learn more about these tools, turn to Part 3 of the six-part Toolkit that follows Chapter 10.

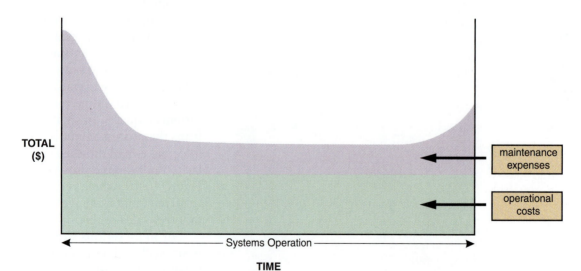

FIGURE 10-7 The total cost of operating an information system includes operational and maintenance costs. Operational costs (green) are relatively constant, while maintenance expenses (purple) vary over time.

Examples of Maintenance Tasks

Corrective Maintenance
- Diagnose and fix logic errors
- Replace defective network cabling
- Restore proper configuration settings
- Debug program code
- Update drivers
- Install software patch

Adaptive Maintenance
- Add online capability
- Create new reports
- Add new data entry field to input screen
- Install links to Web site
- Create employee portal

Perfective Maintenance
- Install additional memory
- Write macros to handle repetitive tasks
- Compress system files
- Optimize user desktop settings
- Develop library for code reuse
- Install more powerful network server

Preventive Maintenance
- Install new antivirus software
- Develop standard backup schedule
- Implement regular defragmentation process
- Analyze problem report for patterns
- Tighten all cable connections

FIGURE 10-8 Corrective maintenance fixes errors and problems. Adaptive maintenance provides enhancements to a system. Perfective maintenance improves a system's efficiency, reliability, or maintainability. Preventive maintenance avoids future problems.

Near the end of a system's useful life, adaptive and corrective maintenance expenses increase rapidly, but perfective maintenance typically decreases when it becomes clear that the company plans to replace the system. Figure 10-9 shows the typical patterns for each of the four classifications of maintenance activities over a system's life span.

Corrective Maintenance

Corrective maintenance diagnoses and corrects errors in an operational system. In addition to errors in the original version of the system, corrective maintenance often is needed to resolve issues created by previous maintenance changes. To avoid introducing new problems, all maintenance work requires careful analysis before making changes. The best maintenance approach is a scaled-down version of the SDLC itself, where investigation, analysis, design, and testing are performed before implementing any solution. Recall that in Chapter 9 you learned about the difference between a test environment and an operational environment. Any maintenance work that could affect the system must be performed first in the test environment, and then migrated to the operational system.

IT support staff can respond to errors in various ways, depending on the nature and severity of the problem. Most organizations have standard procedures for minor errors, such as an incorrect report title or an improper format for a data element. In a typical procedure, a user submits a systems request that is evaluated, prioritized, and scheduled by the system administrator or the systems review committee. If the request is approved, the maintenance team designs, tests, documents, and implements a solution. As you learned in Chapter 2, many organizations use a standard online form for systems requests. In smaller firms the process might be an informal e-mail message similar to the example shown in Figure 10-10, which requests a relatively minor change in a monthly sales report.

For more serious situations, such as incorrect report totals or inconsistent data, a user submits a systems request with supporting evidence. Those requests receive a high priority and a maintenance

	Immediately After Implementation	Early Operational Life	Middle Operational Life	Later Operational Life
Corrective Maintenance	High	Low	Low	High
Adaptive Maintenance (Minor Enhancements)	None	Medium	Medium	Medium
Adaptive Maintenance (Major Enhancements)	None	None	Medium to High	Medium to High
Perfective Maintenance	Low	Low to Medium	Medium	Low
Preventive Maintenance	Low	Medium	Medium	Low

FIGURE 10-9 Information systems maintenance depends on two major factors: the type of maintenance and the age of the system.

team begins work on the problem immediately. Severe errors sometimes occur because the system's developers did not test for certain data combinations or processing situations.

The worst-case situation is a total system failure. If an emergency occurs, the maintenance team bypasses the initial steps and tries to correct the failure immediately. Meanwhile, a written systems request is prepared by a user or a member of the IT department and added to the maintenance log. When the system is operational again, the maintenance team determines the cause, analyzes the problem, and designs a permanent solution. The IT response team updates the test data files, thoroughly tests the system, and prepares full documentation.

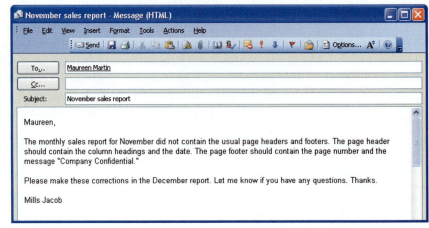

FIGURE 10-10   Example of an e-mail request for the correction of a formatting error in a report.

The process of managing system support is described in more detail on page 481, including an overview of maintenance tasks and a procedural flowchart, which is shown in Figure 10-14 on page 486.

Adaptive Maintenance

Adaptive maintenance adds enhancements to an operational system and makes the system easier to use. An **enhancement** is a new feature or capability. The need for adaptive maintenance usually arises from business environment changes such as new products or services, new manufacturing technology, or support for a new Web-based operation.

The procedure for minor adaptive maintenance is similar to routine corrective maintenance. A user submits a systems request that is evaluated and prioritized by the systems review committee. A maintenance team then analyzes, designs, tests, and implements the enhancement. Although the procedures for the two types of maintenance are alike, adaptive maintenance requires more IT department resources than minor corrective maintenance.

A major adaptive maintenance project is like a small-scale SDLC project because the development procedure is similar. Adaptive maintenance can be more difficult than new systems development because the enhancements must work within the constraints of an existing system.

Perfective Maintenance

Perfective maintenance involves changing an operational system to make it more efficient, reliable, or maintainable. Requests for corrective and adaptive maintenance normally come from users, while the IT department usually initiates perfective maintenance.

During system operation, changes in user activity or data patterns can cause a decline in efficiency, and perfective maintenance might be needed to restore performance. When users are concerned about performance, you should determine if a perfective maintenance project could improve response time and system efficiency.

Perfective maintenance also can improve system reliability. For example, input problems might cause a program to terminate abnormally. By modifying the data entry process, you can highlight errors and notify the users that they must enter proper data. When a system is easier to maintain, support is less costly and less risky. In many cases, you can simplify a complex program to improve maintainability.

In many organizations, perfective maintenance is not performed frequently enough. Companies with limited resources often consider new systems development, adaptive maintenance, and corrective maintenance more important than perfective maintenance. Managers and users constantly request new projects, so few resources are available for perfective maintenance work. As a practical matter, perfective maintenance can be performed as part of another project. For example, if a new function must be added to a program, you can include perfective maintenance in the adaptive maintenance project.

Perfective maintenance usually is cost-effective during the middle of the system's operational life. Early in systems operation, perfective maintenance usually is not needed. Later, perfective maintenance might be necessary, but have a high cost. Most benefits of perfective maintenance are less valuable if the company already plans to discontinue the system.

When performing perfective maintenance, analysts often use a technique called software reengineering. **Software reengineering** uses analytical techniques to identify potential quality and performance improvements in an information system. In that sense, software reengineering is similar to business process reengineering, which seeks to simplify operations, reduce costs, and improve quality — as you learned in Chapter 1.

ON THE WEB

For more information about Software Reengineering, visit **scsite.com/sad6e/ more**, locate Chapter 10, and then click the Software Reengineering link.

Depending on the results of software reengineering, the system might be revised, migrated to a different environment, or replaced altogether. Tominy Services is an example of a firm that specializes in helping business and government agencies migrate applications to new hardware and software platforms, as shown in Figure 10-11. An excellent tutorial and explanation of reengineering by Professor Hausi A. Müller can be found at www.rigi.csc.uvic.ca/UVicRevTut/ F3strat.html.

Programs that need a large number of maintenance changes usually are good candidates for reengineering. The more a program changes, the more likely it is to become inefficient and difficult to maintain. Detailed records of maintenance work can identify systems with a history of frequent corrective, adaptive, or perfective maintenance.

Preventive Maintenance

To avoid problems, preventive maintenance requires analysis of areas where trouble is likely to occur. Like perfective maintenance, the IT department normally initiates preventive maintenance. Preventive maintenance often results in increased user satisfaction, decreased downtime, and reduced TCO. Preventive maintenance competes for IT resources along with other projects, and sometimes does not receive the high priority that it deserves.

FIGURE 10-11 Tominy Services specializes in helping business and government agencies migrate applications to new hardware and software platforms.

CASE IN POINT 10.1: OUTBACK OUTSOURCING, INC.

You are a systems analyst at Outback Outsourcing, a firm that handles payroll processing for many large companies. Outback Outsourcing uses a combination of payroll package programs and in-house developed software to deliver custom-made payroll solutions for its clients. Lately, users have flooded you with requests for more new features and Web-based capability to meet customer expectations. Your boss, the IT manager, comes to you with a question. She wants to know when to stop trying to enhance the old software and develop a totally new version better suited to the new marketplace. How would you answer her?

MANAGING SYSTEM SUPPORT

System support requires effective management, quality assurance, and cost control. To achieve these goals, companies use a variety of strategies, such as a maintenance team, a process for managing maintenance requests and priorities, a configuration management process, and a maintenance release procedure. In addition, firms can use version control and baselines to track system releases and analyze the system's life cycle. These strategies and terms are described in the following sections.

Maintenance Team

A **maintenance team** consists of a system administrator, and one or more systems analysts and programmers. The system administrator should have solid technical expertise, and experience in troubleshooting and configuring operating systems and hardware. Successful analysts need a background in information technology, strong analytical abilities, and a good understanding of business operations and management functions. IT managers have various views on how to organize and staff a maintenance team, and the approach varies depending on the firm.

SYSTEM ADMINISTRATOR A **system administrator** manages computer and network systems. A system administrator must work well under pressure, have good organizational and communication skills, and be able to understand and resolve complex issues in a limited time frame. In most organizations, a system administrator has primary responsibility for the operation, configuration, and security of one or more systems. The system administrator is responsible for routine maintenance of operating systems, networks, and hardware components. The system administrator usually is authorized to take preventive action to avoid an immediate emergency, such as a server crash, network outage, security incident, or hardware failure. Systems administration is a vital function, and various professional associations, such as SAGE, which is shown in Figure 10-12 on the next page, offer a wide variety of technical information and support for system administrators.

SYSTEMS ANALYSTS Systems analysts assigned to a maintenance team are like skilled detectives who investigate and rapidly locate the source of a problem by using analysis and synthesis skills. **Analysis** means examining the whole in order to learn about the individual elements, while **synthesis** involves studying the parts to understand the overall system. A systems analyst must understand the system elements and how to maintain them without affecting the overall system. Analysts also need effective interpersonal and communications skills and they must be creative, energetic, and eager for new knowledge.

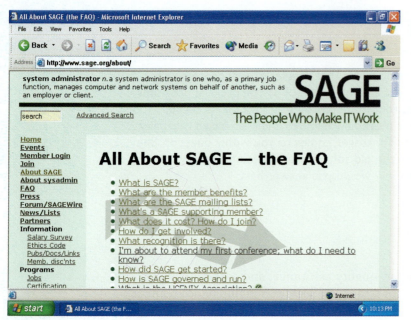

FIGURE 10-12   As stated on its Web site, SAGE seeks to advance the status of system administration as a profession, establish standards of professional excellence and recognize those who attain them, develop guidelines for improving the technical and managerial capabilities of members of the profession, and promote activities that advance the state of the art or the community.

PROGRAMMERS   In a small organization, a programmer might be expected to handle a wide variety of tasks, but in larger firms, programming work tends to be more specialized. For example, typical job titles include an **applications programmer**, who works on new systems development and maintenance; a **systems programmer**, who concentrates on operating system software and utilities; and a **database programmer**, who focuses on creating and supporting large-scale database systems. Many IT departments also use a job title of **programmer/analyst** to designate positions that require a combination of systems analysis and programming skills.

ORGANIZATIONAL ISSUES   IT managers often divide systems analysts and programmers into two groups: one group performs new system development, and the other group handles all maintenance. One advantage of this approach is that the maintenance group develops strong support skills. Some organizations, however, use a more flexible approach and assign IT staff members to various projects as they occur. By integrating development and support work, the people developing the system also assume responsibility for maintaining it. Because the team is familiar with the project, additional training or expense is unnecessary, and members are likely to have a sense of ownership from the onset.

Unfortunately, many analysts feel that maintenance work is less attractive than developing new systems, which they see as more interesting and creative. In addition, an analyst might find it more challenging to troubleshoot and support someone else's work that might have been poorly documented and organized.

Some organizations that have separate maintenance and new systems groups and rotate people from one assignment to the other. When analysts learn different skills, the organization is more versatile and people can shift to meet changing business needs. For instance, systems analysts working on maintenance projects learn why it is important to design easily maintainable systems. Similarly, analysts working on new systems get a better appreciation of the development process and the design compromises necessary to meet business objectives. That knowledge can help them become better maintenance systems analysts.

One disadvantage of rotation is that it increases overhead costs because time is lost when people move from one job to another. When systems analysts constantly shift between maintenance and new development, they have less opportunity to become highly skilled at any one job. Another disadvantage is that with the rotation method, some analysts must spend a substantial amount of time in a job that is less desirable to them personally.

Newly hired and recently promoted IT staff members often are assigned to maintenance projects because their managers believe that maintenance work offers the best learning experience. The opportunity to study existing systems and documentation is an excellent way to gain experience. In addition, the mini-SDLC used in many adaptive maintenance projects is good training for the full-scale systems development life cycle. For a new systems analyst, however, maintenance work might be more difficult than systems development tasks, and it might make sense to assign a new person to a development team where experienced analysts are available to provide training and guidance.

CASE IN POINT 10.2: BRIGHTSIDE INSURANCE, INC.

As IT manager at Brightside Insurance Company, you organized your IT staff into two separate groups — one team for maintenance projects and the other team for new systems work. That arrangement worked well in your last position at another company. Brightside, however, previously made systems assignments with no particular pattern.

At first, the systems analysts in your group did not comment about the team approach. Now, several of your best analysts have indicated that they enjoyed the mix of work and would not want to be assigned to a maintenance team. Before a problem develops, you have decided to rethink your organizational strategy. Should you go back to the way things were done previously at Brightside? Why or why not? Do other options exist? What are they?

Managing Maintenance Requests

Typically, maintenance requests involve a series of steps, as shown in Figure 10-13 on the next page. After a user submits a request, a system administrator determines whether immediate action is needed and whether the request is under a prescribed cost limit. In non-emergency requests that exceed the cost limit, a systems review committee assesses the request and either approves it, with a priority, or rejects it. The system administrator notifies affected users of the outcome.

MAINTENANCE REQUEST Users submit most requests for corrective and adaptive maintenance when the system is not performing properly, or if they want new features. IT staff members usually initiate requests for perfective and preventive maintenance. To keep a complete maintenance log, all work must be covered by a specific request that users submit in writing or by e-mail.

INITIAL DETERMINATION When a user submits a maintenance request, the system administrator makes an initial determination. If the request is justifiable and involves a severe problem that requires immediate attention, the system administrator takes action at once. In justifiable, but non-critical, situations, the administrator determines whether the request can be performed within a pre-authorized cost level. If so, he or she assigns the maintenance tasks and monitors the work.

ROLE OF THE SYSTEMS REVIEW COMMITTEE When a request exceeds a predetermined cost level or involves a major configuration change, the systems review committee either approves it and assigns a priority, or rejects it.

COMPLETION OF THE WORK The system administrator usually is responsible for assigning maintenance tasks to individuals or to a maintenance team. Depending on the situation and the company's policy, the system administrator might consider rotating assignments among the IT staff or limit maintenance tasks to certain individuals or teams, as explained in the previous section.

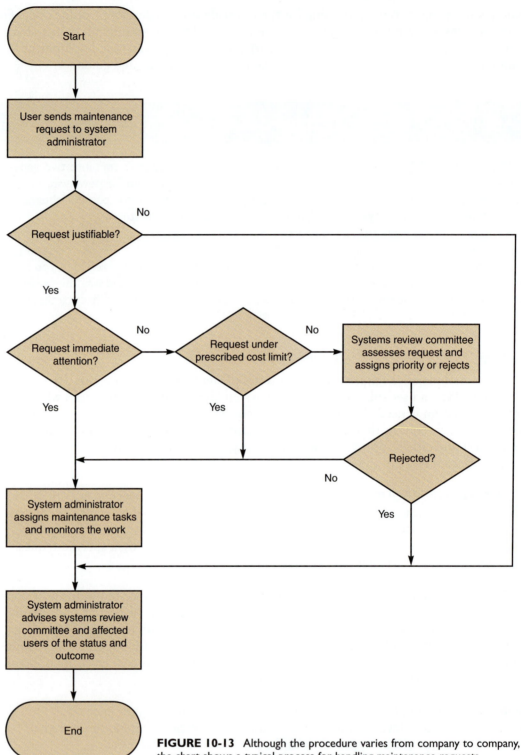

FIGURE 10-13 Although the procedure varies from company to company, the chart shows a typical process for handling maintenance requests.

USER NOTIFICATION Users who initiate maintenance requests expect a prompt response, especially if the situation directly affects their job responsibilities. Even when corrective action cannot occur immediately, users appreciate feedback from the system administrator and should be kept informed of any decisions or actions that affect their maintenance requests.

Establishing Priorities

In many companies, the systems review committee separates maintenance requests from new systems development requests when evaluating requests and setting priorities. In other organizations, all requests for systems services are put into one group and considered together; the most important project then is given top priority, whether it is maintenance or new development.

Many IT managers believe that evaluating all projects together leads to the best possible decisions because maintenance and new development require similar IT department resources. In IT departments where systems analysts and programmers are organized into separate maintenance and new development groups, however, it might make sense to evaluate requests separately. Another advantage of a separate approach is that maintenance is more likely to receive a proportional share of IT department resources.

Neither approach guarantees an ideal allocation between maintenance and new systems development. The most important objective is to have a procedure that balances new development and necessary maintenance work to provide the best support for business requirements and priorities.

Configuration Management

Configuration management (CM) is a process for controlling changes in system requirements during the development phases of the SDLC. Configuration management also is an important tool for managing system changes and costs after a system becomes operational. Most companies establish a specific process that describes how system changes must be requested and documented.

As enterprise-wide information systems grow more complex, configuration management becomes critical. Industry standards have emerged, and many vendors offer configuration management software and techniques. In addition to providing configuration management for complex projects as shown in Figure 10-14 on the next page, AccuRev software claims that its product enables many people to coordinate their actions effectively.

A system implemented in multiple environments often has different versions for each platform, and thus requires different maintenance updates. Configuration management is an effective tool for managing that type of situation. Using a specific configuration management process, the IT staff keeps track of all system versions, installs all maintenance updates, and ensures that all versions of the system work correctly.

Configuration management also helps to organize and handle documentation. An operational system has extensive documentation that covers development, modification, and maintenance for all versions of the installed system. Most documentation material, including the initial systems request, project management data, end-of-phase reports, data dictionary, and the IT operations and user manuals, is stored in the IT department.

Most maintenance projects require documentation changes. You must be especially careful to issue updates whenever you make adaptive changes or perform major corrective maintenance. It is important to avoid surprises for users and IT staff members. Keeping track of all documentation and ensuring that updates are distributed properly are important aspects of configuration management.

Maintenance Releases

Coordinating maintenance changes and updates can be difficult, especially for a complex system with several versions. Many organizations, and especially software vendors, use numbered releases to designate different versions. When a **maintenance release methodology** is used, all noncritical changes are held until they can be implemented at the same time. Each change is documented and installed as a new version of the system called a **maintenance release**.

ON THE WEB

For more information about Configuration Management, visit **scsite.com/sad6e/ more**, locate Chapter 10, and then click the Configuration Management link.

FIGURE 10-14 AccuRev provides configuration management software that helps companies maintain and coordinate complex IT systems. The CM Yellow Pages feature provides a source of information and resources for CM professionals.

For an in-house developed system, the time between releases usually depends on the level of maintenance activity. A new release to correct a critical error, however, might be implemented immediately rather than saved for the next scheduled release. The decision depends on the nature of the error and the possible impact of the release.

When a release method is used, a numbering pattern distinguishes the different releases. In a typical system, the initial version of the system is 1.0, and the release that includes the first set of maintenance changes is version 1.1. A change, for example, from version 1.4 to 1.5 indicates relatively minor enhancements, while whole number changes, such as from version 1.0 to 2.0 or from version 3.4 to 4.0, indicate a significant upgrade.

The release methodology offers several advantages, especially if two teams perform maintenance work on the same system. When a release methodology is used, all changes are tested together before a new system version is released. The release methodology also reduces costs because only one set of system tests is needed for all maintenance changes. This approach results in fewer versions, less expense, and less interruption for users.

Using a release methodology also reduces the documentation burden. Every time a new version of a system is implemented, all documentation must be updated, and some users feel that they spend too much time filing documentation changes. Even worse, some users let the upgrades pile up and eventually ignore them. With a release methodology, all documentation changes are coordinated and become effective simultaneously. Users and IT staff members integrate a package of updates into their documentation for each release.

The release methodology also has some potential disadvantages. Users expect a rapid response to their problems and requests, but with a release methodology, new features or upgrades are available less often. Even when changes would improve system efficiency or user productivity, the potential savings must wait until the next release date, which might increase operational costs.

Commercial software suppliers also provide maintenance releases, often called **service packs**, similar to the Microsoft Service Pack for Windows XP shown in Figure 10-15. As Microsoft explains, a Service Pack contains all the fixes and enhancements that have been made available in the previous year.

Version Control

Version control is the process of tracking system releases, or versions. When a new version of a system is installed, the prior release is **archived**, or stored, along with any other previous versions. In some large organizations, this task is performed by a person called a **systems librarian**. If a new version causes a system to fail, a company can reinstall a prior version to restore operations. In addition to tracking system versions, the IT staff also is responsible for configuring systems that have several modules at various release stages. For example, an accounting system might have a one-year old accounts receivable module that must interface with a brand new general ledger module.

As systems grow more complex, version control becomes an essential part of system documentation necessary to maintain and support the system. In addition to in-house version control procedures, companies can purchase software from vendors such as

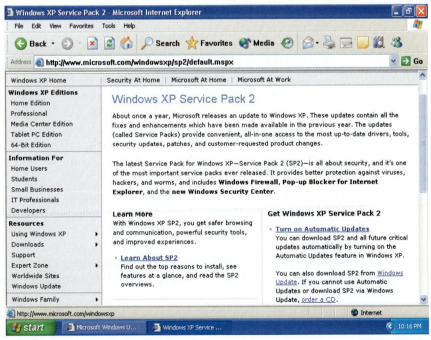

FIGURE 10-15 A Microsoft Service Pack provides access to up-to-date drivers, tools, security patches, and customer-requested product changes.

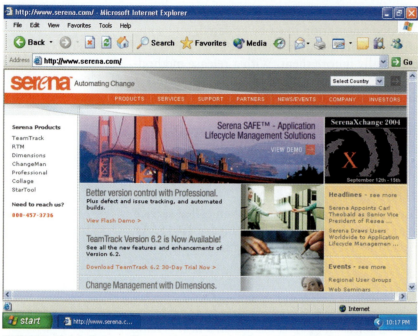

FIGURE 10-16 Serena offers products that provide version control and other software management features.

Serena, which offers products that provide version control and other software management features, as shown in Figure 10-16.

Baselines

A **baseline** is a formal reference point that measures system characteristics at a specific time. Systems analysts use baselines as yardsticks to document features and performance during the systems development process. The three types of baselines are functional, allocated, and product.

The **functional baseline** is the configuration of the system documented at the beginning of the project. It consists of all the necessary system requirements and design constraints.

The **allocated baseline** documents the system at the end of the design phase and identifies any changes since the functional baseline. The allocated baseline includes testing and verification of all system requirements and features.

The **product baseline** describes the system at the beginning of system operation. The product baseline incorporates any changes made since the allocated baseline and includes the results of performance and acceptance tests for the operational system.

MANAGING SYSTEM PERFORMANCE

A system's performance directly affects users who rely on it to perform their job functions. To ensure satisfactory support for business operations, the IT department monitors current system performance and anticipates future needs.

When most firms used a central computer for processing data, it was relatively simple to measure the efficiency of the system. Today, companies use complex networks and client/server systems to support business information needs. A user at a client workstation often interacts with an information system that depends on other clients, servers, networks, and data located throughout the company. Rather than a single computer, it is the integration of all those system components that determines the system's capability and performance.

To measure system performance, companies use **benchmark testing**, which also was discussed in Chapter 5, Development Strategies. In an article on benchmark basics shown in Figure 10-17, authors Bernard Farrell and Brian Butler describe benchmarking as a set of standard tests on one system to compare its performance and capacity to that of other systems. Many software vendors offer benchmark testing software. For example, as shown in Figure 10-18, Benchmark Factory® provides a variety of operational measurements and tests.

System management includes performance and workload management, capacity planning, and CASE tools that perform systems maintenance tasks and analysis.

Performance and Workload Measurement

You already are familiar with several **workload measurements**, including the number of lines printed, the number of records accessed, and the number of transactions processed in a given time period. To measure performance of network-based systems, an analyst also needs to consider response time, bandwidth, and throughput. Analysts also consider turnaround time as a way to measure system performance and user support.

RESPONSE TIME **Response time** is the overall time between a request for system activity and the delivery of the response. In the typical online environment, response time is measured from the instant the user presses the ENTER key or clicks a mouse button until the requested screen display appears or printed output is ready. Response time is affected by the system design, capabilities, and processing methods. If a user requests a batch-processed report, for example, the batch processing schedule determines the response time. Response time includes three elements: the time necessary to transmit or deliver the request to the system, the time that the system needs to process the request, and the time it takes to transmit or deliver the result back to the user. If the request involves network or Internet access, response time is affected by data communication factors.

Online users expect an immediate response, and they are frustrated by any apparent lag or delay. Of all performance measurements, response time is the one that users notice and complain about most.

Benchmark Basics
By Bernard Farell and Brian Butler

Introduction
One can think of benchmarking as the running of a set of standard tests on one system to compare its performance and capacity to that of other systems. Benchmarks measure:

- Performance of an enterprise system
- Performance of a specific subsystem, such as disk, video, CPU, or memory
- Performance of a particular application, such as spreadsheet, database, or CAD/CAM
- Performance of server-based applications, such as database, file, messaging, or Web
- Capacity of an enterprise system

All good benchmarks use a well-defined testing methodology based on real-world use of a computer system. Benchmarks measure system performance in a deterministic and reproducible manner, allowing a user to judge the performance and capacity of their systems properly. When used properly, benchmarks determine:

- Reliability
- Bottlenecks
- Enterprise capacity
- Impartial purchasing information

Why Benchmark?
Reliable enterprise-server performance equates to excellent customer service. Excellent customer service equates to maximized profits. In a highly competitive and unforgiving e-commerce environment, system performance is the defining factor that keeps customers satisfied. Satisfied customers provide higher company revenue and profit. Implementing a well-planned benchmarking program for e-commerce is essential to staying competitive.

FIGURE 10-17 The authors describe benchmarking as a set of standard tests on one system to compare its performance and capacity to that of other systems.

BANDWIDTH AND THROUGHPUT
Bandwidth and throughput are closely related terms, and many analysts use them interchangeably. **Bandwidth** describes the amount of data that the system can transfer in a fixed time period. Bandwidth requirements are expressed in bits per second. Depending on the system, you might measure bandwidth in **Kbps (kilobits per second)**, **Mbps (megabits per second)**, or **Gbps (gigabits per second)**. Analyzing bandwidth is similar to forecasting the hourly number of vehicles that will use a highway in order to determine the number of lanes required.

Throughput measures actual system performance under specific circumstances and is affected by network

FIGURE 10-18 Benchmark Factory® software provides a variety of operational measurements and tests.

loads and hardware efficiency. Throughput, like bandwidth, is expressed as a data transfer rate, such as Kbps, Mbps, or Gbps. Just as traffic jams delay highway traffic, throughput limitations can slow system performance and response time. That is especially true with graphics-intensive systems and Web-based systems that are subject to Internet-related conditions.

As you learned in Chapter 8, System Architecture, slow performance can be as devastating as no performance at all. Users expect reliable, fast responses 24 hours a day, seven days a week. The Computer Measurement Group (CMG®) maintains a site, shown in Figure 10-19, that provides support and assistance for IT professionals concerned with performance evaluation and capacity planning. Many vendors, such as Keynote, offer performance management software tools, as shown in Figure 10-20.

TURNAROUND TIME   **Turnaround time** applies to centralized batch processing operations, such as customer billing or credit card statement processing. Turnaround time measures the time between submitting a request for information and the fulfillment of the request. Turnaround time also can be used to measure the quality of IT support or services by measuring the time from a user request for help to the resolution of the problem.

The IT department often measures response time, bandwidth, throughput, and turnaround time to evaluate system performance both before and after changes to the system or business information requirements. Performance data also is used for cost-benefit analyses of proposed maintenance and to evaluate systems that are nearing the end of their economically useful lives.

Finally, management uses current performance and workload data as input for the capacity planning process.

Capacity Planning

Capacity planning is a process that monitors current activity and performance levels, anticipates future activity, and forecasts the resources needed to provide desired levels of service.

FIGURE 10-19 The Computer Measurement Group is a non-profit organization that primarily is concerned with performance evaluation and capacity management.

FIGURE 10-20 Keynote is a vendor that offers performance management software.

As the first step in capacity planning, you develop a current model based on the system's present workload and performance specifications. Then you project demand and user requirements over a one- to three-year time period and analyze the model to see what is needed to maintain satisfactory performance and meet requirements. To assist you in the process, you can use a technique called what-if analysis.

What-if analysis allows you to vary one or more elements in a model in order to measure the effect on other elements. For example, you might use what-if analysis to answer questions such as: How will response time be affected if we add more PC workstations to the network? Will our client/server system be able to handle the growth in sales from the new Web site? What will be the effect on server throughput if we add more memory?

Powerful spreadsheet tools also can assist you in performing what-if analysis. For example, Microsoft Excel contains a feature called Goal Seek that determines what changes are necessary in one value to produce a specific result for another value. In the

ON THE WEB

For more information about Capacity Planning, visit **scsite.com/sad6e/ more**, locate Chapter 10, and then click the Capacity Planning link.

FIGURE 10-21 Microsoft Excel provides a Goal Seek feature that permits what-if analysis. In the first example, the Web site order processing time is 22.5 seconds per order, and 3,840 orders per day. The analyst asks the program to calculate how much faster the processing must be to handle 9,000 transactions per day rather than 3,840. The second figure shows that the new processing time must be 9.6 seconds per order.

example shown in Figure 10-21, a capacity planning worksheet indicates that the system can handle 3,840 Web-based orders per day, at 22.5 seconds each. The user wants to know the effect on processing time if the number of transactions increases to 9,000. As the Goal Seek solution in the bottom figure shows, order processing will have to be performed in 9.6 seconds to achieve that goal.

When you plan capacity, you need detailed information about the number of transactions; the daily, weekly, or monthly transaction patterns; the number of queries; and the number, type, and size of all generated reports. If the system involves a LAN, you need to estimate network traffic levels to determine whether or not the existing hardware and software can handle the load. If the system uses a client/server design, you need to examine performance and connectivity specifications for each platform.

Most important, you need an accurate forecast of future business activities. If new business functions or requirements are predicted, you should develop contingency plans based on input from users and management. The main objective is to ensure that the system meets all future demands and provides effective support for business operations. Many firms offer capacity planning software and services, as shown in Figure 10-22.

System Maintenance Tools

You can use automated tools that provide valuable assistance during the operation and support phase. Many CASE tools include system evaluation and maintenance features, including the following examples:

- ➡ Performance monitor that provides data on program execution times
- ➡ Program analyzer that scans source code, provides data element cross-reference information, and helps evaluate the impact of a program change

- ➡ Interactive debugging analyzer that locates the source of a programming error
- ➡ Reengineering tools
- ➡ Automated documentation
- ➡ Network activity monitor
- ➡ Workload forecasting tool

In addition to CASE tools, you also can use spreadsheet and presentation software to calculate trends, perform what-if analyses, and create attractive charts and graphs to display the results. Information technology planning is an essential part of the business planning process, and you probably will deliver presentations to management. You can review Part 1 of the Systems Analyst's Toolkit for more information on using spreadsheet and presentation software to help you communicate effectively.

🛠 TOOLKIT TIME

The CASE tools in Part 2 of the Systems Analyst's Toolkit can help you document business functions and processes, develop graphical models, and provide an overall framework for information system development. To learn more about these tools, turn to Part 2 of the six-part Toolkit that follows Chapter 10.

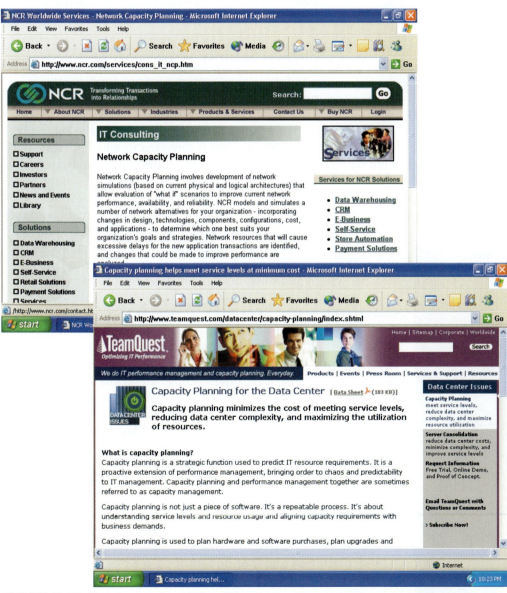

FIGURE 10-22 Many firms, such as NCR and TeamQuest, offer capacity planning software and services.

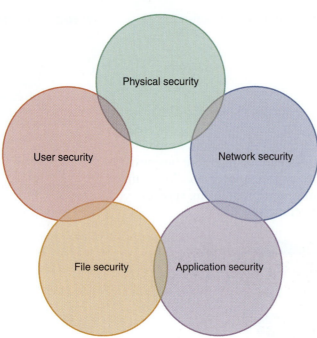

FIGURE 10-23 Overall security involves five separate, but interrelated, levels.

SYSTEM SECURITY

Security is a vital part of every computer system. This section discusses the importance of security and how companies are adapting to new security challenges and risks. Top managers often make the final strategic and budget decisions regarding security, but systems analysts should understand the overall picture in order to make informed recommendations. To assess system security, you must analyze five separate, but interrelated, security levels: physical security, network security, application security, file security, and user security. The following sections describe these levels, which are shown in Figure 10-23, and the issues that must be addressed.

Physical Security

The first level of system security concerns the physical environment, including critical equipment located in a computer room, as well as safeguards for servers and desktops throughout the company. A **computer room** is any area in which servers, network hardware, and related equipment operate. Some companies have a dedicated room built specifically for this purpose. Other firms might use an office, a storage area, or even a closet. Regardless of its size and shape, a computer room requires special protection from unwanted intrusion. In addition to computer room protection, all computers on the network must have some degree of physical security, because each server or workstation can be a potential access point. Physical access to a computer represents an entry point into the system and must be controlled and protected.

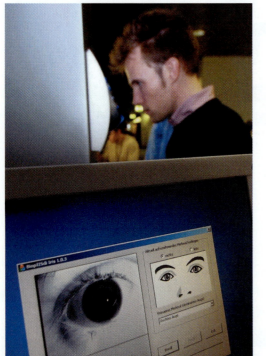

FIGURE 10-24 Companies use biometric scanning to analyze the features of the eye's iris, which has more than 200 points that can be measured and used for comparison.

COMPUTER ROOM SECURITY Perimeter security is essential in any room or area where computer equipment is operated or maintained. Physical access must be controlled tightly, and each entrance must be equipped with a suitable security device. All access doors should have internal hinges and electromagnetic locks that are equipped with a battery backup system to provide standby power in the event of a power outage. When the battery power is exhausted, the doors should fail in a closed position, but it should be possible for someone locked inside the room to open the door with an emergency release.

To enhance security, many companies are installing **biometric scanning systems**, which map an individual's facial features, handprint, or eye characteristics, as shown in Figure 10-24. These systems replace magnetic identification badges, which can be lost, stolen, or altered.

Video cameras and motion sensors can be used to monitor computer room security and provide documentation of all physical activity in the area. A **motion sensor** uses infrared technology to detect movement, and can be configured to provide audible or silent alarms, and to send e-mail messages when it is triggered. Other types of sensors can monitor temperature and humidity in the computer room. Motion sensor alarms can be activated at times when there is no expected activity in the computer room, and authorized technicians should have codes to enable or disable the alarms.

SERVERS AND DESKTOP COMPUTERS If possible, server and desktop computer cases should be equipped with locks. This simple, but important, precaution might prevent an intruder from modifying the hardware configuration of a server, damaging the equipment, or removing a disk drive. Server racks should be locked, to avoid the unauthorized placement and retrieval of keystroke loggers. A **keystroke logger** is a device that can be inserted between a keyboard and a computer. Typically, the device resembles an ordinary cable plug, so it does not call attention to itself. The device can record everything that is typed into the keyboard, including passwords, while the system continues to function normally. Keystroke loggers can be used legitimately to monitor, back up, and restore a system, but if placed by an intruder, a keystroke logger represents a serious security threat.

In addition to hardware devices, keystroke logging software also exists. A keystroke logging program can be disguised as legitimate software and downloaded from the Internet or a company network. The program remains invisible to the user as it records keystrokes and uploads the information to whoever installed the program.

Tamper-evident cases should be used where possible. A tamper-evident case is designed to show any attempt to open or unlock the case. In the event that a computer case has been opened, an indicator LED remains lit until it is cleared with a password. Tamper-evident cases do not prevent intrusion, but a security breach is more likely to be noticed. Many servers now are offered with tamper-evident cases as part of their standard configuration.

Monitor screensavers that hide the screen and require special passwords to clear should be used on any server or workstation that is left unattended. Also, use a **BIOS-level password**, also called a **boot-level password**, or a **power-on password**, that must be entered before the computer can be started. Also, a boot-level password prevents an unauthorized person from booting a computer by using a floppy disk or a CD-ROM.

NOTEBOOK COMPUTERS When assessing physical security issues, be sure to consider additional security provisions for notebook and laptop computers. Because of their small size and high value, notebook computers are tempting targets for thieves and industrial spies. Although the following suggestions are intended as a checklist for notebook computer security, many of them also apply to desktop workstations.

→ Select an operating system, such as Windows XP Professional or Windows 2000 Professional, that allows secure logons and BIOS-level passwords. Older versions of Windows did not offer these protections. Also, log on and work with a user account that has limited privileges rather than an administrator account, and mask the administrator account by giving it a different name that would be hard for a casual intruder to guess.

→ Mark or engrave the computer's case with the company name and address, or attach a tamper-proof asset ID tag. These measures might not discourage a professional thief, but might deter a casual thief, or at least make your computer relatively less desirable because it would be more difficult to use or resell. Security experts also recommend that you use a generic carrying case, such as an attaché case, rather than a custom carrying case that calls attention to itself and its contents. Also be sure to complete and submit all manufacturer registration cards.

→ Many notebook computers have a **Universal Security Slot** (USS) that can be fastened to a cable lock or laptop alarm. Again, while these precautions might not deter professional thieves, they might discourage and deter casual thieves.

→ Back up all vital data before using the notebook computer outside the office. Also, instead of using your computer's hard drive, save and transport highly

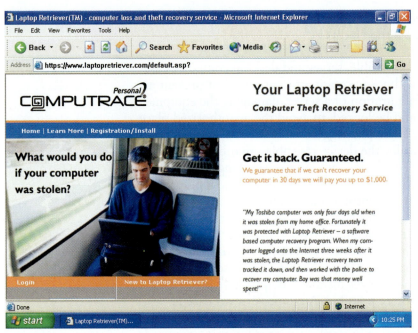

FIGURE 10-25 CompuTrace is a security firm that offers a $1,000 guarantee that it can recover a stolen computer within 30 days

sensitive data on removable media, such as a flash memory device.

➡ Use tracking software that directs your laptop periodically to contact a security tracking center. If your notebook is stolen, the call-in identifies the computer and its physical location. Armed with this information, the security tracking center can alert law enforcement agencies and communications providers. As shown in Figure 10-25, CompuTrace is a security firm that offers a $1,000 guarantee that it can recover a stolen computer within 30 days.

➡ While traveling, try to be alert to potential high-risk situations, where a thief, or thieves, might attempt to distract your attention and snatch your computer. These situations often occur in crowded, noisy places like airport baggage claim areas, rental car counters, and security checkpoints. Also, while traveling by car, store your computer in a trunk or lockable compartment where it will not be visible through a window.

➡ Establish stringent password protection policies that require minimum length and complexity, and set a limit on how many times an invalid password can be entered before the system locks itself down. This feature is called an account lockout threshold, and can be created by clicking Control Panel – Administrative Tools – Security Policy, and following the various menu choices. A specific lockout duration also can be selected. In some situations, you might want to establish file encryption policies to protect extremely sensitive files.

CASE IN POINT 10.3: OUTER BANKS COUNTY

Outer Banks County is a 200-square-mile area in coastal North Carolina, and you are the IT manager. The county has about a hundred office employees who perform clerical tasks in various departments. A recent budget crisis has resulted in a wage and hiring freeze, and morale has declined. The county manager has asked you to install some type of keystroke logger to monitor employees and determine whether they are fully productive. After your conversation, you wonder whether there might be some potential privacy and security issues involved.

For example, does an employer have a duty to notify its employees that it is monitoring them? Should the employer notify them even if not required to do so? From a human resources viewpoint, what would be the best way to approach this issue? Also, does a potential security issue exist? If an unauthorized person gained possession of the keystroke log, he or she might be able to uncover passwords and other sensitive data.

What are your conclusions? Are these issues important, and how would you respond to the county manager's recommendation? Before you answer, you should go on the Internet and learn more about keystroke loggers generally, and specific products that currently are available.

Network Security

A **network** is defined as two or more devices that are connected for the purpose of sending, receiving, and sharing data, which is called network **traffic**. In order to connect to a network, a computer must have a **network interface**, which is a combination of hardware and software that allows the computer to interact with the network. To provide security for network traffic, data can be **encrypted**, which refers to a process of encoding the data so it cannot be accessed without authorization.

ENCRYPTING NETWORK TRAFFIC Network traffic can be intercepted and possibly altered, redirected, or recorded. For example, if an **unencrypted**, or **plain text**, password or credit card number is transmitted over a network connection, it can be stolen. When the traffic is encrypted, it still is visible, but its content and purpose are masked.

Figure 10-26 shows an example of encrypted traffic compared to plain text traffic. In the upper screen, the user has logged on to the SCR Associates case study, using a password of sad6. Notice that anyone who gains access to this data easily could learn the user's password. In the lower screen, the user has logged on to an online bank account and used a password, but the encryption process has made it impossible to decipher the keystrokes.

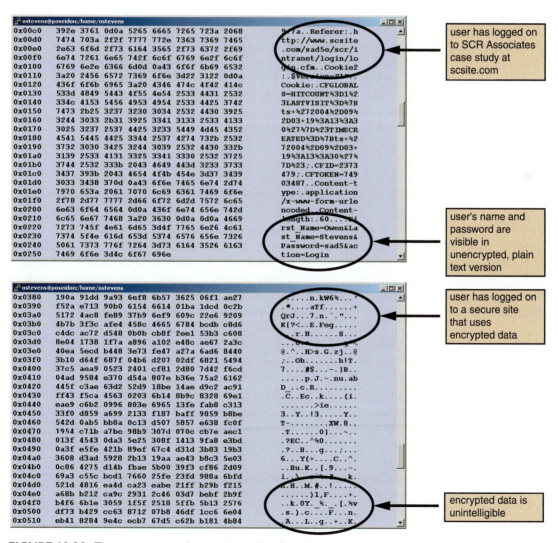

FIGURE 10-26 The upper screen shows an example of unencrypted text, which contains a visible password. In the lower screen, the encrypted text cannot be read.

Message

Encrypted with Public Key

Only can be decrypted with
Private Key

FIGURE 10-27 In a PKE environment, a message encrypted with a public key only can be decrypted with the matching private key.

A common encryption technique is called **public key encryption (PKE)**. In a PKE environment, each user on the network has a pair of keys: a **public key** and a **private key**, as shown in Figure 10-27. A user can send his or her public key to other users, and the recipients can use the public key to encrypt and transmit messages to the original sender, who is the owner of the public key. Data encrypted with that key, however, only can be decrypted with the matching private key. The matching private key is the other half of the key pair, and must be guarded tightly by its owner.

It is especially important to encrypt traffic on a wireless network. Wi-Fi networks present a unique vulnerability, in that traffic interception cannot be prevented. If the traffic is encrypted adequately, any data that is intercepted by an unintended recipient will be useless to the intruder. **Wi-Fi Protected Access (WPA)** and **Wired Equivalent Privacy (WEP)** are the most common methods used to secure a wireless network. This approach requires each wireless client be configured manually to use a special, pre-shared key, rather than key pairs.

PRIVATE NETWORKS It is not always practical to secure all network traffic. Unfortunately, encrypting traffic increases the burden on a network, and can decrease network performance significantly. In situations where network speed is essential, such as a Web server linked to a database server, many firms use a private network to connect the computers. A **private network** is a dedicated connection, similar to a leased telephone line. Each computer on the private network must have a dedicated interface to the network, and no interface on the network should connect to any point outside the network. In this configuration, unencrypted traffic safely can be transmitted because it is not visible, and cannot be intercepted from outside the network.

VIRTUAL PRIVATE NETWORKS Private networks work well with a limited number of computers, but if a company wants to establish secure connections for a larger group, it can create a virtual private network (VPN). A **virtual private network (VPN)** uses a public network, such as the Internet or a company intranet, to connect remote users securely. Instead of using a dedicated connection, a VPN allows remote clients to use a special key exchange that must be authenticated by the VPN. Once authentication is complete, a secure network connection, called a **tunnel**, is established between the client and the access point of the local intranet. All traffic is encrypted through the VPN tunnel, which provides an additional level of encryption and security.

PORTS AND SERVICES A **port**, which is identified by a positive integer, is used for routing incoming traffic to the correct application on a computer. In TCP/IP networks, such as the Internet, all traffic received by a computer contains a **destination port**. Because the destination port determines where the traffic will be routed, the computer sorts the traffic by port number, which is included in the transmitted data. An analogy might be a large apartment building with multiple mailboxes. Each mailbox has the same street address, but a different box number.

A **service** is an application that monitors, or listens on, a particular port. For example, a typical e-mail application listens on port 110. Any traffic received by that port is routed to the e-mail application. Services play an important role in computer security, and they can be affected by port scans and denial of service attacks.

1. Port scans. **Port scans** attempt to detect the services running on a computer by trying to connect to various ports and recording the ports on which a connection was accepted. For example the result of an open port 110 would indicate that a mail server is running. Port scans can be used to draw an accurate map of a network, and pinpoint possible weaknesses.

2. Denial of service. A **denial of service** (**DOS**) attack occurs when an attacking computer makes repeated requests to a service or services running on certain ports. Because the target computer has to respond to each request, it can become bogged down and fail to respond to legitimate requests. A much more devastating attack based on this method is called a **distributed denial of service** (**DDOS**) attack. This attack involves multiple attacking computers that can synchronize DOS attacks on a server, as shown in Figure 10-28.

FIREWALLS A **firewall** is the main line of defense between a local network, or intranet, and the Internet. Firewall software examines all of the network traffic sent to and from the intranet. Preset **rules**, also called **protocols**, determine whether the firewall will allow the traffic to pass. When a matching rule or protocol is found, the firewall automatically accepts or rejects the traffic. Firewalls can be configured to detect and respond to DOS attacks, port scans, and other suspicious activity. For example, a basic set of firewall rules for a company that has a Web server might include the following:

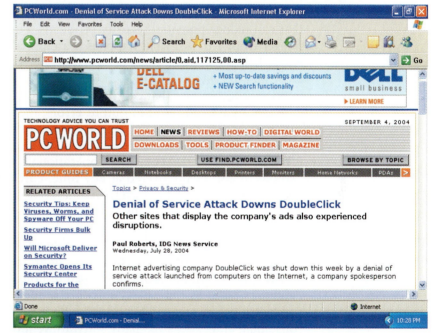

1. Allow incoming traffic (ports 80 and 443) to our Web server

2. Block incoming traffic to any other ports

FIGURE 10-28 The screen shows an example of a denial of service attack.

3. Detect port scans and block all traffic to a scanned port

Application Security

In addition to securing the computer room and shielding network traffic, it is necessary to protect any applications running on a server. The systems analyst should be aware of each server-based application and possible security implications that might arise. To protect the integrity and configuration of an application, the systems analyst must analyze its functions, identify possible security concerns, and carefully study all available documentation. Application security also requires an understanding of services, input validation techniques, and software patches and updates.

SERVICES In the Network Security section, you learned that a service is an application that monitors, or listens on, a particular port. A systems analyst can determine which services are running by conducting a routine port scan, which is a software utility that detects a running application. If a particular application is not needed, it should be disabled. Disabling unnecessary applications and services also improves system performance and reliability. In some cases, a combination of one or more improperly configured services could create a vulnerability called a **security hole**. For example, a Web server and an anonymous FTP (File Transfer Protocol) service could be configured on the same server to use the same files. A malicious user could use the FTP server to upload some destructive code, and then use the Web server to gain access to the malicious code.

Typically, applications are configured to run only as a user has specific rights to access the program. For example, an **administrator**, or **super-user**, account allows essentially unrestricted access to the application. To prevent unauthorized or destructive changes, the application should be configured to be available to users with non-privileged accounts, so that they can access the program but are unable to make changes to built-in functions or configurations. User rights, also called **permissions**, are discussed in more detail in the File Security section, which follows.

INPUT VALIDATION Most applications accept input from other programs, files, or users. When designing an application, it is essential to include input validation features that can reduce potential security problems. For example, if an application requires an integer from 1 to 10, what happens if an alphabetic character, or the number 31 is entered? If the application is designed properly, it will respond with an appropriate error message. As you learned in Chapter 6, data entry and validation checks are important techniques that can help safeguard data integrity and quality. Failure to validate input data can result in output errors, increased maintenance expense, and erratic system behavior.

PATCHES AND UPDATES In an operational system, security holes, also called **exploits**, might be discovered at any time. **Patches** are software modules intended to repair these holes, and reduce the vulnerability of a server or application. Patches should be tested carefully, just as any new software release must be tested as part of the configuration management process. Before applying a patch, an effort should be made to determine the risks of *not* applying the patch, and the possibility that the patch might affect other areas of the system.

An application that is not developed in-house often is called **third-party software**. Patches released by third-party software vendors usually are safe, but research should be conducted before any patch is applied. Because researching and applying patches is time-consuming and expensive, many software vendors offer an **automatic update service** that enables an application to contact the vendor's server and check for a needed patch. If a patch is available, it can be downloaded and installed without human intervention. Depending on the configuration, the update process might be entirely automated, or could require approval by IT managers. Although it is convenient, fully automatic updating carries very substantial risks, and is acceptable only if the change can readily be undone if the patch produces unexpected results or problems.

File Security

Computer configuration settings, users' personal information, and other sensitive data are stored in files. The safety and protection of these files is a vital element in any computer security program, and a systems analyst needs to consider the importance of permissions, which can be assigned to individual users or to user groups.

PERMISSIONS File security is based on establishing a set of permissions, which describe the rights a user has to a particular file or directory on a server. The most common permissions are read, write, and execute. Typical examples of permission include the following:

- Read a file — The user can read the contents of the file
- Write a file — The user can change the contents of the file
- Execute a file — The user can run the file, if it is a program
- Read a directory — The user can list the contents of the directory
- Write a directory — The user can add and remove files in the directory

When assigning file permissions, a system administrator should ensure that each user has only the minimum permissions necessary to perform his or her work — not more. In some firms, the system administrator has broad discretion in assigning these levels; in other companies an appropriate level of management approval is required for any permissions above a standard user level. In any case, a well-documented and enforced permissions policy is necessary to promote file security and reduce system vulnerability.

USER GROUPS Individual users who need to collaborate and share files often request a higher level of permissions that would enable any of them to change file content. A better approach, from a system administrator's viewpoint, might be to create a user group, add specific users, and assign file permissions to the group, rather than to the individuals. Many firms use this approach, because it allows a user's rights to be determined by his or her work responsibilities, rather than by job title or rank. If a person is transferred, he or she leaves certain groups and joins others that reflect current job duties.

User Security

The final level of security involves the identification of system users and consideration of user-related security issues. Regardless of other security precautions and features, security ultimately depends on system users and their habits, practices, and willingness to support security goals. Unfortunately, many system break-ins begin with a user account that is compromised in some way. Typically, an intruder accesses the system using the compromised account, and may attempt a **privilege escalation attack**, which is an unauthorized attempt to increase permission levels. User security involves identity management policies that include a comprehensive password protection policy and awareness of social engineering risks, and an effective means of overcoming user resistance.

IDENTITY MANAGEMENT Identity management refers to controls and procedures necessary to identify legitimate users and system components. Identity management involves a mix of technology, security issues, societal concerns about privacy, and business-related interests in cost effectiveness and user productivity. It is important to recognize that identity management is an evolving technology that is being pursued intensively by corporations, IT associations, and governments on an international basis.

In an excellent paper that can be downloaded at burtongroup.com, the Burton Group describes identity management as a "set of electronic records that represent ... people, machines, devices, applications, and services." This definition of identity management suggests that not just users, but each component in a system, must have a verifiable identity that is based on unique characteristics. For example, user authentication might be based on a combination of a password, a Social Security number, an employee number, a job title, and a physical location. According to the Burton Group, companies are starting to address identity management as an enterprise issue, rather than on a system-by-system basis. The white paper suggests that in the future, identity management technology will stress portable, enterprise-wide authentication and control techniques. Because of the

ON THE WEB

For more information about Identity Management, visit **scsite.com/6e/more**, locate Chapter 10, and then click the Identity Management link.

devastating consequences of intrusion, IT managers are giving top priority to identity management strategies and solutions. The first line of defense for any system is user passwords, but additional levels of password protection can add cost and cause inconvenience for legitimate users. Even without compromising the password protection layer, determined intruders can penetrate system security by using social engineering techniques. These topics are discussed in the following sections.

PASSWORD PROTECTION   Although password issues were discussed earlier in the section on physical security, the following section offers additional suggestions about password protection. Although passwords are a key element in any security program, users often prefer to choose passwords that are easy to recall, and they sometimes resent having to remember complex passwords, or multiple passwords. IT managers should require passwords that have a minimum length and require a combination of case-sensitive letters and numbers. Unfortunately, any password can be compromised if a user writes it down and stores it in an easily accessible location in a desk or on a bulletin board. As a protective measure, many companies establish a password time limit, such as 30 or 60 days, and require users to select a new password when the limit is reached.

In addition to traditional password protection, new technologies are available to secure the company networks and authenticate legitimate users. For example, some firms issue their employees a small handheld device that can generate and display a numeric validation code that the employee enters in addition to his or her normal password. Using this technology, America Online, Inc., recently announced a second level of protection called **AOL® PassCode**, as shown in Figure 10-29. Users who want to take advantage of this feature can obtain a keychain-sized device that displays a unique six-digit code every 60 seconds. After entering his or her primary password, the user then inputs this code, which validates the account.

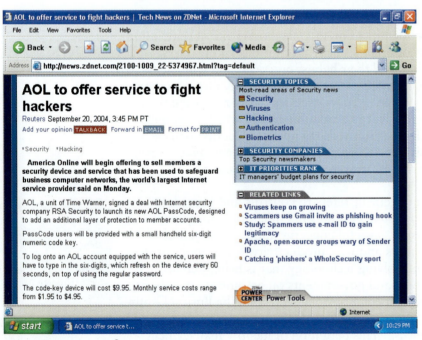

FIGURE 10-29 AOL® PassCode uses a keychain-sized device that generates and displays a unique six-digit validation code.

Unfortunately, new technology sometimes creates new risks. For example, in October 2004, Google announced a downloadable desktop-based search engine with a powerful indexing feature that scans all the files, documents, e-mail, chats, and stored Web pages on a user's computer. In an October 19, 2004, Associated Press article, author Anick Jesdanun noted that several security consultants had expressed concerns about user privacy if the Google software is installed in a multi-user environment, because the program can recall and display almost anything stored on the computer. In addition to privacy concerns, a security risk could occur if an intruder uses the term *password* in a search, because the program might be able to find password reminders that were received and stored in e-mail folders.

In the article, a Google spokesperson is quoted as saying that "… managers of shared computers should think twice about installing the software until Google develops advanced features such as password protection and multi-user support."

SOCIAL ENGINEERING   Even if users are protecting and securing their passwords, an intruder might attempt to gain unauthorized access to a system using a tactic called **social engineering**. In a social engineering attack, an intruder uses social interaction to gain access to a computer system. For example, the intruder might pretend to be a new employee, an outside technician, or a journalist. Through a series of questions, the intruder tries to obtain the information that he or she needs to compromise the system. A common ploy is for the attacker to contact several people in the same organization, and use some information from one source to gain credibility and entry to another source. An intruder also might contact a help desk and say: "Hi. This is Mark Tompkins from accounting. I seem to have forgotten my password. Could you give me a new one?" Although this request might be legitimate, it also might be an attacker trying to access the system. A password never should be given based solely on this telephone call. The user should be required to provide further information to validate his or her identity, such as a Social Security number, employee ID, telephone extension, and company e-mail address.

USER RESISTANCE   Many users, including some senior managers, dislike high security measures because they can be inconvenient and time-consuming. Some users question the need for higher security levels, and resist these initiatives. If a systems analyst is asked whether specific security precautions really are necessary, he or she should remind the user that the company owes the highest possible level of security to its customers, who have entrusted personal information to the firm; to its employees, who also have personal information stored in company files; and to its shareholders, who expect the company to have a suitable, effective, and comprehensive security program that will safeguard company assets and resources. When users understand this overall commitment to security and feel that they are part of it, they are more likely to choose better passwords, be more alert to security issues, and contribute to the overall success of the company's security program.

CASE IN POINT 10.4:   CHAIN LINK CONSULTING, INC.

Chain Link Consulting is an IT consulting firm that specializes in system security issues. The company's president has asked you to help her put together a presentation to a group of potential clients at a trade show meeting next month. First, she wants you to review system security issues, considering all five security levels. Then she wants you to come up with a list of ways that Chain Link could test a client's security practices, in order to get a real-world assessment of vulnerability.

To make matters more interesting, she told you it was OK to be creative in your recommendations, but not to propose any action that would be illegal or unethical. For example, it would be OK to pose as a job applicant with false references to see if they were being checked, but it would not be appropriate to pick a lock and enter the computer room.

Your report is due tomorrow. What will you suggest?

BACKUP AND DISASTER RECOVERY

In Chapter 8, you learned about backup and disaster recovery issues that must be addressed as an integral part of the overall system architecture. Unfortunately, the tragic events of September 11, 2001, and increased concern about global terrorism have forced many companies to upgrade their backup and disaster recovery plans. As shown in Figure 8-39 on page 394, the heightened focus on disaster recovery has spawned a whole new disaster recovery industry, which includes many new tools and techniques. For example, consider the enormous popularity of Web-based data backup, which was

ON THE WEB

For more information about Backup and Disaster Recovery, visit **scsite.com/6e/more**, locate Chapter 10, and then click the Backup and Disaster Recovery link.

described in Chapter 8, as a relatively inexpensive, but highly secure, form of business insurance. Many IT professionals feel that terrorism concerns have raised the awareness level throughout the corporate world, and that will make it easier to obtain top management support for prevention and recovery efforts.

SYSTEM OBSOLESCENCE

Even with solid support, at some point every system becomes obsolete. For example, you might not remember the punch card shown in Figure 10-30, which represented the cutting edge of data management back in the 1960s. It is interesting to note that almost 50 years later, punch card technology still survives in voting systems used in some states, but this method rapidly is being replaced by newer technology.

Constantly changing technology means that every system has a limited economic life span, some longer than others. Analysts and managers must realize that they can anticipate system obsolescence in several ways and it never should come as a complete surprise.

A system becomes **obsolete** when users no longer require its functions or when the platform becomes outmoded. The most common reason for discontinuing a system is that it has reached the end of its economically useful life, as indicated by the following signs:

FIGURE 10-30 Forty years ago, punch cards represented the state-of-the-art in data management. As technology evolved, punch cards quickly became obsolete. To maintain a competitive edge, companies must use the newest, most efficient IT available, and obsolescence never should come as a surprise.

1. The system's maintenance history indicates that adaptive and corrective maintenance are increasing steadily.

2. Operational costs or execution times are increasing rapidly, and routine perfective maintenance does not reverse or slow the trend.

3. A software package is available that provides the same or additional services faster, better, and less expensively than the current system.

4. New technology offers a way to perform the same or additional functions more efficiently.

5. Maintenance changes or additions are difficult and expensive to perform.

6. Users request significant new features to support business requirements.

Type	Activity level
Corrective Maintenance	Low
Adaptive Maintenance (Minor Enhancements)	None
Adaptive Maintenance (Major Enhancements)	None
Perfective Maintenance	None
Preventive Maintenance	None

FIGURE 10-31 All maintenance activities decrease significantly during the final phase of operations as a replacement system is being developed.

Systems operation and support continues until a replacement system is installed. Toward the end of a system's operational life, users are unlikely to submit new requests for adaptive maintenance because they are looking forward to the new release. Similarly, the IT staff usually does not perform much perfective or preventive maintenance because the system will not be around long enough to justify the cost. A system in its final stages requires corrective maintenance only to keep the system operational. Figure 10-31 shows typical levels of maintenance for a system at the obsolescence stage in the SDLC.

User satisfaction typically determines the life span of a system. The critical success factor for any system is whether or not it helps users achieve their operational and business goals. As an IT staff member, you should expect to receive input from users and managers throughout the systems development process. You should investigate and document all negative feedback, because it can be the first signal of system obsolescence.

At some point in a system's operational life, maintenance costs start to increase, users begin to ask for more features and capability, new systems requests are submitted, and the SDLC begins again.

FACING THE FUTURE: CHALLENGES AND OPPORTUNITIES

The only thing that is certain about the future is continuous change. Change itself is neither good nor bad — the real issue is how people and companies deal with the challenges and opportunities that are bound to occur.

No one would start a complex journey without a map and a plan. To navigate the future of information technology, companies require strategic plans, which were discussed in Chapter 2. An individual also needs a plan to guide him or her to a specific goal or destination. This section discusses some predictions and stresses the importance of personal planning and development, including the acquisition of professional credentials.

Predictions

Although no one can foresee the specifics, it is clear that companies will continue to face intense competition and global change, especially in the wake of economic, social, and political uncertainty. For example, prior to the business slowdown that continued during 2003, Gartner Consulting, a prominent forecasting firm, had predicted explosive growth in B2B and Internet-based commence. In 2004, Gartner revised its prediction and suggested that slower, but steady, growth probably would occur. Gartner warned that bottom-line TCO would be the highest priority, surmounted only by corporate concern for safety and security.

Tim Bajarin, an IT consultant and futurist, suggested in a recent article that the fastest growth will take place in customer-oriented applications and supply chain management. According to Mr. Bajarin, many firms will devote substantial resources to dealing with security issues that emerged as a result of the September 11, 2001, attacks. Specific strategies will include more emphasis on distributed computer networks and data storage, worst-case scenario planning, and stronger protection, both physical and electronic, for company and customer data.

What about long-term prospects for IT and the role of the systems analyst? Although disruptions will occur, technology advances will spur business growth and productivity. The technology itself, however, is not the key — the real driving force will be how the technology is harnessed and applied. This point was driven home by Fred Mapp, an AMD executive who is shown in Figure 10-32 on the next page. Mr. Mapp stated that "Technology is only a tool — a walking stick, if you will — to help you get to your destination." He also pointed out that "the best walking stick ever crafted won't find the way for you."

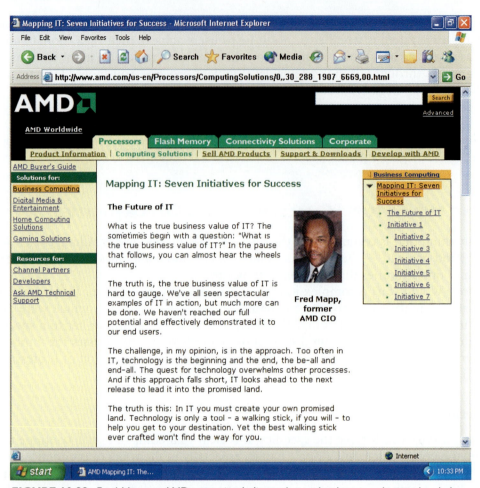

FIGURE 10-32 Fred Mapp, an AMD executive, believes that technology is only a tool to help companies arrive at a destination.

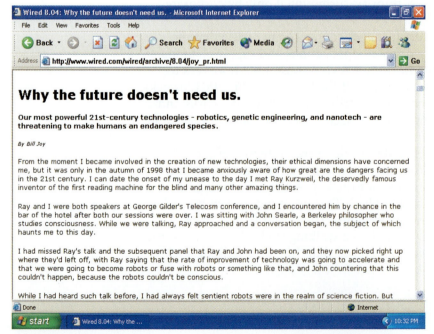

FIGURE 10-33 Some observers wonder whether technology is moving so fast that humans will be left behind.

It is interesting to note that some observers, such as Bill Joy, wonder whether technology is moving so fast that humans will be left behind, as shown in Figure 10-33. What does seem clear is that the future world of IT must be envisioned, planned, and created by skilled professionals. The real challenge is to be ready with the right mix of skills, knowledge, credentials, and experience.

STRATEGIC PLANNING FOR IT PROFESSIONALS

An IT professional should think of himself or herself as a business corporation that has certain assets, potential liabilities, and specific goals. Individuals, like companies, must have a strategic plan in order to achieve their objectives. The starting point is to formulate an answer to the following career planning question: Where do I want to be three, five, or ten years from now, and what do I want to be doing?

Working backwards from your long-term goals, you can develop intermediate milestones and begin to manage your career just as you would manage an IT project. You can even use the project management tools described in Part 4 of the Systems Analyst's Toolkit to construct a Gantt chart or a PERT/CPM chart using months (or years) as time units. Once the plan is developed, you would monitor it regularly to see whether you were still on schedule.

Planning a career is not unlike planting a tree that takes several years to reach a certain height. Once you know the desired height and the annual growth rate, you can determine when you must plant the tree. Similarly, if you want to possess a particular educational credential two years from now, and the credential takes two years to earn, then you need to start on it immediately if you want to adhere to your timetable.

ON THE WEB

For more information about IT Credentials, visit **scsite.com/ sad6e/more**, locate Chapter 10, and then click the IT Credentials link.

IT CREDENTIALS AND CERTIFICATION

In recent years, technical credentials and certification have become extremely important to IT employers and employees. In a broad sense, **credentials** include formal degrees, diplomas, or certificates granted by learning institutions to show that a certain level of education has been achieved successfully. The term **certification** also has a special meaning that relates to specific hardware and software skills that can be measured and verified by examination. For example, a person might have a two- or four-year degree in Information Systems and possess an A+ certification, which attests to the person's computer hardware knowledge and skills.

In addition to Microsoft, as shown in Figure 10-34, many other IT industry leaders offer certification, including Cisco, Novell, Oracle, and Sun Microsystems. To learn more

FIGURE 10-34 Microsoft states that its Microsoft Certified Professional (MCP) credential is for professional who have the skills to implement a Microsoft product or technology as part of a business solution.

about certification generally, you can visit the Web site maintained by the ICCP (Institute for Certification of Computing Professionals), which is shown in Figure 10-35.

FIGURE 10-35 ICCP (Institute for Certification of Computing Professionals) maintains a Web site that provides information about certification opportunities.

CHAPTER SUMMARY

Systems operation, security, and support covers the entire period from the implementation of an information system until the system no longer is used. A systems analyst's primary involvement with an operational system is to manage and solve user support requests.

Corrective maintenance includes changes to correct errors. Adaptive maintenance satisfies new systems requirements, and perfective maintenance makes the system more efficient. Adaptive and perfective maintenance changes often are called enhancements. Preventive maintenance is performed to avoid future problems.

The typical maintenance process resembles a miniature version of the systems development life cycle. A systems request for maintenance work is submitted and evaluated. If it is accepted, the request is prioritized and scheduled for the IT group. The maintenance team then follows a logical progression of investigation, analysis, design, development, testing, and implementation.

Corrective maintenance projects occur when a user or an IT staff member reports a problem. Standard maintenance procedures usually are followed for relatively minor errors, but work often begins immediately when users report significant errors.

In contrast to corrective maintenance, adaptive, perfective, and preventive maintenance projects always follow the organization's standard maintenance procedures. Adaptive maintenance projects occur in response to user requests for improvements to meet changes in the business or operating environments. The IT staff usually initiates perfective maintenance projects to improve performance or maintainability. Automated program restructuring and reengineering are forms of perfective maintenance. In order to avoid future problems, IT staff performs preventive maintenance, which involves analysis of areas where trouble is likely to occur.

A maintenance team consists of one or more systems analysts and programmers. Systems analysts need the same talents and abilities for maintenance work as they use when developing a new system. Many IT departments are organized into separate new development and maintenance groups where staff members are rotated from one group to the other.

Configuration management is necessary to handle maintenance requests, to manage different versions of the information system, and to distribute documentation changes. Maintenance changes can be implemented as they are completed or a release methodology can be used in which all noncritical maintenance changes are collected and implemented simultaneously. A release methodology usually is cost-effective and advantageous for users because they do not have to work with a constantly changing system. Systems analysts use functional, allocated, and product baselines as formal reference points to measure system characteristics at a specific time.

System performance measurements include response time, bandwidth, throughput, and turnaround time. Capacity management uses those measurements to forecast what is needed to provide future levels of service and support. Also, CASE tools that include system evaluation and maintenance features can be used during the systems operation, security, and support phase.

Security is a vital part of every computer system. System security involves five separate, but interrelated, security levels: physical security, network security, application security, file security, and user security. Physical security concerns the physical environment, including critical equipment located in a computer room, as well as safeguards for servers and desktops throughout the company. Network security involves encryption techniques, as well as private networks and other protective measures, especially where wireless transmissions are concerned. Application security requires an understanding of services, input validation techniques, and software patches and updates. File security involves the use of permissions, which can be assigned to individual users or to user groups. User security involves identity management techniques, a comprehensive password protection policy, an awareness of social engineering risks, and an effective means of overcoming user resistance.

All information systems eventually become obsolete. The end of a system's economic life usually is signaled by rapidly increasing maintenance or operating costs, the availability of new software or hardware, or new requirements that cannot be achieved easily by the existing system. When a certain point is reached, an information system must be replaced, and the entire systems development life cycle begins again.

An IT professional should have a strategic career plan that includes long-term goals and intermediate milestones. An important element of a personal strategic plan is the acquisition of IT credentials and certifications that document specific knowledge and skills. Many IT industry leaders offer certification, and the ICCP (Institute for Certification of Computing Professionals) can provide additional information about certification questions and issues.

Key Terms and Phrases

adaptive maintenance 477
administrator 500
allocated baseline 488
analysis 481
AOL PassCode® 502
applications programmer 482
archived 487
automatic update service 500
bandwidth 489
baseline 488
benchmark testing 488
biometric scanning systems 494
BIOS-level password 495
boot-level password 495
capacity planning 490
certification 507
computer room 494
configuration management (CM) 485
corrective maintenance 477
credentials 507
database programmer 482
denial of service (DOS) 499
destination port 498
distributed denial of service (DDOS) 499
encrypted 497
enhancement 479
exploits 500
firewall 499
functional baseline 488
Gbps (gigabits per second) 489
help desk 474
information center (IC) 474
Kbps (kilobits per second) 489
keystroke logger 495
maintenance activities 477
maintenance expenses 477
maintenance release 485
maintenance release methodology 485
maintenance team 481
Mbps (megabits per second) 489
motion sensor 494
network 497
network interface 497
obsolete 504
operational costs 477

patches 500
perfective maintenance 477
permissions 500
plain text 497
port 498
port scans 499
power-on password 495
preventive maintenance 477
private key 498
private network 498
privilege escalation attack 501
product baseline 488
programmer/analyst 482
protocols 499
public key 498
public key encryption (PKE) 498
response time 489
rules 499
security hole 500
service 499
service packs 487
social engineering 503
software reengineering 480
super-user 500
synthesis 481
system administrator 481
systems librarian 487
systems programmer 482
tamper-evident cases 495
third-party software 500
throughput 489
traffic 497
tunnel 498
turnaround time 490
unencrypted 497
Universal Security Slot (USS) 495
user training package 474
version control 487
Virtual Classroom 475
virtual private network (VPN) 498
what-if analysis 491
Wi-Fi Protected Access (WPA) 498
Wired Equivalent Privacy (WEP) 498
workload measurements 489

Learn It Online

Instructions: To complete the Learn It Online exercises, start your browser, click the Address bar, and then enter the Web address **scsite.com/sad6e/learn**. When the Systems Analysis and Design Learn It Online page is displayed, follow the instructions in the exercises below. Each exercise has instructions for saving your results, either for your own records or for submission to your instructor.

1 Chapter Reinforcement

TF, MC, and SA

Below SAD Chapter 10, click the Chapter Reinforcement link. Print the quiz by clicking Print on the File menu for each page. Answer each question.

2 Flash Cards

Below SAD Chapter 10, click the Flash Cards link and read the instructions. Type 20 (or a number specified by your instructor) in the Number of playing cards text box, type your name in the Enter your Name text box, and then click the Flip Card button. When the flash card is displayed, read the question and then click the ANSWER box arrow to select an answer. Flip through the Flash Cards. If your score is 15 (75%) correct or greater, click Print on the File menu to print your results. If your score is less than 15 (75%) correct, then redo this exercise by clicking the Replay button.

3 Practice Test

Below SAD Chapter 10, click the Practice Test link. Answer each question, enter your first and last name at the bottom of the page, and then click the Grade Test button. When the graded practice test is displayed on your screen, click Print on the File menu to print a hard copy. Continue to take practice tests until you score 80% or better.

4 Who Wants To Be a Computer Genius?

Below SAD Chapter 10, click the Computer Genius link. Read the instructions, enter your first and last name at the bottom of the page, and then click the Play button. When your score is displayed, click the PRINT RESULTS link to print a hard copy.

5 Wheel of Terms

Below SAD Chapter 10, click the Wheel of Terms link. Read the instructions, and then enter your first and last name and your school name. Click the PLAY button. When your score is displayed on the screen, right-click the score and then click Print on the shortcut menu to print a hard copy.

6 Crossword Puzzle Challenge

Below SAD Chapter 10, click the Crossword Puzzle Challenge link. Read the instructions, and then enter your first and last name. Click the SUBMIT button. Work the crossword puzzle. When you are finished, click the Submit button. When the crossword puzzle is redisplayed, click the Print Puzzle button to print a hard copy.

Case-Sim: SCR Associates

Background

SCR Associates is a consulting firm that offers IT solutions and training. SCR needs an information system to manage operations at its new training center. The new system will be called TIMS (Training Information Management System). As a newly hired systems analyst, you will report to Jesse Baker, systems group manager. You will work on various tasks and practice the skills you learned in this chapter.

Using the Case

The SCR Associates case study is a Web-based simulation that allows you to practice your skills in a real-world environment. The case study transports you to SCR's company intranet, where you can complete 10 work sessions, each aligning with a chapter. As you work on the case, you will receive e-mail and voice mail messages, obtain information from SCR's online libraries, and perform various tasks. The first time you enter the SCR Case, you should go to the Starting page at **scsite.com/sad6e/scr** for detailed instructions.

Preview: Session 10

You assisted your supervisor, Jesse Baker, in various implementation tasks, and the TIMS system is up and running. Now she wants you to focus on system operation, support, and security tasks. Specifically, she wants you to work on a help desk, version control, configuration management, capacity planning, and system security issues. She also wants you to create a checklist that will help SCR know when the TIMS system is reaching the end of its useful life.

To start a work session, you log on to the SCR intranet. When you enter your name and password, an opening screen displays links to the work sessions, and you select Session 10. At this point, you check your e-mail and voice mail messages carefully. Then you begin working on your task list, which includes the following items:

Tasks: Systems Operation, Support, and Security

1. Jesse wants a recommendation about an SCR help desk. She said that I can get more information on the Internet. She wants any input by early next week. She said there's lots of information out there on this topic. She wants me to suggest a plan for creating an SCR help desk.

2. At our meeting, Jesse asked me how SCR should manage the TIMS system in the future. Search the Internet to learn more about version control, configuration management, and capacity planning, and send her the results of my research.

3. Another important issue: Security! Jesse wants my thoughts on how SCR should manage IT security, and she wants me to consider all five levels.

4. Jesse says that no one likes surprises or problems. She wants me to draft a checklist that SCR can use to detect TIMS obsolescence as early as possible. She also said that I might be receiving some interesting news very soon. Wonder what that's about?

FIGURE 10-36 Task list: Session 10.

Chapter Exercises

Review Questions

1. List and describe the four classifications of maintenance.
2. Which of the four types of maintenance is most likely to generate changes to user documentation?
3. Why are newly hired systems analysts often assigned to maintenance projects?
4. What is configuration management and why is it important?
5. List the typical steps in requesting system maintenance.
6. What is a release methodology and what are the pros and cons of this approach? What is the purpose of version control?
7. Define the following terms: response time, bandwidth, throughput, and turnaround time. How are the terms related?
8. What is the purpose of capacity planning? How is what-if analysis used in capacity planning?
9. What are the five levels of security? Name at least three specific security issues that pertain to each level.
10. List six indications that an information system is approaching obsolescence.

Discussion Topics

1. Assume that your company uses a release methodology for its sales system. The current version is 4.5. Decide whether each of the following changes would justify a version 5.0 release, or be included in a version 4.6 update: (a) Add a new report, (b) add a Web interface, (c) add data validation checks, (d) add an interface to the marketing system, and (e) change the user interface.
2. The four types of IT system maintenance also apply to other industries. Suppose you were in charge of aircraft maintenance for a small airline. What would be an example of each type of maintenance — corrective, adaptive, perfective, and preventive — in this situation?
3. An IT manager assigns programmers and systems analysts to maintenance projects if they have less than two years of experience or if they received an average or below rating in their last evaluation. Do you agree with this practice?
4. What are the most important security issues facing companies today? Have these changed in the last five years, and will they continue to change? How should companies prepare themselves for security threats and problems in the future?

Projects

1. Using the Internet, locate a software package designed to automate version control. List the key features and describe your findings in a brief memo.
2. Develop a process for managing change requests and design a form to handle a generic change request. The process should include a contingency plan for changes that must be resolved immediately.
3. Visit the IT department at your school or at a local company and find out whether performance measurements are used. Write a brief report describing your findings.
4. Using a spreadsheet, print the Help explanation for the what-if analysis feature (called Goal Seek in Microsoft Excel) and create a worksheet that demonstrates this feature.

Apply Your Knowledge

The Apply Your Knowledge section contains four mini-cases. Each case describes a situation, explains your role in the case, and asks you to respond to questions. You can answer the questions by applying knowledge you learned in the chapter.

Premium Publishers

Situation:

Premium Publishers is a small publishing firm that specializes in reprinting classic literature. A year ago the IT staff developed a Web-based order entry system. The system has performed well, but the company would like to add more features and improve performance. So far, most of the maintenance has involved correcting minor errors.

1. What type of maintenance have the IT staff performed? What types of maintenance will they perform if the existing system is retained?
2. If new features are added, what methodology should the IT staff use to add new functions and enhancements?
3. What security measures should the firm consider? Prepare a checklist of items that should be reviewed and monitored.
4. Even though the new system is only a year old, e-commerce changes constantly. At what point should Premium Publishers consider replacing the Web-based system with a new system, and why?

Oceanside Furniture

Situation:

Oceanside Furniture produces indoor and outdoor wicker furniture. The company grew from one store in 1995 to eight locations today. Two years ago, the company's IT department developed an inventory control system to keep track of products and reorder out-of-stock items. The new system was well received by users, and inventory problems have decreased significantly. Since the inventory system became operational, however, users steadily have requested increased functionality and changes in screen forms and reports.

1. Should Oceanside have a specific process to manage future changes and enhancements? What should it be?
2. What about version control? Should Oceanside institute a maintenance release methodology? Why or why not?
3. Suppose that you had to assign specific IT staff members to maintain the inventory control system. How would you accomplish the task? Describe your strategy in a brief memo.
4. What should Oceanside watch for to detect possible obsolescence in the future? Develop a checklist with specific examples that Oceanside management could use.

3 Robin Hood Associates

Situation:

Robin Hood Associates is an IT consulting firm that develops new systems and maintains older systems for its clients. Robin Hood recently was awarded a contract to correct problems with an existing system. The system is three years old, and the consulting firm that initially designed the system did a poor job of documentation. The data dictionary, user manuals, and other reference material never have been updated, and no process exists for version control.

1. As one of the Robin Hood team members, how should you proceed? What steps would you take, and what would be your priorities?
2. Are CASE tools available that you could use on this assignment? What are they?
3. What advice would you give to the client regarding capacity planning for the future?
4. What steps should the client take to ensure that the system is secure? Prepare a checklist with at least 15 security items that the client should evaluate and monitor.

4 Economy Travel

Situation:

Economy Travel specializes in personalized travel packages at popular prices, and the firm operates 12 offices in major U.S. cities. A key selling point is the firm's client management database, which includes preferences such as airline seating choices and favorite hotels. Economy Travel purchased the client management software as an off-the-shelf vendor package and modified the program to meet the company's needs. The package has been operational for one year and has performed well. Economy Travel, however, is in the process of expanding its operation to include six additional locations. You have been called in as a consultant to help the company make some decisions about IT support.

1. What performance and workload measurement issues should the company consider at the present time?
2. What capacity planning issues should the company consider at the present time?
3. Should the company establish a system baseline before the integration of the six new sites? Explain your answer.
4. As an IT consultant, you must understand the client's business. From that perspective, consider the impact of the Internet on the travel agency business. Investigate this topic using the Internet and other sources of information, and decide what issues to discuss with Economy Travel.

Case Studies

Case studies allow you to practice specific skills learned in the chapter. Each chapter contains several case studies that continue throughout the textbook, and a chapter capstone case.

NEW CENTURY HEALTH CLINIC

New Century Health Clinic offers preventive medicine and traditional medical care. In your role as an IT consultant, you will help New Century develop a new information system.

Background

You implemented the new system at New Century Health Clinic successfully, and the staff has used the system for nearly four months. New Century is pleased with the improvements in efficiency, office productivity, and patient satisfaction.

Some problems have surfaced, however. The office staff members call you almost daily to request assistance and suggest changes in certain reports and forms. You try to be helpful, but now you are busy with a major project for a local distributor of exercise equipment. Actually, your contract with New Century required you to provide support only during the first three months of operation. Anita Davenport, New Century's office manager, reported that the system seems to slow down at certain times during the day, making it difficult for the staff to keep up with its workload. Also, you increasingly are concerned about system security. A recent article in the local newspaper described an incident where a disgruntled former employee was about to break into the computer system and destroy or alter data.

Assignments

1. You are willing to charge a lower rate for ongoing support services because you designed the system. You want New Century to use a specific procedure for requesting assistance and changes, however, so that you can plan your activities efficiently. Prepare a complete, written procedure for New Century Health Clinic maintenance change requests. Include appropriate forms with your procedure.
2. What could be causing the periodic slowdowns at New Century? If a problem does exist, which performance and workload measures would you monitor to pinpoint the problem?
3. At the end of the systems analysis phase, you studied the economic feasibility of the system and estimated the future costs and benefits. Now that the system is operational, should those costs and benefits be monitored? Why or why not?
4. You decide to prepare a security checklist for New Century. Prepare a list of security issues that the firm should evaluate and monitor. Be sure to organize the items into categories that match the five security levels.

PERSONAL TRAINER, INC.

Personal Trainer, Inc., owns and operates fitness centers in a dozen Midwestern cities. The centers have done well, and the company is planning an international expansion by opening a new "supercenter" in the Toronto area. Personal Trainer's president, Cassia Umi, hired an IT consultant, Susan Park, to help develop an information system for the new facility. During the project, Susan will work closely with Gray Lewis, who will manage the new operation.

Background

System changeover and data conversion were successful for the new Personal Trainer system. The post-implementation evaluation indicated that users were pleased with the system. The evaluation also confirmed that the system was operating properly. Several users commented, however, that system response seemed slow. Susan Park, the project consultant, wants to meet with you to discuss operation, maintenance, and security issues affecting the new system.

Assignments

1. What might be causing the slow response time? Prepare a brief memo explaining system performance and workload measurement, using nontechnical language that Personal Trainer users can understand easily.

2. Personal Trainer's top management asked you to provide ongoing maintenance for the new system. In order to avoid any misunderstanding, you want to provide a brief description of the various types of maintenance. Prepare a brief memo that does this, and include at least two realistic examples of each type of maintenance.

3. Although the system has been operational for a short time, users already have submitted several requests for enhancements and noncritical changes. Should Personal Trainer use a maintenance release methodology to handle the requests? Why or why not?

4. What are the main security issues that Personal Trainer should address? Prepare a memo that lists the primary concerns and offers a specific recommendation for dealing with each issue.

TARHEEL INDUSTRIES

Tarheel Industries is a medium-sized sporting goods manufacturer located in North Carolina. Tarheel's online production support system was developed in-house and was implemented two months ago. The system runs 24 hours a day in Tarheel's three manufacturing facilities.

Background

Last Monday morning, the production support system developed a problem. When a screen display for certain parts was requested, the displayed values were garbled.

When she was alerted to the situation, Marsha Stryker, Tarheel's IT manager, immediately assigned a systems analyst to investigate the problem. Marsha instructed the analyst, Eric Wu, to resolve the problem and get the system up and running as soon as possible. Eric previously worked on two small maintenance projects for the production control system, so he was somewhat familiar with the application.

Eric worked the rest of the day on the problem, and by 6:30 in the evening, he developed and implemented a fix. After verifying that the production support system again was capable of producing correct part displays, Eric went home. Early the following morning, Marsha called Eric and two other members of the applications maintenance group to a meeting in her office, where she briefed them on a new adaptive maintenance project for another high-priority system. She asked them to begin work on the new project immediately.

Several nights later, the production control system crashed shortly after midnight. Every time the system was reactivated, it crashed again. Finally, around 2:30 a.m., all production lines were shut down and third-shift production workers were sent home. The production support system finally was corrected and full production was restored the following day, but by that time, Tarheel Industries had incurred thousands of dollars in lost production costs. The cause of the production support system crash was identified as a side effect of the fix that Eric made to the system.

Assignments

1. Is the second production support system failure entirely unexpected?
2. Who is most to blame for the second system failure?
3. What might Marsha have done differently to avoid the situation? What might Eric have done differently?
4. Outline a new set of maintenance procedures that will help Tarheel Industries avoid such problems in the future.

MILLS IMPORTS

Mills Imports is a successful importer of gourmet coffees, cheeses, and specialty foods from around the world. Mills Imports recently developed and implemented an online sales information system.

Background

Using a client/server design, the PCs in each of the firm's 12 retail stores were networked with a server located in the sales support center at the main office. Salespeople in the retail stores use the customer sales information system to record sales transactions; to open, close, or query customer accounts; and to print sales receipts, daily sales reports by salesperson, and daily sales reports by merchandise code. The sales support staff uses the system to query customer accounts and print various daily, weekly, and monthly reports.

When the customer sales system was implemented, the IT department conducted extensive training for the salespeople and the sales support center staff. One member of the systems development team also prepared a user manual, but users are familiar with the system so the manual rarely is used.

Two weeks ago, Mills opened two additional stores and hired six new sales representatives. A manager gave the user manual to the new sales representatives and asked them to read it and experiment with the system. Now, salespeople in both new stores are having major problems using the sales system. When a representative from the main office visited the stores to investigate the problem, she discovered that the new people could not understand the user manual. When she asked for examples of confusing instructions, several salespeople pointed to the following examples:

- Obtaining the authorization of the store manager on Form RBK-23 is required before the system can activate a customer charge account.
- Care should be exercised to ensure that the BACKSPACE key is not pressed when the key on the numeric keypad with a left-facing arrow is the appropriate choice to accomplish nondestructive backspacing.
- To prevent report generation interruption, the existence of sufficient paper stock should be verified before any option that requires printing is selected. If not, the option must be reselected.
- The F2 key should be pressed in the event that a display of valid merchandise codes is required. That same key terminates the display.

Assignments

1. What policies or procedures could Mills Imports have established to avoid the situation?
2. Should the sales support staff ask the IT department to rewrite the user manual as a maintenance project, or should they request a training session for the new salespeople? Can you offer any other suggestions?
3. Rewrite the user manual instructions so they are clear and understandable for new users. What steps might you take to ensure the accuracy of the new user manual instructions?
4. In the process of rewriting the user manual instructions, you discover that some of the instructions were not changed to reflect system maintenance and upgrade activities. A request form on the firm's intranet, for example, has replaced Form RBK-23. Mills also has phased out printed reports in favor of online reports, which users can view by entering a user name and password. Rewrite the user manual instructions to reflect the changes.

CHAPTER CAPSTONE CASE: SoftWear, Limited

SoftWear, Limited (SWL), is a continuing case study that illustrates the knowledge and skills described in each chapter. In this case study, the student acts as a member of the SWL systems development team and performs various tasks.

Background

In mid-December 2006, five months after the post-implementation evaluation, the payroll package and the ESIP system were operating successfully and users seemed satisfied with both systems.

During that time, users requested minor changes in reports and screen displays, which the IT staff handled easily. Jane Rossman, manager of applications, continued to assign a mixture of new systems and maintenance tasks to the IT team, and the members indicated that they enjoyed the variety and challenge of both types of work.

Debra Williams, the payroll clerk who prints the ESIP checks, reported the only operational problem. She could not load and align the special check stock in the printer correctly. Becky Evans visited Debra to study the situation and then wrote a specific procedure to solve the problem.

No overtime had been paid in the payroll department since the new system was implemented, and errors in payroll deductions had stopped. Michael Jeremy, SWL's vice president of finance, who initiated the payroll and ESIP projects, is very pleased with the system's operation and output. He recently visited an IT department staff meeting to congratulate the entire group personally.

Some requests for enhancements also occurred. Mike Feiner recently submitted a systems request for the ESIP system to produce an annual employee benefits statement with the current value of all savings plan deductions, plus information on insurance coverage and other benefits data. Mike also indicated that the company would offer several new ESIP choices during 2005, including various mutual funds.

On December 15, Pacific Software announced the latest release of its payroll package. The new version supported full integration of all payroll and human resources functions and data. Ann Hon, director of information systems, was interested in the announcement because she knew that Tina Pham, SWL's vice president of human resources, wanted a human resources information system (HRIS) to support SWL's long-term needs. At Ann's request, Jane Rossman assigned Becky Evans to analyze the new payroll package to determine if SWL could implement the latest version as a companywide client/server application.

Becky began the preliminary investigation by reviewing the current system and meeting with Mike Feiner to learn more about the new ESIP options. Next, she met with Marty Hoctor, a representative from Pacific Software, to review the features of the new release. After describing the new software, Marty mentioned that a large Midwestern retail chain recently implemented the package, and he invited Becky to contact Fred Brown, director of IT at that company, to discuss the new release. Becky spoke with Fred, and he agreed to e-mail her a summary of comments that users had made about the new software.

Becky completed her preliminary investigation, including a cost-benefit analysis, and worked with Jane Rossman and Ann Hon to prepare a report and presentation to SWL's newly formed systems review committee, which was created at Ann's suggestion. In their presentation, the IT team recommended that SWL upgrade to the new release of the payroll package and build a client/server application for all of SWL's payroll and personnel functions, including the ESIP system. They also suggested that a team of IT and human resources people get together to study preliminary economic, technical, and operational factors involved in a human resources information system and report back to the systems review committee. They pointed out that if the project was approved, the same team could handle the systems development using JAD or RAD techniques. After the presentation, the committee approved the request and Ann called an IT department staff meeting for the next morning to start planning the systems analysis phase.

During the meeting, Ann and Jane thanked the entire department for its efforts on the payroll and ESIP projects. Ann pointed out that although the payroll package and the ESIP system support SWL's current needs, the business environment changes rapidly and a successful, growing company must investigate new information management technology constantly. At this point, the systems development life cycle for SWL begins again.

SWL Team Tasks

1. Now that the new ESIP system is operational, Jane Rossman wants you to track system performance using various measurements. At a minimum, she expects you to monitor operational costs, maintenance frequency, technical issues, and user satisfaction. You can add other items if you choose. Write a proposal for Jane that lists each factor you will measure, and make sure that you explain why the item is important and how you plan to obtain the information.

2. Jane also wants you to learn more about human resources information systems (HRISs) that help a company manage information about its people. Many firms have replaced older personnel record-keeping systems with powerful, state-of-the-art HRIS products. You will be assigned to the SWL team that will study the feasibility of a human resources information system. Using the Internet, your task is to identify several commercial packages and the names of firms or consultants who specialize in HRIS implementation. Write a brief memo to Jane with your findings.

3. Jane wants you to prepare a security audit procedure for SWL. Specifically, she wants you prepare a checklist of security issues that need to be evaluated and rated. She said to consider all five security levels, and to include as many specific items as possible that should be assessed.

4. As Ann Hon pointed out in the last meeting, the business environment changes rapidly and a successful, growing company like SWL must investigate new information management technology constantly. Ann has asked you to describe trends in software and hardware that might affect SWL's future IT plans. Perform research on the Internet to identify several technology issues that might represent potential problems or opportunities for SWL, and present the results in a memo to Ann.

THE SYSTEMS ANALYST'S TOOLKIT

The Systems Analyst's Toolkit presents a valuable set of cross-phase skills and knowledge that you can use throughout the systems development process. Part 1 discusses communication tools that can help you write clearly, speak effectively, and deliver powerful presentations. Part 2 describes CASE tools that you can use to design, construct, and document an information system. Part 3 demonstrates financial analysis tools you can use to measure project feasibility, develop accurate cost-benefit estimates, and make sound decisions. Part 4 explains project management tools that can help you organize, plan, and manage IT projects to a successful conclusion. Part 5 describes object-oriented tools that you can use to represent and model an information system. Part 6 explains Internet resource tools that you can use to locate information, obtain reference material, and monitor IT trends and developments.

PART

Communication Tools

In **Part I** of the Systems Analyst's Toolkit, you will learn about written and oral communication skills that you can use as a systems analyst.

INTRODUCTION

OBJECTIVES

When you finish this part of the Toolkit, you will be able to:

- List the guidelines for successful communications
- Explain the importance of effective letters, memos, and e-mail communication
- Explain how to measure the readability of written material
- Describe the organization of written reports that are required during the SDLC and explain each report section
- List the guidelines for effective oral communication
- Organize and plan an oral presentation
- Use speaking techniques to achieve your objectives

A successful systems analyst must have good written and oral communication skills to perform his or her job effectively. Never underestimate the importance of effective communications, whether you are using a memo, e-mail, or an oral presentation to convey your ideas. The following guidelines will help you prepare and deliver effective presentations. Remember, however, that nothing increases your ability to communicate better than practicing these skills.

TOOLKIT INTRODUCTION CASE: Mountain View College Bookstore

Background: Wendy Lee, manager of college services at Mountain View College, wants a new information system that will improve efficiency and customer service at the three college bookstores.

In this part of the case, Florence Fullerton (systems analyst) and Harry Boston (student intern) are talking about communication tools and techniques.

Participants:	Florence and Harry
Location:	Mountain View College Cafeteria, at the beginning of the bookstore information system project
Discussion topics:	Guidelines for successful oral and written communications.

Florence:	Harry, before we start the project for Wendy, let's talk about written and oral communication tools and techniques. We'll be using these throughout the systems development process.
Harry:	*Fine with me. I've always enjoyed my English and writing courses.*
Florence:	Well, everything you learned in school certainly applies in the workplace. The basic principles of good communications apply everywhere. But in a business environment there are some additional issues to keep in mind.
Harry:	*Such as?*
Florence:	For example, you will be preparing documents, slide presentations, and training material for users. In each situation, you have to consider the audience very carefully, including their technical knowledge, organizational level, and experience. You'll need to adjust your approach based on those factors, and be aware of the readability of your written work. Also, you'll be using e-mail as a primary communications tool.
Harry:	*I understand. Are there any special ground rules for using e-mail?*
Florence:	Well, e-mail can be more casual than typical business writing — but not *too* casual. We'll talk about that, along with ways to maximize your online effectiveness using software such as Microsoft Outlook. Also, we'll go over some guidelines for preparing slide presentations.
Harry:	*Sounds good to me. When do we start?*
Florence:	Right now. Here's a task list to get us underway.

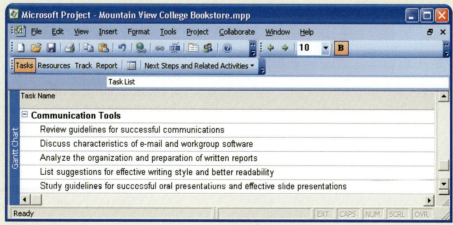

FIGURE TK 1-1

SUCCESSFUL COMMUNICATION STRATEGIES

Successful communication does not just happen. Usually, it is the result of a specific strategy that includes careful planning, hard work, and practice. To be a successful communicator, you must consider five related questions about yourself, your audience, and your objectives: why, who, what, when, and how. You also must consider the cultural context of your communication. Above all, you must know your subject and have confidence in yourself.

Why, Who, What, When, and How

The **why, who, what, when, and how of communications** are important questions that you must answer before you communicate. These five questions are described in the following section.

WHY Know *why* you are communicating, and what you want to accomplish. Ask yourself the question, "Is this communication necessary, and what specific results am I seeking?" Your entire communication strategy depends on the results that you need.

WHO Know *who* your targets are. Chapter 1 describes how the information needs of managers depend on their organizational and knowledge levels. When communicating with management, sometimes a fine line exists between saying enough and saying too much. Each situation is different, so you must use good judgment and be alert for input from your audience.

WHAT Know *what* is expected of you and when to go into detail. This is directly related to knowing who your targets are and the organizational and knowledge levels of your audience. For example, a vice president might expect less detail and more focus on how a project supports the company's strategic business goals. You must design your communications just as carefully as your systems project. For example, will the recipients expect you to address a specific issue or topic? Will they expect cost estimates or charts? Design your communications based on the answers to those questions.

WHEN Know *when* to speak and *when* to remain silent and let others continue the discussion. To be an effective speaker, you must be a good listener — and use audience feedback to adjust your presentation. Good timing is an essential part of every presentation. Your delivery must be paced properly — too fast and you will lose your audience; too slow and they might become bored.

HOW Know *how* to communicate effectively. You can strengthen your communication skills by using Toolkit suggestions, reflecting upon your own experiences, and observing successful and unsuccessful techniques used by others.

Cultural Context

Communication strategy is affected by the cultural context in which the communication takes place, as shown in Figure TK 1-2.

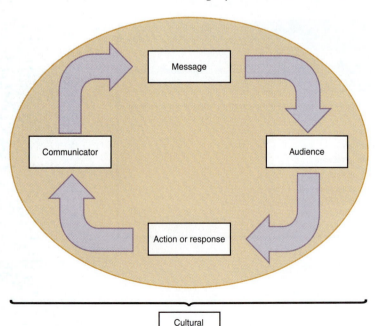

FIGURE TK 1-2 Every communication takes places within an overall cultural context.

Cultural differences can relate to many factors, including geography, background, educational level, societal differences, and so on, and must be taken into account when asking and answering the why, who, what, when, and how of communications.

In addition to these factors, you learned in Chapter 1 that corporate culture is very important. A **corporate culture** is the set of beliefs, rules, traditions, values, and attitudes that define a company and influence its way of doing business. To be successful, a systems analyst must understand, and work within, the corporate culture. For example, if you speak to a group in a company that encourages a highly participative style, you might want to solicit feedback, invite audience comments, or conduct a poll during your presentation. Similarly, if the organization or group is very formal, or very informal, you might want to adjust your style accordingly.

Know Your Subject

No matter how well you plan your communication, you must know your subject inside and out. Your credibility and effectiveness will depend on whether others believe you and support your views. No one can know everything, so it is important to adopt a specific preparation strategy. For example, before a presentation, consider what others expect you to know and what questions they will ask. No matter how well you prepare, however, you will not have an answer for every question. Remember that it is better to say, "I don't know, but I'll find out and get back to you," rather than to guess.

WRITTEN COMMUNICATIONS

Good writing is important because others often judge you by your writing. If you make a mistake while speaking, your audience probably will forget it. Your written errors, however, might stay around for a long time. Grammatical, typographical, and spelling errors distract readers from your message. Your written communications will include e-mail messages, memos, and letters, as well as more formal reports and documents.

Writing Style and Readability

If you have not taken a writing course, you should consider doing so. If you have a choice of courses, select one that focuses on business writing or technical writing. Any writing class, however, is worth the effort. Bookstores and libraries have many excellent books on communicating effectively, and many Internet sites offer writing guidelines, tips, and grammar rules. As you prepare written documents, keep in mind the following suggestions:

1. Know your audience. If you are writing for nontechnical readers, use terms that readers will understand.
2. Use the **active voice** whenever possible. For example, the active voice sentence "Tom designed the system," is better than, "The system was designed by Tom," which is an example of the **passive voice**.
3. Keep your writing concise and well-organized. Use one paragraph to convey a single idea.
4. Use an appropriate style. For example, use a conversational tone in informal documents and a business tone in formal documents.
5. Use lists. When you must enumerate a number of subtopics related to the same topic, lists are an organized way to present them.
6. Use short, easy-to-understand words. Your objective is not to impress your audience with the size of your vocabulary.
7. Avoid repeating the same word too often. Use a thesaurus to locate synonyms for frequently repeated words. Many word processing programs include a thesaurus and other tools to help you write better.

ON THE WEB

For more information about Effective Written Communications, visit **scsite.com/sad6e/ more**, locate Toolkit Part 1 and then click the Effective Written Communications link.

ON THE WEB

For more information about Grammar Checkers, visit **scsite.com/sad6e/ more**, locate Toolkit Part 1 and then click the Grammar Checkers link.

8. Check your spelling. You can use the spell checker in your word processing program to check your spelling, but remember that a **spell checker** is a tool that identifies only words that do not appear in the program's dictionary. For example, a spell checker will not identify instances when you use the word *their*, instead of the word *there*.

9. Check your grammar. Most word processing programs include a **grammar checker**, which is a tool that can detect usage problems and offer suggestions. When you use a grammar checker, you can set various options to match the level and style of the writing and to highlight or ignore certain types of usage. For example, you can set the grammar checker in Microsoft Word to check grammar rules only, or you can configure it to check writing style, as shown in Figure TK 1-3, including gender-specific words, sentence fragments, and passive sentences.

Notice that the user has asked the program to check that 1, and only 1, space is placed at the end of each sentence.

10. Review your work carefully. Then double-check it for spelling, grammatical, and typographical mistakes. If possible, ask a colleague to proofread your work and suggest improvements.

All writers must consider **readability**, which analyzes ease of comprehension by measuring specific characteristics of syllables, words, and sentences. Two popular readability tools are the Flesch Reading Ease Score and the Flesch-Kincaid Grade Level Score.

The **Flesch Reading Ease score** measures the average sentence length and the average number of syllables per word and rates the text on a 100-point scale using the formula shown in Figure TK 1-4. With this tool, the higher the score, the easier it is to understand. Notice that Microsoft suggests that for most standard documents, you should aim for a score of 60-70.

The **Flesch-Kincaid Grade Level score** uses the same variables, but in a different formula that produces a rating keyed to a U.S. grade-school level. For example, a score of 8.0 would indicate material easily understood by a person at an eighth-grade reading level. With this tool, Microsoft suggests that for most standard documents, you should aim for a score of 7.0 to 8.0.

E-Mail, Memos, and Letters

E-mail is the primary form of communication in most companies. Many companies use **workgroup software** because it offers many features in addition to basic e-mail capability. These features include calendars, task lists, schedules, contact lists, and document management, among others.

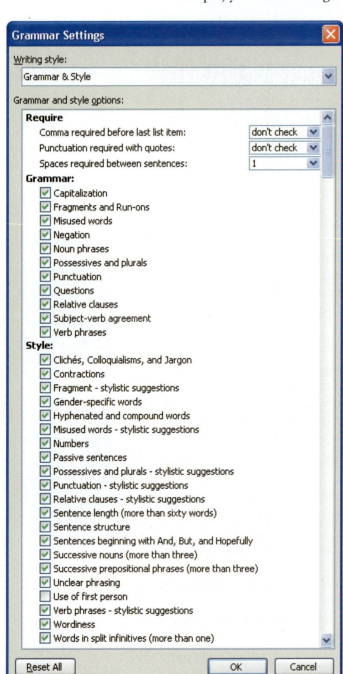

FIGURE TK 1-3 You can set the grammar checker in Microsoft Word to check grammar rules only, or you can configure it to check your writing style.

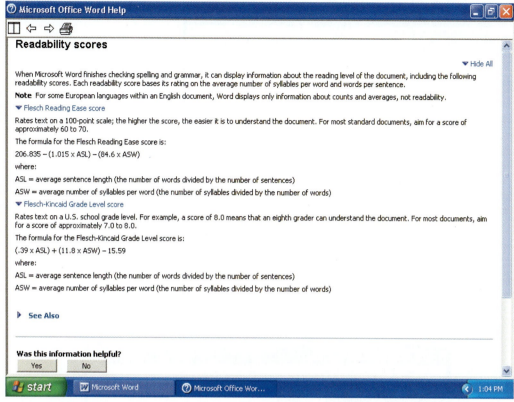

FIGURE TK 1-4 Two popular readability measurement tools are the Flesch Reading Ease Score and the Flesch-Kincaid Grade Level Score.

Examples of workgroup software are Microsoft Outlook and Novell's GroupWise, which is shown in Figure TK 1-5 on the next page. Notice that a GroupWise user can collaborate with other users by sharing documents and folders, and can even create a discussion group to exchange and record ideas.

Although e-mail and workgroup software have become the main form of internal communication, in-house memos still are important, and external communications often require letters printed on company letterhead.

Most companies have a standard format, or template, for internal memos and external letters. If your company stores those on a network, you can download and use the templates. If you want to create your own designs, you can use a word processor to create templates with specific layouts, fonts, and margin settings. A **template** gives your work a consistent look and makes your job easier. Word processing programs also provide a feature that allows you to design your memos as forms and fill in the blanks as you work.

Most companies now use **e-mail** as the standard form of written correspondence. E-mail usually is less formal than other written communication, but you still must follow the rules of good grammar, correct spelling, and clear writing.

Although many authors use a more conversational style for e-mail, you should remember that e-mail messages often are forwarded to other recipients or groups, and so they are as important as any other form of written communication. If you regularly exchange messages with a specific group of users, most e-mail programs allow you to create a distribution list that includes the members and their e-mail addresses. For

ON THE WEB

For more information about Readability, visit **scsite.com/sad6e/ more**, locate Toolkit Part 1 and then click the Readability link.

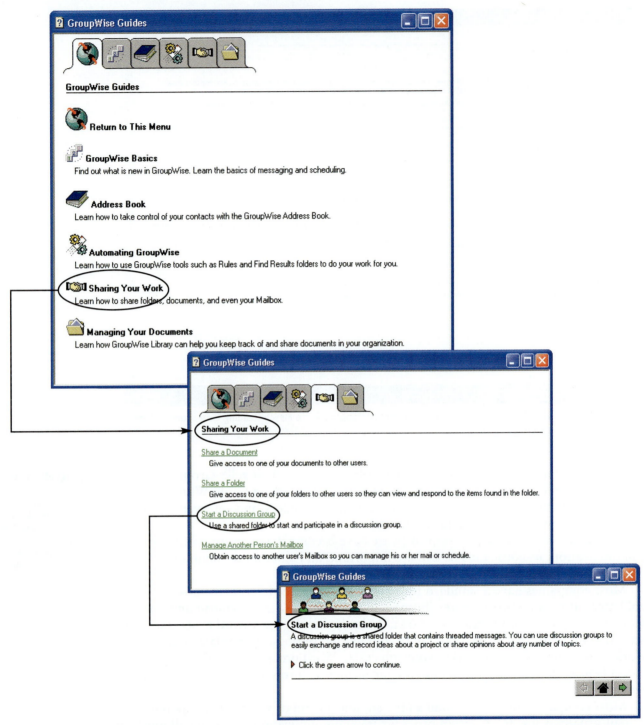

FIGURE TK 1-5 Workgroup software, such as Novell's GroupWise, allows a user to collaborate with others by sharing documents and folders, and creating discussion groups to exchange and record ideas.

example, Figure TK 1-6 shows how to use Microsoft Outlook to send an e-mail to a six-person systems development team.

Reports

You must prepare many reports during the systems development life cycle, including the preliminary investigation report, the system requirements document at the end of the systems analysis phase, the system design specification at the end of the system design

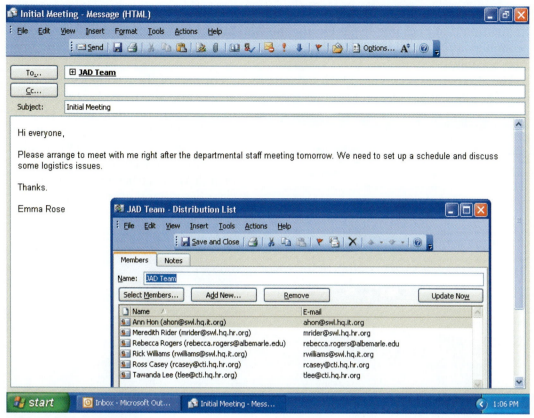

FIGURE TK 1-6 Microsoft Outlook allows users to create distribution lists for sending e-mail messages.

phase, and the final report to management when the system goes into operation. You also might submit other reports, such as status reports, activity reports, proposals, and departmental business plans. You will create your reports as electronic documents, so you can attach them to e-mails and print them, if desired.

In some cases, you must present reports more formally. The example in Figure TK 1-7 on the next page shows a binder for a system requirements document, which includes an introduction, executive summary, findings, recommendations, time and cost estimates, expected benefits, and an appendix.

You can use a **cover memo,** or an e-mail message similar to the one shown in Figure TK 1-7, when you send a report, and you can set a date, time, and place for an oral presentation. You also can request that the recipients read the report in advance of the presentation.

The **introduction** usually includes a title page, table of contents, and brief description of the proposal. The title page should be clean and neat and contain the name of the proposal, the subject, the date, and the names of the development team members. If the project already has a recognized name or acronym, use it. Include a **table of contents** when the report is long or includes many exhibits. Many word processing programs include a tool that can generate a table of contents automatically.

The **executive summary** is used to summarize the entire project, including your recommendations, in several paragraphs. Generally, the executive summary should not exceed 200 words or one page.

Use the **findings section** to describe the major conclusions that you or the team reached during the systems analysis phase. You can make the findings section detailed or summarized, depending on the project. You must explain the logical design of the new system in a way that nontechnical managers can understand clearly. With a management audience, the most important task is to explain how the proposed system supports the company's business needs.

The **recommendations section** presents the best system alternative, with a brief explanation that does not disparage anyone who favors a different alternative. Your recommendation should mention the essential factors of economic, technical, and operation feasibility.

The **alternatives section** can be a separate section or part of the recommendations section. The alternatives section identifies various strategies and alternatives, as discussed in Chapter 5. In the alternatives section, you should list the advantages and disadvantages of each major system alternative. In this section, you should include the cost-benefit results, with a clear description of the economic

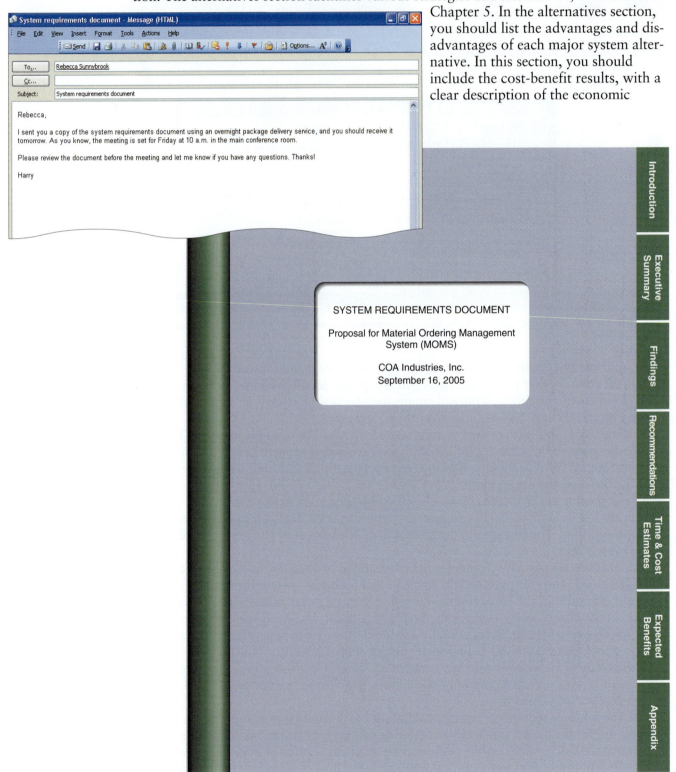

FIGURE TK 1-7   Typical binder for a system requirements document, with an explanatory e-mail message that notes the date, time, and place for the presentation.

analysis techniques that were used. You can use tables or graphs to support and clarify your alternatives when necessary.

When you have a large number of supporting documents such as questionnaires or sampling results, you should put those items in an **appendix** located at the end of the document. Make sure you include only relevant information, and provide references for interested readers.

ORAL COMMUNICATIONS

An **oral presentation** is required at the end of the preliminary investigation and again at the conclusion of the systems analysis phase. You might need to give more than one presentation in some situations to present technical material to members of the IT department or to present an overview for top managers. When preparing an oral presentation, you should perform six important tasks: define the audience, define the objectives for your presentation, organize the presentation, define any technical terms you will use, prepare your presentation aids, and practice your delivery.

ON THE WEB

For more information about Effective Presentations, visit **scsite.com/sad6e/more**, locate Toolkit Part 1 and then click the Effective Presentations link.

Define the Audience

Before you develop a detailed plan for a management presentation, you must define the audience. Senior managers often prefer an executive summary rather than a detailed presentation, but that is not always the case, especially in smaller companies where top management is more involved in day-to-day activities. If you consider the expectations of your audience and design your presentation accordingly, you will improve your chances of success.

Define the Objectives

When you communicate, you should focus on your objectives. In the management presentation for the systems analysis phase, your goals are the following:

- ➡ Inform management of the status of the current system
- ➡ Describe your findings concerning the current system problems
- ➡ Explain the alternative solutions that you developed
- ➡ Provide detailed cost and time estimates for the alternative solutions
- ➡ Recommend the best alternative and explain the reasons for your selection

Organize the Presentation

Plan your presentation in three stages: the introduction, the information, and the summary. First, you should introduce yourself and describe your objectives. During the presentation, make sure that you discuss topics in a logical order. You should be as specific as possible when presenting facts — your listeners want to hear your views about what is wrong, how it can be fixed, how much it will cost, and when the objectives can be accomplished. In your summary, briefly review the main points, and then ask for questions.

Define Any Technical Terms

You should avoid specialized or technical terminology whenever possible. If your audience might be unfamiliar with a term that you plan to use, either define the term or find another way to say it so they will understand your material.

ON THE WEB

For more information about Presentation Software, visit **scsite.com/sad6e/more**, locate Toolkit Part I and then click the Presentation Software link.

Prepare Presentation Aids

Much of what people learn is acquired visually, so you should use helpful, appropriate visual aids to help the audience follow the logic of your presentation and hold their attention. Visual aids also can direct audience attention away from you, which is helpful if you are nervous when you give the presentation. You can use a visual aid with an outline of topics that will help you stay on track. You can enhance the effect of your presentation with visual aids that use various media and software, as explained in the following sections.

VISUAL AIDS Visual aids can help you display a graphical summary of performance trends, a series of cost-benefit examples, or a bulleted list of important points. You can use whiteboards, flip charts, overhead transparencies, slides, films, and videotapes to enhance your presentation. When preparing your visual aids, make sure that the content is clear, readable, and easy to understand. Verify ahead of time that the audience can see the visual material from anywhere in the room. Remember that equipment can fail unexpectedly, so be prepared with an alternate plan.

PRESENTATION SOFTWARE With a computer and a projection system, you can use **presentation software**, such as Microsoft PowerPoint, to create slides with sounds, animation, and graphics. Figure TK 1-8 provides more information about hardware and software requirements that you need to broadcast a slide presentation on the Internet. Using this technique, a presentation can be viewed from any location with Internet access. When you broadcast a live presentation, if you also have a conference call to connect the viewers, you can take questions and gather feedback. If it is impractical to have all viewers attend at the same time, you can store the presentation on a server so it can be downloaded whenever convenient. As Microsoft points out, the presentation is saved in HTML (hypertext markup language) format. Then, all your audience needs in order to see the presentation is a browser and access to the server or computer where you are storing the presentation or from which you are broadcasting it live.

Preparing an effective slide presentation requires time and effort, and personal experience is the best teacher. There is no

FIGURE TK 1-8 You can broadcast a multimedia PowerPoint presentation on the Internet, if you have the required hardware and software. The presentation can be viewed live, or stored on a server so it can be downloaded at a convenient time.

universal agreement about how to prepare a slide show, and many sources of information exist. Some overall guidelines include the following:

➡ Your first step (and perhaps the most important) is to prepare an overall outline that will be the foundation of your presentation. You should focus on the content and structure of your presentation before you consider visual issues.

➡ Remember that a fine line exists between providing too little information and too much.

➡ Display one topic per slide, and try to follow the rule often called the 7 **by 7 rule**: no more than seven items per slide, and no more than seven words per item. Some presenters believe that a **6 by 6 rule** is even more effective.

➡ When displaying a list of items, consider using a series of slides to add each point sequentially, especially if you want to focus attention on the item being discussed.

➡ Use bullets rather than numbers, unless you are showing a specific sequence or order.

➡ Choose easily readable fonts. Use sans serif styles, such as Arial, for all body text. If you do use a serif style (such as Times Roman), apply it only in titles.

➡ Use appropriate point sizes for titles and body text. Your goal is to prepare slides that are readable and visually attractive. Although point size selection depends on individual judgment and experience, here are some suggestions to get you started: for titles, try either 40- or 36-point fonts; for body text, 32- or 24-point fonts usually work well.

➡ Select special effects carefully — too many graphics, colors, sounds, or other special effects will distract your audience.

➡ You can include tables or graphics, but keep them simple and easy to understand. Also, you can use a special effect, such as boldface, italics, underlining, or a different color, to highlight an important word or phrase.

➡ Strive for a consistent look and feel among your slides, and position visual elements in the same place on each slide. You should use a master template to assure uniformity and conform to company-wide standards that might apply, such as a copyright notice, a confidentiality statement, or placement of the company name and logo. Choose colors carefully, and keep them consistent. Usually, light letters on a dark background are easiest to read. Presentation software normally has predefined color palettes that provide background and text colors that ensure readability. Use these palettes as a guideline for selecting colors when possible.

➡ Be sure to check spelling and grammar!

➡ During the presentation, do *not* read your slides to the audience! They can read the slides on their own. Your slide presentation is an outline that provides structure and emphasis — it is not the presentation itself.

➡ It is important to deliver a presentation that can be viewed easily from anywhere in the room. When setting up, consider the size of the room, the number of people attending, the size and location of your visual aids, and the characteristics of any projection equipment you will be using.

Practice

The most important part of your preparation is practice. You should rehearse several times to ensure that the presentation flows smoothly and the timing is correct. Practicing will make you more comfortable and build your confidence.

Do not be tempted to write a script. If you read your presentation, you will be unable to interact with your audience and adjust your content based on their reactions.

Instead, prepare an outline of your presentation and practice from the outline. Then, when you deliver the actual presentation, you will not have to struggle to remember the exact words you planned to say, and you will be able to establish a good rapport with your audience.

The Presentation

When you give the presentation, the following points will help you succeed:

SELL YOURSELF AND YOUR CREDIBILITY To have a successful presentation, you must sell yourself and your credibility. A brilliant presentation will not convince top managers to approve the system if they are not sold on the person who gave the presentation. On the other hand, many systems projects are approved because the systems analyst did an excellent sales job.

Your presentation must show confidence about the subject and your recommendations. You should avoid any conflicts with the people attending the presentation. If anyone directs critical remarks to you, address the issues honestly and directly. You will have a successful presentation only if you know the material thoroughly, prepare properly, and sell yourself and your credibility.

CONTROL THE PRESENTATION During the presentation, you must control the discussion, maintain the pace of the presentation, and stay focused on the agenda — especially when answering questions. Although you might be more familiar with the subject material, you must not appear to have a superior attitude toward your listeners. Maintain eye contact with the audience and use some humor, but do not insert irrelevant jokes or make a joke at someone else's expense.

ANSWER QUESTIONS APPROPRIATELY Let your audience know whether you would prefer to take questions as you go along or have a question and answer session at the end. Sometimes the questions can be quite difficult. You must listen carefully and respond with a straightforward answer. Try to anticipate the questions your audience will ask so you can prepare your responses ahead of time.

When answering a difficult or confusing question, repeat the question in your own words to make sure that you understand it. For example, you can say, "If I understand your question, you are asking if …" This will help avoid confusion and give you a moment to think on your feet. To make sure that you gave a clear answer, you can say, "Have I answered your question?" Allow follow-up questions when necessary.

USE EFFECTIVE SPEAKING TECHNIQUES The delivery of your presentation is just as important as its content. You can strengthen your delivery by speaking clearly and confidently and projecting a relaxed approach. You also must control the pace of your delivery. If you speak too fast, you will lose the audience, and if the pace is too slow, people will lose their concentration and the presentation will not be effective.

Many speakers are nervous when facing an audience. If this is a problem for you, keep the following suggestions in mind:

1. Control your environment. If you are most nervous when the audience is looking at you, use visual aids to direct their attention away from you. If your hands are shaking, do not hold your notes. If you are delivering a computer slide show, use the keyboard to advance to the next slide instead of using the mouse. Concentrate on using a strong, clear voice. If your nervousness distracts you, take a deep breath and remind yourself that you really do know your subject.

2. Turn your nervousness to your advantage. Many people do their best work when they are under a little stress. Think of your nervousness as normal pressure.

3. Avoid meaningless filler words and phrases. Using words and phrases such as okay, all right, you know, like, um, and ah are distracting and serve no purpose.

4. Practice! Practice! Practice! Some people are naturally gifted speakers, but most people need lots of practice. You must work hard at practicing your presentation and building your confidence. Many schools offer speech or public speaking courses that are an excellent way of practicing your skills. It also can be advantageous to preview your presentation with one or more people and ask for input.

TOOLKIT SUMMARY

Your success as a systems analyst depends on your ability to communicate effectively. You must know why you are communicating, what you want to accomplish, who your targets are, what is expected of you, and when to go into detail. You must know your subject and how to use good written and oral communications techniques.

You will be judged by your written work, so it must be free of grammatical, spelling, and punctuation errors. You should write e-mail, letters, and memos clearly, and the writing style should match the situation. Many firms have standard formats for letters and memos, and you can use templates to achieve consistency.

Your writing must be clear and understandable. You can use readability measurement tools such as the Flesch Reading Ease score and the Flesch-Kincaid Grade Level score.

You will prepare various reports during the SDLC, and the format will vary depending on the nature of the report. Your reports should have a cover memo and might include an introduction, an executive summary, findings, recommendations, time and cost estimates, expected benefits, and an appendix.

In addition to written communications, you must communicate effectively in person. You might have to deliver several presentations to different audiences at different times during the SDLC. Presentations are an important form of oral communication, and you should follow specific guidelines in preparing your presentation. You prepare by defining your audience, identifying your objectives, and organizing the presentation itself. You also need to define technical terms and prepare visual aids to help your audience understand the material. Most important, you must practice your delivery to gain confidence and strengthen your presentation skills.

When you develop slide presentations, you should follow the 6 by 6 rule or 7 by 7 rule and other guidelines that will make your slide easy to read and understand. You should select fonts and point sizes carefully, and strive for a consistent look and feel throughout the presentation. Special effects can be interesting, but do not overuse them.

When you give the presentation, you are selling your ideas and your credibility. You must control the discussion, build a good rapport with the audience, answer all questions clearly and directly, and try to use good speaking techniques. Again, the best way to become a better speaker is to practice.

Key Terms and Phrases

Toolkit Exercises

Review Questions

1. Describe the why, who, what, when, and how of communications. Explain each term and give an example. Also, what is a corporate culture and why is it important?
2. Mention five specific techniques you can use to improve your written documents.
3. What is the role of e-mail communication? What techniques can you use to become an effective e-mail communicator?
4. What are the main sections of a written report to management, and what is the purpose of each section?
5. When preparing an oral presentation, what six tasks should you perform?
6. When you organize the presentation, what three stages do you plan?
7. Why are visual aids important? Give at least three examples of different types of visual aids, with a specific example of how you would use each type in an actual presentation. You can use the SWL case or make up your own scenario.
8. What should you do during the delivery of your presentation to improve the success of the presentation?
9. Name three specific strategies you can use if you get nervous during a presentation.
10. Why is practice so important when preparing a presentation?

Discussion Topics

1. When is a casual e-mail style *too* casual? Most people would agree that business e-mail can be more conversational than formal written documents, but even e-mail has its limits. Suppose you were the manager of a staff group with 25 employees. What guidance would you give them regarding e-mail style and usage?
2. Is it possible to over-communicate in some situations? For example, in the discussion about interviewing in Chapter 3, you learned that it is best to avoid leading questions, which might suggest an answer to the interviewee. Can you think of other examples, like writing newspaper headlines, where "less is more"?
3. Many articles have been written about the importance of body language. Do you believe that physical behavior is a reliable means of communication? Think of examples where you were conscious of a person's body language. Did the body language relate to something they were trying to communicate to you — or something they were trying *not* to communicate?
4. The issue of workplace privacy affects all employees. Electronic monitoring of e-mail, especially, has been the subject of many news articles, discussion, and debates. How do you feel about this issue? Should e-mail monitoring be always permissible, never permissible, or does the answer depend on specific factors? If so, what are they? Perform research on the Internet and defend your position.

Projects

1. "The Elements of Style" by William Strunk, Jr. and E. B. White is a popular reference manual for proper English usage. The book identifies many words and phrases that are commonly misused, including the following examples: *between* and *among*, *affect* and *effect*, *different from* and *different than*, *like* and *as*, and *infer* and *imply*. Using "The Elements of Style" or another source, investigate each of the usage examples listed above, and write a brief memo that explains how each word or phrase should be used.

2. If you have access to Microsoft PowerPoint or another presentation tool, prepare a slide presentation. The topic of your presentation is "How to Prepare an Effective Slide Presentation." Assume that your audience is familiar with presentation software, but never has considered guidelines for style or effectiveness. Your presentation should represent a good example of the guidelines on pages 532–533.

3. Refer to the description of readability measurements on page 526. Now try your skill as a training manual writer. Choose a simple hardware or software task and write a two- or three-paragraph description of how to perform the task. When you are finished, check the readability statistics. Assume that you are writing for technical novices, so try to keep the Flesch Reading Ease score above 60, and the Flesch-Kincaid Grade Level score to 8.0 or less.

4. View at least three examples of public speaking. You can investigate TV network news broadcasts, C-SPAN, or any other source. The speakers can be elected officials, newscasters, or others. Your objective is to develop a profile for each speaker. Your profile should include six specific characteristics of the speaker: gestures, expressions, voice levels, inflections, timing, and eye contact. Briefly summarize the results, and add comments on how you would rate the effectiveness of each speaker. Be sure to list your reasons.

PART 2 CASE Tools

In **Part 2** of the Systems Analyst's Toolkit, you will learn how CASE tools can help you perform systems development and maintenance tasks.

INTRODUCTION

OBJECTIVES

When you finish this part of the Toolkit, you will be able to:

- Explain CASE tools and the concept of a CASE environment
- Trace the history of CASE tools and their role in a fourth-generation environment
- Define CASE terms and concepts, including a repository, modeling tools, documentation tools, engineering tools, and construction tools
- Explain an integrated development environment
- Provide examples of CASE tools features
- Describe future trends for CASE tools, including new developments and the emerging role of object-oriented analysis and design

Computer-aided systems engineering (CASE), also called **computer-aided software engineering**, is a technique that uses powerful software, called **CASE tools**, to help system developers design and construct information systems. In this part of the Systems Analyst's Toolkit, you will learn about the history, characteristics, and features of CASE tools. You will see specific examples of CASE tools and how they are used in various development tasks. In addition, you will learn about integrated software development environments.

TOOLKIT INTRODUCTION CASE: Mountain View College Bookstore

Background: Wendy Lee, manager of college services at Mountain View College, wants a new information system that will improve efficiency and customer service at the three college bookstores.

In this part of the case, Florence Fullerton (systems analyst) and Harry Boston (student intern) are talking about CASE tools and concepts.

Participants:	Florence and Harry
Location:	Florence's office, early in the systems planning phase
Discussion topics:	CASE tools, integrated development environments, CASE terms and concepts.

Florence:	Harry, before we get too far into the project, let's talk about CASE tools and concepts and how we can use them in the development process.
Harry:	*Sure. I saw examples of CASE tools in my systems analysis course. CASE stands for computer-aided systems engineering, right?*
Florence:	Yes. Some people say CASE stands for computer-aided *software* engineering instead of computer-aided *systems* engineering. There's really no difference. Either way, CASE tools are an integral part of the systems development process.
Harry:	*Will we use CASE tools on the bookstore project?*
Florence:	Yes. We'll start by identifying and modeling business functions and processes. That information will become part of a central repository, which is a database that stores all the characteristics of the information system.
Harry:	*Then what?*
Florence:	We'll use CASE tools to draw various diagrams, including DFDs, UML diagrams, functional decomposition diagrams, and structure charts. You'll learn about these as we go along. We might also use CASE tools to generate program code, screens, and reports. Also, depending on the software environment we select, we might use an integrated development environment.
Harry:	*What's that?*
Florence:	An integrated development environment is a built-in CASE tool that a vendor integrates into a software product.
Harry:	*Anything else?*
Florence:	Well, before we decide on a CASE tool, we'll take a look at two specific examples: Visible Analyst and System Architect. Here's a task list to get us started.

FIGURE TK 2-1

OVERVIEW OF CASE TOOLS

If you ask a carpenter for an example of a tool, the response might be a hammer, drill, or screwdriver. Put the same question to a chef, and the answer might be a measuring cup, knife, or spatula. Every type of work requires specific tools to do the job properly, and system development is no different. CASE tools can reduce costs, speed up development, and provide comprehensive documentation that can be used for future maintenance or enhancements. System developers also use CASE tools to plan business-driven systems starting with the company's operational needs and future requirements.

The Carnegie Mellon Software Engineering Institute, a leader in software standards and quality management, suggests that a **CASE environment** is more than a set of CASE tools — it includes any use of computer-based support in the software development process. As Figure TK 2-2 shows, the Carnegie Mellon definition includes managerial, administrative, and technical support for a software project.

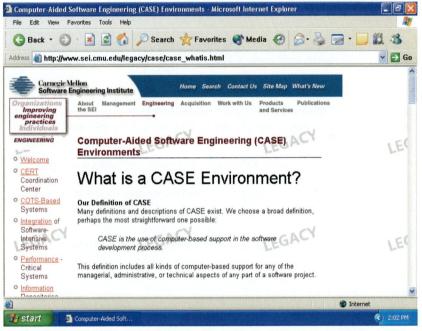

FIGURE TK 2-2   The Carnegie Mellon definition of a CASE environment includes any software-based managerial, administrative, and technical support for a software project.

CASE Tools History

As early as the 1960s, programmers used tools such as editors and code debuggers to write programs for mainframe computers. Today, in our software-driven world, CASE tools have evolved into powerful resources that systems analysts need to build and maintain complex information systems.

Forty years ago, virtually all code was written in **procedural** languages such as COBOL, which required a programmer to create code statements for each processing step. In contrast, modern languages such as Visual Basic or Java are called **non-procedural**, or **event-driven**, languages because instead of writing a series of sequential instructions, a programmer defines the actions that the program must perform when certain events occur. Because non-procedural languages are **object-oriented programming languages (OOPL)**, they are especially valuable in implementing an object-oriented system design. You can learn more about object-oriented analysis and design concepts in Part 5 of the Systems Analyst's Toolkit.

Another trend involves powerful programming languages called **fourth-generation languages (4GLs)** that are part of the **fourth-generation environment** described in Figure 5-30 on page 230. In a fourth-generation environment that includes modern CASE tools, system developers can develop accurate prototypes, cut development time, and reduce expense.

The Marketplace for CASE Tools

The CASE tool marketplace includes a wide variety of vendors and products, and no one tool dominates the market. You can use a site such as the one shown in Figure TK 2-3 to locate CASE tool products and vendors. Depending on their features, some CASE tools can

🌐 ON THE WEB

For more information about Fourth-Generation Languages, visit **scsite.com/sad6e/ more**, locate Toolkit Part 2 and then click the Fourth-Generation Languages link.

cost thousands of dollars, while others are available as shareware, or even as freeware, as shown in Figure TK 2-4.

How do you select a CASE tool? The answer depends on the type of project, its size and scope, possible budgetary and time constraints, and, importantly, the preferences and experience of the system development team. After you study the terms, concepts, and examples in this part of the Toolkit, you will be able to evaluate various products and make an informed decision. The first step in learning about CASE tools is to understand basic CASE terms and concepts.

FIGURE TK 2-3 This site lists many CASE tool products and vendors.

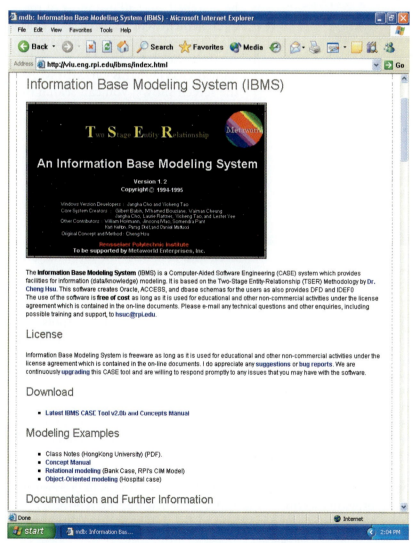

FIGURE TK 2-4 Information Base Modeling System (IBMS) is a freeware CASE tool that can be downloaded and used for educational purposes.

ON THE WEB

For more information about The CASE Tool Marketplace, visit **scsite.com/sad6e/more**, locate Toolkit Part 2 and then click The CASE Tool Marketplace link.

CASE Terms and Concepts

A typical CASE tool is actually a set of individual tools that share a repository of information.

The important terms and concepts are explained in the following sections.

Repository

A **repository** is a database that serves as a central storage location for all information about the system being developed. Once a data element has been defined in the repository, it can be accessed and used by processes and other information systems. For example, your sales processing, accounts receivable, and shipping systems all might require data about customers. After the CUSTOMER data element is entered in the repository, all three systems can share a consistent, up-to-date definition.

FIGURE TK 2-5 A Visible Analyst repository search for the data element named CUSTOMER NUMBER. The results will show all instances of the data element.

When you define a data element in the repository, you can assign a data type and format, a range of acceptable values, and one or more aliases. An **alias** is an alternative name for a data element. The repository can be searched, and all instances of the data element will be listed. For example, Figure TK 2-5 shows a Visible Analyst search for the data element named CUSTOMER NUMBER. As the screen shows, you can search the entire repository, or among specific types of diagrams, and the results will show all instances of the data element.

Individual Tools

An integrated set of CASE tools can be used to model, document, engineer, and construct the information system, as explained in the following sections.

MODELING TOOLS Throughout the SDLC, system developers use modeling tools and diagrams to represent the system graphically. The textbook describes many examples, including Unified Modeling Language diagrams and functional decomposition diagrams (Chapter 3), data flow diagrams (Chapter 4), entity-relationship diagrams (Chapter 7), structure charts (Chapter 8), and many types of object-oriented diagrams (Toolkit Part 5). Most popular CASE products offer these modeling tools, among others. One of the most important benefits of a CASE environment is that it provides an overall framework that allows a developer to create a series of graphical models based on data that has already been entered into a central repository.

DOCUMENTATION TOOLS The main source of system documentation is the repository, which was explained in the previous section. In most CASE software, the repository automatically identifies the new entries and adds them to the database. In addition to the repository itself, many CASE products provide tools that check automatically for inconsistent or incomplete information in forms, reports, and diagrams. This is especially important in large, complex systems.

ENGINEERING TOOLS   Engineering tools include forward engineering and reverse engineering tools. **Forward engineering** means translating business processes and functions into applications. Some CASE tools allow you to build the system either by editing objects and code directly, or by modifying graphical representations such as DFDs and UML diagrams. As you learned in Chapter 1, CASE tools such as System Architect and Visible Analyst allow you to develop a business model that can be translated into information system components. **Reverse engineering** allows you to examine an existing application and break it down into a series of diagrams, structure charts, and source code. Using a reverse engineering CASE tool, an analyst can transform existing application source code into a working model of the system. This can be especially important when integrating new systems with legacy systems or systems that were developed in different environments. Figure TK 2-6 shows examples of reverse engineering tools built into two CASE tools.

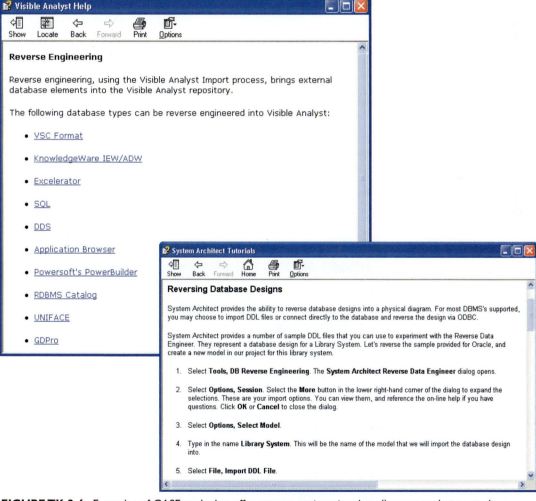

FIGURE TK 2-6   Examples of CASE tools that offer reverse engineering that allows an analyst to study an application or database from a design viewpoint.

CONSTRUCTION TOOLS A full-featured CASE tool can handle many program development tasks, such as generating application code, screens, and reports.

- → An **application generator**, also called a **code generator**, allows you to develop computer programs rapidly by translating a logical model directly into code. As shown in Figure TK 2-7, Popkin's System Architect uses information stored in the data repository to generate applications in languages such as Java, C++, and Visual Basic.

- → A **screen generator** is an interactive tool that helps you design a custom interface, create screen forms, and handle data entry format and procedures. The screen generator allows you to control how the screen will display captions, data fields, data, and other visual attributes. Modern CASE tools usually include a screen generator that interacts with the data dictionary. As shown in Figure TK 2-8, Gillani Software's FourGen® CASE tool set includes a screen generator, along with many other powerful features.

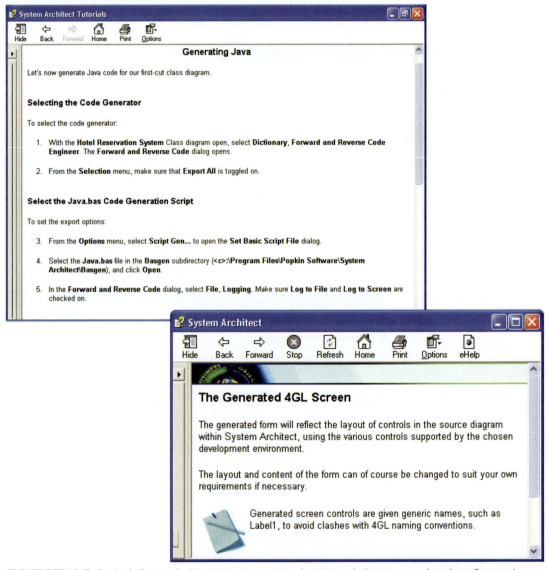

FIGURE TK 2-7 Popkin's System Architect can generate application code languages such as Java, C++, and Visual Basic.

→ A **report generator**, also called a **report writer**, is a tool for designing formatted reports rapidly. Using a report generator, you can modify a report easily at any stage of the design process. When you are satisfied with the report layout, the report writer creates a report definition and program code that actually produces the report. You also can input sample field values to create a **mock-up report** for users to review and approve.

FIGURE TK 2-8 FourGen® offers a screen generator that can create data entry screens and forms, and a report generator that creates the program code necessary to produce the report.

INTEGRATED DEVELOPMENT ENVIRONMENTS

ON THE WEB

For more information about Integrated Development Environments, visit **scsite.com/sad6e/ more**, locate Toolkit Part 2 and then click the Integrated Development Environments link.

An **integrated development environment** (IDE) uses a built-in CASE tool that a software vendor includes to make it easier to plan, construct, and maintain a specific software product. Many large firms such as Microsoft, Oracle, and IBM offer IDEs that relate to their family of products. The following sections explain how these tools are used.

Examples of Integrated Development Environments

Although generic CASE tools can be used to plan and design any type of information system, it usually is easier to use an integrated tool that the vendor has provided. For example, as shown in Figure TK 2-9, Oracle provides **Oracle Designer**, which is packaged with Oracle's application software. According to the company, Oracle Designer models business processes, data entities, and relationships — and can transform these models into designs that generate complete applications. Other leading firms, such as SAP and Sybase, also offer powerful development tools.

Figure TK 2-10 shows Microsoft's **Visual Studio .NET**, which is another example of an integrated development environment. Visual Studio .NET includes various application development tools that are specifically designed to support Microsoft's Web-based application development strategy. Notice that Microsoft describes the product as a rapid application development (RAD) tool, as well as an integrated development environment.

Pros and Cons of Integrated Development Tools

In a specific software environment, an integrated development tool is highly effective because it is an integral part of the vendor's software package. The only possible disadvantage is that each IDE is different, and requires a learning curve and skills that

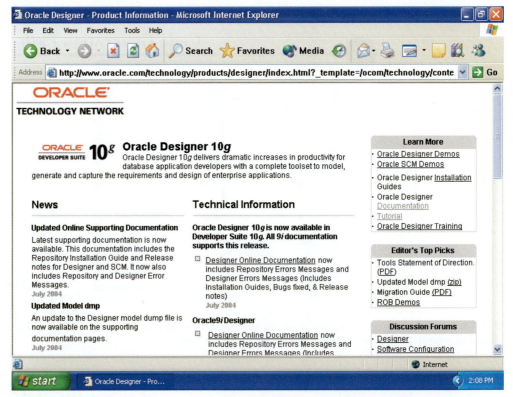

FIGURE TK 2-9 Oracle Designer is a modeling and application development tool packaged with Oracle's application software.

might or might not be readily transferable. In contrast, non-specific CASE tools such as Visible Analyst or System Architect can be used in any development environment. Given the dynamic changes in IT, a systems analyst should seek to learn as many development and CASE tools as possible.

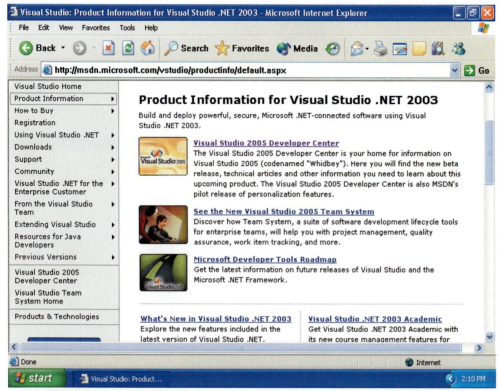

FIGURE TK 2-10 Visual Studio .NET is an integrated development environment that supports Microsoft's Web-based application strategy.

CASE TOOL EXAMPLES

You can choose from dozens of vendors and CASE tools that offer a wide range of functions, characteristics, and appearance. The following sections illustrate several features of products offered by three leading CASE tool suppliers: Visible Systems Corporation, Popkin Software, and Rational Software.

Visible Analyst

Visible Systems Corporation is an important player in the software development market. Visible offers tools for data and application modeling, code generation, and software configuration management.

The **Visible Analyst®** CASE tool can generate many types of models and diagrams. Figure TK 2-11 on the next page shows three sample diagrams for a library system: an entity-relationship diagram, a data flow diagram, and a structure chart. All three examples are integrated with a central data repository.

ON THE WEB

For more information about The Visible Analyst CASE Tool, **scsite.com/sad6e/ more**, locate Toolkit Part 2 and then click the Visible Analyst CASE Tool link.

FIGURE TK 2-11 Three sample Visible Analyst diagrams are integrated with the central data repository for a library system.

ON THE WEB

For more information about The System Architect CASE Tool, visit **scsite.com/ sad6e/more**, locate Toolkit Part 2 and then click the System Architect CASE Tool link.

Visible Analyst also provides a full range of Help features, including the error message analysis screen shown in Figure TK 2-12. When a user clicks an alphabetic letter, he or she can learn more about a specific error message that the program has displayed.

System Architect

On its Web site, Popkin Software claims that it leads the market for modeling and design tools that can build enterprise systems in full alignment with business

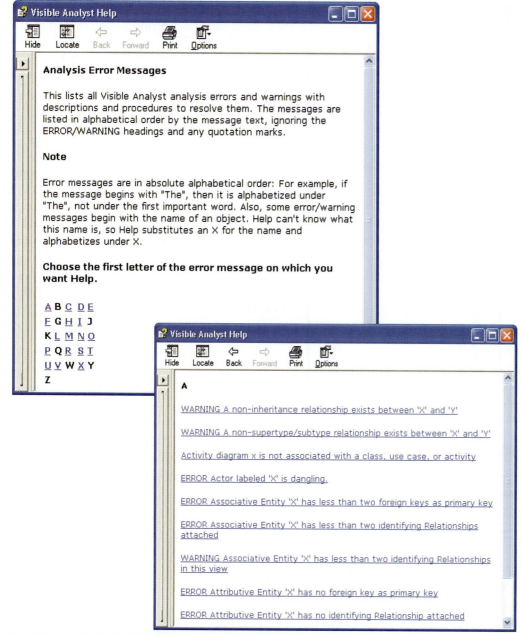

FIGURE TK 2-12 Visible Analyst provides error message analysis. When a user clicks an alphabetic letter, he or she can learn more about a specific error message.

requirements. Popkin states that its product, **System Architect**®, is the first fully integrated modeling tool to unify the enterprise with complete business and systems information management.

Popkin's emphasis on business modeling is apparent. In addition to the framework concept, which is described in the next section, Popkin offers numerous diagrams and definitions, all keyed to a particular view of the system. For example, as shown in Figure TK 2-13 on the next page, when a user wants to model the system from a specific viewpoint, he or she can create a new diagram or definition from an extensive list.

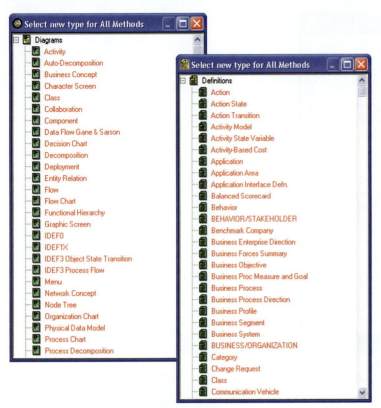

Popkin also offers extensive tutorials with its System Architect product. For example, as shown in Figure TK 2-14, a user can use an international hotel business model to learn the features of the program.

Rational Software

IBM's Rational Software offers a wide range of systems development and modeling products, including a powerful tool called **Rational Software Architect**. As the upper screen in Figure 2-15 shows, Rational Software Architect uses model-driven development and the UML to produce applications and services. By visiting the Rational Web site, you can view and download an online publication called the **Rational Edge**, a sample of which is shown in the lower screen in Figure 2-15.

FIGURE TK 2-13 System Architect provides a wide choice of diagrams and definitions for users who want to model a particular view of the system.

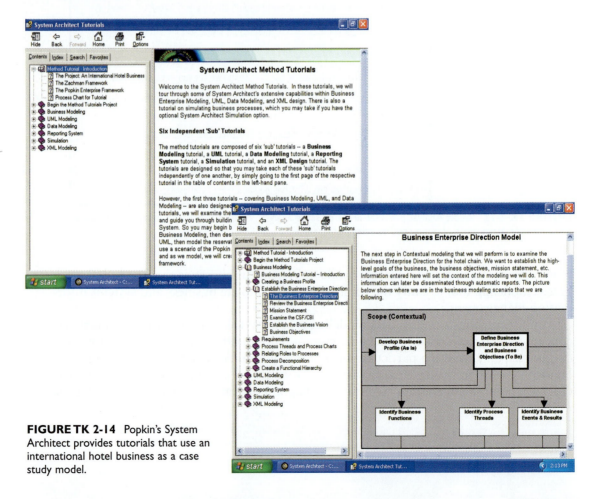

FIGURE TK 2-14 Popkin's System Architect provides tutorials that use an international hotel business as a case study model.

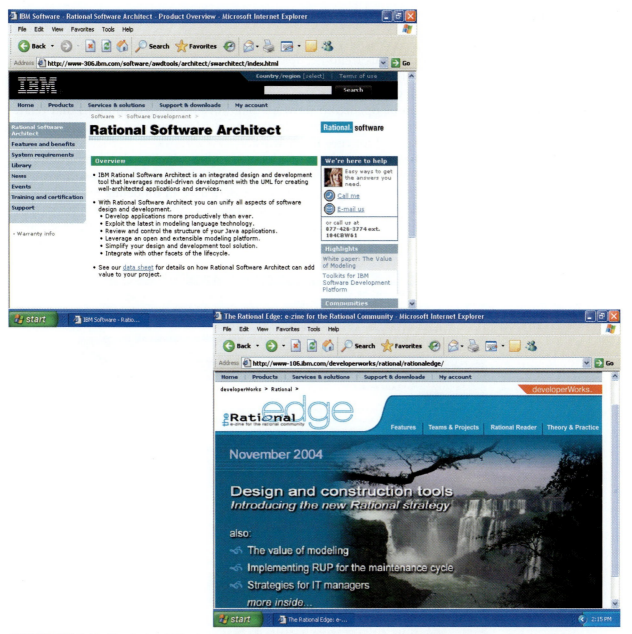

FIGURE TK 2-15 The Rational Edge is an online publication that contains news and information about Rational Software.

FUTURE TRENDS

Traditional CASE software evolved from functional tools, such as code editors, to cross-life cycle tools to help developers envision and construct an entire information system. The next generation of CASE software will go even further; it will consist of cross-platform tools that are capable of working with data and business processes both within the enterprise and from outside customers and suppliers.

Just as modern spacecraft could not have been built without specialized, high-technology tools, software of the future will undoubtedly be planned, constructed, and maintained with a new generation of CASE tools. Although it is difficult to predict the future, two trends seem clear: CASE tool vendors will continue to include powerful new features, and the popularity of object-oriented tools will continue to grow.

New Features

In each new version, CASE tool vendors seek to provide more features and greater flexibility. An example of this trend is Popkin Software's **Framework Manager**, which is shown in Figure TK 2-16. This feature enables a company to develop a multi-cell business model, where each cell represents a specific business operation or process. According to Popkin, each cell can be opened to show all diagrams and data definitions that relate to that cell. The program also supports industry-specific frameworks, such as the U.S. Department of Defense Architecture Framework.

Also, as software becomes more powerful and complex, the lines between traditional CASE tools and other modeling tools continue to blur. For example, **Microsoft Visio** generally is regarded as a charting tool, but it is widely used in modeling networks, business processes, and many types of special diagrams. Visio also offers a variety of online tutorials and training sessions, some of which include self-assessment, as shown in Figure TK 2-17. If you want to use Visio to learn about flowcharts, you can start

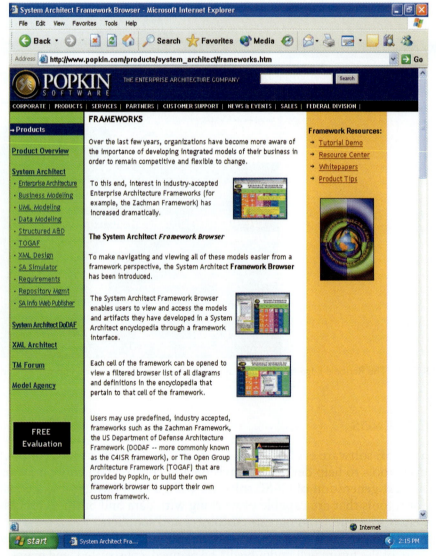

FIGURE TK 2-16   Each cell in Popkin Software's Framework Manager represents a specific business operation or process and can be opened to show the diagrams and data definitions that relate to that cell.

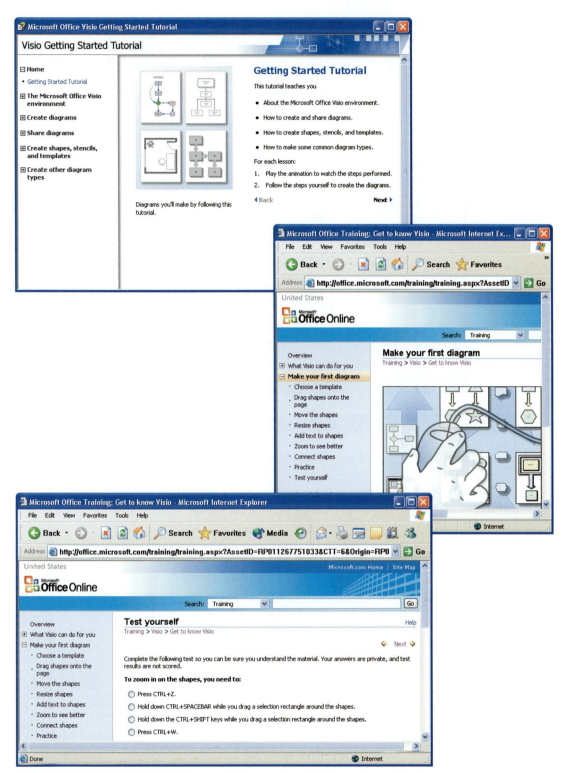

FIGURE TK 2-17 Microsoft Visio scan model networks and business processes and can create special diagrams such as cross-functional flowcharts.

with the simple example shown in Figure TK 2-18 on the next page, and progress to more powerful tools, such as cross-functional flowcharts that provide a three-dimensional view of a process or function.

Another trend is represented by Microsoft's Visual Studio .NET, which was discussed in an earlier section. Visual Studio .NET represents an enormous shift in emphasis to

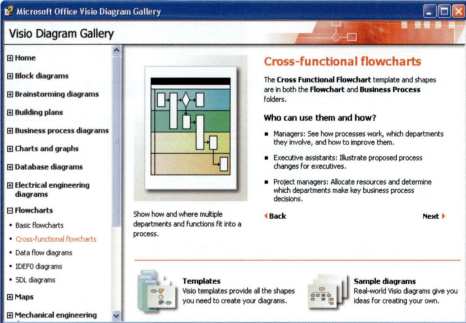

FIGURE TK 2-18 You can take advantage of built-in tutorials to learn about various types of flowcharts, from simple to complex.

Web-based development. According to Microsoft, Visual Studio .NET is capable of designing, building, testing, and deploying its Web services and applications.

The Emerging Role of Object-Oriented Analysis and Design

As you learned in Chapter 1, **structured analysis** uses a series of phases, called the **systems development life cycle (SDLC)**, to plan, analyze, design, implement, and support an information system. Although structured analysis continues to be a dominant methodology, **object-oriented analysis and design** (**OOAD**) is gaining popularity. Using an object-oriented approach, a developer creates objects called actors, which represent the human users who interact with the system. This approach allows the developer to visualize a system through the eyes of the people who will work with it. A major trend toward object-oriented languages has spurred interest in O-O CASE tools, which can provide a seamless development sequence that includes planning, analysis, design, and actual coding.

Other attractive features of an O-O approach include modular design and reusable code that easily can be combined and reassembled into new components. This offers a significant potential for cost reduction and faster development times. Unfortunately, these benefits are not always achieved, but that will change as more systems are developed using O-O. To learn more about object-oriented analysis and design, you can go to Part 5 of the Systems Analyst's Toolkit.

TOOLKIT SUMMARY

CASE stands for computer-aided systems engineering. CASE tools are software programs that system developers use to help them design and construct information systems. CASE tools can reduce costs, speed up development, and provide comprehensive documentation that can be used for future maintenance or enhancements.

Older systems used program code that was written in procedural languages such as COBOL, which required a programmer to create code statements for each processing step. Modern languages such as C++ and Java are non-procedural, or event-driven, languages because a programmer defines the actions that the program must perform when certain events occur.

Non-procedural languages, called 4GLs, are object-oriented programming languages (OOPL). 4GLs are important components of a fourth-generation environment that allows system developers to develop accurate prototypes, cut development time, and reduce expense.

A repository is a database that serves as a central storage location for all information about the system being developed. Once a data element has been defined in the repository, it can be accessed and used by processes and other information systems. An alias is an alternative name for a data element. The repository can be searched, and all instances of the data element will be listed.

An integrated set of CASE tools can be used to model, document, engineer, and construct the information system. Modeling tools represent the system graphically by using various types of diagrams, including data flow diagrams (DFDs), Unified Modeling Language (UML) diagrams, functional decomposition diagrams, structure charts, and network diagrams.

The main source of system documentation is the repository, which identifies new elements and adds them to the database. Additional documentation is provided by tools that check automatically for inconsistent or incomplete information in forms, reports, and diagrams.

Forward engineering means translating business processes and functions into applications. Reverse engineering allows you to examine an existing application and break it down into a series of diagrams, structure charts, and, in some cases, source code.

A CASE tool can handle many program development tasks, such as generating application code, screens, and reports.

An integrated development environment (IDE) uses a built-in CASE tool that a software vendor includes to make it easier to plan, construct, and maintain a specific software product. Examples of IDEs include Oracle Designer and Microsoft's Visual Studio .NET.

Two trends seem clear: CASE tool vendors will continue to include powerful new features, and the popularity of object-oriented tools will continue to grow.

Key Terms and Phrases

alias *542*

application generator *544*

CASE environment *540*

CASE tools *538*

code generator *544*

computer-aided software engineering *538*

computer-aided systems engineering (CASE) *538*

event-driven *540*

forward engineering *543*

fourth-generation environment *540*

fourth-generation languages (4GLs) *540*

Framework Manager *552*

integrated development environment (IDE) *546*

Microsoft Visio *552*

mock-up report *545*

non-procedural *540*

object-oriented analysis and
   design (OOAD) *555*

object-oriented programming
   languages (OOPL) *540*

Oracle Designer *546*

procedural *540*

Rational Edge *550*

Rational Software Architect *550*

report generator *545*

report writer *545*

repository *542*

reverse engineering *543*

screen generator *544*

structured analysis *554*

System Architect® *549*

systems development life cycle (SDLC) *554*

Visible Analyst® *547*

Visual Studio .NET *546*

Toolkit Exercises

Review Questions

1. Define CASE, CASE tools, and a CASE environment.
2. Explain the difference between procedural and non-procedural languages.
3. Describe 4GLs and their characteristics.
4. Define a repository, and explain its role in the systems development process.
5. What are forward and reverse engineering tools, and how are they used?
6. Provide an example of an application generator and a screen generator.
7. How is a report generator used, and what is a mock-up report?
8. Explain the concept of an integrated development environment and provide two examples of IDEs.
9. What are some features of Popkin's Framework Manager and Microsoft's Visio?
10. What is the emerging role of object-oriented analysis and design?

Discussion Topics

1. Would a systems analyst be better off in a position where he or she works with an integrated application environment, or in a job where a variety of generic CASE tools are used? Defend your conclusion.
2. Review the examples of System Architect and Visible Analyst in the preceding sections, and then visit the Internet sites for both companies. What are your impressions of the companies and the products they offer? Share your views with other students, and see whether you agree or disagree with their impressions.
3. If you were a programmer, would you prefer to work with procedural or non-procedural languages? Explain your reasons.
4. If the trend toward more powerful CASE tools continues, many of the tedious program development tasks might be performed automatically by the CASE software. Is there a limit to the capabilities of future CASE software? Could complete information systems be designed by describing a business operation and specifying certain inputs, outputs, and procedures? Why or why not? Explain your answer.

Projects

1. Go to the site shown in Figure TK 2-3 on page 541 and locate an example of a CASE tool. Visit the vendor's site and learn all you can about the product. Write a brief report that describes your experience.
2. Go to the site shown in Figure TK 2-4 on page 541 and download the IBMS CASE tool. Experiment with the software, and write a brief report that describes your experience.
3. Search the Internet and locate an example of a screen generator. Visit the vendor's site and learn all you can about the product. Write a brief report that describes your experience.
4. Go to the site shown in Figure TK 2-16 on page 552 and learn more about Popkin Software's Framework Manager. Write a brief report summarizing your findings.

PART

3 Financial Analysis Tools

In **Part 3** of the Systems Analyst's Toolkit, you will learn how to use financial analysis tools during the planning, analysis, design, implementation, and maintenance of an information system.

INTRODUCTION

OBJECTIVES

When you finish this part of the Toolkit, you will be able to:

- Define economic feasibility
- Classify costs and benefits into various categories, including tangible or intangible, direct or indirect, fixed or variable, and developmental or operational
- Understand chargeback methods and how they are used
- Use payback analysis to calculate the length of time that it takes for a project to pay for itself
- Use return on investment analysis to measure a project's profitability
- Use present value analysis to determine the value of a future project measured in current dollars

Part 3 of the Systems Analyst's Toolkit shows you how to use various tools to calculate a project's costs and benefits. As a systems analyst, you need to know how to calculate costs and benefits when you conduct preliminary investigations, evaluate IT projects, and make recommendations to management.

Financial analysis tools are important throughout the systems development life cycle. For example, in Chapter 2 you learn that economic feasibility depends on a comparison of costs and benefits. A project is economically feasible if the future benefits outweigh the estimated costs of developing or acquiring the new system. In Chapter 5, when you analyze development strategies, you apply financial analysis tools and techniques as you examine various options. Then, as Chapter 10 explains, you use these tools again to recognize the end of a system's useful life.

TOOLKIT INTRODUCTION CASE: Mountain View College Bookstore

Background: Wendy Lee, manager of college services at Mountain View College, wants a new information system that will improve efficiency and customer service at the three college bookstores.

In this part of the case, Florence Fullerton (systems analyst) and Harry Boston (student intern) are talking about financial analysis tools and techniques.

Participants:	Florence and Harry
Location:	Mountain View College Cafeteria, during the systems planning phase
Discussion topics:	Economic feasibility, chargeback methods, cost-benefit classification, payback analysis, return on investment analysis, and net present value analysis.

Florence: Hi, Harry. Before we go any further with the preliminary investigation, I wanted to meet with you to discuss financial analysis tools and techniques, and how we will apply them.

Harry: *Fine with me. Where do we start?*

Florence: Well, because economic feasibility depends on a project's costs and benefits, the first step is to classify those costs and benefits into specific categories. For example, costs can be tangible or intangible, direct or indirect, fixed or variable, and developmental or operational.

Harry: *Okay, I understand. What do we do after we classify everything?*

Florence: Then we use one or more financial analysis tools: payback analysis, return on investment analysis, and net present value analysis. We'll learn how to use them to evaluate the system and compare alternatives. We'll also talk about chargeback methods.

Harry: *What are they?*

Florence: A chargeback method is just a way to allocate costs for an IT system. We'll have to talk to Wendy about that. Meanwhile, here's a task list we can work on:

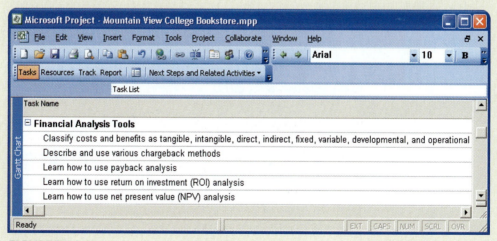

FIGURE TK 3-1

DESCRIBING COSTS AND BENEFITS

As a systems analyst, you must review a project's costs and benefits at the end of each SDLC phase so management can decide whether or not to continue the project. Before you can use the economic analysis tools described in this section of the Toolkit, you must learn how to identify and classify all costs and benefits.

As you learned in Chapter 2, **economic feasibility** means that the projected benefits of the proposed system outweigh the projected costs. When you determine economic feasibility, you must consider the project's benefits compared to the project's **total cost of ownership** (**TCO**), which includes ongoing support and maintenance costs, as well as acquisition costs. As you learned earlier, TCO is a comprehensive yardstick for making project decisions. Figure TK 3-2 shows a TCO Snapshot Tool that Compaq uses when proposing information systems solutions.

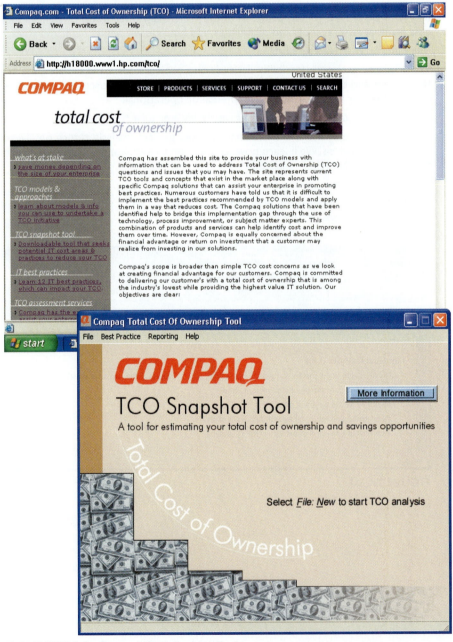

FIGURE TK 3-2 Compaq's TCO Snapshot Tool.

Cost-benefit analysis is used by business and government as a decision-making tool. For example, Figure TK 3-3 shows the Web site of the Center for Information Technology (CIT), which is a support division for the National Institutes of Health. Notice that CIT's standard for assessing an IT project is net present value, which is an analytical tool that is described later in this part of the Toolkit.

Cost Classifications

Costs can be classified as tangible or intangible, direct or indirect, fixed or variable, and developmental or operational. **Tangible costs** are costs for which you can assign a specific dollar value. Examples of tangible costs include employee salaries, hardware and software purchases, and office supplies. Tangible costs also include the interest charges that firms must pay when they need to borrow money for working capital or to finance new projects. In times of high interest rates, these costs can be significant and must be considered.

In contrast, **intangible costs** are costs whose dollar value cannot be calculated easily. The cost of customer dissatisfaction, lower employee morale, and reduced information availability are examples of intangible costs.

FIGURE TK 3-3 The Center for Information Technology (CIT), a support division for the National Institutes of Health, uses cost-benefit analysis as a decision-making tool.

If the analyst examines an intangible item carefully, however, it sometimes is possible to estimate a dollar value. For example, users might dislike a system because it is difficult to learn. Their dissatisfaction is an intangible cost, but if it translates into an increase in errors that must be corrected, you probably could assign a tangible dollar cost. You should try to work with tangible costs whenever possible.

Direct costs are costs that can be associated with the development of a specific system. Examples of direct costs include the salaries of project team members and the purchase of hardware that is used only for the new system. In contrast, **indirect costs**, or **overhead expenses**, cannot be attributed to the development of a particular information system. The salaries of network administrators, copy machine rentals, and insurance expenses are examples of indirect costs.

Fixed costs are costs that are relatively constant and do not depend on a level of activity or effort. Many fixed costs recur regularly, such as salaries and hardware rental charges. **Variable costs** are costs that vary depending on the level of activity. The costs of printer paper, supplies, and telephone line charges are examples of variable costs.

Developmental costs are incurred only once, at the time the system is developed or acquired. Those costs might include salaries of people involved in systems development, software purchases, initial user training, and the purchase of necessary hardware or furniture. **Operational costs** are incurred after the system is implemented and continue while the system is in use. Examples of operational costs include system maintenance, ongoing training, annual software license fees, and communications expense.

Some costs apply to more than one category of expenses. For example, overtime pay for clerical staff during the systems analysis phase would be classified as developmental, variable, and direct. A monthly fee for maintaining the company's Web site would be regarded as operational, fixed, and indirect.

Managing Information Systems Costs and Charges

Management wants to know how much an information system costs, so it is important for the systems analyst to understand direct costs, indirect costs, and methods of allocating IT charges within the company.

Direct costs usually are easier to identify and predict than indirect costs. For example, the salaries of project team members and the purchase of hardware, software, and supplies for the new system are direct costs. After a new information system goes into operation, other direct costs might include the lease of system-specific hardware or software.

Many IT department costs cannot be attributed directly to a specific information system or user group. Those indirect costs can include general hardware and software acquisition expenses; facility maintenance, air conditioning, security, rent, insurance, and general supplies; and the salaries of operations, technical support, and information center personnel.

A **chargeback method** is a technique that uses accounting entries to allocate the indirect costs of running the IT department. Most organizations adopt one of four chargeback methods: no charge, a fixed charge, a variable charge based on resource usage, or a variable charge based on volume.

1. **No charge method.** Some organizations treat information systems department indirect expenses as a necessary cost of doing business, and IT services are seen as benefiting the entire company. Thus, indirect IT department costs are treated as general organizational costs and are not charged to other departments. In this case, the information systems department is called a **cost center**, because it generates accounting charges with no offsetting credits for IT services.

2. **Fixed charge method.** With this method, the indirect IT costs are divided among all the other departments in the form of a fixed monthly charge. The monthly charge might be the same for all departments or based on a relatively constant factor such as department size or number of workstations. By using a fixed charge approach, all indirect costs are charged to other departments, and the IT group is regarded as a profit center. A **profit center** is a department that is expected to break even or

show a profit. Under the profit center concept, company departments purchase services from the IT department and receive accounting charges that represent the cost of providing the services.

3. **Variable charge method based on resource usage. Resource allocation** is the charging of indirect costs based on the resources used by an information system. The allocation might be based on connect time, server processing time, network resources required, printer use, or a combination of similar factors. **Connect time** is the total time that a user is connected actively to a remote server — some Internet service providers use this as a basis for charges. In a client/server system, **server processing time** is the time that the server actually responds to client requests for processing. The amount a particular department is charged will vary from month to month, depending not only on that department's resource usage, but also on the total resource usage. The information systems department is considered a profit center when an organization uses the resource allocation method.

4. **Variable charge method based on volume.** The indirect information systems department costs are allocated to other departments based on user-oriented activity, such as the number of transactions or printing volume. As with the resource allocation method, a department's share of the costs varies from month to month, depending on the level of activity. In this case, the information systems department is considered a profit center.

Benefit Classifications

In addition to classifying costs, you must classify the benefits that the company expects from a project. Like costs, benefits can be classified as tangible or intangible, fixed or variable, and direct or indirect. Another useful benefit classification relates to the nature of the benefit: positive benefits versus cost-avoidance benefits. **Positive benefits** increase revenues, improve services, or otherwise contribute to the organization as a direct result of the new information system. Examples of positive benefits include improved information availability, greater flexibility, faster service to customers, higher employee morale, and better inventory management.

In contrast, **cost-avoidance benefits** refer to expenses that would be necessary if the new system were not installed. Examples of cost-avoidance benefits include handling the work with current staff instead of hiring additional people, not having to replace existing hardware or software, and avoiding problems that otherwise would be faced with the current system. Cost-avoidance benefits are just as important as positive benefits, and you must consider both types when performing cost-benefit analysis.

COST-BENEFIT ANALYSIS

Cost-benefit analysis is the process of comparing the anticipated costs of an information system to the anticipated benefits. Cost-benefit analysis is performed throughout the SDLC to determine the economic feasibility of an information system project and to compare alternative solutions. Many cost-benefit analysis techniques exist. This section covers discussion of only the three most common methods: payback analysis, return on investment analysis, and present value analysis. Each of the approaches analyzes cost-benefit figures differently, but the objective is the same: to provide reliable information for making decisions.

 ON THE WEB

For more information about Payback Analysis, visit **scsite.com/ sad6e/more**, locate Toolkit Part 3 and then click the Payback Analysis link.

Payback Analysis

Payback analysis is the process of determining how long it takes an information system to pay for itself. The time it takes to recover the system's cost is called the **payback period**. To perform a payback analysis, you carry out the following steps:

1. Determine the initial development cost of the system.

2. Estimate annual benefits.

3. Determine annual operating costs.

4. Find the payback period by comparing total development and operating costs to the accumulated value of the benefits produced by the system.

When you plot the system costs over the potential life of the system, you typically see a curve such as the one shown in Figure TK 3-4. After the system is operational, costs decrease rapidly and remain relatively low for a period of time. Eventually, as the system requires more maintenance, costs begin to increase. The period between the beginning of systems operation and the point when operational costs are rapidly increasing is called the **economically useful life** of the system.

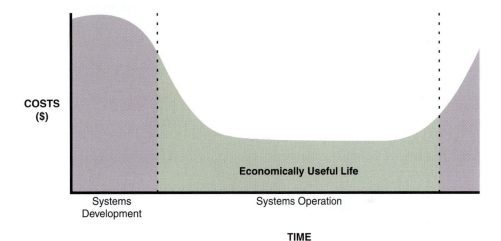

FIGURE TK 3-4   The costs of a typical system vary over time. At the beginning, system costs are high due to initial development expense. Costs then drop during systems operation. Maintenance costs begin to increase until the system reaches the end of its economically useful life. The area between the two dashed lines shows the economically useful life of this system.

When you plot the benefits provided by an information system against time, the resulting curve usually resembles the one shown in Figure TK 3-5. Benefits start to appear when the system becomes operational, might increase for a time, and then level off or begin to decline.

When conducting a payback analysis, you calculate the time it takes for the accumulated benefits of an information system to equal the accumulated costs of developing and operating the system.

In Figure TK 3-6, the cost and benefit curves are plotted on the same graph. The dashed line indicates the payback period. Notice that the payback period is not the point when current benefits equal current costs, where the two lines cross. Instead, the payback period compares accumulated costs and benefits. If you graph current costs and benefits, the payback period corresponds to the time at which the areas under the two curves are equal.

FIGURE TK 3-5 The benefits of an information system change over time. Benefits are not realized until the system becomes operational. Then, benefits usually increase rapidly at first before leveling off.

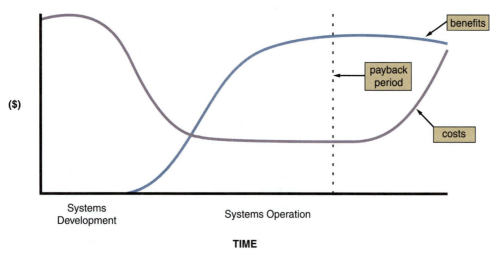

FIGURE TK 3-6 A system's costs and benefits can be plotted on the same graph. The dashed line indicates the payback period, when accumulated benefits equal accumulated costs.

Figure TK 3-7 on the next page contains two cost-benefit tables. The tables show the anticipated annual costs, cumulative costs, annual benefits, and cumulative benefits for two information systems projects. Year 0 (zero) corresponds to the year in which systems development begins. The development of Project A takes less than one year, so some benefits are realized in Year 0. Systems development for Project B requires more than one year, so the benefits do not begin until some time in Year 1.

In Project A, by the end of Year 4, the cumulative costs are $135,700, which slightly exceeds the $132,000 cumulative benefits. By the end of Year 5, however, the cumulative benefits of $171,000 far exceed the cumulative costs, which are $157,700. Therefore, at some point in time during Year 5, the accumulated costs and benefits are equal, and the payback period is established. In Project B, a similar situation exists. By the end of Year 4, Project B's cumulative costs are $191,000, which is greater than the cumulative benefits of $156,000. At some point during Year 5, cumulative benefits will exceed cumulative costs, and the system will have paid for itself.

If more specific information is available regarding the timing of costs and benefits during a year, you can calculate the payback period more precisely. Another approach is

PROJECT A:

YEAR	COSTS	CUMULATIVE COSTS	BENEFITS	CUMULATIVE BENEFITS
0	60,000	60,000	3,000	3,000
1	17,000	77,000	28,000	31,000
2	18,500	95,500	31,000	62,000
3	19,200	114,700	34,000	96,000
4	21,000	135,700	36,000	132,000
5	22,000	157,700	39,000	171,000
6	23,300	181,000	42,000	213,000

PROJECT B:

YEAR	COSTS	CUMULATIVE COSTS	BENEFITS	CUMULATIVE BENEFITS
0	80,000	80,000	——	——
1	40,000	120,000	6,000	6,000
2	25,000	145,000	26,000	32,000
3	22,000	167,000	54,000	86,000
4	24,000	191,000	70,000	156,000
5	26,500	217,500	82,000	238,000
6	30,000	247,500	92,000	330,000

FIGURE TK 3-7 Payback analysis data for two information systems proposals: Project A and Project B.

to create a chart that shows the exact point when cumulative benefits exceed cumulative costs, as shown in Figure TK 3-9 on page 368.

Some managers are critical of payback analysis because it places all the emphasis on early costs and benefits and ignores the benefits received after the payback period. Even if the benefits for Project B in Year 6 soared as high as $500,000, the payback period for that project still occurs during the fifth year of operation. In defense of payback analysis, the earlier cost and benefit predictions usually are more certain. In general, the further out in time that you extend your projections, the more unsure your forecast will be. Thus, payback analysis uses the most reliable of your cost and benefit estimates.

Payback analysis rarely is used to compare or rank projects because later benefits are ignored. You would never decide that Project A is better than Project B simply because the payback period for A is less than that for B; considering all the costs and all the benefits when comparing projects makes more sense.

Even with its drawbacks, payback analysis is a widely used tool. Many business organizations establish a minimum payback period for approved projects. If company policy requires a project to begin paying for itself within three years, then neither project in Figure TK 3-7 would be approved, though both are economically feasible.

Using a Spreadsheet to Compute Payback Analysis

You can use a spreadsheet to record and calculate accumulated costs and benefits, as shown in Figure TK 3-8. The first step is to design the worksheet and label the rows and columns. After entering the cost and benefit data for each year, you enter the formulas. For payback analysis, you will need a formula to display cumulative totals, year by year. For example, the first year in the cumulative costs column is the same as Year 0 costs, so the formula in cell C6 is =B6. The cumulative cost total for the second year is Year 0 cumulative total + Year 1 costs, so the formula for cell C7 is =C6+B7, and so on. The first worksheet shows the initial layout and the second worksheet shows the finished spreadsheet.

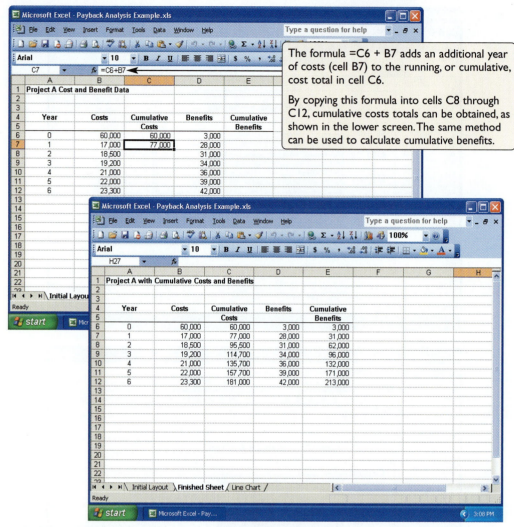

FIGURE TK 3-8 A Microsoft Excel worksheet displays payback analysis data for Project A in the upper screen. When cumulative cost and benefit formulas are entered, the finished worksheet in the lower screen appears.

After you verify that the spreadsheet operates properly, you can create a line chart that displays the cumulative costs, benefits, and the payback period, which is identified by the intersection of the cost and benefit lines, as shown in Figure TK 3-9 on the next page.

Return on Investment Analysis

Return on investment (ROI) is a percentage rate that measures profitability by comparing the total net benefits (the return) received from a project to the total costs (the investment) of the project. ROI is calculated as follows:

ROI = (total benefits – total costs) / total costs

Return on investment analysis considers costs and benefits over a longer time span than payback analysis. ROI calculations usually are based on total costs and benefits for a period of five to seven years. For example, Figure TK 3-10 on page 569 shows the ROI calculations for Project A and Project B. The ROI for Project A is 17.7 percent, and the ROI for Project B is 33.3 percent.

In many organizations, projects must meet or exceed a minimum ROI. This minimum ROI can be an estimate of the return the organization would receive from investing its

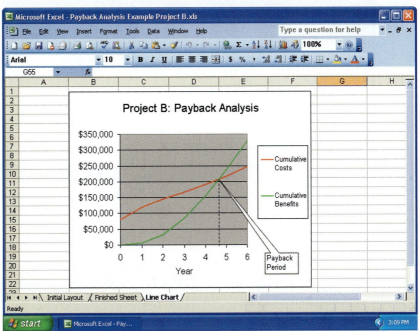

FIGURE TK 3-9 Microsoft Excel can be used to show the payback period by creating a chart of cumulative costs and benefits. Note that Project A has a shorter payback period than Project B.

ON THE WEB

For more information about Return on Investment Analysis, visit **scsite.com/ sad6e/more**, locate Toolkit Part 3 and then click the Return on Investment Analysis link.

money in other investment opportunities such as treasury bonds, or it can be a higher rate that the company requires for all new projects. If a company requires a minimum ROI of 15 percent, for example, then both Projects A and B would meet the criterion.

You also can use ROI for ranking projects. If Projects A and B represent two different proposed solutions for a single information systems project, then the solution represented by Project B is better than the Project A solution. If Projects A and B represent two different information systems projects, and if the organization has sufficient resources to pursue only one of the two projects, then Project B is the better choice.

Critics of return on investment analysis raise two points. First, ROI measures the overall rate of return for the total period, and annual return rates can vary considerably. Two projects with the same ROI might not be equally desirable if the benefits of one project occur significantly earlier than the benefits of the other project. The second criticism is that the ROI technique ignores the timing of the costs and benefits. This concept is called the time value of money, and is explained in the section on the present value analysis method.

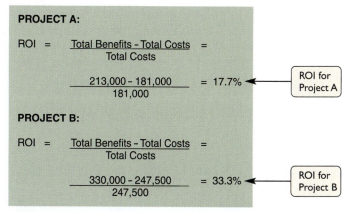

FIGURE TK 3-10 Return on investment analysis for Project A and Project B shown in Figure TK 3-7 on page 566.

Using a Spreadsheet to Compute ROI

You also can use spreadsheet programs to calculate the ROI. To do so for Project A, first set up the worksheet and enter the cost and benefit data. You can use cumulative columns (as you did in payback analysis) but you also will need two overall totals (one for costs and one for benefits), as shown in Figure TK 3-11.

The last step is to add a formula to calculate the ROI percentage rate, which is displayed in cell B16 in Figure TK 3-11. As stated previously, the ROI calculation is total benefits minus total costs, divided by total costs. Therefore, the formula that displays the ROI percentage in cell B16 is =(D13 - B13)/B13.

A major advantage of using a spreadsheet is if your data changes, you can modify your worksheet and calculate a new result instantly.

FIGURE TK 3-11 The worksheet for ROI analysis for Project A.

Present Value Analysis

A dollar you have today is worth more than a dollar you do not receive until one year from today. If you have the dollar now, you can invest it and it will grow in value. For example, would you rather have $100 right now or a year from now? The answer should be obvious. If you receive the $100 now, you can invest it in a mutual fund that has an annual return of eight percent. One year from now, you will have $108 instead of $100.

Alternatively, you might start from a different point of view. Instead of asking, "How much will my $100 be worth a year from now?" you can ask, "How much do I need to invest today, at eight percent, in order to have $100 a year from now?" This concept is known as the **time value of money**, and it is the basis of the technique called **present value analysis**.

The **present value** of a future dollar is the amount of money that, when invested today at a specified interest rate, grows to exactly one dollar at a certain point in the future. The specified interest rate is called the discount rate. In present value analysis, a company uses a discount rate that represents the rate of return if the money is put into relatively risk-free investments, such as bonds, instead of being invested in the project.

PERIODS	6%	8%	10%	12%	14%
1	0.943	0.926	0.909	0.893	0.877
2	0.890	0.857	0.826	0.797	0.769
3	0.840	0.794	0.751	0.712	0.675
4	0.792	0.735	0.683	0.636	0.592
5	0.747	0.681	0.621	0.567	0.519
6	0.705	0.630	0.564	0.507	0.456
7	0.665	0.583	0.513	0.452	0.400
8	0.627	0.540	0.467	0.404	0.351
9	0.592	0.500	0.424	0.361	0.308
10	0.558	0.463	0.386	0.322	0.270

FIGURE TK 3-12 Portion of a present value table showing adjustment factors for various time periods and discount rates. Values in the table are calculated using the formula shown in the text. Notice how the factors decrease as time and percentages increase.

Most companies require a rate of return that is higher than the discount rate because of the degree of risk in any project compared with investing in a bond. Companies often reject projects that seem attractive because the risk is not worth the potential reward.

To help you perform present value analysis, adjustment factors for various interest rates and numbers of years are calculated and printed in tables called **present value tables**. Figure TK 3-12 shows a portion of a present value table, including values for 10 years at various discount rates.

Many finance and accounting books contain comprehensive present value tables, or you can obtain this information on the Internet, as shown in Figure TK 3-13.

ON THE WEB

For more information about The Time Value of Money, visit **scsite.com/sad6e/ more**, locate Toolkit Part 3 and then click The Time Value of Money link.

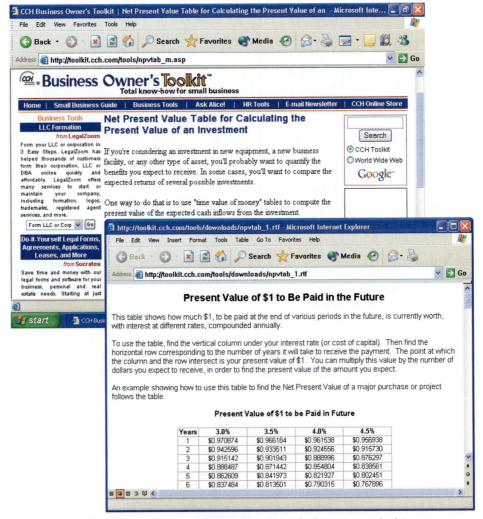

FIGURE TK 3-13 The CCH Web site provides a variety of information to the business community, including present value tables.

To use a present value table, you locate the value in the column with the appropriate discount rate and the row for the appropriate number of years. For example, to calculate the present value of $1 at 12 percent for five years, you look down the 12 percent column in Figure TK 3-12 until you reach the row representing five years. The table value is 0.567. To determine what the present value of $3,000 will be in five years with a discount rate of 12 percent, multiply the present value factor from the table by the dollar amount; that is, PV = $3,000 × 0.567 = $1,701.

To perform present value analysis, you must time-adjust the cost and benefit figures. First, you multiply each of the projected benefits and costs by the proper present value factor, which depends on when the cost will be incurred or the benefit will be received. The second step is to sum all the time-adjusted benefits and time-adjusted costs. Then, you calculate the **net present value** (**NPV**) of the project, which is the total present value of the benefits minus the total present value of the costs. Figure TK 3-14 on the next page shows the calculation of net present value for two sample projects.

In theory, any project with a positive NPV is economically feasible because the project will produce a larger return than would be achieved by investing the same amount of money in a discount rate investment. Remember that risks are associated with any project, however, and management typically insists on a substantially higher return for high-risk projects. For example, both projects in Figure TK 3-14 have positive net present values and appear economically worthwhile. Suppose, however, that you knew one of the projects had a 90 percent probability of achieving its goals, while the other project had only a 70 percent chance. To be attractive, the project with the higher risk would have to offer a corresponding higher reward.

Net present value also can be used to compare and rank projects. All things being equal, the project with the highest net present value is the best investment. Figure TK 3-14 shows that Project B is a better investment than Project A because it has a higher net present value.

Present value analysis provides solutions to the shortcomings of payback analysis and return on investment analysis. Unlike payback analysis, present value analysis considers all the costs and benefits, and not just the earlier values. In addition, present value analysis takes into account the timing of costs and benefits, so their values can be adjusted by the discount rate that provides a common yardstick and recognizes the time value of money. Even so, companies often use all three methods to get more input for making decisions. Sometimes a project will score higher on one method of analysis and lower on another.

Using a Spreadsheet to Calculate Present Value

You can use a worksheet such as the one shown in Figure TK 3-15 on page 573 to calculate the present value based on the data for Project A. You begin by entering the unadjusted cost and benefit values and the discount factors for each year. Next, enter a formula to produce an adjusted value for each cost and benefit entry. To produce an adjusted value, you multiply the cost or benefit value by the discount factor. You start with cell B12 by entering the formula =B10*B11. Because the factor is 1.000, the 3,000 amount remains unchanged.

Now, you copy the formula from cell B12 to cells C12 through H12, and the adjusted values will display. You total the adjusted benefits in cell I12 with the formula =SUM(B12:H12), and then use the same method for the cost figures. Your final step is to calculate the net present value in cell D18 by subtracting the adjusted costs in cell I16 from the adjusted benefits in cell I12.

PROJECT A: **NET PRESENT VALUE**

	Year 0	Year 1	Year 2	Year 3	Year 4	Year 5	Year 6	Total
Benefits:	3,000	28,000	31,000	34,000	36,000	39,000	42,000	
Present Value Factor (12%):	1.000	0.893	0.797	0.712	0.636	0.567	0.507	
Present Value:	3,000	25,004	24,707	24,208	22,896	22,113	21,294	143,222
Costs:	60,000	17,000	18,500	19,200	21,000	22,000	23,300	
Present Value Factor (12%):	1.000	0.893	0.797	0.712	0.636	0.567	0.507	
Present Value:	60,000	15,181	14,745	13,670	13,356	12,474	11,813	141,239
Net Present Value:							net present value of Project A →	1,983

PROJECT B: **NET PRESENT VALUE**

	Year 0	Year 1	Year 2	Year 3	Year 4	Year 5	Year 6	Total
Benefits:	——	6,000	26,000	54,000	70,000	82,000	92,000	
Present Value Factor (12%):	——	0.893	0.797	0.712	0.636	0.567	0.507	
Present Value:	——	5,358	20,722	38,448	44,520	46,494	46,644	202,186
Costs:	80,000	40,000	25,000	22,000	24,000	26,500	30,000	
Present Value Factor (12%):	1.000	0.893	0.797	0.712	0.636	0.567	0.507	
Present Value:	80,000	35,720	19,925	15,664	15,264	15,026	15,210	196,809
Net Present Value:							net present value of Project B →	5,377

FIGURE TK 3-14 Net present value analysis for Project A and Project B.

There is one more way to use a worksheet in present value analysis. Most spreadsheet programs include a built-in present value function that calculates present value and other time-adjusted variable factors. The program inputs the formula and then you input the investment amount, discount rate, and number of time periods. You can use your spreadsheet's Help function to find out more about using these functions.

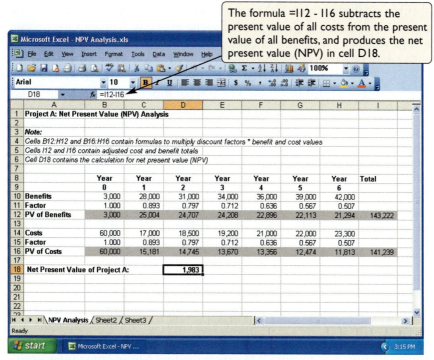

FIGURE TK 3-15 A Microsoft Excel worksheet can be used to calculate net present value (NPV).

TOOLKIT SUMMARY

As a systems analyst, you must be concerned with economic feasibility throughout the SDLC, and especially during the systems planning and systems analysis phases. A project is economically feasible if the anticipated benefits exceed the expected costs. When you review a project, you work with various feasibility and cost analysis tools.

You must classify project costs as tangible or intangible, direct or indirect, fixed or variable, and developmental or operational. Tangible costs are those that have a specific dollar value, whereas intangible costs involve items that are difficult to measure in dollar terms, such as employee dissatisfaction. Direct costs can be associated with a particular information system, while indirect costs refer to overhead expenses that cannot be allocated to a specific project. Fixed costs remain the same regardless of activity levels, while variable costs are affected by the degree of system activity. Developmental costs are one-time systems development expenses, while operational costs continue during the systems operation and use phase.

Every company must decide how to charge or allocate information systems costs and the chargeback method. Common chargeback approaches are no charge, a fixed charge, a variable charge based on resource usage, or a variable charge based on volume.

Some companies use a no charge approach because IT services benefit the overall organization. This method treats the IT group for accounting purposes as a cost center that offers services without charge. In contrast, if management imposes charges on other departments, the IT department is regarded as a profit center that sells services that otherwise would have to be purchased from outside the company.

You also must classify system benefits. Many benefit categories are similar to costs: tangible or intangible, fixed or variable, and direct or indirect. Benefits also can be classified as positive benefits that result in direct dollar savings or cost-avoidance benefits that allow the firm to avoid costs that they would otherwise have incurred.

Cost-benefit analysis involves three common approaches: payback analysis, return on investment (ROI) analysis, and present value analysis. You can use spreadsheet programs to help you work with those tools.

Payback analysis determines the time it takes for a system to pay for itself, which is called the payback period. In payback analysis, you compare total development and operating costs to total benefits. The payback period is the point at which accumulated benefits equal accumulated costs. A disadvantage of this method is that payback analysis analyzes only costs and benefits incurred at the beginning of a system's useful life.

Return on investment (ROI) analysis measures a system by comparing total net benefits (the return) to total costs (the investment). The result is a percentage figure that represents a rate of return that the system offers as a potential investment. Many organizations set a minimum ROI that all projects must match or exceed and use ROI to rank several projects. Although ROI provides additional information compared with payback analysis, ROI expresses only an overall average rate of return that might not be accurate for a given time period. Also, ROI does not recognize the time value of money.

Present value analysis adjusts the value of future costs and benefits to account for the time value of money. By measuring all future costs and benefits in current dollars, you can compare systems more accurately and consistently. Present value analysis uses mathematical factors that you can derive or look up in published tables. You also can use a spreadsheet function to calculate present value. Many companies use present value analysis to evaluate and rank projects.

Key Terms and Phrases

chargeback method *562*

connect time *563*

cost center *562*

cost-avoidance benefits *563*

cost-benefit analysis *563*

developmental costs *562*

direct costs *562*

economic feasibility *560*

economically useful life *564*

fixed charge method *562*

fixed costs *562*

indirect costs *562*

intangible costs *561*

net present value (NPV) *571*

no charge method *562*

operational costs *562*

overhead expenses *562*

payback analysis *564*

payback period *564*

positive benefits *563*

present value *569*

present value analysis *569*

present value tables *570*

profit center *562*

resource allocation *563*

return on investment (ROI) *567*

server processing time *563*

tangible costs *561*

time value of money *569*

total cost of ownership (TCO) *560*

variable charge method based on
    resource usage *563*

variable charge method based on volume *563*

variable costs *562*

Toolkit Exercises

Review Questions

1. What is economic feasibility? How do you know if a project is economically feasible?
2. How can you classify costs? Describe each cost classification, and provide a typical example for each category.
3. What is a chargeback method? What are four common chargeback approaches?
4. How can you classify benefits? Describe each benefit classification, and provide a typical example for each category.
5. What is payback analysis, and what does it measure? What is a payback period, and what is the formula to calculate the payback period?
6. What is return on investment (ROI) analysis, and what does it measure? What is the formula to calculate ROI?
7. What is present value analysis, and what does it measure?
8. What is the meaning of the phrase, time value of money?
9. Why is it difficult to assign a dollar figure to an intangible cost? When and how can it be done? Provide an example with your explanation.
10. What is a system's economically useful life, and how is it measured?

Discussion Topics

1. Suppose your supervisor asks you to inflate the benefit figures for an IT proposal, in order to raise the priority of his or her favorite project. Would this be ethical or not? Does internal cost-benefit analysis affect company shareholders? Why or why not?
2. In Part 3 of the Toolkit, you learn how to use payback analysis, ROI, and NPV to assess IT projects. Can these tools also be used in your personal life? Give an example of how you might use each one to help you make a decision.
3. Is there a role for intuition in the decision-making process, or should all judgments be made strictly on the numbers? Provide specific reasons for your answer.
4. The time value of money is an important factor when analyzing a project's NPV. Is the time value of money more important, less important, or of the same importance in periods of low inflation compared to high inflation periods? Explain your answer.

Projects

1. Suppose you are studying two hardware lease proposals. Option 1 costs $4,000, but requires that the entire amount be paid in advance. Option 2 costs $5,000, but the payments can be made $1,000 now and $1,000 per year for the next four years. If you do an NPV analysis assuming a 14 percent discount rate, which proposal is less expensive? What happens if you use an eight percent rate?
2. Assume the following facts:
   A project will cost $45,000 to develop. When the system becomes operational, after a one-year development period, operational costs will be $9,000 during each year of the system's five-year useful life. The system will produce benefits of $30,000 in the first year of operation, and this figure will increase by a compound 10% each year. What is the payback period for this project?
3. Using the same facts as in Project 2, what is the ROI for this project?
4. Using the same facts as in Project 2, what is the NPV for this project?

4 Project Management Tools

PART

In **Part 4** of the Systems Analyst's Toolkit, you will learn about project management tools that you can use to plan, schedule, monitor, and manage IT projects.

INTRODUCTION

OBJECTIVES

When you finish this part of the Toolkit, you will be able to:

- Describe project management tools and how they are used

- Describe the steps used in project planning, scheduling, monitoring and controlling, and reporting

- Explain techniques for estimating task completion times and costs

- Describe various scheduling tools, including Gantt charts and PERT/CPM charts

- Calculate completion times, start dates, and end dates for a project

- Explain the steps involved in software change control

- Understand the reasons why projects sometimes fail

Part 4 of the Systems Analyst's Toolkit explains project management, cost estimating, and change control for information systems projects. You will learn about project planning, scheduling, monitoring, reporting, and the use of project management software. You will learn how to use Gantt charts and PERT/CPM techniques to schedule and monitor projects. You also will learn how to control and manage project changes that typically occur.

TOOLKIT INTRODUCTION CASE: Mountain View College Bookstore

Background: Wendy Lee, manager of college services at Mountain View College, wants a new information system that will improve efficiency and customer service at the three college bookstores.

In this part of the case, Florence Fullerton (systems analyst) and Harry Boston (student intern) are talking about project management tools and techniques.

Participants:	Florence and Harry
Location:	Mountain View College Cafeteria, during the systems planning phase
Discussion topics:	Project planning and estimating, Gantt charts, PERT/CPM charts, Microsoft Project software, project monitoring, and software change control.

Florence:	Hi, Harry. Glad I ran into you. If you have time, I'd like to talk with you about project management, which we'll be using as we plan and execute the bookstore information system project.
Harry:	*Sure. I've read a little about project management, but I don't know the specifics.*
Florence:	Well, we manage business and personal projects every day, but we don't always give it much thought. When it comes to larger-scale IT projects, you need specific tools and techniques to do the job. You also need a project manager, who is responsible for planning, leading, organizing, and controlling all the tasks.
Harry:	*I guess that's you?*
Florence:	Sure is. No matter which tools you use, the idea is to break the project down into individual tasks, determine the order in which the tasks need to be performed, and figure out how long each task will take. With this information, you can use Gantt charts or PERT/CPM charts to schedule and manage the work.
Harry:	*I've seen Gantt charts — they're the ones that look like horizontal bar charts?*
Florence:	Right. In addition to Gantt charts, we'll use PERT/CPM charts, which look like network diagrams that show all the tasks, patterns, and calculations that we'll need. We'll learn how to create PERT/CPM charts manually, and we'll also experiment with Microsoft Project, which is a powerful project management tool.
Harry:	*Anything else we need to know?*
Florence:	Yes. After we have a specific plan, we need to monitor it carefully, report the progress, and employ a process called software change control. If you are ready, here's a task list to get us started.

FIGURE TK 4-1

PROJECT MANAGEMENT OVERVIEW

ON THE WEB

For more information about Project Management, visit **scsite.com/sad6e/more**, locate Toolkit Part 4 and then click the Project Management link.

Project management is the process of planning, scheduling, monitoring and controlling, and reporting upon the development of an information system. Project management is important throughout the entire SDLC but is especially vital during systems implementation, which usually is the longest and most costly phase.

The goal of project management is to deliver an information system that is acceptable to users and is developed on time and within budget. The acceptability, deadline, and budget criteria all must be met for a project to be considered successful. To meet those requirements, you must manage the project carefully and effectively.

Every successful project must have a leader. The **project manager**, or **project leader**, usually is a senior systems analyst or an IT department manager if the project is large. An analyst or a programmer/analyst might manage smaller projects. In addition to the project manager, most large projects also have a project coordinator. The **project coordinator** handles administrative responsibilities for the development team and negotiates with users who might have conflicting requirements or want changes that would require additional time or expense.

Project managers typically perform four main tasks: project planning, scheduling, monitoring and controlling, and reporting:

- **Project planning** includes identifying project tasks and estimating completion time and costs.

- **Project scheduling** involves the creation of a specific timetable, usually in the form of charts that show tasks, task dependencies, and critical tasks that might delay the project. Scheduling also involves selecting and staffing the project team and assigning specific tasks to team members. Project scheduling uses Gantt charts and PERT/CPM charts, which are explained in the following sections.

- **Project monitoring and controlling** requires guiding, supervising, and coordinating the project team's workload. The project manager must monitor the project's progress, evaluate the results, and take corrective action when necessary to control the project and stay on target.

- **Project reporting** tasks include regular progress reports to management, users, and the project team itself. Effective reporting requires strong communication skills and a sense of what others want and need to know about the project.

PROJECT PLANNING

The project plan provides an overall framework for managing costs and schedules. Project planning takes place at the beginning and end of each SDLC phase to develop a plan and schedule for the phases that follow.

The planning process starts with a list of tasks or activities. A **task**, or **activity**, is any work that has a beginning and an end and requires the use of company resources such as people, time, or money. Examples of tasks include conducting interviews, designing a report, selecting software, waiting for the delivery of equipment, or training users. Tasks are basic units of work that the project manager plans, monitors, and tracks, so tasks should be relatively small and manageable.

In addition to tasks, every project has events, or milestones. An **event**, or **milestone**, is a recognizable reference point that can be used to monitor progress and manage the project. For example, an event might be the start of user training, conversion of system data, or completion of interviews. A milestone such as *Complete 50 percent of program testing* would not be useful information unless you could determine exactly when that event should occur.

Project managers must begin by identifying all tasks and developing time and cost estimates for each task. The next step is to determine the order in which the tasks must be performed and assign tasks to specific members of the project team. As the work is performed, the project manager leads and coordinates the team, monitors events, and reports on progress.

Event or Milestone

Task

FIGURE TK 4-2 Using a questionnaire requires a series of tasks and events to track the progress. The illustration shows the relationship between the tasks and the events, or milestones, that mark the beginning and end of each task.

Identifying Tasks

When identifying tasks, a project manager must consider many factors. One of the most important variables is the size of the project, because the amount of work does not relate directly to the size of the project. If one project is twice the size of another project, the larger project will take more than twice as many resources to develop.

For example, consider Figure TK 4-3 and Figure TK 4-4 on the next page. Each figure shows two projects, labeled as Project A and Project B.

In Figure TK 4-3, Project A has two development team members working on a system with three programs and four users. Project B has four team members assigned to a system with six programs and eight users. At first glance, it might appear that Project B is twice as large as Project A and will require twice as many resources. This, however, is not the case. Project B actually will require considerably more than twice as many resources as Project A.

Figure TK 4-4 shows all the possible interactions among the team members, illustrating how the amount of work does not relate directly to the size of the project. As you can see, only one interaction exists in Project A.

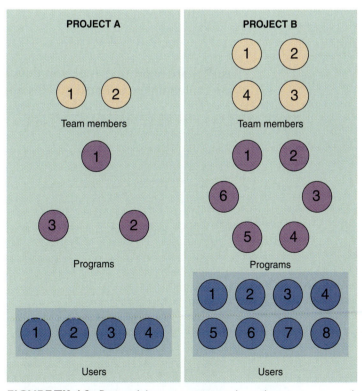

FIGURE TK 4-3 Project A has two team members, three programs, and four users. Project B has twice as many team members, programs, and users. Is Project B twice as large as Project A?

Project B, however, has a four-member team, so as many as six different interactions can take place. Six times as many relationships can mean more delay, misunderstanding, and difficulty in coordinating tasks.

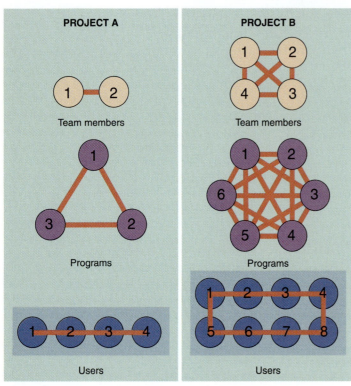

FIGURE TK 4-4 Now the relationships have been drawn. Notice that Project B has six team member interactions, 15 possible program interfaces, and eight users to satisfy. Project B clearly is more than twice as large as Project A.

In addition, look at the interfaces among programs, which were discussed in the systems analysis phase. Project A has three programs, so only three possible interfaces exist. In contrast, Project B has six programs, so it has fifteen possible interfaces, each with its own set of specifications, requirements, and potential problems. Finally, the analysts working on Project B know that it is more complex to satisfy twice as many users and to balance conflicting priorities.

Figure TK 4-5 shows the relationship between project resources and project size. Notice that the dashed line indicates a linear forecast. Most analysts would agree, however, that the solid line forecasts actual requirements more accurately.

The capabilities of project team members also affect time requirements. A less experienced analyst usually will need more time to complete a task than an experienced team member will. Other factors that can affect project time requirements include the attitudes of users, the degree of management support, and the priority of the project compared with other projects within the organization.

Estimating Task Completion Time and Cost

Task completion times and related cost estimates usually are expressed in **person-days** that represent the amount of work that one person can complete in one day. This approach, however, can present some problems. For example, if it will take one person 20 days to perform a particular task, it might not be true that two people could complete the same task in 10 days or that 10 people could perform the task in two days.

Some tasks can be divided evenly so it is possible to use different combinations of time and people, up to a point. For instance, if it takes two person-days to install the cables for a new local area network, one person might do the task in two days, two people in one day, or four people in half a day. In most systems analysis tasks, however, time and people are not interchangeable. If one analyst needs two hours to interview a user, two analysts also will need two hours to do the same interview.

Many project managers use a weighted formula for calculating the estimated duration of each task. The project manager first makes three time estimates for each task: an optimistic, or **best-case estimate** (B), a **probable-case estimate** (P), and a pessimistic, or **worst-case estimate** (W). The manager then assigns a **weight**, which is an importance value, to each estimate. The weight can vary, but a

FIGURE TK 4-5 As the size of a project grows, the resources needed to develop it will grow even faster. Notice the difference between the linear forecast (dashed line) and the actual forecast (solid line).

common approach is to use a ratio of B = 1, P = 4, and W = 1. The expected task duration is calculated as follows:

$$\frac{(B+4P+W)}{6}$$

For example, a project manager might estimate that a file-conversion task could be completed in as few as 20 days or could take as many as 34 days, but most likely will require 24 days. Using the formula, the expected task duration is 25 days, calculated as follows:

$$\frac{(20+(4*24)+34)}{6} = 25$$

Factors Affecting Time and Cost Estimates

When developing time and cost estimates, project managers must consider four main factors:

→ Project size and scope

→ IT resources

→ Prior experience with similar projects or systems

→ Applicable constraints.

PROJECT SIZE AND SCOPE You learned in Chapter 1 that information systems have various characteristics that affect their complexity and cost. In addition to considering those factors, a project manager must estimate the time required to complete each project phase. To develop accurate estimates, a project manager must identify all project tasks, from initial fact-finding to system implementation. Regardless of which systems development methodology he or she uses, the project manager must determine how much time will be needed to perform each task. In developing an estimate, the project manager must allow time for meetings, project reviews, training, and any other factors that could affect the productivity of the development team.

IT RESOURCES Companies must invest heavily in cutting-edge technology and Web-based systems to remain competitive in a connected world. In many areas, skilled IT professionals are in great demand, and firms must work hard to attract and retain the talent they need. A project manager must assemble and guide a development team that has the skill and experience to handle the project. If necessary, additional systems analysts or programmers must be hired or trained, and this must be accomplished within a specific time frame. After a project gets under way, the project manager must deal with turnover, job vacancies, and escalating salaries in the technology sector — all of which can affect whether or not the project can be completed on time and within budget.

PRIOR EXPERIENCE WITH SIMILAR PROJECTS OR SYSTEMS A project manager can develop time and cost estimates based on the resources used for similar, previously developed information systems. The experience method works best for small- or medium-sized projects where the two systems are similar in size, basic content, and operating environment. In large systems with more variables, the estimates are less reliable.

In addition, you might not be able to use experience from projects that were developed in a different environment. For example, when you use a new Web-based database application, you might not have previous experience to measure in this environment. In this situation, you can design a prototype or pilot system to gain technical and cost estimating experience. A pilot system is a small system that is developed as a basis for understanding a new environment. The concept is similar to pilot operation, which is one of the four system changeover methods that you learned about in Chapter 9, but it takes place much earlier in the systems development life cycle.

CONSTRAINTS You learned in Chapter 2 that constraints must be defined as part of the preliminary investigation of a project. A constraint is a condition, restriction, or requirement that the system must satisfy. For example, a constraint might involve maximums for one or more resources, such as time, dollars, or people. Given those limitations, the project manager must define the system requirements that can be achieved realistically within the required constraints. In the absence of constraints, the project manager calculates the resources needed. In contrast, if constraints are present, the project manager either must adjust other resources or must change the scope of the project. This approach is similar to the what-if analysis that is described in Chapter 10.

OVERVIEW OF PROJECT SCHEDULING

Project scheduling involves the creation of a specific timetable, usually in the form of charts that show tasks, task dependencies, and critical tasks that might delay the project. Scheduling also involves selecting and staffing the project team and assigning specific tasks to team members.

When scheduling a project, the project manager must know the duration of each task, the order in which the activities will be performed, the start and end times for each task, and who will be assigned to each specific task.

Once the time for each task is estimated, the project manager determines if certain tasks are dependent on other activities. A **dependent task** cannot be started until one or more other tasks are completed. You cannot tabulate questionnaires, for example, until they have been developed, tested, approved, distributed, and returned. After the project manager identifies all the task dependencies, he or she arranges the tasks in a logical sequence.

The next step is to set starting and ending times for each task. A task cannot start until all preceding activities on which it depends are completed. The ending time for a task is its start time plus whatever time it takes to complete the task.

When scheduling a project, project managers must decide how they will assign people to the work. Assignments should not overload or underutilize team members, and alternate periods of inactivity followed by intense effort can cause problems and should be avoided. Although scheduling can be a difficult task, a project manager must balance task time estimates, sequences, and personnel assignments to achieve a workable schedule.

Several graphical planning aids can help a project manager in the scheduling process. We will examine two of those tools: Gantt charts and PERT/CPM charts.

ON THE WEB

For more information about Gantt Charts, visit **scsite.com/sad6e/more**, locate Toolkit Part 4 and then click the Gantt Charts link.

PROJECT SCHEDULING WITH GANTT CHARTS

Gantt charts were developed many years ago by Henry L. Gantt as a production control technique and still are in common use. A **Gantt chart** is a horizontal bar chart that represents a series of tasks. In the Gantt chart shown in Figure TK 4-6, the analyst displays time on the horizontal axis and arranges the activities

FIGURE TK 4-6 A Gantt chart for the implementation phase of a project. The chart shows 11 activities on the vertical axis and the elapsed time on the horizontal axis.

vertically, from top to bottom, in the order of their start dates. The horizontal position of the bar shows the start and end of a task, and the length of the bar indicates its duration. On the horizontal axis, time can be shown as elapsed time from a zero starting point, or as actual calendar dates.

Medium-sized projects can have dozens of tasks, and larger projects might have hundreds, or even thousands, of tasks and activities. A detailed Gantt chart for a very large project might be quite complex and hard to understand. To simplify the Gantt chart, a project manager can combine related activities into one task. For example, in Figure TK 4-6 the activities labeled Programming, Write User Manual, and Program Testing actually are **task groups**, where each task represents several activities.

A Gantt chart can be used to track and report progress in several ways, as shown in Figure TK 4-7. For example, bars can be fully or partially darkened to show completed tasks, as shown in the top chart. Arrowheads can be used to indicate the completed portion of a task, as shown in the second chart. Finally, progress can be shown by including a second bar under the schedule bar, as shown in the bottom chart. In all cases, a vertical line indicates the current, or reporting, date. Notice that all three charts show how much of the task has been completed and determine whether or not the work is on schedule. In Figure TK 4-7, for example, task 2 is about 80 percent complete, although 100 percent of the time allotted for the task has passed. Similarly, Task 4 appears to be about 25 percent finished, although the task has used about only five percent of the time allotted for the task.

Gantt charts are used to report progress because they present an overview of the project's status; however, they are not an ideal tool for controlling a complex project because they do not provide enough detailed information.

PROJECT SCHEDULING WITH PERT/CPM CHARTS

The **Program Evaluation Review Technique (PERT)** was developed by the U.S. Navy to manage very complex projects, such as the construction of nuclear submarines. At approximately the same time, the **Critical Path Method (CPM)** was developed by private industry to meet similar project management needs. The important distinctions between the two methods have disappeared over time, and today the technique is called either PERT, CPM, or PERT/CPM.

Overview of PERT/CPM

PERT/CPM is called a **bottom-up technique**, because it analyzes a large, complex project as a series of individual tasks, called **project tasks**.

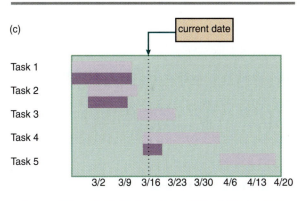

FIGURE TK 4-7 Three different ways to show the status of a project on a Gantt chart. All three charts show a current date of March 16. In the chart at the top, the completed portion of each bar is shaded. In the middle chart, a triangle or arrowhead indicator is used. In the chart at the bottom, a second bar shows the completed work. All three methods show that Task 1 is completed, Task 2 is about 80 percent finished but behind schedule, Task 3 has not yet started, Task 4 is ahead of schedule, and Task 5 has not yet begun.

![ON THE WEB]

For more information
about PERT/CPM, visit
scsite.com/sad6e/
more, locate Toolkit
Part 4 and then click
the PERT/CPM link.

To prepare a PERT/CPM chart, you first identify all the project tasks and estimate how much time each task will take to perform. Next, you must determine the logical order in which the tasks must be performed. For example, some tasks cannot start until other tasks have been completed. In other situations, several tasks can be performed at the same time.

Once you know the tasks, their duration, and the order in which they must be performed, you can calculate the time that it will take to complete the project. You also will be able to identify the specific tasks that will be critical to the project's on-time completion. These techniques are explained in the following sections.

PERT/CPM Chart Format

In a PERT/CPM chart, project tasks are shown as rectangular boxes, arranged in the sequence in which they must be performed. Each rectangular box, called a **task box**, has five sections, as shown in Figure TK 4-8. Each section of the task box contains important information about the task, including its duration, earliest start, earliest finish, latest finish, and latest start. Before you start to work with PERT/CPM charts, you must learn about these terms and concepts, which are described in the following sections:

→ T (**task duration** or **time**) is the predicted duration of a task. All tasks must use the same time units, which can be hours, days, weeks, or months — depending on the project. Every project starts at zero (0) time, because no preceding events exist.

→ ES (**earliest start**) is the earliest time that a task can begin. For example, the first task can begin at zero (0) time. The next task, however, cannot begin until the first task is completed, so the ES for the following task is the EF (earliest finish) of the preceding task.

→ EF (**earliest finish**) is the earliest time that a task can be completed. To calculate EF, you add the task duration (T) to the ES for that task. For example, if a task has an ES of 15, and the duration (T) for the task is 3 days, then the EF will be 18. When you use PERT/CPM, you first calculate the ES and EF for all tasks, working from left to right across the diagram until the final (rightmost) task is reached. It is important to understand that the EF for the final task in a project represents the **expected project duration** for the project — in other words, the earliest finish for the final task.

→ LF (**latest finish**) is the latest time that a task can be completed without delaying the overall project. After you work from left to right and enter the ES and EF for each task, you start to work your way backward, from right to left. The LF for the final task is the same as the EF for that task, because it also represents the project's final completion date. As you work your way to the left, the LS (latest start) for a following task becomes the LF for the preceding task. For example, if the latest that a task can start (LS) is the 16th week, then the latest finish (LF) for the preceding task also is the 16th week.

→ LS (**latest start**) is the latest time that a task can begin without delaying the overall project. Before you can calculate LS, you must know the task's LF (latest finish). Then, you subtract T (task duration) from LF in order to know when the task must start (LS).

TEXT BOX FORMAT

Task ID and Name   Task ID and Name

| T | ES | EF | | T | ES | EF |
| | LS | LF | | | LS | LF |

Task Box Terms and Symbols

T   Task Duration (the time the task will take in hours, weeks, months, etc.)

ES   Earliest Start (the earliest time that this task can begin)

EF   Earliest Finish (the earliest time that this task can finish)

LS   Latest Start (the latest time that this task can begin without delaying the overall project)

LF   Latest Finish (the latest time that this task can finish without delaying the overall project)

➡   Indicates logical flow of dependent tasks

FIGURE TK 4-8 Two tasks are shown. The format for a task box consists of five sections. Each section contains important information about the task, including its duration, earliest start, earliest finish, latest finish, and latest start. The arrow indicates the logical flow of dependent tasks.

Task Patterns

In any project, large or small, tasks depend on each other and must be performed in a sequence, not unlike the commands in a software program. **Task patterns** can involve sequential tasks, multiple successor tasks, and multiple predecessor tasks. In larger projects, these patterns can become quite complex, and an analyst must study the logical flow carefully.

SEQUENTIAL TASKS When tasks must be completed one after another, they are called **sequential tasks**. Figure TK 4-9 shows two sequential tasks with the values for T, ES, and EF entered. Notice that task B depends on task A because task B cannot start until task A is completed.

MULTIPLE SUCCESSOR TASKS When several tasks can take place at the same time, each is called a **concurrent task**. Often, two or more concurrent tasks depend on a single prior task, which is called a **predecessor task**. In this situation, each of the concurrent tasks is called a **successor task**. Both successor tasks can start as soon as the predecessor task is completed.

In the example shown in Figure TK 4-10, successor tasks C and D both can begin as soon as task B is finished. Notice that the EF for task B becomes the ES for both tasks C and D. In other words, the earliest that task B can finish is 40, so 40 is the earliest that tasks C and D can start.

MULTIPLE PREDECESSOR TASKS
Suppose that a task requires two or more prior tasks to be completed before it can start. Figure TK 4-11 shows an example of this situation, where task E cannot begin until tasks C and D are finished. Because they are unlikely to end at the same time, the longest (latest) predecessor task becomes the controlling factor. Notice that the ES for task E is 65, not 45. Why is this so? Because task E depends on two predecessor tasks, C and D, task E cannot begin until the later of those tasks is complete. Therefore, the ES for a successor task must be the latest (largest) EF for any of its preceding tasks. In the example shown, task D's EF (65) is the controlling factor, so it becomes the ES for task E.

Complex Task Patterns

When various task patterns combine, you must study the facts carefully in order to understand the logical sequence of tasks. For

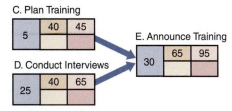

FIGURE TK 4-9 An example of sequential tasks. Task B cannot start until task A is finished. In the example, the EF (earliest finish) for each task is determined by adding T (task duration) to the ES (earliest start) for the task. Notice that the ES for task B is the same as the EF for task A.

FIGURE TK 4-10 An example of multiple successor tasks. Tasks C and D can start as soon as task B is completed. Notice that the ES for tasks C and D are the same as the EF for task B.

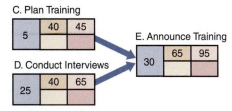

FIGURE TK 4-11 An example of multiple predecessor tasks. Task E cannot start until tasks C and D are finished. Notice that the ES for tasks D is 65, which is the largest (latest) EF of the predecessor tasks.

example, consider the following sample fact statements and the task patterns they represent, which are shown in Figure TK 4-12:

- Sample of sequential tasks: Perform task A. When task A is complete, perform task B.

- Sample of sequential tasks and multiple successor tasks: Perform task A. When task A is complete, perform task B. When task B is finished, start two tasks: task C and task D. When task C is complete, start two more tasks: task E and task F.

- Sample of sequential tasks, multiple successor tasks, and multiple predecessor tasks: Perform task A. When task A is complete, perform task B. When task B is finished, start two tasks: task C and task D. When task C is complete, start two more tasks: task E and task F. When tasks E and F are done, start task G. Then, when tasks G and D are finished, perform task H.

A systems analyst must understand that project calculations will not be accurate unless the underlying task pattern is logically correct.

A PERT/CPM Example with Five Tasks

Figure TK 4-13 shows a PERT/CPM chart with five tasks. Notice that tasks A and B are sequential tasks, task B has multiple successor tasks, and task E has multiple predecessor tasks. In this figure, T, ES, and EF have been entered, and the project duration is 95 days.

Perform task A. When task A is complete, perform task B.

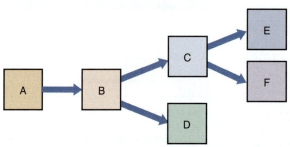

Perform task A. When task A is complete, perform task B. When task B is finished, start two tasks: task C and task D. When task C is complete, start two more tasks: task E and task F.

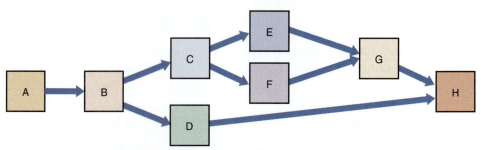

Perform task A. When task A is complete, perform task B. When task B is finished, start two tasks: task C and task D. When task C is complete, start two more tasks: task E and task F. When tasks E and F are done, start task G. Then, when tasks G and D are finished, perform task H.

FIGURE TK 4-12 Examples of three fact statements and the task patterns they represent.

EXAMPLE OF ES-EF CALCULATION FOR MULTIPLE PREDECESSOR AND SUCCESSOR TASKS

FIGURE TK 4-13 Example of a PERT/CPM chart with five tasks. Tasks A and B are sequential tasks, task B has multiple successor tasks, and task E has multiple predecessor tasks. Notice that T, ES, and EF have been entered and the project duration is 95 days.

Now you must calculate LS and LF. Your first step is to enter an LF of 95 days for the final task, which is the same as the EF. That is because the last event is the overall project completion date, and there is no room for slippage.

Remember that LS and LF work just the opposite from ES and EF — now you start from the right and work your way back toward the first task. As you go along, you *subtract* T instead of adding it, as you did earlier. Figure TK 4-14 shows the final version with LS and LF entered. Notice that the LF of task B is 40. Why is this so? The LF for a task with two successor tasks must be the *smallest* LS of the successor tasks. This is exactly the opposite of the ES – EF calculations, where the ES of a successor task is the largest preceding ES. In other words, the latest a preceding task can end is determined by the earliest task that is waiting for it to be completed. In the example, the LS for task D is 40, so task D *must* start by the fortieth day, while task C does not have to start until the sixtieth day. Therefore, task B must be finished by the fortieth day or else it will delay task D's start.

FIGURE TK 4-14 The final version of the chart shown in Figure TK 4-13. Now the LS (latest start) and LF (latest finish) for all tasks have been entered. Notice that the LF for a task with two successor tasks must be the *smallest* LS of the successor tasks. In the example, the LS for task D is 40, so task D *must* start by the fortieth day, while task C does not have to start until the sixtieth day. Therefore, task B must be finished by the fortieth day or else it will delay task D's start. Also notice that the critical path (A-B-D-E) is highlighted.

Critical Path

In Figure TK 4-14, notice that the ES and LS are identical in tasks A, B, D, and E. Also notice that the EF and LF are the same in these tasks. Tasks A, B, D, and E represent the critical path, which has been highlighted in the figure. A **critical path** is a series of tasks with no slack time. **Slack time** is the difference between a task's EF and LF. For example, if EF is 65 and LF is 75, 10 days of slack time exist. In other words, that particular task could be as much as 10 days late before it would have an impact on the overall project completion date. In Figure TK 4-14, 20 days of slack time exist for task C, so task C could start up to 20 days late and still not affect the overall project completion date.

If any task along the critical path falls behind schedule, the entire project is delayed. As the name implies, a critical path includes all tasks that are vital to the project schedule. Project managers always must know what the critical path is, so they can monitor progress and make prompt decisions to keep the project on track.

Transforming a Task List into a PERT/CPM Chart

Figure TK 4-15 shows a list of 11 tasks. Notice that each task has a description, a duration, and a reference to predecessor tasks, if any, which must be completed before the task can begin. To construct a PERT/CPM chart from this task list, you must develop three versions:

VERSION 1: BASIC STRUCTURE In the first version, shown in Figure TK 4-16, you identify all tasks, determine task dependencies, draw and label each task, use arrows to show the logical flow and task dependencies, and enter the task duration for each task. Notice that there are sequential tasks, tasks with multiple successor tasks, and tasks with multiple predecessor tasks.

TASK	DESCRIPTION	DURATION (DAYS)	PREDECESSOR TASKS
A	Develop Plan	1	-
B	Assign Tasks	4	A
C	Obtain Hardware	17	A
D	Programming	70	B
E	Install Hardware	10	C
F	Program Test	30	D
G	Write User Manual	25	E
H	Convert Files	20	E
I	System Test	25	F
J	User Training	20	G, H
K	User Test	25	I, J

FIGURE TK 4-15 Example of a table listing 11 tasks, together with their descriptions, durations, and predecessor tasks.

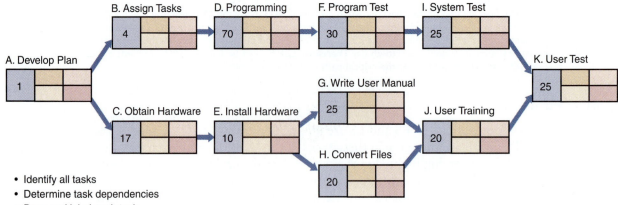

- Identify all tasks
- Determine task dependencies
- Draw and label each task
- Use arrows to show the logical flow and task dependencies
- Enter the task duration (T) for each task

FIGURE TK 4-16 In the first version of the chart, you identify all tasks, show task dependencies, draw and label each task, use arrows to show the logical flow and task dependencies, and enter the task duration for each task.

VERSION 2: ENTER ES AND EF VALUES In the second version, as shown in Figure TK 4-17, you enter the ES for task A as zero (0), then you enter 1 as the ES for succeeding tasks B and C. Continuing from left to right, you add the task duration (T) for each task to its ES to determine its EF. As you proceed, there are two important rules you must keep in mind:

→ If a successor task has more than one predecessor task, use the highest EF of the predecessor tasks as the ES for the successor task.

→ If a predecessor task has more than one successor task, use the predecessor task's EF as the ES for all successor tasks.

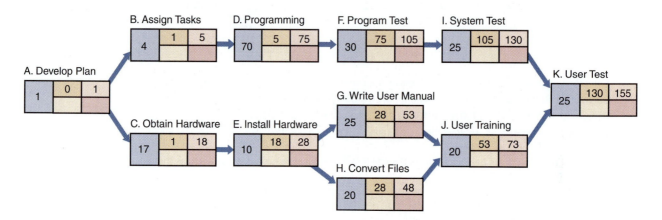

- Enter the ES for task A as zero (0)
- Add the task duration (1) for task A to the ES (0) and enter the EF in the top right box (1)
- Because the EF for task A is 1, enter 1 as the ES for succeeding tasks B and C
- Continuing from left to right, add the task duration (T) for each task to its ES to determine and enter its EF
  Note: If a predecessor task has more than one successor task, use the predecessor task's EF as the ES for all successor tasks
  If a successor task has more than one predecessor task, use the **highest** EF of the predecessor tasks as the ES for the successor task
- The EF of the rightmost task is the earliest that the project can be completed

FIGURE TK 4-17 In the second version of the chart, you enter the ES for task A as zero (0), then you enter 1 as the ES for succeeding tasks B and C. Continuing from left to right, you add the task duration (T) for each task to its ES to determine its EF. As you proceed, remember to apply the rules noted in the figure.

VERSION 3: ADD LF AND LS VALUES In the third version, as shown in Figure TK 4-18 on the next page, you enter an LF of 155 for the final task (task K). The LF for the final task always is the same as the EF, because it represents the project completion date. Then you subtract the task duration (25) for task K from the LF (155) and enter the LS (130) in the lower left-hand box. You continue from right to left, subtracting the task duration for each task from its LF to determine the LS, until you reach the leftmost task. Now enter the LF for the final task (task K) — it will be the same as the EF — the project completion date. Here again, bear in mind two rules:

→ If a predecessor task has more than one successor task, you use the lowest LS of the successor tasks as the LF for the predecessor task.

→ If a successor task has more than one predecessor task, you use the successor task's LS as the LF for all predecessor tasks.

After you enter the LS and LF figures, you will be able to identify the critical path. As you learned earlier, the critical path is the sequence of tasks with no slack time — ES and LS are identical, and EF and LF are identical. Therefore, the critical path in the example is A-B-D-F-I-K.

- Enter the LF for the final task (task K) — it will be the same as the EF — the project completion date
- Subtract the task duration (25) for task K from the LF (155) and enter the LS (130) in the lower left-hand box
- Because the LS for task K is 130, enter 130 as the LF for preceding tasks I and J
- Continuing from right to left, subtract the task duration (T) for each task from its LF to determine and enter its LS, until you reach the leftmost task

  Note: If a successor task has more than one predecessor task, use the successor task's LS as the LF for all predecessor tasks

  If a predecessor task has more than one successor task, use the **lowest** LS of the successor tasks as the LF for the predecessor task

- The critical path is the sequence of tasks with no slack time — ES and LS are identical, and EF and LF are identical (tasks A-B-D-F-I-K in the example)

FIGURE TK 4-18 In the final version of the chart, you enter an LF of 155 for task K. Because this is the final task, the EF and LF represent the project completion date. Then you continue from right to left, subtracting the task duration for each task from its LF to determine the LS, until you reach the leftmost task. As you proceed, remember to apply the rules noted in the figure. Notice that the critical path, which is the sequence of tasks with no slack time, is A-B-D-F-I-K.

Comparing Gantt Charts and PERT/CPM

One significant advantage of PERT/CPM charts is that, unlike Gantt charts, all individual tasks and dependencies are shown. Most project managers find PERT/CPM charts very helpful for scheduling, monitoring, and controlling projects. A project manager would convert the ES, EF, LS, and LF information to actual dates by laying out the entire project on a calendar. Then, on any given day, the manager can compare what should be happening to what is taking place, and react accordingly.

PERT/CPM charts differ from Gantt charts in several ways. First, a PERT/CPM chart displays the critical path for the overall project and the slack time, if any, for each task. This information can be very valuable to a manager who is trying to address the highest priority issues. Although a PERT/CPM chart provides more detailed information about a project, a Gantt chart offers a rapid overview that graphically displays the timing, duration, and progress of each task. PERT/CPM and Gantt charts are not mutually exclusive techniques. Project managers often use both methods.

PROJECT MONITORING AND CONTROLLING

A project must be planned and scheduled before the work actually starts. After the project tasks begin, the project manager concentrates on monitoring and controlling the project.

Monitoring and Control Techniques

Regardless of whether the project was planned and scheduled with project management software or in some other manner, the project manager must keep track of the tasks and progress of team members, compare actual progress to the project plan, verify the completion of project milestones, and set standards and ensure that they are followed. To help ensure that quality standards are met, many project managers institute structured walkthroughs. A **structured walkthrough** is a review of a project team member's work by other members of the team. Generally, systems analysts review the work of other systems analysts, and programmers review the work of other programmers, as a form of peer review. Structured walkthroughs take place throughout the SDLC and are called **design reviews**, **code reviews**, or **testing reviews**, depending on the phase in which they occur.

Maintaining a Schedule

Maintaining a project schedule can be a challenging task, and most projects run into at least some problems or delays. By monitoring and controlling the work, the project manager tries to anticipate problems, avoid them or minimize their impact, identify potential solutions, and select the best way to solve the problem.

The better the original plan, the easier it will be to control the project. If clear, verifiable milestones exist, it will be simple to determine if and when those targets are achieved. If enough milestones and frequent checkpoints exist, problems will be detected rapidly.

A project that is planned and scheduled with PERT/CPM can be tracked and controlled using these same techniques. As work continues, the project manager revises the plan to record actual times for completed tasks and revises times for tasks that are not yet finished. Project managers often spend most of their time tracking the tasks along the critical path, because delays in those tasks have the greatest potential to delay or jeopardize the project. Other tasks cannot be ignored, however. For example, suppose that a task off the critical path takes too long and depletes the allotted slack time. At that point, the task actually becomes part of the critical path, and any further delay will push back the overall project.

It is mathematically possible for a project to have more than one critical path. In these situations, you must identify any path that has a continuous chain of tasks with no slack time.

PROJECT REPORTING

Members of the project team regularly report their progress to the project manager, who in turn reports to management and users. As shown in Figure TK 4-19, the project manager collects, verifies, organizes, and evaluates the information he or she receives from the team. Then the manager decides which information needs to be passed along,

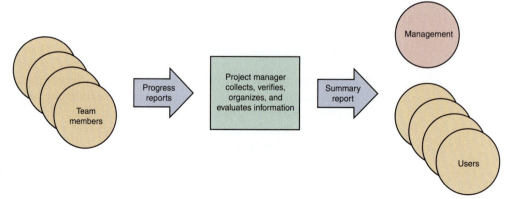

FIGURE TK 4-19 Members of the project team regularly report their progress to the project manager, who in turn reports to management and users.

prepares a summary that can be understood easily, adds comments and explanations if needed, and submits it to management and users.

Project Status Meetings

Although team members constantly use e-mail to communicate, most project managers schedule regular status meetings with the entire project team. At those meetings, each team member updates the group and identifies any problems or delays. Although meetings can be time-consuming, most project managers believe it is worth the effort. The sessions give team members an opportunity to share information, discuss common problems, explain new techniques, and offer comments that can be extremely valuable to team members working on other areas of the project. The meetings also give the project manager an opportunity to update the entire group, seek input, and conduct brainstorming sessions.

Project Status Reports

A project manager must report regularly to his or her immediate supervisor, upper management, and users. Although a progress report might be given verbally to an immediate supervisor, reports to management and users usually are written. Gantt charts often are included in progress reports to show project status graphically.

Deciding how to handle potential problems can be difficult. At what point should you inform management about the possibility of cost overruns, schedule delays, or technical problems? At one extreme is the overly cautious project manager who alerts management to every potential snag and every slight delay. The danger here is that the manager loses credibility over a period of time, and management might ignore potentially serious situations. At the other extreme is the project manager who tries to handle all situations single-handedly and does not alert management until a problem is serious. By the time management learns of the problem, little time might remain in which to react or devise a solution.

A project manager's best course of action lies somewhere between the two extremes, but is probably closer to the first. If you are unsure of the consequences, you should be cautious and warn management about the possibility of a problem. When you report the situation, you also should explain what you are doing to handle and monitor the problem. If you believe the situation is beyond your control, you might want to suggest possible actions that management can take to resolve the situation. Most managers recognize that problems do occur on most projects; it is better to alert management sooner rather than later.

ON THE WEB

For more information about Project Management Software, visit **scsite.com/ sad6e/more**, locate Toolkit Part 4 and then click the Project Management Software link.

PROJECT MANAGEMENT SOFTWARE

Project management software can assist you in project planning, estimating, scheduling, monitoring, and reporting. Powerful project management packages offer many features, including PERT/CPM, Gantt charts, resource scheduling, project calendars, cost tracking, and cost-benefit analysis. The analyst can select output in the form of printed reports, screen displays, or graphical plots.

Project Management Example Using Microsoft Project

The first step in project management is to identify the tasks, task duration, and task dependencies. Typically, an analyst must review the results of planning and fact-finding in order to extract this information. For example, suppose you receive the following summary from the IT manager:

> "Please study the following plan: First, we will review the systems request. That will take three days. Then, two tasks can begin at once: we can review the documentation, which will take three days, and review the Internet access delays, which will take two days.
>
> When the documentation and the Internet access delays have been analyzed, we can contact managers about the interviews, which will take two days. After we contact the managers, we can plan the interview schedule, which will take two days. Next, we can prepare the preliminary investigation report, which will take two days. When the report is ready, we can deliver our presentation to the committee, which will take two days.
>
> After the presentation, three tasks can begin at once: we plan the interview questions, which will take one day; contact the interviewees, which will take one day; and send out the questionnaire, which will be returned in five days. When the interview questions are ready and the interviewees have been contacted, we can conduct the interviews, which will take three days. Finally, when the interviews have been conducted and the questionnaire results are back, we can tabulate all results, which will take one day."

Your manager now wants you to create a Gantt chart and a PERT chart that show all tasks, dependencies, dates, and total project duration.

Your first step is to create a Gantt chart showing the necessary information. You decide to use Microsoft Project 2003, a powerful project management program, to construct the chart shown in Figure TK 4-20. As you enter each of the 12 tasks, you also enter the task duration and the predecessor tasks that must be completed before the task can begin.

When you are finished entering the tasks, the program displays the Gantt chart, which consists of 12 horizontal bars, connected with arrows that indicate the task dependencies. Notice that Saturdays and Sundays are shown as shaded columns because no work will be performed on those days. The program makes these adjustments automatically. For example, Task 1, which has a duration of three days, starts on a Thursday and ends on a Monday.

After you complete the Gantt chart, you decide to view the data in the form of a PERT chart. In Microsoft Project 2003, a PERT chart is referred to as a **network diagram**. When you select this option on the View menu, the upper screen in Figure TK 4-21 on the next page displays. An expanded view of the diagram is shown in the lower screen of Figure TK 4-21. You study the diagram and see that the program has calculated the calendar dates for each task, including a beginning and ending date. Notice that the diagram displays the

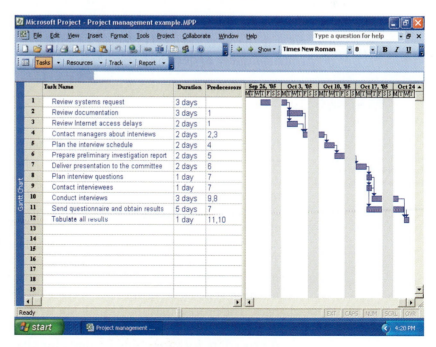

FIGURE TK 4-20 The Microsoft Project screen shows an example of a systems development project in the form of a Gantt chart.

FIGURE TK 4-21 Two views of the PERT chart, or network diagram, that was generated by Microsoft Project 2003. The chart displays the same information as the Gantt chart shown in Figure TK 4-20, including task dependencies, and it also includes a red line that indicates the project's critical path.

same information as the Gantt chart, including task dependencies, and also includes a red line that indicates the project's critical path. According to the diagram, if the project remains on schedule, the last task will be completed on Wednesday, October 26, 2005.

Notice that several differences exist between the computer-generated diagram and the PERT chart that appears in Figure TK 4-20 on the previous page. The task boxes in Microsoft Project are similar to PERT/CPM task boxes, but the information is displayed in a somewhat different manner. In Microsoft Project, each task box contains the task description, task identification number, task duration, start date, and end date. The critical path is indicated by a bold line. Also, using Microsoft Project, you can assign each task to one or more people, assign budget targets, produce progress reports, and readjust schedule and deadlines as necessary.

You learned that project schedules, task estimates, and personnel assignments all are interrelated. Therefore, project planning is a dynamic task and involves constant change. One significant advantage of integrated interactive project management software is that it allows the project manager to adjust schedules, estimates, and resource assignments rapidly to develop a workable plan.

SOFTWARE CHANGE CONTROL

Software change control is the process of managing and controlling changes requested after the system requirements document has been submitted and accepted. Software change control can be a real problem because the development process involves many compromises, and users are never entirely satisfied with the results. Changes to an information system's requirements are inevitable. The issue, therefore, is how to create an effective process for controlling changes that protects the overall project, but allows those changes that are necessary and desirable.

The project coordinator, rather than the project manager, has primary responsibility for change control because requests for change most often are initiated by someone outside the information systems department. A specific process must be in place for handling requested changes. The process must be formal, but flexible enough to incorporate desired changes promptly with minimal impact to the overall project.

A procedure for processing requests for changes to an information system's requirements consists of four steps: complete a change request form, take initial action on the

ON THE WEB

For more information about Software Change Control, visit **scsite.com/sad6e/more**, locate Toolkit Part 4 and then click the Software Change Control link.

request, analyze the impact of the requested change, and determine the disposition of the requested change.

1. Complete a change request form. The person requesting the change completes a System Requirements Change Request form similar to the one shown in Figure TK 4-22. On the form, which can be stored in an online network library, the requester describes and justifies the desired changes. The requester attaches helpful documents and pertinent information, such as new calculations, copies of government regulations, and memos from executives specifying new strategies and directions.

2. Take initial action on the request. The project coordinator enters a sequential control number and the date on the change request form, reviews the specific change, and then determines if the change should be deferred to a later date, rejected for specific reasons, or investigated further. If the request is deferred or rejected, the project coordinator sends a copy of the request back to the requester. If the change is to be investigated further, then the request is reviewed for impact by the project manager or a systems analyst.

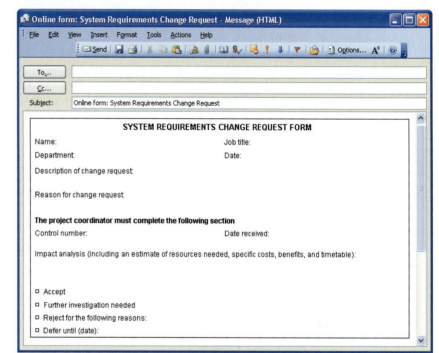

FIGURE TK 4-22 Sample of a System Requirements Change Request form that can be stored in an online library. Notice the Impact analysis section. If a system has a great number of changes, what does that indicate?

3. Analyze the impact of the requested change. The project manager or a systems analyst must review the request and determine the impact of incorporating the change into the information system's requirements. Then, the manager or analyst prepares an impact analysis that describes the effect of the change on the information system's requirements and on costs and schedules. The analysis should address the impact of incorporating the change immediately versus incorporating the change after the currently configured information system has been implemented.

4. Determine the disposition of the requested change. Based on the impact analysis and the project coordinator's recommendation, the change might be accepted, deferred, or rejected. In each of the three cases, the project coordinator informs the requester of the action taken.

KEYS TO PROJECT SUCCESS

To be successful, an information system must satisfy business requirements, stay within its budget, be completed on time, and — most important of all — be managed effectively. When a project develops problems, the reasons typically involve business, budget, or schedule issues, as explained in the following sections. In addition to planning and managing the project, a project manager must be able to recognize problems and deal with them effectively.

Business Issues

The major objective of every system is to provide a solution to a business problem or opportunity. If the system does not do this, then it is a failure — regardless of positive reaction from users, acceptable budget performance, or timely delivery. When the information system does not meet business requirements, causes might include unidentified or unclear requirements, inadequately defined scope, imprecise targets, shortcuts or sloppy work during systems analysis, poor design choices, insufficient testing or inadequate testing procedures, and lack of change control procedures. Systems also fail because of changes in the organization's culture, funding, or objectives. A system that falls short of business needs also produces problems for users and reduces morale and productivity.

Budget Issues

Cost overruns typically result from one or more of the following:

- Unrealistic estimates that either were too optimistic or were based on incomplete definitions of the work to be done.
- Failure to develop an accurate TCO forecast that considered all cost elements.
- Poor monitoring of progress and inadequate reaction to early signs of problems.
- Schedule delays due to unanticipated factors.
- Human resource factors, including turnover, inadequate training, and motivation issues.

Schedule Issues

Problems with timetables and project milestones can indicate a failure to recognize task dependencies, confusing effort with progress, poor monitoring and control methods, personality conflicts among team members, or turnover of project personnel.

The failure of an IT project also can be caused by poor project management techniques. If the project manager fails to plan, staff, organize, supervise, communicate, motivate, evaluate, direct, and control properly, then the project is certain to fail. Even when factors outside his or her control contribute to the failure, the project manager is responsible for recognizing the early warning signs and handling them effectively.

Successful Project Management

Project management is a challenging task. Project managers must be alert, technically competent, and highly resourceful. They also must be good communicators with strong human resources skills. A project manager rightly can be proud when he or she handles a successful project that helps the company achieve its business objectives. Unfortunately, projects can and do get derailed for a wide variety of reasons. When problems occur, the project manager's ability to handle the situation becomes the critical factor.

When a project manager first recognizes that a project is in trouble, behind schedule, or out of control, what options are available? Alternatives can include trimming the project requirements, adding to the project resources, delaying the project deadline, and improving management controls and procedures.

Sometimes, when a project experiences delays or cost overruns, the system still can be delivered on time and within budget if several less critical requirements are trimmed. The system can be delivered to satisfy the most necessary requirements, and additional features can be added later as a part of a maintenance or enhancement project.

If a project is in trouble because of a lack of resources or organizational support, management might be willing to give the project more commitment and higher priority. For example, management might agree to add more people to a project that is behind schedule. Adding staff, however, will reduce the project's completion time only if the additional people can be integrated effectively into the development team.

If team members lack experience with certain aspects of the required technology, temporary help might be obtained from IT consultants or part-time staff. Adding staff can mean training and orienting the new people, however. In some situations, adding more people to a project actually might increase the time necessary to complete the project. More staff also means increased costs and the potential for exceeding budget limits.

When a project is behind schedule, a typical response is to push back the completion date. This is an option only if the original target date is flexible and the extension will not create excessive costs or other problems.

Toolkit Summary

Project management is the process of planning, scheduling, monitoring and controlling, and reporting upon the development of an information system. Project management is important throughout the SDLC, but is especially vital during the implementation phase of a project. The primary objective of project management is to deliver a system that meets all requirements on time and within budget. Although the project manager can use a variety of software tools that make the job easier, he or she must have a clear understanding of project management concepts and techniques.

Project management begins with identifying and planning all specific tasks or activities. Projects also have events or milestones that provide reference points to monitor progress. After identifying the tasks, project managers develop a work schedule that assigns specific tasks to project team members.

Time and cost estimates for tasks usually are made in person-days. A person-day represents the work that one person can accomplish in one day. Estimating the time for project activities is more difficult with larger systems. Project managers must consider the project size and scope, IT resources, prior experience with similar projects or systems, and applicable constraints.

In project scheduling, the project manager develops a specific time for each task, based on available resources and whether or not the task is dependent on other activities being accomplished earlier. The project manager can use graphical tools such as Gantt charts and PERT/CPM charts to assist in the scheduling process.

A Gantt chart is a horizontal bar chart that represents the project schedule with time on the horizontal axis and tasks arranged vertically. It shows individual tasks and task groups, which include several tasks. In a Gantt chart, the length of the bar indicates the duration of the tasks. A Gantt chart can display progress, but does not show task dependency details or resource assignment unless the chart was created with a project management program that supports dependency linking and the entry of other information.

A PERT/CPM chart shows the project as a network diagram with tasks connected by arrows. Using a prescribed calculation method, the project manager uses a PERT/CPM chart to determine the overall duration of the project and provide specific information for each task, including the earliest start (ES), earliest finish (EF), latest start (LS), and latest finish (LF). With this information, the manager can determine the critical path, which is the sequence of tasks that have no slack time and must be performed on schedule in order to meet the overall project deadline.

A project manager uses a variety of techniques to monitor, control, and report project tasks. The methods include structured walkthroughs, which are reviews of a team member's work by other team members. A project manager also keeps team members and others up-to-date with regular reports and periodic meetings.

Software change control is concerned with change requests that arise after the system requirements document has been approved, and most companies establish a specific procedure for managing such requests. A typical change control procedure consists of four steps: completion of a change request form, initial action, impact analysis, and final disposition.

In the end, every successful information system must support business requirements, stay within budget, and be available on time. Sound project management involves the same skills as any type of management. The project manager must be perceptive, analytical, well-organized, and a good communicator. If the project manager senses that the project is off-track, he or she must take immediate steps to diagnose and solve the problem.

Key Terms and Phrases

activity *580*

best-case estimate *582*

bottom-up technique *585*

code reviews *593*

concurrent task *587*

critical path *589*

Critical Path Method (CPM) *585*

dependent task *584*

design reviews *593*

earliest finish (EF) *586*

earliest start (ES) *586*

event *580*

expected project duration *586*

Gantt chart *584*

latest finish (LF) *586*

latest start (LS) *586*

milestone *580*

network diagram *595*

person-days *582*

PERT/CPM *585*

predecessor task *587*

probable-case estimate *582*

Program Evaluation Review Technique (PERT) *585*

project coordinator *580*

project leader *580*

project management *580*

project management software *594*

project manager *580*

project monitoring and controlling *580*

project planning *580*

project reporting *580*

project scheduling *580*

project tasks *585*

sequential tasks *587*

slack time *589*

software change control *596*

structured walkthrough *593*

successor task *587*

task *580*

task box *586*

task duration (T) *586*

task groups *585*

task patterns *587*

testing reviews *593*

time *586*

weight *582*

worst-case estimate *582*

Toolkit Exercises

Review Questions

1. What is project management, and what are its main objectives?
2. What is the relationship between tasks and events, or milestones?
3. If Project A has twice as many resources as Project B, will Project A be twice as complex as Project B? Why or why not?
4. What is the difference between sequential and concurrent tasks?
5. Compare the characteristics, advantages, and disadvantages of a Gantt chart to those of a PERT/CPM chart.
6. Define the following terms: best-case estimate, probable-case estimate, and worst-case estimate, and describe how a project manager can use these concepts to estimate task duration.
7. How does a project manager calculate EF, ES, LS, and LF?
8. What is a critical path, and why it important to project managers?
9. What are some project reporting and communication techniques?
10. What is software change control, and what are the four steps typically involved?

Discussion Topics

1. In Poor Richard's Almanac, Benjamin Franklin penned the familiar lines: "For the want of a nail the shoe was lost, for the want of a shoe the horse was lost, for the want of a horse the rider was lost, for the want of a rider the battle was lost, for the want of a battle the kingdom was lost — and all for the want of a horseshoe nail." Looking at the outcome in hindsight, could project management concepts have avoided the loss of the kingdom? Explain your answer and share your views with other students.
2. Microsoft Project 2003 is an example of software that is very powerful, but quite expensive. As a project manager, how would you justify the purchase of this software?
3. Suppose you have a limited budget for software and are unable to purchase project management software. Think about how you might use a spreadsheet program or a database program to manage the project. Share your ideas with the class.
4. Many managers claim to have "seat of the pants" intuition when it comes to project management. In your view, does this kind of intuition actually exist? Can you think of examples to support your views?

Projects

1. Microsoft Project is a popular project management program, but other alternatives exist. Perform research on the Internet and identify another project management software option. Submit a brief report with the results of your research, including price, major features, and your recommendation.
2. Think of all the tasks that you perform when you purchase a car. Include any research, decisions, or financial issues that relate to the purchase. Draw a Gantt chart that shows all the tasks and the estimated duration of each.

3. At Lightfoot Industries, where you work as a systems analyst, you have been asked to lead a JAD session similar to the one described in Chapter 3. You must develop a specific schedule for the tasks listed below (the estimated task duration for each is shown in parentheses):

   - First, you need to contact the participants and explain their roles (1 day). Then you must obtain approval from their department managers (5 days).

   - After you obtain the approval, two tasks can begin at the same time: you can arrange the meeting room (4 days) and prepare an agenda for the initial session (11 days).

   - When the agenda is ready, you can start two more concurrent tasks: prepare the information packets (4 days) and create visual aids (8 days).

   - When the meeting room is arranged and the information packets are ready, you can send out an e-mail to participants (1 day).

   - Finally, after the e-mail is sent to participants and the visual aids are ready, you can conduct the JAD sessions (5 days).

   Using PERT/CPM techniques, develop a chart that shows ES, EF, LS, and LF for the project. Be sure to highlight the project's critical path. Use a format similar to Figure TK 4-18 on page 592. If project management software is available, use it to develop the chart.

4. At Riverside Financial, where you work as a project manager, you have been asked to conduct user training sessions during the implementation phase for a new information system. You must develop a specific schedule for the tasks (the estimated task duration for each is shown in parentheses):

   - First, you need to send an e-mail message to all department managers announcing the training sessions (1 day).

   - After the e-mail message goes out, two tasks can begin at the same time: you can develop the training material (4 days) and confirm arrangements for the training facility you plan to use (11 days).

   - As soon as the training material is complete, you can work on two tasks at once: arrange to have copies of handout material printed (3 days) and develop a set of PowerPoint slides (4 days).

   - When the PowerPoint slides are ready, you conduct a practice training session with the instructor who will assist you (1 day).

   - Finally, when the practice session is over, the handout material is ready, and the training facility is confirmed, you conduct the user training sessions (3 days).

   Using PERT/CPM techniques, develop a chart that shows ES, EF, LS, and LF for the project. Be sure to highlight the project's critical path. Use a format similar to Figure TK 4-18. If project management software is available, use it to develop the chart.

PART 5 Object-Oriented Tools

In **Part 5** of the Systems Analyst's Toolkit, you will learn about object-oriented analysis tools and techniques. In addition to structured analysis, object-oriented analysis is another way to represent and model an information system.

INTRODUCTION

OBJECTIVES

When you finish this part of the Toolkit, you will be able to:

- Explain how object-oriented analysis can be used to describe an information system
- Define object modeling terms and concepts, including objects, attributes, methods, messages, classes, and instances
- Explain relationships among objects and the concept of inheritance
- Draw an object relationship diagram
- Describe Unified Modeling Language (UML) tools and techniques, including use cases, use case diagrams, class diagrams, sequence diagrams, state transition diagrams, and activity diagrams
- Explain the advantages of using CASE tools in developing the object model
- Explain how to organize an object model

Part 5 of the Systems Analyst's Toolkit describes object-oriented analysis. In this section, you will learn how to use object-oriented methods to document, analyze, and model an information system. As you learned in Chapter 1, several systems development methodologies exist. Although traditional structured analysis is the most popular approach, the use of object-oriented analysis and design is growing rapidly.

TOOLKIT INTRODUCTION CASE: Mountain View College Bookstore

Background: Wendy Lee, manager of college services at Mountain View College, wants a new information system that will improve efficiency and customer service at the three college bookstores.

In this part of the case, Florence Fullerton (systems analyst) and Harry Boston (student intern) are talking about object-oriented concepts, tools, and techniques.

Participants: Florence and Harry
Location: Mountain View College Cafeteria, during the systems analysis phase
Discussion topics: Object-oriented concepts, tools, and techniques.

Florence:	Hi, Harry. I want to chat with you about object-oriented analysis before we finish the systems analysis phase. Would this be a good time to talk?
Harry:	*Sure. I know that object-oriented analysis is a different way of looking at things, but I don't know much about how it works.*
Florence:	Well, object-oriented analysis describes an information system by identifying things called objects. An object represents a real person, place, event, or transaction. For example, in the bookstore, when a student purchases a textbook, the student is an object, the textbook is an object, and the purchase transaction itself is an object.
Harry:	*That sounds a little like the entities we identify in structured analysis.*
Florence:	Yes, but there's a big difference — in structured analysis we treat data and the processes that affect the data separately. Objects, on the other hand, contain the data *and* the processes, called methods, that can add, modify, or change the data. To make it even more interesting, one object can send a message to another object to request some action or response. For example, a driver object adjusts the cruise control, which sends one or more messages to the car object telling it to maintain a steady speed.
Harry:	*I get it. So objects can be people, things, or events?*
Florence:	Yes. To show how the system works, we use a special modeling language called the UML. We even show human actors as stick figures that interact with business functions called use cases.
Harry:	*I'd like to give it a try.*
Florence:	No problem. Although we'll still use structured analysis, it will be interesting to model the system in object-oriented terms. Let's get started on our task list:

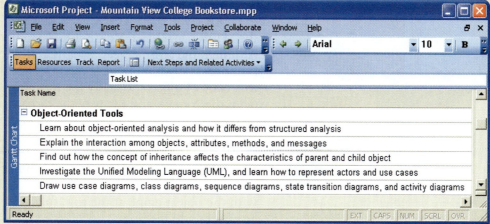

FIGURE TK 5-1

OBJECT-ORIENTED TERMS AND CONCEPTS

ON THE WEB

For more information about Object-Oriented Analysis, visit **scsite.com/ sad6e/more**, locate Toolkit Part 5 and then click the Object-Oriented Analysis link.

Object-oriented (O-O) analysis describes an information system by identifying things called objects. An **object** represents a real person, place, event, or transaction. For example, when a patient makes an appointment to see a doctor, the patient is an object, the doctor is an object, and the appointment itself is an object.

Object-oriented analysis is a popular approach that sees a system from the viewpoint of the objects themselves as they function and interact. The end product of object-oriented analysis is an **object model**, which represents the information system in terms of objects and object-oriented concepts. Later, during the implementation phase of the SDLC, system developers can translate O-O designs directly into O-O program code modules using languages such as C++ and Java.

Overview of O-O Analysis

In Chapter 3, you learned that the **Unified Modeling Language (UML)** is a widely used method of visualizing and documenting an information system. In this chapter, you use the UML to develop object models. Your first step is to understand basic object-oriented terms, including objects, attributes, methods, messages, classes, and instances. In this chapter, you will learn how systems analysts use those terms to describe an information system.

An object represents a person, place, event, or transaction that is significant to the information system. In Chapter 4, you created DFDs that treated data and processes separately. An object, however, includes data *and* the processes that affect that data. For example, a customer object has a name, an address, an account number, and a current balance. Customer objects also can perform specific tasks, such as placing an order, paying a bill, and changing their address.

ON THE WEB

For more information about The Unified Modeling Language, visit **scsite.com/ sad6e/more**, locate Toolkit Part 5 and then click The Unified Modeling Language link.

An object has certain **attributes**, which are characteristics that describe the object. For example, if you own a vehicle, it has attributes such as make, model, and color. An object also has **methods**, which are tasks or functions that the object performs when it receives a **message**, or command, to do so. For example, your vehicle performs a method called *turn on wipers* when you send a message by moving the proper control. Figure TK 5-2 shows examples of attributes, methods, and messages for a vehicle object.

A **class** is a group of similar objects. For example, PT Cruisers belong to a class called CAR. An **instance** is a specific member of a class. *Your* red PT Cruiser, therefore, is an instance of the CAR class. At an auto dealership, you might observe many instances of the CAR class, the TRUCK class, the MINIVAN class, and the SPORT UTILITY VEHICLE class, among others. Although the term, object, usually refers to a particular instance, systems analysts sometimes use the term to refer to a class of objects. Usually the meaning is understood from the context and the way the term is used.

Objects

Consider how the UML describes a family with parents and children. The UML represents an object as a rectangle with the object name at the top, followed by the object's attributes and methods.

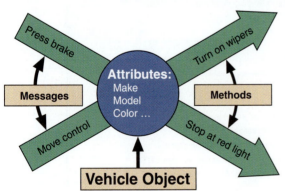

FIGURE TK 5-2 A vehicle object has attributes, can perform methods, and receive messages.

Figure TK 5-3 shows a CHILD object with certain attributes such as name, age, sex, and hair color. If the family has three children, there are three instances of the CHILD object. A CHILD object performs certain methods, such as picking up toys, eating dinner, playing, cooperating, and getting ready for bed. To signal the CHILD object to perform those tasks, you send certain messages that the CHILD object could understand. For example, the DINNER'S READY message tells a CHILD object to come to the table and eat a meal, while the SHARE WITH YOUR BROTHER/SISTER message tells a CHILD object to cooperate with other CHILD objects.

Continuing with the family example, the PARENT object in Figure TK 5-4 possesses the same attributes as the CHILD object and an additional attribute defining the parent as a biological, step-, or adoptive parent. The PARENT object also can perform methods, such as reading a bedtime story, driving the car pool van, or preparing a school lunch. The message GOOD NIGHT tells the PARENT object to read a bedtime story, while the message DRIVE signals that it is the PARENT object's turn to drive the car pool van.

FIGURE TK 5-3 The CHILD object includes four attributes and five methods. James Smith, Amelia Ali, and Misty Greene are instances of the CHILD object.

FIGURE TK 5-4 The PARENT object includes five attributes and three methods. Mary Smith, Ahmed Ali, and Anthony Greene are instances of the PARENT object.

The family also might have a DOG object, as shown in Figure TK 5-5. That object can have attributes such as name, breed, age, color, sex, and favorite food. The DOG object can perform methods such as wagging its tail, eating, fetching, and sleeping. The message GOOD DOG, when directed to the DOG object, signals it to wag its tail. Similarly, the DINNER'S READY message signals the DOG object to run to its food bowl.

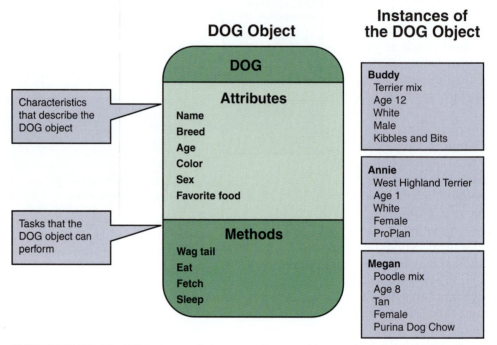

FIGURE TK 5-5 The DOG object includes six attributes and four methods. Buddy, Annie, and Megan are instances of the DOG object.

STUDENT Object

STUDENT

Attributes
Student number
Name
Address
Telephone
Date of birth
Fitness record
Status

Methods
Add fitness-class
Drop fitness-class
Change address
Change telephone
Change status
Update fitness record

INSTRUCTOR Object

INSTRUCTOR

Attributes
Instructor number
Name
Address
Telephone
Fitness-classes taught
Availability
Private lesson fee
Status

Methods
Teach fitness-class
Change availability
Change address
Change telephone
Change private lesson fee
Change status

Now consider an example of a fitness center, and the objects that interact with the fitness center's enrollment system. A typical fitness center might have students, instructors, fitness-class schedules, and a registration process.

STUDENT and INSTRUCTOR objects are shown in Figure TK 5-6. Each STUDENT object has the following attributes: student number, name, address, telephone, date of birth, fitness record, and status. In addition, a STUDENT can add a fitness-class; drop a fitness-class; change an address, telephone, or status; and update his or her fitness record.

The INSTRUCTOR object in Figure TK 5-6 has the following attributes: instructor number, name, address, telephone, fitness-classes taught, availability, private lesson fee, and status. An INSTRUCTOR object

FIGURE TK 5-6 The STUDENT object includes seven attributes and six methods. The INSTRUCTOR object includes eight attributes and six methods.

can teach a fitness-class, and change his or her availability, address, telephone, private lesson fee, or status.

The FITNESS-CLASS SCHEDULE object shown in Figure TK 5-7 includes data about fitness-classes, including fitness-class number, date, time, type, location, instructor number, and maximum enrollment. The FITNESS-CLASS SCHEDULE object includes the methods that can add or delete a fitness-class, or change a fitness-class date, time, instructor, location, or enrollment.

The REGISTRATION RECORD object shown in Figure TK 5-8 includes the student number, fitness-class number, registration date, fee, and status. The REGISTRATION RECORD object includes methods to add a REGISTRATION instance when a student enrolls, or drop a REGISTRATION instance if the fitness-class is canceled or for nonpayment. Notice that if a student registers for three fitness-classes, the result is three instances of the REGISTRATION RECORD object. The REGISTRATION RECORD object also includes a method of notifying students and instructors of information.

Attributes

If objects are similar to nouns, attributes are similar to adjectives that describe the characteristics of an object. How many attributes are needed? The answer depends on the business requirements of the information system and its users. Even a relatively simple object, such as an inventory item, might have a part number, description, supplier, quantity on hand, minimum stock level, maximum stock level, reorder time, and so on. Some objects might have a few attributes; others might have dozens.

Systems analysts define an object's attributes during the systems design process. In an object-oriented system, objects can inherit, or acquire, certain attributes from other objects. When you learn about relationships between objects and classes, you will understand how that occurs.

Objects can have a specific attribute called a **state**. The state of an object is an adjective that describes the object's current status. For example, depending on the state, a student can be a future student, a current student, or a past student. Similarly, a bank account can be active, inactive, closed, or frozen.

Methods

A method defines specific tasks that an object can perform. Just as objects are similar to nouns and attributes are similar to adjectives, methods resemble verbs that describe *what* and *how* an object does something.

FITNESS-CLASS SCHEDULE Object

FIGURE TK 5-7 The FITNESS-CLASS SCHEDULE object includes seven attributes and seven methods.

REGISTRATION RECORD Object

REGISTRATION RECORD

Attributes

Student number
Fitness-class number
Registration date
Fee
Status

Methods

Add student
Drop student
Notify instructor of add
Notify instructor of drop
Notify all of fitness-class cancellations

FIGURE TK 5-8 The REGISTRATION object includes five attributes and five methods.

Method: MORE FRIES	Steps:
	1. **Heat oil**
	2. **Fill fry basket with frozen potato strips**
	3. **Lower basket into hot oil**
	4. **Check for readiness**
	5. **When ready raise basket and let drain**
	6. **Pour fries into warming tray**
	7. **Add salt**

FIGURE TK 5-9 The MORE FRIES method requires the server to perform seven specific steps.

Method: ADD STUDENT	Steps:
	1. **Add a new student instance**
	2. **Record student number**
	3. **Record student name**
	4. **Record student address**
	5. **Record student telephone number**
	6. **Record student date of birth**
	7. **Record sex of student**
	8. **Record state of student**
	9. **Save new student data**

FIGURE TK 5-10 In the fitness center example, the ADD STUDENT method requires the STUDENT object to perform nine specific steps.

Consider a server who prepares fries in a fast-food restaurant. A systems analyst might describe the operation as a method called MORE FRIES, as shown in Figure TK 5-9. The MORE FRIES method includes the steps required to heat the oil, fill the fry basket with frozen potato strips, lower it into the hot oil, check for readiness, remove the basket when ready and drain the oil, pour the fries into a warming tray, and add salt.

Figure TK 5-10 shows another example of a method. At the fitness center, an ADD STUDENT method adds a new instance of the STUDENT class. Notice that nine steps are required to add the new instance and record the necessary data.

Messages

A message is a command that tells an object to perform a certain method. For example, the message ADD STUDENT directs the STUDENT class to add a STUDENT instance. The STUDENT class understands that it should add the student number, name, and other data about that student, as shown in Figure TK 5-11. Similarly, a message named DELETE STUDENT tells the STUDENT class to delete a STUDENT instance.

The same message to two different objects can produce different results. The concept that a message gives different meanings to different objects is called **polymorphism**. For example, in Figure TK 5-12, the message GOOD NIGHT signals the PARENT object to read a bedtime story, but the same message to the DOG object tells the dog to sleep. The GOOD NIGHT message to the CHILD object signals it to get ready for bed.

Message: ADD STUDENT Tells the STUDENT class to perform all the steps needed to add a STUDENT instance.

Message: DELETE STUDENT Tells the STUDENT class to perform all the steps needed to delete a STUDENT instance.

STUDENT

Attributes

Student number
Name
Address
Telephone
Date of birth
Fitness record
Status

Methods

Add student
Delete student
Add fitness-class
Drop fitness-class
Change address
Change telephone
Change status
Update fitness record

FIGURE TK 5-11 The message ADD STUDENT signals the STUDENT class to perform the ADD STUDENT method. The message DELETE STUDENT signals the STUDENT class to perform the DELETE STUDENT method.

Message: GOOD NIGHT

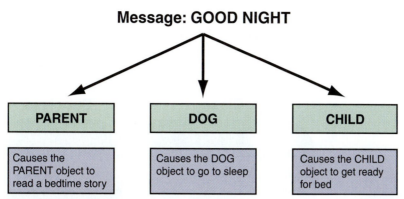

FIGURE TK 5-12 In an example of polymorphism, the message GOOD NIGHT produces different results, depending on which object receives it.

You can view an object as a **black box**, because a message to the object triggers changes within the object without specifying how the changes must be carried out. A gas pump is an example of a black box. When you select the economy grade at a pump, you do not need to think about how the pump determines the correct price and selects the right fuel, as long as it does so properly.

The black box concept is an example of **encapsulation**, which means that all data and methods are self-contained. A black box does not want or need outside interference. By limiting access to internal processes, an object prevents its internal code from being altered by another object or process. Encapsulation allows objects to be used as modular components anywhere in the system, because objects send and receive messages but do not alter the internal methods of other objects.

Object-oriented designs typically are implemented with object-oriented programming languages. A major advantage of O-O designs is that systems analysts can save time and avoid errors by using modular objects, and programmers can translate the designs into code, working with reusable program modules that have been tested and verified. For example, in Figure TK 5-13, an INSTRUCTOR object sends an ENTER GRADE message to an instance of the STUDENT RECORD class. Notice that the INSTRUCTOR object and STUDENT RECORD class could be reused, with minor modifications, in other school information systems where many of the attributes and methods would be similar.

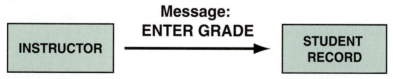

FIGURE TK 5-13 In a school information system, an INSTRUCTOR object sends an ENTER GRADE message to an instance of the STUDENT RECORD class.

Classes

An object belongs to a group or category called a class. All objects within a class share common attributes and methods. Objects within a class can be grouped into **subclasses**, which are more specific categories within a class. For example, TRUCK objects represent a subclass within the VEHICLE class, along with other subclasses called CAR,

MINIVAN, and SCHOOL BUS, as shown in Figure TK 5-14. Notice that all four subclasses share common traits of the VEHICLE class, such as make, model, year, weight, and color. Each subclass also can possess traits that are uncommon, such as a load limit for the TRUCK or an emergency exit location for the SCHOOL BUS.

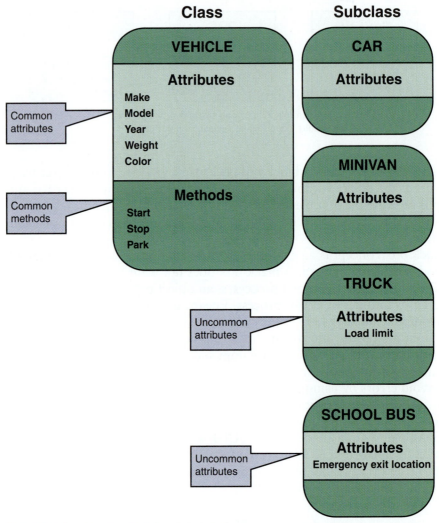

FIGURE TK 5-14 The VEHICLE class includes common attributes and methods. CAR, TRUCK, MINIVAN, and SCHOOL BUS are instances of the VEHICLE class.

In the fitness center example shown in Figure TK 5-15, INSTRUCTOR objects represent a subclass within the EMPLOYEE class. The EMPLOYEE class also can contain MANAGER and OFFICE STAFF subclasses, because a manager and staff members are employees. All INSTRUCTOR, MANAGER, and OFFICE STAFF objects contain similar information (such as employee name, title, and pay rate) and perform similar tasks (such as getting hired and changing an address or telephone number).

A class can belong to a more general category called a **superclass**. For example, a NOVEL class belongs to a superclass called BOOK, because all novels are books. The

NOVEL class can have subclasses called HARDCOVER and PAPERBACK. Similarly, as shown in Figure TK 5-16, the EMPLOYEE class belongs to the PERSON superclass, because every employee is a person, and the INSTRUCTOR class is a subclass of EMPLOYEE.

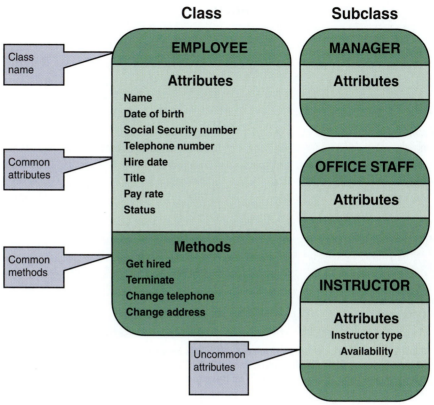

FIGURE TK 5-15 The fitness center EMPLOYEE class includes common attributes and methods. INSTRUCTOR, MANAGER, and OFFICE STAFF are subclasses within the EMPLOYEE class.

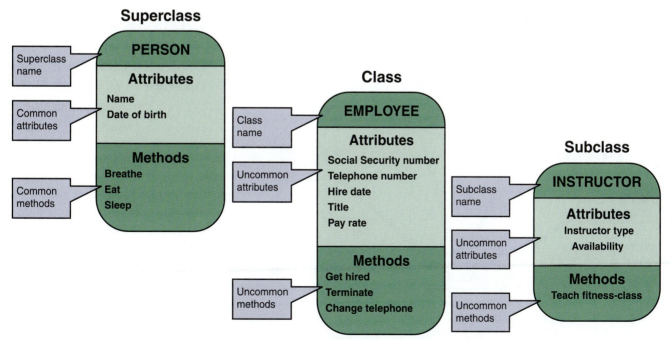

FIGURE TK 5-16 At the fitness center, the PERSON superclass includes common attributes and methods. EMPLOYEE is a class within the PERSON superclass. INSTRUCTOR is a subclass within the EMPLOYEE class.

Inheritance

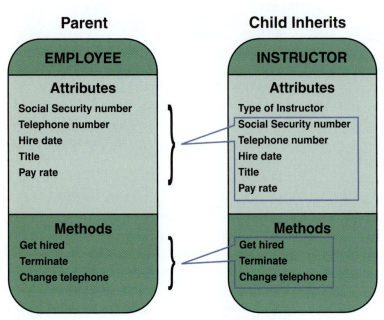

FIGURE TK 5-17 An inheritance relationship exists between the INSTRUCTOR and EMPLOYEE objects. The INSTRUCTOR (child) object inherits characteristics from the EMPLOYEE (parent) class and can have additional attributes of its own.

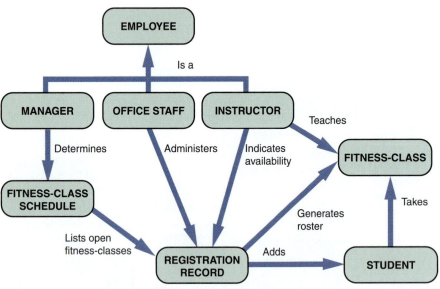

FIGURE TK 5-18 Object relationship diagram for the fitness center.

RELATIONSHIPS AMONG OBJECTS AND CLASSES

Relationships enable objects to communicate and interact as they perform business functions and transactions required by the system. Relationships describe what objects need to know about each other, how objects respond to changes in other objects, and the effects of membership in classes, superclasses, and subclasses. Some relationships are stronger than others (just as a relationship between family members is stronger than one between casual acquaintances). The strongest relationship is called inheritance. **Inheritance** enables an object, called a **child**, to derive one or more of its attributes from another object, called a **parent**. In the example in Figure TK 5-17, the INSTRUCTOR object (child) inherits many traits from the EMPLOYEE object (parent), including SOCIAL SECURITY NUMBER, TELEPHONE NUMBER, and HIRE DATE. The INSTRUCTOR object also can possess additional attributes, such as TYPE OF INSTRUCTOR. Because all employees share certain attributes, those attributes are assumed through inheritance and do not need to be repeated in the INSTRUCTOR object.

Object Relationship Diagram

After you identify the objects, classes, and relationships, you are ready to prepare an object relationship diagram that will provide an overview of the system. You will use that model as a guide as you continue to develop additional diagrams and documentation. Figure TK 5-18 shows an object relationship diagram for a fitness center. Notice that the model shows the objects and how they interact to perform business functions and transactions.

OBJECT MODELING WITH THE UNIFIED MODELING LANGUAGE

Just as structured analysis uses DFDs to model data and processes, systems analysts use the Unified Modeling Language (UML) to describe object-oriented systems.

In Chapter 3, you learned that the UML is a popular technique for documenting and modeling a system. The UML uses a set of symbols to represent graphically the various components and relationships within a system. Although the UML can be used for business process modeling and requirements modeling, it mainly is used to support object-oriented system analysis and to develop object models.

ON THE WEB

For more information about Use Case Modeling, visit **scsite.com/sad6e/ more**, locate Toolkit Part 5 and then click the Use Case Modeling link.

Use Case Modeling

A **use case** represents the steps in a specific business function or process. An external entity, called an **actor**, initiates a use case by requesting the system to perform a function or process. For example, in a medical office system, a PATIENT (actor) can MAKE AN APPOINTMENT (use case), as shown in Figure TK 5-19.

PATIENT (Actor)

MAKE APPOINTMENT (Use Case)

FIGURE TK 5-19 In a medical office system, a PATIENT (actor) can MAKE APPOINTMENT (use case).

Notice that the UML symbol for a use case is an oval with a label that describes the action or event. The actor is shown as a stick figure, with a label that identifies the actor's role. The line from the actor to the use case is called an association, because it links a particular actor to a use case. Figure TK 5-20 shows use case examples of a passenger making an airline reservation, a customer placing an order, and a bus dispatcher changing a student's pickup address.

Use cases also can interact with other use cases. When the outcome of one use case is incorporated by another use case, we say that the second case **uses** the first case. The UML indicates the relationship with a hollow-headed arrow that *points at* the use case being used. Figure TK 5-21 on the next page shows an example where a student adds a fitness-class and PRODUCE FITNESS-CLASS ROSTER *uses* the results of ADD FITNESS-CLASS to generate a new fitness-class roster. Similarly, if an instructor changes his or her availability, UPDATE INSTRUCTOR INFORMATION *uses* the CHANGE AVAILABILITY use case to update the instructor's information.

Passenger

Make Airline Reservation

Customer

Place Order

Bus Dispatcher

Change Pickup Address

FIGURE TK 5-20 Three use case examples. The UML symbol for a use case is an oval. The actor is shown as a stick figure.

FIGURE TK 5-21   When a student adds a class, PRODUCE FITNESS-CLASS ROSTER uses the results of ADD CLASS to generate a new class roster. When an instructor changes his or her availability, UPDATE INSTRUCTOR INFORMATION uses the CHANGE AVAILABILITY use case to update the instructor's information.

To create use cases, you start by reviewing the information that you gathered during the requirements modeling phase. Your objective is to identify the actors and the functions or transactions they initiate. For each use case, you also develop a **use case description** in the form of a table. A use case description documents the name of the use case, the actor, a description of the use case, a step-by-step list of the tasks and actions required for successful completion, a description of alternative courses of action, preconditions, postconditions, and assumptions. Figure TK 5-22 shows an example of the ADD NEW STUDENT use case.

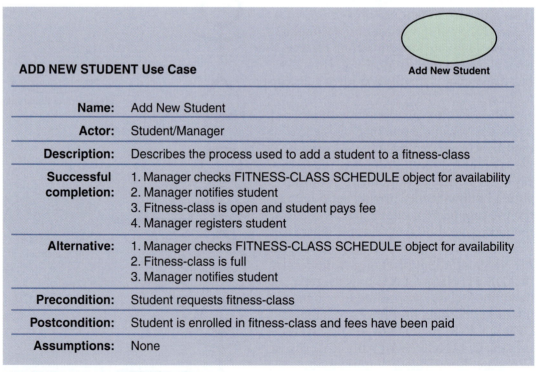

FIGURE TK 5-22   The ADD NEW STUDENT use case description documents the process used to add a current student into an existing class.

When you identify use cases, try to group all the related transactions into a single use case. For example, when a hotel customer reserves a room, the reservation system blocks a room, updates the occupancy forecast, and sends the customer a confirmation. Those events are all part of a single use case called RESERVE ROOM, and the specific actions are step-by-step tasks within the use case.

Use Case Diagrams

A **use case diagram** is a visual summary of several related use cases within a system or subsystem. Consider an auto service department which involves customers, service writers who prepare work orders and invoices, and mechanics who perform the work. Figure TK 5-23 shows a possible use case diagram for the auto service department.

When you create a use case diagram, the first step is to identify the system boundary, which is represented by a rectangle. The **system boundary** shows what is included in the system (inside the rectangle) and what is not included in the system (outside the rectangle). After you identify the system boundary, you place the use cases on the diagram, add the actors, and show the relationships. Figure TK 5-24 shows a use case diagram for a school bus system that creates a new bus route.

Use Case Diagram: Auto Service Department

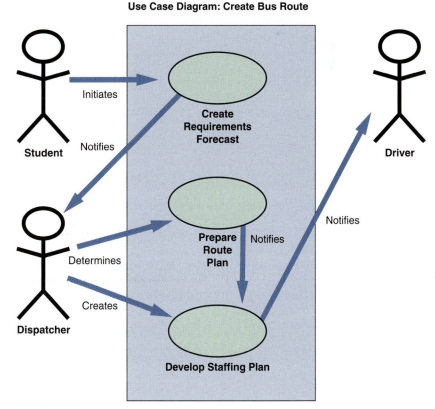

FIGURE TK 5-23   A use case diagram to handle work at an auto service department.

Use Case Diagram: Create Bus Route

FIGURE TK 5-24   A use case diagram to create a school bus route.

Class Diagrams

A **class diagram** represents a detailed view of a single use case, shows the classes that participate in the use case, and documents the relationship among the classes. Like a DFD, a class diagram is a logical model, which evolves into a physical model and finally becomes a functioning information system. In structured analysis, entities, data stores, and processes are transformed into data structures and program code. Similarly, class diagrams evolve into code modules, data objects, and other system components.

In a class diagram, each class appears as a rectangle, with the class name at the top, followed by the class's attributes and methods. Lines show relationships between classes and have labels identifying the action that relates the two classes. When you construct the diagram, the first step is to review the use case and identify the classes that participate in the underlying business transaction.

The class diagram also includes a concept called **cardinality**, which describes how instances of one class relate to instances of another class. You learn about cardinality in Chapters 4 and 6 of the textbook. For example, an employee might have earned no vacation days or one vacation day or many vacation days. Similarly, an employee might have no spouse or one spouse. Figure TK 5-25 shows various UML notations and cardinality examples. Notice that in Figure TK 5-25, the first column shows a UML notation symbol that identifies the relationship shown in the second column. The third column provides a typical example of the relationship, which is described in the last column. In the first row of the figure, the UML notation $0..*$ identifies a *zero or many* relation. The example is that an employee can have no payroll deductions or many deductions.

Cardinality also is important during structured analysis data design, which is discussed in Chapter 6.

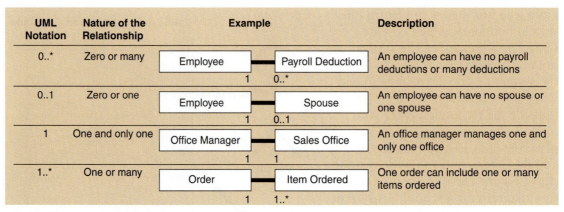

UML Notation	Nature of the Relationship	Example		Description
0..*	Zero or many	Employee — Payroll Deduction 1 0..*		An employee can have no payroll deductions or many deductions
0..1	Zero or one	Employee — Spouse 1 0..1		An employee can have no spouse or one spouse
1	One and only one	Office Manager — Sales Office 1 1		An office manager manages one and only one office
1..*	One or many	Order — Item Ordered 1 1..*		One order can include one or many items ordered

FIGURE TK 5-25 Examples of UML notations that indicate the nature of the relationship between instances of one class and instances of another class.

Figure TK 5-26 shows a class diagram for a sales order use case. Notice that the sales office has one sales manager who can have anywhere from zero to many sales reps. Each sales rep can have anywhere from zero to many customers, but each customer has only one sales rep.

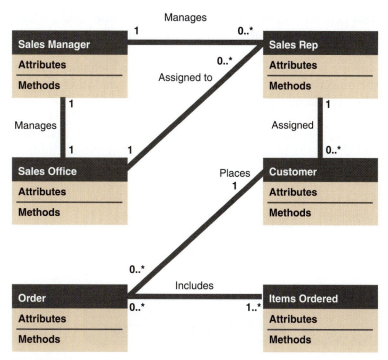

FIGURE TK 5-26 Class diagram for a sales order use case (attributes and methods omitted for clarity).

Sequence Diagrams

A **sequence diagram** is a dynamic model of a use case, showing the interaction among classes during a specified time period. A sequence diagram graphically documents the use case by showing the classes, the messages, and the timing of the messages. Sequence diagrams include symbols that represent classes, lifelines, messages, and focuses. These symbols are shown in Figure TK 5-27.

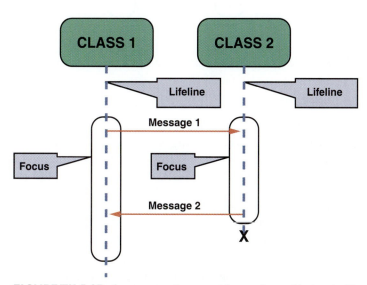

FIGURE TK 5-27 A sequence diagram with two classes. Notice the X that indicates the end of the CLASS 2 lifeline. Also notice that each message is represented by a line with a label that describes the message, and that each class has a focus that shows the period when messages are sent or received.

CLASSES   A class is identified by a rectangle with the name inside. Classes that send or receive messages are shown at the top of the sequence diagram.

LIFELINES   A lifeline is identified by a dashed line. The **lifeline** represents the time during which the object above it is able to interact with the other objects in the use case. An X marks the end of the lifeline.

MESSAGES   A message is identified by a line showing direction that runs between two objects. The label shows the name of the message and can include additional information about the contents.

FOCUSES   A focus is identified by a narrow vertical shape that covers the lifeline. The **focus** indicates when an object sends or receives a message.

The fitness center example shown in Figure TK 5-28 shows a sequence diagram for the ADD NEW STUDENT use case. Notice that the vertical position of each message indicates the timing of the message.

FIGURE TK 5-28   The sequence diagram for the ADD NEW STUDENT use case. The use case description for ADD NEW STUDENT is shown in Figure TK 5-21 on page 616.

State Transition Diagrams

Earlier in this chapter you learned that state refers to an object's current status. A **state transition** diagram shows how an object changes from one state to another, depending on events that affect the object. All possible states must be documented in the state transition diagram, as shown in Figure TK 5-29. A bank account, for example, could be opened as a NEW account, change to an ACTIVE or EXISTING account, and eventually become a CLOSED or FORMER account. Another possible state for a bank account could be FROZEN, if the account's assets are legally attached.

In a state transition diagram, the states appear as rounded rectangles with the state names inside. The small circle to the left is the initial state, or the point where the object first interacts with the system. Reading from left to right, the lines show direction and describe the action or event that causes a transition from one state to another. The circle at the right with a hollow border is the final state.

FIGURE TK 5-29 An example of a state transition diagram for a bank account.

Activity Diagrams

An **activity diagram** resembles a horizontal flowchart that shows the actions and events as they occur. Activity diagrams show the order in which the actions take place and identify the outcomes. Figure TK 5-30 shows an activity diagram for a cash withdrawal at an ATM machine. Notice that the customer initiates the activity by inserting an ATM card and requesting cash. Activity diagrams also can display multiple use cases in the form of a grid, where classes are shown as vertical bars and actions appear as horizontal arrows.

FIGURE TK 5-30 An activity diagram shows the actions and events involved in withdrawing cash from an ATM machine.

Sequence diagrams, state transition diagrams, and activity diagrams are dynamic modeling tools that can help a systems analyst understand how objects behave and interact with the system.

CASE Tools

Object modeling requires many types of diagrams to represent the proposed system. Creating the diagrams by hand is time-consuming and tedious, so systems analysts rely on CASE tools to speed up the process and provide an overall framework for documenting the system components. In addition, CASE tools ensure consistency and provide common links so that once objects are described and used in one part of the design, they can be reused multiple times without further effort. Part 2 of the Systems Analyst's Toolkit describes CASE tools that can be used in object-oriented analysis.

ORGANIZING THE OBJECT MODEL

In this chapter, you learned how to use object-oriented tools and techniques to build a logical model of the information system. Now you are ready to organize your diagrams and documentation so the object model is easily read and understood. If you used a CASE tool to develop the design, much of this work will be performed automatically by the CASE software.

There are many ways to proceed with the task of organizing the object model, and experience will be your best teacher. After you identify the system's objects, classes, and relationships, you should develop an object relationship diagram that provides an overview of the system. If you do not use a CASE-generated model, each diagram or object definition should be supported by clear, relevant documentation that can be accessed easily by anyone who reviews the object model. For example, you should organize your use cases and use case diagrams so they can be linked to the appropriate class, state transition, sequence, and activity diagrams. Your diagrams and documentation are the foundation for the system's design, so accuracy is important. Remember that it is much easier to repair a diagram now than to change the software later.

TOOLKIT SUMMARY

This chapter introduces object modeling, which is a popular technique that describes a system in terms of objects. Objects represent real people, places, events, and transactions. Unlike structured analysis, which treats data and processes separately, objects include data and processes that can affect the data. During the implementation process, systems analysts and programmers transform objects into program code modules that can be optimized, tested, and reused as often as necessary.

Object-oriented terms include classes, attributes, instances, messages, and methods. Classes include objects that have similar attributes, or characteristics. Individual members of a class are called object instances. Objects within a class can be grouped into subclasses, which are more specific categories within the class. A class also can belong to a more general category called a superclass.

Objects can send messages, or commands, that require other objects to perform certain methods, or tasks. The concept that a message gives different meanings to different objects is called polymorphism. An object resembles a black box, with encapsulated, or self-contained, data and methods. The strongest relationship between objects is inheritance.

After you identify the objects, classes, and relationships, you prepare an object relationship diagram that shows the objects and how they interact to perform business functions and transactions.

The Unified Modeling Language (UML) is a widely used method of visualizing and documenting an information system. UML techniques include use cases, use case diagrams, class diagrams, sequence diagrams, state transition diagrams, and activity diagrams.

A use case describes a business situation initiated by an actor, who interacts with the information system. Each use case represents a specific transaction, or scenario. A use case diagram is a visual summary of related use cases within a system or subsystem. A class diagram represents a detailed view of a single use case, showing the classes that participate in the underlying business transaction, and the relationship among class instances, which is called cardinality. A sequence diagram is a dynamic model of a use case, showing the interaction among classes during a specified time period. Sequence diagrams include lifelines, messages, and focuses. A state transition diagram shows how an object changes from one state to another, depending on events that affect the object. An activity diagram resembles a horizontal flowchart that shows actions and events as they occur in a system.

CASE tools provide an overall framework for system documentation. CASE tools can speed up the development process, ensure consistency, and provide common links that enable objects to be reused.

At the end of the object modeling process, you organize your use cases and use case diagrams and create class, sequence, state transition, and activity diagrams.

Key Terms and Phrases

activity diagram *621*

actor *615*

attributes *606*

black box *611*

cardinality *618*

child *614*

class *606*

class diagram *618*

encapsulation *611*

focus *620*

inheritance *614*

instance *606*

lifeline *620*

message *606*

methods *606*

object *606*

object model *606*

object-oriented (O-O) analysis *606*

parent *614*

polymorphism *610*

relationships *614*

sequence diagram *619*

state *609*

state transition *620*

subclasses *611*

superclass *612*

system boundary *617*

Unified Modeling Language (UML) *606*

use case *615*

use case description *616*

use case diagram *617*

uses *615*

Toolkit Exercises

Review Questions

1. What is object-oriented analysis, and what are some advantages of using this technique?
2. Define an object, and give an example.
3. Define an attribute, and give an example.
4. Define a method, and give an example.
5. Define encapsulation, and explain the benefits it provides.
6. Define polymorphism, and give an example.
7. Define a class, subclass, and superclass, and give examples.
8. Define an actor, and give an example.
9. Define a use case and a use case diagram, and give examples.
10. Define the term, black box, and explain why it is an important concept in object-oriented analysis.

Discussion Topics

1. The chapter mentioned that systems analysts and programmers transform objects into program code modules that can be optimized, tested, and reused. Modular design is a very popular design concept in many industries. What other examples of modular design can you suggest?
2. You are an IT consultant, and you are asked to create a new system for a small real estate brokerage firm. Your only experience is with traditional data and process modeling techniques. This time, you decide to try an object-oriented approach. How will you begin? How are the tasks different from traditional structured analysis?
3. You are creating a system for a bowling alley to manage information about its leagues. During the modeling process, you create a state transition diagram for an object called LEAGUE BOWLERS. What are the possible states of a league bowler, and what happens to a bowler who quits the league and rejoins the following season?
4. A debate is raging at the IT consulting firm where you work. Some staff members believe that it is harder for experienced analysts to learn object-modeling techniques, because the analysts are accustomed to thinking about data and processes as separate entities. Others believe that solid analytical skills are easily transferable and do not see a problem in crossing over to the newer approach. What do you think, and why?

Projects

1. Search the Internet for information about the history and development of UML.
2. Contact the IT staff at your school or at a local business to learn whether the organization uses object-oriented programming languages. If so, determine what languages and versions are used and why they were selected.
3. Search the Internet for information about groups and organizations that support and discuss object-oriented methods and issues.
4. Search the Internet for information about CASE tools that provide UML support.

PART 6 Internet Resource Tools

In **Part 6** of the Systems Analyst's Toolkit, you will learn about Internet resource tools that can help you perform your duties and achieve your professional goals.

INTRODUCTION

OBJECTIVES

When you finish this part of the Toolkit, you will be able to:

- Describe the characteristics of the Internet and the World Wide Web

- Formulate an Internet search strategy, and evaluate your requirements, choose a proper tool, assess the quality of the results, and download virus-free results

- Explain how to use search engines, subject directories, and the invisible Web to locate the information you require

- Demonstrate advanced search techniques, including Boolean logic and Venn diagrams

- Describe other Internet communication resource tools, including newsgroups, newsletters, mailing lists, Web-based discussion groups, chat rooms, and instant messaging

- Provide examples of IT community resources and their value to a systems analyst

- Explain the benefits and disadvantages of online learning opportunities

The Internet offers a wealth of information about every conceivable subject. Without a good road map, however, it is easy to become overwhelmed by the sheer volume of material. Part 6 of the Systems Analyst's Toolkit will describe various Internet resources, assist you in formulating an effective information gathering strategy, and explain Internet resource tools and techniques that you can use to access the information you need.

TOOLKIT INTRODUCTION CASE: Mountain View College Bookstore

Background: Wendy Lee, manager of college services at Mountain View College, wants a new information system that will improve efficiency and customer service at the three college bookstores.

In this part of the case, Florence Fullerton (systems analyst) and Harry Boston (student intern) are talking about Internet resource tools.

Participants: Florence and Harry
Location: Mountain View College Cafeteria, near the end of the systems analysis phase
Discussion topics: Internet resource tools.

Florence: Hi, Harry. Did you get a chance to try that new search engine?

Harry: *I sure did. First, I formulated an Internet search strategy, as you suggested, and then I did a search using the logical operators that we talked about. I liked the way the search engine organized the results for me. I also followed your suggestions about checking out the quality of the results.*

Florence: Sounds good. But remember — sometimes it might be better not to start your search with a search engine.

Harry: *Why not?*

Florence: Well, the Internet is a huge place. In some situations, you might want to get a broad overview of a topic before plunging into a specific search. If so, you might want to use a subject directory like Yahoo! or the Librarians' Index to the Internet. Another important resource is called the invisible Web, which is a collection of searchable databases that usually are not accessed by search engines.

Harry: *Okay. What about using other tools, like newsgroups, newsletters, mailing lists, Web-based discussion groups, chat rooms, and instant messaging?*

Florence: They all are important ways to get online information. Also remember that the IT community has many resources that can help you locate information, keep up with IT developments, and advance your career with knowledge and training.

Harry: *It seems like the more I know about the Internet, the more I have to learn.*

Florence: I feel the same way. Let's see what else we can learn about Internet resource tools. Here's a task list to get us started.

FIGURE TK 6-1

OVERVIEW

As a systems analyst, you will perform a variety of tasks and functions. You will rely on your knowledge, skills, and experience as you respond to a variety of short- and long-term challenges.

It is obvious that the rate of technological change precludes any one person from having all the answers. Fortunately, you have access to the Internet, where an enormous storehouse of information is available to you at little or no cost. The **Internet** is a worldwide network that integrates many thousands of other networks, which in turn link millions of government, business, educational, and personal users around the globe. The Internet can assist you in your daily work by helping you solve technical problems and can help you advance your career by offering access to training, education, and communication with other IT professionals.

The Internet allows you to visit the **World Wide Web**, usually referred to as the **Web**, which contains billions of text and multimedia documents called **Web pages**. A collection of related Web pages is called a **Web site** and is stored on a computer called a **Web server**. A **Web browser**, or **browser**, is a software program that allows you to access and display Web pages that are delivered to you by a Web server. Internet Explorer and Netscape are popular browsers that offer powerful graphic interfaces to help you navigate the Web and use other Internet services, such as e-mail and other types of online communication.

ON THE WEB

For more information about The World Wide Web, visit **scsite.com/sad6e/ more**, locate Toolkit Part 6, and then click The World Wide Web link.

FIGURE TK 6-2 This representation of the Internet shows the need for an effective navigation strategy. Without a reliable map, it is easy to get lost or overwhelmed by the information.

Some Characteristics of the Internet

Before exploring the Internet, it is helpful to learn more about its size and characteristics. Internet growth has been spectacular in recent years, and the trend is expected to continue.

According to a recent Federal Communications Commission estimate, the Internet has more than 40 million Web sites. How much information is stored on these sites? A recent article in *Competia Online Magazine* stated that almost one trillion individual documents are stored on the Web. Assuming a world population of about six billion, there would be about 160 Web pages for every man, woman, and child on earth.

Another view is offered by Lumeta Corporation, a firm that offers software designed to examine and describe large-scale networks, including the Internet. On its Web site, the company describes the history of **Internet mapping**, which is a method of probing the paths to each registered Internet entity. These paths are depicted as a map, which is shown in Figure TK 6-2. According to Lumeta, this data makes it possible to analyze, document, and predict the Internet's growth and behavior. As Lumeta points out, the maps themselves are interesting and visually appealing.

Summary of Internet Resources and Tools

As you journey on the Internet, many navigation tools are available to you. Sometimes, one tool works best; in other situations, you might find that a combination of tools is more useful. Internet search resources and tools include search engines, subject directories, and a collection of searchable database resources called the invisible Web. Internet communication tools, such as newsgroups, newsletters, mailing lists, Web-based discussion groups, chat rooms, and instant messaging also are available. These resources and tools are described briefly in the next section and explained in more detail in following sections.

SEARCH ENGINES A **search engine** is an application that uses keywords and phrases to locate information on the Internet and list the results of the search. **Meta-search engines** are tools that can apply multiple search engines simultaneously. For most people, search engines are the workhorses of information gathering. Search engines employ a variety of approaches to gathering information, and although they are extremely valuable tools, users should be aware of potential problems. For example, search results can be affected if the search engine permits commercial users to achieve higher priority based on payment of fees. Also, search engines access only a portion of the Internet.

SUBJECT DIRECTORIES A **subject directory** is a Web site that allows you to access topics by using a hierarchy, starting with general headings and proceeding to more specific topics. A subject directory is an excellent starting point when you want an overview of a particular topic before proceeding to specific Web sites.

THE INVISIBLE WEB The **invisible Web** refers to a vast store of documents, databases, and Web pages that are not detected by search engines. A recent article in the *Journal of Electronic Publishing* estimates that public information on the invisible Web is 500 times larger than the commonly defined World Wide Web. The invisible Web includes numerous university and government libraries and other searchable resources.

INTERNET COMMUNICATION RESOURCES To tap the full potential of the Internet, users must be effective communicators. In addition to the tools already mentioned, a systems analyst might acquire valuable information by using newsgroups, newsletters, mailing lists, Web-based discussion groups, chat rooms, and instant messaging. These tools are described in the following sections.

FORMULATING AN INTERNET RESEARCH STRATEGY

An Internet research strategy is necessary to avoid frustration and wasted time. A pilot or ship captain would not begin a journey without knowing his or her destination. Similarly, you should develop a strategy that will allow you to navigate efficiently and confidently toward your objectives. To be effective, you should consider a four-step approach:

1. Evaluate your information requirements
2. Match your information requirements to the proper tool
3. Assess the quality of the results
4. Download the results and perform a virus scan

Over time, you will gain experience and develop your own preferences for using the Internet. You should remember that each research situation is unique, and several tools and techniques might be necessary to achieve the results you require.

Evaluate Your Information Requirements

The first step to finding the information you need is to make sure you really understand what you are seeking. You need to spend time thinking about the topic to ensure that you are casting an appropriate net. For example, a colleague or supervisor may ask you to help decide between two specific CASE products. Your initial inclination might be to find a review of various CASE applications. Upon reflection, however, you realize it would be more useful to understand CASE tools in a general sense before comparing product statistics. This realization leads you to start with a more generalized search instead of going directly to vendor sites.

Match Your Information Requirement to the Proper Tool

Once you feel that you understand the information required, it is time to pick an initial tool. At this point, you face a difficult decision. Should you use search engines or subject directories, or should you try to access the invisible Web? Should you seek commercial sites, IT publications, professional associations, newsgroups, or other areas to explore?

As you gain experience and apply the skills explained in this part of the Systems Analyst's Toolkit, you will be able to handle a wide range of Internet tools and resources. As with most skills, the more you use them, the more expertise you acquire. In time, you will work with a wide range of tools, and you probably will develop your own list of favorite sites and resources.

Assess the Quality of the Results

By definition, the Internet is essentially open and unregulated. On the plus side, a huge diversity of information is available. The quality of content, however, varies greatly. Unlike published journals or textbooks, almost anyone can post **content**, or material, on the Web. This means that the searcher must review the information very carefully. Questions to ask when accessing content include:

SOURCE Is the author identifiable? Does the author have expertise on the subject? You may need to trace back through Web site addresses or URLs to find biographical information, or do a separate search on the author's name.

ACCURACY Does the information come from a commercial source that is offering its own solution? Is it from an association with an inherent bias? Often, it is very difficult to find completely objective information. Identifying biases and finding information from a variety of sources is a way to address this problem.

SCOPE Is the information specific enough? If not, you should narrow and refine your search and seek additional resources until you locate the information you need. When you use a search engine, one way to do this is to perform a **sub-search** using the results of the initial search as a starting point.

CURRENCY How old is the information? Is the topic static or dynamic? In the IT world, technology changes very quickly. If you locate information that appears to be out of date, you might seek more recent data to ensure that your results are valid.

LOOK AND FEEL Is the information easy to access and navigate? If the site is designed in a logical manner and offers value-added links to worthwhile pages and resources, do not be overly concerned with style — some excellent material is created by authors and producers who focus on content, not design.

If you find the content useful, be sure to credit the source properly when you use it. You must observe legal and ethical standards when you deal with Internet material. To learn more about proper citation and to view specific examples of how to cite electronic material, you can visit the Library of Congress site at *http://memory.loc.gov/learn/start/cite/index.html*.

Download the Results and Perform a Virus Scan

Once you have discovered the appropriate information, you can save it to your hard drive or network, depending on the content and purpose. The information you found may be in one of many formats, including Microsoft Office documents, spreadsheets, and databases; Adobe PDF files; and multimedia material with file extensions such as jpeg, mpeg, and pcx.

Many sites allow you to click a link and download the file directly to your hard drive. If this option is not offered explicitly, you can try right-clicking a link or embedded object. This action usually displays a list of choices that includes downloading the selected information.

It is important to protect your network and computer system from any unwanted viruses. Unlike intellectual content, which is easy to evaluate, it is impossible for you to determine the integrity and validity of the internal file structure and format without the use of a virus detection tool. As Figure TK 6-3 shows, many thousands of viruses are identified each day. Viruses cost businesses many millions of dollars in lost data and additional effort. Without proper protection, you run the risk of not only corrupting your own files or hard drive, but bringing your entire company network down.

The following sections offer additional explanations of search engines, subject directories, the invisible Web, and other Internet tools.

FIGURE TK 6-3 According to its Web site, Trend Micro is a global leader in network antivirus and Internet content security software and services. Notice the daily and weekly virus statistics, which reflect the enormous number of viruses detected.

SEARCH ENGINES

A search engine often is the best starting point for gathering information. A well-planned search will narrow the range of content to a manageable level and will allow you to explore the choices or execute a sub-search within the focused results. As with any tool, it is important to understand the intended use and limitations of a search engine before applying it to a task.

 ON THE WEB

For more information about Search Engines, visit **scsite.com/sad6e/more**, locate Toolkit Part 6 and then click the Search Engines link.

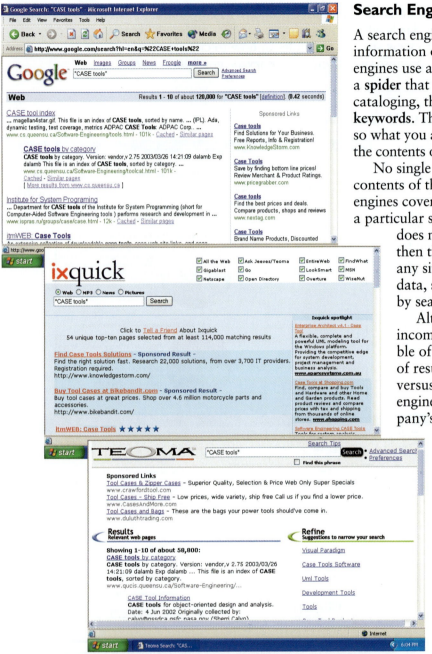

Search Engine Basics

A search engine is a tool that helps people find information on the World Wide Web. Search engines use a specialized computer program called a **spider** that travels from site to site **indexing**, or cataloging, the contents of the pages based on **keywords**. The results are compiled into a database, so what you are searching is not the Web itself, but the contents of the search engine's database.

No single search engine can catalog the shifting contents of the Web, and even the most powerful engines cover a fraction of known Web content. If a particular site is not widely linked, or its author does not submit it to major search engines, then the material is invisible to them. Also, any site that requires a visitor to type in data, such as a name, cannot be accessed by search engines.

Although search engine indexes are incomplete and often dated, they are capable of delivering an overwhelming number of results, or **hits**. The real issue is quality versus quantity. When comparing search engines, it is important to know the company's policy toward allowing commercial sites to boost their ranking in a **pay for performance** arrangement. Links that are subsidized by companies are called **sponsored links**.

Not all search engines work the same way. By understanding the underlying algorithms, or specific rules, that drive these information engines, it is possible to better target your search. For example, some sites, like Google, rank their pages by analyzing the number of other sites that link to that page. Other sites, like Ask Jeeves.com, organize results by concepts or intended meanings. Teoma.com uses an interesting approach called **Subject-**

FIGURE TK 6-4 Google is an example of an indexed search engine, and ixquick is an example of a meta-search site. Teoma is a combination engine that includes ranked pages, suggestions to refine or narrow the search, and an expert-compiled resources section.

Specific Popularity™, which ranks a site based on the number of same-subject pages that reference it, not just general popularity, to determine a site's level of authority.

You usually can determine an engine's approach by clicking the About tab or link on the search site. The following section describes several examples of search engines, which are shown in Figure TK 6-4.

INDEXED SEARCH ENGINES Google, like most other popular research tools, is an **indexed search engine** that organizes and ranks the results of a search. Although they have much in common, each tool has its own search algorithms, features, and user interface. Other examples of indexed search engines include AltaVista, Ask Jeeves, and Dogpile, among many others.

META-SEARCH ENGINES Meta-search engines can apply multiple search engines simultaneously. A meta-search engine examines the indexed results of several search engines to provide broader coverage. In addition to ixquick, other examples of meta-search engines include Metacrawler and Teoma, which has a feature that offers suggestions to help you refine and narrow your search.

Search Techniques

Consider the following suggestions when you begin a search:

- → Refine your topic. Unless you limit the scope of your topic, you might be overwhelmed by the number of results. If you are looking for general information on a broad topic, consider a subject directory site.

- → Translate your question into an effective search query. Searches are executed on keywords. You will improve your success if you pick the proper keywords. Try to find unique words or phrases and avoid those with multiple uses. For example, search for *external hard drive* (a computer hardware device), rather than *hard drive* (also might refer to a difficult auto trip). Consider using advanced search techniques, which are described in the following section.

- → Review the search results and evaluate the quality of the results. If the search needs refinement or additional material, you can either use the site's advanced search techniques or select a different Internet resource altogether.

To be effective, you should understand the mechanics of the search engine, use proper spelling, find unique phrases, and experiment with a variety of approaches. If you are consistently returning too many results, try using topic-specific terms and advanced search techniques. Conversely, if too few results are returned, eliminate the least important terms or concepts, broaden your subject, or use more general vocabulary when you select terms.

Advanced Search Techniques

Many search engines offer powerful features that allow you to refine and control the type of information returned from searches. These features can include the option to search within returned results and the ability to search within specific areas, such as newsgroups. Perhaps the most powerful advanced feature is the option to use Boolean logic.

Boolean logic is a system named after British mathematician George Boole and refers to the relationships among search terms. You can use various combinations of the **logical operators** OR, AND, and NOT to improve your search success greatly. Figure TK 6-5 on the next page graphically illustrates the use of the operators with search terms. The circles shown in the figure are called Venn diagrams. A **Venn diagram** uses circular symbols to illustrate Boolean logic. Venn diagrams are named after John Venn, a nineteenth-century scholar who devised a scheme for visualizing logical relationships. In the sample diagrams, the shaded area indicates the results of the search.

LOGICAL OPERATORS	EXAMPLE	VENN DIAGRAM (SHADED AREA INDICATES RETURNED RESULTS)
A **or** B	Baseball **or** Football	Baseball ⬤ Football
A **and** B	Baseball **and** Football	Baseball ⬤ Football
A **not** B	Internet **not** Web	Internet ⬤ Web
A **or** B **or** C	Colorado **or** Mining **or** Gold	Colorado ⬤ Mining — Gold
A **and** B **and** C	Colorado **and** Mining **and** Gold	Colorado ⬤ Mining — Gold
A **and** B **not** C	Colorado **and** Mining **not** Gold	Colorado ⬤ Mining — Gold

FIGURE TK 6-5 Examples of logical operators OR, AND, and NOT. The shaded area represents the returned results. OR is the most inclusive term, returning results if any of the terms appear; AND requires all keywords to appear; and NOT excludes results even if they are found in the same document.

To learn more about how logical operators work, consider the following diagrams:

OR The first diagram at the top of Figure TK 6-5 shows that the **OR** term will retrieve all results containing either term. Notice that the shaded area includes both circles. The OR operator can be used when you need a wide search net.

AND The second diagram in Figure TK 6-5 shows that the **AND** term will retrieve only those results in which all terms linked by the AND operator are present. Notice that the shaded area includes only the overlapping portion of the two circles. The more terms or concepts combined in an AND search, the fewer pages will be returned. The AND operator often is used to narrow a set of search results.

NOT The third diagram in Figure TK 6-5 shows how the NOT operator can be used to exclude certain records. In this diagram, consider the closely related terms, Internet and Web. It is likely that these terms both appear in many Web pages. The **NOT** operator will strip out the results containing the unwanted term. For example the search string, Internet NOT Web, will return only those pages with the term, Internet. You should use the NOT operator carefully, because the term you want to exclude may be intertwined with the term you seek in many documents that would be useful to you.

The next three diagrams in Figure TK 6-5 illustrate other combinations of logical operators where three search terms are involved.

USING PHRASES Suppose you want to find sites that sell board games that require players to use strategy, such as Monopoly®. In your search, you could specify both terms, *strategy* AND *game*, but your results probably would include many documents that describe game strategies used in various sports, which is not what you are seeking. A much better approach would be to search using the phrase "strategy game" enclosed in quotes. A **phrase** is more specific than an AND operator, because it specifies an exact placement of terms. In this example, the phrase "strategy game" will not retrieve any documents unless they contain that exact phrase.

The implementation of Boolean logic varies by search engine. Some engines require the use of full Boolean searching using the complete operators (OR, AND, NOT) in the search window. Others use implied Boolean logic with keyword searching. In **implied Boolean logic**, symbols are used to represent Boolean operators, such as a plus sign (+) for AND, and a minus sign (-) for NOT. If two search terms are entered in the search window with a space between them, some search engines may assume an OR; others assume an AND. You need to consult the site's Help files to understand the underlying rules.

Most search engines provide an **advanced search** feature that offers a fill-in form similar to the example shown in Figure TK 6-6. Notice that a user can narrow the search by entering search terms in the upper part of the form, or they can enter the actual Boolean expression in the lower part of the form.

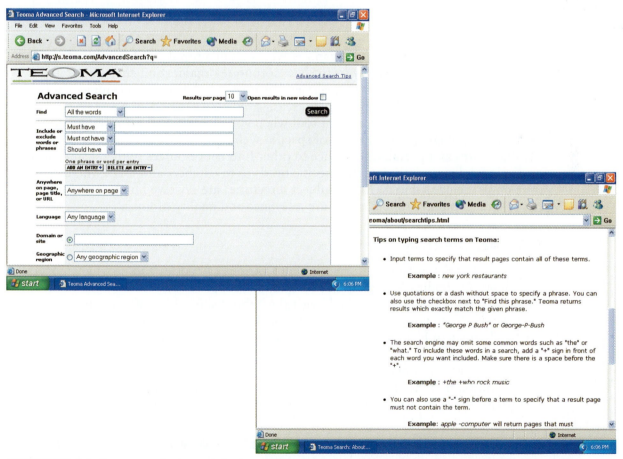

FIGURE TK 6-6 For users unfamiliar with Boolean terms, many search engines offer an advanced search feature with convenient fill-in templates. In this case "all of these words" is equivalent to the AND operator, "any of these words" is the same as the OR operator, and "none of these words" is equivalent to NOT. "This exact phrase" is useful if your topic is identified by technical phrases or terms.

A Search Checklist

Many people find it helpful to prepare for an Internet search by using a checklist similar to the following.

1. Does the topic have any unique words, phrases, or acronyms? If so, use these terms in the search.

2. Do any of the search terms have other spellings or names? If so, include these with an OR operator in the search.

3. Are certain additional words or phrases likely to appear in any Web document? If so, consider adding an AND operator to narrow the search.

4. Is there any unrelated material that my search terms might pick up? If so, consider using the NOT operator to exclude these documents.

5. Are any organizations, publications, or institutions likely to have an interest in my topic? If so, try to locate their Web sites and then conduct a further search using the site indexes and databases available on the site.

6. Is the search returning results too numerous to examine? If so, keep adding additional terms to narrow the search and reduce the number of hits until a reasonable number is achieved.

SUBJECT DIRECTORIES

A subject directory collects and organizes Web sites in a top-down format, based on subjects and topics. An analogy might be a corporate organization chart, where you could go to the top person for an overview, then visit with lower-level employees to obtain specific information about their areas.

A subject directory is an excellent tool when you want general information about a topic before plunging into an array of specific Web sites. Yahoo! is a popular directory site that serves as a **portal**, or entrance to other Internet resources. Other academic and professional directories target the specific needs of researchers and users who concentrate on particular subjects. Many subject directories are reviewed by human experts, rather than computer robots, to ensure relevance and quality of links.

A Subject Directory Example

Subject directories organize information into various categories and provide an overall framework for finding information. For example, suppose you wanted to learn more about Internet magazines. You could visit the Yahoo! site, which offers a subject directory search. When you click the *Internet* topic link on the main page, as shown in the left-hand screen in Figure TK 6-7, a screen would display various categories, or subtopics, as shown in the middle screen. When you click the *Magazines* link, the right-hand screen would display with a list of Internet magazines.

In addition to Yahoo!, other popular subject directories include About.com and the Librarians' Index to the Internet, which maintains a site at lii.org.

Advantages and Disadvantages of Subject Directories

The main advantage of a subject directory is that it provides an overview when you are not sure of the size and scope of your topic. Later, when you have a better understanding of your subject, you can use a search engine to seek additional information and examples.

Subject directories also have shortcomings. Many subject directories use human expertise to formulate the subject organization and determine the placement of links. This process involves subjective decisions that might affect the quality of search results. Some subject directories are updated continually; others might not be current. Also, unlike a search engine, a subject directory forces you to work your way through a series of levels, rather than using specific words and phrases to locate directly the material you seek.

FIGURE TK 6-7 Yahoo! is an example of a subject directory that organizes information into various categories to provide an overall framework. In the example shown, the user has visited the Yahoo! site, clicked the *Internet* topic link, and then clicked the *Magazines* link, which causes the list of Internet magazines to display.

THE INVISIBLE WEB

Most of us are familiar with what is called the **visible Web**, which refers to Web sites that are indexed by the major search engines and are publicly accessible. As discussed earlier, much more information is available on the Internet that is not indexed. The terms, invisible Web, **hidden Web**, or **deep Web**, are used to describe this valuable information source, which includes numerous text, graphics, and data files stored in collections that are unreachable by search engines.

The invisible Web includes searchable databases that contain an enormous amount of information in university and government libraries, as well as thousands of specialized databases that are maintained by institutions and organizations around the world.

Much of the invisible Web is open to the public, but some databases are password protected. Many sites allow guest access, but some areas can be accessed only by members of a specific group.

In an article in the *Journal of Electronic Publishing*, author Michael K. Bergman compared Internet searching to dragging a net across the surface of the ocean. He stated that "While a great deal may be caught in the net, there is still a wealth of information that is deep, and therefore, missed. The reason is simple: Most of the Web's information is buried far down on dynamically generated sites, and standard search engines never find it." Mr. Bergman pointed out that traditional search engines create their indices by **spidering**, or crawling, through many millions of Web pages. He pointed out that "To be discovered, the page must be static and linked to other pages.... Because traditional search engine crawlers cannot probe beneath the surface, the deep Web has heretofore been hidden."

ON THE WEB

For more information about The Invisible Web, visit **scsite.com/ sad6e/more**, locate Toolkit Part 6 and then click The Invisible Web link.

Invisible Web Examples

A few examples of information on the invisible Web include the following:

- ➡ Specialized topic databases: subject-specific collections of information, such as corporate financial filings and reports, genealogy records, or Ellis Island immigration data

- ➡ Hardware and software vendors: searchable technical support databases for large sites such as Microsoft's or Oracle's knowledge bases

- ➡ Publications: databases of published and archived articles

- ➡ Libraries: searchable catalogs for thousands of libraries, including the Library of Congress and numerous university and institutional libraries

- ➡ Government databases: census data, statutes, patents, copyrights, and trademarks

- ➡ Auction sites: searchable listing of items, bidders, and sellers

- ➡ Locators: telephone numbers, addresses, and e-mail addresses

- ➡ Career opportunities: job listings and resume postings

Navigation Tools for the Invisible Web

You can access the invisible Web in several ways. One approach is use a search engine to locate a portal, or entrance, to a searchable database by including the word, database, as a required search term. For example, if you are searching for information about printer drivers, you could specify "printer drivers" AND database. The additional term will narrow the search results and increase the likelihood of finding searchable collections of printer drivers.

You also can access the invisible Web by using specialized portals that list and organize searchable databases. An example of an invisible Web portal is completeplanet.com, which is shown in the upper screen in Figure TK 6-8. Completeplanet.com claims to access over 70,000 invisible Web databases that are frequently overlooked by traditional searching, and also offers a special search tool called the Deep Query Manager™. A similar set of tools is available at the State University of New York site shown in the lower screen in Figure TK 6-8. This site offers a Deep Web tutorial and a Database Finder that can locate databases that might not be visible otherwise.

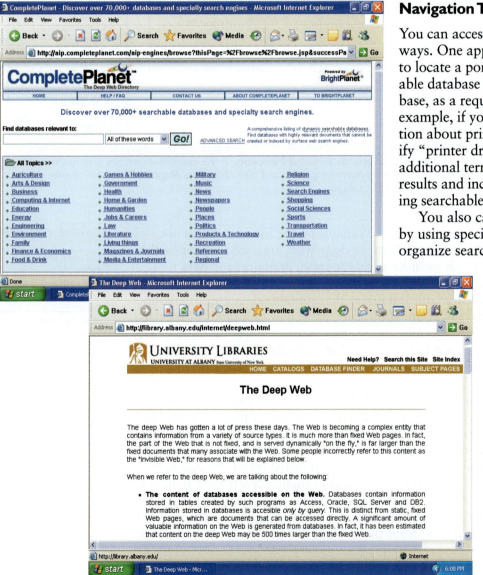

FIGURE TK 6-8 The sites shown are organized by topic and have links to many searchable databases whose contents cannot be indexed by traditional search engines.

If you spend a significant amount of time searching the invisible Web, you might want to use special navigation software to assist you. For example, EndNote is an application offered by ISI ResearchSoft, a division of Thomson Corporation, as shown in Figure TK 6-9.

EndNote uses a special information transfer method called the **Z39.50 protocol** that allows a user to connect directly to hundreds of government and university databases. The top screen in Figure TK 6-9 shows a sample of available databases. In the middle screen, the user has selected the Library of Congress catalog and is ready to enter specific search terms and logical operators. The bottom screen shows that the user has connected to the remote database.

FIGURE TK 6-9 EndNote is an application that uses a special information transfer method called the Z39.50 protocol that allows you to connect directly to hundreds of government and university databases. In the example shown, the user has selected the Library of Congress catalog and is ready to enter specific search terms and logical operators. The bottom screen shows that the user has connected to the remote database.

Figure TK 6-10 shows a recap of the Internet tools and resources: search engines, subject directories, and the invisible Web. Notice that each has advantages and disadvantages.

Recap of Internet Search Resources

RESOURCE	POSSIBLE USES	ADVANTAGES	DISADVANTAGES	NOTES
Search Engines	Good initial starting point, especially if you have an overall understanding of the topic. Search engines can lead you to important government, professional, or commercial sites.	Flexibility. You can choose from many different engines with various features. Some allow newsgroup access as well. Meta-search engines can return and rank results from multiple sources. Advanced search techniques can be used.	Frequently produces information overload. Can return many irrelevant or out-of-date links. Without a refined search, it is impossible to examine results carefully. Some sites allow companies to improve their hits by "pay for performance."	You can improve search effectiveness significantly by using advanced search techniques based on logical operators.
Subject Directories	Good way to get a broad overview of a topic before accessing specific sites.	With a subject directory, you can maintain broader focus and perspective, and work from the general to the specific without getting lost in a maze of Web sites.	Material is organized by human intervention; quality, currency, and accuracy might vary.	Once you work your way through the various levels, you might be able to bookmark the resource for more direct future access.
Invisible Web	Information from non-indexed databases and searchable directories such as company financial reports, library holdings, industry reports, and government information.	Very diverse resource. Many more pages on the Web are non-indexed rather than indexed.	Can be difficult to access unless you know where to look. Navigating a searchable database can be more difficult than using a traditional search engine, because no common interface exists.	Portal sites are available to help you navigate the invisible Web. You can use a general search engine to locate searchable databases by searching a subject term and the word *database*.

FIGURE TK 6-10 A recap of the three main Internet search resources: search engines, subject directories, and the invisible Web. Notice that each option has advantages and disadvantages.

INTERNET COMMUNICATION RESOURCES

Suppose that you are asked to analyze your organization's virus protection requirements. As part of your research you would want to learn about relevant news, developments, and the latest virus threats. You also might want to suggest several specific products. Assume that you performed your research using a search engine. Now you want to check your conclusions by getting feedback from other IT professionals. You can consider using newsgroups, newsletters, mailing lists, Web-based discussion groups, chat rooms, and instant messaging.

Newsgroups

Most people are familiar with bulletin boards they see at school, at work, and in their communities. Using thumb tacks or tape, people post information and read what others have posted. A **newsgroup** is the electronic equivalent of the everyday bulletin board. Newsgroups offer online discussion forums that address every conceivable subject and interest area. A newsgroup can put you in touch with the knowledge, experience, and opinions of a large online community.

Newsgroups are part of the **Usenet**, which is a discussion system that consists of Internet-based bulletin boards. The Usenet was designed to allow users to communicate quickly and effectively in the early days of the Internet. Many newsgroups are open to the public; others are closed and can be accessed only with a username and password.

Articles or messages are posted to the appropriate newsgroups by users, and posted topics are broken down into **threads**, or subtopics. To view and post messages to a newsgroup, you need a program called a **newsreader**. You can use a stand-alone news-reader, such as Forté software's popular Agent program, or you can work with newsreaders that are built into browsers such as Internet Explorer and Netscape.

ON THE WEB

For more information about Newsgroups, visit **scsite.com/sad6e/more**, locate Toolkit Part 6 and then click the Newsgroups link.

Some search engines and subject directories allow you to conduct a specific search among newsgroups. The upper screen in Figure TK 6-11 shows categories of newsgroups that can be searched by the Google search engine. When the user clicks the *Computers* link, the lower screen displays. This portal would provide a convenient entry point for a systems analyst who wants to explore and participate in computer-related newsgroups.

To understand how newsgroups work, consider the following example. In your research on virus protection, which was mentioned in the previous section, assume that you have narrowed the product choices down to two. You are having trouble, however, differentiating between them and would like feedback from current users. You might want to visit individual product sites for user testimonials, but you

FIGURE TK 6-11 Google provides an easy way to access Usenet discussion forums. The screen shows categories of newsgroups, and a search engine that can browse for newsgroups that meet the search criteria.

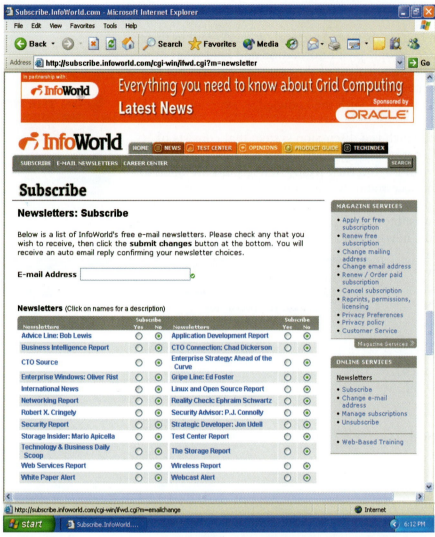

FIGURE TK 6-12 *InfoWorld* magazine offers free e-mail newsletters to IT professionals.

would be unlikely to find a negative opinion on a vendor's site. You also could poll your professional colleagues, but you want to survey a variety of users that goes beyond your limited circle.

At this point, you might decide to tap into an appropriate newsgroup and see if there have been any postings that are relevant to you. Some newsgroups are moderated, in which articles are sent to a person who approves them before they are posted for the group. Before you post, you should read the FAQ files associated with each newsgroup. The term **FAQs** stands for **frequently asked questions**. FAQs are a common method of providing guidance on questions that users are likely to ask. In many cases, FAQs describe the particular **netiquette**, or Web guidelines for protocol and courtesy, that exist on a particular newsgroup or site.

As you gain experience, you might decide to subscribe to newsgroups that address topics of interest to you, including some of the ones listed in Figure TK 6-11 on the previous page.

Newsletters

Newsletters are published by numerous commercial and non-profit groups that offer membership subscriptions to users who are interested in specific topics. In the example shown in Figure TK 6-12, *InfoWorld* magazine offers free e-mail newsletters to IT professionals interested in a wide range of topics. Notice that some newsletters are published daily, others weekly. Although newsletters are not interactive, they can provide a convenient way to keep current on subjects of interest and developments of interest to the subscriber.

Mailing Lists

A **mailing list**, also called a **listserv**, is similar to a newsgroup in that it provides a forum for people who want to exchange information about specific topics. Like a newsgroup, users can post messages and view postings made by others. Instead of a bulletin board approach, however, a mailing list uses e-mail to communicate with users. A computer called a **list server** directs e-mail to people who subscribe to, or join, the mailing list.

When a person subscribes to a list, he or she can receive e-mail messages as they are posted. Subscribers also can access a collection of messages called a **digest**. Many mailing lists maintain Web sites where users can search message archives.

A systems analyst would be interested in mailing lists that focus on information technology. To locate IT-related mailing lists, you can visit the Web sites of professional organizations, and you can try adding the phrase, mailing list or listserv, to your search topic. Also, as shown in Figure TK 6-13, you can visit Web sites such as lsoft.com and tile.net that organize mailing lists by name and subject.

Web-Based Discussion Groups

Another online communication resource is called a **Web-based discussion group**, which is an online community that combines features of mailing lists and newsgroups. Most Web-based discussion groups can be accessed through a portal, such as Yahoo!. Group members can receive messages either individually or in digest form like a mailing list, and they can browse messages stored on the group's Web site. In addition to text messages, group Web sites often include membership lists and contact information, photo galleries, and links of interest to members.

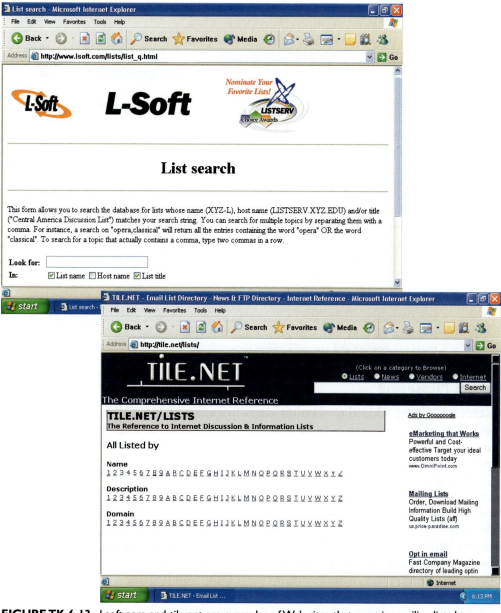

FIGURE TK 6-13 Lsoft.com and tile.net are examples of Web sites that organize mailing lists by name and subject.

Web-based discussion groups are popular because they offer a convenient and free meeting place with a graphical interface that makes it easy for users to access information and exchange messages.

Chat Rooms

A **chat room,** also called a **channel,** is an online meeting place where users can interact and converse in real time. The chat room concept originated with **IRC,** which stands for **Internet Relay Chat.** IRC is a multichannel system supported by servers that enable conversations, group or individual, on a worldwide basis. You can learn more about IRC at the Web site at www.irc.org, and you can follow links to see a list of available IRC channels that might be of interest to you.

Various companies also provide chat rooms that are available to IT professionals interested in specific topics. For example, Microsoft offers a wide variety of technical chat rooms, as shown in Figure TK 6-14.

FIGURE TK 6-14 Microsoft offers a wide variety of technical chat rooms where users can interact and converse in real time.

Instant Messaging

Instant messaging (IM) allows online users to exchange messages immediately, even while they are working in another program or application. Users are alerted that other members of their group are available online, and users can send and receive messages or enter into a chat with other users.

Although instant messaging began as a popular feature in home-oriented services such as AOL and Yahoo!, it has become an important business communications tool. Corporate use of IM, however, raises serious security and privacy concerns because it is relatively uncontrolled. Also, certain industries such as banking and health care must observe legal regulations that govern all their communications, including IM, which must be logged and documented. As shown in Figure TK 6-15, firms such as Blue Coat offer software that can manage instant messaging and provide necessary security and controls.

ON THE WEB

For more information about Instant Messaging, visit **scsite.com/sad6e/ more,** locate Toolkit Part 6 and then click the Instant Messaging link.

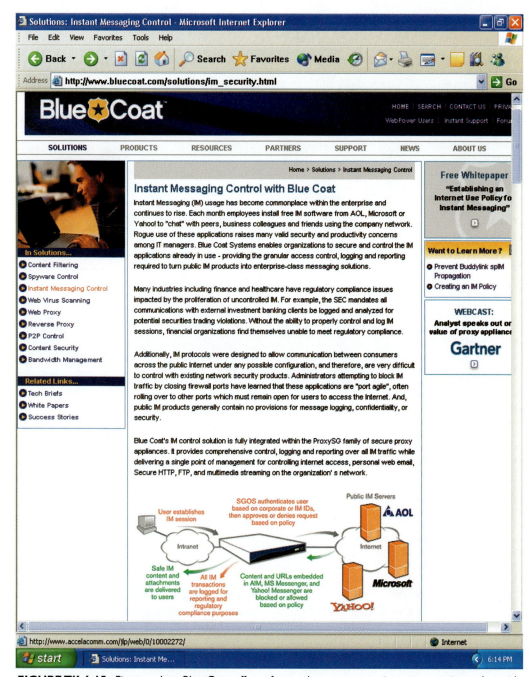

FIGURE TK 6-15 Firms such as Blue Coat offer software that can manage instant messaging and provide necessary security and controls.

Figure TK 6-16 on the next page shows a recap of Internet resources that can assist a systems analyst in online research and communication: newsgroups, newsletters, mailing lists, Web-based discussion groups, chat rooms, and instant messaging. Notice that each resource has advantages and disadvantages.

Recap of Internet Communication Resources

RESOURCE	POSSIBLE USES	ADVANTAGES	DISADVANTAGES	NOTES
Newsgroups	Answers to technical questions, advice, and support.	Can find information on every conceivable subject — good place to exchange views with other systems analysts. Many search engines can search newsgroup postings.	Cumbersome to search through message threads. Need to assess quality of information carefully.	Some major search engines allow newsgroup access, which provides a convenient way to participate.
Newsletters	Good way to follow trends and developments regarding specific IT topics.	Newsletters often are free to users who can subscribe to specific topics.	Not interactive, and amount of information might be overwhelming. Difficult to filter the important from the unimportant.	Some newsletters are published daily; others weekly or monthly.
Mailing Lists	Members can exchange information with others about specific topic of interest.	Messages arrive by e-mail, rather than in the form of bulletin board postings.	Amount of material might be difficult to read and analyze.	Some mailing lists, or listservs, allow members to search archived messages.
Web Discussion Groups	Members form a Web-based community regarding topics of common interest.	Combine many convenient features of newsgroups and mailing lists.	Although free, these groups usually must be accessed through a Web portal.	Web discussion groups have become very popular because they offer an attractive combination of features and convenience.
Chat Rooms	Online meeting places where users can interact and converse.	Many IT chat rooms are visited by professionals who are willing to help each other solve problems.	Discussions take place in real time, which might not be convenient. Dialog might be unfocused, and non-specific to the information you need.	Many large vendors, such as Microsoft, offer technical chat rooms.
Instant Messaging	A way to exchange messages immediately, even while working in other applications.	Highly efficient means of real-time communication on topics of interest. Good way to collaborate on team projects.	Can be distracting to a busy user, and sheer volume of non-essential messages can be a problem.	The Gartner Group predicts that by 2005, 60 percent of real-time communication will be driven by instant messaging technology.

FIGURE TK 6-16 A recap of Internet communication resources that can assist a systems analyst in online research and communication. Notice that each option has advantages and disadvantages.

INFORMATION TECHNOLOGY COMMUNITY RESOURCES

If you were asked to check a stock price or research the weather in a distant city for a business trip, you probably would not use a search engine. Instead, you would visit a favorite site you use regularly to access specific information. Similarly, when you require IT information, you can access a huge assortment of sites and resources that can be called the **information technology (IT) community**. This vast collection includes many sites that IT professionals can use to research specific questions or obtain background information. As a systems analyst, you are a member of this community. Like most communities, it offers you resources and support, including answers to technical questions, updates on new products and services, and information about training opportunities. The IT community includes numerous publications and online magazines, searchable databases, Web-based discussion groups, and mailing lists.

Four important components of the IT community are corporate resources, government resources, professional resources, and online learning resources, which are described in the following sections.

Corporate Resources

Corporate resources can provide general IT knowledge and background, as well as help solve specific business challenges. It is very important to evaluate corporate content carefully, because some sites are developed by companies with an interest in selling you a specific solution or product. Figure TK 6-17 shows an example of a site that offers product reviews and information.

If you are looking for help on a software application, it is a good idea to start by reviewing the software documentation. In many cases, technical support is included free of charge for a specific period of time. If you are working with an application with expired technical support, the software provider's Web site will describe support options that are available to you, including various fees and charges. Common problems often are addressed in the FAQ section.

An important corporate resource to systems analysts is their own internal company Web site or intranet. An intranet must be easy to access and provide access to valuable information. Companies increasingly are using intranets as a means of sharing information and working towards common solutions. Intranets can contain company policies and procedures, lessons-learned files, and financial information. They also enable employees to access and update their personal benefit information. In many organizations, the intranet is reducing the volume of paper memos and reports by serving as an enterprise-wide library and clearinghouse.

FIGURE TK 6-17 CNET.com is an example of a site that offers product reviews and information.

Government Resources

The IT needs of the federal government are enormous. Not surprisingly, a number of excellent federal IT resources are available on the Internet. Many sites offer comprehensive, non-biased information and valuable advice for IT professionals. For example, recent General Accounting Office (GAO) reports on the IT industry have covered everything from an analysis of the information security practices to a framework for assessing IT investments. Additionally, government sites can provide information on federal, state, and local business policies and regulations. The General Services Agency (GSA) site depicted in Figure TK 6-18 is a good source for federal policies and regulations, especially for firms that do business with the government.

FIGURE TK 6-18 The GSA site contains information about federal IT policies, news, and related links. The screen shows a sample from the IT Regulations, Guidelines and Laws section.

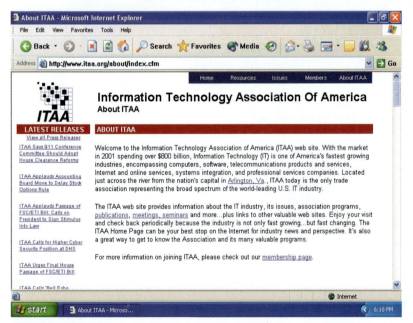

FIGURE TK 6-19 The ITAA site is one of many resources that a systems analyst can use to keep up with current issues, trends, and opportunities.

Professional Resources

The sites of professional associations are another resource worth consideration. Many associations focus on a specific topic such as project management, software engineering, or information security. Some of these associations are free, though most require you to provide basic information in order to access the complete site. The links provided by these sites often are quite useful. Professional organizations, such as the **Information Technology Association of America (ITAA)** site shown in Figure TK 6-19, also sponsor seminars and training. Many associations offer electronic newsletters that relate to your area of interest and are delivered to you by e-mail on a periodic basis.

Online Learning Resources

It is impossible for an individual to be an expert in all areas of the constantly changing IT landscape. Targeted professional development is a way for IT workers to remain focused and current in their chosen areas. In the past, this goal often meant attending lengthy and expensive off-site training courses. Advances in bandwidth and processing power have made online learning an increasingly attractive option for many IT professionals.

Online learning, also referred to as **e-learning**, is a term that refers to the delivery of educational or training content over the public Internet or an intranet. You can locate learning opportunities by searching the Web or through various professional associations. Many schools and colleges have seen a tremendous increase in demand for online learning and have increased their course offerings accordingly. The **Gov Online Learning Center** shown in Figure TK 6-20 is a government site with many online learning information and opportunities for federal employees.

Online learning can take many forms, ranging from individual self-paced instruction with little or no instructor involvement, to interactive, instructor-led groups with streaming audio and video capability. When choosing an online learning method, your learning goals and the quality of the content are the most important considerations. You need to think about your personal learning preferences. For example, you may learn better in a collaborative environment rather than working alone. If that is the case, consider options that include an interactive peer community. Below are some advantages and disadvantages that apply to the use of online resources:

BENEFITS OF ONLINE LEARNING

Benefits of online learning include the following:

- Convenient. You can participate in training when and where you want.

- Economical. Online learning options generally are less expensive than traditional face-to-face learning.

- Customizable. Generally, you can tailor the learning experience to your interests and needs.

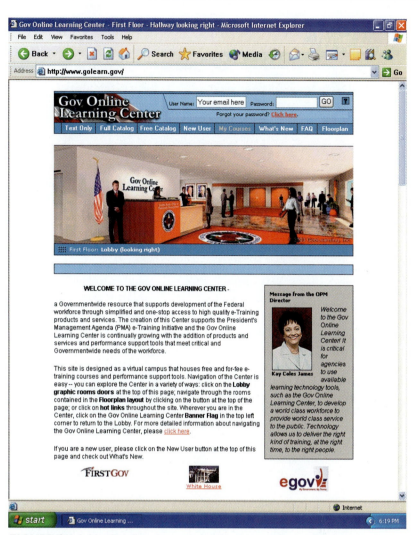

FIGURE TK 6-20 The Gov Online Learning Center offers a wide range on online training for federal employees.

DISADVANTAGES OF ONLINE LEARNING

Disadvantages of online learning include the following:

- Interaction. Although online learning can be highly collaborative, it lacks the face-to-face component that some learners find necessary. Additionally, you are less likely to receive the focused feedback that you would get when participating in traditional classroom training.

- Interface. Although bandwidth and computing power have increased greatly in recent years, the interface in an online learning experience may be a limitation. For example, you might experience slower processing performance, especially if the training uses interactive video, audio, or high-resolution graphics.

- Suitability. Online learning may not be the best option, particularly if the content is complicated and unfamiliar to you.

Figure TK 6-21 on the next page shows a recap of IT community resources, including commercial resources, government and professional resources, and online learning opportunities. Notice that each resource has advantages and disadvantages.

Recap of IT Community Resources

RESOURCE	POSSIBLE USES	ADVANTAGES	DISADVANTAGES	NOTES
Corporate Resources	Specific technical hardware or software help, training opportunities.	First stop for troubleshooting proprietary software or hardware.	Very often an agenda is associated with the site — for example, advocating a particular product or service.	Vendor sites contain valuable specific product or solution information (check the site's FAQs). Many offer newsletters for interested visitors.
Government Resources	Information on IT regulations.	Wide variety of general topics — from congressional studies to industry-relevant government regulations.	Not all information can be accessed via the Web — sometimes sites refer the searcher to a document number for ordering. Information tends to be general and not always relevant to the commercial sector.	Suggested sites — Library of Congress, General Accounting Office, Government Computer News.
Professional Resources	Information on professional skills and standards, IT career advice, and job opportunities.	Very specific IT interest items. Sites often provide valuable links and information on training opportunities.	Quality of sites varies. Many very specialized sites.	These sites often are worth bookmarking and using as central IT portal sites.
Online Learning Resources	An IT professional needs to stay current in a constantly changing technology environment. Online learning can provide job-specific skills and support for career advancement.	Convenient, economical, and customizable. You can participate in training when and where you want, and online learning options are generally less expensive than traditional face-to-face learning. Also, you generally can tailor the learning experience to your interests and needs.	Online learning lacks the face-to-face component that some learners find necessary. Learners are less likely to receive focused feedback. Also, the interface in an online learning experience may be a limitation. Overall, online learning may not be the best option, particularly if the content is complicated and unfamiliar to you.	When considering online learning, you must know your personal learning style and what works best for you. You should examine the entire range of options, from individual self-paced instruction with little or no instructor involvement, to interactive, instructor-led groups with streaming audio and video capability. Your goals and the quality of the content are the most important considerations.

FIGURE TK 6-21   A recap of IT community resources that a systems analyst can use to keep up with current issues and trends in IT. Notice that each option has advantages and disadvantages.

TOOLKIT SUMMARY

The Internet is a worldwide network that integrates many thousands of other networks, which in turn link millions of government, business, educational, and personal users around the globe. The Internet can assist you in your daily work by helping you solve technical problems and in the ongoing development of your career by providing access to training and professional education.

The Internet allows access to the World Wide Web, usually called the Web, which refers to the global collection of electronic documents stored on the Internet. These documents are referred to as Web pages, which are organized and stored on individual Web sites.

The primary research tools include search engines, subject directories, and a collection of searchable database resources called the invisible Web. A search engine uses keywords and phrases to locate information on the Internet and list the results of the search. Users should be aware that results can be affected if the search engine permits commercial users to achieve higher priority based on payment of fees. Also, search engines access only a portion of the Internet. Meta-search engines are tools that can apply multiple search engines simultaneously.

A subject directory is a Web site that allows you to access topics by using a hierarchy, starting with general headings and proceeding to more specific topics. A subject directory is an excellent starting point when you want an overview of a particular topic before proceeding to specific Web sites.

The invisible Web, or hidden Web, describes numerous text, graphics, and data files stored in collections that are unreachable by search engines.

An Internet research strategy should use a four-step approach: evaluate your information requirements, match your information requirements to the proper tool, assess the quality of the results, and download the results and perform a virus scan. Many people find it helpful to prepare for an Internet search by using a checklist to identify key terms, phrases, and characteristics of the topic.

Other Internet tools that might be of value to a systems analyst are newsgroups, newsletters, mailing lists, Web-based discussion groups, chat rooms, and instant messaging. Newsgroups, which are part of the Usenet, are online discussion groups that address every conceivable subject and interest area. Newsletters are published by numerous commercial and nonprofit groups that offer membership subscriptions to users who are interested in specific topics. A mailing list, or listserv, allows subscribing members to post and receive messages forwarded to them by a list server. A Web-based discussion group, usually accessed through a portal such as Yahoo!, combines features of newsgroups and mailing lists for its members. A chat room is an online meeting place where users can interact and converse in real time. Instant messaging allows online users to exchange messages immediately, even while they are working in another program or application.

When an IT professional needs to research a topic or seek background information, he or she can turn to an assortment of sites and resources called the information technology (IT) community. The IT community includes corporate, government, professional, and online learning resources.

Professional development through online learning is a way for IT workers to remain current in their chosen areas. Online learning refers to the delivery of educational or training content over the Internet or an intranet. Online learning is convenient, economical, and customizable. Some disadvantages, however, include a lack of face-to-face interaction, limitations of the interface, and the fact that not everyone works well with this type of training.

Key Terms and Phrases

advanced search *635*

AND *634*

Boolean logic *633*

browser *628*

channel *644*

chat room *644*

content *630*

deep Web *637*

digest *642*

e-learning *648*

FAQs (frequently asked questions) *642*

Gov Online Learning Center *649*

hidden Web *637*

hits *632*

implied Boolean logic *635*

indexed search engine *632*

indexing *632*

Information Technology Association of America
   (ITAA) *648*

information technology (IT) community *647*

instant messaging (IM) *644*

Internet Relay Chat *644*

Internet *628*

Internet mapping *628*

invisible Web *629*

IRC *644*

keywords *632*

listserv *642*

list server *642*

logical operators *633*

mailing list *642*

meta-search engines *629*

netiquette *642*

newsreader *641*

newsgroup *641*

newsletters *642*

NOT *634*

online learning *648*

OR *634*

pay for performance *632*

phrase *635*

portal *636*

search engine *629*

spider *632*

spidering *637*

sponsored links *632*

sub-search *630*

subject directory *629*

Subject-Specific Popularity™ *632*

threads *641*

Usenet *641*

Venn diagram *633*

visible Web *637*

Web *628*

Web-based discussion group *643*

Web browser *628*

Web pages *628*

Web server *628*

Web site *628*

World Wide Web *628*

Z39.50 protocol *639*

Toolkit Exercises

Review Questions

1. Describe the size and characteristics of the Internet and the World Wide Web.
2. How do search engines differ from subject directories? Provide examples of search engines and subject directories.
3. What is the invisible Web, and how can it be accessed?
4. What steps should you follow when formulating an Internet research strategy?
5. What questions should you ask when evaluating the quality of Internet research results?
6. What are sponsored links, and how can they affect the quality of your search results?
7. What is Boolean logic? Provide three examples.
8. How do Venn diagrams show the effect of the three logical operators?
9. Describe newsgroups, newsletters, mailing lists, Web-based discussion groups, chat rooms, and instant messaging. How can these tools be used in an Internet research task?
10. What is the information technology community, and what resources does it offer for Internet research tasks?

Discussion Topics

1. The textbook explains that some companies pay to obtain a higher ranking when search results are displayed. Is this good, is it bad, or does it not matter to you as a user? Explain your position.
2. Some people rely heavily on instant messaging to communicate with friends and business colleagues; others find it to be a distraction. Do you use instant messaging? Why or why not?
3. Could Boolean logic and Venn diagrams be useful in everyday life? How might they be used?
4. The Internet has affected many aspects of our society. What are the most important benefits of the Internet, and what problems have been created by it?

Projects

1. Use a search engine and enter the following words: presidential candidates in 2008. Run the search and notice how many results appear. Now place quote marks around the phrase and run the search again. Explain the difference in the results.
2. Will the search phrase, commercial television, return the same results as the phrase, television commercial? Experiment with a search engine, and explain the results you obtain.
3. Use the Yahoo! subject directory to identify two or three dictionaries of technical terms. Begin with the subject Computers and Internet, and then follow the appropriate links until you obtain results. Describe the results of your research. What other research strategies could you use for this task? Would they be better? Why or why not?
4. Locate a computer-related newsgroup and review a sample of several recent postings. Report your results.

INDEX

1:1: A type of entity relationship. A one-on-one relationship, abbreviated 1:1, exists when exactly one of the second entity occurs for each instance of the first entity. 318

1:M: A type of entity relationship. A one-to-many relationship, abbreviated 1:M, exists when one occurrence of the first entity can be related to many occurrences of the second entity, but each occurrence of the second entity can be associated with only one occurrence of the first entity. 318, 319

24/7: 24 hours a day, 7 days a week. The term, 24/7, often is used in an IT context to describe the requirement for information systems to be continually up and running. 368

6 by 6 rule: The 6 by 6 rule suggests that on a slide, no more than six items should be placed on each slide, and each item should have no more than six words. 533

7 by 7 rule: The 7 by 7 rule suggests that on a slide, no more than seven items should be placed on each slide, and each item should have no more than seven words. 533

802.11 High Rate: A popular version of the 802.11 network standard for wireless networks, with a nominal transmission rate of 11 million bits per second within a 100-meter range. 391

802.11 network standard: A family of wireless network specifications developed by the IEEE. 391

802.11b: A popular version of the 802.11 network standard for wireless networks, with a nominal transmission rate of 11 million bits per second within a 100-meter range. Also known as 802.11 High Rate or Wi-Fi. 391

AAAI (American Association for Artificial Intelligence), 270, 271

abbreviation codes: Abbreviation codes are alphabetic abbreviations. For example, standard state codes include NY for New York, ME for Maine, and MN for Minnesota. 334. *See also* **codes**

absolute date: An absolute date is the total number of days from some specific base date. To calculate the number of days between two absolute dates, you subtract one date from the other. For example, using a base date of January 1, 1900, August 13, 2001 has an absolute date value of 37116 and April 27, 2002 has an absolute date of 37373. If you subtract the earlier date value from the later one, the result is 257 days. 346

acceptable values, 169

acceptance tests: Also known as a system test. Acceptance testing involves the entire information system. An acceptance test includes all typical processing situations. During an acceptance test, users enter data, including samples of actual, or live data, perform queries, and produce reports to simulate actual operating conditions. All processing options and outputs are verified by users and the IT project development team to ensure that the system functions correctly. 433

account lockout threshold: A limit on how many times an invalid password can be entered before the system locks itself down. 496

accuracy, information, 630

AccuRev, 486

action codes: Action codes indicate what action is to be taken with an associated item. For example, a student records program might prompt a user to enter or click an action code such as D (to display the student's record), A (to add a record), and X (to exit the program). 335

Action Office Products case study, 79-80

active voice: Active voice refers to using sentences where the actor is the subject of the sentence. For example, "Tom designed the system" is in active voice. 525

activities: An activity, or task, is any work that has a beginning and an end, and requires the use of company resources, including people, time, and/or money. Examples include conducting a series of interviews, designing a report, selecting software, waiting for the delivery of equipment, and training users. 580

activity diagrams: An activity diagram resembles a horizontal flow chart that shows the actions and events as they occur. Activity diagrams show the order in which actions take place and identify the outcome. 621

actor: An external entity with a specific role. In a use-case model, actors are used to model interaction with the system. 99

adaptive maintenance: Adaptive maintenance adds new capability and enhancements. 477, 478-79. *See also* maintenance

activities, 477
    expenses, 478
    minor, 479
    procedures, 479
    task examples, 478

administrators: In certain types of applications, an administrator is an account type that allows essentially unrestricted access to the application. 500

advanced search: An advanced search can include the option to search within returned results and the ability to search within specific areas, such as newsgroups. 635. *See also* **search engines**

aesthetics: Aesthetics focuses on how an interface can be made attractive and easy to use. 268

alias: Term used in various data dictionaries to indicate an alternate name, or a name other than the standard data element name, that is used to describe the same data element. 168
    data element, 168
    data flow, 169
    data store, 170
    entity, 171
    record, 172

allocated baseline: The allocated baseline documents a system at the end of the design phase and identifies any changes since the functional baseline. The allocated baseline includes testing and verification of all system requirements and features. 488

alphabetic codes: Alphabetic codes use alphabet letters to distinguish one item from another based on a category, an abbreviation, or an easy-to-remember value, called a mnemonic code. 334. *See also* **codes**

alternatives section: In a report, an alternatives section is recommended. The alternatives section lists the advantages and disadvantages of each major system alternative. This section also includes the cost-benefit results, with a clear description of the economic analysis techniques that were used. Tables or graphs can be used to support and clarify the alternatives when necessary. 530-31. *See also* reports

American Association for Artificial Intelligence (AAAI), 270, 271

American National Standards Institute (ANSI): ANSI developed a standard set of symbols for systems flowcharts. 231

value. The daily hours worked by an employee, for example, must fall within the range of 0 to 24. 281

range-of-response questions: Closed-ended questions that ask the person to evaluate something by providing limited answers to specific responses or on a numeric scale. 108

rapid application development (RAD): A team-based technique that speeds up information systems development and produces a functioning information system. RAD is similar in concept to joint application development (JAD), but goes further by including all phases of the SDLC. 19, 49, 93, 95-97. *See also* **joint application development (JAD)**
  activities, 96
  advantages, 97
  construction, 96
  cutover, 96
  disadvantages, 97
  group approach, 95
  objectives, 96-97
  phases, 96
  phases illustration, 97
  prototyping, 96
  requirements planning, 96
  use, 95-96
  user design, 96
  user involvement, 96

Rapid Economic Justification (REJ): REJ is a Microsoft product. It includes a method for measuring total costs and benefits to help IT professionals analyze and optimize IT investments. 104

Rational Edge, 550-51

Rational Software Architect, 550

readability: Readability analyzes ease of comprehension by measuring specific characteristics of syllables, words, and sentences. 526

read-only properties: Elements of an application that can configured so users can view, but not change, the data. 210

reasonableness check: A type of data validation check that identifies values that are questionable, but not necessarily wrong. For example, input payment values of $0.05 and $5, 000, 000.00 both pass a

simple limit check for a payment value greater than zero, and yet both values could be errors. 281

recommendations section: The recommendations section of a report presents the best system alternative, with a brief explanation. 530

records: A record, also called a tuple, is a set of related fields that describes one instance, or member of an entity, such as one customer, one order, or one product. A record might have one or dozens of fields, depending on what information is needed. 167, 314
  aliases, 172
  attributes, 172
  data flow, 169
  description, 172
  documenting, 172
  logical, 343, 344
  physical, 343

records retention policy: A records policy that is designed to meet all legal requirements and business needs for keeping records. 284

recovery procedures: Recovery procedures involve restoring data and restarting a system after an interruption. Recovery procedures can be used to restore a file or database to its current state at the time of the last backup. 348, 393, 395-96

redundancy, DBMS, 307

referential integrity: A type of validity check. Referential integrity is a set of rules that avoids data inconsistency and quality problems. 316-17
  building, into design, 317
  deletion prevention, 317
  example, 316-17
  rules specification, 317

relational model: A model used in relational databases. The relational model was introduced during the 1970s and became popular because it was flexible and powerful. 338-40

relationships: Relationships enable objects to communicate and interact as they perform the business functions and transactions required by a system. Relationships

describe what objects need to know about each other, how objects respond to changes in other objects, and the effects of membership in classes, superclasses, and subclasses. 318-20, 614
  identifying, 424-26
  inheritance, 614
  many-to-many, 318-19
  object and class, 614
  one-to-many, 318
  one-to-one, 318

repeating groups: A repeating group is a set of data items that can occur any number of times in a single record. A repeating group can be thought of as a set of subsidiary records contained within the main record. 323

report analysis form: A report analysis form contains information about the fields, data types and lengths, report frequency and distribution, and other comments. 257

report footer: The report footer, which appears at the end of the report, can include grand totals for numeric fields and other end-of-report information. 254

report generators: A report generator, also called a report writer, is a tool for designing formatted reports rapidly. 209, 229, 545

report header: A report header appears at the beginning of a report and identifies the report, as well as the report title, date, and other necessary information. 254

report writer: A report writer, also called a report generator, is a tool for designing formatted reports rapidly. 545

reports, 251-57
  alternatives section, 530-31
  appendix, 531
  character-based, 257
  column heading alignment, 254
  column spacing, 254-55
  control break, 251
  cover memo, 529
  data dictionary, 172-73
  design, user involvement, 253-54
  design issues, 256-57
  design principles, 254-56, 257
  detail, 251-53

  detail lines, 251, 256
  exception, 253
  executive summary, 529
  field order, 254-55
  findings section, 529
  introduction, 529
  length calculations, 258
  management, final, 453
  mock-up, 254, 545
  preliminary investigation, 70-71
  printer spacing chart, 257
  printing, 258-59
  project status, 594
  recommendations section, 530
  summary, 253
  time calculations, 259
  volume, 258
  as written communications, 528-31

repository: A repository is a database that serves as a central storage location for all information about a system being developed. 542

request for proposal (RFP): A request for proposal (RFP) is a written list of features and specifications given to prospective vendors before a specific product or package has been selected. 214
  complexity, 215
  evaluation model, 215
  illustrated, 214
  preparing, 214-15
  response evaluation, 215
  size, 215

request for quotation (RFQ): A request for quotation (RFQ) is used to obtain a price quotation or bid on a specific product or package. 216

requirements model: A requirements model describes the information that a system must provide. 16

requirements modeling: Modeling that is used in the systems planning phase of the SDLC. It involves fact-finding to describe the current system and identify the requirements for the new system. 22, 90-123
  introduction, 90
  sample questions, 105

requirements planning phase: A phrase that combines elements of the systems planning and systems analysis phases of the SDLC. 96

PHOTO CREDITS

Figure 1-5 (c), Mars Rover, Courtesy NASA/JPL-Caltech; Figure 1-7 (d), server room, Courtesy of Sun Microsystems; Figure 1-13 (b), Motorola microcontroller, Courtesy of Motorola; Figure 1-18, RFID in use (warehouse), Courtesy of Texas Instruments, RFID Systems; Figure 2-7, Hand Recognition System in place at Johnson & Wales, Courtesy of IR Recognition Systems; Figure 2-10, Man driving forklift, ©Alistair Berg/PhotoDisc; Figure 2-20, business interview, ©Comstock Images/Getty Images; Figure 2-21, high tech presentation, ©Tim Brown/Getty Images; Figure 3-3, business meeting with whiteboard, ©Masterfile; Figure 3-17, businessmen drinking coffee outside with laptop, ©Kevin Dodge/Masterfile; Figure 3-20, FedEx observation, ©Mark Richards/Photo Edit; Figure 3-26, RIM Blackberry 957 in hand, Courtesy of Research in Motion; Figure 4-2, businesspeople with smart board, Courtesy of Luidia, Inc.; Figure 4-4, network wires jumbled, ©Royalty-Free/CORBIS; Figure 4-24, clean room, Courtesy of Texas Instruments; Figure 4-41, woman with laptop giving presentation, ©Dennis MacDonald / Photo Edit; Figure 5-10, couple checking into hotel with computer at front desk, ©Masterfile; Figure 5-22, current computer magazines on rack, ©Gary Herrington; Figure 5-26, RFID scanner (keg with tag), Courtesy of TrenStar; Figure 5-27, wind tunnel photo, Courtesy of NASA; Figure 6-13, shredding documents, © Spencer Grant/Photo Edit; Figure 6-14, diskless workstations, © Reuters/Kamal Kishore/Landov; Figure 6-18, working on computer, © Steve Cole/Masterfile; Figure 6-33, customer signature stored in digital form, © Courtesy of Interlink Electronics, Inc.; Figure 7-50, control room, ©James Leynse/CORBIS; Figure 7-27, student and faculty advising, ©David Young-Wolff/Photo Edit; 7-38, video store, ©Spencer Grant/Photo Edit; Figure 8-6, password, ©Comstock/Getty Images; Figure 8-8, online retailer operations, ©Bloomberg News/Landov; Figure 8-30, POS terminal in use, ©Karlheinz Schindler/Landov; Figure 8-43, business presentation, ©Michael Newman/Photo Edit; Figure 9-5, international street signs, ©Bob Daemmrich/Photo Edit; Figure 9-24, group around computer, ©H. Prinz/CORBIS; Figure 9-30, training-manufacturing, ©Spencer Grant/Photo Edit; Figure 9-32, group training, ©PhotoDisc Collection/Getty Images; Figure 10-2, woman training male factory worker on circuit board, ©Walter Hodges/Getty Images; Figure 10-3, female executive wearing telephone headset, using computer, ©Walter Hodges/Getty Images; Figure 10-6, maintenance, DoD photo by Airman Charlie Whetstine, U.S. Navy; Figure 10-24, biometric device, ©Boris Roessler/Landov